**TOXICOLOGY
of DRUGS
and CHEMICALS**

Toxicology of Drugs and Chemicals

BY

WILLIAM B. DEICHMANN, Ph.D.

PROFESSOR AND CHAIRMAN
DEPARTMENT OF PHARMACOLOGY
AND
DIRECTOR OF THE
RESEARCH AND TEACHING CENTER OF TOXICOLOGY
UNIVERSITY OF MIAMI, SCHOOL OF MEDICINE
CORAL GABLES, FLORIDA

AND

HORACE W. GERARDE, M.D., Ph.D.

ASSOCIATE CLINICAL PROFESSOR
DEPARTMENT OF ENVIRONMENTAL MEDICINE
NEW YORK UNIVERSITY
NEW YORK, NEW YORK
AND
ADJUNCT PROFESSOR IN BIOCHEMISTRY
SCHOOL OF DENTISTRY
FAIRLEIGH DICKINSON UNIVERSITY
TEANECK, NEW JERSEY

1969

ACADEMIC PRESS   New York   San Francisco   London
A Subsidiary of Harcourt Brace Jovanovich, Publishers

ACADEMIC PRESS, INC.
111 Fifth Avenue, New York, New York 10003

United Kingdom Edition published by
ACADEMIC PRESS, INC. (LONDON) LTD.
24/28 Oval Road, London NW1

LIBRARY OF CONGRESS CATALOG CARD NUMBER: 69-12282

PRINTED IN THE UNITED STATES OF AMERICA

Dedicated to our wives
Hedy and Dotty

"PARTS PER MILLION"

1 ppm is equal to 1 inch in 16 miles,
1 ppm is 1 minute in 2 years,
1 ppm is a 1-gram needle in a ton of hay,
1 ppm is 1 penny in $10,000.00,
1 ppm is 1 ounce (30 gm) of salt in 62,500 pounds (28,375 kg) of sugar,
1 ppm is 1 large mouthful of food when compared with the food a person will eat in a lifetime,
1 ppm is the theoretical concentration that 1 teaspoon of DDT will impart to the hay when spread on 5 acres of alfalfa,
1 ppm is 1 drop in 16 gallons, or in 80 "fifths," a very dry martini indeed!

FOREWORD

Since the publication four years ago of "Symptomatology and Therapy of Toxicological Emergencies" by W. B. Deichmann and Horace W. Gerarde, great strides have been made in scientific technology, medicine, agriculture, and insect control, which have led to the development of many new products. Some of these products, especially drugs, can be toxic to man, particularly to children and the elderly, and to animals as well.

With the complicated structure of many of these substances and the various symptoms which develop following exposure to them, it is no longer possible to utilize a few old-fashioned remedies which formerly were sufficient to relieve the symptoms. Moreover, it is not possible to recall the symptoms and therapy of overdoses of more than a few of these toxic products. Therefore, it has become urgently necessary to revise and up-date the information pertaining to toxicology from the world literature.

In the previous three editions authored by W. B. Deichmann and his able colleague, Horace W. Gerarde (who co-authored the second and third editions), it was found necessary to increase the number of compounds discussed with each edition. This edition has proved to be no exception—a great many new drugs and chemicals have been added and some older and now obsolete products have been deleted.

In spite of its necessary enlargement, the format, found so convenient for speedy reference in emergencies, has been maintained so that the book can still be carried in a physician's bag or kept at hand in the hospital emergency ward, the poison control center, or the doctor's office.

We congratulate Dr. W. B. Deichmann and Dr. Horace W. Gerarde on their accomplishment, and hope this fourth edition will be as eagerly accepted as the previous ones were.

M. JAY FLIPSE, M. D.
Clinical Associate
Professor of Medicine
University of Miami

Miami, Florida
January, 1969

PREFACE

The fourth edition, as the previous one ("Symptomatology and Therapy of Toxicological Emergencies"), is designed to present, as a ready reference, data on side effects of drugs and toxicity of industrial chemicals, and recommendations for the treatment of undesirable effects and overdoses.

Practically every section has been rewritten to include information which has appeared in the medical literature since 1964. Since most of our colleagues and students acquired the habit of referring to our third volume as the "Toxicology Book," we have decided to follow their lead and title the fourth edition "Toxicology of Drugs and Chemicals." This volume, too, is not intended to be a text of pharmacology; therefore, no attempt has been made to cover every drug. The book also contains information on the degree of animal toxicity and the pharmacological effects of new industrial chemicals. Plant toxins have been given particular consideration, and we are indebted to Dr. K. Lampe, Professor of Pharmacology, University of Miami, for placing at our disposal his chapters and bibliography on plants. Unlike the third edition, in which plants were listed by their Latin names, we have, in this edition, listed plants by their English names, with Latin identification in parentheses.

For ready reference, the compounds and nonproprietary names of drugs are listed alphabetically in Chapter IV. The index lists the drugs under their proprietary names. The index also includes those organs or systems primarily affected by a particular drug or industrial chemical. Many references are included in the text directing the physician or toxicologist to the sources of the data in the event that more detailed information is desired. The format of the work and the large print are maintained since these features were found to be helpful in emergency situations.

It is our hope that the fourth edition will be accepted as was the third by teachers of chemistry, biochemistry, pharmacology, toxicology, radiation medicine, industrial hygiene, etc., by the members of the Poison Control Centers, as well as by those whose responsibility involves the health of workers in the chemical industry and public health in general.

Primarily, this volume was prepared for the physician who requires toxicological-type information on a drug or chemical.

As pointed out by Richard P. Bergen:

If a particular drug is known to have side effects which may prove dangerous to the patient, the physician should make a reasonably full disclosure to the patient of the risks involved before obtaining the consent of the patient to the administration of the drug (*JAMA* **181**, 1022, 1962).

It is our belief that this volume will provide the physician with such information at a moment's notice.

W. B. DEICHMANN

January, 1969

H. W. GERARDE

ACKNOWLEDGMENTS

In the preparation of the fourth edition we have again relied heavily on our colleagues to provide authoritative current information. We acknowledge our deep appreciation to the following contributors:

A. H. Banner, Ph.D., Professor of Zoology, University of Hawaii—for his contribution to the chapter on *Fish*.

H. C. Hodge, Ph.D., Professor and Chairman, Department of Pharmacology, University of Rochester—for reviewing and updating the section on *Fluorides*.

J. E. Kiley, M.D., Professor of Medicine and Head of the Division of Kidney Diseases, Albany Medical College—for up-dating his chapter, *Dialytic Therapy of Poisoning*, which appeared also in the third edition.

A. J. Lehman, M.D., Ph.D., Director, Division of Pharmacology, Bureau of Scientific Research, Food and Drug Administration—for adding to our understanding of the significance of *"Parts Per Million"* and *Sodium Nitrite* in meat.

J. F. Palmer, M.D., Assistant to the Director for Scientific Coordination, Bureau of Medicine, Food and Drug Administration—for providing the list of *drugs* that have been withdrawn from the market.

H. F. Smyth, Jr., Ph.D., Professor of Industrial Toxicology, Graduate School of Public Health, University of Pittsburgh—for his eloquent description of 1 ppm in terms of a *very dry martini*.

F. E. Shideman, M.D., Ph.D., Professor and Head, Department of Pharmacology, University of Minnesota—for review and contributions to Chapter III, *Supportive Treatment*: Respiration, Circulation, Gastroenteric Tract, Central Nervous System, Liver, Kidneys, Electrolytes, and Water Balance.

C. C. Snyder, M.D. (formerly University of Miami), Professor and Chairman, Division of Plastic Surgery, University of Utah—for rewriting the section on *Snakebite Treatment*.

F. W. Sunderman, M.D., Director, Institute for Clinical Science, Inc., Philadelphia—for contributions to the sections on *Nickel* and *Copper*.

H. E. Tebrock, M.D., Medical Director, General Telephone and Electronics Corporation, New York—for his chapter on *Prevention of Coronary Heart Disease*.

We are equally grateful to our colleagues in the University of Miami School of Medicine for their contributions:

R. J. Boucek, M.D., Professor of Medicine—for rewriting the section on *Digitalis*.

H. R. Gilmore III, M.D., Associate Professor of Medicine—for recommendations of *Drug Dosages* to Increase Blood Pressure, Reduce Blood Pressure in a Hypertensive Crisis, Stimulate Cardiac Contractile Force, Lower Cerebrospinal Fluid Pressure, and Counteract Respiratory Depression.

M. H. Kalser, M.D., Ph.D., Professor of Medicine and Physiology—for recommendations of *Drug Dosages* to Reduce Central Nervous System Stimulation, for Disturbances of the Digestive Tract, to Counteract Convulsions and Extrapyramidal Reactions Induced by Tranquilizers.

K. F. Lampe, Ph.D., Professor of Pharmacology and Anesthesiology—for valuable assistance and for making available his files on the *Pharmacology and Toxicology of Plant Poisons*.

W. Lindau, M.D., Clinical Associate Professor of Pharmacology and Clinical Assistant Professor of Medicine—for reviewing the sections on *Shock, Diarrhea of Travelers, Heparin, Bishydroxy-coumarin, Warfarin,* and *Vitamin K*.

J. B. Mann, M.D., Assistant Professor of Medicine—for recommendations of *Drug Dosages* for Replacement of Potassium, to Counteract Acidosis, and to Induce Diuresis of an Alkaline Urine.

E. L. Nagel, M.D., Assistant Professor of Anesthesiology—for reviewing the section on *Narcotics*.

W. L. Nyhan, M.D., Ph.D., Professor and Chairman, Department of Pediatrics—for rewriting the chapter: Treatment of *Acetylsalicylic Acid Intoxication*.

R. E. Parks, M.D., Professor and Chairman, Department of Radiology—for reviewing and up-dating the chapter on *Radiation*.

J. L. Radomski, Ph.D., Professor of Pharmacology—for his valuable contributions to the sections on the individual *Antibiotics*.

B. Sallman, Ph.D., Professor and Chairman, Department of Microbiology—for reviewing of the section on *Food Poisoning*.

K. Savard, Sc.D., Professor of Biochemistry and Medicine—for up-dating the sections on *Adrenocortical Hormones, Corticotropin, Estrogens, Anovulatory Steroids,* and *Testosterone*.

S. M. Shafey, M.D., Assistant Professor of Neurology—for review of *Central Nervous System Drug Dosages*.

T. R. Struhl, M.D., F.A.C.S., Clinical Instructor in Anatomy and General Surgery—for reviewing and up-dating the sections on *Diving, Artificial Respiration,* and *Cardiac Massage*.

We are grateful to Charlotte Honderick and Dotty Gerarde for valuable editorial assistance, and to typists Frances Fernandez, Sherry Joret, Janet McLaughlin, Judy Snyder, Aletha Thompson, Dorothy Morin, and Eleanor Walls. Their conscientious work has contributed much toward the fourth edition.

CONTENTS

First Aid and General Suggestions for Treatment

Drugs and Adult Dosages for the Treatment of Intoxications

Supportive Treatment

Drugs and Chemicals: Signs, Symptoms, and Treatment of Intoxications

Tabular Summaries

TOXICOLOGY
of DRUGS
and CHEMICALS

CHAPTER I

FIRST AID AND GENERAL SUGGESTIONS FOR TREATMENT

General Recommendations and Advice via Telephone

The primary purpose of first aid is to keep the patient alive. When in doubt as to what to do, it is best to do nothing; *call a physician.* Be sure there is good reason for administering any treatment or drug. Heroic measures may do more harm than good. If you know what to do, give first aid and have someone call a physician or an ambulance.

In a case of acute poisoning, a physician's advice via telephone to a frantic individual may be lifesaving and prevent permanent injury. Instructions must be brief, explicit, and practical; and they must take into consideration the condition of the patient at the moment, the nature of the chemical, and whether it was ingested, inhaled, spilled on the skin, splashed into the eyes, or injected.

The following recommendations are suggested:

1. If the patient is gasping for breath or if breathing has stopped, immediately begin artificial respiration; have someone call the police department, fire department, or rescue squad for a resuscitator.

2. If unconscious, in shock, deeply cyanotic, or in convulsions, take the patient to the hospital at once.

3. If a patient who has ingested a toxic substance is conscious, make him drink as much tap water, salt water, or milk as possible; then induce vomiting. If it is definitely known that a strong alkali (lye, Drano, ammonia), a strong acid, or a petroleum solvent (kerosene) has been swallowed, do *not* induce vomiting, but take the patient immediately to the hospital.

4. After filling the stomach with liquids, induce vomiting by placing a spoon or finger into the patient's mouth and touching the back of the throat. If the pa-

tient is a child, do this while holding him across your knees in a "spanking position," with head lower than trunk and hips.

5. Collect vomitus in a suitable container. Again fill the stomach with fluids and induce vomiting. Repeat several times.

6. Save the toxic substance (poisonous plant, drug, chemical) and the container from which it (the chemical, drug, or household poison) was taken.

7. Take the patient, the regurgitated material, and the container to the hospital.

8. For skin contamination *drench* affected parts with water (hose, tub, or shower) and remove contaminated clothing under the shower.

9. For eye contamination, wash eyes for 15–20 minutes with running water.

10. Keep calm and try to reassure the victim.

Transportation of Injured

After *ingestion* of a toxic plant or chemical, transport the patient in such a way that he maintains an open airway to prevent the aspiration of vomitus. Remove false teeth. Place him on the stretcher in a prone position with head lower than hips, or (particularly in the case of a child) on the back seat of a car or station wagon on his side or abdomen with head turned to the side.

Narcotics should *not* be given to a patient who is unconscious or suffering from a head injury, respiratory difficulty, or shock.

Mouth-to-Mouth or Mouth-to-Nose Breathing for Adults and Children

"Head-Tilt Oral Resuscitation": [J. O. Elam *et al.*, *JAMA* **172**, 812 (1960)].

1. Lift neck (Fig. 1).

2. Tilt the head back as far as possible by holding crown of head with one hand. Sufficient tilting usually opens the victim's mouth.

3. Pull the chin upward with the other hand (Fig. 2).

4. Inflate the lungs through the nose or mouth (if through the mouth, the nose must be pinched closed); or, in an infant, through the nose and mouth (Fig. 3).

5. Remove your mouth to let the victim exhale passively (Fig. 4). (If necessary, let him exhale through his mouth, momentarily separating his lips.)

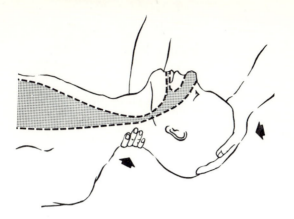

Fig. 1

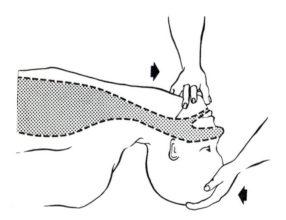

Fig. 2

Fig. 3

3

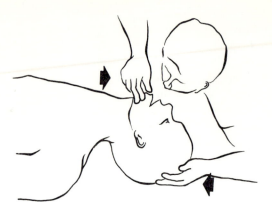

Fig. 4

Continue until victim breathes, or until rigor mortis is evident.

"The position of the rescuer's hands and the wide area of the oral seal must be emphasized for successful performance of this method. Both of the rescuer's hands continuously maintain maximum extension of the head [Fig. 5, bottom]. Nasal inflation is preferred, to avoid gastr   ilatation. Inflation through the vic   event of nasal blockage merely requires separation of his lips with the rescuer's thumb, which is already in place on the victim's chin [Fig. 5, center]. In babies and children, care must be taken to pull the chin upward without exerting pressure on the soft tissues, which could encroach on the air passages [Fig. 5, top].

"An important modification is the optional use of the semilateral position for the victim. The victim's shoulder may rest continuously on the rescuer's knee during resuscitation [Fig. 6]. From this position, the victim's head is easily tilted to provide gravity drainage of fluid from the pharynx [Fig. 7]. Small victims, particularly after submersion in water or obstruction by a foreign body in the upper airway, should be inverted and, if necessary, sharp blows applied between the shoulder blades to help clear the obstruction [Fig. 8].

"The head-tilt oral method fulfills the need for a simple and effective universal procedure for resuscitating children and adults. Maximum extension of the victim's head opens and keeps open the air passages by the simplest maneuver, without involving insertion of the finger or equipment into the mouth (J. O. Elam *et al.*, cited above)."

Tubes and masks are not recommended because the average rescuer (1) does not carry them and, in an emergency, time should not be taken to find a substitute; (2) is not able to judge the reflex response of an unconscious person and may cause serious injury when inserting an instrument; and (3) lacks the skill and experience required to use the artificial oral airway properly.

"Red Cross data and that from other sources show that, if resuscitation is begun within one minute after breathing stops, 98 % will survive; two minutes, 92 %; three minutes, 72 %; four minutes, 50 %; and five minutes, 25 %. Heart action is said to cease five to six minutes after breathing has stopped. Severe brain damage and irreversible central nervous system changes will have occurred after eight minutes of apnea or four minutes of cardiac arrest [J. F. Tomashefski, *JAMA*, **175**, 639 (1961)]."

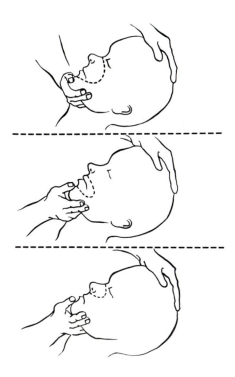

Fig. 5

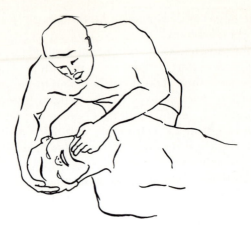

Fig. 6

"Two rescuers can do *Mouth-to-Mouth and External Cardiac Resuscitation* simultaneously instead of alternately. However, in cases where there is liquid or semi-liquid material in the lungs, air passages or stomach (i.e., drowning, pulmonary edema, vomiting, etc.), simultaneous application results in stomach and pulmonary contents being discharged into the face of the rescuer performing direct mouth-to-mouth resuscitation. This is avoided *when chest compression and*

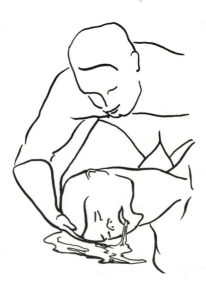

Fig. 7

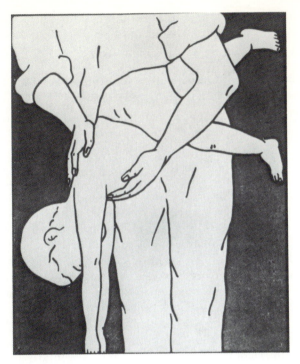

Fig. 8

lung inflation are alternated [Fig. 9]. Better pulmonary ventilation is also provided without any significant sacrifice in the effectiveness of circulation.

"In an emergency a single individual can alternately inflate the lungs and compress the chest. In this case it may be desirable to follow each lung inflation

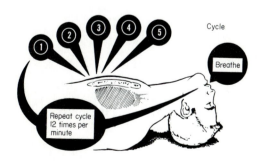

Fig. 9

with a series of six cardiac compressions, instead of five [A. S. Gordon, *J. Occup. Med.*, 4, 27 (1962)]." (See Fig. 10.)

Combination Silvester Method for Artificial Respiration with External Cardiac Massage

In a patient with a suspected contagious disease, the Silvester method may be preferred, combined with external cardiac resuscitation to provide *Silvester heart-lung resuscitation* (Fig. 10). "The victim is placed on a firm surface with a towel, block, or some other slight elevation under his shoulders so that his head will drop back into maximum extension. The rescuer kneels at the victim's head, grasps both of his wrists, places them on top of each other in the center of the chest over the lower half of the breastbone and rocks forward, using the weight of his body *to deliver a series of cardiac compressions*. He then rocks backward, raising the victim's arms above his head to produce lung inflation. The complete cycle is then repeated 12–15 times per minute [A. S. Gordon, *J. Occup. Med.* 4, 27 (1962)]."

External Cardiac Massage

External cardiac massage is not for the unskilled since it involves certain hazards. Training in the technique is necessary for its use with maximum safety and effectiveness.

If a person is not breathing, and in addition, is unconscious, pulseless, and apparently dying or dead, initiate immediately mouth-to-nose or mouth-to-mouth breathing and cardiac massage. According to the Ad Hoc Committee on Cardiopulmonary Resuscitation of the Division of Medical Sciences, National Academy of Sciences-National Research Council, emergency cardiopulmonary resuscitation involves the following steps:

1. Airway opened (Fig. 11)
2. Breathing restored (Fig. 12)
3. Circulation restored (Fig. 13)
4. Definitive therapy

These measures should always be started as quickly as possible, and always in the order shown [*JAMA* 198, 138 (1966)].

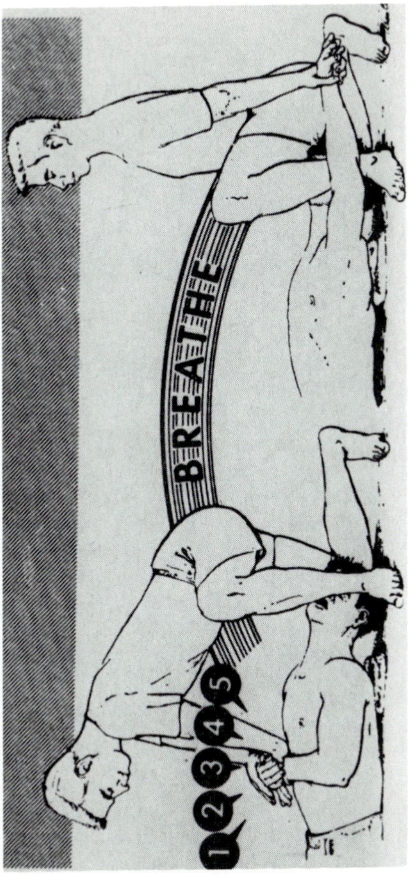

Fig. 10

9

A Airway

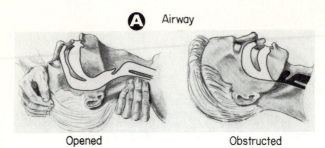

Opened   Obstructed

Fig. 11

B Breathing

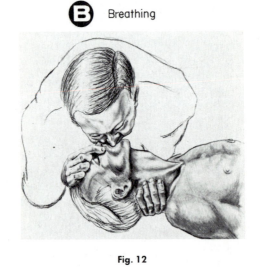

Fig. 12

C Circulation

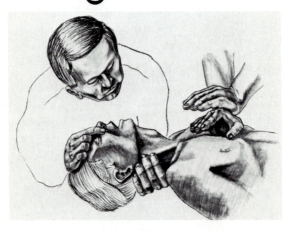

Fig. 13

Proceed as follows to restore circulation [taken from an editorial in *J. Occup. Med.* **3**, 39 (1960), based on studies by W. B. Kouwenhoven, J. R. Jude, and C. G. Knickerbocker, "Closed-Chest Cardiac Massage," *JAMA* **173**, 1064 (1960)]:

1. Place person on a firm surface, face up, and have someone else proceed with oral resuscitation.

2. Kneel beside the victim, facing his head (Fig. 14).

3. Apply the heel of one hand on the lower 5 cm (2 inches) of the chest plate (sternum). The heel of the other hand is brought on top of the first (Fig. 14).

4. Now push down rhythmically (not more than 2 inches), using your full body weight, at the rate of 60 times per minute. Be sure to ease up after every compression.

5. Continue until the patient shows signs of life, such as spontaneous gasping respiration, contraction of the pupils, or palpable brachial, carotid, or femoral pulses, or until rigor mortis is evident. In most patients, spontaneous cardiac activity and respiration return within 20 minutes.

"Epinephrine, 0.5 mg intravenously or directly into one of the chambers of the heart, should be given as soon as possible. Other cardiotonic drugs that may be used include: 25–50 mg ephedrine; 45 mg mephentermine; or 0.1–0.2 mg isoproterenol hydrochloride. Continued massage will distribute the drug evenly throughout the myocardium and the body. Calcium chloride or calcium gluconate is beneficial if

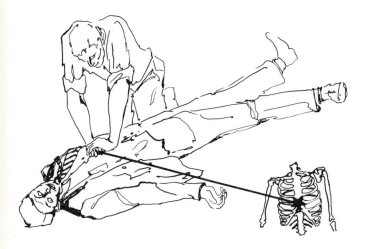

Fig. 14

weak cardiac action returns. One-half or 1 gm of a 10%
solution is given intravenously or into the heart blood
[J. R. Jude *et al.*, *JAMA* **178**, 1063 (1961)]."

Management after Cardiac Arrest

Hospital treatment may include the following:

1. *Induced hypothermia* to reduce oxygen requirements of the central nervous system. To initiate hypothermia, an intravenous infusion of 200 mg of 0.04%
meperidine and 50 mg of 0.01% promethazine in 500
ml of fluid is given at a rate not inducing shivering,
and not so quickly as to depress respiratory or cardiovascular activities. Further sedation is added in the
form of intramuscular phenobarbital and diphenylhydantoin sodium (Dilantin) every 4 hours. These drugs
act synergistically to reduce shivering and control
convulsions. Diphenylhydantoin also prevents ventricular arrhythmias which may occur during hypothermia. As these drugs become effective, the dosage of
meperidine-promethazine is reduced. Subsequent
convulsions may be controlled with repeated small
doses of intravenous 2.5% thiopental. For long-term
management, paraldehyde I.M. is useful. If cardiac
arrest has been prolonged, the patient's temperature
should be rapidly lowered to 30°C by means of a cooling blanket. Maintain this temperature for 2 or 3 days,
or until signs of central nervous system damage have
disappeared.

2. Mannitol (50 ml of a 25% solution I.V.) or urea
(1.0 gm/kg) by I.V. infusion *to lower cerebral spinal
fluid pressure and cerebral edema;* this drug to be
given if cerebral circulation has been inadequate for 4
minutes or more [W. A. Dodds *et al.*, *Can. Anaes. Soc.
J.*, **8**, 561 (1961); *Mod. Med.*, **30**, 136, (1962)]. According to D. E. Hutcheon, in congestive heart failure,
mannitol and urea are usually contraindicated because
they further increase plasma volume. For more detailed information refer to "Water and Salt Balance"
by D. E. Hutcheon in "Drill's Pharmacology in Medicine" (third edition), The Blakiston Division, Mc-
Graw-Hill Book Company, New York.

Prevention of Coronary Heart Disease

Physicians are becoming increasingly active in the
prevention of coronary heart disease. The periodic

examination affords a uniquely propitious time to evaluate the relative risk that a particular individual will develop symptomatic coronary disease in the future, and to guide him toward the steps he should take to reduce that risk.

Among those who seem healthy, the physician looks for the following characteristics as indicative of an excess risk of developing overt coronary heart disease:

1. Familial occurrence of coronary disease at an early age.

2. Sustained blood pressure over 160/95 mm Hg.

3. Serum cholesterol of more than 260 mg %, a fasting triglyceride of more than 250 mg %, or a prominent electrophoretic pre-beta lipoprotein band.

4. Body weight 30% or more above standards listed in tables of desirable weight.

5. Fasting blood sugar of more than 120 mg %, decreased glucose tolerance or significant glycosuria.

6. History of gout or a uric acid level over 7.5 mg %.

7. Electrocardiographic abnormalities.

8. Heavy cigarette smoking.

9. Lack of physical activity.

10. Excessive exposure to emotional stress and tension.

When an individual has been identified by the industrial physician as having greater than average proneness to coronary disease, he should be referred to his personal physician for any additional studies that may be indicated, and for the establishment of a long-term program that includes repeated evaluation of the cardiovascular system and measures to remove or neutralize the coronary risk factors (H. E. Tebrock, University of Miami).

Tracheostomy

This procedure may be lifesaving, but *it should not be attempted unless a real emergency exists.*

Signs of obstruction include noisy breathing or absence of breathing, straining of neck, cyanosis, and unconsciousness. Remove foreign bodies from the mouth, and pull the lower jaw forward to prevent obstruction of the pharynx by the tongue. This simple maneuver of hyperextension will establish a clear air-

evaluation of the case. He must make the decision to induce vomiting, perform gastric lavage, or leave the material in the stomach. If the decision is emesis or gastric lavage, it is imperative that aspiration of gastric contents be avoided. This cannot be overemphasized, for even a teaspoonful of an irritant material (kerosene) may cause fatal chemical pneumonitis if aspirated into the lungs.

The physician may wish to repeat (*once*) the administration of 15 ml of *syrup* of ipecac. Vomiting is facilitated by giving fluid, approximately 200 ml of water or milk. According to A. B. Coleman, apomorphine, later neutralized by levallorphan, given parenterally has been used successfully at Duke University Hospital and other centers. Use of this drug requires skill and experience at dosage estimation [*New Engl. J. Med.*, **277**, 1135, (1967)].

Gastric lavage should be considered even if several hours have elapsed after ingestion of the poison. Warm tap water is as effective as any other material. To be thorough, 2 gallons should be used for an adult in portions of about 200–400 ml. Charcoal may be added to the lavage water to obtain a thin suspension. The child should be restrained with an encircling, tightly drawn sheet or blanket. The tube should be passed through the nose. A catheter with extra holes in it can be used. It is advisable to wash with 20–40 ml at a time. A large syringe (50–100 ml) may help if the tube tends to block. If the quantities of water used are too large, some of the contents of the stomach may be driven into the intestine; this is undesirable. Even a "successful" gastric lavage should not give the physician a feeling of security. Neither gastric lavage nor emesis should be attempted in a child who is comatose or convulsing.

In a comatose patient, the passing of a naso-gastric tube is extremely dangerous and should be done only by one familiar with the technique and under direct visualization. Testing must be done to make certain that the tube is not in the trachea or lungs. Lavage should not be attempted until it is certain that the tube is in the stomach.

Unless one is dealing with a chemical that has a marked corrosive action, elimination of the toxic material from the enteric tract should be followed by a cathartic. Administer 250 ml of 10% sodium or magnesium sulfate (for a child up to age three, give one-third of this dose). Stimulation of other excretory functions is desirable. The intravenous injection of 5% dextrose is always in order, but excessive quantities must be avoided.

"When a corrosive agent has been swallowed, it is imperative, early in the course of treatment, to have the patient swallow a weighted string, the proximal end of which is subsequently taped to the side of the face. This is important for the later treatment by dilatation when stricture of the esophagus ensues. If one delays too long, edema of the esophagus will make swallowing of the string impossible (John J. Farrell, University of Miami, personal communication)."

Coins, keys, needles, pins, etc., swallowed by children and adults rarely become lodged, but it may take 2 weeks, and in exceptional cases several months, before the object is excreted. Only in exceptional instances will surgery be indicated. Do *not* give a cathartic to force excretion of these items.

Food Poisoning

Poisoning by microorganisms that multiply in food and produce exo- and endotoxins prior to ingestion (*Staphylococcus aureus, Clostridium botulinum, C. perfringens, Streptococcus faecalis, Proteus vulgaris, Escherichia coli*) or by those that produce intoxication via infection after ingestion of contaminated food (*Salmonella typhimurium, S. enteritidis, S. cholerae-suis*) must be differentiated from intoxications by drugs and other chemicals (see Table 1, p. 667).

Treatment: Induce vomiting (give 500 ml of warm water containing from 5 to 10 teaspoonfuls of sodium chloride), or perform gastric lavage. In the absence of diarrhea, give a saline cathartic. Maintenance of respiration and adequate circulation are most important. Treat dehydration, nausea, and persistent diarrhea or persistent vomiting [G. M. Dack, *JAMA* **172,** 929 (1960)].

Intoxications by *Clostridium botulinum* Maintain respiration, protect against aspiration of stomach contents, and induce vomiting. Hypoventilation and asphyxia may require tracheostomy or the use of a

17

mechanical respirator [H. S. Davis, *JAMA* **173**, 87 (1960)]. Maintain fluid and electrolyte balance (dextrose, sodium chloride). If indicated, administer the following: oxygen, artificial respiration, whole blood or plasma, antibiotics, and sulfonamides.

Intoxications by Staphylococci This is the most common type encountered in the United States. In severely poisoned individuals, hypotension, shock, and, in rare cases, death may follow. If vomiting and diarrhea are severe, emetic drugs need not be given. For pain, give codeine sulfate (30–60 mg), or morphine sulfate (10–15 mg). Give caffeine sodium benzoate (500 mg parenterally) for severe prostration. Restore fluid balance by feeding rice water, clear broth, or tea or by the I.V. administration of plasma or blood. Broad-spectrum antibiotics should *not* be given. It is important not to interfere with the normal microbial flora.

Infections by *Salmonella* The predominant clinical picture is mild gastroenteritis. Occasionally certain strains invade the circulation and cause infections which may last many days. Some fatalities have occurred. Treatment is similar to that described for staphylococcic food poisoning. Antibiotic therapy should be withheld until specific diagnosis for *Salmonella* infection has been made.

Poisoning by *B. cereus* and *C. perfringens* No specific treatment is indicated since the symptoms are mild and of short duration. The diarrhea removes the organisms from the gastroenteric tract.

Poisoning by Streptococci Poisoning by α-hemolytic *Streptococcus* and *Streptococcus faecalis* induces the same symptoms as *B. cereus* and *C. perfringens*. No specific treatment is indicated.

Poisoning by Plants

Parts of plants are sometimes ingested accidentally, but more frequently they are swallowed thoughtlessly by both adults and children. An intoxication should always be suspected if a healthy person suddenly becomes ill.

Plants that will induce hypersensitivity or an intoxication when ingested are listed under the plant's name in Chapter IV.

Safe Handling and Use of Pesticides

The more extensively used synthetic pesticides include organochlorine compounds (OCC), organic phosphates (OP), carbamates (C), nitro compounds (N), and a miscellaneous group (M). See Table 2, p. 669.

Precautionary Measures for the Home Owner, Agricultural Sprayer, and Pest Control Operator Extreme caution must be exercised in the handling and use of all pesticides, but particularly the organic phosphates. Before using these pesticides:

1. Read and follow precisely the directions on the label.

2. Mix or prepare the pesticide solution (or dust) outdoors where free movement of air exists and in an upwind position to reduce exposure hazard.

3. Before spraying near dwellings, inform the occupants and instruct them to close windows and keep children and pets indoors until further notice. (In some instances, permission to spray will be required.)

4. Never smoke or eat while handling or spraying a pesticide preparation.

5. Wear adequate protective clothing: (a) Home owners (for backyard use of pesticides)—protect hands with rubber gloves, and wear a rubber apron. (b) Pest control operators and agricultural sprayers—*each morning* don clean cotton shirt, shorts, rubberized overalls, rubberized jacket, rubber boots, rubber gloves, sou'wester, tight-fitting goggles, and protective nose mask.

During the spraying operation:

1. No worker or sprayer should work alone when spraying. Walk upwind—walk or drive *away from* the cloud.

2. Watch for changes in wind direction.

3. Do *not* spray area near wells, cisterns, canals, or other sources of water supply.

4. Never smoke or eat while spraying or dusting.

5. If a pesticide solution should spill onto oilcloth-type clothing, rinse off as promptly as possible with a flood of water. If conventional clothing becomes contaminated, remove immediately and wash affected parts of the body with a flood of water. If spilled into

the eyes, rinse eyes with clean water for at least 15 minutes.

6. If a pesticide solution should be accidentally swallowed, try to vomit immediately. Drink a pint of water, milk, tea, coffee, or any soft drink, and vomit again. (Children should be given half this volume.) See p. 15.

7. Signs and symptoms of illness: see Organic Phosphates, p. 438; Organochlorine Compounds, p. 20; PAM, p. 448; or individual pesticides.

8. Before eating lunch, rinse off oilcloth and rubberized clothing, rubber boots, and rubber gloves with water from a hose. Wash face, hands, and arms thoroughly with soap and water. Before resuming work, replace filter in nose mask.

Following completion of daily spraying operation:

1. Return the pesticides to their proper storage place, making certain they are stored in tightly closed and clearly labeled containers, *out of reach* of all unauthorized people, particularly children, and pets.

2. Properly dispose of all empty containers—wash them repeatedly with running water from a hose before taking them to a dump. If possible, burn pesticide bags in a "hot" incinerator. Never reuse pesticide bags or other pesticide containers.

3. Decontaminate all equipment by washing with a flood of water. Make certain that the wash water does not drain into ditches, canals, or ponds.

4. Hose off all protective oilcloth-type clothing, using plenty of water. Store clothing properly for reuse. Don street clothes before leaving work area.

Responsibilities of Management

1. *Know the identity of the pesticide preparations purchased.* The pesticide manufacturer may modify or change the type or concentration of "inert" ingredients. The term "inert" found on the labels of commercial products *should not be taken literally.* Solvents and other vehicles used for this purpose may significantly influence the rate of absorption of a pesticide in man, animals, and plants, thereby intensifying or decreasing its toxicity.

2. *Know the laws of your state or county with regard to:* (a) Pesticides permitted for specific uses (county agents or agricultural commissioners can al-

ways be contacted for advice concerning the ever-changing laws and safe spraying practices). (b) Employment regulations as they relate to age, sex, physical condition, etc., of employees. (NOTE: Regardless of existing laws, individuals with known liver or blood diseases, or central nervous system disorders, should not work with pesticides).

3. *Assume the primary responsibility* for the supervision of all operations related to the storage, handling, and use of pesticides by personnel (sprayers and farm workers) and bystanders. As a rule, the labor contractor takes little responsibility for the immediate working conditions.

4. *Arrange for medical supervision* for the protection of both management and workers. The name of a physician experienced in pesticide toxicology and treatment can be secured from the local County Medical Association or Public Health Department. Medical supervision is "just good business," regardless of the size of the agricultural operation, and should include the following three services: (a) Preemployment physical examination. (b) Permission for a worker to consult the physician whenever he experiences symptoms suggestive of poisoning. (c) Permission for the physician to request the reexamination of a worker and to schedule certain tests at specific intervals, at his discretion.

5. *Have all pesticide containers carefully examined* for proper labeling, breaks or leaks, defective valves or fittings, as soon as a shipment is received. If a container is found to be damaged, or if bags are found to be too "dusty," it is important that the shipper (railroad or trucking company) be notified at once. Severe intoxication has resulted from the contamination of various other materials or articles transported in a freight car or truck used for the transport of organic phosphates.

6. *Store all pesticides* in the original tightly closed containers, in a restricted area, securely locked. Select the location of a storeroom (or building) removed from all dwellings, and consider the direction of prevailing winds in order to protect nearby residents from accidental leakage or spillage from broken containers. In an air-conditioned building, make certain that the total air supply system does not become contaminated and

that the effluent air is ejected high enough for ready dilution.

7. *Education of workers.* Obviously, acquainting the worker with the dangers associated with the handling of these compounds must be in language he understands. It should be made clear to him that these toxic agents can be safely handled and used as long as specific precautionary measures are strictly observed.

8. *Protective clothing* must be worn at all times. The degree of protection required varies with the operation, and with atmospheric and other conditions.

a. Indoor workers. In areas with efficient hood ventilation, the following is required: ¾-length rubber gloves, rubber work shoes or boots, full-length latex rubber apron, approved respirator or mask, and protective goggles. No worker or sprayer should work alone when handling these hazardous materials.

b. Field sprayers. Field workers may suffer total body exposure to vapor or dust clouds unless properly protected. Each morning don: clean cotton shirt and shorts, rubberized overalls, rubberized jacket, rubber boots, rubber gloves, sou'wester, tight-fitting goggles, and protective nose mask.

c. Pilot of spray plane. Generally speaking, the ground crew is more likely to suffer exposure than the pilot of a spray plane. Nevertheless, the pilot must observe specific precautions to avoid exposure. He should wear: freshly laundered underwear, socks, and clothing every day; approved mask or respirator when spraying parathion or other organic phosphate of this toxic group; goggles and rubber gloves. The motor of the plane should be "off" when the dust is being loaded. The pilot should observe the "no smoking" and "no eating" regulations. Dust should emerge well behind the pilot and, as with the ground crew, he must make certain he does not return through the dust cloud.

All personnel handling organic phosphates should change to clean underwear and clothing daily. Regardless of the degree of pesticide exposure, work clothes should never be worn home, nor street clothes at work.

Thorough washing with soap and water is a must before eating, drinking, or smoking. At the completion of the work day, all parts of the body should be washed under a shower with plenty of soap.

9. *Atmospheric conditions*

a. In hot weather. Management and supervisory personnel must exercise additional care and caution, since intoxications are more likely to occur. Frequent clothing changes or rinsing off of protective rubber garments is particularly important for sprayers operating in subtropical or tropical climates.

b. In windy weather. It is best not to spray at all, since drift is likely to become a problem, contaminating homes, ponds, and streams.

10. *The safe handling of organic phosphates* is best instituted and supervised by a trained crew.

a. Drums should be opened either outdoors or under a ventilated hood. Bungs must be unscrewed *slowly* to release internal pressure.

b. A closed pipe system should be used to transfer liquid organic phosphates from a storage tank to a dust-impregnating unit. Similarly, concentrates to be blended with "inert" materials should be handled in a *closed* system with exhaust ventilation and a dust collector. The scrubber should be checked routinely for organic phosphate content.

c. Mechanical exhaust ventilation should be provided for all weighing, bagging, dumping, and loading locations, unless these operations are performed in the open air.

d. Before disposal, empty bottles or drums should be washed with a flood of water from a hose, or better yet, with a solution of caustic soda. Punch holes in drums and take both bottles and drums to a private or city dump. At the end of each day, collect all empty pesticide bags and take them to the dump. They may be burned there if the polluted air will not create a hazard; they are best disposed of in a "hot" incinerator.

e. If an organic phosphate is spilled, add sawdust or soil and remove to a disposal area. If spillage occurs in a building, thoroughly wash area with soap or soda ash, and flush thoroughly.

11. *Responsibility of management to the population.*

a. Contact the Food and Drug Administration with

regard to the limits of contamination permitted by law in raw agricultural products or in finished foods.

b. Plant contamination. For some reason not fully understood, retention of organic phosphate pesticides or their metabolites may continue in plants for much longer than the calculated period. Areas sprayed with certain organic phosphates should not be entered for 30 days without protective clothing. It is important that residents in or near agricultural areas be warned of the danger of entering such contaminated fields.

c. Contamination of waters. Directions to operating personnel must be explicit regarding measures to be used to avoid contamination of wells, creeks, canals, ponds, and rivers. If accidental contamination should occur in spite of all precautionary measures, the Public Health Service should be notified immediately.

Medical Supervision of Workers Handling Pesticides The physician will render medical supervision of employees. To fulfill his responsibility he may request:

1. Preemployment physical examination of all employees.

2. Certain hematologic, chemical, or other tests (RBC cholinesterase and plasma pseudocholinesterase activities) to determine individual suitability for specific work.

3. Permission for the employee to see him whenever symptoms suggestive of a pesticide intoxication are experienced or observed.

4. Permission to request the employee to reappear for examination or for certain tests as indicated by the employee's job or physical condition.

5. Notification from the employer, in writing, whenever an employee is to be dismissed, so that he may request a final examination and/or certain tests if he wishes.

6. Opportunity to acquaint himself with the occupational operation, so that he may better advise the employees regarding personal hygiene and the protection required for specific jobs.

The physician in turn may agree to keep the employer informed, in writing, of the status of the employees. He will assist the employer in outlining first-aid measures and emergency procedures. He will assume responsibility for arranging hospital and/or other services in the event that the employee should require such care as a result of an intoxication or injury related to his job.

The physician must, of course, be thoroughly familiar with all phases of pesticide toxicology and with the methods of treating intoxications caused by these compounds.

Proof of an intoxication by a pesticide is dependent upon: (a) history of a positive exposure, (b) clinical findings consistent with the picture of intoxication, including response to accepted treatment, and (c) corroborative laboratory findings.

Exposure by Inhalation: Choking and Suffocation

An asphyxiated child suspected of having a foreign body in the airway (coughing, gagging, dyspnea) should be suspended momentarily by the ankles or inverted over one arm and given a sharp blow between the shoulder blades to dislodge the obstructing material (Fig. 8). Persistent severe cyanosis may require tracheostomy.

An adult should be placed on his side and a sharp blow administered between the shoulders. The dislodged material can then usually be removed from the victim's mouth (Fig. 16).

If choking was caused by exposure to fumes, smoke, etc., remove the patient from the contaminated atmosphere. If he is unconscious, keep the airway open (remove foreign bodies from mouth and throat and pull the tongue forward) and loosen or remove all tight

Fig. 16

clothing. Watch the patient constantly. If there are indications that he will vomit, then place him in a prone (face down) position so that fluid, such as vomitus, will flow out and not obstruct the airway. Administer artificial respiration if necessary.

A burn of the respiratory tract may follow exposure to irritating gases or hot vapors. Fluid may subsequently collect in the lungs (pulmonary edema). This may not appear for several hours after the burn. These patients should be taken to a hospital for proper treatment and observation. During transport keep the patient in a sitting position and administer oxygen if necessary.

Skin Exposure

Materials spilled on the skin are removed most effectively by thorough washing with soap and plenty of water. Do *not* waste time looking for solutions to neutralize or solubilize the chemical. If a considerable portion of the body has been exposed, remove all clothing under the shower and *flood with water*. The oily sap of certain fruits, leaves, stems, or bark of a number of plants, bushes, or trees produces dermatitis in sensitive people. After contact, wash hands and exposed skin thoroughly with laundry soap and water. See also Poison Ivy, p. 484 and p. 350.

Eye Exposure

Copious irrigation with water for at least 10 minutes will usually remove irritating vapors, acids, alkalis, or solvents splashed into the eye.

Eye injuries should be treated immediately, and all but the most trivial should be referred to an ophthalmologist for more definitive treatment.

Treatment of Burns

Chemical burn (acid, alkalies, creosote): Wash affected parts with water for at least 15 minutes. Acid burns may be subsequently washed with 0.5% sodium bicarbonate; alkali burns with 1% acetic acid or 1% citric acid. Cover with a dry cloth. If burns are due to hydrofluoric acid, continue irrigation for three to five or even 12 hours. If quicklime (particles of calcium oxide) is the offending agent, remove all solid particles *before* the application of water, then use a *stream* of water under pressure to remove the remaining particles before they dissolve with the liberation of heat.

Do not use a grease, powder, or ointment in the first aid treatment of burns, *except* for sunburn or other minor burns. For these a skin cream or oil may be applied. For treatment of shock, see p. 29.

Hospital treatment includes sedation, cleansing of the wound with a bland soap and water, removal of dead tissue, grafting, fluid therapy, tetanus prophylaxis (booster dose of toxoid or antitoxin), and the administration of antibiotics and vitamins (moderate doses of vitamin B complex I.V. during the first few days, followed by vitamin C, 1000–1500 mg daily until the wound has healed). For eye burns, see Eye Exposure, p. 26. If pain is a problem, see Scalded and burned skin.

Scalded and burned skin: First aid treatment for thermal, electrical, and chemical burns includes *immediate* cooling. If immersion of the affected part in ice water is not possible, apply ice water, ice cubes, or cold compresses. This method, practiced by the Eskimos for many years, reduces pain and decreases the edema and blistering (probably through vasoconstriction and reduction of capillary permeability and oxygen requirements of the involved tissues). Immersion or cold application should be continued for at least 30 minutes, or up to 5 hours or more, depending on the severity and area involved. Immersion should be repeated if pain recurs, thus reducing the need for analgesic drugs.

Subsequent treatment depends on the individual case. Superficial burns heal faster when exposed to air, but exposure retards the healing time of deep burns [D. Eastwood *et al., Acta Chir. Scand.* **131**, 205 (1966)]. Application of a dressing of 0.5% aqueous silver nitrate has also been recommended. (This is about $\frac{1}{20}$ the concentration of silver nitrate used 50 years ago for this purpose.) They caution that silver nitrate is potentially dangerous, extreme care must be used, and continuous attention paid to the dressings and moisture loss. If the dressing is permitted to dry, silver nitrate will precipitate as silver chloride and silver bicarbonate on the wound surface; it will also form sodium nitrate and probably cause depletion of electrolytes

leading to hyponatremia and hypochloremia. Therefore, it is important that dressings be changed frequently and kept soaked with the silver nitrate
solution. Monitoring of serum sodium chloride and
potassium is important in all burn cases, but particularly when silver nitrate is being applied. This is
particularly important in the treatment of children
[C. C. Bondoc *et al.*, *J. Pediat. Surg.* **2**, 22 (1967)]. In
extensive burns treated for a week or longer with 0.5 %
silver nitrate, bacteria (*Aerobacter cloacal*) that reduce
nitrate to nitrite may grow, resulting in the production
of methemoglobin. [This is a new complication reported by J. L. Ternberg and F. Luce, *Surgery* **63**, 328
(1968).]

"Several Medical Letter consultants prefer cephal-
othin for initial treatment of bacterial sepsis, pending
culture and sensitivity results, because of its bacteri-
cidal activity against many organisms, including penicillinase-producing staphylococci. Other clinicians
have successfully used penicillin G combined with a
semi-synthetic penicillin such as cloxacillin or
methicillin (for penicillinase-producing staphylococci). For suspected Gram-negative infections,
streptomycin, chloramphenicol or kanamycin can be
used pending laboratory studies. For *Pseudomonas*
infections, polymyxin B or colistimethate must be
used [Medical Letter, May 20, 1966]."

Pain

For pain, give two tablets of aspirin, Bufferin, Em-
perin Compound, or Pyramidon dissolved in water. If
necessary, give the same dose in 20 minutes, but do
not give more than eight tablets per day.

For a variety of reasons, it is not recommended that
an opiate be used routinely in First Aid treatment. A
patient with a moderately severe burn is usually in
shock; therefore, a narcotic, if administered, may not
appear to affect the patient. The physician, unless
experienced in this type of treatment, may consider
giving a second dose; this is likely to influence unfa-
vorably the patient's respiration and circulation.

Apply an icebag to painful areas. Pain due to burns
is treated by *immediate* immersion in cold water
(5-10°C). See Burns, p. 26. For cooling of the skin by

ethyl chloride or by a new fluoromethane compound, see *Brit. Med. J.*, **1**, 250 (1961).

Caution: Large doses of aspirin, Bufferin, and certain related drugs, will make a person on Dicumarol or warfarin therapy sensitive to capillary damage and to internal hemorrhages.

Shock

Shock may be recognized by cold and clammy skin, dulling of sensibilities, a pale complexion, and a weak and rapid pulse. The individual's temperature and blood pressure will be low.

Treatment: Do not move the patient more than is necessary. Loosen tight clothing, prevent sweating, and keep him slightly cool. Avoid drafts. He may lie on his back or side, with pillows or clothing under his head and legs. A patient with head or chest injuries should be placed with two or three pillows under his shoulders and head (Fig. 17).

If the patient is conscious and thirsty, help him to sit up and give him lukewarm water, or lukewarm coffee or tea. If medical help is delayed, give him a pint of water containing ¾ teaspoon of baking soda and ¼ tea-

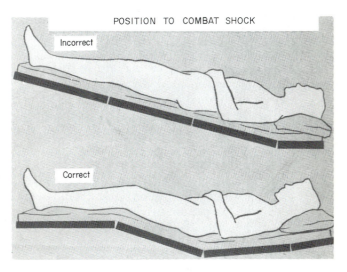

POSITION TO COMBAT SHOCK

Incorrect

Correct

Fig. 17

Taken from M. K. Mendenhall and J. A. Jenicek, *Texas J. Med.* **56**, 76, 1960

spoon of table salt. Do *not* give alcohol. If the patient is semiconscious, or if he has abdominal injuries, do *not* give any fluids. Oxygen is beneficial.

Wounds

Cleanse the injured area (abrasion, incision, or laceration) with a hexachlorophene soap (pHisoHex) and water. Leave some of the suds on the wound and apply a loose bandage.

To remove grease from a wound, carefully wipe off as much as possible with sterile gauze pads. Follow by gentle scrubbing with a mild soap. Remove remaining grease with isopropyl alcohol, acetone (flammable), or methyl chloroform (trichlorethane) (nonflammable). Because acetone and chloroform may be irritating to the skin, apply with caution when such treatment is needed.

There is always the danger of tetanus with a puncture wound, particularly in southern states. Therefore, cleanse with soap and water, bandage, and report to a physician for possible immunization. (See also Tetanus, p. 33.)

Hemorrhage

To stop bleeding, apply pressure directly to the wound by firmly pressing with sterile gauze pads or, if none are available, a clean cloth. Once bleeding has stopped, bandage the wound fairly tightly with 6–10 layers of 2-inch gauze pads. In case of severe laceration, a tourniquet may be needed.

If a tourniquet (which may be a 2-inch bandage, stocking, belt, or necktie) is required, apply it a few centimeters above the wound edge, or slightly above the joint if the laceration is just below the elbow or knee. Apply it only tightly enough to arrest bleeding; take care not to obliterate completely the pulse in the part distal to the tourniquet. A tourniquet should *never* be covered. Take the patient to a hospital or physician immediately. See also Snakes for use of the tourniquet, p. 532.

Itching

While itching is most often a mild disorder of brief duration, it is sometimes a severe, prolonged, and agonizing disorder resistant to therapy. Corticosteroids, administered systemically or topically, often relieve itching. Some of the over-the-counter preparations containing phenol or menthol are sometimes helpful. Oral antihistamines, because of their sedative effects, as well as other sedative drugs will at times give relief. Topical preparations containing antihistamines are of little value, and repeated use can cause sensitization reactions. Ice packs can sometimes be helpful, but frequently none of the agents presented here give substantial relief. A variety of lotions, creams and other topical preparations may be helpful.

In some persons and in some localized conditions, including atopic dermatitis, poison ivy and other contact dermatoses, and insect bites, the brief application of very hot water to the affected area has brought immediate and complete relief lasting as long as several hours [*Med. Letter* (July 1, 1966)].

Caution: The water should be hot enough to cause considerable discomfort when it is applied, but not hot enough to burn (the range of 50 to 60°C – 120 to 140° F – is suggested, subject to cautious trial). If the water is too hot, damage can, or course, result; especially where a chronic or recurrent condition is to be treated, the patient would be well advised to purchase a suitable thermometer. If the water is not hot enough, it may aggravate the itching instead of relieving it. The hot water treatment is most suitable for localized itching; if large areas are to be treated, the water should be applied to a small area at a time. The required temperature is much too high to be used safely in a bath or shower.

Diving

Overbreathing is sometimes practiced by the free diver or skin diver. During hyperventilation, a diver "blows off" carbon dioxide, replacing it with oxygen, in other words, he fills his lungs to capacity with air. The danger point is reached when the oxygen level drops below a certain point, or when the carbon dioxide level rises above a certain level. In either case, when this occurs he *must* start breathing, and at this moment, as he inhales water, he is likely to drown (T. R. Struhl, University of Miami).

Diving with scuba or other compressed air equipment may lead to poisoning by oxygen, nitrogen, carbon dioxide, carbon monoxide, or air. As the diver is

31

exposed to the increased water pressure, nitrogen, helium, and oxygen go in solution in blood and other tissues. The nitrogen in the inhaled air may become an anesthetic producing narcosis ("rapture of the deep"). Oxygen breathed at a partial pressure greater than 2 atmospheres may cause convulsions, and the physiological or toxic action of carbon dioxide and carbon monoxide are potentiated because of their increased partial pressures.

For a diver who has spent more than an hour at a depth exceeding approximately 12 meters (40 feet), a too rapid ascent presents no oxygen hazard because this gas can be used by the tissues, but in changing from the liquid to the gaseous state, nitrogen emboli will block the circulation or inflate the tissues producing a variety of symptoms referred to as bends, or caisson disease. When the bubbles of nitrogen enter the pulmonary capillary bed, they can readily pass to the left chambers of the heart and into the arterial circulation, thereby inducing aeroembolism. When the bubbles enter the poorer circulation around the joints, they produce emboli in the end arteries causing pain in the joints. The name "bends" describes the position assumed to ease the pain. Skin diving usually denotes diving without compressed air equipment, and if this is so, there is no possibility of the person developing the bends.

Caution: Any type of diving should not be undertaken by anyone suffering from an infection in the nasal passages, sinuses, or eustachian tubes, or from pulmonary tuberculosis, chronic bronchitis, emphysema, asthma, or a cardiovascular disease. The obese and the elderly should also refrain from diving. Use of ear plugs is dangerous because the external pressure may drive them into the ear. Gas-forming foods and beverages should not be consumed prior to diving. Breath-holding by any diver (when using compressed air equipment) during rapid ascent may rupture the alveoli, resulting in subcutaneous emphysema and air embolism. The diver should exhale *continuously* during rapid ascent. Failure to observe this precaution from a depth of about 10 meters (33 feet; pressure of 2 atmospheres), and even from a depth of 10 feet, has caused fatalities (T. R. Struhl, University of Miami, personal communication). Chewing of gum to "pop the ears" will cause gastroenteric pain due to expansion of the swallowed gas. Never dive alone, and do not fail to use a buddy-line.

The mechanism of death from immersion in salt water is different from that in fresh water. The osmotic pressure of sea water is greater than that of extracellular fluid, and the presence of any quantity of it in the lungs results in an osmotic pressure gradient. Sodium chloride diffuses into the extracellular fluid, and water is drawn rapidly through the pulmonary endothelium into the lungs. This may lead to massive pulmonary edema, hypoxia, increased viscosity of the blood, electrolyte imbalance, and cardiac failure.

By contrast, the inhalation of fresh water creates an osmotic gradient in the opposite direction. Water is rapidly drawn into the circulation causing rupture of the red blood cells. Blood may be diluted 50% within two or three minutes. Because of these changes, the heart is subjected to hypoxia, overfilling, potassium excess, and sodium deficit leading to ventricular fibrillation [*Lancet* **1**, 468 (1962); *JAMA*, **203**, 337 (1968)].

Treatment: In caisson disease and air embolism, recompression should be initiated promptly even if not absolutely required, since it is not hazardous to the patient, and after 48 hours it is rarely helpful. If the patient has to be flown to a recompression chamber, the flight should be made at the lowest safe altitude. If recompression facilities are not available, administer oxygen for several hours. This will promote shrinkage of the air bubbles and promote elimination of the inert gases (particularly nitrogen) from the body. See also Nitrogen, p. 424, and Oxygen, p. 442.

Tetanus (Lockjaw)

A person with a deep puncture wound should see a physician promptly for evaluation and possible immunization.

The administration of a reinforcing ("booster") dose of tetanus toxoid is indicated if the individual has received active immunization during the past 15 years. This booster dose of tetanus toxoid, given at the time of injury, rapidly produces protective antibody levels.

"Passive immunization with tetanus immune globulin (human) at the time of injury is advisable in those patients who have not received prior immunization with tetanus toxoid and in whom the risk of reactions to equine tetanus antitoxin must be avoided ("New

Drugs," American Medical Association, Chicago, 1966)."

Tetanus immune globulin (Homo-Tet; Hyper-Tet; Hu-Tet) prepared from *human* blood plasma is virtually free from the risk of inducing hypersensitivity; it is therefore preferable to the tetanus antitoxin of animal origin.

"All authorities agree that active immunization with tetanus toxoid should be instituted in those patients who receive passive immunization with tetanus immune globulin. However, some feel that the initiation of such a program should be delayed for one month after the administration of a tetanus immune globulin, whereas other authorities believe that interference with antibody response from the passively acquired material is not sufficiently great to outweigh the advantage of beginning active immunization when the patient is at hand [*JAMA* **192**, 471 (1965)]."

Dosage: For passive immunization, the usual intramuscular dose of tetanus immune globulin (*human*) for adults and children is 4 units per kilogram body weight, although larger doses may be used (250 units may be given to an adult).

Treatment of tetanus: The administration of 3000–6000 units of tetanus immune globulin (human) has produced satisfactory results. Higher doses have also been used, but the optimal therapeutic dosage has not yet been established [*JAMA*, **192**, 471 (1965)].

Note: "Tetanus antitoxin of human origin, which carries no risk of complications, more quickly confers a higher degree of immunity than equine antitoxin. The cost of treating reactions to horse serum, together with the financial loss incurred by work absence, far outweighs the cost of human antitoxin. The use of antitoxin of animal origin is no longer medically or legally defensible [B. J. F. Perey, *Can. Med. Assoc. J.* **94**, 437 (1966)]."

It is of interest to note that the U.S. Army now immunizes against tetanus only once every 6 years and is trying to stretch the time to once every 10 years. In line with this is the remark by G. Edsall *et al.*, that routine boosters in individuals known to have had primary immunization, including a reinforcing dose, be given only at 10-year intervals, and that emergency boosters be given no closer than 1 year apart [*JAMA* **202**, 111 (1967)].

CHAPTER II

DRUGS AND ADULT DOSAGES
for the
TREATMENT OF INTOXICATIONS

Gastric Lavage

Water.

Milk.

Tea.

Tannic acid, 2 % solution.

Vegetable oil (after ingestion of a corrosive agent).

U.S.P. Powdered Charcoal (10 gm) in water (consistency of a moderately thick soup). (Supplier: S. B. Penick Co., 100 Church Street, New York.) Charcoal may be administered after vomiting or lavage and left in the stomach to reduce absorption of toxic material. The so-called "universal antidote," composed of charcoal, tannic acid and magnesium oxide (also "burned toast") is essentially useless. [D. Henschler, and P. Kreutzer, *Deut. Med. Wochschr.* **50**, 2241 (1966)].

Disturbances of the Digestive Tract

Stimulants

Pilocarpine NO_3, dose 5 mg P.O.

Neostigmine Br, dose 15 mg P.O.

Neostigmine methylsulfate, dose 0.5 mg S.C.

Methacholine Cl (Mecholyl), dose 10 mg S.C.; 0.2 gm P.O.

Bethanechol Cl (Urecholine), dose 5–15 mg P.O.

Mild laxatives.

Antispasmodics

Atropine sulfate, dose 0.5 mg P.O.

35

Tr. of belladonna, dose 0.6 ml P.O.

Paregoric (Tr. of opium camphorated), dose 2–4 ml.

Adiphenine HCl (Trasentine), dose 50–100 mg P.O.

Papaverine HCl, dose 0.1 gm, P.O.; 30 mg I.M., I.V.

Propantheline Br (Pro-Banthine Br), dose 15–30 mg P.O.

Diphemanil methylsulfate (Prantal), 50 mg–0.2 gm, P.O.

Calcium gluconate, 10% solution 10–20 ml, I.V.

Calcium lactate, 10% solution 10–20 ml, I.V.

Diphenoxylate HCl (Lomotil) 2.5 mg, P.O.

To Induce Central Nervous System Stimulation

Caffeine and sodium benzoate, dose 0.5 gm P.O., I.M.

Amphetamine sulfate (Benzedrine), dose 5 mg P.O.

Pentylenetetrazol (Metrazol), dose 5 ml of a 10% solution I.V., as diagnostic test (return of reflexes indicates that no other analeptics are required).

To Counteract Convulsions

Mephenesin, dose 0.5–1.0 gm by *slow* I.V. injection, or 1.0–3.0 gm by I.V. drip.

Phenobarbital, dose 30–60 mg P.O. or parenteral.

Amobarbital (Amytal), dose 0.5–0.75 gm I.V.

Thiopental Sodium (Pentothal), dose 50–75 mg. I.V.

Diphenylhydantoin (Dilantin), dose 100 mg P.O., I.M.

Paraldehyde, dose 4 ml P.O. (If paraldehyde is to be administered I.M., make certain that the drug is prepared for I.M. use).

Tribromoethanol (Avertin), dose 60 mg/kg by rectum. Total dose not to exceed 8 gm for women, or 10 gm for men.

Extrapyramidal Reactions or Tremors Induced by Tranquilizers (Parkinsonian Syndrome, Tetanus-like Syndrome, Chorea)

For tremors of parkinsonism (paralysis agitans)

Trihexyphenidyl HCl (Artane). Begin with 1 mg P.O. daily or twice daily and gradually increase to 2 mg 4 times daily, if needed.

Benztropine methanesulfonate (Cogentin). Begin with 1 mg for first 24 hours, I.V. slowly, increase to 1–2 mg twice daily.

For muscular rigidity

Diphenhydramine HCl (Benadryl) dose 25 mg P.O. or
I.V. 4 times daily.

To Increase Blood Pressure

Ephedrine sulfate, dose 10–25 mg, I.V., I.M.

Neo-Synephrine HCl, dose 2–4 mg I.V.

Levarterenol bitartrate (Levophed), dose 2–4 μg/
minute by continuous I.V. infusion (0.5–1 ml/min-
ute of solution containing 4 ml of commercial
solution diluted to 1000 ml with 5% dextrose or
0.9% sodium chloride). Caution must be employed
if a dose of 0.5–1 mg of the base is administered as a
single I.M. injection.

Isoproterenol (Isuprel), 0.5 mg in 500 ml 5% dextrose
in water, or in 0.9% aqueous NaCl. (Drug may improve circulation in conditions of diminution of
myocardial contractility or an exceptionally low
pulse rate).

To Increase Cardiac Rate

Epinephrine (Adrenalin). See Anaphylactic Drug
Reaction, p. 56.

Isoproterenol (Isuprel). See To Increase Blood Pressure, p. 37.

Ephedrine sulfate, 25–50 mg I.M., or 15 mg I.V.

To Reduce Blood Pressure in a Hypertensive Crisis

Reserpine, 2.5–5.0 mg I.M. or I.V.; repeat, if needed,
at 8-hour intervals. Give also an antacid to neutralize the excess gastric acidity induced by this drug.
(Dose for mild hypertension: 0.25–1.0 mg/day in
divided doses.)

Trimethaphan camphorsulfonate (Arfonad). Dilute 10
ml vial containing 500 mg in 500 ml of saline for
continuous I.V. infusion, adjust rate as required.

Methyldopa (Aldomet). Dosage is 250 mg, 2 to 4 times
a day P.O.

To Stimulate Cardiac Contractile Force

Digoxin. Initial dose 1.5–2 mg I.V., I.M., or P.O., followed by 0.25–0.75 mg daily.

Lanatoside C (Cedilanid). Initial dose 0.8 mg I.V., followed by 0.2 to 0.4 mg every 2–4 hours. (This drug is
not used for maintaining digitalization.)

Digitalis. Except for contractile force, digitalis is usually a myocardial depressant.

To Lower Cerebrospinal Fluid Pressure

Urea. Give I.V. 0.1–1.0 gm per kilogram body weight as a 30% solution in 5% dextrose at a rate of 3 ml/minute. The whole dose should be given over a period of 1 to 1½ hours.

Mannitol, 1 gm/kg, as a 25% solution in 1000 ml water given over a period of 6 hours.

To Counteract Respiratory Depression

Oxygen.

Artificial respiration.

Curare antagonists.

Neostigmine methylsulfate, dose 0.5 mg S.C. or I.M.

Edrophonium Cl (Tensilon), dose 5–10 mg repeatedly I.V., dose not to exceed 30 mg.

(Atropine to lessen excessive side effects of these drugs.)

To Replace Potassium

Potassium chloride. Oral dose: 1 gm, 1–6 times per day. Intravenous, 250 mg–2 gm, *slowly* as an infusion. Injection rate should not exceed 10 ml/minute, with a concentration of 80 mEq/liter. If potassium deficit is not severe, use vials containing 20 ml of 15% potassium chloride (each vial contains 40 mEq of potassium diluted with proper solutions of dextrose or sodium chloride to 1000 ml). Potassium gluconate (Kaon) and elixir potassium bicarbonate (K-Lyte) may also be used.

Foods high in potassium (mg/100 gm) include the following*:

Yeast, brewers, dry	1700
Apricots, dry	1700
Bran flakes	1200
Potato chips	880
Peanut butter	820
Dates and figs, dry, approx.	790
Almonds, dry	710
Prunes, dry	600

* Taken from "Nutrition Data," 4th Edition, published by H. J. Heinz Co.

Bananas	400
Carrots, raw	410
Red beet, raw	350
Meats, cooked, approx.	300
Cantaloupe	230
Grapefruit, raw	200
Orange juice, fresh	182

To Counteract Acidosis

Sodium bicarbonate. If CO_2 combining power is 20–40 vol. %, give P.O. 5 gm of $NaHCO_3$ every 20–40 minutes until CO_2 combining power is above 45 volumes percent or until urine is alkaline. If CO_2 combining power is below 20 volumes percent, give P.O. or slowly I.V., 0.8 gm/kg of $NaHCO_3$ (5% aqueous solution, or 5% $NaHCO_3$ added to 5% aqueous dextrose).

Sodium lactate. If CO_2 combining power is below 20 volumes percent, give P.O., or slowly I.V. $\frac{1}{6}M$ sodium lactate, 60 ml/kg.

If cathartic was administered, initiate I.V. treatment for combating acidosis; continue P.O. medication as soon as feasible.

To Induce Diuresis of an Acid Urine

Ammonium chloride. Dose: 1 gm P.O. 4 times a day for a few days (at this time the diuretic action of the drug ceases).

To Induce Diuresis of an Alkaline Urine

Sodium lactate, $\frac{1}{6}M$ solution plus 5 volumes of 5% dextrose, at a rate of 100-200 ml/kg during the first 24 hours.

Sodium bicarbonate. Dose: 2 gm P.O. up to 4 times a day.

Acetazolamide (Diamox), 0.5-1.0 gm P.O. 3 or 4 times daily. I.V. dose: 0.5 gm 3 or 4 times daily.

To Treat Metal Intoxications

Dimercaprol (BAL), see p. 224
Calcium disodium edetate (Calcium Disodium Versenate), see p. 236.
Desferrioxamine (Desferal), see p. 334.
Dithiocarb, see p. 583.
D-Penicillamine, see p. 452.

To Reduce Hyperthermia (Fever)

Wet towel.
Ice bath.
Alcohol sponge.
Promethazine HCl (Phenergan) and meperidine HCl, see p. 12.
Acetylsalicylic acid and related drugs.

To Counteract Methemoglobinemia

Blood.
Oxygen.
Methylene blue. Dose 0.15 gm I.V. (1–2 mg/kg as a 1.0% solution).
Ascorbic acid. 0.5–1.0 gm P.O. or S.C. as needed.

Narcotic Agents

Of Plant Origin
Codeine phosphate (methylmorphine). Adult dose: 30 mg P.O., S.C.
Pantopon (containing 50% morphine) (Omnipon). Adult dose: 20 ml P.O., S.C.
Morphine sulfate. Adult dose: 10 mg S.C., I.M.
Opium (paregoric). Adult dose: 5 ml P.O.
Dimethylmorphine (thebaine). Clinically not useful.
Marihuana (cannabis). Clinically not useful.

Synthetics Chemically Related to Morphine or Codeine
Dihydrocodeine (Parzone; Paracodin). Adult dose: 30 mg P.O. and parenterally.
Ethylmorphine HCl (Dionin). Adult dose: 15 mg P.O.
Dihydrocodeinone bitartrate (Hycodan; Dicodid). Adult dose: 10 mg P.O.
Oxymorphone HCl (Numorphan). Adult dose: 5 mg P.O., 1.5 mg I.M., 0.75 mg I.V.
Methyldihydromorphinone (Metopon). Adult dose: 3 mg P.O.
Levorphanol tartrate (Levorphan; Levo-Dromoran). Adult dose: 2 mg P.O., S.C.
Dihydromorphinone HCl (Dilaudid). Adult dose: 2 mg P.O., S.C.
Apomorphine HCl. Adult dose: 2–6 mg S.C.
Diacetylmorphine (heroin). Clinically not useful.

Synthetics Chemically Not Related to Morphine

Meperidine HCl (Demerol; Dolantin; Pethidine). Adult dose: 50 mg P.O., I.M.

Alphaprodine HCl (Nisentil). Adult dose: 40 mg S.C., 20 mg I.V.

Anileridine HCl (Leritine). Adult dose: 25 mg P.O.

Piminodine ethylate (Alvodine). Adult dose: 25 mg P.O., 10 mg S.C., I.M.

Methadone HCl (Amidone; Dolphine). Adult dose: 5 mg P.O., I.M., S.C.

Phenazocine HBr (Prinadol; NIH-7519). Adult dose: 1 mg I.M., I.V.

Antagonists for Opiates

Nalorphine HCl (Nalline). 5.0 mg (parenteral). Usual total dose 2–40 mg in divided doses. Doses for newborn infant 0.2 mg. (*This is a narcotic.*)

Levallorphan tartrate (Lorfan). 1.0 mg, then 0.5 mg (parenteral) as required. Total dose *not* to exceed 5 mg. Dose for newborn infant 0.05 mg. (This is not a narcotic.)

Note: For a complete list of the Drugs Subject to Federal Narcotic Laws, see General Circular No. 262 published by the Treasury Department, Bureau of Narcotics, Washington, D. C. 20225.

CHAPTER III
SUPPORTIVE TREATMENT

Respiration

Respiratory embarrassment must be recognized and corrected promptly.

1. If there is obstruction to breathing, establish airway by pulling tongue forward, inserting an airway tube, or doing a tracheostomy.

2. Begin artificial respiration as outlined on p. 2.

3. If difficulty in breathing is a result of pulmonary edema, the problem is limitation of respiratory exchange by accumulation of fluid in the alveoli. In this case, treatment should be carried out with the patient in the sitting position. Administration of oxygen is most important.

Pulmonary edema may result from the inhalation, ingestion, injection, or skin absorption of chemicals. Chemicals that cause pulmonary edema by inhalation cause local irritation of the alveolar epithelium resulting in permeability changes that allow passage of fluid into the air spaces. The edema may be delayed for hours after the exposure to some chemicals (nickel carbonyl, oxides of nitrogen, and phosgene) so that an individual may be well enough to go home but awakens gasping for breath in the night. In general, any chemical vapor, fume, or mist that is carried deep into the lung tissue may cause pulmonary edema. Signs and symptoms include dyspnea, cyanosis, rapid respiration, noisy wet breathing (rales), and in severe cases, foaming from the nose and mouth. Primary treatment involves rest and oxygen. See also pages 245, 318.

Circulation

Peripheral hypotension of vasomotor origin usually responds to pure vasoconstrictors (Wyamine) or to drugs that cause vasoconstriction and have an inotropic effect on the myocardium (Levophed, Aramine). Occasionally the inotropic effects are of primary importance, especially if vasoconstriction is already a major problem, in which case neosynephrine or Isuprel are drugs of choice. Selection of the proper drugs for individual patients requires the highest degree of knowledge and sophistication on the part of the physician.

Whole blood or blood plasma are the replacement fluids of choice in oligemic shock. If they are not readily available, use human serum albumin or dextran. For more information on the choice of transfusion material, see *JAMA*, **180**, 230 (1962).

Congestive heart failure usually responds to digitalis (or a related glycoside) I.V. or P.O. and a diuretic. Digitalizing doses: for a *most rapid* effect, use ouabain, 0.3–0.75 mg I.V., peak effects within 2 hours; a *most useful* drug is digoxin, 0.75–2.0 mg I.V., peak effect within 5 hours. Diuretics: meralluride (Mercuhydrin) 1–2 ml I.M.; mercaptomerin (Thiomerin) (Diucardyn) 0.5–2.0 ml S.C.; ethacrynic acid 25–50 mg; and furosemide (Lasix) 40 mg P.O.

For cardiac arrhythmias, consider using quinidine hydrochloride or gluconate, or procainamide (Pronestyl) P.O. or I.M. For arrhythmias K^+ I.V., lidocaine (Xylocaine) I.V., or diphenylhydantoin (Dilantin) I.M. are also very important (R. J. Boucek, University of Miami, personal communication).

Only in extreme emergencies is the feebly beating heart an indication for the use of epinephrine. Inject directly into the heart muscle 0.5-2 ml of a 1:1000 solution of epinephrine previously diluted with 10 volumes of isotonic saline. This treatment must be carried out with the full realization that it might precipitate ventricular fibrillation in a heart that is damaged by a chemical or by intrinsic cardiac pathology (coronary artery disease, etc.). This is particularly true in a heart sensitized by halogenated hydrocarbons, benzene, cyclopropane, or certain other chemicals. If circulatory arrest (either ventricular fibrillation or cardiac arrest) prevails for a period beyond three minutes, serious neurological sequelae or death may result. The following procedures should be used.

1. Apply cardiac massage immediately, as described on p. 8 with or without accompanying artificial respiration.

2. Use a Pneophore-positive pressure device (Mine Safety Devices, Pittsburgh, Pa.) to inflate the lungs until an anesthesia machine can be obtained. At that time, insert an endotracheal tube and assist the respiratory attempts of the patient by administering pure oxygen.

3. If ventricular fibrillation is present, use electric defibrillation after previously massaging the heart. If the heart is in arrest, inject 1 ml of 1:1000 solution of epinephrine into the left ventricular cavity and continue massage. Intracardiac epinephrine may produce ventricular fibrillation in a previously arrested heart. If this occurs, defibrillate as described above. (See also External Cardica Massage, p. 8).

Gastroenteric Tract

Nausea, vomiting, local irritation, and diarrhea are the most frequent signs and symptoms associated with acute intoxications. The symptoms will usually subside after removal of the toxicant by vomiting, gastric lavage, or the use of a cathartic. Antiemetics, such as chlorpromazine HCl (Thorazine) P.O. or I.M., or prochlorperazine (Compazine) rectally may be useful. Saline preparations are the most dependable and harmless agents for removal of a compound from the enteric tract by catharsis. Drugs and other measures which help to restore normal gastroenteric function include withholding all food for a limited period of time; ingestion of tea, milk, or gruel; oral administration of paregoric, atropine sulfate, Lomotil (atropine plus diphenoxylate), dihydromorphinone (Dilaudid), or morphine sulfate for treatment of hyperactivity. Meperidine (Demerol) I.M. or another narcotic analgesic may be required to treat pain. Give physostigmine or neostigmine for intestinal relaxation or distention. All of these measures should be supported by rest and by the restoration of water and electrolyte balance. Infusions of modified Ringer solutions have been life-saving when there has been excessive loss of fluid from the gastroenteric tract.

Central Nervous System

The judicious use of analeptics, depressants, or analgesics may prevent additional injury to the central nervous system. Analeptics are indicated *only* when a true drug depression exists. The following usually give the desired effect: caffeine and sodium benzoate P.O. or I.M., amphetamine sulfate and related drugs P.O., pentylenetetrazol I.V., and others. Anoxia and asphyxia are *not* indications for the administration of analeptics. Adequate pulmonary ventilation with 100% oxygen is the treatment of choice (see Oxygen, p. 442).

When induced by chemical agents, convulsions, hyperexcitability, and tremors respond to injectable thiopental sodium I.V., pentobarbital sodium I.V. or P.O., paraldehyde P.O., or ether.

Other drugs that induce relaxation of skeletal muscle include methaminodiazepoxide (Librium) P.O., promazine HCl (Sparine) P.O., and the citric acid salt of orphenadrine (Norflex) P.O., as well as succinylcholine I.V., and decamethonium bromide (Syncurine) I.V. Succinylcholine has been found useful in the treatment of tetanus and the black widow spider bite. It has also been given as an adjuvant to anticonvulsive drugs. Succinylcholine and Syncurine must be administered with great caution, since positive pressure respiration is the *only* antidotal measure for these agents. Neostigmine and edrophonium (Tensilon) partially antagonize the effects of tubocurarine and related drugs. Neostigmine and Tensilon do not antagonize, and indeed they may potentiate the effects of succinylcholine and Syncurine.

Pain can often be alleviated with topical anesthetics, atropine sulfate, salicylates, and related drugs. The anti-spasmodics give relief if the symptoms are due to gastroenteric hyperactivity or spasms. Fortunately, severe pain is not a frequent symptom in chemical intoxications, and opiates are best avoided. In the event that opiates are used, it is wise to recall the side effects that these compounds may induce.

Liver

The essential features of therapy include: (1) discontinuation of exposure to the hepatotoxic agent and to ethyl alcohol; (2) ingestion of a diet high in carbohydrates, moderately rich in proteins, low in fat content, and supplemented with vitamin C and B complex. Choline and methionine are two of the many lipotropic agents which have maintained some popularity, but their effectiveness in the laboratory has never been equalled in clinical practice; (3) during the initial period of treatment, absolute bed rest is equally as important as the dietary regimen; this to be followed by a period of moderate activity. Should failure of liver function become acute and severe, reduce protein intake promptly, maintaining the content of carbohydrate, fat, and supplements unaltered. Management of this condition is a special problem. It may require transfusions. Drug therapy, even with agents that do not affect the liver, should be greatly curtailed. The doses administered must be carefully adjusted to the ability of the liver to metabolize or detoxify. Barbiturates should be avoided.

Kidneys, Electrolytes, and Water Balance

Direct or indirect injury to the kidneys and/or derangement of water and electrolyte balance is produced in many acute intoxications.

Simple dehydration, that is, the loss of water with minimal loss of electrolytes, is not very common. The condition is corrected by replacement of water by mouth or by I.V. injection of 5% aqueous glucose. Marked loss of water by perspiration, vomiting, or diarrhea in anuric patients treated with electrolyte-free fluids may result in water intoxication, which is characterized by cramps in legs and abdomen and possibly convulsions and death (see Water, p. 627). Sodium chloride will promptly reverse this condition. Loss of water and electrolytes may be corrected by ingestion or infusion of normal saline, or when due to excessive vomiting or sweating, by the administration of a hypertonic solution of sodium chloride and glucose in water.

In renal injury due to shock, hemorrhage, or intravascular hemolysis, the underlying condition must be treated as vigorously as possible. Blood, plasma, and electrolytes should be used to correct anemia, shock, dehydration, acidosis, or alkalosis. Five or more liters of fluid may be needed in the first few hours. This volume may be given without fear if the type and quantity required are determined by a careful analysis of the clinical and chemical aspects of the case.

During the phase of anuria, which may last from 2 to 14 days, the clinical picture depends largely on therapy. If fluid balance is maintained, the patient is relatively asymptomatic; but if fluids are given in excess, edema, hypertension, dyspnea, and cerebral symptoms of confusion, irritability, and coma appear. Patients have died of pulmonary edema during the first few days due to the administration of excessive parenteral fluids.

Emphasis during the phase of anuria should be directed towards prevention of overhydration and potassium intoxication. The desire to correct blood chemical abnormalities should be resisted. Since breakdown of tissue protein is the chief source of potassium, measures should be taken to prevent this. Antibiotics should be administered to control or prevent infection. Adequate nonprotein calories should be given to meet energy requirements and prevent protein catabolism. Oral intake of low protein diets should be instituted as soon as possible, since sufficient calories to meet total body requirements cannot be given parenterally in a volume small enough to avoid overhydration.

For hyperpotassemia, the intravenous administration of 10–20 ml of 10% calcium chloride or gluconate will oppose the action of potassium on the myocardium.

The phase of diuresis is characterized by a urine output of up to 5–10 liters per day and by a urinary excretion of sodium chloride up to 20–40 gm per day. It is essential to replenish water and salt during this phase. This can best be managed on an 8-hour basis, for the amounts involved are so large and the rapidity of change so great, that if 24-hour values were used a serious state of salt depletion and dehydration might result. Ringer's solution or physiological saline should be given I.V. until oral intake is possible. At this time, after each voiding, a 0.5% solution of sodium chloride and sodium bicarbonate of equal concentration in a volume equal to the urine volume should be given orally at once to maintain fluid and electrolyte balance. The serum chloride should be checked during this period to detect hypochloremia or, rarely, hyperchloremia. See also Water, p. 627.

Dialytic Therapy of Poisoning

Removal of a poison from the body has always been one of the objectives of treatment. It is now possible to remove poisons from the blood by using the artificial kidney (hemodialysis) or by peritoneal dialysis.

Generally, the artificial kidney removes poisons from the blood more rapidly and reliably than peritoneal dialysis. Many functioning artificial kidney units are distributed throughout the country and transportation of patients to such units is usually feasible when necessary. Transportation of seriously poisoned patients nevertheless is often hazardous. Patients with respiratory impairment should not be moved unless respiratory function can be reasonably guaranteed during the trip. The state of circulation should be good enough so that circulatory collapse does not occur en route. The referring physician is responsible for meticulous medical attention until the patient reaches the artificial kidney unit. If the patient cannot be transported, peritoneal dialysis may often be substituted for hemodialysis. The major factor in successful application of dialytic techniques is not the method of dialysis or the type of equipment, but the experience of the personnel. Success in dialytic treatment requires a physician experienced with dialysis.

In addition to its role in removal of poison from the body, dialytic therapy may be life-saving in maintaining a patient through a period of acute temporary renal failure resulting from intoxication by such agents as carbon tetrachloride, bichloride of mercury, and ethylene glycol.

Dialysis has proved effective in the removal of about one hundred types of poisons including the following compounds: acetylsalicylic acid, bromides, ethanol, ethchlorvynol (Placidyl), glutethimide (Doriden), methanol, methyl salicylate (oil of wintergreen), and thiocyanate, as well as barbiturates such as amobarbital sodium (Amytal sodium), barbital, butabarbital sodium, cyclobarbital calcium (Cyclobarbitone), pentobarbital (Nembutal), phenobarbital, and secobarbital (Seconal). Table 9, p. 684, lists compounds which are dialyzable, but the degree to which dialysis is clinically effective is not yet definitely established. Poisoning from barbiturates, salicylates, and glutethimide produces more than 75% of the cases requiring dialytic treatment and of these three types of poisoning, barbiturate intoxication is by far the most frequently encountered.

Hemodialysis is particularly effective in removing long-acting barbiturates (phenobarbital) but is also helpful in cases of poisoning from intermediate or short-acting barbiturates (pentobarbital), although removal of these compounds is less rapid. We have found that if the patient responds to pain, he will survive barbiturate intoxication with careful supportive treatment unless he has other serious complications. If, after several hours of satisfactory supportive therapy with special attention to respiration and circulation, the patient does not respond to pain, then resort to dialysis, since such patients remain in coma for days with severe impairment of respiration and circulation and pneumonia. Quantitative blood barbiturate levels are helpful in defining the need for dialytic therapy. Blood concentrations exceeding 9 mg% of long-acting, 6 mg% of intermediate, and 3 mg% of short-acting barbiturates usually require dialytic treatment. Over 95% of cases of barbiturate coma recover on a program of supportive therapy, augmented by dialysis when indicated.

In cases of serious salicylate intoxication, the improvement seen with hemodialysis is often dramatic. When the blood salicylate concentration is over 75 mg%, patients often manifest hyperthermia, tachypnea, tachycardia, derangement of blood pH and electrolyte composition, delirium and coma. A blood salicylate level above 75 mg% associated with such symptoms requires dialysis as soon as possible.

In glutethimide poisoning, hemodialysis has been disappointing. We have seen patients who have been dialyzed 48 hours after ingestion of about 10 gm of glutethimide die of hypotension and shock, even though the glutethimide blood concentration was reduced to levels not usually indicating serious toxicity. Experience suggests that dialysis is helpful when patients have ingested over 10 gm and have a blood concentration of over 3.0 mg%—the sooner dialysis is begun after ingestion, the more helpful it seems to be. It appears that the longer glutethimide is in the body, the less hemodialysis improves the outcome, and patients poisoned by glutethimide, if not dialyzed within 24 hours of ingestion, generally seem to benefit less from dialysis than do those with barbiturate or salicylate intoxication.

For detailed and up-to-date reviews of the dialysis of poisons and drugs, see J. F. Maher, and G. E. Schreiner, *Trans. Am. Soc. Artificial Internal Organs* **13**, 369 (1967). (John Kiley, The Albany Medical College of Union University.)

Blood Dyscrasias

Drug-Induced Aplastic Anemia. A. J. Erslev [*JAMA* **188**, 531, (1964)] reported that aplastic anemia is a frequent manifestation of drug toxicity and is characterized by pancytopenia and a fatty hypoplastic bone marrow.

In about one-half the cases reported, it is believed that a drug or chemical plays an etiological role. Chloramphenicol appears to be by far the most important offender; however, published case reports and reports sent to the AMA Registry on Blood Dyscrasias attest to the potential bone marrow toxicity of mephenytoin (Mesantoin), sulfonamides, phenylbutazone (Butazolidin), some insecticides and solvents, and many other compounds. It is difficult to separate drug-induced from idiopathic cases. There is no test which provides proof of an etiological relationship. Therefore, a conclusion must be drawn on the basis of personal judgment and statistics.

Caution: The mortality rate, even in well treated cases of aplastic anemia, is about 50%; therefore, the logical approach is prevention. Patients who require treatment with these drugs should have a white blood cell count and differential, an estimation of platelets, a reticulocyte count, and a hemoglobin determination at the onset of treatment and at reasonable intervals thereafter.

Treatment: Since recovery, whether spontaneous or in response to the removal of an etiological agent, is very slow, the goal of therapy is to prevent death from complications during the intervening period. To maintain a hemoglobin level sufficient for reasonable activity, transfusions should be given sparingly. The patient should be instructed to report promptly any signs or symptoms of infection. The prophylactic use of antibiotics is not recommended. If an infection does develop, it should be treated quickly, vigorously, and persistently. In severe infections, transfusion of fresh blood from donors with high leukocyte counts (chronic myeloid leukemia or myelofibrosis) has been claimed to be beneficial. Likewise, fresh blood from donors with high platelet counts (polycythemia vera) may be helpful in counteracting severe hemorrhagic episodes. Testosterone in pharmacologic doses, prednisone, and splenectomy have occasionally appeared to induce permanent remissions. (See Table 3, p. 670.)

Drug-Induced Agranulocytosis. C. M. Huguley, Jr. [*JAMA* **188**, 817 (1964)] reported that granulocytopenia is the most common hematological adverse reaction to drugs. If infection develops as a result of a severe neutropenia (agranulocytosis), the mortality rate ranges from 20–50%, even when early and effective treatment is instituted.

Acute agranulocytosis is characterized by a severe drop in the total leukocyte count with almost complete disappearance of granulocytes. The red blood cell and platelet counts are not affected. There is a reduction of the granulocytic series in the bone marrow, with a lack of more mature forms (maturation arrest), or even complete absence of granulocytes. With recovery, there is frequently a "compensatory" increase in immature forms. Lymphadenopathy and splenomegaly are not present in acute agranulocytosis, but toxic hepatitis sometimes occurs. A skin rash is observed in about 10% of these patients.

Drug-induced agranulocytosis may occur after a single dose if a drug is given to a patient who has been receiving occasional doses of that drug for a period of months or even years. However, agranulocytosis is more likely to occur in patients who have received continuous treatment for 2–8 weeks, or even for many months.

Prophylaxis consists of knowing the drugs that most frequently produce agranulocytosis and using these drugs with caution. The patient must be warned to discontinue taking the drug and to report immediately to the physician if he should develop any evidence of infection, particularly fever or sore throat, or if he should develop a skin rash or show evidence of jaundice. As a further precaution, a white blood cell and differential count should be performed before a patient is treated with a drug known frequently to produce agranulocytosis. These tests should be repeated at any hint of an infection, rash, or jaundice.

Treatment consists of discontinuing the drug and treating any infection present appropriately, immediately, and massively. (See Table 3, p. 670.)

Drug-Induced Hemolytic Anemia. E. Beutler [*JAMA* **189**, 143 (1964)] reported that drug-induced hemolytic anemia can occur as the result of several different mechanisms. Administration of "oxidant" drugs such as primaquine phosphate, nitrofurantoin (Furadantin), and acetanilid will regularly produce hemolysis in individuals with a sex-linked inborn error of metabolism, G-6-PD deficiency. This abnormality is probably the most common single cause of sensitivity to "oxidant" drugs.

Many drugs have been found to cause hemolysis of G-6-PD-deficient red blood cells. Drugs most frequently implicated are naphthalene, nitrofurantoin, salicylazosulfapyridine (Azulfidine), sulfamethoxypyridazine (Kynex, Midicel), aminosalicylic acid, and sodium sulfoxone (Diasone Sodium). Most of these drugs are capable of producing hemolysis of normal red blood cells when administered either in doses larger than usual or when given to subjects who, because of impaired renal function, develop unusually high blood levels of such a drug.

Only in rare cases will drug-induced hemolysis result from the development of antibodies that, in the presence of the drug, agglutinate red cells. Drugs implicated in hemolytic anemias include stibophen (Fuadin), penicillin, quinine, quinidine, acetophenetidin (Phenacetin), and others. (See Table 3, p. 670.)

Treatment depends first of all on recognition of the fact that a drug-induced hemolysis has occurred. In this case, withdraw the drug immediately. Hematinics such as iron, liver, or vitamins are of no benefit, and whenever possible, transfusions are to be avoided because of their inherent risks. In Negroes with G-6-PD deficiency, most drug-induced hemolysis is self-limiting and will usually subside even though drug administration is continued. This may not be the case in Caucasians, though hemolysis will cease within a few days after withdrawal of the drug. A good reticulocyte response suggests that recovery will be prompt.

Drug-Induced Thrombocytopenia. The following was taken from W. H. Crosby and R. M. Kaufman [*JAMA* **189**, 417 (1964)]. Thrombocytopenia, because of drug sensitization, is a serious but not common complication of drug therapy, since it may cause serious bleeding or lead to death due to brain hemorrhage. Although thrombocytopenia is present when the platelet count falls below the normal range of 200,000–400,000/mm³ (direct method), a significant bleeding tendency is usually not encountered in otherwise healthy persons unless the platelet count is less than 20,000/mm³.

In a person previously sensitized to a drug, re-exposure may provoke a fulminant thrombocytopenia and purpura. Allergic manifestations such as wheezing, skin rash, and chills and fever also may develop. The more important sensitizing drugs include quinidine, chlorothiazide, acetazolamide, sulfisoxazole, and phenylbutazone. The thrombocytopenia results from immunological damage to circulating platelets, leading to their premature removal from the blood; bone marrow examination reveals numerous megakaryocytes which appear normal morphologically.

The antibiotic ristocetin causes thrombocytopenia by a different mechanism—it is directly toxic to platelets. This is a dose-related phenomenon. Lowering the dose ameliorates the thrombocytopenia.

There are other drugs that may cause thrombocytopenia by depressing the production of platelets. Since this disorder is often irreversible, the outlook is necessarily grave. Some agents that have been associated with the induction of thrombocytopenia by affecting either the production or life-span of platelets, or both, are listed in Table 3, p. 670.

Treatment: Discontinue the drug. Recovery will usually be rapid and complete.

Corticosteroids are of no value in the treatment of thrombocytopenia caused by drug sensitization. As a matter of fact, the use of these compounds can complicate the differential diagnosis. Idiopathic thrombocytopenia purpura may be improved by the administration of steroids, whereas drug-related purpura is improved when the administration of the responsible drug is stopped, and it is sometimes unwise to take both measures at once.

Patients with drug-related purpura must be instructed about the nature of their illness and the importance of avoiding the offending drug in the future. They must also be warned about possibilities that the drug may be present in patented mixtures.

Photosensitivity

R. L. Baer and L. C. Harber [*JAMA* **192**, 989 (1965)] report that drug-induced photosensitivity reactions are unique in that exposure to both light and a drug is required for the adverse cutaneous reaction to occur. The usual light source is direct sunlight; however, diffuse light and artificial light are also capable of eliciting this reaction. The photosensitizing drug may have been administered topically, orally, or parenterally.

Drug-induced photosensitivity reactions may occur by at least two mechanisms—phototoxic or photoallergic.

A phototoxic drug reaction is induced by a nonimmunological mechanism. In a significant percentage of individuals, and under appropriate conditions, this reaction occurs upon the *first* exposure to light of sufficient intensity in people who have received previously adequate doses of the drug. Clinically, such a reaction is often of the exaggerated sunburn type. The majority of drugs causing phototoxic reactions are resonating aromatic rings with a molecular weight ranging from 200 to 500.

The pattern of a photoallergic drug reaction is similar to that of other forms of allergic hypersensitivity. Frequently, there is a history of induction, and an intervening incubation period between the sensitizing exposure and the development of the patient's capacity to react clinically to a subsequent exposure. A flare-up of the reaction at distant previously exposed sites can occur. The concentration of the drug necessary to elicit a photoallergic reaction is much lower than that needed to produce a phototoxic reaction. As with other types of allergic sensitization, only a small percentage of the population is genetically susceptible to the development of the sensitization. Therefore, the incidence of photoallergic reactions is much lower than that of phototoxic ones.

When a photosensitizing drug is involved in both a phototoxic and a photoallergic reaction, then the wavelengths of the photoallergic action spectrum usually exceed those of the phototoxic ones. Some photoallergens produce ordinary allergic contact dermatitis in the absence of light. (See Table 4, p. 674.)

Treatment: Discontinue drug therapy and avoid sunlight. In the majority of cases, this will lead to rapid improvement. Treatment otherwise is symptomatic and supportive. Some patients with a resistant form of drug-induced photosensitivity have benefitted from a one- to two-week stay in a darkened room.

Anaphylactic Drug Reaction

Anaphylactic shock has been reported following the injection of penicillin, insulin, local anesthetics, mercurials, and a multitude of drugs; after injection of pollen or other extracts; after bee and wasp stings; after inhalation of castor bean dust, and upon the mere tasting of cottonseed-flavored candy.

Individuals who are to be treated with horse serum or with drugs known to have caused hypersensitivity reactions should be questioned *before* treatment regarding previous injections of horse serum or allergic reactions (asthma, hay fever, eczema, or hives). (See Tetanus, p. 33.) Since serum shock is sudden and severe, it may be fatal unless one is prepared to treat it immediately.

Signs and symptoms of an anaphylactic reaction may include: respiratory distress (because of bronchospasm or angioneurotic edema involving the larynx), pallor, restlessness, pruritus, vomiting, cramps, apprehension, tachycardia, convulsions, coma, and vascular collapse.

Prevention:
1. Avoid unnecessary sensitization.
2. Do not use penicillin in trifling infections.
3. Avoid penicillin in lozenges and troches.
4. Do not use antibiotics routinely before operations or tooth extractions in normal persons.

5. Do not use any drugs with a history of sensitization in patients with an allergic history. (See Table 5, p. 675.)

Precautions include:

1. Use of *oral* medication (topical applications are the most dangerous).

2. An injection should be given in the distal part of an extremity to permit use of a tourniquet if necessary.

3. Administration of a drug and antihistamine in the same syringe offers no protection.

4. The skin scratch test, which may be followed but not preceded by a conjunctival test, should be made even though they may have limited value in detecting drug sensitivity [R. A. Kern, *JAMA* **179**, 19 (1962)].

5. "In the event that a therapeutic agent is to be used despite a positive history, a positive skin test, or both, the precautionary measures should include starting an intravenous infusion to facilitate the prompt administration of epinephrine, diphenhydramine hydrochloride, or both in the event of vascular collapse, and having a tracheostomy set available. The agent should be administered in the distal portion of an extremity so that a tourniquet can be applied and epinephrine injected locally immediately if a significant local reaction develops. It (the drug) should first be administered intracutaneously, then subcutaneously, and finally intramuscularly in increasing doses, and the initial dose by any route should not exceed the final dose by the previous route. To minimize the possibility of an appreciable accumulation of antigen, the intervals between injections should be 20–30 minutes. It is apparent from the studies with penicillin that neither a positive history nor a positive skin test necessarily indicates that a systemic reaction will occur [K. F. Austen, *JAMA* **192**, 108 (1965)]."

Treatment:

1. Have available at all times a tray with a tourniquet, airways, sterile syringes and needles, and ampoules of diphenhydramine hydrochloride and epinephrine.

2. At the first sign of a severe reaction, inject 0.1 ml of epinephrine into the site to inhibit absorption of the agent and apply the tourniquet to further delay absorption (loosen it every 15 minutes). See also Bee Stings, p. 124.

3. Keep the airway open and give oxygen.

4. Give sympathomimetic drugs. Epinephrine (0.2–0.5 ml of a 0.1% solution) may be given S.C. in repeated doses or may even be given I.V. (slowly in 10 ml of saline). Diphenhydramine hydrochloride (50–80 mg) may be administered I.M. or I.V. (K. F. Austen).

5. Do not stop treatment when the patient seemingly improves after epinephrine; it is short-acting and the patient may slip back into shock when the effect of this drug wears off.

6. Continue with hydrocortisone by intravenous drip: 100–250 mg initially, up to 1000 mg in 25 hours.

7. Steroids taken orally may be used in protracted delayed mild to moderate reactions [R. A. Kern, *JAMA* **179**, 19 (1962)].

8. If bronchospasm occurs and is not otherwise controlled, aminophylline (0.25–0.5 gm) may be given slowly intravenously. In the event of intractable hypoxia or inability to insert an endotracheal tube, a tracheostomy is advisable [K. F. Austen, *JAMA* **192**, 108, (1965)]. See Table 5, p. 675.

CHAPTER IV

DRUGS AND CHEMICALS: SIGNS, SYMPTOMS, AND TREATMENT OF INTOXICATIONS

ABBOMEENS

Abbomeen E-2 (N,N-di(2-hydroxyethyl)cyclohexylamine) has an oral LD_{50} (male rats) of 2.6 gm/kg. Female guinea pigs exposed for 1 hour to an aerosol of 2 mg/liter died during exposure or within the hour following. Autopsy showed small hemorrhagic spots on the lungs. Moderate to severe corneal opacity, iritis, and conjunctivitis were found after instillation of 0.1 ml into the eyes of rabbits. Abbomeen E-2 is a mild skin irritant at doses of 632 mg/kg or below (rabbit). Higher doses may cause damage and systemic intoxication.

Abbomeen E-25 (N,N-(2-hydroxyethyl)$_{25}$ cyclohexylamine) has an oral LD_{50} (male rats) of 38.3 gm/kg. Male guinea pigs exposed for 1 hour to an aerosol of 2 mg/liter survived the exposure. One died on the sixth day. When 0.1 ml was instilled into the eyes of rabbits, only slight conjunctivitis occurred. No skin irritation was found after application to the skin of rabbits.

Treatment: For skin and eye contact, irrigate the affected parts with large volumes of water. For ingestion, induce vomiting and follow with gastric lavage. In case of inhalation, remove the victim to an adequately ventilated area. Give artificial respiration, if necessary [*Abbott Lab. Tech. Bull.* **13** (1966)].

ACETALDEHYDE (Ethanal; Acetic Aldehyde; Ethyl Aldehyde)

The vapors are irritating to mucous membranes. Large doses may cause coughing, headache, weakness, paralysis of the respiratory center, and finally loss of consciousness. It is less toxic than formaldehyde. Paraldehyde is a trimer of acetaldehyde. See Aldehydes, p. 81.

Treatment: See Formaldehyde, p. 278, and Paraldehyde, p. 450.

ACETAMINOPHEN

This compound (N-acetyl-p-aminophenol or p-hydroxyacetanilid) is the primary metabolite of acetanilid and acetophenetidin. It is used alone and sold as Tylenol, Tempra, Apamide, or Lyteca as well as in combination with many other drugs as an analgesic and antipyretic. Its therapeutic potency and side effects are similar to those of aspirin. Like the parent drugs, acetaminophen is devoid of anti-inflammatory or antirheumatic properties, but unlike aspirin, acetaminophen does not depress plasma prothrombin. It does not readily produce methemoglobinemia. Apparently only one instance of neutropenia, two of pancytopenia, and three of leukopenia have been reported.

Caution: Acetaminophen and related drugs should be administered to the newborn with caution and only by the physician since the detoxifying mechanisms are not fully functioning at this age. For treatment of an overdose, see Acetylsalicylic Acid, p. 67, and Acetanilid, p. 62.

ACETANILID (Antifebrin)

This analgesic is a constituent of several headache powders and tablets. Prolonged daily use of 1 gm or more has resulted in gastroenteric disturbances, drowsiness, hemolytic anemia, methemoglobinemia, reticulocytosis, cyanosis, antipyresis, acute renal failure, and collapse. Death is due to nephritis and uremia. Of the postmortem findings, advanced degenerative changes of the kidneys are particularly apparent. See Blood Dyscrasias, p. 51, also Acetaminophen, p. 61.

Treatment: In case of an overdose administer gastric lavage, cathartics, enema, oxygen and, if required, articial respiration. Transfusions are indicated if methemoglobinemia is severe. See p. 40. This drug is contraindicated in renal disease.

ACETAZOLAMIDE (Diamox)

This diuretic, as well as dichlorphenamide (Daranide) and methazolamide (Neptazane), are carbonic anhydrase inhibitors. Diamox in particular is useful in the treatment of glaucoma and in cor pulmonale. Side effects, which have a tendency to disappear with continued use, include drowsiness, paresthesia, and metabolic acidosis. There are a few isolated reports of skin reaction, fever, acute myopia, thrombocytopenia, and fatal agranulocytosis. See Blood Dyscrasias, p. 51 and p. 670. This drug, in high doses, has produced teratogenic effects in rats [*Science* **149**, 306 (1965)].

Treatment: An overdose requires symptomatic and supportive treatment. See also Chlorothiazides, p. 170, Furosemide, p. 281, and Ethacrynic Acid, p. 244.

ACETIC ACID

Vinegar is 4–6% acetic acid. Glacial acetic acid (100%) is extremely corrosive; ingestion will cause local destruction of mucous membranes of the mouth, esophagus, and stomach, severe pain, vomiting, bloody diarrhea, and pulmonary disturbances. See Table 54, p. 742.

Treatment: For ingestion lavage the stomach with water and follow with demulcents. In cases of pulmonary involvement use oxygen.

ACETIC ANHYDRIDE

This compound is toxicologically comparable to glacial acetic acid. It reacts exothermically with water to form acetic acid. See Acetic Acid, p. 63, and Table 54, p. 742.

ACETOACETARYLAMIDES

These chemicals have a relatively low order of toxicity. Prolonged or repeated breathing of vapors may be harmful. Repeated or prolonged contact with the skin may cause skin irritation.

Treatment: Gastric lavage in case of ingestion. For skin or eye contact, flood affected part with water.

ACETOHEXAMIDE (Dymelor)

This is a relatively new drug for the treatment of diabetes. Like the related sulfonylureas, it is capable of reducing the blood level only as long as the pancreas produces insulin. Its therapeutic period of activity lies between that of tolbutamide and chlorpropamide. Side effects or signs of toxicity have been minimal. They have been noted in an occasional hypersensitive patient or in persons who received excessive dosages.

Caution: Since this drug has not yet been fully evaluated, close supervision of the patient is in order. A case of prolonged hypoglycemia and coma was reported in a diabetic with renal insufficiency. According to the Council on Drugs of the American Medical Association, acetohexamide should *not* be used in pregnant patients. Insulin remains the therapy of choice for diabetics during pregnancy [*JAMA* **191**, 127 (1965)]. Montgomery *et al.* reported a rise in serum alkaline phosphatase in 48% of diabetics treated with acetohexamide. This may be suggestive of a possible deleterious effect of the drug on the liver [M. J. Goldstein and A. J. Rothenberg, *New Engl. J. Med.* **275**, 97 (1966)].

J. B. Field *et al.* reported that phenylbutazone (Butazolidin) can potentiate the hypoglycemic effects of acetohexamide [*New Engl. J. Med.* **277**, 889 (1967)].

Treatment: In the diabetic with renal insufficiency, the repeated administration of 50% glucose failed to prevent recurrence of hypoglycemia and coma. Peritoneal dialysis was successful in removing acetohexamide and its metabolites [W. T. Lampe, *Arch. Internal Med.* **120**, 239 (1967)]. For additional precautions and treatment of overdoses, see Sulphonylurea Drugs, p. 563.

ACETONE

Ingestion of a toxic dose causes gastroenteric irritation, narcosis, and injury to the kidneys and liver. Some adults have taken 20 ml orally without ill effects. A 42-year-old man who drank 200 ml of acetone lapsed into coma for 12 hours. He recovered, but renal glucosuria was noted for 5 months [S. Gitelson *et al.*, *Diabetes* **15**, 810 (1966)]. Depending on the concentration in the air and the duration of the exposure, inhalation produces central nervous system depression, dizziness, narcosis, and coma. After application of a plaster cast with acetone setting fluid, a child was comatose for 6 hours but recovered in 24 hours [P. K. Renshaw and R. M. Mitchell, *Brit. Med. J.* **1**, 615 (1956)]. See p. 712.

Treatment: For ingestion, gastric lavage, oxygen if necessary, and a low-fat diet. For inhalation, remove promptly from contaminated atmosphere to fresh air. Administer oxygen and artificial respiration if required. Subsequent treatment is symptomatic and supportive.

ACETONE CYANHYDRIN (AC)

Acetone cyanhydrin decomposes into acetone and hydrogen cyanide in an alkaline medium (such as perspiration). A case of cyanide poisoning has been described in a worker whose clothes were contaminated with acetone cyanhydrin [J. Lang and F. Stintzy, *Arch. Maladies Professionnelles* **21**, 652 (1960)].

Treatment: See Cyanides, p. 191.

ACETONES, PERHALOGENATED

See: Trichlorotrifluoroacetone, p. 603, dichlorotetrafluoroacetone, p. 213.

ACETONITRILE (Methyl Cyanide; Ethanenitrile)

Exposure to 160 ppm for 4 hours causes flushing of the face and a feeling of constriction in the chest; 500 ppm for brief periods is irritating to the nose and throat. Severe exposures cause irritability, skin eruptions, confusion, delirium, convulsions, paralysis, and death due to central nervous system depression. The clinical manifestations of overexposure are due to thiocyanate rather than to cyanide.

Treatment: Remove the victim from the contaminated atmosphere. Give artificial respiration and oxygen if respiration is impaired. In two cases M. L. Amdur used oxygen, fluids, whole blood, ascorbic acid, and sodium thiosulfate [*J. Occupational Med.* **1**, 627 (1959)]. Vasodilators are contraindicated.

ACETOPHENAZINE (Tindal)

This drug is a member of the piperazine group of the phenothiazines. For general effects and side effects, see Chlorpromazine, p. 171, and Phenothiazines, p. 464. S. D. Witton reported on paradoxical hypertension in 8% of 67 patients receiving Tindal. This reaction was manifested by a sudden rise of both systolic and diastolic blood pressure, with malaise, headache, drowsiness, dizziness, and sometimes fever. According to Witton, paradoxical hypertension tends to occur more frequently in the elderly and in patients with a history of hypertension [*Am. J. Psychiat.* **121**, 387 (1964)].

ACETOPHENETIDIN (Phenacetin)

This drug has analgesic and mild antipyretic properties. In addition, therapeutic doses cause relaxation, drowsiness, and reduction of mental activity. In some countries, this drug is popular for the treatment of tension or anxiety. Acetophenetidin is largely metabolized to N-acetyl-p-aminophenol (acetaminophen), which is responsible for the therapeutic effects. Traces of aniline, phenetidin, or p-aminophenol may also be produced as metabolites. Its misuse has resulted in systemic intoxications (cyanosis, giddiness, profuse perspiration, hematuria, coma). On rare occasions, skin rashes and hemolytic anemia have been reported. Prolonged and continuous use has led to depression of bone marrow activity, insomnia, tremors, cyanosis, yellow vision, and renal injury ("Phenacetin nephritis"). Since acetophenetidin is usually taken in combination with other drugs, it is impossible to state whether the untoward effects noted are caused by this drug alone, by other drugs, or by the total analgesic preparation.

Caution: Children under three months should not be given Phenacetin. To prevent kidney lesions and disease, avoid administration of larger than therapeutic doses and regular use for more than 10 days without approval of a physician. If used more than 10 days for the treatment of arthritis or rheumatism, the physician should be consulted promptly if pain persists. Children under 12 years of age receiving this drug should remain under close medical supervision. Hypersensitivity may be related to a genetic effect that is rare in Caucasians but is found in about 10% of American Negroes.

Treatment: See Acetanilid, p. 62.

ACETYLCYSTEINE (Mucomyst)

Acetylcysteine is used as a mucolytic agent. It appears to be useful as an adjunct in the management of cystic fibrosis. Due to the absence of controlled studies, assessment of its value in the treatment of other respiratory tract diseases has been difficult. The drug may cause bronchospasm, especially in asthmatic patients [*JAMA* **190**, 147 (1964)].

ACETYLENE (Ethyne)

Exposure to 20% in air may cause dyspnea and headache; 40% causes collapse.

A worker inhaled acetylene gas from a leaking torch and was admitted to the hospital 18 hours later because of severe respiratory distress and chest pain. The respiratory rate was 60–70 per minute. Breathing was diaphragmatic; rhonchi and wheezes were heard throughout both lung fields. A chest film showed extensive pulmonary edema, bronchopneumonia, and pleural effusion in both lungs.

Although acetylene has been used as an anesthetic agent, pulmonary changes of the type described above have not been reported. It is believed that some impurity in the commercial acetylene was probably responsible for the pulmonary irritation. See Hydrocarbon Gases, p. 316.

Treatment: Under supportive treatment the patient described above gradually recovered. No residual changes were seen by repeated X-ray examination 2 weeks after admission.

ACETYLSALICYLIC ACID (Aspirin)

Aspirin is a most useful and widely used drug for the alleviation of pain, headache, and neuralgia. In a small percentage of patients, dermatitis and other allergic reactions bar its use. In some individuals requiring large or prolonged dosage, gastroenteric side effects, such as pain or heartburn limit its use. Bleeding partially due to a systemic effect inhibiting mucus production by the stomach may occur [*Surg. Gynecol. Obstet.* **120**, 92 (1965)]. Hypoglycemia following salicylate treatment may be more common than recognized [*Am. J. Diseases Children* **109**, 165 (1965); *Am. J. Diseases Children* **112**, 558 (1966)].

An oral overdose produces gastric irritation, tinnitus, perspiration, severe dehydration, thirst, fever, and lethargy. Hyperventilation is followed by respiratory alkalosis; metabolic acidosis soon occurs followed by coma and death. Death is due to oligemic shock resulting from the disturbance in acid base balance and dehydration. In an adult, definite symptoms of salicylism may be expected after ingestion of one dose of approximately 10 gm which produces a serum salicylate level in excess of 35 mg/100 ml [H. D. Greer *et al.*, *JAMA* **193**, 555 (1965)]. In rats acetylsalicylic acid administered rectally (LD_{50}, 0.79 gm/kg) is less toxic than when given orally (LD_{50}, 0.2 gm/kg) [B. B. Caldwell and E. M. Boyd, Queen's University, Kingston, Ontario (1966)].

Systemic intoxications occasionally result from the cutaneous application of ointments and oils containing 3–6% of a salicylate. Percutaneous intoxication is a potential hazard in patients with psoriasis treated with ointments containing this drug. Salicylates readily pass the placental barrier. A pregnant woman ingested about 16 gm of acetylsalicylic acid 27 hours before delivery. Twelve hours after birth, the infant's serum salicylate level was 35 mg/100 ml.

An overdose of this drug acts as an anticoagulant inducing hypoprothrombinemia similar to that produced by bishydroxycoumarin (Dicumarol) and related compounds.

Prolonged use of acetylsalicylic acid causes anemia. A report in *Lancet* [**II**, 768 (1966)] describes pancytopenia in 5 patients who ingested from 1.5–20 kg over periods up to 50 years.

Caution: Use aspirin with caution in patients with active peptic ulcers. The therapeutic or toxic effects of enteric-coted or delayed-action aspirin (*Relax, Measurin*, and other preparations) are frequently erratic or greatly delayed. (See Buffered aspirin, p. 143.) An editorial in *JAMA* [**190**, 1064 (1964)] points out that oral administration of sodium bicarbonate is indicated as a prophylactic measure in patients with extensive psoriasis treated over a long period of time with a salicylic acid ointment.

Treatment: After ingestion of an overdose of acetylsalicylic acid, induce vomiting promptly. This measure is contraindicated, however, if the patient is unconscious. Vomiting, which may be induced by *syrup* of ipecac, is much more effective than gastric lavage in removing gastric contents. The standard dose of syrup of ipecac is 15 ml. The process is facilitated by giving fluid (approximately 200 ml of milk or water) just after the syrup. Ipecac may be repeated if vomiting does not occur in 20 minutes. If this does not induce vomiting, gastric lavage is performed and both the salicylate and the ipecac are removed.

The degree of intoxication should always be assessed by determination of the concentration of salicylate, sodium, potassium, chloride, and carbon dioxide in the blood. The blood sugar should also be measured routinely.

Mild salicylate poisoning can be managed by the provision of water and electrolytes by mouth; in general, fluids must be given parenterally. Most patients are seen quite early and clinical signs of dehydration are not present. Nevertheless, they must all be given large amounts of fluid. It should be recognized that patients who develop acute renal shutdown must be treated in other ways. Exchange transfusions and peritoneal dialysis have been employed successfully in these patients. The use of 5% albumin in the fluid used for dialysis results in more effective removal of salicylate that is bound to protein. In the usual patient, initial hydration is performed by using 20 ml/kg of Ringer's lactate or a balanced salt solution (⅔ physiological saline, ⅓ of M/6 sodium lactate). This is given in the first ½–1 hour. If urine flow has not begun, 5–10% glucose may be infused rapidly in the amount of 20 ml/kg. In the presence of overt shock, initial hydration with a sodium-containing fluid is often enough to reverse the shock; if not, plasma or whole blood are administered.

After urine flow is established, 40 ml/kg of a balanced salt solution is infused composed of one volume of Ringer lactate and one volume of 5% glucose and containing 1 mEq of potassium acetate or potassium chloride per kilogram. This is administered for about 6 hours, after which 15 ml/kg of isotonic $NaHCO_3$ is infused. From about 7 to 24 hours 100 ml/kg is given of a mixture of 40 ml Ringer lactate, 45 ml 5% glucose, 15 ml isotonic $NaHCO_3$ and 2 mEq potassium acetate. In 24 hours, this regimen provides 195 ml/kg and 15, 3, and 9 mEq of sodium, potassium, and chlorine, respectively. Flow should be adjusted to provide urine flow rates of approximately 0.5 ml per minute in the average patient, or 60 ml/kg/24 hours. In the presence of dropping urine flow rates, the BUN should be determined and the amount of 5% glucose infused should be increased. Rarely, more intensive alkalinization may be necessary, but this must be carefully monitored with blood pH determinations. Sodium bicarbonate may be given to such patients in increments of 3–5 mEq per kilogram of body weight over intervals of 2–4 hours, the need for each dose being determined by the clinical response and pH of the blood.

Salicylate is excreted more rapidly in an alkaline urine, and for this reason, the early administration of sodium bicarbonate has been recommended. However, it is extremely difficult to alkalinize the urine of patients with advanced ketoacidosis and very large and potentially dangerous quantities may be given if urinary pH is used as the only indicator. Possible complications of this treatment, especially in severely poisoned individuals, include hypernatremia and hypokalemia. "The administration of potassium often is more effective in alkalinizing the urine of such individuals [Alan K. Done, *JAMA* **192,** 770 (1965)]." Oral potassium citrate has been used for this purpose with apparent success but controlled studies have not yet been reported. Patients so treated should be carefully monitored for signs of potassium intoxication.

All patients are given 1–5 mg of vitamin K_1 oxide to prevent or combat hypoprothrombinemia. The rate of administration of glucose or the concentration of glucose in the infusion fluid should be adjusted to deal with hypoglycemia. Supportive treatment may include oxygen or assisted respiration. Opiates are contraindicated. Stimulants are equally undesirable, since respiratory stimulation is already marked. In contrast to experience with other ototoxic drugs, hearing loss usually improves rapidly after withdrawal of the drug. (William L. Nyhan, University of Miami). For additional information on acetylsalicylic acid, refer to A. K. Done, *JAMA* **192,** 770 (1965) and to R. H. Moser, *Clin. Pharmacol. Therap.* **8,** 333 (1967).

ACID CHLORIDES (Acyl Chlorides)

These compounds react with water to form carboxylic acids and hydrochloric acid. In general, they are strong irritants, particularly the lower molecular weight group—acetyl, propionyl, butyryl. As a class they are toxicologically similar to the corresponding acid anhydrides.

Treatment: See Acetic Acid, p. 63.

ACIDS, ALIPHATIC DI- and TRICARBOXYLIC (Acids, Aliphatic Di- and Tribasic)

Sebacic, adipic, glutaric, succinic, pimelic, and citric acids have a low order of toxicity. Many of these acids are found in edible fruits and vegetables.

Maleic acid is extremely irritating to mucous membranes and skin. Instillation of 1 and 5% solutions into the conjunctival sacs of the eyes of rabbits caused cloudiness of the cornea, hyperemia of the conjunctiva, and edema of the nictitating membrane in a few minutes.

Fumaric acid, the geometric isomer of maleic acid, is much less toxic.

Tartaric acid is a dihydroxy dicarboxylic acid which occurs naturally in fruits and vegetables. Tartrates are used as cathartics, since they are poorly absorbed from the intestinal tract.

Tartaric acid dust eroded the teeth of employees working in an atmosphere containing a mixture of tartaric acid, sucrose, magnesium sulfate, and sodium bicarbonate. It was calculated that clinical erosion of the teeth resulted from a 6-month exposure to 1.1 mg of tartaric acid per cubic meter of air [E. V. Henson, *J. Occupational Med.* **1**, 339 (1959)]. See also Oxalic Acid, p. 441.

Treatment: See Acetic Acid, p. 63.

ACIDS, AROMATIC MONO- AND DICARBOXYLIC (Benzene Mono- and Dicarboxylic Acids)

The monocarboxylic acids—benzoic, phenylacetic, diphenylacetic, cinnamic, and phenylstearic—are solids at room temperature. They have a low order of toxicity. The dicarboxylic acids *ortho-*, *meta-* (isophthalic), and *para*-phthalic acid (terephthalic), have a low to moderate order of toxicity. The toxicity decreases in the order listed above. Overexposure to finely divided powders of the aromatic acids may cause skin and mucous membrane irritation.

Treatment: Discontinue exposure. For skin or eye contact, flood affected part with water.

ACIDS, FATTY (Acids, Organic; Acids, Monocarboxylic Acids, Aliphatic)

The short-chain acids (formic, acetic) in concentrated liquid form are corrosive to the body surfaces, and the vapors are extremely irritating to mucous membranes. In general, the short-chain unsaturated acids are more toxic than the corresponding saturated acids. See Acrylic Acid, p. 76. The long-chain members are much less irritating. Systemic intoxication from exposure to fatty acids is rare [E. V. Henson, *J. Occupational Med.* **1**, 339 (1959)].

Treatment: See Acetic Acid, p. 63.

ACIDS, NAPHTHENIC (Cylic Carboxylic Acids; Cycloparaffinic Carboxylic Acids)

At ordinary temperature these are liquids having a relatively high acidity and a characteristic penetrating, persistent odor. Based on animal experiments, they are regarded as slightly toxic. Excessive contact with skin and mucous membranes will cause irritation.

Treatment: Remove from skin, eyes, or mucous membranes by flooding affected parts with water. In case of ingestion induce vomiting and follow with gastric lavage.

ACKEE; AKEE (*Blighia sapida*)

The active ingredients (hypoglycin A and B) in the unripe fruit and seeds of this tree are potentially dangerous hepatotoxins. Poisonings have occurred periodically on the island of Jamaica, where it is known as the "vomiting sickness." The significant acute symptoms are vomiting and coma. Death is preceded by convulsions. In areas outside the continental United States there are certain species of *Senecio* and *Crotalaria* which cause cirrhosis of the liver.

Treatment of ackee poisoning is symptomatic. Glucose I.V. and the restoration of electrolyte balance are important.

ACONITINE

This is the active principle of *Aconitum napellus*. Ingestion may produce marked gastroenteric distress, diarrhea, and generalized central excitation, followed by depression. The lethal dose for an adult is 20–40 ml of a 10 % solution in alcohol (tincture).

Treatment: Vomiting or gastric lavage, artificial respiration, oxygen if required and central nervous system depressants for the control of convulsions are recommended.

ACRISORCIN (Akrinol)

This drug is a useful antifungal agent for topical use in the treatment of tinea versicolor (pityriasis versicolor). Since this is a new agent, it has not yet been established whether it produces a permanent cure. No adverse reactions have been reported.

ACROLEIN (Acrylaldehyde; Acrylic Aldehyde; Propenal)

This is a colorless liquid with a sharp penetrating odor detectable at 1 ppm in air; 5.5 ppm causes mucous membrane irritation. Inhalation of air containing 10 ppm may be fatal in a few minutes. The threshold limit is 0.5 ppm. See Aldehydes, p. 81, and Table 22, p. 699.

Treatment: For vapor exposure, remove victim immediately from the contaminated atmosphere. If breathing has stopped, give artificial respiration and oxygen. Keep the exposed person under observation for 24 hours for possible development of delayed pulmonary edema. See Pulmonary Edema on p. 43. In case of ingestion, gastric lavage, saline cathartics, and demulcents are recommended.

ACROLEIN DIMER (3,4-Dihydro-2*H*-pyran-2-carboxaldehyde)

Acrolein dimer is the product of a reaction between two molecules of acrolein. It is a colorless mobile liquid with an unpleasant, acrolein-like odor. In the presence of heat, light, or air, the pure dimer tends to polymerize. Acrolein dimer is practically nontoxic by oral ingestion, and animals survive 8 hours of exposure to the saturated vapor at room temperature. The liquid is not irritating to rabbit skin but it causes severe injury when instilled and permitted to remain in contact with the rabbit's eye. Acrolein dimer has found limited use in industry and human use experience is not available.

Treatment: Prompt treatment of contaminated skin by washing with soap and water will prevent skin injury. In case of accidental eye contamination, wash the affected tissues with flowing water for 15 minutes.

ACRYLAMIDE

This is a white solid which melts at 84–85° C. It has been found to produce system disorders in animals.

"There appear to be several gradations of severity of this syndrome: muscular weakness, ataxia, and atrophy due to disuse, depending upon the size of the dose and the period of administration. No evidence of sensory involvement was found nor was there definite evidence as to the site of involvement of the central nervous system. An extensive neurohistological study in two dogs disclosed nothing abnormal in the central or peripheral nervous system.

"The acute oral LD_{50} for mice has been found to be 170 mg/kg. With single oral doses of 100 mg/kg, dogs developed the characteristic motor syndrome within 24 hours. When dogs were given smaller doses administered daily for a month, no toxicity was observed. With repeated oral administration to smaller animals, there was an inverse relation between the size of the dose and the time of onset. Toxic doses were in about the same range as in dogs. Inhalation of acrylamide dust and dermal application of aqueous solutions behaved in a similar manner. In rabbits, 50 daily applications of 1 ml/kg of a 1% solution (10 mg/kg) were without effect, but when a 5% solution (50 mg/kg) was used, the characteristic syndrome appeared during the third week. When doses of 0.1 ml of a 50% aqueous solution (50 mg) were placed in the eyes of rabbits daily for 10 days, one of six animals developed the syndrome.

"A dose as small as 1 mg/kg, when given daily by intravenous and/or intraperitoneal injection, will produce the syndrome in about six months. In this species signs of poisoning consist chiefly of dysmetria, disturbances of equilibrium, weakness and tremors. The intravenous LD_{50} is 85 mg/kg. Results of studies to date indicate that the pathological process is probably limited to the brain and is reversible. If poisoning is permitted to progress to a severe state, recovery may be greatly prolonged. In mild cases, recovery is usually rapid. The site and mechanism of action within the brain have not been determined. Extensive histopathological studies of the central nervous system in severely poisoned cats have not disclosed significant abnormalities. A 19-year-old worker who had handled acrylamide for three months in a chemical factory suffered from dermatitis, excessive sweating, tiredness, weight loss, muscle pain and marked weakness in the legs, ataxia, slurred speech, and attacks of generalized tremors.

"Acrylamide is a primary skin irritant of moderate intensity. Forty-four per cent of human subjects patch tested with a 1% solution experienced dermal irritation. It is also an irritant to the eye [D. McCollister, *Toxicol. Appl. Pharmacol.* **6** 172 (1964)]."

Treatment: In the case of the 19-year-old worker, although no therapy was given after removal from exposure, there was gradual improvement; however, recovery was still incomplete after 3 months. The neurological lesions in chronic acrylamide poisoning appears to be a midbrain disturbance and peripheral neuropathy [T. O. Garland and M. W. H. Patterson, *Brit. Med. J.* **4**, 134 (1967)]. Remove from the skin and eyes promptly by flooding the affected parts with water. In case of ingestion, induce vomiting.

ACRYLATES (Acrylic Monomers; Acrylic Esters)

The acrylates used in industry are: methyl, ethyl, butyl, ethylbutyl, and ethylhexyl esters of acrylic acid. The lower molecular weight monomeric esters are lachrymators and irritants. Methyl acrylate at 75 ppm is irritating to the eyes, nose and throat. The same effects are produced by ethyl acrylate at 50 ppm. Rabbits treated with these compounds had elevated concentrations of blood porphyrins. The acrylates are also skin irritants. Allergic reactions (headache, skin eruption, eye irritation) have been reported following contact with methyl methacrylate liquid monomer. In general, the toxicity of these esters decreases with increasing molecular weight. Higher methacrylates (from alcohol with eight or more carbon atoms) have a relatively low order of toxicity. See Table 34, p. 715. 1, 3-Butylene dimethacrylate (BDMA) is slightly toxic. Its acute oral toxicity for rats is approximately 15.0 gm per kilogram of body weight. The corresponding value for methyl methacrylate is 8.0−9.0 gm/kg. See Plastic Fingernails, p. 480.

Treatment: In case of inhalation, remove the victim promptly from the contaminated atmosphere and give artificial respiration and oxygen if necessary. For ingestion, use gastric lavage, demulcents, and cathartics. For skin or eye contact, flood affected tissues with water for 15 minutes.

ACRYLIC ACID (Propenic Acid; Vinylformic Acid)

This is a strong corrosive organic acid. The oral LD_{50} (rat) is 0.25–0.5 gm/kg. Brief skin or eye contact may cause severe chemical burns. Vapors are irritating to the skin, eyes, and mucous membranes. See Table 54, p. 742.

Treatment: Same as Acetic Acid, p. 63.

ACRYLONITRILE (Vinyl Cyanide; Propenenitrile)

This chemical is toxic by ingestion, by absorption through intact skin, and by inhalation. Overexposure causes headache, weakness, nausea, vomiting, and abdominal cramps. The threshold limit is 15–20 ppm. Severe exposure may cause unconsciousness, convulsions, and death. The onset and development of symptoms is much slower in comparison with exposure to inorganic cyanide. See p. 191.

Contrary to earlier belief, the high toxicity of acrylonitrile does not result from liberation of cyanide ions. Acrylonitrile acts as a selective poison of the central and peripheral nervous system.

If the nitrile link (stable *in vitro*) is broken *in vivo*, cyanide ions are not released in sufficient amounts to constitute a cyanide risk. For example, after administration of 50 mg/kg acrylonitrile I.V. (24 mg CN/kg), only 3.8% CN was excreted in urine in three days; with NaCN 65% CN was excreted. Administration of p-aminopropiophenone to form methemoglobin did not protect animals against acrylonitrile; it did protect against high doses of cyanide.

Treatment: Death (from shock and hypothermia) was delayed and symptoms were controlled by sodium thiosulphate and anesthetics, phenobarbitone or reserpine [G. Paulet *et al., Arch. Maladies Professionelles Med. Travaux* **27**, 849 (1966)].

ADHESIVE TAPE (Surgical Tape)

Some sensitive individuals develop eczematous reactions following application of adhesive tape. Severe skin reactions were elicited by contact with diamylhydroquinone, an antioxidant formerly used in such types of tape. The development of sensitization is enhanced by frequent repeated stripping and reapplication of adhesive tape.

Treatment: Discontinue exposure.

ADRENOCORTICAL HORMONES

Overdoses of mineralo-corticosteroids (11-desoxy-corticosterone, DCA, DOCA, Aldosterone) will cause an increase in plasma volume and interstitial fluid, edema, pulmonary congestion, arterial hypertension, and cardiac dilatation.

Overdoses of glucocorticosteroids [cortisone (Compound E), corticosterone (Compound B), and hydrocortisone or cortisol (Compound F)] over a prolonged period may produce some or all of the following effects which are related, to some extent, to hyperadrenalism—breakdown of peripheral tissue protein, wasting of muscles, increased gluconeogenesis, hyperglycemia, glycosuria, decrease in circulating eosinophils and lymphocytes, rounding of the face ("moon face"), hirsutism in women (androgen effect), acne, weakness, headache, euphoria, psychoses, and convulsions. There may also occur a reactivation of a gastric ulcer, salt and water retention with an increase in body weight, hypertension, aggravation of spinal osteoporosis, exacerbation of tuberculosis, formation of cataracts, and suppression of endogenous ACTH. This effect on ACTH frequently leads to exacerbation of symptoms if the treatment is stopped abruptly.

ACTH produces the same therapeutic and side effects as cortisol and cortisone through its effect on the patient's adrenals. Though rarely used as replacement therapy in patients with no pituitary function, ACTH produces important changes in fat metabolism (mobilization of fat depots, increased fat oxidation, enhanced ketogenesis) and enhanced glucose tolerance. In addition, it may cause increased pigmentation of the skin and hypersensitivity reactions.

Steroid preparations, because of their anti-inflammatory reaction, induce both therapeutic and side effects. Suppression of inflammation is associated with reduction in tissue repair. The analgesic effect permits overuse of a joint, frequently resulting in painless damage. According to Rinehart, 24 of 92 recently examined rheumatic patients under steroid therapy showed clinical evidence of steroid toxicity. Steroids should *never* be administered for prolonged periods, and *always* under close medical supervision [*Northwest. Med.* **61**, 749 (1962)]. Cataracts were observed in 14 of 38 patients with rheumatoid arthritis who received systemic treatment with moderate to high doses of corticosteroids for periods exceeding 1 year [*JAMA* **182**, 719 (1962)]. The FDA published contraindications and side effects associated with the use of corticosteroid ophthalmic preparations, and their combinations with antimicrobial drugs. Among the contraindications listed are the following: (a) acute herpes simplex, vaccinia, varicella, and most other virus diseases of the cornea and conjunctiva; (b) tuberculosis of the eye; (c) fungal diseases of the eye; and (d) acute purulent untreated infections of the eye, which, like other diseases caused by microorganisms, may be masked or enhanced by the presence of the steroid. Important side effects include: (a) increased intraocular pressure in certain individuals after extended use and (b) perforation of the cornea in those diseases which cause its thinning.

Sudden cessation of prolonged therapy (cortisone, cortisol) with doses exceeding 25 mg per day frequently leads to withdrawal symptoms (headache, vomiting, nausea, pains in muscles and joints). These effects subside in 2–5 days [Henneman *et al.*, *JAMA* **158**, 384 (1955)]. More lasting effects, such as peripheral neuropathy (polyneuropathy), were reported in patients who received cortisone for rheumatoid arthritis [R. H. Ferguson and C. H. Slocumb, *Sci. News Letter* (Dec. 24, 1960)].

Paramethasone acetate (Haldrone), betamethasone (Celestone), and dexamethasone (Decadron) appear to have a greater tendency than other steroids to produce marked mental stimulation and increased appetite. Prednisone (Meticorten) has produced several fatalities from generalized peritonitis due to perforated ulcers. A few other patients developed muscle weakness, dyspnea, and edema. In an occasional patient triamcinolone (Aristocort) has produced striking muscular cramps, weakness, and atrophy, or diplopia, bilateral papilledema, and retinal hemorrhage. In two children, eye changes were followed by complete recovery in eight days after discontinuation of therapy.

Caution: ACTH or corticotropin, cortisol, cortisone and many of the related drugs *should not be used* in a patient suffering from renal or cardiovascular disease, peptic ulcer, osteoporosis, tuberculosis, and psychotic or convulsive disorders. Under certain circumstances the physician will consider taking the calculated risk accompanying the use of these drugs. In any patient, discontinuation of steroid therapy should be gradual; even a marked reduction in dose should be avoided.

Diets high in calcium may prevent osteoporosis in rheumatoid arthritis patients receiving corticosteroids [*Mod. Med.* **29**, 46 (1961)].

It is doubtful that, as yet, a steroid has been discovered that has marked anti-inflammatory effects without producing some of the following side effects: insomnia, "moon face," psychoses, exacerbation of diabetes, decreased resistance to infection, peptic ulceration, osteoporosis, and fractures.

Use of the Thorn test (ACTH) in two patients with suspected adrenocortical insufficiency caused their death. These fatalities might have been avoided if, as a precaution, the following drug had been used: 9-α-fluorohydrocortisone, 1–2 mg daily, during the test, using 500 ml of isotonic sodium chloride as a diluent for the ACTH [*Arch. Internal Med.* **107**, 372 (1961)].

AEROSOL 22

A 35% solution of Aerosol 22 is considered to be practically nontoxic by ingestion in single doses on the basis of the acute oral LD_{50} for male albino rats (18.7 ml/kg). In terms of solid content, this dosage is equivalent to 6.5 gm/kg.

Dosages up to 10 ml/kg of the 35% solution held in contact with the closely clipped abdomen of albino rabbits for a period of 24 hours caused no deaths nor any gross signs of systemic toxicity. Only slight transient irritation of the skin resulted from such applications. Similarly, the solution was only mildly irritating in the rabbit eye.

The product fed to rats at dietary concentrations of 0.05%, 0.25%, and 1.25%, in terms of solid content of the 35% solution, had no effect on survival, food intake, or weight gain over a period of 28 days.

The capacity of Aerosol 22 to irritate the skin, by either primary irritation or sensitization, has been investigated in human subjects. The undiluted product (35% concentration) caused no irritation when held in contact with the skin under an occlusive dressing for several days. In the sensitization test the undiluted product was applied to denuded skin for 15 days under an occlusive dressing; after a rest period of 3 weeks, a challenging test with 35% material was applied for 48 hours. This test was negative in all 100 volunteers tested.

Treatment: In case of eye contact, flood with water.

AG 246 (MEMPP)

This is a new analgesic compound which also has antiinflammatory and anticonvulsive properties. Chemically, it is the chlorohydrate of morpholino-ethyl-2-methyl-4 phenyl-6 pyridazone-3. Little is known about this drug [*Time* p. 62 (November 12, 1965)].

AIR

Venous air embolism is a rare but preventable cause of death. It may occur whenever air is injected under pressure as in some radiological procedures, but it is most common during rapid transfusion with pumping devices. It may also occur during head, neck, and pelvic operations. A precordial stethoscope should always be used in such situations. Diagnosis is established by hearing the "mill wheel" murmur.

Durant and associates [*Am. Heart J.* **33**, 269 (1947)] have shown that there are four important factors in determining the prognosis in venous air embolism: (1) the volume of air that gains admission to the circulation, (2) the speed with which air is administered, (3) the position of the body at the time of the embolism accident, and (4) the efficacy of the respiratory mechanism in eliminating the gas via the lungs. Death is due to circulatory obstruction resulting from an air trap in the right ventricular outflow tract or ventricular fibrillation provoked by the intracardiac air. Ten to 20 ml of air were injected slowly into the jugular vein of a dog without evidence of injury.

Treatment: Success depends on rapid diagnosis, as 90% of untreated cases will die. Treatment formerly consisted of administering oxygen and vasopressors and placing the patient in the left lateral decubitus position. Closed chest cardiac massage has recently proved effective, and the use of this technique allows therapy to begin as soon as air embolism is suspected and before other therapeutic measures are instituted

[J. D. Gottlieb, *et al., Anesthesia Analgesia Current Res.* 44, 773 (1965)].

ALCOHOLS

The saturated alcohols, in general, are central nervous system depressants which have a low to moderate degree of toxicity. The corresponding unsaturated alcohols tend to be more toxic (See Allyl Alcohol, p. 86). Repeated contact of the lower molecular weight alcohols with the skin may cause dermatitis due to dehydration and removal of protective skin lipids. The aspiration of undiluted low molecular weight *n*-primary alcohols into the lung causes pulmonary edema and hemorrhage [H. Gerarde and D. Ahlstrom, *Arch. Environ. Health* 13, 457 (1966)]. Methanol is known to cause blindness following ingestion. See Methyl Alcohol, p. 383 and Table 21, p. 695 for quantitative toxicological information. See also Ethyl Alcohol, p. 249; Isopropyl Alcohol, p. 339; and *n*-Butyl Alchol, p. 144.

Treatment: Remove from the skin, mucous membranes, or eyes with copious volumes of water. In case of ingestion, induce vomiting and follow with gastric lavage and cathartics. For acute vapor inhalation, remove individual from the contaminated atmosphere. If necessary, administer artificial respiration and give oxygen. Subsequent treatment is supportive and symptomatic.

ALDEHYDES

As a class, aldehydes are irritating substances. The unsaturated aldehydes are more toxic than the corresponding saturated compounds. The following are listed in order of decreasing toxicity: acrolein, crotonaldehyde, acetaldehyde, propionaldehyde, isobutyraldehyde, and *n*-butyraldehyde. *n*-Valeraldehyde and isovaleraldehyde are relatively nontoxic. Particular care should be taken in the handling of acrolein, methacrolein, propionaldehyde, acetaldehyde, acetaldol, ethylbutyraldehyde, and ethylhexaldehyde. See Table 22, p. 699. Many higher molecular weight aldehydes are normally present in natural products [H. Salem and H. Cullumbine, *Toxicol. Appl. Pharmacol.* 2, 183 (1960)].

Treatment: See Formaldehyde, p. 278.

ALDRIN

Ingestion, inhalation, or skin absorption of a toxic dose will induce nausea, vomiting, hyperexcitability, tremors, epileptiform convulsions, and ventricular fibrillation. Aldrin may cause temporary reversible kidney and liver injury. Symptoms may be seen after ingestion of less than 1 gram in an adult; ingestion of 25 mg has caused death in children. See also Endrin, p. 238, and Chlorinated Hydrocarbons, p. 648.

Treatment: Give oxygen and artificial respiration if necessary. Prompt and thorough removal from the skin by flooding with water and from the stomach by vomiting or gastric lavage are indicated. Use phenobarbital or bromides for the control of central nervous system stimulation. Calcium gluconate has been reported to control convulsions. Avoid all noise, jarring, etc. Keep patient quiet. Do not use oily cathartics. Do not use epinephrine since it may induce ventricular fibrillation.

ALKALIES

Alkalies include the following: Ammonium hydroxide, p. 96, calcium hydroxide, calcium oxide, p. 149, potassium carbonate (potash), potassium hydroxide, sodium carbonate (soda lime), p. 543, and sodium peroxide, p. 546.

ALKA-SELTZER

An Alka-Seltzer tablet contains acetylsalicylic acid 0.32 gm, sodium bicarbonate 1.90 gm, citric acid 1.05 gm, and monocalcium phosphate 0.19 gm. When Alka-Seltzer is dissolved in water, carbon dioxide is evolved and acetylsalicylic acid is converted into the soluble sodium salt, sodium acetylsalicylate. The sodium content totals 521 mg or approximately 22.7 mEq per tablet. The pH lies between 6 and 7. See Acetylsalicylic Acid, p. 67.

ALKYL ACID PHOSPHATES

These chemicals are not cholinesterase inhibitors. They are strong acids and should be handled as mineral acids. See Phosphoric Acid, p. 472.

ALKYL-ALUMINUM COMPOUNDS

The aluminum alkyls and certain halide derivatives (aluminum triethyl, diethyl, trimethyl, diisobutyl, tri-isobutyl, and chloride derivatives) burst into flame and decompose spontaneously in air forming white fumes that have a musty odor. Persons exposed to these fumes should be examined for possible lung or bronchial injury. The fumes are known to cause "metal fume fever." See Metal Fumes, p. 376. Contact with the skin, eyes, or mucous membranes will cause severe burns which are slow to heal.

Treatment: For skin, eye, or mucous membrane contact, wash with copious volumes of running water for 15 minutes. For pain, local application of ice water and morphine are recommended. Treat subsequently as thermal burn. See p. 26. In cases of inhalation, remove from exposure; if needed, give artificial respiration and oxygen. Keep under observation for evidence of pulmonary injury.

ALKYL-ARYL SULFONATES (Sodium Alkyl-Aryl Sulfonates)

These are anionic surfactants having a moderate degree of toxicity. Toxicologically, they may be compared with sodium alkyl sulfates. See Alkyl Sodium Sulfates, p. 85.

ALKYLATE

This is high-octane aviation and motor gasoline blending stock. Chemically, it consists of saturated, branched-chain paraffin hydrocarbons in the C_5–C_9 range with C_8 hydrocarbons predominating. See Gasoline, p. 285.

ALKYLBENZENES

Vapors of toluene, xylenes, styrene, and alkylbenzenes may produce irritation of the upper respiratory tract, disturbance of vision, dizziness, nausea, collapse, and coma. Direct contact with skin and eyes has resulted in intense burning. Unlike benzene, these compounds do not affect hemopoietic tissue.

Treatment: Remove from the eyes and skin by thorough washing with water. In case of ingestion administer saline cathartics and demulcents. *Do not induce vomiting.* Subsequent treatment is symptomatic and supportive.

ALKYL BORIC ACIDS (Alkyl Dihydroxy Boranes)

Chloropropyl boric acid, nonyl boric acid, and dodecyl boric acid are examples of this class of chemicals. They are very weak acids. Toxicologically, they belong in the same class as boric acid. See Boric Acid, p. 138.

ALKYL-2-CYANOACRYLATES

This is a family of chemicals currently under investigation as tissue adhesives for "sutureless" surgical procedures. The histotoxicity of these compounds is due to the heat evolved during polymerization *in situ* and the release of toxic compounds during their degradation.

The methyl derivative is decidedly more toxic to nerve cells than the other cyanoacrylate homologs tested. Unlike the other homologs, it produces considerable necrosis in the surrounding tissue.

N-butylcyanoacrylate is more neurotoxic than the *N*-heptyl, *N*-octyl, and isobutyl homologs.

Long-term implantations in the soft tissue of thirteen chimpanzees for an average of eleven months have failed to reveal any evidence of tumor formation [R. Lehman *et al.*, *Arch. Surg.* **93**, 441 (1966)].

ALKYL DISULFIDES (Dithioalkanes)

Dimethyl, diethyl, dipropyl, and dibutyl disulfide are liquids at room temperature. Unlike mercaptans and alkyl sulfides, these compounds have very little odor. Limited toxicological information is available. A feeding study on di-*n*-propyl disulfide (dogs) indicates a high order of toxicity.

Treatment: For inhalation, remove from the contaminated atmosphere and give artificial respiration and oxygen if needed. In case of ingestion, induce vomiting, follow with gastric lavage and cathartics. Subsequent treatment is symptomatic and supportive.

ALKYLENE OXIDES

See Ethylene Oxide, p. 258; Propylene Oxide, p. 502.

ALKYLPHENOLS

2-Ethylhexylphenol: rat oral LD_{50}, 2.46 gm/kg; rabbit skin LD_{50}, 2.52 ml/kg.

2,6-Dimethyl-4-heptylphenol: rat oral LD_{50}, 1.6 gm/kg; rabbit skin LD_{50}, 2.14 ml/kg.

The concentrated vapor of either of the two compounds at room temperature was not fatal to rats on 4-hour exposure. Both substances are corrosive and irritating to the skin. One-tenth ml of either material in contact with rabbit skin for 24 hours caused necrosis.

Treatment: See Phenol, p. 463.

ALKYL SODIUM ISOTHIONATES

These are anionic surfactants having a moderate degree of toxicity. They are used in detergent formulations. See Alkyl Sodium Sulfates, p. 85.

ALKYL SODIUM SULFATES (Sodium Alkyl Sulfates)

These compounds are extensively used as detergents. Chemically, they are sodium salts of the sulfate esters of high molecular weight alcohols (anionic detergents). In general, these chemicals have a moderate order of toxicity. Repeated skin contact with concentrated solutions may cause dermatitis. Gastrointestinal irritation, vomiting, and diarrhea may follow ingestion of a large dose. See Detergents, p. 201.

Treatment: In case of ingestion of a toxic dose induce vomiting, and follow with gastric lavage. Remove from the skin with water.

ALLAMANDA (A. *cathartica*)

The ingestion of this plant will induce catharsis. No treatment is required.

ALLETHRIN (Allyl Cinerin)

This is a botanical insecticide having a low order of toxicity. See Rotenone, p. 521.

ALLOPURINOL (Zyloprim)

Allopurinol inhibits the production of uric acid. It has therefore found use in the therapy of hyperuricemia associated with gout. The most common side effects noted, in about 3% of patients, included skin rash, fever, alopecia, or gastroenteric symptoms. A few cases of reversible hepatotoxicity and asymptomatic rise in serum alkaline phosphatase or serum transaminase have been reported. Some investigators have found an increase in acute attacks of gout during early stages of therapy (even when subnormal levels of serum uric acid had been attained), a rise in blood urea nitrogen in patients with pre-existing renal disease, asymptomatic leukopenia, and formation of cataracts.

Caution: According to the manufacturer, this drug is presently contraindicated for use in (a) nursing mothers, (b) children, except in patients with hyperuricemia secondary to malignancy, and (c) patients who have developed a severe reaction to allopurinol. Fluid intake should be sufficient to yield a daily output of at least 2 liters; the urine should be alkaline (Burrows Wellcome & Co., October 1966).

ALLYL ALCOHOL (Propenol)

The vapors of allyl alcohol are irritating to the eyes, nose, and mucous membranes. An hour's exposure to 1000 ppm is fatal to laboratory animals; a saturated atmosphere is lethal in a few minutes. Allyl alcohol is extremely irritating to the skin and is readily absorbed through the intact skin in toxic, even lethal amounts. Absorption results in injury to the viscera. It is highly toxic by ingestion. Small quantities contaminating cigarettes, food, and hands could cause injury.

Treatment: For inhalation exposure, remove the individual to fresh air and give artificial respiration if necessary. In case of eye contact, flush thoroughly with water for at least 15 minutes. For skin contact, immediately remove all contaminated clothing and shoes and wash affected area with water for at least 15 minutes. In case of ingestion, induce vomiting and follow with gastric lavage and demulcents.

ALLYL CHLORIDE

Inhalation of a saturated atmosphere could cause death in a few minutes. Exposure to 3000 ppm might be lethal in an hour, and inhalation of concentrations in the range of 300 ppm for an hour can cause serious effects. High concentrations of the vapors are irritating to the eyes and nose.

Allyl chloride is irritating to the skin. There is also a possibility that it can be absorbed through the skin in toxic quantities.

Allyl chloride has a moderate to high degree of toxicity by ingestion. Small quantities found on contaminated cigarettes, food, and hands could cause injury, particularly from repeated contact.

Treatment: For inhalation, remove the individual to fresh air; if breathing stops, give artificial respiration and oxygen. Subsequent treatment is symptomatic and supportive. In case of eye contact, flush with water for at least 15 minutes. For skin contact, immediately remove all contaminated clothing and shoes under the shower. Flush the skin with water for at least 15 minutes. If the material is swallowed, induce vomiting and follow with gastric lavage, demulcents, and saline cathartics.

ALMONDS

Bitter almonds contain the glycoside amygdalin. This is hydrolyzed to cyanide in the gastroenteric tract. F. Kerdel-Vegas reported a case of generalized hair loss following the ingestion of 70 to 80 Coco de Mono (*Lecythis ollaria*) almonds. Nervousness and anxiety, violent chills, watery diarrhea, and anorexia were followed in 8 days by a sudden extensive loss of scalp and body hair. Within a month, the patient had lost 4 kg in body weight. Experiments in mice confirmed the results seen in man. Elucidation of the toxic mechanism will require further work [*J. Invest. Dermatol.* **42**, 91 (1964)].

Treatment: See Cyanide p. 191.

ALPHAPRODINE (Nisentil)

This synthetic narcotic is chemically related to meperidine. The undesirable effects (respiratory depression, alteration in gastroenteric, cardiovascular, and renal functions) and the tendency to cause addiction are similar to morphine and related potent analgesics, except that the side effects are of shorter duration.

Treatment: Respiratory depression is promptly antagonized by nalorphine or by levallorphan. When given with alphaprodine, levallorphan and nalorphine will counteract the rise in cerebrospinal fluid pressure caused by alphaprodine.

ALPHAZURINE

This is a blue dye that stains only viable tissue. It is used in lymphography and to guide debridement in severe burns. Recently, three patients treated with this new agent suffered anaphylactic shock. One of these patients experienced paroxysms of sneezing, severe respiratory distress and bronchospasm followed by shock, a generalized seizure and cardiac arrest after one-third of the calculated dose of 0.1 mg/kg had been injected I.V. Emergency treatment resulted in some improvement. The patient suffered several additional episodes of bronchospasm until his condition deteriorated, and death followed on the fifth postinjection day.

Caution: This dye should be used with caution until more is known about it. Obviously, a positive skin test contraindicates its use [*New Engl. J. Med.* **272,** 1281 (1965); *JAMA* **198,** 668 (1966)].

ALUMINUM

A sliver of aluminum penetrating the skin will form aluminum salts which induce local irritation and possibly cause secondary infection. The soluble aluminum salts have a marked astringent and antiseptic action; they are moderately irritating in concentrated solutions. Excessive use of aluminum hydroxide results in the formation of aluminum chloride, which has an astringent action on the gastroenteric mucosa. Crystalline alum is used as a styptic. Prolonged inhalation of dusts containing high concentrations of aluminum have produced emphysema, non-nodular pulmonary fibrosis, and fatalities. Pulmonary changes induced by inhaled aluminum dust constitute a new type of pneumoconiosis, designated as an "aluminosis" [*Intern. Arch. J. Gewerbepathol. Gewerbehyg.* **19,** 131 (1962)]. The ingestion of traces of aluminum, through the use of cooking utensils, is harmless.

Treatment: For ingestion of an overdose of a soluble aluminum salt, administer milk and induce vomiting; continue with symptomatic and supportive treatment. Treat eye exposure by thorough flushing with water. For inhalation, see Metal Fumes, p. 376.

ALUMINUM-ALKYLS

See Alkyl–Aluminum Compounds, p. 83.

AMANTADINE HYDROCHLORIDE (Symmetrel)

This new antiviral agent is indicated *only* in patients of all ages for whom an *influenza A2* infection would entail a grave risk, particularly when a vaccine cannot be used. The drug has no therapeutic properties [Council on Drugs, *JAMA* **201**, 372 (1967)].

Nausea, anorexia, and vomiting have been reported occasionally. The most common adverse reactions are hyperexcitability, tremors, slurred speech, ataxia, psychic depression, insomnia, lethargy, and dizziness. Doses as high as four times the recommended dose have caused convulsions.

Caution: The recommended daily dosage should not be exceeded. Amantadine should not be given to patients who are being treated with central nervous stimulants or psychopharmacological agents. This drug should not be administered to patients with a history of epilepsy, and only under close medical supervision [Council on Drugs, *JAMA* **201**, 374 (1967)].

AMBENONIUM CHLORIDE (Mytelase)

This is one of the drugs used in the treatment of myasthenia gravis. Its beneficial action is due primarily to inhibition of acetylcholinesterase and other esterases leading to an augmented concentration of acetylcholine at the neuromuscular junction, and secondly to a direct excitatory action on the neuromuscular junction. The side effects of Mytelase are those related to marked or excessive parasympathetic stimulation, which, after high doses, will include neuromuscular blockade. When used in relatively low doses for the treatment of urinary retention and bowel atony, this drug was responsible for cholinergic crises in two patients. A similar incident resulted from the combined administration of this drug and mecamylamine hydrochloride (Inversine).

Caution: Mytelase is contraindicated in patients receiving ganglionic blocking agents, as for instance Inversine [*New Engl. J. Med.* **271**, 1260 (1964)].

AMIDES (Saturated Fatty Acid Amides)

The saturated fatty acid amides are bland and nonirritating substances having a low order of toxicity.

Treatment: None is required.

AMINE BORANES (Dimethylamine Borane; Trimethylamine Borane; Pyridine Borane)

These chemicals are less toxic than the borohydrides. Dimethylamine borane is about one-half as toxic as decaborane. Systemic intoxication is manifested principally as central nervous system depression. See Boranes, p. 137.

AMINES, ALIPHATIC (Alkyl Amines; Alkylene Amines)

These alkaline substances cause irritation and severe burns on contact with the skin and mucous membranes. A sensitization type of dermatitis has been reported following exposure to certain amines used in resin manufacture. Hivelike swelling involving the eyes, face, and neck occurs in sensitive individuals. The sensitivity appears to be permanent. Once a person becomes sensitized, a minimal exposure can cause symptoms. Myocardial, vascular, and muscular lesions have been produced in animals exposed to allylamines. See Table 23, p. 702.

Treatment: See Ammonia, Aqueous, p. 95.

AMINES, AROMATIC

The following substances and their salts are carcinogenic for the urinary bladder of man and the dog: 4-aminobiphenyl (Xenylamine), 4-nitrobiphenyl, 2-naphthylamine, and benzidine. Malignancies in man have been reported after exposure of only a few weeks and a latent period of several years. Three other compounds have the same potentialities, since they induced bladder tumors in dogs. These are 2-acetylaminofluorene, *N,N*-dimethyl-4-aminoazobenzene, and 4-amino-3,2'-dimethylazobenzene (*o*-aminoazotoluene).

Caution: Stringent precautions must be taken to avoid exposure to these substances. They may produce cancer by inhalation (either vapors or dust), ingestion, or by absorption through the skin. For details see "Bladder Cancer, a Symposium," Wm. B. Deichmann *et al.*, Aesculapius Publishing Company, Birmingham, Alabama, 1967.

2-AMINOBENZENETHIOL (o-Aminothiophenol)

Five hundred mg/kg of 2-aminobenzenethiol administered orally is acutely lethal to rats. It produces methemoglobin. An oral dose of 50 mg/kg had no effect on nine out of ten rats tested. Severe dermatitis may result from skin contact.

Treatment: For skin and eye contact, flood affected parts with water for 15 minutes. In case of ingestion, induce vomiting and follow with gastric lavage. See Methemoglobinemia, p. 40.

AMINOCAPROIC ACID (EACA)

This systemic blood coagulant is a monoaminocarboxylic acid related to lysine. It is used in conditions of excessive bleeding from systemic hyperfibrinolysis and urinary fibrinolysis. Side effects such as hypotension, nausea, and diarrhea are common. In patients with poor renal function, serum potassium may become elevated. There have been several reports of thrombosis, some of them fatal. It is not clear whether the thrombosis was caused by this drug or due to preexisting intravascular clotting.

Caution: This drug should be considered an adjunct to and not a substitute for blood or blood component replacement. The drug is contraindicated in pregnancy until more is known about it [*Med. Letter* 9, 9 (1967); M. Goulian, *Ann. Internal Med.* 65, 782, (1966)].

AMINOGLUTETHIMIDE (Elipten)

This drug has been used for the management of various types of seizures. Side effects or symptoms of toxicity have appeared in approximately every second patient and included a morbilliform rash (most frequently) or ataxia, drowsiness, mental confusion, headache, and periorbital edema. Occasionally, behavioral difficulties, transient leukopenia, hypothyroidism, goiter, and masculinization were noted [*J. Clin. Endocrinol. Metab.* 26, 1014 (1966); 27, 265 (1967)]. The A.M.A. Council on New Drugs (1966 Edition) recommends that therapy with this drug be discontinued if the rash does not disappear in 1 week.

AMINOHYDROXY COMPOUNDS (2-Amino-1-butanol; 2-Amino-2-methyl-1-propanol; 2-Amino-2-methyl-1,3-propanediol; 2-Amino-2-ethyl-1,3-propanediol)

This is a moderately toxic class of chemicals similar in action to mono- and diethanolamine and morpholine. Since they are mildly alkaline, prolonged or frequently repeated exposure of the skin may result in irritation. See Ethanolamines, p. 246.

2-AMINOINDANE

This non-narcotic analgesic is a mild central stimulant. Side effects may include slow respiration, euphoria, dreaminess, and addiction.

Treatment is symptomatic.

AMINOPHYLLINE (Theophylline with Ethylenediamine)

This drug is most toxic when given I.V. and S.C. (dose, 3.5 mg/kg), less toxic when administered P.O. (5.0 mg/kg), and least toxic when given rectally in a dose of 6.0 mg/kg at 8- or preferably at 12-hour intervals. Many children are sensitive to aminophylline. Severe intoxications and death have followed rectal administration because of hypersensitivity or overdosage. Rectal absorption of aminophylline is unreliable, and the possible cumulative effect of prolonged treatment by this route of administration must be kept in mind. Parents should be acquainted with the side effects and warned not to give this drug indiscriminately to asthmatic children and to call the doctor when anorexia, irritability, vomiting, and thirst become apparent. Signs and symptoms of intoxication include nausea, vomiting, restlessness, tremors, convulsions, fever, marked thirst, respiratory acidosis, and vasomotor collapse. The simultaneous administration of aminophylline and ephedrin is contraindicated.

Treatment: When side effects appear, discontinue treatment immediately and, if necessary, treat symptomatically for central nervous system stimulation, dehydration, hyperthermia, and shock. Restore the acid-base balance with lactate or bicarbonate. Oxygen and antibiotics provide supportive therapy.

AMINOPTEROYLGLUTAMATE (Aminopterin)

Because of toxicity, this anti-leukemic drug has been withdrawn from the market. When used as an abortifacient, it produced a fetus with multiple abnormalities [*Am. J. Obstet. Gynecol.* **84**, 356 (1962)].

3-AMINOPYRIDINE HYDROCHLORIDE

No human toxicity has been reported. For animals, the Approximate Lethal Doses are: rats, 79 mg/kg as a 1.0% aqueous solution; dogs, 23 mg/kg per se in capsule; 14–21 day old chicks, 325 mg/kg as a 1.0% aqueous solution of the free base. The percutaneous lethal dose for rabbits is 327 mg/kg as a paste in tap water. Signs of toxicity include central nervous system stimulation and respiratory difficulties. 3-Aminopyridine has a higher vapor pressure than 4-aminopyridine.

Treatment: See 4-Aminopyridine Hydrochloride.

4-AMINOPYRIDINE HYDROCHLORIDE

No human toxicity has been reported. For animals, the Approximate Lethal Oral Doses are: rats, 28 mg/kg as a 0.5% aqueous solution; dogs, 4 mg/kg in capsule, 12 mg/kg as 0.25% on grain; swine, 18 mg/kg as 0.25% on grain; 14–21 day old chicks, 15 mg/kg as a 1.0% aqueous solution. The acute percutaneous lethal dose for rabbits is 327 mg/kg as a paste in tap water. It is moderately irritating to the rabbit's eye but not to the skin. Signs of toxicity include ataxia, salivation, central nervous system stimulation, labored breathing, convulsions, and coma.

Treatment: In case of contact with skin, eye, or mucous membrane, flood affected area with water. For ingestion, induce vomiting and follow with gastric lavage. Subsequent treatment is symptomatic and supportive.

AMINOPYRINE (Amidopyrine, Pyramidon)

An acutely toxic dose produces central nervous system stimulation (tremors and convulsions). In a hypersensitive patient, ingestion of therapeutic doses of this analgesic and antipyretic drug may produce leukopenia and agranulocytosis. These effects may appear without warning after the drug has been used for some time without harmful effects.

Prolonged use of aminopyrine has occasionally induced skin rash, fever, inflammation and ulceration of the throat and mouth, renal complications, jaundice, anemia, and prostration. In many foreign countries, this drug is sold over the counter in combination with other drugs. (See also Blood Dyscrasias, p. 51.)

Treatment: At the first undesirable sign or symptom, discontinue therapy immediately. In case of accidental ingestion of a toxic dose, induce vomiting or perform gastric lavage, give a saline cathartic and, if necessary, administer oxygen and a central depressant. Maintain an adequate fluid balance. Also consider giving transfusions of whole blood.

AMINOSALICYLIC ACID (PAS; Pasem; Pamisyl; Parasal)

This drug is used together with streptomycin or isoniazid to treat tuberculosis. Occasionally, PAS will induce loss of appetite, nausea and vomiting, and severe effects involving the liver and kidney. Three children developed acute hemolytic anemia with methemoglobinemia. It is believed that these children were treated with the drug after it had undergone decomposition.

Caution: PAS should not be administered if this drug shows signs of chemical decomposition. The amount dispensed should not exceed one week's supply [*Am. J. Diseases Children* **108**, 425 (1964)]. Gastroenteric side effects are reduced or eliminated when the drug is taken at mealtime.

AMITRIPTYLINE (Elavil)

Side effects and signs of toxicity of this tranquilizer include autonomic reactions, behavioral abnormality, drug potentiation, dyskinesia, hyperflexia, seizures, cardiovascular involvement and skin lesions. An overdose produces marked central nervous system stimulation. See Phenothiazines, p. 464. Recently reported side effects involved a 50-year-old woman who developed paresthesia of the left side of the face and body, and slurred speech after amitriptyline therapy for 2 weeks [*Lancet* **I**, 426 (1968)].

Symptoms simulating a cerebrovascular accident were reported by Brown in 4 patients [*Practitioner* **200**, 288 (1968)]. Recovery followed withdrawal of the drug.

Caution: The risk of convulsions in amitriptyline-treated patients should be seriously considered. The drug should be used with extreme caution in patients with a presumed low seizure threshold, such as those with brain damage, previous or present epilepsy, epileptic family history, or epileptogenic activity in the EEG [T. A. Betts, *et al.*, *Lancet* **I**, 390 (1968)].

AMMONIA, ANHYDROUS

This is a stable, pungent, colorless gas—50 ppm detectable by odor; 700 ppm causes eye irritation, and permanent injury may result if prompt remedial measures are not taken; 5000 ppm can cause immediate death from spasm, inflammation, or edema of the larynx. Contact of the liquid with skin freezes the tissue and then produces a caustic burn. Small cuts and scratches on skin burn intensely in the presence of small amounts of ammonia.

Treatment: For skin or eye contact, flood immediately with running water for 15 minutes. Treat subsequently as thermal burn. See p. 26. For inhalation, remove the victim from contaminated atmosphere and, if necessary, give artificial respiration and oxygen. Observe for laryngeal spasm and perform tracheostomy if indicated. See Ammonia, Aqueous, p. 95.

AMMONIA, AQUEOUS (Ammonium Hydroxide)

Liquid or vapor produces marked local irritation at the point of contact with skin, mucous membranes, lungs, or gastroenteric tract. The ingestion of household ammonia causes burning pain in the mouth, throat, stomach, and thorax, constriction in the throat and coughing. This is soon followed by vomiting of blood or by passage of loose stools containing blood. The local and systemic effects produced may lead to respiratory difficulties, convulsions, and shock. A brief exposure to 5000 ppm or the ingestion of 3–4 ml may be fatal.

Treatment: Removal from the eyes or skin is best accomplished by a copious flow of water. For ingestion, lavage stomach with water or lemon juice, milk, or demulcents. The longer the interval between the ingestion of ammonia and gastric lavage the greater is the hazard of perforating the esophagus or stomach. Severe edema of the glottis may require tracheostomy. Give artificial respiration and oxygen if needed. Rest is most important. Do not give emetics. See "Removal from Alimentary Tract," p. 15.

AMMONIA, ENDOGENOUS

Hyperammonemia of endogenous origin may occur in patients with partial cirrhosis and gastrointestinal hemorrhage, surgical shunts, acute or chronic hepatic insufficiency, congestive heart failure, in states of shock, diabetic coma, and chronic pulmonary emphysema. The abnormally increased blood concentration of ammonium ions produces symptoms progressing from stupor to coma (hepatic coma, hepatocerebral intoxication, "meat poisoning," "ptomaine poisoning") and death. One of the earliest signs may be a flapping tremor of the hands ("liver flap") when the arms and fingers are extended forcibly by the patient.

Treatment: Withdraw protein from the diet. In the case of a patient with bleeding esophageal varices, make an early and vigorous effort to control the bleeding. Use cathartics and enemas to eliminate the pool of nitrogenous material in the gastroenteric tract. Administer broad-spectrum antibiotics orally in order to eliminate, as much as possible, the bacterial flora which form ammonia from ingested "nitrogen" in the enteric tract. Give glutamic acid parenterally because of its known ammonia-binding capacity. Administer arginine because of its apparent effect in lowering the blood ammonia and increasing the blood urea nitrogen.

AMMONIUM CHLORIDE

Ammonium chloride, in oral doses of 0.5–1 gm 3–4 times a day, is used as an acidic diuretic. Even though its effectiveness as a diuretic diminishes or ceases after a few days, it occasionally causes acidosis and demineralization of bony structures. Since it potentiates the action of other diuretics, it is frequently used in combination with these compounds. In the treatment of bromism, ammonium chloride is occasionally used instead of sodium chloride when it is desirable to support and augment the excretion of bromide and to keep tissue sodium from increasing. The compound finds some use as an expectorant.

Unpublished single 6-hour inhalation studies conducted in our laboratory with mice, rats, guinea pigs, and rabbits indicate that a concentration of 50 mg/m³ of ammonium chloride vapors induces no signs of intoxication during the exposure. Post mortem examination immediately after exposure demonstrated congestion of the trachea and bronchial mucosa with increased mucus; the lungs were somewhat distended and emphysematous with petechial hemorrhages and hyperemia. The liver was enlarged, the spleen brownish red in color, and the adrenal medulla was hemorrhagic. Animals sacrificed 8 days after exposure showed the same type and severity of histopathological tissue change. Exposure to higher concentrations caused even more marked gross and histopathological tissue changes.

Treatment: Treat acidosis with sodium lactate or sodium bicarbonate, P.O., I.V., or by gastric intubation. I.V. sodium glutamate (25 gm) in 5% dextrose (500 ml) and L-arginine hydrochloride (25 gm) in 10% dextrose (500 ml) may be beneficial. Hemodialysis should also be considered in cases of severe intoxication.

AMMONIUM O,O-DIETHYL PHOSPHORODITHIOATE

This is a slightly toxic organic phosphate. The lethal oral dose for rats is about 7.9 gm/kg. A 25% aqueous solution applied to the skin and eyes of rabbits showed only a mild degree of irritation, comparable to that produced by many soaps and detergents.

Treatment: In case of ingestion of a large dose, induce vomiting.

AMOBAM (Diammonium Ethylene Bisdithiocarbamate)

This compound is used as a fungicide, a "short stop" for liquid soaps, slimicide and mildew preventative, and as a chemical intermediate. The oral LD_{50} for rats is greater than 450 mg/kg. This compound is less toxic than Nabam, the corresponding disodium salt, and less irritating to the skin due to its lower alkalinity. See Thiocarbamates, p. 585.

Treatment: In case of skin and eye contact, flood affected parts with water for 15 minutes. For ingestion, induce vomiting and follow with gastric lavage and demulcents.

AMODIAQUINE (Camoquin)

This synthetic antimalarial agent is closely related to chloroquin in its action and usage. Gastroenteric symptoms have been noted in a few patients. Toxic doses produce central nervous system effects such as spasticity, incoordination, or convulsions. Review of the literature since 1953 reveals that there have been isolated incidents of severe reactions with some fatalities (leukopenia, pancytopenia, agranulocytosis, diplopia, anorexia, jaundice) [K. Booth *et al., Brit. Med. J.* **3**, 32 (1967)].

Treatment: Perry *et al.* [*JAMA* **179**, 598 (1962)] described a patient who suffered hepatitis and agranulocytosis following amodiaquine therapy; the patient responded favorably to adrenocorticotropin and prednisone. They considered these drugs to be lifesaving. Booth *et al.* point out that it is important that physicians familiarize themselves with correct dosage schedules for antimalarials since some of the toxic effects can be related directly to overtreatment.

AMPHETAMINE (Benzedrine)

The primary effects of amphetamine and amphetamine-like drugs include stimulation of the central nervous system, a vasopressor response, mydriasis and inhibition of gastroenteric activity. Excessive use has been reported to induce insomnia, irresponsible and irrational behavior, increased blood pressure, angina, cardiac arrhythmia, shock and possibly tremors, convulsions, coma, and death. Considering the widespread use of these drugs, the incidence of fatalities has been rare [*Arch. Internal Med.* **112**, 822 (1963)].

A 42-year-old male drank a "benzedrine cocktail" prepared by dissolving the contents of a benzedrine inhaler in Coca Cola. An hour later he felt weak and confused, developed severe headache, and was unable to walk home. Two days later he had a left hemiplegia with almost complete paralysis of the left side of the face, arm, and leg. Benzedrine inhalers contain approximately 300 mg of free amphetamine [*Brit. Med. J.* **1**, 26 (1956)].

The most serious complications result from the repeated or prolonged use of oral, but particularly I.V., doses of these drugs, since this leads to tolerance, dependence, and withdrawal symptoms — in other words, to addiction. The drugs primarily implicated include amphetamine (Benzedrine), dextroamphetamine (Dexedrine), diethylpropion (Tenuate;

Tepanil), and methamphetamine, which is available under a number of trade names (see "American Drug Index," p. 36. J. B. Lippincott Company, Philadelphia, 1968).

The chronic oral use of amphetamines is common among "show-business types" and some adolescents, while the "hippies," middle class neurotics, former heroin addicts, and "outlaw" motorcycle groups are said to be large users of amphetamines for injection [J. C. Kramer et al. JAMA **201**, 305 (1967)]. According to J. C. Kramer et al., chronic use of these drugs induces physiological and biochemical adaptations which are analogous to the changes hypothesized to explain the abstinence syndromes due to opioids or barbiturates. Tolerance is rapidly acquired and the addict may take immense doses for 5 or 6 days, during which he may not sleep. During this time, he becomes paranoid and disorganized. He discontinues drug use and finally falls into a prolonged semi-comatose state. The sleep lasts 12–18 hours, but semi-comatose states lasting for 4–5 days have also been reported. Upon awakening he is lethargic and feels the need to resume his drug for a new round. For details, see the reports by J. C. Kramer et al. and the Committee on Alcoholism and Addiction and Council on Mental Health [JAMA **197**, 1023 (1966)]. "Doping with amphetamines is much more dangerous in warm weather [Sci. News **91**, 353 (1967)]." Dextroamphetamine has produced teratogenic effects in mice [Lancet **II**, 1021 (1965)].

Treatment: Symptomatic therapy is directed toward antagonizing central nervous system stimulation and hypertension. Chlorpromazine (Thorazine) in high therapeutic doses is very effective. A. K. Done suggests a dose of 15 mg I.M. for a 2-year-old child [Clin. Pharmacol. Therap. **2**, 750 (1961)]. Barbiturates are less desirable; to be effective, they have to be given in relatively large doses. According to A. K. Done, a particularly difficult problem is posed by cases of poisoning involving preparations which combine an amphetamine (or one of its derivatives) with a barbiturate. In such instances, the stimulant effects may predominate early despite the presence of large amounts of a barbiturate. The excretion of amphetamines is markedly affected by the pH of the urine. Excretion is slow when the urine is alkaline, rapid in acidosis. The acidosis of starvation — during an amphetamine "run" — may thus create conditions which favor excretion, thereby increasing the dose required (J. C. Kramer *et al.*).

AMPHOTERICIN B (Fungizone)

This antibiotic is administered by I.V. infusion. Because of its toxicity, it should be used only when clearly indicated. It is likely to produce chills, fever, vomiting, headache, renal damage, and thrombophlebitis at the site of injection. Anaphylaxis, thrombocytopenia, anemia, convulsions, and irreversible renal damage have been produced in a few isolated patients.

The intrathecal injection of this drug may produce similar side effects and in addition palsies (including foot drop), chemical meningitis, and difficulty in micturition.

Caution and treatment: Fresh solutions should be prepared for each injection. The total daily dose infused over a period of 6 hours should not exceed 1.5 mg/kg. Prior to injection, patients may be given 0.6 gm of aspirin and an antiemetic to reduce some of the undesirable effects. Hydrocortisone sodium succinate (25 mg), injected directly into the I.V. tubing at the time of injection, has also been effective in reducing side effects.

AMPICILLIN

This is a semisynthetic penicillin for oral and parenteral use. Hypersensitivity reactions and toxicity are similar to the undesirable effects induced by penicillin G.

Caution: The drug should not be administered to a patient with a history of penicillin allergy.

AMYL NITRITE

This drug induces generalized vasodilatation and a prompt fall in blood pressure. Since amyl nitrite dilates the coronary arteries it is used to relieve the pain of angina pectoris. It is also useful in the treatment of cyanide intoxication. The methemoglobin formed by amyl nitrite binds cyanide as cyanmethemoglobin. A toxic dose produces severe headache, vertigo, visual disturbances, marked methemoglobinemia, and cyanosis.

Treatment: Place patient in recumbent position for inhalation of amyl nitrite. If necessary administer oxygen. Do *not* apply heating pads since they may promote collapse. For the treatment of severe methemoglobinemia, transfuse with whole blood or give I.V. or I.M. a dose of 1–2 mg/kg methylene blue or an oral dose of 3-5 mg/kg. See Methylene Blue, p. 390 and Sodium Nitrite, p. 543.

ANESTHETIC HYPERTHERMIA

According to C. R. Stephen [*Mod. Med.* **36**, 129 (1968)] fulminating hyperthermia from unknown cause during anesthesia is a growing source of concern and may justifiably be considered a new syndrome. Fourteen cases have been reported in the literature. In 12 additional patients, the condition was observed within an average of 90 minutes after induction of anesthesia in a controlled air-conditioned environment; it was irreversible in 10 patients. Halothane was the principal anesthetic used.

Treatment: Patient survival depends largely on immediate drastic measures to reduce body heat, providing high concentrations of oxygen with hyperventilation, combatting metabolic acidosis, and supporting failing circulation. Prevention is the best treatment, however, and a recording thermometer connected to an esophageal or rectal thermocouple provides time to act before the elevation becomes irreversible.

ANGIOTENSIN AMIDE (Hypertensin)

When renin (a proteolytic enzyme formed only in renal tissue) reacts with hypertensinogen, a serum globulin octapeptide is formed having marked pressor and vasoconstrictor properties. This has been named angiotensin. Two fractions are known, angiotensin I and angiotensin II. Angiotensin amide is the name for a synthetic compound which, chemically, is a minor structural variant of the natural angiotensin II. The compound is several times more potent than levarterenol; its primary action appears to be on the arteriolar side of the microcirculation of visceral blood vessels.

Caution: This drug is still under investigation; hence it should be used with caution. It should not be used in the treatment of shock following myocardial infarction since it does not exert a direct cardiac stimulating effect. High doses should be avoided since they are likely to induce ventricular irregularities (New Drugs, evaluated by the A.M.A. Council on Drugs, 1966, Chicago, Illinois).

ANHYDRIDES, ORGANIC

These compounds react readily with water, sometimes violently, liberating heat to form the corresponding organic acids. See Table 54, p. 742.

ANILERIDINE (Leritine)

This analgesic narcotic is related to meperidine. Its side effects are less common, less severe, and of shorter duration than those produced by equivalent doses of morphine sulfate. This drug is addictive. It differs from meperidine in that it apparently does not liberate histamine.

Treatment: Nalorphine and levallorphan are effective respiratory depression antagonists. See Narcotic Agents, p. 40, and Opiates, p. 435.

ANILINE (Aminobenzene; Phenylamine)

Commercial aniline (mixture of aniline, toluidine, nitrobenzene, and other benzene derivatives) is often the active ingredient of shoe dyes, hair dyes, insoluble marking ink, lithograph ink, mimeograph ink, and floor polishes. In severe cases of intoxication, symptoms include marked cyanosis, a slow, bounding pulse, symptoms of air hunger, nausea and vomiting, low blood pressure, sudden and extreme prostration, and sometimes convulsions. Most intoxications have occurred as the result of accidental contact with shoe dyes or marking inks or the ingestion of contaminated liquor. The primary clinical pathological changes are: (1) The excessive formation of methemoglobin with resulting cyanosis and anoxemia. (2) The effects of anoxemia, aniline, and nitrobenzene on the central nervous system. (3) The hemolytic effect of nitrobenzene. See Table 25, p. 707.

Treatment: In case of ingestion, induce vomiting, perform gastric lavage, and follow with a saline cathartic. Oxygen therapy and transfusion are effective. Intravenous fluids, particularly 10% glucose in isotonic saline, promote the elimination of aniline, nitrobenzene, and related compounds. To treat methemoglobinemia, see p. 40. Aniline spots on the skin may be removed with 5% acetic acid followed by lukewarm water.

ANISINDIONE (Miradon)

This is a long-acting oral anticoagulant which has no advantages over warfarin sodium. Occasionally, hematuria and chromaturia have been noted.

Treatment: The effect of this drug may be rapidly counteracted by vitamin K_1 (phytonadione, U.S.P.). Precautions, side effects, and contraindications are the same as for other systemic anticoagulants. See Warfarin, p. 626.

ANOVULATORY DRUGS: Norethnodrel with Mestranol (Enovid, Conovid); Norethindrone with Mestranol (Norinyl; Ortho-Novum); Ethynodiol Diacetate with Mestranol (Ovulen-21); ("The Pill")

These are synthetic, progesterone-like drugs consisting of a progestin plus estrogen. They inhibit cyclic ovulation and are used for oral contraception. These drugs are potent. Oral contraceptives distributed in the United States now carry a new warning ordered by the Food and Drug Administration. In essence, this warning cites the findings of British investigators who found that women taking such preparations increase their chances of death or disease from blood clots by 7 to 10 times. In May, 1967, the British Research Council concluded that "... there can be no reasonable doubt that some types of thrombotic disorders are associated with the use of oral contraceptives." In more recent reports, the Council's Statistical Research Unit and the British Committee on Safety of Drugs confirm the association between the use of oral contraceptives and deep-vein thrombosis and pulmonary embolism. Oral contraceptives may also cause cerebral thrombosis. On the other hand, an association between oral contraceptives and other thromboses on the arterial side, notably coronary thrombosis, remains unproved [*Brit. Med. J.* **2,** 193, 199 (1968); *Clin-Alert* (May 31, 1968)].

Temporary side effects may include nausea, depressive symptoms, headache (frequently migrainous in type), gastroenteric disturbances, vaginal "spotting," discomfort in the breasts, or a mild weight gain. F. E.

Cormia recently reported 5 cases of diffuse alopecia during or following administration of contraceptive drugs [*JAMA* **201**, 635 (1967)]. L. R. Erickson and E. S. Peterka reported sunlight hypersensitivity similar to polymorphic light eruptions in a 31-year-old Negro woman who was taking Enovid E. Lesions and symptoms cleared after drug withdrawal only to reappear after trial with other oral contraceptives [*JAMA* **203**, 980 (1968)]. Recently it was reported that two young women developed reversible vascular damage of the colon while on Enovid or Norlestrin therapy. The symptoms cleared upon discontinuation of use of these contraceptives [*New Engl. J. Med.* **278**, 452 (1968)]. For a summary on menstrual dysfunction and oral contraceptive drugs, see E. T. Tyler's report [*JAMA* **203**, 611 (1968)].

Caution: These drugs and related steroid preparations should not be used in the presence of breast or genital cancer. It may be prudent to avoid these agents if there is a family history of such malignancies. These drugs should be used with caution in the presence of vascular disease, hypertension, or migraine in women who have experienced marked postpartum disturbances [*Lancet* **II**, 444 (1967)], and in women with known abnormalities of glucose tolerance [*Lancet* **II**, 776 (1967)]. J. J. Schrogie, *et al.* reported that in young healthy women treated with oral contraceptives, the hypoprothrombinemia response to bishydroxycoumarin decreased. Therefore, women taking oral contraceptives may need increased doses of the anticoagulant [*Clin. Pharmacol. Therap.* **8**, 670 (1967)]. If conception is believed to have occurred, use of an anovulatory drug should be discontinued to avoid the possibility of masculinizing a female fetus. Restraint should be exercised in prescribing drugs for adolescent girls until experience has demonstrated that no permanent effects or spontaneous ovulation are caused by their use at an early age.

The anovulatory drugs, used for contraceptive purposes *may have the opposite effect* if the drug is discontinued after a period of ingestion (rebound of suppressed pituitary function).

Since little is known of the effects of prolonged administration, the health status of the user should be thoroughly appraised prior to the use of any of these drugs and reevaluated at intervals of 6–12 months [Council on Drugs, American Medical Association, *JAMA* **202**, 306 (1967)]. Current oral contraceptive labeling includes the following statement: "Discontinue medication pending examination if there is sudden partial or complete loss of vision, or if there is a sudden onset of proptosis, diplopia or migraine. If examination reveals papilledema or retinal vascular lesions, medication should be withdrawn. (*Clin-Alert*, No. 200, 1968)."

There have been two reports that indicate that extreme caution should be exercised in the morphological diagnosis of mammary or cervical cancer in young women taking oral contraceptives [*Am. J. Clin. Pathol.* **49**, 52 (1968); *Obstet. Gynecol.* **31**, 190 (1968)]. One final point: reports of side effects due to the use of "the pill" will continue to be published. As pointed out in an editorial, the purpose of publishing case reports is not to sound an alarm of what may have been merely fortuitous events, but to encourage physicians to ask young ladies about their medicinal and dietary habits. *Any intervening illness in a young lady taking an anovulatory agent must be interpreted etiologically against the likelihood of the same illness affecting the same patient were she not "on the pill"* [*New Engl. J. Med.* **278**, 452 (1968).

ANTACIDS

Studies conducted in 3 normal volunteers, 2 patients with hypoparathyroidism and 1 patient with pseudohypoparathyroidism showed that prolonged, excessive ingestion of nonabsorbable antacids containing magnesium-aluminum hydroxide results in depletion of body phosphorus by rendering dietary phosphorus nonabsorbable. This syndrome is characterized by hypophosphatemia, hypophosphaturia, increased gastroenteric absorption of calcium, hypercalciuria, increased absorption of skeletal calcium and phosphorus, and debility with anorexia, weakness, bone pain, and malaise. The frequency of the syndrome is unknown. Treatment of phosphorus depletion is a matter of supplying adequate dietary phosphorus [M. Lotz *et al. New Engl. J. Med.* **278**, 409 (1968)].

Antacids containing magnesium and/or aluminum

hydroxides include: Alkets, Aludrox, Aluscop, Alzi-nox, Amphojel, Co-Gel, Gelusil, Kudrox, Maalox, Magnatril, Marblen, Oxaine, Riopan, Robalate, Silain-Gel, Trevidal, Trisogel, and WinGel [*Clin-Alert* (March 21, 1968)].

ANTIBIOTICS, CUTANEOUS REACTIONS

Reactions from topical use: Penicillin and strepto-mucin (p. 453) should not be used topically because of their high potential for producing sensitization. It is possible that sensitization of the patient may preclude later use of these agents. When used topically, tetra-cycline, chlortetracycline, and oxytetracycline (p. 578) rarely sensitize. Neomycin may cause a persistent con-tact dermatitis; however, this is relatively rare, and lasting forms of exfoliative dermatitis have not been noted (p. 418). Chloramphenicol rarely produces con-tact dermatitis (p. 164).

Systemic reactions: Due to its extensive use, peni-cillin produces a great number of serious reactions, various cutaneous and serious anaphylactoid reac-tions, particularly in asthmatic patients (p. 418). A few of the reactions to be expected are erythema multi-forme, urticaria, eruptions due to light sensitivity, moniliasis, black hairy tongue, and pruritus ani. Urti-caria and other reactions in a penicillin-sensitive pa-tient may be the result of exposures to this antibiotic in milk and milk products, Roquefort and blue cheese, and poliomyelitis vaccine (Salk).

The routine systemic use of novobiocin is not rec-ommended because of the high incidence of drug eruptions. Morbilliform and scarlatiniform eruptions are common, and yellow discoloration of the sclera may also result (p. 433).

Chloramphenicol may produce blood dyscrasias and should be used only for serious disorders. Chloram-phenicol may induce moniliasis and pruritus ani, and it can be retinotoxic. Contact dermatitis from the exter-nal use of chloramphenicol occurs only rarely.

The oral administration of broad-spectrum anti-biotics may cause moniliasis, gastroenteritis, and pruritus ani.

Griseofulvin, the antifungal agent, may produce urticarial, morbilliform, and petechial eruptions or photosensitivity (p. 293). Demethylchlortetracycline causes photosensitivity, as well as a unique photo-onycholysis; photosensitivity is produced by a dose of about 600 mg per day, and is more likely to occur in bright summer sun (p. 55).

Fixed drug eruptions have been reported in association with the use of broad-spectrum antibiotics.

Treatment: Cutaneous reactions to antibiotics can generally be controlled by colloid baths, cold compresses, topical application of corticosteroids, and the systemic administration of corticosteroids or corticotropin for brief periods [Rees B. Rees, *JAMA* **189**, 658 (1964)].

ANTIHISTAMINES

The antihistamines compete with histamine for certain cell receptors; therefore, they do not neutralize or antagonize all of the pharmacological effects of histamine. The many antihistaminic preparations vary considerably in their effectiveness in reducing the intensity of allergic or related reactions, for the treatment of motion sickness, or as local anesthetics. In spite of differences in chemical constitution and pharmacological action, certain general statements can be made.

There is a fairly wide margin between a therapeutic and a toxic dose in adults, but not in small children. Fatalities have resulted in young children from ingestion of 100 and 180 mg of diphenhydramine (Benadryl) and from 100 mg of pyrilamine maleate (Mepyramine) [*Arch. Toxicol.* **18**, 93 (1959)]. Following therapeutic doses, the common side effects in 20–50 % of adult patients may include *sedation, dizziness*, gastroenteric irritation, and "dry mouth." These effects are sometimes followed by nervousness and increased heart rate. In hypersensitive individuals, application of an antihistamine to the skin or mucous membranes has induced sensitivity reactions, and applications to the eye have induced allergic and irritating conjunctival reactions. Serious side effects such as bone marrow depression are rare.

The primary effects of an overdose in adults are drowsiness and coma in some individuals, followed occasionally by tremors and convulsions. Small children are much more susceptible—overdoses lead quickly to central excitation. In some children, ataxia, tremors, fixed dilated pupils, fever, and flushing of the face were followed by severe convulsions, coma, and death in 60–90 minutes. A recent report describes the production of an acute psychosis with amnesia and marked atropine-like effects following ingestion of an overdose of Benadryl [S. A. Nigro, *JAMA* **203**, 301 (1968)].

Caution: Antihistamine solutions applied to the eye or nose are, as a rule, more irritating than beneficial. Ointments or creams can also be irritating; in addition, they may be sensitizing and should therefore not be used repeatedly. These drugs should be avoided during pregnancy [*Brit. Med. J.* **2**, 1446 (1962)]. Antihistamines should not be used by anyone whose work involves public safety except after returning home and before retiring.

Treatment: There is no specific antidote. The toxic effects of antihistamines differ in children and adults. The pharmacological effects of the individual antihistamines are also different. *Prompt and repeated vomiting after ingestion of water, milk, or tea is most important* and more effective in removing gastric contents than gastric lavage in the physician's office 30–60 minutes later. Follow with the *cautious* administration of drugs for symptomatic treatment. The convulsive phase is a critical one, since the patient may pass at any moment into the depressed stage. Mild sedatives [paraldehyde or thiopental (Pentothal)] may be helpful during the excitatory stage. In the depressed state, caffeine and/or nikethamide (Coramine) are indicated in certain patients. Oxygen and artificial respiration should be administered if necessary. The blood Benadryl concentration dropped from 0.55–0.32 mg per 100 ml immediately following an exchange transfusion of 1500 ml of whole blood in a 15-month-old child. [R. F. Huxtable and J. Landwirth, *Am. J. Diseases Children* **106**, 496 (1963)]. Histamine is not an antagonist nor an antidote for antihistamines. See also Tripelennamine, p. 610, and Paregoric, p. 451.

ANTIMONY

Ingestion of toxic doses of antimony salts will promptly induce severe gastroenteric distress (abdominal cramps, diarrhea, vomiting), followed by jaundice, muscular pain, dizziness, and prostration. Death is the result of circulatory and respiratory failure. Skin and eye contact may result in dermatitis, keratitis, and ulceration. Vapors of antimony hydride (stibine) are extremely toxic. Inhalation may produce some or all of the following: nausea, headache, weakness, trembling, destruction of red blood cells and hemoglobinuria, anuria, jaundice, coma, and death. Upper respiratory tract irritation, pneumonitis, gastroenteric effects, and dermatitis have also been reported after overexposure to vapors of antimony oxide contaminated with arsenic. Antimony potassium tartrate (tartar emetic) is occasionally used as an expectorant. Antimony trichloride ("butter of antimony") caused an acute intoxication in men exposed to vapors [*Brit. J. Ind. Med.* **23**, 318 (1966)]. The use of Astiban (antimony dimercaptosuccinate) for the treatment of schistosomiasis caused electrocardiographic changes in 9 of 38 patients. Women were more severely affected than men [*Am. J. Cardiol.* **10**, 829 (1962)].

Treatment: After ingestion, induce vomiting and perform gastric lavage; follow with cathartics, diuretics and demulcents. After inhalation exposure, remove victim promptly from the site of exposure and administer oxygen. Skin burns caused by antimony trichloride should be treated by copious irrigation with water. Replacement transfusions are indicated in antimony hydride poisoning. In animal experiments, BAL was found effective in increasing the urinary excretion of antimony.

ANTIPYRINE (Phenazone)

This drug is closely related in its use to aminopyrine. For side effects and symptoms of intoxication, see Aminopyrine, p. 93.

ANT STING (Fire Ant Bite)

In some southern states, stings (not bites) of red fire ants are becoming a health problem. Sensitivity to the sting varies, but a single sting may induce a local wheal, formation of a pustule surrounded by a red halo, and an edematous painful area. Systemically there may be nausea, vomiting, trembling, dizziness, perspiration, cyanosis, asthma, shortness of breath, temporary blindness, shock, and/or coma. A few anaphylactoid reactions have been reported, and one or two deaths. There are also reports that fire ants have killed small pigs and a calf.

Treatment: There is no effective local treatment. Use a tourniquet, if it is possible. The pustules usually clear up in 3 to 7 days (steroids, antibiotics, or antihistamines locally are of no value). For systemic effects, give epinephrine and Benadryl or another antihistamine [*JAMA* **172,** 1221 (1960)]. Give children an antihistamine orally and 1:1000 epinephrine parenterally in doses ranging from 0.1 ml in infants to 1.0 ml in children weighing 50 kg (100 pounds). For emergency measures use oxygen, steroids, and possibly tracheostomy. See also Anaphylactic Drug Reaction, p. 56, and Snake Bite, for use of tourniquet, p. 532.

ANTU (α-Naphthyl Thiourea)

This is less toxic than DDT and safer to handle than sodium fluoroacetate. It is relatively nontoxic for man (no fatalities reported), rabbits, and chickens, but much more toxic for cats and dogs. It kills by producing a drowning pulmonary edema resulting from its action on lung capillaries.

Treatment: After ingestion, induce vomiting and administer gastric lavage and a saline cathartic. Absolute rest and the administration of oxygen under positive pressure are important. See Pulmonary Edema, p. 43. Massive doses of cysteine have been recommended I.P. (up to 1 gm/kg). The compound is effectively removed from the skin by washing with soap and water.

APOMORPHINE

This is a centrally acting emetic. It is used less frequently in the United States than in certain countries for the removal of stomach contents in cases of poisoning. Apomorphine is available in ampules for S.C. injection in doses of 2–8 mg/ml. The dosage for children is 0.5–2 mg; for adults 3–10 mg. Depending on the sensitivity of the individual, severe nausea and vomiting is produced within 10–15 minutes. T. A. Hanson reports that repeated vomiting occurred within 15 minutes after administration of apomorphine in 42 of 46 children [*Southern Med. J.* **60,** 603 (1967)]. The drug is not effective in individuals with marked depression of the central nervous system; they should not receive this drug. Solutions of apomorphine deteriorate and turn green on standing at room temperature. These green solutions should not be used. Apomorphine side effects are prolonged nausea, weakness, pallor, irregular respiration, tachycardia, and hypotension.

This drug is not reliable after ingestion of phenothiazines, since these components are potent antiemetics.

Treatment: If vomiting or retching continues after the stomach has been emptied, the use of levallorphan (Lorfan) or nalorphine (Nalline) is indicated (see p. 41).

APPLE PACKERS NOSEBLEED

In the state of Washington nasal congestion, irritation, and hemorrhages were induced in more than 1000 people engaged in the apple-packing industry who used "blue paper trays" made from salvaged newspaper.

In approximately 1 % of cases, septic ulcers developed severe enough to require packing, cautery, or other treatment. The causative agent(s) in the newspaper has not yet been identified. Recovery followed removal from exposure [G. E. Quinby *JAMA* **197**, 165 (1966)].

APRICOT KERNELS (Apricot Jam)

A 6-year-old Swiss girl was found unconscious by a neighbor who thought she was "merely drunk." Later, emesis and convulsions made this diagnosis questionable. The odor of hydrogen cyanide on her breath suggested cyanide poisoning.

The child had carefully extracted and eaten 10 to 20 dried apricot kernels which were added for flavor to a jar of apricot jam. One apricot kernel on assay had 0.143 gm% HCN; her intake was calculated to be 14–28 mg HCN; the fatal dose for a child is about 20 mg [*Med. Hyg. Geneve* **16**, 306 (1958)]. Persic oil is the same as apricot kernel oil.

Treatment: Gastric lavage and charcoal were effective in this case. See Cyanides, p. 191.

ARAMITE

This compound has a low order of acute toxicity. The probable lethal oral dose is 30 gm for an adult. It is irritating to the skin, mucous membranes, and eyes. Ingestion of a toxic dose causes central nervous system depression and possibly liver and kidney injury. Prolonged ingestion of 200 ppm produced enlargement of the liver and kidneys in rats and dogs; at 400 ppm Aramite was carcinogenic to the liver.

Treatment: Wash skin, eyes, and mucous membranes with copious amounts of water. For ingestion, induce vomiting and follow with gastric lavage, saline cathartics, and forcing of fluids. Subsequent treatment is symptomatic and supportive.

ARBOR VITAE (*Thuja* species)

Extracts of this and several related evergreens [white cedar (*Chamaecyparis thyoides*), tansy (*Tanacetum vulgare*), juniper (*Juniperus sabina*)] have been used as an abortifacient. The effects of a large dose are vomiting and diarrhea. Repeated ingestion of low doses of these extracts has caused personality changes and convulsions.

Treatment: No specific information is available on the treatment of such intoxications. The induction of vomiting followed by a saline cathartic are indicated. Further treatment is symptomatic.

ARMAZIDE

This algicide and sanitizer consists of 12% w/v each of dodecylamine hydrochloride, trimethyl alkyl ammonium chloride, and methyl alkyl dipolyoxypropylene ammonium methyl sulfate.

The oral LD_{50} for rats is 2.28 ml/kg. Rats fed 0.125 and 0.4 ml/kg for a 4-week period showed no deleterious effects. 1.25 ml/kg caused 70% mortality.

The undiluted preparation was found to be a moderate skin irritant. A 1:80,000 aqueous dilution produced no irritation of the intact or abraded skin of rabbits. A 1:80,000 aqueous dilution produced no ocular irritation when instilled into the conjunctival sac of rabbits.

Treatment: See Detergents, p. 201.

AROMATIC AMINES

Absorption of the aromatic amines 4-aminobiphenyl, 2-naphthylamine, benzidine; and 4-nitrobiphenyl has led to hemorrhagic cystitis, recurrent papillomata, and cancer of the urinary bladder in man and dog. For further information see "Bladder Cancer, a Symposium," by Wm. B. Deichmann *et al.*, Aesculapius Publishing Company, Birmingham, Alabama (1968).

Treatment Periodic cystoscopic examination will detect early anatomic changes in the urinary bladder. Surgery may be considered as well as radiotherapy.

ARSENIC

The minimum lethal oral dose of arsenic trioxide for an adult is about 180 mg. Within 30–60 minutes, ingestion of a toxic dose causes severe burning of the mouth and throat, gastroenteric pain, vomiting, diarrhea with hemorrhage, hematuria, dehydration, jaundice, oliguria, and collapse. Central nervous system symptoms (headache, dizziness, and hyperexcitability) may be present, obscuring gastroenteric complaints. Shock may develop rapidly as a consequence of paralysis and increased permeability of the capillaries. Breath and stools may have a garlicky odor. Arsenic is found in the skin, hair, nails, urine, blood, and feces for weeks or months after the ingestion of a toxic dose.

Cancer mortality was investigated in a 7500 km^2 area of the province of Cardoba, Argentina, which has artesian well water with a high arsenic content. During the years 1949–1959, 23.84% of all deaths were due to cancer (372 men, 183 women); the average age was 58.1 years. In areas where the living and health standards were similar, but where arsenic-free water was consumed, cancer mortality was 10.3% (R. M. Bergoglio, *Prensa. Med. Arg.* **51**, 994, 1964).

Potassium arsenite (Fowler's solution) is a well-known cause of skin cancer. Cancer of the mucosa of the mouth, esophagus, and urogenital tract, with metastases to the lungs, has been reported in patients treated with potassium arsenite.

Vaginal use of Acetarsol pessaries is known to have resulted in death due to absorption of arsenic. Arsphenamine has been implicated in the production of blood dyscrasias. For hematological effects in arsenic poisoning, see Kyle and Pease, *New Engl. J. Med.* **273**, 18 (1965). Inhalation of calcium arsenate dust (used to kill crabgrass) has produced upper respiratory tract irritation. Arsine is the most dangerous form of arsenic. See Arsine, p. 641.

Treatment: Gastric lavage with 1% sodium thiosulfate in water or milk, emesis, and saline cathartics are recommended. BAL (Dimercaprol) is the antidote of choice. See Dimercaprol, p. 224. Administer I.V. fluids for dehydration. Two cases of oral lead arsenate poisoning were successfully treated at the Jackson Memorial Hospital, Miami, Florida, by the *cautious* administration of BAL for 1 or 2 days, followed by Calcium EDTA the third or fourth day.

ASBESTOS

Four fibrous silicates with the generic name asbestos are in commercial use. These are crocidolite (blue); amosite (brown); anthophyllite (white); and chrysotile (white), which is by far the most common. Asbestos is in increasing demand for many industrial uses, especially in shipyards and for pipe-lagging. The material must be mined, milled, and fabricated, and at each stage a fine penetrating dust is produced. Asbestosis refers to a type of lung fibrosis in workers who have suffered extensive exposure to asbestos dust. This may or may not be associated with a recognizable disease during the lifetime, and is produced by all types of asbestos [R. T. P. De Treville *et al.*, *JAMA* **203**, 1142 (1968)]. To date, only the dusts from crocidolite and chrysotile have been definitely implicated as carcinogenic. With crocidolite, the relationship was established in the 1950's in South Africa where this blue asbestos mine is located. It was found that the disease takes 40–50 years to develop, but that fatal exposure could be as brief as 3 months in childhood. More than half of those investigated had not worked in the asbestos industry, but had been subjected to only environmental exposure. M. C. Godwin and G. Jagatic reported on mesotheliomas caused by the inhalation of chrysotile, which is mined extensively in Canada [*JAMA* **204**, 1009 (1968)]. For a report on the first epidemiological study in the United States, see paper by T. F. Mancuso and E. J. Coulter, *Arch. Environ. Health* **6**, 210 (1963).

The tumor associated with both crocidolite and chrysotile dust is a mesothelioma. It is a tumor of the lung lining (and occasionally the peritoneum) and can reach remarkable dimensions. While these lesions have not been known to develop following exposure

114

to amosite and anthophyllite dusts, it is well to avoid their exposure [*Nature* **215**, 855 (1967)].

R. T. P. De Treville *et al.*, in referring to experimentally produced bodies with nonasbestos materials, find that they have an appearance *very* similar to asbestos bodies. They sound a word of caution, and suggest that bodies seen in the lungs of normal persons not be assumed to be asbestos bodies until their mineral core has been definitely identified by electron diffraction.

Dipping asbestos boards in a cementing solution before hammering and sawing is the most effective means of reducing dust exposure ("Occupational Health Activities," U.S. Department of Health, Education, and Welfare, No. 2, December 1967).

ASTHMADOR

This is a nonprescription mixture of belladonna and stramonium for the relief of bronchial asthma by burning and inhaling the smoke [M. H. Keeler and F. J. Kane, Jr., *Am. J. Psychiat.* **124**, 852, (1967)].

A confused, disoriented, and uncoordinated 18-year-old boy was brought to the emergency room. His symptoms subsided within 24 hours. He later admitted to ingesting $1\frac{1}{2}$ teaspoonfuls of Asthmador. Several individuals required emergency treatment after ingesting beer or cola containing 1 or 2 teaspoonfuls of Asthmador. Another young man suffered an intoxication a few hours after smoking four Asthmador cigarettes. The clinical picture was that of an atropine intoxication. He had slurred speech and an ataxic gait and was markedly confused; he also had a dry, red skin, tachycardia, dilated pupils, fever, and a severely swollen uvula and palate. Thirty-six hours later, all symptoms cleared and he remembered little of his intoxication [W. F. Wilcox, *New Engl. J. Med.* **277**, 1209 (1967); *Clin-Alert* (January 12, 1968)]. See Atropine, p. 116, and Scopolamine, p. 524.

ATRAZINE

The active ingredient of Atrazine herbicides is 2-chloro-4-ethylamino-6-isopropylamino-*s*-triazine. Atrazine 50W, a wettable powder containing 50 % 2-chloro-4-ethylamino-6-isopropylamino-*s*-triazine, is whitish in color, virtually odorless, and has a low toxicity for man and animals. The acute oral LD_{50} of Atrazine is 1.75 gm/kg (mice) and 3.08 gm/kg (rats). Fifty per cent of the animals survived after 400 mg/kg were administered orally 6 days a week for 4 weeks.

Treatment: Remove from the skin and eyes with water. Induce vomiting in case of ingestion.

ATROPINE SULFATE

Intoxications have occurred following therapeutic overdosage and ingestion of plants containing atropine. The lethal dose of atropine is approximately 15 mg for a child, 100 mg for an adult. Signs and symptoms of atropine intoxication depend primarily on dose and individual susceptibility.

The following oral dose-symptom relationship was experienced by an adult:

0.5 mg: slight dryness of throat.

0.5–1 mg: "dry mouth," thirst, mydriasis.

2 mg: marked mydriasis, some loss of accommodation, tachycardia.

3–5 mg: headache, muscular weakness, dysphagia, alteration of voice, hot and dry skin, retention of urine, and inability to urinate.

7–8 mg: severe mydriasis and disturbances of vision, fever, hyperexcitability, muscular incoordination, and elevated blood pressure.

10 mg: mania, delirium, hallucinations, circulatory and respiratory failure.

The average U.S.P. dose of atropine sulfate for an adult is 0.5 mg. An individual suffering from an organic phosphate intoxication can tolerate large doses.

Jahnke pointed out that children and adults living in the tropics or subtropics are particularly sensitive to atropine. Severe and fatal intoxications have been reported in children after instillation (aqueous) or application (salve) of 1–2 mg to the eyes, and after the oral administration of 0.2–2 mg doses. Ataxia, restlessness, delirium, fright, and aggressive behavior were noted early [W. Jahnke, *Arch. Toxikol.* **16**, 243 (1957)].

The *routine* use of atropine preoperatively has been questioned, since according to P. J. Tomlin *et al.* this drug causes a definite degree of hypoxemia [Lancet, **I**, 14 (1964)].

Treatment: After ingestion of a plant material containing atropine or related compound (see Jimson

Weed, p. 341), induce vomiting *promptly* and repeatedly, or perform gastric lavage with water, 2% tannic acid, or tea. The true parasympathetic drugs, pilocarpine or methacholine (Mecholyl), antagonize the peripheral effects of atropine but are of little value against the central effects which are more serious. For central excitation give a short-acting barbiturate, chloral hydrate, or paraldehyde. Large doses of sedatives should be avoided. Also administer dextrose I.V. In a severe intoxication, artificial respiration and oxygen are indicated. Jahnke recommends cooling or sponging with *water* to reduce the body temperature. After mild or severe intoxication, recovery is usually complete within a few days, except for muscular weakness which may persist for 2 weeks, and partial loss of accommodation which may persist for a month or two. Chlorpromazine should not be administered since there is evidence that the effects of atropine or related drugs may be intensified by this tranquilizer [Science **158**, 669 (1967)].

AZOBISISOBUTYRONITRILE ("VAZO")

"VAZO" is a white crystalline solid which is stable at room temperature and can be stored and handled safely. It is used as a vinyl polymerization catalyst. The approximate lethal dose (ALD) of "VAZO" administered orally to rats is 670 mg/kg. The ALD of tetramethyl succinitrile (TMSN), one of the possible decomposition products of VAZO, is 60 mg/kg. TMSN is nonvolatile (m.p. 168°C).

Treatment: Avoid breathing air containing "VAZO" dust. Under circumstances where dust is noticeable and exposure is more than transient, wear a clean dust mask. Avoid contact with eyes, skin, and clothing. In case of contact, wash skin with plenty of soap and water; flush eyes with water for at least 15 minutes. Since some of the potential decomposition products are highly toxic, it is strongly recommended that *all operations* be carried out with adequate ventilation.

BACITRACIN (Baciguent Ointment)

This antibiotic is administered topically, P.O., or I.M., but not I.V. High I.M. doses of 60,000–80,000 units per day in divided doses should be administered only under close medical supervision, because signs of nephrotoxicity have been noted after I.M. and P.O. use, but not after topical use of local injection into areas of infection. Hypersensitivity reactions may follow oral and parenteral use of the drug; gastroenteric symptoms (including rectal itching) may follow oral use.

Caution: The drug should be used I.M. only when clearly indicated. Its administration should be discontinued promptly when the urinary output drops to 600 ml with adequate fluid intake (which should be no less than 2.5 liters per day for an adult), or when there is evidence of excessive nitrogen retention or progressive azotemia. Signs of renal irritation such as proteinuria, casts, or reduced specific gravity of the urine, according to R. Lich, Jr., do not constitute an indication for drug interruption, since these changes tend to reverse after cessation of therapy ("Drugs of Choice, 1966–1967" C. V. Mosby, St. Louis, Missouri, 1966).

BACTINE

This is a formulation which exhibits antibacterial, antifungal, cleansing, and deodorizing actions. The active ingredients are methylbenzethonium chloride, polyethylene glycol, monoisooctyl phenyl ether, chlorothymol, and alcohol. The inert ingredients, comprising 95 % of the formulation by weight, are propylene glycol, essential oils, and water.

Since Bactine has a bitter taste, it is doubtful if much would be accidentally consumed by humans or domesticated animals. In rats and cats the oral LD_{50} for Bactine is approximately 55 ml/kg.

Cutaneous tests on 151 subjects, using either closed patches or uncovered applications, gave no evidence of skin sensitization.

Treatment: In case of ingestion induce vomiting.

BANANA PEEL

The "high" feeling that some youths have reported after smoking banana skin is psychological.

BARBADOS NUT (*Jatropha curcas*)

The seeds of this herbaceous plant (also known as physic nut, purge nut or curcas bean) contain curcin (a toxalbumin) and other compounds, including an alkaloid, a resin, and a glycoside. Ingestion of three seeds

118

has resulted in gastroenteric symptoms similar to those described for crabs-eye. Severe spasms, intense polypnea, rapid respiration, electrocardiographic changes, and hypotension have been reported in cases of severe or fatal intoxications. Usually an intoxication runs its course in 24–48 hours. The resin has caused dermatitis in sensitive individuals.

The seeds of closely related *Jatropha* species contain the same or a similar toxalbumin. These include *J. gossypiifolia* (bellyache bush), *J. hastada* (perregrina), and *J. multifida* (coral plant or physic nut).

Treatment: See Crabs-eye, p. 188.

BARBITURATES (Goof-Balls; Red-Birds; Yellow-Jackets; Blue-Heavens)

The barbiturates are general depressants. The degree of depression depends primarily on the barbiturate used, the dosage, mode of administration, degree of tolerance, and state of excitability of the individual. Persons who have ingested large therapeutic doses may show poor judgment, emotional instability, and at times may have a toxic psychosis. Neurological signs may include nystagmus, dysarthria, and ataxia.

Potentially fatal oral doses of barbiturates are: 5 gm (long-acting) or 3 gm (short-acting). Potentially fatal blood levels are 8 mg % of a long-acting, or 3.5 mg % of a short-acting barbiturate, indicating that short-acting barbiturates are more toxic [L. B. Berman *et al., JAMA* **161**, 820 (1956)]. However, it is recognized that considerable individual variation exists. Recovery has been reported following the ingestion of 33 gm of phenobarbital [*Acta Med. Scand.* **139** (suppl), 253 (1951)]. L. D. Vandam and W. L. Collins reported what is probably the longest known recorded coma—192 hours—following the ingestion of an unknown quantity of phenobarbital [*JAMA* **184**, 239 (1963)]. Death is due to central and peripheral failure of respiration and circulation; frequently renal failure is a contributing factor.

The sudden or abrupt withdrawal of barbiturates from one who is physically dependent on these drugs will result in the abstinence syndrome. Symptoms may include anxiety, headache, tremors, weakness, vomiting, cardiovascular changes, and grand mal convulsions. These may be followed by confusion, disorientation, tremors, and hallucinations. The delirium may last up to 5 days and end with prolonged sleep. Usually the entire withdrawal syndrome is self-limiting with no organic sequelae. However, patients have died during uncontrolled, untreated barbiturate withdrawal syndromes [Committee on Alcoholism and Addiction and Council on Mental Health, *JAMA* **193**, 673 (1965)].

Caution: Barbiturates should be administered with caution to patients with hepatic damage, to alcoholics, and to those under Dicumarol therapy. By stimulating microsomal enzyme activity, phenobarbital has been found to decrease the half-life of a number of drugs given subsequently, including bishydroxycoumarin, hexobarbital, diphenylhydantoin, and griseofulvin [*Med. Ann. District Columbia* **34**, 578 (1965)]. A recent editorial warns that barbiturates should *not* be administered for at least 5 hours after anticoagulant medication is taken [*JAMA* **201**, 877 (1967)]. Patients receiving Dicumarol and phenobarbital fail to attain a clinically desirable state of anticoagulation, while discontinuation of barbiturate therapy in a patient receiving Dicumarol is liable to cause severe hemorrhage [*Med. Ann. District Columbia* **34**, 578 (1965)]. When phenobarbital is combined with diphenylhydantoin, the cardiac antiarrhythmic activity of diphenylhydantoin is potentiated [P. H. Blachly *JAMA* **202**, 155 (1967)]. See also Chloral Hydrate, p. 163.

Treatment: First in importance is the maintenance of respiration and circulation. Keep air passages clear. Use positive pressure oxygen when necessary. Follow with gastric lavage if the patient is treated in less than 2 hours after ingestion of the drug. It has been recommended that 60 gm of magnesium sulfate in solution be allowed to remain in the stomach after gastric lavage. (In a recent paper W. G. Johanson raises the question whether surgical gastrostomy might not be indicated when a roentgenogram discloses a large mass of tablets in the stomach of a comatose patient. [*JAMA* **202**, 1106 (1967).]

Treatment otherwise is symptomatic. L. W. Henderson and J. P. Merrill emphasize that *"conservative management is the best initial treatment to date for all forms of barbiturate intoxication"* [*Ann. Intern. Med.* **64**, 876 (1966)]. F. Plum and A. G. Swanson

[*JAMA* **163**, 827 (1957)] treated 243 barbiturate patients; 160 of these were comatose and all but 4 recovered. Their treatment was directed toward the following:

(1) *maintaining circulatory activity*
(2) *maintaining respiratory exchange*
(3) *preventing complications of coma*

Pressor agents and artificial respiration were used liberally. Electrical stimulation was found unreliable in patients in deep coma. Drs. Plum and Swanson concluded that *no method of general systemic stimulation provided an adequate substitute for direct physiological treatment of depressed respiration or circulation.* [See also report by C. Clemmesen and E. Nilsson and their description of the "Scandinavian Method" of treatment, *Clin. Pharmacol. Therap.* **2**, 220 (1961).] J. C. Strickler, in his recent editorial, pointed out that "Hemodialysis and, to a lesser extent, peritoneal dialysis remove barbiturates from the body more rapidly than any of the reported forced diuretic regimens. Hemodialysis quite efficiently eliminates short-acting barbiturates, whereas forced diuresis does not." However, since hemodialysis cannot be easily employed for periods longer than approximately 8 hours, a greater total clearance may be achieved in the end by diuresis, which can be continued for several days. Dr. Strickland suggests that hemodialysis should, therefore, be used in profoundly comatose patients in whom the initial hours of therapy appear crucial, particularly those who have ingested short-acting barbiturates [*Clin. Pharmacol. Therap.* **6**, 693 (1965)]. "Forced diuresis" has been effective by infusing an osmotically active agent such as urea or mannitol. Even though there is no general agreement, it nevertheless appears that the concurrent administration of sodium bicarbonate or lactate further increases excretion of the barbiturate [A. L. Linton *et al.*, *Lancet* **II**, 377 (1967)]. Other drugs that have been used to force diuresis include glucose, saline, THAM, chlorothiazide, organic mercurials, furosemide (Lasix), and combinations of these. [An extracorporeal device, utilizing anion-exchange resins, for the treatment of experimental (dog) barbiturate intoxication was recently reevaluated by T. F. Nealon *et al.*, *JAMA* **197**, 118 (1966).]

Symptomatic or prophylactic treatment may include administration of vitamin B complex, antibiotics, and serum albumin (2 ml/kg body weight, maximum of 60–85 ml) to reduce edema. Analeptics such as pentylene tetrazol (Metrazol), Bemigride, nikethamide (Coramine), or caffeine should be used with caution. After the use of these stimulants one must anticipate convulsions, vomiting with aspiration of gastric contents, cardiac arrhythmias, as well as an increase in the cerebral oxygen demand in excess of the available oxygen supply, and possible irreversible brain damage [J. E. Eckenhoff and W. Dam, *Am. J. Med.* **20**, 912 (1956)].

BARIUM

Water-soluble barium salts are readily absorbed from the gastroenteric tract and are extremely toxic, inducing local irritation, peripheral vasoconstriction, digitalis-like action on the heart, violent peristalsis, and paralysis of the central nervous system. Barium-containing depilatory preparations should be used with caution, since dermatitis is produced in approximately 30% of users. Kunwar and Nath reported eleven cases of poisoning when rodent poison containing barium carbonate was inadvertently mixed with flour. One patient died as a result of respiratory paralysis. The taste of the contaminated food was unaltered. Symptoms consisting of giddiness, nausea, vomiting, abdominal pain, headache, and generalized weakness began about half an hour after the meal. Treatment was symptomatic since the identity of the poison was not known [*Current Med. Pract.* **4**, 234 (1960)].

Barium sulfate is insoluble in water and, as a rule, is harmless when administered by mouth or by enema. Bashour and Pierce reported the case of a 9-month-old infant with ileocolonic intussusception who suffered two perforations when given a barium enema. The infant survived because surgery was performed *immediately* [*Am. J. Surg.* **112**, 787 (1966)]. Berman *et al.* warn that in some of the older patients a barium enema presents a distinct hazard. Ten of 62 patients with a history of previous heart disease showed electrocardiographic changes while undergoing routine barium enema examinations. One patient died after developing arrhythmia [*J. Am. Geriat. Soc.* **13**, 672 (1965); *Radiology,* **89**, 250 (1967)].

Treatment of an oral poisoning consists primarily of oral administration of an aqueous 10% solution of magnesium or sodium sulfate, resulting in the precipitation of insoluble barium sulfate and the production of catharsis. In a severe intoxication, calcium or a magnesium salt may have to be given I.V. with caution. Treatment otherwise is supportive and symptomatic.

BARLEY

Brownlee reports that twelve young steers given sudden access to ample stores of coarsely crushed barley suffered from malaise and loss of appetite. Six animals scoured profusely, and one died 7 days later [*Vet. Rec.* **78**, 606 (1966)]. Rox reports that two heifers and five cows, after consuming an excess of moist barley meal, exhibited an acute alcoholic poisoning syndrome with hepatitis, staggering gait, and general incoordination. The animals recovered in 4–5 days [*Vet. Rec.* **78**, 574 (1966)].

BAYER 28589 (2,6-Di-*tert*-butyl-4-nitrophenol)

Bayer 28589 has an oral LD_{50} for rats of 250 mg/kg. Doses of 100 mg/kg were administered to a cat and a rabbit without producing signs of toxicity. When 1.0 mg/kg of the compound was applied in the form of an oil suspension to the shaved bellies of rats, no irritation occurred and there was no indication that the compound was absorbed. No irritation or signs of toxicity occurred when the compound was applied to the ear of a rabbit for 24 hours or to the forearms of six men.

In an inhalation study, one rabbit, one guinea pig, two rats, and four mice were placed in a 400 liter chamber. The animals were exposed to a concentration of 1 mg of Bayer 28589 per liter of air for 2 hours daily for 5 days. Signs of toxicity began to appear after the fifth exposure. When the animals were sacrificed and examined, no gross internal changes were observed.

Treatment: See Phenols, p. 463.

BAYER 29493 O,O-Dimethyl-O-[4-methylthio-m-tolyl] phosphorothioate)

This insecticide is in the intermediate mammalian toxicity class for organic phosphates. The LD_{50} for rats is 325 mg/kg by the intraperitoneal route and 310 mg/kg by the oral route. In a subacute feeding study, Bayer 29493 was fed to rats at the rate of 6.25 mg/kg per day. In 3–4 days 50% depression of cholinesterase occurred. In 15 days the cholinesterase was depressed to about 80% of its normal value.

Treatment: See Organic Phosphates, p. 438.

BAYER 30686 (2,3-Quinoxalinedithiol Cyclic Trithiocarbonate)

This compound is a miticide. Bayer 30686 has an oral LD_{50} for rats of 2.0 gm/kg. The acute intraperitoneal toxicity for rats is approximately 250 mg/kg. The dermal toxicity was determined by applying 1.0 gm/kg of the compound as an aqueous suspension to the shaved bellies of rats for four hours. No signs of intoxication or irritation occurred. The compound did not cause skin irritation when applied to the ear of a rabbit for a 24-hour period. When placed in a rabbit's eye, the compound caused a temporary reddening of the conjunctiva. When the compound was applied to the forearm of human subjects, an irritation was produced in two out of eight people treated.

The inhalation toxicity of Bayer 30686 was tested by placing one rabbit, one guinea pig, two rats, and four mice in a 400 liter chamber. A suspension of 400 mg of the compound in 10 ml of water was sprayed into the room at hourly intervals for 4 hours on each of 4 successive days. No signs of toxicity were observed.

Treatment: See Organic Phosphates, p. 438.

BEE STINGS

The signs and symptoms following stings by bees, wasps, yellow jackets, and hornets depend on the number and location of the stings and the susceptibility of the victim. Usually, there is only a local reaction, but in sensitive individuals generalized reactions occur, and the effects may be fatal.

Local effects include erythema, itching, pain, and swelling at the site of the sting. Generalized reactions such as apprehension, precordial oppression, dyspnea, and vertigo usually develop within 5 minutes. In severe cases, there may be loss of consciousness lasting several minutes, often followed by severe coughing, rapid respiration, tachycardia, cyanosis, generalized urticaria, shivering, hyperpyrexia, and headache. Occasionally, there will be nausea, vomiting, and diarrhea followed by epileptiform convulsions. The patient may suffer complete exhaustion, falling into a deep sleep lasting several hours. This is usually followed by gradual recovery associated with headaches and fatigue. Leukopenia and eosinophilia may be marked. The systemic effects usually last for only a few hours or at most several days. There are a few isolated cases of encephalopathy [*JAMA* **188**, 1083 (1964)].

Bee and wasp stings may be fatal within a very short time. A sting on the base of the tongue, palate, or pharynx is liable to produce suffocation because of the marked swelling of the mucous membranes. However, death may also result from a single sting on the neck, face, or even the hand if the venom enters the circulation directly or reaches an area where it is quickly absorbed.

The severe symptoms, as well as the fatalities caused by a single sting, are mainly due to anaphylaxis or to pronounced capillary damage (multiple hemorrhages in the mucous membranes of the stomach, duodenum, trachea, liver, and central nervous system).

Treatment: Local effects may be treated by applying ice, dilute ammonia, laundry soap, menthol solution, or wetted sodium bicarbonate under a loose bandage. A handful of wet mud may be used if the accident occurs in the field. For wasp stings, vinegar has also been recommended. Remove the stinger carefully, so as not to squeeze the venom sac. If the sting is on an extremity, apply a tourniquet and report to a physician promptly. (Loosen tourniquet every 15 minutes).

Systemic effects, if severe, need *immediate* treatment including epinephrine S.C. (up to 1 ml of a 1:1000 solution repeatedly), establishment of a free airway, administration of oxygen, and artificial respiration, if needed. Calcium, as calcium lactate (10 ml of a 10% solution), or as the gluconate, should be injected slowly I.V. at the earliest possible moment. Use smaller doses for children. The injection of a readily ionizable calcium salt may be preceded or followed by 10–20 mg of Benadryl, I.V. or I.M. Miller reported dramatic improvement in a child who was "dying" (severe cyanosis, respiration, heart beat, and pulse undetectable) who received 2 ml of 10% calcium lactate I.V. followed by a second injection of 4.5 ml (University of Louisville, Kentucky). Analeptic and vasopressor drugs should be considered if respiration and vasomotor centers are involved. ACTH and steroid therapy have also been used, but they act too slowly to be of value in treating the immediate anaphylactic reaction [*Schweiz. Med. Wochschr.* **95**, 1731 (1965)]. See also Anaphylactic Drug Reaction, p. 56.

Isoproterenol (Isuprel) should be used instead of epinephrine in individuals suffering from high blood pressure or a heart condition. (Isoproterenol is not a vasoconstrictor and does not counteract shock symptoms.) Place one tablet of 10 mg under the tongue and let it dissolve. If symptoms persist, give another tablet in 5–10 minutes; if breathing becomes difficult, use the epinephrine spray without delay. Give 3 or 4 whiffs, repeat at intervals of 3–5 minutes [J. H. Shaffer, *JAMA* **177**, 473 (1961)].

Consider immunization in individuals sensitive to insect stings. Following hyposensitization, reactions to subsequent stings are reduced in about 90% of persons. Protection may be lost in less than a year, or may be maintained for years [*JAMA* **193**, 115 (1965); **196**, 259 (1966); **197**, 598 (1966)].

BEMEGRIDE (Megimide)

This drug has found some use as a respiratory and circulatory stimulant. A toxic dose produces exaggerated reflexes, muscular twitchings, tremors, hyperventilation, and convulsions.

Treatment of an overdose is largely symptomatic. In an exceptional instance, it may be necessary to give a barbiturate or an inhalation anesthetic to control convulsions.

BENACTYZINE (Sauvitil; Phobex)

This diphenylmethane tranquilizer has potent atropine-like properties. In an occasional patient, this drug will induce a peculiar mental state consisting of mental blocking, a feeling of intoxication, depersonalization, and changes in body image [S. Cohen, *Mod. Treat.* **2**, 505 (1965)]. Excessive doses are likely to aggravate an incipient psychosis associated with depression.

Treatment: Reduce dose or discontinue therapy; if necessary, continue with symptomatic treatment.

BENOQUIN

Erythema and edema of the face developed promptly in a Mexican woman who used a Benoquin-petrolatum ointment for the treatment of hyperpigmentation on both cheeks. The use of the preparation was continued at a reduced concentration and rate of application for 4 months. After 1 year "white spots" appeared on the face, neck, arms, and hands. Further use of the preparation for about 5 months resulted in complete depigmentation of the face [*Arch. Dermatol.* **92**, 211 (1965)].

Treatment: Reduce the dose or discontinue treatment.

BENORTERONE

Benorterone (17-α-methyl-B-nortestosterone) induced breast enlargement in 12 of 13 young men given the anti-androgen for acne. Benorterone, currently available for experimental use only, is devoid of estrogenic activity as judged by standard laboratory procedures. It has not been subjected to assay for breast-stimulating effect (R. M. Caplan, *J. Clin. Endocrinol. Metab.* **27**, 1348 (1967); *Clin-Alert* (Oct. 20, 1967)].

BENZALKONIUM (Zephiran)

This is a cationic detergent and a potent antiseptic. (Soap is an anionic detergent and will antagonize or neutralize the disinfectant properties of benzalkonium.) In the dilutions used, the drug is nonirritating and has a moderate order of toxicity. Gauze sponges and cotton pledgets should not be kept in a 1:1000 solution of Zephiran. These sponges will absorb the drug and reduce the bacteriocidal properties of the solution to such an extent that *Pseudomonas achromobacteriaceae* will grow and multiply. Severe and fatal infections have been reported following venipuncture in areas of skin cleansed with these solutions [*New*

Engl. J. Med. **263**, 800 (1960)]. See also Quaternary Ammonium Compounds, p. 508.

BENZENE (Benzol)   See page 642.

BENZENE HEXACHLORIDE (Lindane; BHC; Hexachlorocyclo-hexane)   See page 643.

BENZENE PHOSPHORUS DICHLORIDE (Benzene Phosphonic Dichloride; Phenylphosphorus Dichloride)

This is a highly reactive acid chloride which should be handled with caution. See Acid Chlorides, p. 71.

BENZENE PHOSPHORUS OXYDICHLORIDE (Phenylphosphonic Dichloride)

A reactive acid chloride. Handle with great care. See Acid Chlorides, p. 71.

BENZOCAINE (Ethyl Aminobenzoate)

There is little evidence that benzocaine in any concentration, applied to the intact or burned skin, is effective in relieving either pain or itching. Many local anesthetic preparations are effective when applied to mucous membranes, but 5% benzocaine (the concentration in the NF preparation and in many commercial formulations) is almost completely ineffective even on mucous membranes [J. Adriani and R. Zepernick, *JAMA* **188**, 711 (1964)]. A 20% preparation of benzocaine was found to be effective for only a few minutes [J. Adriani *et al.*, Clin. Pharmacol. Therap. **5**, 49 (1964); Med. Letter, **6**, 86 (1964)].

A 24-year-old man complained of hoarseness and sore throat of 10 to 12 hours duration. When examined, he showed signs of laryngitis and pharyngitis but was afebrile and had no signs of respiratory obstruction. Immediately after the examination, he took a lozenge containing 10 mg of benzocaine, 1 mg of tyrothricin, and chlorophyll. Acute and increasing respiratory distress appeared promptly, and he was pronounced dead 20 minutes later. Analysis of the postmortem findings and other data indicated that the fatality was due to sensitivity to benzocaine or tyrothricin [D. J. Hesch, *JAMA* **172**, 62/12 (1960)].

Several incidents of severe methemoglobinemia due to rectal absorption of benzocaine have been reported in infants and in a 6-year-old girl [*New Engl. J.*

Med. **263**, 454 (1960); *J. Pediat.* **66**, 797 (1965)]. Recently benzocaine intoxication resulted from topical application [*J. Pediat.* **67**, 509 (1965)].

Treatment: See Anaphylactic Shock, p. 56.

BENZQUINAMIDE (Quantril)

This agent was introduced as an antianxiety drug. Little clinical information is available at this time. High oral doses in animals induced emesis, anorexia, elevation of blood pressure, tachycardia, and miosis.

Caution: Administer this drug with caution until more data have become available. Atropine reduced the mortality or prolonged the life of animals given lethal dosages [*JAMA* **184**, 276 (1963)].

BENZYL CHLORIDE

This compound is intensely irritating to the skin, eyes, and mucous membranes.

Treatment: Drench affected part with water for at least 15 minutes. In case of eye contact, flood with water and consult an ophthalmologist if there is any indication that injury may have resulted. For ingestion, induce vomiting and follow with gastric lavage and demulcents. Subsequent treatment is symptomatic and supportive.

BERYLLIUM

The severity of an acute intoxication is determined by the magnitude of the inhalation exposure. There is usually a short latent period between exposure and the onset of illness, and one or more weeks may elapse before an X-ray finding of pneumonitis. Workers who suffer an "acute chemical pneumonitis," as a rule, recover if removed promptly from the site of exposure. Those who suffer a "delayed or chronic chemical pneumonitis" must be considered cases of chronic beryllium poisoning; in these individuals the liver and spleen may be involved [A. Hamilton and H. L. Hardy, "Industrial Toxicology," Harper (Hoeber), New York, (1949)].

Exposure to oxides of beryllium may cause a chronic lung disease which may make its first appearance as late as 25 years after the last exposure. This condition often may be mistaken for sarcoidosis or miliary tuberculosis.

Treatment: Immediate removal from the site of exposure and rest are essential. Symptomatic treatment involves a short, high-level course of corticotropin succeeded by long-term oral cortisone in dosages sufficient to control dyspnea, cough, and fatigue. Supportive therapy with oxygen, bronchodilators, and antibiotics is indicated. The steroids may reduce the size of the enlarged spleen, liver, and hilar nodes. Liver function often improves and lung densities may lighten; both of these are reversible upon discontinuance of the drug. Symptomatic relief may be obtained, however, without improvement in the chest roentgenogram, and the disease may progress to wide-spread chronic fibrosis and emphysema despite treatment (H. L. Hardy; H. E. Tebrock, University of Miami, personal communication). Aurin tricarboxylic acid was found moderately effective in the treatment of a beryllium intoxication in monkeys, but not in dogs or humans [*Ind. Med. Surg.* **33**, 566 (1964)]. (For a review of toxicity and safety procedures, see H. M. Donaldson, *Arch. Environ. Health* **10**, 554 (1965); J. Cassuto, *J. Occupational Med.* **7**, 261 (1965)].

BETHANECHOL CHLORIDE (Urecholine)

This drug has pharmacologic properties similar to those of methacholine (Mecholyl) and carbachol (Doryl). As true parasympathomimetic agents, these compounds are used in situations where an effect mimicking parasympathetic stimulation is desirable; for instance, for slowing of the heart, for inducing urination, or for stimulating gastroenteric activity. They do not stimulate the autonomic ganglia or skeletal muscle. A 41-year-old patient with marked urinary retention received subcutaneous doses of 7.5 mg of bethanechol every 4 hours for 1 day, then 5 mg every 4 hours for 2 days. This led to profuse sweating and, within 24 hours, to eruption of numerous superficial small lesions on legs and arms. These disappeared promptly after withdrawal of the drug [*Arch. Dermatol.* **95**, 499 (1967)].

Caution: These drugs are contraindicated in conditions of asthma, gastroenteric obstruction, and in patients in whom hypertension is undesirable or dangerous.

Treatment of an overdose requires atropine sulfate promptly.

BICYCLOHEPTADIENE DIBROMIDES

The medical histories of three chemists who worked with a mixture of bicycloheptadiene dibromides indicate that these compounds are highly toxic. Two of the subjects developed an illness characterized by progressive, intractable bronchial asthma which resulted in death, despite all forms of therapy. One of these patients had a pancytopenia and multiple hemorrhages at the time of his death. The third subject had persistent auscultatory wheezes and evidence of loss of pulmonary function.

Although the mechanism of action of the chemicals is unknown, certain features of the illness suggest a hypersensitivity response. It is recommended that these and other compounds of unknown toxicity be considered potentially hazardous until proved otherwise [J. F. Murray and A. Fink, *Arch. Environ. Health* **5**, 5 (1962)].

Treatment: Discontinue exposure and treat symptomatically.

BIS(DICHLOROACETYL)DIAMINE

This compound (WIN 18,446) inhibits spermatogenesis and causes disappearance of seminal epithelium. Since it has a very high Antabuse-like action, it cannot be used with safety in any male population where consumption of alcoholic beverages is encountered. The compound is not used as a drug.

BIS(2-ETHYLHEXYL) HYDROGEN PHOSPHITE

A dose of 0.071 mg/kg applied to the skin of rabbits caused a noticeable erythema for several days. This has been confirmed in humans. No evidence of interference with blood cholinesterase could be demonstrated in rabbits or dogs exposed to this chemical.

Treatment: For skin, eye, or mucous membrane contact, flood affected parts with water. For ingestion induce vomiting and follow with gastric lavage.

BISHYDROXYCOUMARIN (Dicumarol)

In contrast to heparin, which acts immediately after parenteral administration, bishydroxycoumarin is administered P.O. and acts much more slowly, requiring 24–72 hours for its anticoagulant action to develop fully. Phenprocoumon (Liquamar), diphenadione (Dipaxin), and anisindione (Miradon) are also recognized as "long-acting" anticoagulants. Warfarin sodium (Coumadin; Panwarfin) and acenocoumarol (Sintrom) are termed "intermediate-acting." "Short-acting" anticoagulants of this group include ethyl biscoumacetate (Tromexan) and phenindione (Danilone, Dindevan, Eridone, Hedulin) ("New Drugs, Evaluated by the A.M.A. Council on Drugs", 1967). Overdoses of these anticoagulants cause hemorrhages; however, it is recognized that, in individuals with metabolic deficiencies, hemorrhages may occur with doses that do not depress prothrombin activity excessively. In addition to the hazard of bleeding, the indandione group may cause hypersensitivity phenomena such as glomerulonephritis, thrombocytopenia, etc. An abstract in *Clin-Alert* (March 30, 1968) calls attention to coumarin necrosis. Of 2493 patients who received coumarin in the Bremen medical clinics, 0.2% experienced these difficulties. Lesions appeared suddenly, usually from 3 to 10 days after initiation of anticoagulant therapy. The sites of predilection were the thigh, breast, abdominal wall, buttock, and calf. It is believed that the true incidence of coumarin necrosis is likely to be much higher than the reported 0.2%. According to Nudelman and Kempson [*Clin-Alert*, No. 143 (1966)], the lesions are progressive even after drug withdrawal and administration of vitamin K, but in the patients of C. H. Viets and D. Gebauer at the Bremen clinic, the lesions ceased to progress and healed spontaneously. A prominent feature in their cases was an abnormal anticoagulant responsiveness to coumarin drugs [*Deut. Med. Monatsh.* **13**, 23 (1968)].

Caution: Dicumarol and related drugs are contraindicated in the following: patients suffering from kidney or liver disease, ulcerative lesions of the gastroenteric tract, cerebral hemorrhage, blood dyscrasias with bleeding tendencies, subacute bacterial endocarditis, threatened or incomplete abortions, pregnancies near term, vitamin C deficiency, individuals in poor nutritional state, or individuals given daily large doses of salicylates. "Purple toes," an uncommon sequela of dicumarol and warfarin therapy, has been reported; the discoloration appeared after several weeks of treatment. Patients on anticoagulant therapy should avoid exposure to carbon tetrachloride and other hepatotoxic and nephrotoxic agents. Luton described a patient on

Dicumarol therapy, who accidentally ingested 0.1 ml of carbon tetrachloride. He suffered marked hypo-prothrombinemia 2 days later [*JAMA* **193**, 1386 (1965)]: Administration of Dicumarol and diphenylhydantoin (Dilantin) to a 59-year-old man resulted in an increased serum Dilantin concentration and symptoms of Dilantin toxicity [*Lancet* **II**, 640 (1966)].

Outpatients on long-term treatment should carry several 5 mg tablets of vitamin K to be taken in case of an accident resulting in bleeding, and a card to alert the surgeon who might be involved in an emergency operation.

The response to Dicumarol-type anticoagulants is influenced by a variety of other drugs or chemicals, which, largely through microsomal activity, either increase or decrease the metabolism of these anticoagulants. For example, Dicumarol requirements are *increased* during concommittant phenobarbital (Dorsital, Luminal), butabarbital (Butisol), and secobarbital (Seconal) therapy. Withdrawal of the barbiturate, if not followed rather promptly by a lower dose of the anticoagulant, will result in hemorrhages, and has caused death [*JAMA* **197**, 366 (1966); *Current Therap. Res.* **10**, 70 (1968)]. Chloral hydrate and oral Enovid-type contraceptives behave similarly and tend to lead to an increased requirement (decrease in half-life) of Dicumarol [*Clin. Pharmacol. Therap.* **8**, 670 (1967)]. The metabolism of biscoumacetate (Tromexin) is accelerated after administration of glutethimide (Doriden). Obviously, it is advisable to administer with caution all Dicumarol-type anticoagulants, and for that matter also the indandione-type compounds if they have to be given with other drugs (see below). E. Turdey *et al.* add another note of caution: they found that the inhibition of coumarin action by phenobarbital was not related to the dosage of either drug. Evidently it is the status of the patient's liver detoxifying mechanism which plays a vital role [*Muench. Med. Wochschr.* **109**, 1272 (1967)].

When administered concommittantly with Dicumarol and related drugs, certain compounds will increase the half-life of the anticoagulants, requiring a *reduction* of Dicumarol dosage. These include: diphenylhydantoin (Dilantin), clofibrate (Atromid S), norethandrolone (Nilevar) [*Circulation* **34**, 210 (1966)], phenylbutazone and oxyphenbutazone [*Clin-*

Alert No. 122 (1964)], tolbutamide (Orinase), and phenyramidol (Analexin) [*Metabolism* **16**, 1029 (1967)].

Treatment: Discontinue the administration of the Dicoumarol-type drug immediately and give a transfusion of fresh whole blood to correct the hypoprothrombinemia. If indicated, follow with the I.V. administration of vitamin K_1 (phytonadione) 25–100 mg I.V. at a rate not exceeding 10 mg/minute, which should result in a normal prothrombin level in 12–24 hours. See also Vitamin K, p. 625. Vitamin K should be given only if hemorrhage has actually occurred or if blood prothrombin levels are so low as to make hemorrhage appear imminent. Give the *minimum* dose that will return the prothrombin time to a safe level. An unnecessarily large dose results in the prothrombin time becoming refractory to therapeutic response for as long as 1 or 2 weeks.

BISMUTH

"In the last 45 years there have been numerous reports of toxic effects of bismuth, which was once a widely used drug in the treatment of syphilis. Bismuth sodium triglycollamate (Bistrimate) is marketed as oral therapy for *verruca vulgaris*, the common wart, and other dermatoses. Several current textbooks of dermatology recommend this therapy for verrucae even though there is evidence that bismuth is ineffective. Since the drug is available, is prescribed, and is thus a potential source of poisoning, it seems advisable to reemphasize the toxicity of bismuth compounds. . . . Acute renal failure developed in an eight-year old boy who had been taking Bistrimate for the treatment of multiple warts [R. Urizar and R. L. Vernier, *JAMA* **198**, 187 (1966)]."

A boy who received bismuth thioglycollate (Thio-Bismol) (one S.C. dose of 1.3 mg/kg) for the treatment of small warts on his hands "developed emesis two or three times a day for a week, loss of appetite, swelling of the face, enlargement of the abdomen, renal damage, and a skin rash on the head and extremities." He recovered in 1 month.

Bacteria in the gastroenteric tract may change bismuth subnitrate to nitrite with the resultant production of methemoglobinemia. The probable lethal oral dose of this compound for an infant is 5 gm. In pre-scribing bismuth preparations for gastroenteric upsets, the risk involved should always be kept in mind.

Use of bismuth succinate suppositories for the treat-ment of sore throat in infants and small children has resulted in the production of systemic effects includ-ing fever and skin lesions. Bismuth salts should no longer be used for pediatric disorders.

Ingestion of certain salts of bismuth induces effects similar to those produced by salts of arsenic. These include changes in the skin, disturbances of the gas-troenteric tract, and injury to the liver and kidney. Some organic bismuth compounds have a high order of toxicity comparable to that of lead tetraethyl.

Caution: Because of the risk involved in the use of bismuth compounds, they should *never* be used in the management of benign lesions. [*JAMA* **198**, 187 (1966)].

Treatment: BAL has been recommended [W. F. von Oettingen, "Poisoning, A Guide to Clinical Diagnosis and Treatment," Saunders, Philadelphia, 1958]. How-ever, treatment consists largely in the management of the complications, primarily renal and hepatic failure. The 8-year-old boy responded to hemodialysis and supportive measures. (See Dimercaprol. p. 224).

BISPHENOL [4,4′-Isopropylidenediphenol;2,2-Bis (p-hydroxyphenyl)propane]

Bisphenol is moderately irritating to the skin. The oral LD_{50} is 6.5 gm per kilogram of body weight. Bisphenol is not hazardous to handle, but direct contact should be avoided.

Treatment: Remove from the skin and eyes by flush-ing the affected areas with water.

BITHIONOL (Actamer)

All preparations containing Bithionol [2,2′-thio bis(4,6-dichlorophenol)] have been withdrawn or are in the process of being removed from the market. They induced marked photosensitivity. The following are included: Coco-Borax Powdered Hand Soap con-taining Bithionol; Cutitone Acne Cream containing Bithionol; Degerm with Actamer containing Bi-thionol; Dial Deodorant Soap containing Bithionol; Lan-O-Kleen containing Bithionol; Rexall Medicated Dusting Powder containing Bithionol; Surginol Surgical Soap containing Bithionol; Thylox Sulfur Cream and Soap containing Bithionol.

BITUMEN (Asphalt, Petroleum Pitch)

Prolonged skin contact may cause dermatitis and acne-like lesions as well as keratoses similar to those caused by tar, but less severe. The greenish-yellow fumes given off when asphalt is boiled can cause photosensitization and melanoses. [*Brit. Med.* **2**, 99 (1966)].

BL-353

BL-353 contains approximately 70 % *N,N'*-dimethyl-*N,N'*-dinitrosoterephthalamide (NTA) and 30 % white mineral oil, by weight. Limited tests on laboratory animals indicate that BL-353 has very low acute toxicity. Such tests also indicate that BL-353 is a minor skin irritant. For this reason, skin contact should be avoided.

DMT (dimethyl terephthalate), the white residue formed by thermal decomposition of BL-353, has a low order of toxicity. Tests for skin irritation indicate that the white needle crystals are nonirritating to the intact skin and only slightly irritating to broken skin. No allergic skin sensitization was observed in these tests.

Treatment: In case of skin contact, the exposed area should be washed promptly and thoroughly with soap and copious amounts of water.

"BLACKLIGHT"

The possible hazards of "blacklight" in a night club were investigated. It was found that the wavelengths were in a range not harmful to the eyes ("Occupational Health Activities," No. 2, U. S. Dept. of Health, Education and Welfare, December, 1967).

BLACK LOCUST (*Robina pseudoacacia*)

The bark, seeds, and leaves (but not the flowers) of this tree, also known as black acacia, contain the toxalbumins phasin and robin. Ingestion of plant material induces, after about 1 hour, gastric distress followed by symptoms similar to those described for crabs-eye (except for diarrhea). In nonfatal cases, recovery is usually complete in 2 to 3 days. Fatalities have been rare.

Treatment: See Crabs-eye, p. 188. Treat constipation if this develops.

BORANES (Hydroborons; Boronhydrides; Borohydrides; Exotic Fuels; High Energy Fuels; HEF)

The boranes are an extremely toxic class of compounds. Based on animal experimentation, borane toxicity appears to be comparable to phosgene, chlorine, fluorine, and arsine. Liquid boranes will irritate the skin and cause acute local inflammation with the formation of small blisters, redness, and swelling. These compounds can be absorbed through the skin and membranes of the mouth and eyes. Vapor concentrations below the levels harmful on inhalation are not irritating to the eyes.

Diborane hydrolyzes rapidly in the lungs causing pulmonary edema and hemorrhage. It is only slightly soluble in water and the amount absorbed by the blood is low.

Early symptoms of exposure are tightness of chest, coughing, and respiratory difficulties. Brief exposure produces minor pulmonary irritation with congestion of the trachea and lungs; prolonged exposure may cause damage to the kidneys and liver.

Pentaborane and decaborane on acute exposure affect the central nervous system primarily. Early symptoms are dizziness, headache, drowsiness, incoordination, nausea, and vomiting. In severe poisoning, abnormal muscular contractions or twitching are followed by convulsions and coma. This may be followed by hiccups, difficulty in breathing, skin pallor, poor muscular coordination, and visual, auditory, and speech difficulties. In chronic exposure, liver and kidney damage are likely to occur; central nervous system symptoms are less prominent. See Table 26, p. 707.

Treatment: Remove the victim from the contaminated atmosphere. Give artificial respiration and oxygen if necessary. Use intermittent positive pressure oxygen for pulmonary edema. If muscle spasm or muscle tremor is present, use barbiturates to prevent convulsions. Severely poisoned patients have made spontaneous complete recovery with symptomatic and supportive treatment.

BORIC ACID (Boracic Acid)

Absorption of boric acid through the denuded, inflamed, or normal skin, from body cavities, and from the gastroenteric tract has resulted in gastroenteric and circulatory disturbances and in injury to the kidneys. Fatalities have resulted from skin absorption of boric acid (or borax) when used as dusting powder on diapers. Some infants have only fever or a subnormal temperature before becoming comatose. In 120 reported cases of poisoning, the mortality was 52.5% [*Conn. Med. J.* **18**, 745 (1954); *Brit. Med. J.* **1**, 237 (1955)]. The ingestion of 1 gm of boric acid caused the death of an infant. The probable lethal oral dose for an adult is 5–15 gm for boric acid, borax (sodium tetraborate), and sodium perborate. G. B. Skipworth *et al.* warn against the use of "medicated" talcum powders containing boric acid. Repeated local application of this preparation to the skin of a 3-year-old child caused a severe systemic intoxication and a generalized erythematous desquamation of the skin. The child survived the acute intoxication. The specific gravity of the urine remained low for 9 months [*Arch. Dermatol.* **95**, 83 (1967)].

Treatment: There is no specific antidote. Induce vomiting promptly or lavage the stomach and colon; administer demulcents and large volumes of alkali-water to counteract acidosis and to promote diuresis. Continuous peritoneal dialysis for 24–48 hours is much more effective than exchange transfusion. Peritoneal dialysis is the treatment of choice for critically ill infants.

Note: Boric acid has doubtful therapeutic value. It should be *completely* eradicated from hospitals, dispensaries, and the pharmacopeia [L. C. Wong, *Can. Med. Assoc. J.* **90**, 1018 (1964)].

BOROHYDRIDES (Sodium and Potassium)

These are white solids that react slowly with water to form an alkaline solution. The reaction with acids is rapid, liberating hydrogen. Ingestion will result in violent reaction on contact with gastric acid.

Treatment: See Sodium Hydroxide, p. 543.

BORON OXIDE

This has a low order of toxicity by ingestion or inhalation of aerosols containing high concentrations of the oxide. Skin and eye contact causes irritation due to conversion of the oxide to boric acid. See Boric Acid, p. 138.

BORON TRICHLORIDE

This is a colorless gas that fumes in moist air forming hydrochloric acid. See Hydrochloric Acid, p. 317.

BORON TRIFLUORIDE

This colorless gas fumes in air and has a sharply acidic odor. It causes skin burns similar to hydrofluoric acid burns. Inhalation causes irritation of the respiratory tract. It is available also in liquid form as complexes of ether (boron fluoride etherate, 48% BF_3), phenol (26% BF_3), and acetic acid (40% BF_3).

Treatment: See Hydrofluoric Acid, p. 317.

BRETYLIUM TOSYLATE

This is an antihypertensive agent. Serious side effects have not been noted, although muscular weakness and digestive disturbances were reported in some patients.

Caution: The possible production of hyperchlorhydria from release of vagal predominance should be kept in mind.

"BRIGHTENERS"

"Brighteners" include the following chemicals: Disodium 4,4'-bis(4-p-methoxyanilino-6-morpholino-1,3,5-triazin-2-ylamino)stilbene-2,2'-disulfonate; disodium 4,4'-bis(2,4-dimethoxybenzamido)stilbene-2,2'-disulfonate; disodium 4,4'-bis [(4,6-dianilino-1,3,5-triazin-2-yl)amino]stilbene-2,2'-disulfonate; 1-benzimidazolyl-2-(N-hydroxyethyl)benzidazolylethylene; and sodium 4-(2H-naphtho(1,2-d)triazol-2-yl)stilbene-2-sulfonate.

"Brighteners," or "optical bleaches," are used at levels varying from a few hundredths of 1% to a maximum of 0.2% in detergent products. They are deposited in minute amounts on fabrics during laundering and improve the appearance of whiteness or brightness in the fabric. The brighteners listed above have been thoroughly tested. Under the exaggerated test conditions used, these materials appear to be innocuous, and they should therefore be completely safe at the concentrations normally found in soaps and detergents [F. H. Snyder *et al.*, *Toxicol. Appl. Pharmacol.* **5**, 176 (1963)].

BROMIDES

Ingestion of sodium or potassium bromide is followed by depression of sensory and motor areas of the cortex. After absorption of toxic doses, effects usually include gastroenteric distress, constipation, skin rash, and severe central nervous system depression. Psychoses have been observed following the prolonged use of bromides and preparations containing bromides and other hypnotics and sedatives, such as Nervine or Carbrital [*Brit. Med. J.* **4**, 806 (1967); *Med. J. Australia* **2**, 763 (1966)]. A dose of 4 ml of Bromo Seltzer contains 320 mg of sodium bromide and 160 mg of acetanilid [*Delaware Med. J.* **26**, 205 (1954)]. Individuals with a history of addiction to alcohol or barbiturates frequently use bromides. Physicians should avoid prescribing bromide-containing medications and caution patients about self-medication. Typical signs of bromide intoxication may be absent with blood bromide levels exceeding 200 mg/100 ml. Chemical analysis will establish the diagnosis.

Treatment: After ingestion of an overdose, induce vomiting by use of salt water (table salt), or administer gastric lavage with isotonic saline followed by oral administration of sodium chloride. A regimen frequently recommended includes ammonium chloride (furnishing chloride and acting as a diuretic), 6 gm/day P.O. in divided doses, together with 2 ml of meralluride (Mercuhydrin) I.M. every second or third day [*JAMA* **20**, 100 (1956)].

Ethacrynic acid has been recommended to promote the elimination of bromide ion. This compound is four times as effective as mannitol diuresis. In one patient with bromide intoxication, saline loading increased the bromide clearance fivefold; ethacrynic acid added to the saline produced an added sevenfold increase [*J. Lab. Clin. Med.* **68**, 913 (1966)]. See also Hemodialysis, p. 49.

BROMINE   See page 645.

9-BROMOFLUORENE

Two hundred fifty students were given the preparation of 9-bromofluorene from *N*-bromosuccinimide and fluorene as a laboratory exercise and 24 students developed a blistering rash 10–20 days later. A postgraduate student who had prepared 9-bromofluorene developed a blistering rash on the face, limbs, and upper half of the trunk. During 3 weeks in the hospital under stringent treatment, healing occurred. In order to be sure of the involvement of 9-bromofluorene in the skin eruption, a small quantity of the pure, dry material was placed on a small area of skin and left for 24 hours. The subject of this test had no previous contact with halogenofluorene compounds. There was an initial, mild irritation which healed in a few days, but 10 days after application of the compound, a severe local reaction began to develop. This response to a single application of the substance indicates that 9-bromofluorene is a powerful sensitizing agent.

Individuals differ considerably in the ease with which they become sensitized, but aromatic compounds with reactive halogens are powerful sensitizers. 1-Chloro-2,4-dinitrobenzene has been used for many years in experimental studies of man as a potent agent for producing sensitization. Such sensitization may persist for at least 3 years in some individuals. The test subject is still sensitive to a 0.5% solution of 9-bromofluorene in hexane some 2 years after his previous contact with the material. More recently, a skin rash has been seen in a postgraduate student who had prepared 1,2-dibromoacenaphthene, and a skin sensitivity to this substance was demonstrated. Cyano compounds may behave similarly and 4-cyanobenzyl-mesobenzanthrone is known to have caused a particularly severe skin reaction (E. W. Powell, *Chem. Ind. London* p. 2080 (1967).

Treatment: Discontinue exposure. Treat as thermal burn. Severe cases may require hospitalization and corticosteroid medication.

BROMOFORM

Ingestion of an overdose leads to respiratory difficulties, tremors, and loss of consciousness. The probable lethal oral dose for an adult is 10 gm.

Treatment: Gastric lavage, oxygen, and cathartics are recommended.

BROMO SELTZER

A measuring cupful (approx. 5.2 grams) contains 130 mg phenacetin, 195 mg acetaminophen, 162.5 mg potassium bromide, and 32.5 mg caffeine, plus sodium bicarbonate and citric acid to yield 2.0 gm sodium citrate.

Treatment: For treatment of an overdose, see individual compounds.

BRONZE POWDER (Copper and Zinc)

Inhalation of a large quantity of bronze powder used for gilding Christmas cards has caused a necrotizing suppurative bronchitis, pulmonary edema, and pleuritis. The powder is in the form of thin flakes and consists of 70% copper, 30% zinc, and a trace of stearate lubricant.

Treatment: A 2-year-old boy died despite treatment with oxygen, antibiotics, aminophylline, BAL, and adrenocortical extract [*New Engl. J. Med.* **256**, 40 (1957)].

BUBBLE BATH

Irritation of the lower urinary tract has been produced in children and adults following bubble baths. The female urethra is especially vulnerable. The cause is exposure to a concentrated solution of the soap preparation. Roberts encountered five women in whom long-standing urethral and bladder irritation was precipitated or aggravated by the habitual use of bubble bath soap preparations [*JAMA* **201**, 207 (1967)].

Caution: Adequate dilution before bathing usually prevents this problem.

BUBBLE GUM

This consists principally of synthetic rubber, polymer mixture, and flavor additives. Ingestion of large quantities may lead to bezoar formation. See Bezoars, p. 643.

BUCKTHORN (Rhamus cathartica)

The bark and the fruit in particular of buckthorn trees contain a number of anthraquinone (emodin) compounds which are the active ingredients of cascara sagrada. Ingestion of the plant material has resulted in marked gastroenteric effects, kidney damage, and electrolyte imbalance.

When used as a drug, the cathartic action of cascara sagrada (and also senna) is restricted to the colon, hence the latent period of approximately 6 hours. Severe intoxications have followed ingestion of the bark as an abortifacient.

Treatment: See Tung Nut, p. 613, and Poinciana, p. 483.

BUCKWHEAT

Fagopyrism is a cattle and sheep disease. The occurrence of fagopyrism in man is doubtful despite the belief by some that buckwheat eaten during summer months may cause "buckwheat rash." Susceptibility to buckwheat may be manifested as increased light sensitivity. Animals fed buckwheat and kept in semidarkness do not develop the disease. Exposure to sunlight may cause pulmonary and intestinal hemorrhages, enteritis, and emaciation. See Phototoxicity, p. 55.

Treatment: Discontinue ingestion of buckwheat and avoid sunlight.

BUCLIZINE (Softran)

This diphenylmethane derivative is a weak tranquilizer. It is teratogenic in the rat, and should not be used in pregnancy [*Am. J. Obstet. Gynecol.* **95**, 109 (1966)].

BUFFERED ASPIRIN

It is doubtful that buffered aspirin is less likely to induce side effects than acetylsalicylic acid (aspirin). Conclusive evidence is lacking that the amount of alkaline agents contained in buffered aspirin is sufficient to affect appreciably the absorption or excretion of this drug. Several related drugs (Calurin, Ecotrin, Relay, Measurin, and Stendin) have been promoted with claims that they act more rapidly than aspirin, or that they have a desirable delayed action; that they are less likely to cause gastroenteric hemorrhage; and that they are, therefore, safer. Convincing evidence is lacking that these drugs are superior to acetylsalicylic acid. As far as enteric bleeding is concerned, it must be remembered that this is partially induced by

central action. Experience has shown that some enteric-coated aspirins do not disintegrate until they
have passed through most of the bowel. Because of
FDA action, Relay and Stendin (December 14, 1966)
have been removed from the market "because of lack
of evidence to support claims made for these products." For symptoms of an overdose and treatment of
an intoxication, see Acetylsalicylic Acid, p. 67.

BUNAMIODYL SODIUM (BUN; Orabilex)

This gallbladder contrast medium for cholecystography has been withdrawn because of serious toxic
reactions.

BUSULFAN (Myleran)

This is the preferred drug in the treatment of
chronic myelocytic leukemia. It is administered orally
in doses of 2–6 mg/day. The toxicity of this drug is of a
low order. Side effects after prolonged use may include hyperpigmentation and adrenal insufficiency.
Only rarely have bone marrow depression and diffuse
pulmonary interstitial fibrosis been noted [*Ann. Internal Med.* **64**, 154 (1966)].

Caution: The daily dose should be adjusted or treatment discontinued according to the response; the
white blood cell count is the best guide for modification of dosage. Treatment should be continued until
the drug is no longer effective. Appearance of severe
side effects necessitates cessation of therapy.

n-BUTYL ALCOHOL (n-Butanol)

n-Butyl Alcohol is more acutely toxic (anesthetic)
than the lower alcohol homologs. The vapors are irritating to mucous membranes at concentrations exceeding 25 ppm. Excessive exposure may induce headache,
dizziness, drowsiness, eye irritation, and sensitivity
to light. The threshold limit is 100 ppm. See Table 21,
p. 695.

Treatment: See Alcohols, p. 81.

n-BUTYL NITRITE

This chemical causes vasodilatation, hypotension,
and throbbing headache. In general, its effects are
similar to those caused by amyl nitrite. See Amyl Nitrite, p. 100.

p-tert-BUTYLTOLUENE (p-TBT)

This alkyl derivative of benzene has a threshold limit of 10 ppm based on local irritation, odor, and sensory effects. Systemic effects from exposure to higher concentrations are similar to those induced by toluene, styrene, or ethylbenzene.

Treatment: See Toluene, p. 663.

BYSSINOSIS

Byssinosis is a pneumoconiosis resulting from inhalation of cotton, flax, hemp, jute, sisal, and manila fibers. R. S. F. Schilling *et al.* and others indicate that this disabling disease is not caused primarily by mechanical irritation but by pharmacologically active substances which produce edema or contraction of the smooth musculature of the airways. Among the compounds extracted from the dusts are: histamine, 5-hydroxytryptamine, a histamine-releasing factor, and an unidentified smooth muscle constrictor. Pre-existent bronchitis, general atmospheric pollution, and tobacco smoking will aggravate this disease.

Caution: Use of protective devices and face masks will help to reduce exposure. A provisional value of 1 mg/m^3 for total dust is recommended as the maximum allowable concentration of cotton dust. The routine use of antihistamine drugs is not recommended (R. S. F. Schilling *et al., Excerpta Med., Intern. Congr. Ser., No. 62, Madrid, Sept. 1963*).

CACODYLIC ACID (Dimethylarsinic Acid)

This is a hygroscopic crystalline substance. The oral LD$_{50}$ for mice is $>$ 184 mg/kg. See Arsenic, p. 113.

CADMIUM

Ingestion of inorganic salts of cadmium will cause gastroenteric distress, pain, and prostration. Sensory disturbances, liver injury, and convulsions have been observed in severe intoxications. In animals, hypochromic anemia was also noted. Acute intoxications have followed ingestion of fruit juices or milk kept in cadmium-plated containers. Accidental ingestion of silver polish containing cadmium carbonate has also caused intoxications.

Cadmium fumes and dusts are highly toxic; they may produce metal fume fever or a more severe intoxication involving the lungs (pulmonary inflammation, edema, pleurisy, emphysema). Christensen and Olson reviewed the literature and reported on effects from inhalation of cadmium oxide fumes.

Immediate symptoms: weakness, nausea, vomiting, dryness or soreness of the throat, cough, chest pain, shortness of breath, headache, and dizziness; *12–36 hours later:* severe constricting chest pain and marked dyspnea. If the exposure is sufficiently severe, death is likely to occur 5 to 7 days after the exposure. Pathological changes include severe pulmonary edema, cellular proliferation into the alveolar spaces, epithelial hyperplasia of the cells lining the alveoli, intraalveolar hemorrhages, and lung damage in the form of perivascular and peribronchial fibrosis [*Reinl. Arch. Toxikol.* **19**, 152 (1961)]. D. C. Beton *et al.* reported on 5 individuals exposed to cadmium oxide. Four recovered but one died on the fifth day. Autopsy showed, in addition to severe pulmonary changes, bilateral cortical necrosis of the kidneys [*Brit. J. Ind. Med.* **23**, 292 (1966)]. Two deaths occurred from inhalation of silver solder vapors containing cadmium [*JAMA* **196,** 37, (1967)]. Animal experiments indicate that there is an antagonistic action between cadmium and zinc. Abnormal zinc metabolism was found to contribute significantly to the toxicity syndrome following the prolonged ingestion of cadmium [W. C. Supplee, *Science* **139,** 119 (1963)]. See also *Science News,* **95,** 471, (1969).

A 1% suspension of cadmium sulfide (Capsebon) has been used for the treatment of seborrheic dermatitis. The compound does not appear to be absorbed percutaneously to any appreciable extent. No reports of systemic toxicity following topical administration have come to our attention.

Caution: Pneumonitis or pulmonary edema may develop after a patient appears to be well on the way to recovery. While zinc fume fever usually subsides in 12 hours, cadmium intoxication cases progress to a prolonged phase of pulmonary reaction resulting in death in about 1 week. Obviously, individuals who have suffered exposure to cadmium vapors should be kept under observation.

Treatment: If the intoxication occurred by inhalation, remove the individual promptly from the site of exposure and, if required, administer artificial respiration and oxygen. For ingestion of a cadmium salt, induce vomiting and follow with gastric lavage, a saline cathartic, and demulcents. Consider using atropine, opiates, and fluid therapy. $CaNa_2$ EDTA was found effective in acutely poisoned animals and in a few humans. BAL has been found sufficiently effective in animal experiments to justify its use in human intoxication. Since the BAL-cadmium complex has a nephrotoxic action, the physician will have to decide whether or not to use this drug.

CAFFEINE

A cup of regular coffee contains 100–120 mg of caffeine. Instant and "freeze-dried coffee" contain approximately 80 mg of caffeine per cup. Tea contains approximately 60 mg per cup; 180 ml (6 oz.) of coca cola contains 36 mg; and decaffeinated coffee, approximately 3 mg of caffeine per cup. The "calorie-free" drinks contain approximately half the allowable amount of caffeine, approximately 18 mg per 180 ml [*JAMA* **191**, 514 (1965)].

Excessive consumption of caffeine-containing beverages will induce gastroenteric distress and marked diuresis, and has been known to cause photophobia, premature systoles (due to myocardial irritability), tremors, convulsions, and hallucinations. Fever is also a symptom of caffeinism [H. A. Reimann, *JAMA* **202**, 1105 (1967)]. The precise single human lethal dose of caffeine is not known. In one instance, death followed the I.V. administration of 3.2 gm of caffeine [J. M. Peters, *J. Clin. Pharmacol.* **7**, 131 (1967)]. For more extensive reports on the toxicity of caffeine, see papers by E. M. Boyd, *Toxicol. Appl. Pharmacol.* **1**, 250 (1959); *Can. J. Physiol. Pharmacol.* **43**, 995, (1965). Allergy (vasomotor rhinitis, asthma, angioneurotic edema) due to occupational exposure to coffee has been noted occasionally. Boiling the coffee appears to destroy the allergen.

Coffee and tea contain a substance (or substances) that elevates blood fats in susceptible persons. Based on epidemiological studies, a positive relationship exists between intake of coffee and coronary artery disease [*JAMA* **196**, 603 (1966); *Lancet* **I**, 732 (1966)].

In studies with rats, B. R. Zeitlin found that a high level of caffeine intake raised the cholesterol level whether the source was coffee, tea, or free caffeine. The presence of sucrose exacerbates the elevation of serum cholesterol. (B. R. Zeitlin, personal communication.)

Caution: Excessive consumption of caffeine-containing beverages should be avoided. Adding milk to coffee will reduce somewhat the gastroenteric irritation. One half cup, instead of one full cup, of coffee provides all the central nervous system stimulant effect ordinarily required. Caffeine drinks should be avoided by patients suffering from gastric hyperacidity or ulcers of the gastroenteric tract.

*Treatment:*Recovery from gastroenteric and related effects follows rather promptly when ingestion is discontinued.

CALCIUM

Signs and symptoms of hypercalcemia in infants include: failure to thrive, anorexia, lethargy, constipation, nausea, vomiting, fever, and severe dehydration. Hypercalcemia should be suspected when subcutaneous fat necrosis develops during the first week of life.

Skin contact with calcium chloride will cause marked irritation and extensive necrosis, depending on concentration, area, and the duration of contact. If injected I.V. for the control of acute symptoms, it must be given *slowly* and with caution to avoid fatal arrhythmia; this is of particular importance in digitalized patients. Calcium gluconate, calcium lactate, and calcium glucoheptonate may be injected safely in doses of 10 ml of a 10% solution, *if* administered at a rate not exceeding 1.0 ml per minute. For the control of muscular spasms in hypocalcemic tetany, and in magnesium poisoning, administer *slowly* by I.V. injection 5–20 ml of 5% calcium chloride, or 10–20 ml of a 10% solution of calcium gluconate.

The short stature of the Japanese seems to have been caused mainly by a low calcium diet. The high incidence of cerebrovascular lesions among Japanese may be due to the long-term effect of a low calcium diet.

Treatment: In infants, recovery from hypercalcemia was rapid when vitamin D intake was stopped and when a low-calcium diet was administered. Corticosteroids may be helpful [*Am. J. Diseases Children* **104**, 235 (1962)]. Effective reduction of elevated serum calcium levels was achieved in 2 patients with para-thyroid adenomas and 8 patients with carcinoma by treatment with inorganic phosphate (Neutra-Phos) infusions [*JAMA* **201**, 721 (1967)].

A. Alveryd *et al.* treated moderate hypercalcemia in patients with hyperparathyroidism and one case of severe hypercalemia by a daily oral dose of 15 gm of acid sodium phosphate in water. The serum calcium concentration decreased rapidly in all patients [*Nord. Med.* **78**, 1395 (1967)].

Skin contact with calcium chloride requires immediate removal with water. In case of eye contact, flood the eye promptly with water, and continue washing for at least 15 minutes; then consult an ophthalmologist. For ingestion, induce vomiting and treat symptomatically.

CALCIUM ACETYLSALICYLATE CARBAMIDE (Calurin)

This acetyl ester of salicylic acid is highly soluble in water. Overdoses will produce effects similar to those produced by aspirin.

Treatment of an oral overdose, see Acetylsalicylic Acid, p. 67.

CALCIUM CYANAMIDE

This compound does not liberate cyanide when acidified and is not metabolized to cyanide *in vivo*. It has a comparatively low order of toxicity. The probable lethal oral dose for an adult is 40 gm. Ingestion or inhalation of fumes or mists containing this chemical causes throbbing headache, flushing, dizziness, rapid breathing, and collapse. The vasomotor reaction is known as "cyanamide flush" or "mal rouge." Fumes and particulates cause irritation of mucous membranes of the respiratory tract. Alcohol potentiates the action of cyanamide after relatively small doses.

Treatment: For ingestion, gastric lavage, saline cathartics, mild central nervous system sedation, rest, oxygen, and artificial respiration if necessary. For inhalation, discontinue exposure. Subsequent treatment is symptomatic.

CALCIUM HYDROXIDE (Slaked Lime; Hydrated Lime)

This is a weak alkali. Water solutions (limewater) are noncorrosive. No fatal cases of human intoxication have been reported.

Treatment: None required.

CALIFORNIA PRIVET (Ligustrum ovalifolium)

A 5-year-old boy died after ingesting a number of berries of this hedge shrub. The primary effects in non-fatal poisonings are gastroenteric disturbances.

Treatment: See Tung Nut, p. 613, and Poinciana, P. 483.

CAMPHOR (Gum Camphor; 2-Camphanone)

d-Camphor, the primary constituent of oil of camphor, is a central nervous system stimulant and rubefacient. It is not used as an analeptic, since its effects are not sufficiently predictable. The lethal dose of the oil is estimated to be 1 ml for a 1-year-old child; 2 ml is a toxic dose for an adult. Absorption of a toxic dose induces tremors and convulsions. Death is due to collapse and asphyxia.

A 19-month-old infant died after swallowing 1 teaspoonful of 20% camphor in cottonseed oil in spite of the fact that he vomited a few minutes later. A 1-year-old boy who ingested 120 ml of camphorated oil convulsed in 15 minutes; prompt gastric lavage and mouth-to-mouth artificial respiration were responsible for his survival. H. E. Ginn *et al.* reported that a 77-year-old man, who mistakenly ingested 60 ml of a 20% solution of camphorated oil, vomited and suffered several grand mal seizures 30 minutes later.

Treatment: For an oral intoxication, administer gastric lavage, cathartics, diuretics, and sedatives. Control convulsions with a short-acting barbiturate, chloral hydrate, or ether. Do *not* use analeptics or opiates. Hospital treatment of the 77-year-old consisted primarily of 4.5 hours of lipid hemodialysis. Eight liters of soybean oil, warmed to 39–40°C. was recirculated as dialyzate through a Klung dialyzer at 300 ml/minute. Blood from the left radial artery was pumped through the dialyzer at 300 ml/minute and returned to a superficial forearm vein. The patient became alert and had no seizures after 3 hours of dialysis [*JAMA* **203**, 230 (1968)].

CANDICIDIN (Candeptin)

This antibiotic is useful for the *local* treatment of candidal vaginitis. Adverse reactions thus far observed are of little consequence.

CAPTAN (Orthocide)

This chemical has a low order of toxicity. No human experience with overdosage has been reported. The probable lethal oral dose for an adult is 75 gm.

Treatment: For ingestion, gastric lavage and saline cathartics. Subsequent treatment is symptomatic.

CARBAMATES, ALKYL and ARYL

Ethyl carbamate is urethane. See p. 616. Homologs of urethane [methyl, isopropyl, butyl, 2-ethylhexyl, dodecyl (lauryl), allyl, methallyl, and phenyl] are extensively used as agricultural chemicals and in plastics manufacture. Sevin, a broad spectrum insecticide, is 1-naphthyl-N-methyl carbamate. It has a low order of toxicity.

CARBAMAZEPINE (Tegretol)

S. Livingston *et al.* found this anticonvulsive drug—used largely outside the United States—particularly useful in the treatment of psychomotor (temporal lobe) epilepsy. In a total group of 87 patients, the drug was withdrawn in 8 patients: in 3 because of leukopenia, in 4 because of a rash, and in 1 because of resulting abnormal liver function. The most common side effect was diplopia (18%); 5 patients complained of transient blurred vision and a "heavy feeling in the eyes." Drowsiness, disturbances of equilibrium, nausea, vomiting, paresthesias, neutropenia, and recurrence of symptoms of systemic lupus erythematosus were noted to a lesser extent [*JAMA* **200**, 204 (1967)]. British clinicians recently reported two fatalities due to aplastic anemia following Tegretol therapy. A third patient, a 45-year-old woman who suffered from trigeminal neuralgia and who took Tegretol for nine months (a total dose of 180 gm), developed severe pancytopenia. She recovered upon discontinuation of treatment followed by transfusions [*Brit. Med. J.* **1**, 108 (1966)]. A lupus-like syndrome has been reported in association with the administration of hydralazine, hydantoin derivatives, griseofulvin, sulfonamides, and penicillin. Tegretol must now be added to this list. A 63-year-old woman developed symptoms suggestive of lupus erythematosus after being treated with Tegretol for several months with doses of 200 mg two or three times a day for 2 months. She recovered when the drug was discontinued. Two months later the patient resumed Tegretol therapy, and the rash, malaise, and pain recurred within a few days. When the drug was again withdrawn all symptoms subsided [Simpson, *Brit. Med. J.* **2**, 1434 (1966)].

Caution: Reduction in dose or discontinuation of therapy brought about recovery from most side effects. According to A. J. Arieff and M. Mier, this anticonvulsant and psychotropic drug is very dangerous and should be used only under careful supervision. This drug should not be used routinely [*Neurology* **16**, 107 (1966)].

CARBIMAZOLE

This antithyroid agent is used in Europe. Papadopoulos and Harden reported on five women who experienced diffuse loss of scalp hair during carbimazole therapy [*Brit. Med. J.* **2**, 1502 (1966)]. Lee and Dyer reported two additional cases [*Brit. Med. J.* **1**, 760 (1967)]. Loss of hair may occur in hypothyroidism induced by overtreatment with antithyroid drugs; however, Papadopoulos and Harden's patients were euthyroid, all were receiving full replacement doses of thyroxine.

Treatment: Regrowth of hair occurred promptly in the cases reported by Papadopoulus and Harden when the drug was withdrawn; Lee and Dyer reported regrowth of hair in spite of continuation of therapy.

CARBOMYCIN (Magnamycin)

The principal side effect reported in some patients is nausea. Diarrhea is infrequent. Moniliasis may occur.

Treatment: Decrease the dose or discontinue therapy. Subsequent treatment is symptomatic.

CARBON DIOXIDE

The syndrome of carbon dioxide intoxication is frequently unrecognized, since the symptoms and findings simulate a neurologic disorder and may result in a mistaken diagnosis of stroke or brain tumor.

Patients with chronic lung disease, congestive heart failure, muscular dystrophy, or acute respiratory acidosis are prone to carbon dioxide intoxication. Initially, there may be overbreathing, but as retention progresses underbreathing results.

Signs and symptoms of carbon dioxide retention range from drowsiness to deep coma and from elevated blood pressure to severe circulatory collapse with hypotension and shock. Irritability, depression, hallucination, hypomania, euphoria, paranoid tendencies, twitching, tremors, convulsions, and flaccid or spastic paralysis may also be present.

The use of carbon dioxide for angiocardiography is considered to be a safe procedure. The fatal case reported by H. I. Meyers and G. Jacobson appears to be the first reported. The patient was suffering from extensive pulmonary disease and possibly from pericardial effusion. Cardiac action ceased 3 minutes after an I.V. injection of 100 ml of carbon dioxide [*Radiology* **77**, 295 (1961)].

The lack of oxygen, rather than carbon dioxide excess, is the cause of asphyxiation in individuals descending into tanks, etc. For handling carbon dioxide frozen foods, see *JAMA* **168**, 1962 (1958).

Treatment: The appropriate use of mechanical respirators, bronchoscopic drainage, bronchodilators, respiratory stimulants, expectorants, oxygen, steroids, antibiotics, and anticongestive failure therapy is sometimes lifesaving. Standard treatment for a patient with an apparent lack of oxygen is to place him in an oxygen tent. However, in carbon dioxide intoxication, this may initiate a vicious cycle: as more oxygen is absorbed, breathing becomes more and more depressed, causing more carbon dioxide to be retained. If placed in an iron lung, oxygen administration can be adjusted to the needs of the patient [R. J. O'Reilly, *Diseases Chest* **37**, 185 (1960)].

F. Manfredi *et al.* treated three patients with the buffer THAM for severe carbon dioxide intoxication resulting from chronic pulmonary insufficiency. The drug was given I.V. as a 0.33 M solution in 0.2 % sodium chloride (pH of 10.38) at the rate of 300 ml/hour. [For details and supportive treatment see *JAMA* **173**, 999 (1960)]. Improvement was dramatic in one patient; in another THAM treatment was of supportive value; while the third patient died in 20 minutes.

CARBON DISULFIDE (Carbon Bisulfide)

Absorption from the gastroenteric tract, lungs, and skin may produce blurring of vision, nausea, vomiting, headache, hallucinations, injury to the auditory and vestibular apparatus, psychosis, and coma. Skin contact may cause blistering and second degree burns. The probable lethal oral dose for an adult is 30 ml. A 1-hour exposure to 1000 ppm is dangerous to life.

For a pretoxicosis test for carbon disulfide poisoning, see publication by H. E. Stokinger [*J. Occupational Med.* **9**, 537 (1967)].

Treatment: For inhalation exposure, remove the victim promptly from the contaminated area. Administer oxygen and artificial respiration if needed. In case of skin contact, wash affected areas with copious quantities of water. For ingestion, induce vomiting and follow with gastric lavage and saline cathartics.

CARBON MONOXIDE

This odorless, tasteless, colorless gas combines with hemoglobin to form carboxyhemoglobin. Signs and symptoms of intoxication are due primarily to anoxia. The earliest symptoms include loss of brightness perception and fine coordination of ocular muscles. Large doses produce aching limbs, increased pulse rate, frontal headache, nausea, vomiting, and finally collapse and death.

The concentration, exposure time, and physical activity of an individual determine the percentage conversion of hemoglobin to carboxyhemoglobin. The effects produced depend on the degree and duration of saturation of blood with carbon monoxide. Exposure to 4,000 ppm for 1 hour may be fatal.

Treatment: Remove victim promptly from site of exposure. Administer artificial respiration if necessary, and give oxygen. A mixture of 5 % carbon dioxide in oxygen is more likely to facilitate recovery from carbon monoxide poisoning than oxygen alone, but there is no advantage to increasing the amount of carbon dioxide beyond 5 %.

The use of hyperbaric oxygen for the treatment of carbon monoxide poisoning is now well established. Benefits to the patient are twofold. First, the decreased oxygen-carrying capacity resulting from the displacement of oxygen by formation of carboxyhemoglobin can be overcome by the increased content of dissolved oxygen in plasma when the oxygen pressure of the inspired mixture is raised. Second, the elimination of carbon monoxide is markedly increased by hyperbaric oxygenation.

Extensive work in this field has been done in Glasgow, where there has been a systematic effort to insure the prompt transport of carbon monoxide victims to a hyperbaric facility and immediate treatment. Seventy patients with severe carbon monoxide poisoning have been treated at 2 atmospheres absolute oxygen for varying durations, with 95% survival. The success of treatment of carbon monoxide poisoning depends not only on the use of hyperbaric oxygen facilities to provide adequate oxygenation and elimination of carboxyhemoglobin, but also in prompt and intensive therapy to avoid irreversible tissue damage (T. A. Douglas *et al.*, "Clinical Application of Hyperbaric Oxygen," Elsevier, 1964).

CARBON TETRACHLORIDE

Carbon tetrachloride is readily absorbed from the gastrointestinal tract after ingestion and through the lungs during exposure to vapor. In the body, the highest concentrations are found in fat, liver, bone marrow, blood, brain, and kidney. The compound is slowly eliminated from the body, over 50% being exhaled unchanged.

Marked individual differences in susceptibility to carbon tetrachloride characterize the cases reported in the medical literature. Although death after ingestion of 90–150 ml had been reported frequently, ingestion of as little as 5 ml has proved fatal. Several of the factors influencing this variation in toxicity are concomitant ingestion of ethanol, the patient's age, obesity, and prior renal or hepatic disease.

Acute exposure results in a clinical complex manifesting varying degrees of central nervous system depression followed by hepatic and renal damage. The earliest symptoms of intoxication are nausea, dizziness, headache, blurred vision, ataxia, and weakness, with progression to coma and convulsions. The rapidity of onset and severity of symptoms are related to the magnitude of the exposure. Fulminant deaths probably have been caused by excessive CNS depression.

When central nervous system symptoms have subsided, the patient often will experience abdominal pain, nausea, and vomiting. Fever and diarrhea are commonly present during this phase of the illness. Liver dysfunction begins soon after ingestion of carbon tetrachloride, and maximum malfunction occurs within 48–72 hours. The average length of time for development of jaundice is 4 days, and death during the first week after CNS symptoms have subsided is generally attributable to excessive liver damage. The majority of deaths reported, however, have resulted from renal failure. Anuria commonly has developed in 3 days. Successful management of the renal and hepatic phases usually has resulted in recovery.

Treatment: There is no specific antidote; the cornerstone of treatment is prompt supportive therapy. For ingestion, induce vomiting and follow with gastric lavage. In respiratory depression, give artificial respiration. The decision as to whether or not to initiate mannitol therapy should be made early. Fifty gm are given intravenously as a loading dose over a 6-hour period. Thereafter, 25 gm are given every 6 hours for at least 5 days, or until carbon tetrachloride in the expired breath has been reduced to a low concentration.

In view of the probability of hepatocellular injury, the patient should receive adequate rest and a high-caloric, low-fat diet. The use of methionine or choline and the B-complex vitamins has been advocated.

Renal failure, should it develop, is treated in the accepted manner of restricting protein and fluids and establishing isolation precautions [R. D. Stewart *et al.*, *JAMA* **183**, 994 (1963)].

CARBONYL FLUORIDE (COF₂)

This is a colorless, pungent, toxic gas which is highly irritant to the skin, eyes, mucous membranes, and respiratory tract. It hydrolyzes rapidly to hydrogen fluoride and phosgene.

Treatment: See Hydrogen Fluoride, p. 317, and Phosgene, p. 471.

CARBONYL SULFIDE

This is a toxic flammable gas which decomposes to hydrogen sulfide and carbon dioxide on contact with moisture; 0.89% is fatal to mice in 45 seconds; 0.29% caused death in 90 seconds.

Treatment: See Hydrogen Sulfide, p. 320.

CARISOPRODOL (Soma; Rela)

This mild, central-acting, skeletal muscle relaxant is a derivative of meprobamate. It is given orally. Common side effects include drowsiness and urticarial rash; occasionally, weakness and lassitude are noted. "Fixed" drug eruptions and cross-sensitization with meprobamate have also been reported [*JAMA* **180,** 691 (1962)].

Treatment: Reduce dose or discontinue therapy.

CARMINE DYE

Cochineal is a powder derived from dried and ground scale insects and is the source for carmine dye, the active pigment in carminic acid. Recently, dried insects used in the manufacture of this dye imported from Peru and the Canary Islands were found to be contaminated with *Salmonella cubana.* As a result a number of salmonella outbreaks occurred in several hospitals where patients were given capsules of carmine powder as a stool marker [*New Engl. J. Med.* **276,** 850, 829 (1967)].

Caution: These outbreaks of infections suggest the need for instituting procedures in hospitals to ensure the absence of pathogenic microorganisms from stool markers as well as from foods [*New Engl. J. Med.* **274,** 1453 (1966)].

CARPHENAZINE (Proketazine)

This is a relatively new piperazine-type phenothiazine tranquilizer. When compared with related drugs its action is shorter, and it induces a mild stimulating effect making it particularly useful for the treatment of apathetic or withdrawn schizophrenic patients. Information available indicates that it must be used with the same precautions afforded related phenothiazines. According to a 1963 report, carphenazine "has not been shown to be better than other phenothiazines, among them chlorpromazine (Thorazine), still the drug of first choice in many institutions . . . it provides one more drug which can be tried in patients who have not responded to other agents [*Med. Letter* 5, 66, 1963]."

Side effects, precautions, contraindications and treatment: see Chlorpromazine, p. 171, and Phenothiazines, p. 464.

CASTOR BEAN (Ricinus communis)

This tree-like plant is also known as Palma Christi, koli (Hawaii), and castor-oil plant. Signs and symptoms of allergy (dermatitis, bronchial asthma, and conjunctivitis) have followed handling of the castor bean and certain of its products. Severe and fatal intoxications have followed the ingestion of five or more of the beans. The active ingredient is ricin. The lethal dose of this toxalbumin (phytotoxin) for a child is about 0.5 mg/kg.

The systemic effects are similar to those described for crabs-eye, except that the gastroenteric effects may become apparent within a few minutes after chewing a number of the beans. The early effect is a burning sensation in the mouth and throat, followed by severe gastroenteric disturbance, headache, dizziness and generalized depression. Later effects may include liver and kidney damage, electrocardiographic changes, hypotension and circulatory collapse.

Treatment: Gastric lavage is indicated if vomiting is not marked. Further treatment is similar to that outlined under crabs-eye, see p. 188.

CATANAC SP ANTISTATIC AGENT

The LD_{50} of a 35% aqueous solution in single doses by mouth to male albino rats is 8.1 gm/kg. The chemical is not absorbed through the intact rabbit skin, and it does not produce primary irritation of the skin. Single applications of the solid at dosages of 8.0 gm/kg on the clipped skin of the rabbit for a 24-hour period were tolerated with no signs of systemic toxicity and only minimal local irritation. The undiluted compound produced severe injury in the rabbit eye. Feeding studies resulted in no significant effects at a concentration of 0.1% in the diet of rats for a 28-day period. At a concentration of 1%, equivalent to a daily dose of 1 gm/kg, there was marked retardation of growth, although the food intake was maintained at approximately the control level. No characteristic signs of toxicity have been observed after a single dose or repeated doses of the product.

Skin tests on 100 human subjects revealed no evidence of sensitization. A 35% solution was used in these tests. In addition, 100 subjects wore cotton shorts and T-shirts treated with 6% Catanac SP Antistatic Agent (by weight in the fabric) for 30 days without laundering. No dermatitis resulted in these trials.

Except for the danger of eye injury by direct contact, this product is not considered to present a health hazard in ordinary industrial use.

Treatment: In case of eye contact, flood with water for 15 minutes.

CELANDINE (Chelidonium majus)

This medicinal plant was used extensively for its cathartic and diuretic action. The sap of the leaves or stem was used to remove warts and corns. Two fatalities have occurred following ingestion of overdoses. The primary effects include severe gastroenteritis, fever, and shock.

Treatment: See Tung Nut, p. 613, and Poinciana, p. 483.

CELERY BURNS (Celery Blisters; Celery Itch)

Vesicular and bullous lesions followed by depigmentation and hyperpigmentation on exposed areas of the body are commonly noted among celery harvesters in the Michigan celery-growing regions. Mexican and Negro harvesters are definitely less affected by this disease. Florida celery growers have experienced similar cases of dermatitis from handling celery, but it is the white foreman who is affected, rather than the Negro harvester.

Pink-rot celery contains a photoreactive material that can produce vesicular and bullous lesions on human skin after the sites of application are irradiated by natural sunlight or a carbon arc lamp emitting wavelengths between 3200 Å. and 3700 Å. Erythematous, edematous, and pigmentary lesions can be produced on human and animal skin if the sites of pink-rot application are irradiated with a Wood's light emitting wavelengths concentrated at 3650 Å.

Two compounds were isolated from diseased celery and were shown to have a high order of biological activity as determined by the bioassay method. These compounds were 4,5',8-trimethylpsoralen and 8-methoxypsoralen [L. D. Scheel *et al.*, *Biochemistry* **2**, 1127 (1963)].

Prevention: Trousers and long-sleeve shirts provide the most efficient method of protection. Physical sunscreens containing at least 5% titanium dioxide and a chemical sunscreen containing 10% dihydroxybenzophenone-in-oil were effective preventives in laboratory tests [D. J. Birmingham *et al.*, *Arch. Dermatol.* **83**, 73 (1961)].

CEMENT, WET

Portland and similar cements used in the building trade for reinforced concrete, mortar, plaster, etc., consist of lime, clay, and silica in varying proportions. "Cement itch" or dermatitis is common among workers handling these products.

Long-term exposure to high concentrations of "raw" and "mixed" cement dusts may result in micronodulation of the lungs due to the retention of dust in the lymphatics. With "finished" cement, the dust is largely absorbed and there is little or no retention and no resulting fibrosis.

Of 246 cement workers, patch tests for cobalt were positive in 14%, and in 6.5% for nickel. This suggests a correlation between the concentration of cobalt in cement and the incidence of sensitivity to cobalt in cases of cement eczema [V. Pirilä, and H. Kajanne, *Acta Dermato-Venereol.* **45**, 9 (1965)].

See Silicates, p. 530.

CEPHALOTHIN (Keflin)

This parentally administered drug is a cephalosparin, which is effective against many gram-negative and gram-positive organisms. Side effects are similar to those caused by penicillin, but its systemic toxicity is of a low order. Cross-allergenicity with penicillin has occurred with serious consequences [Thoburn *et al.*, *JAMA* **198**, 345 (1966)].

Caution: The drug should be administered by deep muscular injection to reduce local pain and to prevent sloughing of the tissues. I.V. injections must be given with caution to reduce the possibility of thrombophlebitis.

CHEESE

In 1963, two British physicians received the following letter from a MAO-treated patient: "I thought I had better tell you that all my life I have eaten cheese. Now I find if I do so, something in my system objects to it, I get an attack similar to what I call 'migraine' — heart thumping, head racked with pain, and sickness within half an hour. Other patients receiving MAO inhibitors experience this after cheese but the doctors laughed at the idea." The British clinicians regretfully acknowledged that they were among the physicians who laughed [*Clin-Alert*, No. 243 (1963)]. For the "cheese reaction," see Monoamine Oxidase Inhibitors, p. 404.

CHEMAGRO D-113 [1,2-Dichloro-1-(methylsulfonyl)ethylene]

This is a fungicide and nematocide. The intraperitoneal LD_{50} (mice, rats and guinea pigs) ranges from 12.5 to 17 mg/kg. No appreciable sex or species differences were noted. The oral LD_{50} for female rats and male guinea pigs is 61 and 40 mg/kg, respectively.

D-113 is not well absorbed from the skin. Doses of 50 and 250 mg/kg applied to the shaved backs of rats did not produce any evidence of systemic toxicity. Dermal application of 0.5 gm/kg caused 50% mortality in a group of four rats. Dermal application of D-113 results in a severe irritation and corrosive action on the skin.

The tissue injured by dermal application heals slowly. The lesion is similar to that produced by the sulfur and nitrogen mustards. The local effect is much less severe when a 20% powdered formulation is applied to the skin of rabbits for 24 hours.

Treatment: For skin, eye, and mucous membrane contact, flood affected area with water. In case of ingestion, induce vomiting, and follow with saline cathartics. Further treatment is supportive and symptomatic.

CHEMAGRO B-1843 [trans-1,2-Bis(n-propylsulfonyl)ethylene]

This is a seed and soil fungicide. The intraperitoneal LD_{50} (rats, mice, and guinea pigs) ranges from

11.5 to 16.5 mg/kg. No appreciable sex or species differences in susceptibility were noted. The oral LD_{50} for female rats and male guinea pigs is greater than 200 mg/kg. No local irritant effects or evidence of systemic toxicity occurred after application of 0.5 gm/kg to the shaved backs of rats.

Treatment: For skin, eye, and mucous membrane contact, flood affected area with water. In case of ingestion, induce vomiting and follow with saline cathartics. Subsequent treatment is supportive and symptomatic.

CHEMICAL MACE

The active ingredient of Chemical Mace is chloroacetophenone (CN; phenylchloromethylketone), which is the same as standard tear gas. Chemical Mace is packaged in a push-button aerosol pressure can which delivers a spray. The other components in Chemical Mace are solvents and a Freon propellent commonly found in pressurized products used in the home. These chemicals are trichlorotrifluoroethane, 1,1,1-trichloroethane, and cosmetic grade kerosene. l,l,l-Trichloroethane is the primary solvent for CN which is a solid at room temperature. The trichlorotrifluoroethane serves as the propellent and the secondary solvent for the other chemicals. The kerosene also acts as a solvent, but in addition forms a semi-permeable film that prevents intimate contact between CN and the skin.

Contact of Chemical Mace with the skin, eyes, and mucous membranes causes a burning and stinging sensation. A small squirt in the face can incapacitate a man in several seconds and render him confused and powerless. The effects wear off spontaneously in about half an hour leaving no lasting effect or disability. According to Alan Litman, M.D., who first developed Chemical Mace in 1962, there has never been a documented case of permanent injury from contact with this product (*New York Times*, May 11, 1968).

Treatment: Wash with water from the skin, eyes, and mucous membranes as soon as possible.

CHIGGERS

Chigger bites are at first scarcely noticeable, but a

162

mild itching soon becomes quite intense on scratching which produces local edema and a denuded area 1–2 mm in diameter. Marked itching continues for 1–2 weeks; finally a scale forms.

Prevention: Apply a mixture of sublimed sulfur in vanishing cream to the legs up to the knees. Dusting socks, feet, legs, and the inside of trousers with sulfur is also moderately effective, at least as long as perspiration does not become marked.

Treatment: Various proprietary preparations containing benzyl benzoate are recommended [H. K. Gouck, *Arch. Dermatol.* **93**, 112 (1966)].

CHINESE INCENSE SMOKE

The high incidence of naso-pharyngeal cancer among the Chinese may be related to carcinogens present in incense smoke. Several polycyclic aromatic hydrocarbons, including 3,4-benzpyrene, have been detected in the smoke. The 3,4-benzpyrene content is of the order of 0.4 μg per stick of incense. The free-radical content of the tar condensates was estimated to be approximately 1.3×10^{15} stable electrons per gram. This is comparable with the figure of 1×10^{15} per gram for cigarette tar [P. Schoental and S. Gibbard, *Nature* **216**, 612 (1967)].

CHLORACETOPHENONE

This is a potent lacrimator used in tear gas formulations. A fatality has been reported following exposure to high concentrations of vapor (less than 20 minutes exposure to 5.4 gm in a 34 m^3 room). Death was due to pulmonary edema and bronchiolitis. See Tear Gases, p. 574.

Treatment: Remove at once from contaminated atmosphere. Give artificial respiration and oxygen, if necessary. Treat subsequently for pulmonary edema. See p. 43, and Chemical Mace, p. 162.

CHLORAL HYDRATE

The probable lethal oral dose of chloral hydrate for an adult is 10 gm. A toxic dose of this hypnotic induces marked esophageal and gastroenteric irritation, hemorrhages, distress, and central nervous system disturbances. G. J. Gleich *et al.* recently reported an esophageal stricture which became acute approximately 3 months after the ingestion of 18 gm of this compound [*JAMA* **201**, 266 (1967)].

The hypnotic effects of chloral hydrate are particularly marked when this compound is ingested with alcohol, but the effects may not exceed those of summation. Such mixtures are referred to as "knockout drops" or "Mickey Finn."

S. A. Cucinell *et al.* reported the death of a patient who was treated with chloral hydrate and bishydroxycoumarin. Discontinuation of chloral hydrate therapy reduced the effectiveness of the anticoagulant and contributed to the death of the patient [*JAMA* **197**, 366 (1966)]. Chloral hydrate, like phenobarbital, glutethimide, and certain other compounds, increases the metabolism of drugs given at the same time or subsequently, significantly shortening their half-life [*Lancet* **II**, 1027 (1966)].

Drug-withdrawal symptoms resembling delirium tremens were reported in a chloral hydrate addict by I. P. James [*Am. J. Psychiat.* **119**, 880 (1963)].

Chloral-betaine (Beta-Chlor) has sedative and hypnotic effects like those of chloral hydrate, but the gastroenteric side effects are said to be produced less frequently [*JAMA* **190**, 1123 (1964)].

Treatment: The corrosive effects of chloral hydrate on the esophageal and gastric mucosa are considerably reduced if the drug is given as an elixir, in capsules, or dissolved in milk. In case of an overdose, induce vomiting or perform gastric lavage. Further treatment is symptomatic and supportive. Follow the same principles as outlined under Barbiturates, p. 119.

CHLORAMPHENICOL (Chloromycetin)

Administration of therapeutic doses of this antibiotic may be followed by side effects such as nausea, diarrhea, disturbances of the gastroenteric flora, or hypersensitivity reactions, including skin rashes, hemorrhages in the skin, mouth, enteric tract, and urinary bladder, fever and the Herxheimer reaction. Because of a non-dose related hypersensitivity in an occasional patient, the bone marrow may be affected, resulting in leukopenia, thrombopenia, aplasia of the bone marrow, or even in fatal pancytopenia. Fortunately, these hypersensitivity reactions, including fatal blood dyscrasias have been relatively uncommon.

They have been observed almost entirely in patients who received chloramphenicol in small doses over a long period of time [L. E. Cluff, "Drugs of Choice 1966–1967," V. C. Mosley, Saint Louis, Missouri, 1966; *Am. J. Med.* **43**, 762 (1967)]. Effects that are dose-related and that are seen occasionally include optic neuritis and blurring of vision. Digital paresthesias may be produced on rare occasions.

Administration of large or excessive doses of chloramphenicol to newborn infants has caused the "gray baby syndrome"—vomiting, abdominal distention, cyanosis, diarrhea, and fatal peripheral vascular collapse. These undesirable effects have become apparent in some infants after 2 to 4 days of treatment with doses of 200 mg/kg/day. The mortality is high, about 40%; death has occurred most frequently on the fifth day.

Caution: It is desirable that a patient treated with chloramphenicol be hospitalized. The I.V. route is not recommended. Intravenous chloramphenicol sodium succinate, if used, should be changed to the oral drug as soon as practicable. Baseline blood studies should be followed by blood tests every second day during therapy which should be discontinued promptly upon appearance of reticulocytopenia, leukopenia, thrombocytopenia, or anemia.

The drug must not be used in the treatment of trivial infections or where it is not distinctly indicated, as for instance in colds, influenza, or infections of the throat, nor should it be used as a prophylactic agent to prevent bacterial infection. Consult the manufacturer's recommendations for dosages (children and adults), precautions, contraindications, and adverse effects such as blood dyscrasias, the "Gray syndrome," and gastroenteric, neurotoxic and hypersensitivity reactions.

Administration of chloramphenicol to women during pregnancy should be avoided. Lesions of the skin or mucous membranes should be suspected as signs of monoliasis. Prolonged dosage, repeated courses of treatment, or high dosage levels should be considered *only* in the case of the gravest therapeutic necessity.

J. F. Wallace *et al*, caution against continued use of chloramphenicol and penicillin in the treatment of pneumococcal meningitis. They report that "the most hazardous situation clinically is one in which a broad spectrum drug is given for the treatment of vague upper respiratory symptoms which so often antedate meningitis, particularly in children. The thoughtless and frequently unnecessary use of antimicrobials in this situation may make the meningeal infection relatively refractory to drugs and conceivably could result in death, slow recovery, or neurological damage [*J. Lab. Clin. Med.* **70**, 408 (1967)]."

Treatment: Administration of phenylalanine seems to be capable of reversing vacuolization of the bone marrow and has been suggested as a prophylactic for chloramphenicol toxicity. Evidence for its effectiveness in preventing or reversing the serious toxic effects of chloramphenicol has *not* been published.

CHLORCYCLIZINE (Perazil; Di-Paralene)

This antihistaminic is teratogenic in the rat [*Am. J. Obstet. Gynecol.* **95**, 109 (1966)]. See Antihistamines, p. 107.

CHLORDANE (chlordan)   See page 648.

CHLORDIAZEPOXIDE (Librium)

This benzodiazepine tranquilizer has a low order of toxicity. Dizziness, nausea, and skin eruptions have been reported following doses below 75 mg/day. Doses in excess of 1 mg/kg/day have occasionally induced ataxia, grogginess, and increased appetite. Infrequently, liver dysfunction [*Brit. Med. J.* **2**, 52 (1967); *New Engl. J. Med.* **274**, 1449 (1966)], photosensitization [*Arch. Dermatol.* **91**, 362 (1965)], and cerebellar symptoms such as dysarthria, vertigo, and impaired execution of movements requiring skill have been reported [S. Cohen, Mod. Treat. **2**, 505 (1965)]. S. E. Svensen and R. G. Hamilton recently reviewed 287 clinical reports involving 18,000 patients who received this drug. The computed incidence of each reported side effect ranged from 0.16 % (syncope) to 3.9 % (drowsiness). This report confirmed that high initial doses or excessive doses were the prime factors responsible for untoward reactions [*Current Therap. Res.* **8**, 455 (1966)]. Isolated instances of addiction with withdrawal symptoms on discontinuation of the drug have also been observed [*Can. Med. Assoc. J.* **95**, 416 (1966)].

Treatment: The side effects disappeared after adjustment of dose. Overdosage must be carefully avoided in the elderly and in patients who must drive cars, operate-machines, or in those who require mental alertness. Hemodialysis effectively lowered the blood Librium level in a patient who took an overdose of this and related drugs [*JAMA* **202,** 438 (1967)].

CHLORINATED CYANURIC ACIDS (ACL)

These are white crystalline materials used in household and commercial laundry dry bleaches, dishwashing and sanitizing compounds, and scouring powders. ACL-85 is trichloroisocyanuric acid, ACL-70 is dichloroisocyanuric acid, ACL-60 and ACL-59 are the sodium and potassium salts, respectively, of dichloroisocyanuric acid. The probable lethal oral dose for an adult is estimated to be about 250 gm. Their toxicity is due to injury to the lining of the stomach rather than systemic intoxication due to absorption from the gastrointestinal tract. These compounds show no detectable irritation when applied in dry form to the intact skin of rabbits. On abraded skin the dry powders are moderately severe irritants. If a concentrated solution of any of these products is applied to the intact skin of rabbits, moderate skin irritation develops. All of the dry powders are moderately severe irritants in the eyes of rabbits. These materials are irritating to moist skin and the upper respiratory tract. Bronchospasm may occur in individuals sensitive to chlorine.

Treatment: In case of skin or eye contact, flood the affected part with water. For inhalation of dust, treat victim as for chlorine inhalation. See Chlorine, p. 650 [Monsanto Chemical Co., *Technical Bulletin* 1–177 (January 1960)].

CHLORINATED HYDROCARBONS See page 648.

CHLORINE See page 650.

CHLORMEZANONE (Trancopal)

This tranquilizer is used to alleviate mild to moderate anxiety and tension. Side effects noted (drowsiness, dizziness, flushing, dryness of mouth, and nausea) have not been significant. This is a relatively new drug which should be administered with caution.

Treatment: Reduce dose if side effects appear.

CHLOROBENZENE (Monochlorobenzene; Chlorbenzol; Phenyl Chloride)

This is a clear, colorless liquid with a sweet, aromatic, almond-like odor barely perceptible at 60 ppm. Severe vapor exposure in animals caused eye, nose and mucous membrane irritation, drowsiness, incoordination, unconsciousness, and death. Autopsy revealed liver, lung, and kidney injury. Repeated exposure to 500 and 1000 ppm caused liver, lung, and kidney injury in animals, but no effects were noted in the peripheral blood or hemopoietic tissue. Human experience and animal data indicate that chlorobenzene is not readily absorbed through the skin in sufficient quantity or rate to cause systemic intoxication. Prolonged or repeated skin contact will cause a mild chemical burn. The oral LD_{50} is 2.91 gm/kg for rats and 2.83 gm/kg for rabbits.

Treatment: For vapor exposure, remove the victim to an uncontaminated atmosphere. Give artificial respiration and oxygen if necessary. In case of eye and skin contact, flood affected parts with water. Accidental ingestion is treated by the induction of vomiting and followed with gastric lavage, saline cathartics, and demulcents.

o-CHLOROBENZYLIDENE MALONONITRILE

This compound has been reported to have a high degree of potency as a sternutator and lacrimator. A controlled study of the effects on man was conducted to test this compound's possible use in riot control. The eyes were affected by instantaneous and severe conjunctivitis accompanied by burning and pain that persisted for 2–5 minutes and usually disappeared abruptly rather than gradually. The conjunctivitis itself remained intense for up to 25–50 minutes, but the subjects were asymptomatic after 5 minutes.

Inhalation caused "burning" beginning in the throat and progressing down the respiratory tract; this was occasionally associated with coughing. As the exposure continued, this burning became painful and was rapidly followed by a "constricting sensation" throughout the chest. This latter symptom, if present, invariably produced incapacitating effects for several minutes. Sometimes fear accompanied and accentuated this symptom and persons so affected appeared unable to either inhale or exhale.

Burning occurred on exposed skin areas and was greatly accentuated by perspiration, lacrimation, or rhinorrhea. The burning continued for several hours and recurred upon washing the exposed areas or the hair. Heavy exposures produced vesiculation and erythema on exposed areas that at times resembled second-degree burns. These studies indicate that the compound is relatively nontoxic but is highly irritating to both the eyes and respiratory tract. It has produced no adverse effects when used repetitively [C. L. Punte *et al.*, *A.M.A. Arch. Environ. Health* **6**, 366 (1963)].

Treatment: No therapy other than fresh air and encouragement has been found necessary to reduce the respiratory symptoms. For skin or eye contact flood the affected parts with water.

CHLOROMETHYLPHOSPHONIC DICHLORIDE

Chloromethylphosphonic dichloride is a highly reactive chemical. Vapors are extremely irritating to the eyes and lungs. See Acid Chlorides, p. 70.

CHLORONITROBENZENES (Isomers)

Absorption of a toxic dose will lead to central nervous system stimulation, methemoglobinemia, respiratory, and circulatory difficulties.

Treatment: Oxygen, fluid therapy, glucose I.V., and transfusions are recommended. See Methemoglobinemia, p. 40.

CHLORONITROPHENOL (2-Chloro-4-nitrophenol)

2-Chloro-4-nitrophenol is slightly toxic by ingestion. Oral LD_{50} (rat) is 0.9 gm/kg. Inhalation of dusts, vapors, or absorption of the compound through the intact skin will cause methemoglobinemia. In this regard it is not as hazardous as aniline or nitrobenzene.

Treatment: See Aniline, p. 102.

CHLOROPICRIN (Trichloronitromethane; Nitrochloroform; Picfume)

This is a highly toxic odoriferous lacrimator; 2 mg/liter may be fatal if inhaled for 10 minutes. It is highly irritating to the skin, eyes, and mucous membranes of the respiratory tract.

Treatment: See Chlorine, p. 650.

CHLOROTHIAZIDES

These drugs are of importance in the treatment of cardiovascular diseases as well as in many types of edema. Included in this group are chlorothiazide (Diuril); hydrochlorothiazide (Hydro-Diuril; Oretic; Esidrix), flumethiazide (Rautrax), bendroflumethiazide (Naturetin), polythiazide (Renese), and others.

Side effects and signs of toxicity have been reported primarily for chlorothiazide and hydrochlorothiazide. The other drugs of this group have not been used as extensively. It may therefore be well to consider that all of them—until proven otherwise—could induce the following undesirable effects: potassium deficiency, precipitation of an acute attack of gout (reduction of urate excretion), yellow vision, renal colic with hematuria, uric acid crystalluria, sensitivity reactions, skin rash, photosensitization, aggravation of diabetes, glomerulonephritis, and disturbance of carbohydrate metabolism precipitating diabetes mellitus. A few cases of thrombocytopenia and leukopenia have been reported. (See Blood Dyscrasias, p. 51.)

An overdose of chlorothiazide or related drugs can be expected to induce a profound diuresis, severe electrolyte imbalance, and hypotension. One patient, following 4 years of chlorothiazide therapy, developed hyperuricemia with acute gouty arthritis and, shortly thereafter, hyperglycemia with coma [*Arch. Internal Med.* **111**, 465 (1963)]. There have been several reports calling attention to small-bowel ulcerations caused by thiazide potassium (HydroDiuril-Ka) that may progress to actual perforation even after the medication is withdrawn [*Am. J. Surg.* **112**, 97 (1966)].

Caution: Diuril and related drugs have been reported to enhance the hypotensive action of drugs used in the treatment of hypertension; hence the dosage requires frequent re-evaluation. Caution must be exercised when thiazides are administered to diabetics or to those with a prediabetic tendency. The incidence of diabetes is about 30% in patients receiving long-term thiazide therapy [*Lancet* **II**, 328 (1965)]. A glucose tolerance test in a patient on chlorothiazide therapy is unreliable. According to the Council on

Drugs of the American Medical Association, "the hyperglycemic action of these drugs should not preclude their use in diabetic patients, but only the minimal effective dose should be given [*JAMA* **188**, 994 (1964)]." Hydro Diuril-Ka therapy should be discontinued if abdominal pain, nausea, distention, or gastroenteric bleeding occurs.

Treatment is largely symptomatic following induced vomiting and/or gastric lavage. Administer potassium chloride and I.V. fluids. For chlorothiazide overdose consider use of a supplement of 2–6 gm/day of potassium chloride in tablet or syrup form, or a diet high in potassium (lima beans, apricots, peaches, dates, figs, raisins, almonds, prunes, and bananas) (see p. 38). Probenecid has been found to protect against hyperuricemia in nonazotemic hypertensive patients treated with thiazide drugs [E. D. Freis and R. F. Sappington, *JAMA* **198**, 127 (1966)]. See also Furosemide, p. 281, Ethacrynic acid, p. 244, and Digitalis, p. 218.

CHLORPHENESIN CARBAMATE (Maolate)

This new centrally-acting skeletal muscle relaxant is related pharmacologically to mephenesin (Tolserol). After daily oral doses of 1.6–2.4 gm in adults, side effects reported most frequently were drowsiness and dizziness. Occasional gastroenteric symptoms, headache, nervousness, insomnia, and weakness have been noted, and only rarely pruritus and rash.

Caution: This drug should be used with caution in patients with impaired renal or hepatic function. Patients on prolonged therapy should have periodic liver function tests and blood counts. No information is available on the safety of this drug during pregnancy. Chlorphenesin must be used with the same precautions as other agents which in therapeutic doses induce drowsiness.

CHLORPROMAZINE (Thorazine; Largactil)

"What is true for chlorpromazine is generally true for all other ataractic phenothiazines" [J. Kinross-Wright, *JAMA* **200**, 461 (1967)]. Another statement by the same author: "It is a truism that those who need chlorpromazine the most tolerate it the best. This is exemplified by the apparently heroic quantities the psychotic patient can take with few ill effects . . . Some people excrete it for as long as six weeks after a single dose."

By causing peripheral dilatation, this tranquilizer increases heat loss from the body; in addition, it interferes centrally with heat conservation. When given I.V., it may cause a sudden drop in blood pressure because of central and peripheral action. Side and toxic effects following P.O. treatment may include sedation, weakness, orthostatic hypotension, jaundice, hepatitis, leukopenia, tremors, rigidity (parkinsonism), collapse, coma, and dermatitis on hands of individuals handling the drug. (See Blood Dyscrasias, p. 51). In rare cases, lactation, gynecomastia, and gastroenteric withdrawal symptoms (nausea and vomiting) have been induced [*Am. J. Psychiat.* **121**, 491 (1964)].

The latest, but probably not the last, startling side effect of the phenothiazines is the skin-eye syndrome — also known as "purple people" (J. Kinross-Wright). Pigmentation of the skin ranging from a marked suntan to a dark purplish-brown color of the skin, cataract formation, and melanosis of some of the internal organs have been produced in patients who took 0.3–1.5 gm chlorpromazine for 3–10 years [*Lancet* **II**, 111 (1965); *Am. J. Psychiat.* **122**, 331 (1965); *JAMA* **193**, 7 (1965); *Med. J. Australia* **1**, 481 (1966)] (see Phenothiazines, p. 464). Chlorpromazine intensifies the toxic effects of atropine and related compounds.

N. M. Dilworth *et al.* reported the death of a 3-year-old who ingested an unknown amount of chlorpromazine. The symptoms included mydriasis, decreased respiration, cyanosis, drop in body temperature to 31° C, paralytic ileus, rise of blood urea nitrogen to 82 mg%, hyperglycemia (256 mg%), coma, peripheral circulatory failure, and death on the fourth day [*Lancet* **I**, 137 (1963)].

There is no evidence of permanent residual damage to the liver, even though it may take weeks, months, or a year for jaundice to disappear.

In 1964, Greiner and Berry described for the first time oculocutaneous changes induced by chlorpromazine. Other similar reports quickly followed. A recent investigation by Cameron concerns 28 patients with lens or lens and corneal changes that can reasonably be ascribed to chlorpromazine toxicity. A significant association was found between total dosage of the drug and lens changes. Minimal to marked changes were observed in 13% of patients who had received a total dose below 750 gm; and in 87% of those who received a total dosage exceeding 750 gm. One patient showed moderate lens changes with a total dosage of only 99 gm of chlorpromazine (equivalent to 150 mg per day for about 2 years). [*Brit. J. Ophthalmol.* **51**, 295 (1967); *Clin-Alert* (July 1967)].

Caution: Chlorpromazine therapy should be discontinued immediately if the patient becomes severly agitated or depressed. A light-sensitive dermatitis with pruritus or pigmentation of the skin requires reduction or discontinuation of therapy and/or protection from sunlight. A type of window glass that admits a minimum of ultraviolet light should be installed in mental hospitals. Hypotension must be guarded against, since the response to vasopressor drugs is poor. Since there is some indication that phenothiazine-induced lens and corneal changes are not always reversible, patients receiving these drugs should receive periodic eye examinations [*JAMA* **193**, 10 (1965); *Am. J. Psychiat.* **122**, 331 (1965); *Sci. News* **89**, 235 (1966)].

Treatment: As a rule neurological complications following the prolonged use of chlorpromazine diminish or disappear in a few days after reduction of the dose, with or without the support of antiparkinsonian drugs.

Induce vomiting and/or gastric lavage promptly and repeatedly for ingestion of a toxic dose. Further treatment is symptomatic and supportive. Maintain body temperature and electrolyte balance. Since respiration may fail suddenly, suitable respiratory emergency equipment should be immediately available. Exchange transfusion has been advocated for children.

CHLORPROPAMIDE (Diabinese)

A. Gervantes-Amezcua *et al.*, who administered chlorpropamide to 479 diabetic patients during a 6-year period, achieved satisfactory response in 58% and noted unsatisfactory control in the remaining diabetics. Untoward effects reported in 5.1% included, in decreasing order, gastroenteric distress with nausea and vomiting, skin rash, and hypoglycemia. In most instances, these effects appeared during the first 4 weeks of therapy [*JAMA* **193**, 759 (1965)]. Lichenoid eruption in the mouth of a 53-year-old diabetic resulting from chlorpropamide therapy was reported by R.

C. W. Dinsdale *et al.* [*Brit. Med. J.* **1**, 100 (1968)]. The patients of E. J. Benner *et al.* showed a somewhat lower incidence of failure or undesirable effects. This may have been due to the fact that these diabetics "were motivated, cooperative, private patients who (had) received intensive training in the principles of the management of diabetes [*JAMA* **193**, 763 (1965)]."

Diabinese sensitizes many patients to alcohol, inducing an Antabuse-alcohol type of response. A few severe reactions have been reported, including jaundice, liver injury, leukopenia, pancytopenia, thrombocytopenia, agranulocytosis, and exfoliative dermatitis [*Brit. Med. J.* **1**, 148 (1966)]. (See also Blood Dyscrasias, p. 51). The ingestion of a toxic dose (eighteen tablets by a child; thirty 250 mg tablets by a 17-year-old girl) induced severe hypoglycemic coma [Davies *et al.*, *Lancet* **1**, 363 (1967)].

Treatment: Reduce dose or discontinue chlorpropamide therapy if side effects become apparent. Otherwise, treatment is symptomatic. When chlorpropamide therapy is discontinued, readjust the diet and consider the use of insulin, other sulfonylureas, DBI, or a combination of these drugs. Except for induced vomiting or gastric lavage, an overdose of Diabinese is treated like an overdose of insulin. In the Davies *et al.* case, attempts to elevate the blood sugar failed until glucagon was given in addition to glucose.

CHLORTHALIDONE (Hygroton)

Chlorthalidone is one of the congeners of chlorothiazide. When taken in a single dose, 50 mg of chlorthalidone P.O. is equal to approximately 100 mg of hydrochlorthiazide. Both are effective hypotensive agents [W. E. Bowlus and H. G. Langford, *Clin. Pharmacol. Therap.* **5**, 708 (1964)]. M. Klein described one instance of pancytopenia and one case of agranulocytosis believed to have been due to chlorthalidone therapy [*JAMA* **184**, 310 (1963)]. Green reported that approximately half of 23 well-controlled diabetics on long-term chlorthalidone therapy showed a significant rise in blood sugar and urinary adrenal steroid excretion [*Clin-Alert* (Sept. 5, 1964)]. A case of fatal diabetic coma in a patient receiving chlorthalidone and reserpine was reported by Moret [*Deut. Med. Wochschr.* **90**, 1136 (1965)].

Caution: The usual side effects of thiazide diuretics

—hypokalemia, hyperuricemia, and decreased glucose tolerance—may accompany chlorthalidone therapy. An increase in the serum urate level may be reduced by sulfinpyrazone (Anturane) [*JAMA* **33**, 408 (1962)]. See Chlorothiazide, p. 170.

CHLORTHION

This is an organic phosphate which produces parasympathetic effects. It is much less toxic than parathion. See Organic Phosphates, p. 438.

α-CHLOR-p-XYLENE

This is a skin irritant and lacrimator.
Treatment: See Benzyl chloride, p. 129.

CHOLESTEROL

Approximately 5 out of 6 patients with a history of definite myocardial infarction at ages 40 to 69 have serum cholesterol levels of approximately 210 mg% or greater. J. Stamler recognizes 200 or 210 mg% as the upper limit of "normal," while 230 mg% is more generally accepted as the upper normal limit. While it is generally accepted that the risk of coronary heart disease increases in proportion to the rise in serum cholesterol (*Continued Education Series No. 119*, University of Michigan, School of Public Health, 1964), there have been few controlled studies showing that reduction of cholesterol affects the frequency or severity of attacks of coronary heart disease or other complications of atherosclerosis. In one well-controlled study [P. Leren, *Acta Med. Scand. Supp.* **466** (1966)], 206 male patients with myocardial infarction on a cholesterol-lowering diet for 5 years had fewer infarctions and recurrences of angina than a matched control group on a conventional diet. But, the reductions were significant only in patients below the age of 60. Apparently, there have been no controlled trials showing the effects of reduction of serum lipids on mortality or morbidity in persons without a history of coronary disease.

Dietary Measures: Dietary measures remain the method of choice for lowering serum lipids when reduction is desirable. For patients in the high-risk groups, (see Clofibrate, p. 180) *Medical Letter* consultants endorse the suggestions made by the Committee on Nutrition of the American Heart Association in the 1965 pamphlet *Diet and Heart Disease:* (1) Eat less animal (saturated) fat. (2) Increase the intake of unsaturated vegetable oils and other polyunsaturated fats, substituting them for saturated fats wherever possible. (3) Eat less food rich in cholesterol. (4) If overweight, reduce caloric intake to achieve and maintain desirable weight. In addition, we suggest keeping the intake of caffeine-containing beverages at a low level (see Caffeine, p. 147). High triglyceride levels often respond to a lowered carbohydrate intake. Where dietary means are unsuccessful in reducing serum lipids, *Medical Letter* consultants consider clofibrate the drug of choice [*Med. Letter* 9, 103 (1968)].

CHRISTMAS TRIMMINGS

For angel hair, see Glass Wool, p. 285; for bubbling lights, see Christmas Tree Candle Light; p. 653, for fire salts, see Copper, p. 185; Snow Sprays, p. 538; Icicles, p. 323.

CHROMIUM

Skin contact with hexavalent chromium compounds, (chromates, bichromates) may cause dermatitis and slow-healing ulcers. Fair-haired persons are particularly sensitive. Prolonged or repeated inhalation of mists or dusts will result in perforation of the nasal septum. Chromates are recognized today as a group of chemicals capable of inducing pulmonary carcinoma in man. Ingestion of a toxic dose of a chromate will induce severe gastroenteric symptoms and distress. The probable lethal oral dose of a soluble salt for an adult is 5 gm or less.

A 1-year-old Negro girl ingested an unknown quantity of ammonium bichromate from a container brought home from a high school chemistry laboratory. Apparently, the infant thought this was an orange juice preparation and accidentally ingested it. When first seen, she was severely dehydrated, semiconscious, and caustic burns were noted on the mouth and pharynx. She was frothing from the mouth and nose and this area was stained bright yellow-orange. She vomited pale liquid mucous with coffee-brown material and passed rice-water type stools. She died $12\frac{1}{2}$ hours after admission in spite of I.V. saline, vitamin K, and DTPA (calcium trisodium diethylenetriaminepentacetate) [T. E. Reichelderfer, *Southern Med. J.* **61**, 96 (1968)].

Trivalent salts of chromium, such as the phosphate or carbonate, have a low order of toxicity.

Treatment: After ingestion, induce vomiting promptly or administer gastric lavage. Give demulcents and fluid therapy (BAL was found effective in animal experiments). Chronic ulcers heal more readily if the affected areas are cleansed with a dilute solution of sodium hyposulfite or if this drug is applied in the form of a wet dressing. $CaNa_2EDTA$ is useful in treating chrome ulcers but is not effective in systemic intoxications, (See p. 236).

CHRYSANTHEMUMIC ACID
(Chrysanthemummonocarboxylic Acid; 2,2-Dimethyl-3-(2-methylpropenyl)cyclopropanecarboxylic Acid)

This organic acid, which is present in pyrethrum flowers, has a low order of toxicity. See Rotenone, p. 521.

CHYMOTRYPSIN (Buccal; Chymar; Chymolase)

This proteolytic enzyme, administered P.O. and I.M., has been recommended in ophthalmic surgery and as an anti-inflammatory agent. Kirsch reported that a dose of 0.25 ml of α-chymotrypsin produced transient elevation of the intraocular pressure in 55% of 80 nonglaucomatous eyes subjected to intracapsular cataract extraction with enzymatic zonulolysis [*Arch. Ophthalmol.* **75**, 774 (1966)].

Caution: The anti-inflammatory effects of this drug, and hence its usefulness for this purpose, is controversial. A physician contemplating use of this enzyme should know that in a suit against the manufacturer, testimony was presented that allergic effects were noted in 10 of 100 patients. One patient went into acute anaphylactic shock after an I.M. injection of chymotrypsin.

CINCHOPHEN (Atophan)

The effects of this drug resemble those of the salicylates, except that it produces more marked irritation and hemorrhages of the gastroenteric tract. (Large doses readily produce gastric or duodenal ulcers in dogs.) The probable lethal oral dose for an adult is 15 gm.

Treatment: In a case of oral poisoning, administer fluids and induce vomiting promptly; or administer gastric lavage followed by a saline cathartic. Calcium gluconate I.V. and carbohydrates by mouth or I.V., and insulin have been recommended.

CITRATE

Citrate intoxication may arise during replacement of a large volume of blood in exchange transfusions. Several fatalities have occurred in patients receiving infusions of citrated blood under hypothermia during surgery. The clinical warning signs are electrocardiographic changes due to the decreased ionized calcium level in the blood. Cardiac acidosis also appears to play a role [*Surg. Gynecol. Obstet.* **113**, 40 (1961)]. D. E. Argent, after an unsuccessful attempt to reverse ventricular fibrillation with a defibrillator, gave 2.0 ml of 10% calcium chloride intracardially; the heart responded immediately with normal rhythm [*Brit. J. Anaesthesia* **29**, 136 (1957)]. Citrate intoxication rarely impairs the blood coagulation mechanism [*JAMA* **162**, 1534 (1956)].

Treatment: Administer 5 ml of 10% calcium chloride I.V. Argent suggests that 10 ml of calcium gluconate per 1500 ml of blood be transfused to prevent citrate toxicity from massive transfusions. W. A. Sayman recommends separate I.V. infusions of calcium chloride or, preferably, calcium gluconate 1.0 gm as a 10% solution for every 3 transfusions given in 1 hour or less. It has been recommended that patients with hypothermia or impaired liver function receive 1.0 gm of calcium gluconate after every second transfusion, or after every single transfusion of 500 ml of plasma [*Med. Clin. N. Am.* **39**, 133 (1959)].

CITRONELLA

Oil of citronella is a distillation product of *Cymbopogon nardus* or *C. winterianus*. It is used in perfumes, as an insect repellent, and in the preparation known as Antinate for application to bitches in heat to deter male dogs. A 21-month-old child drank "some" Antinate and was admitted to the hospital 1 hour later, pulseless and retching continuously. Cyanosis, convulsions, and finally death occurred 5 hours after ingestion of the material. See also Masking Odorants, p. 365.

Treatment: The induction of vomiting and gastric lavage are recommended in case of ingestion. Treatment otherwise is symptomatic.

CLAMS, OYSTERS

Most clams (molluscs or shellfish) are edible. At certain times, molluscs, soft-shell and other clams, as well as fish, may feed on poisonous microscopic marine animals. Ecological and epidemiological studies have strongly implicated two dinoflagellates, *Gonyaulax catenella* and *G. tamarensis*, as causes of shellfish poisoning along the Pacific and Atlantic coasts of North America. *G. breve* is believed to have caused a mild illness, suggestive of a paralytic poisoning, in individuals who ingested oysters taken from Sarasota Bay, Florida, during the occurrence of a "red tide" [*Science* **148**, 1748 (1965)]. According to P. J. Scheuer, the toxic agent saxitoxin appears to originate in the phytoplankton [*Science* **155**, 1267 (1967)]. The signs or symptoms of intoxication may include allergic reaction, gastroenteric disturbances, muscular paralysis, loosening of the teeth, numbness of the face, lips, tongue and fingers, and respiratory difficulties. (See also Ciguatera Poisoning, p. 265.)

Caution: Because of the increased danger of bacterial contamination, avoid ingesting oysters harvested during the warm months, or during the occurrence of "blooms" (red tides) of dinoflagellates. Unfortunately, poisonous shellfish cannot be recognized by any of the household methods. Before cooking, soak or wash clams thoroughly in water. The water in which shellfish are boiled should *never* be ingested. Steamed clams may harbor the agent responsible for infectious hepatitis, at least in the New England region. Shells open during the first minute of steaming, but 4 to 6 minutes are required for clam-tissue temperatures to approach 100°C. It is safe, therefore, to ingest clams that have been sterilized [R. S. Koff and H. S. Sear, *New Engl. J. Med.* **276**, 737 (1967)]. In the United States, shellfish are produced under the control of the Public Health Service. Raw and frozen oysters, clams, and mussels from Canada and Japan are sold in this country, subject to the same sanitary controls, including shipper identification and a number on each package [Editorial, *JAMA* **200**, 788 (1967)].

Treatment is the same as that outlined under Fish Poisoning, p. 263.

CLOFIBRATE (Atromid-S)

This new drug (ethyl-*p*-chlorophenoxyisobutyrate) has been introduced for reducing elevated plasma cholesterol and triglyceride levels. Its half-life in plasma is about 12 hours. Occasional adverse effects include urticaria, stomatitis, and pruritus. Weight increase occurs in 40 % of patients.

Caution: The drug prolongs the prothrombin time in patients receiving prothrombin-depressant drugs (dicumarol, warfarin, phenindione, diphenadione, and aspirin in large doses). The manufacturer cautions against the use of clofibrate in patients suffering from renal or hepatic impairment and advises that the use of this drug be discontinued several months *before* conception. Since the incidence of pancreatitis in women with familial hyperlipemia is high during pregnancy, some *Medical Letter* consultants believe it safer to continue clofibrate than to risk an attack of pancreatitis.

In the recent evaluation of clofibrate, consultants of *Medical Letter* concluded that clofibrate can be used prophylactically in high-risk patients *who cannot achieve sustained reduction of plasma lipid levels by dietary means alone.* Such patients include those with hyperlipemia and either a history of coronary disease, a high incidence of coronary disease in the family, or tendon xanthoma, or persons without previous coronary disease but with both hyperlipemia and either moderate or severe diabetes or hypertension. Experimental work now in progress may show that it is also desirable to include in this high-risk group persons with high lipid levels but without coronary disease or a family history of hyperlipidemia [*Med. Letter* **9**, 45 (1967)].

A 15-year-old boy who took 49 capsules of clofibrate appears to be the first known attempted suicide with this medication. He showed no clinical or laboratory evidence of harm from this large amount, and remained asymptomatic except for headache, pain in both arms, and inability to walk. The boy remarked "I don't know where my legs are." [A. H. Greenhouse, *JAMA* **204**, 402 (1968)].

CLOMIPHENE CITRATE (Clomid)

This new drug stimulates ovulation in sterile women. Clomid is less expensive, less potent, and less risky than Perganol, a natural hormone containing gonadotrophins. According to E. Tyler, the number of pregnancies following Perganol is higher than after the use of Clomid, but the number of premature infant deaths is also higher. Both Perganol and Clomid produced ovarian cysts — noncancerous, liquid-filled sacs on the ovary — in 15–20 % of patients. Most of the cysts disappeared within a few weeks; one woman required surgery [*Sci. News* **90**, 539 (1966)]. Four of 58 women given Clomid developed ocular symptoms [Roch *et al.*, *Arch. Ophthalmol.* **77**, 14 (1967); *Obstet. Gynecol.* **30**, 699 (1967)].

Caution: As with all known fertility drugs, Clomid carries some risk of multiple births [*Sci. News* **91**, 181 (1967)].

CLOROX

This is a liquid bleach composed of sodium hypochlorite 5.25%, sodium carbonate 0.2% and sodium chloride 4.0%. Since it is commonly included among substances known to cause corrosive esophagitis, such as household ammonia, lye, phenol and acetic acid, esophagoscopy is usually performed on children who take this substance. One hundred twenty-nine cases of Clorox ingestion seen in 1954–1962 were reviewed by Pike *et al.* In the last 65 cases an esophagoscopy was done, but no remarkable lesions were seen. These esophagoscopies were done within 96 hours of ingestion. The amount ingested ranged from approximately 15 gm to a "cupful." Often the amount was unknown. Ingestion was assumed because of the smell of Clorox on the child's mouth. None of these cases developed dysphagia. Only two cases showed a slight esophageal injury just above the cardia. These injuries were mild, excluding the possibility of the late development of stricture.

Treatment: In case of ingestion, induce vomiting and follow with gastric lavage. Direct examination of the esophagus is not indicated after Clorox ingestion because significant esophageal injury is improbable [D. G. Pike *et al.*, *J. Pediat.* **63**; 303 (1963)].

COBALT

Acute intoxications by salts of cobalt are rare. A 19-month-old boy died 5 hours after ingesting 30 gm of a cobalt chloride solution. The symptoms included vomiting, restlessness, drowsiness, and marked cyanosis of the lips and of the nail beds. Antithyroid effects were noted in children and in one adult given enteric-coated cobaltous chloride for the treatment of anemia. All patients had hyperplasia of the thyroid. Weaver and co-workers reported that 8-month-old twin sisters developed thyroid enlargement while receiving cobalt-iron therapy for anemia. One twin developed midline thyroid enlargement which impeded swallowing. Postoperative reinstitution of cobalt-iron therapy was followed by the development of a second mass in spite of treatment with Lugol's iodine and desiccated thyroid [*Calif. Med.* **85**, 110 (1956)].

Cobalt-60 is a source of gamma radiation. Symptoms following exposure to cobalt-60 include nausea, vomiting, and diarrhea, in that order. For details, see Radiation, p. 512.

Recently, in the United States, "beer drinker's disease" or "Münchener Bierherz" (myocardial insufficiency) is believed to have caused 20 deaths in men who drank excessive volumes of beer. The cobalt acetate added to beer in trace amounts to give it a more stable "head" was suspected, but this has not been proven.

Treatment: Cessation of therapy with cobalt containing hematinics is expected to bring about complete regression of symptoms within 2 weeks to 2 months. CaNa$_2$EDTA was found to be an effective antidote in experimental intoxications; see p. 236.

COBALT HYDROCARBONYL

Cobalt hydrocarbonyl decomposes rapidly in air to cobalt carbonate or one of the hydrated oxides.

The LD$_{50}$ for rats for a 30 minute exposure is approximately 165 mg cobalt per cubic meter. A high incidence of pulmonary edema was found in rats exposed to concentrations above 90 mg of cobalt per cubic meter.

Repeated daily exposure for 3 months (71 6-hour periods) to concentrations averaging 9 mg cobalt per cubic meter resulted in no chronic pathological changes in rats, guinea pigs, and dogs. Early deaths were due to acute effects. The lungs of animals sacrificed immediately after exposure contained nodules and aggregates of foam cells which were not found in animals 3 and 6 months later. A single exposure 6 months later caused eosinophilic pneumonia in one of 3 guinea pigs.

Treatment: Discontinue exposure. Administer oxygen if necessary. Subsequent treatment is symptomatic. Observe for premonitory signs and symptoms of pulmonary edema.

COCAINE

Cocaine is derived from the leaves of *Erythroxylon coca.* Chewing the leaves induces mild anesthesia of the mouth, cortical stimulation, and a rise in blood pressure. Intoxications have resulted from ingestion, injection, and skin absorption of cocaine. Doses of 20 and 30 mg applied to mucous membranes have caused death in two susceptible individuals. Premonitory signs included pallor, apprehension, restlessness, followed by tachycardia, muscular spasm, gastroenteric pain, vomiting, convulsions, and coma.

Treatment: Remove drug from skin or mucous membrane, with water. In case of ingestion, vomiting, gastric lavage, and demulcents are recommended. Administer oxygen and artificial respiration if necessary. Use ether or a barbiturate to control convulsions. If heart action has stopped, apply cardiac massage without delay.

COCKROACH POISON

Some insecticides commonly employed in cockroach control are Bayer 29493, chlordane, DDVP, dieldrin, Diazinon, dicapton, malathion, ronnel.

See Table 2, p. 668.

COCOA

Because of the high fat content, ingestion of excessive amounts of cocoa may interfere with digestion and cause gastroenteric distress.

CODEINE (Methylmorphine)

This narcotic causes less severe side effects than morphine. Several clinicians have recommended it for the treatment of post-operative pain, but as L. Lasagna points out, it is amazing how little reliable information there is about its efficacy, particularly by the parenteral route [*Pharmacol. Rev.* **16**, 47 (1964)]. In effective doses, codeine, like other narcotics, depresses respiration and causes morphine-like symptoms such as constipation, nausea, and itching.

On a body weight basis, infants and small children are much more susceptible to codeine than adults [W. Rumler and W. Weigel, *Kinderheilk.* **111**, 241 (1963)]. Withdrawal symptoms were produced in an infant whose mother had taken 6–8 gm of codeine daily for 2 months. The child responded to I.M. codeine (0.4 mg every 3 hours). Eventually, phenobarbital replaced the narcotic. The child recovered [G. Van Leeuwen *et al.*, *Pediatrics* **36**, 635 (1965)].

Caution: W. Rumler and W. Weigel recommend replacing codeine with other remedies (dextromethorphan) in children.

Treatment: Nalorphine and levallorphan are effective antagonists. See Narcotic Agents, p. 40, and Opiates, p. 435.

COLCHICINE

This compound is used because of its antineuralgic and antirheumatic properties. Side effects are frequent. It is the most effective drug for the treatment of acute gouty arthritis. Repeated ingestion of low but toxic doses has caused blood dyscrasias, severe gastroenteric disturbances, nephritis, fever, hepatic damage, tremors, or respiratory difficulties. A single oral dose of 6 mg has proved fatal. Desacetylmethylcolchicine (Colcemide) caused alopecia in a number of cases. Oral administration of 14 mg resulted in total loss of scalp hair within a 24-hour period [*New Engl. J. Med.* **255**, 769 (1956)].

Treatment: In case of diarrhea discontinue therapy or reduce the dose immediately. Since this is a dangerous drug, patients receiving it — particularly those with impaired renal function — should remain under close medical supervision. Administer parenteral doses with *extreme caution* [*Arch. Internal Med.* **115**, 29

(1965)]. In case of an oral overdose, administer fluids and induce vomiting. Further treatment is symptomatic and supportive.

COLISTIN (Colymycin; Coly-Mycin-M)

Colistin is available as the sulfate for oral administration (not absorbed). Intramuscular administration of sodium colistimethate (Coly-Mycin-M) for the treatment of severe urinary tract infections caused by coliform organisms and *Pseudomonas* may produce signs and symptoms of neurotoxicity and nephrotoxicity [*JAMA* **190**, 421 (1964)].

Caution: Since the colistins are potentially nephrotoxic, they should be reserved for infections caused by the *Pseudomonas* species, *E. coli*, and *A. aerogenes*, which are resistant to other antibacterial drugs. The prophylactic use of these drugs is not recommended.

CONCH POISONING

According to *Sea Secrets* [3, No. 10 (1959)] of the International Oceanographic Foundation, the first factual account of conch poisoning (except for the Samba) was reported in 1959. Symptoms included "cramps and pains." Samba is distinguished by its nearly black skin. When ingested, it causes a severe intoxication. For treatment, see Fish Poisoning, p. 263.

CONGO RED

This dye is used I.V. as a diagnostic test for amyloidosis. Harstenmeyer reported that a 38-year-old man collapsed almost immediately after receiving 10 ml. He died 4 days later. Autopsy revealed multiple disseminated fibrin thrombi in the capillaries of the cerebral cortex and fresh hemorrhages in the subarachnoid space.

Because reactions to congo red, including fatalities, continue to be reported, the test should be replaced by biopsy of the rectal mucosa, a far less dangerous and more reliable procedure [*Deut. Med. Wochschr.* **89**, 1845 (1964)].

COPPER

Ingestion of a toxic dose of copper sulfate may induce severe gastroenteric distress (vomiting, gastroenteric pain, and local corrosion and hemorrhages), prostration, anuria, hematuria, anemia, increase in white blood cells, icterus, coma, respiratory difficulties, and circulatory failure. Two men who ingested 60 and 80 gm in solution died in 6 and 9 days, respectively. The minimal lethal oral dose for an adult appears to be 10 gm.

Acute copper poisoning (doses of 5–50 mg) can be expected following ingestion of fruit juices or food acids (acetic, citric, malic, tartaric, oleic, etc.) that have remained in contact with a copper container for any length of time. Tea prepared in a corroded copper water heater caused acute poisoning within minutes after ingestion. The ingestion of copper oxide caused a recent intoxication aboard ship. The oxide present in water stored in a tank was partially converted to copper chloride by gastric juice [*Ned. Tijdschr. Geneesk.* **109**, 978 (1965)]. The widespread use of copper for plumbing, kitchen utensils, beer-brewing kettles, and whiskey-stills, and the infrequency of poisoning would indicate that ingestion and absorption of copper from these sources is of a low order. (An acid reaction must be avoided, since this will dissolve the copper.) A concentration up to 0.2 mg of copper per liter is considered safe in water supplies.

Inhalation of mists of inorganic salts of copper will cause irritation of the upper respiratory tract. In patients suffering from Wilson's Disease, it is important to maintain a significant negative copper balance by intake of a low copper diet and vigorous copper removal. G. A. Nicolson *et al.* suggest that schizophrenics may retain too much copper. These patients, when treated with penicillamine, excreted copper in the urine and showed general improvement and reduction in pigmentation [*Lancet* **I**, 344 (1966)].

Copper naphthenate and quinolinolate have a low order of toxicity.

Treatment: After ingestion, induce vomiting and administer gastric lavage. Give a saline cathartic, fluid therapy, and transfusions if required. Calcium disodium EDTA has been found moderately effective. The usefulness of BAL in copper intoxications has not been fully substantiated. For exposure to skin and eyes wash affected tissues with water.

D-Penicillamine, Ca EDTA, BAL, and sodium diethyldithiocarbamate (Dithiocarb) have been found useful in the treatment of Wilson's Disease [F. S. Sunderman, *J. New Drugs* **4**, 154 (1964)]. See Dimercaprol, p. 224, EDTA, p. 236, Penicillamine, p. 452, Dithiocarb, p. 583, and Heavy Metal Poisoning, p. 39.

CORAL POISONING

Coral lacerations are generally the result of brushing against, or carelessly handling, exoskeletons of various species of dead stony corals. These wounds often become secondarily infected.

Injuries produced by contact with the living coral polyps resemble the effects of stings from the Portuguese man-of-war and the virulent sea-wasp. See Jellyfish, p. 340.

Treatment: The area involved requires prompt cleansing with soap and water, removal of foreign particles, and debridement if necessary. Give symptomatic treatment only if indicated. (For details see B. W. Halsted, "Dangerous Marine Animals," Cornell Maritime Press, Cambridge, Maryland, 1958.)

CORK DUST

Exposure to cork dust has been reported to cause an occupational pneumoconiosis known as suberosis. After 20 or more years of exposure, the chronic stage develops which is seldom totally disabling or fatal. Clinically, the chronic stage is characterized by bronchitis and emphysema associated with pronounced pulmonary function changes. Much of the damage relates to mechanical impairment, but specific pulmonary injury is induced by some unknown factor. Cor pulmonale is a rare sequela and subsequent malignancy is practically unknown.

Treatment: There is no specific therapy. Preventive measures at the present time are the only means of avoiding this disease.

COTTON (Surgical Sponges)

Particles of lint from gauze sponges are capable of inducing adhesions and granulomas. Fragments originate from both gauze sponges and laparotomy sponges. Both are composed of bleached cotton. Gauze was considered the etiological agent in 23 of 32 clinical cases of foreign body granuloma involving the peritoneal cavity [Sturdy *et al.*, *Ann. Surg.* **165**, 128 (1967)].

The common cotton plant (including the seeds) contains gossypol, which is toxic to some animals. Cattle and sheep are unaffected by gossypol. A recently introduced method of pressing and cooking inactivates gossypol so that commercial cottonseed meal may be fed safely to cattle, sheep, chickens, and broilers, but not to laying hens or to pigs.

CRABS-EYE (Abrus Precatorius)

This slender, woody vine is also known as precatory bean, jequirity bean, prayer bead, rosary pea, mienie-mienie Indian bead, seminole bead, weather plant, and lucky bean.

Severe intoxications and fatalities have occurred in children after *chewing* and ingesting a single unripe or ripe bean. Swallowing of the whole ripe seed with its hard coating intact is harmless since it is not decomposed in the gastroenteric tract. The active principle is a thermolabile toxalbumin (abrin), which is extremely toxic; its estimated lethal dose for a child is 0.01 gm/kg.

Signs and symptoms of an intoxication (severe gastroenteritis with nausea, vomiting, and bloody diarrhea) may be delayed for several hours to several days. In a severe intoxication, mydriasis, hypotension, muscular weakness, tremors, tetany, flushing of the skin, tachycardia, hallucinations, convulsions, and coma may follow. Death is due to circulatory collapse and cardiac failure. Severe and prolonged vomiting or diarrhea, if not corrected, will cause electrolyte imbalance, dehydration, hypotension, tachycardia, and cardiac arrhythmias.

Treatment: If it is known that the seed has been ingested, induce vomiting and administer gastric lavage. After the long latent period, when gastroenteric effects are evident, gastric lavage is of little value. There is no known antidote. Symptomatic treatment supported by excellent nursing care should be initiated as early as possible. Bismuth subcarbonate or magnesium trisilicate have been recommended for treatment of the gastroenteric effects. Administer fluids and electrolytes, and calcium gluconate for tetany; treat circulatory disturbances and convulsions symptomatically. A high carbohydrate diet is recommended.

CREOSOTE

This is a mixture of phenols. Prolonged or repeated skin contact may produce dermatoses and skin cancer. Photosensitivity seems to be a factor in the production of skin lesions.

Treatment: Remove from the skin by thorough flushing with water. See Phenol, p. 463.

CROCUS; AUTUMN CROCUS (*Colchicum autumnale*)

All parts of this plant, and also of the glory lily, or climbing lily (*Gloriosa superba*), contain colchicine. Ingestion of these plants produces effects similar to those produced by an overdose of colchicine. Effects appear following a latent period of 2 hours or more and include a severe burning sensation in the mouth and throat and general malaise. These early symptoms may be followed by intensive and prolonged vomiting, colic, severe diarrhea, and tenesmus. In a severe intoxication there is hematuria, oliguria, bloody stools, and shock. Death is due to respiratory and circulatory paralysis.

Treatment: If it is known that the plant material has been ingested, induce vomiting or administer gastric lavage. Follow with a saline cathartic if signs of an intoxication have not yet appeared. Further treatment is supportive and symptomatic.

CROTON (Purging Croton; *Croton tiglium*)

The toxic principle is croton resin, which is present throughout the plant. Ingestion will cause burning in the mouth and stomach and drastic purging, possibly leading to collapse and death. Externally, it may induce severe skin irritation, inflammation, swelling, and pustule formation. Absorption through the skin may cause purging.

Treatment: For gastrointestinal symptoms use demulcents. Further treatment is symptomatic.

CROTONIC ACID

Crotonic acid causes moderate primary skin irritation and severe eye injury. It has been found by animal experimentation to resemble ethylacetoacetate in skin irritation and to be similar to acetic anhydride in eye sensitization. The intraperitoneal LD_{50} is 100 mg/kg in rats and 60 mg/kg in guinea pigs. The oral LD_{50} is 1.0 gm/kg in rats.

Treatment: See Acetic Anhydride, p. 63.

CURARE

Toxic doses of curare, *d*-tubocurarine, dimethyltubocurarine, Intocostrin, gallamine triethiodide (Flaxedil), benzoquinonium (Mytolon), and Laudolissin will produce paralysis of all skeletal muscles. Death is due to paralysis of the thoracic muscles and the diaphragm. As drugs, these compounds are generally given I.V. Oral doses have an extremely low degree of toxicity.

Treatment: Give artificial respiration supported by neostigmine I.V. in doses of 1 ml of 1:1,000 to 2,000 neostigmine, or the methylsulfate solution (up to 4 doses for an adult). Edrophonium chloride (Tensilon), 5–10 mg I.V., is an alternate drug. Ephedrine (30–50 mg SC) is indicated if the blood pressure is low. These drugs are not antidotes. They will, however, reduce the intensity and the duration of peripheral paralysis. Atropine is effective in preventing the bradycardia that may follow the injection of a parasympathetic drug. [Neostigmine and edrophonium chloride (Tensilon) are dangerous in a patient under decamethonium bromide (Syncurine; C_{10}), or succinylcholine chloride (Anectine) therapy].

CYANAMIDE

This is a colorless, deliquescent, crystalline material melting at 45–46°C. Administered as an aqueous dispersion at a constant volume of 20 ml/kg, it has an LD_{50} for rats of 280 mg/kg. The LD_{50} of an aqueous paste in continuous 24-hour contact with the shaved skin of rabbits is 590 mg/kg; an aqueous paste was corrosive to rabbit skin. Small quantities of the dry product produced a severe degree of irritation when introduced into the conjunctival sac of the rabbit eye.

The ingestion of alcoholic beverages a few hours after exposure causes a vasomotor reaction known as "cyanamide flush" or "mal rouge."

Treatment: In case of ingestion, empty the stomach by inducing vomiting. For skin or eye contact, flood the affected tissues with water.

CYANIDES, INORGANIC

Vomiting, convulsions, and unconsciousness occur promptly after ingestion or skin absorption of a toxic dose of sodium or potassium cyanide, or after inhalation, skin absorption, or ingestion of hydrogen cyanide. The lethal oral adult dose of sodium or potassium cyanide ranges from 200 to 250 mg. Exposure to 200 ppm of hydrogen cyanide for three minutes may be fatal.

Treatment: Speed is of the essence. After ingestion of cyanide: inhalation of amyl nitrite followed by *immediate* vomiting or gastric lavage, and the subsequent I.V. injection of sodium nitrite (3% solution at a rate of 2.5–5 ml per minute) and sodium thiosulfate (approximately 50 ml of a 25% solution I.V.), or sodium tetrathionate *plus* the inhalation of oxygen [J. L. Way *et al.*, *J. Pharmacol. Exptl. Therap.* **153**, 381 (1966)]. Repeat injections, if signs of toxicity persist, using similar or smaller doses. Use water copiously if skin exposure is evident. Supportive treatment may include external cardiac massage, artificial respiration and oxygen, warmth, and other symptomatic measures. The stomach may be washed with 5% aqueous sodium thiosulfate leaving 200 ml of this solution in the stomach at completion of lavage [N. K. Chen, and C. L. Rose, *JAMA* **149**, 113 (1952); **162**, 1154 (1956)]. Recovery is possible as long as the vital functions are maintained, even in the face of apparent death. Consider giving a blood transfusion in the event of excessive production of methemoglobinemia (deepening cyanosis in the presence of recovery).

Excessive hypotension is avoided by constant readjustment of the dose of nitrite or thiosulfate as well as by placing the patient in the Trendelenburg position. "There is good reason to utilize the interrupted schedule of administration" of amyl nitrite, namely, 15–30 seconds per minute. This will lessen the danger of inadequate oxygenation [A. K. Done, *Clin. Pharmacol. Therap.* **2**, 750 (1961)].

Recent reports deserve to be given careful consideration. K. D. Friedberg *et al.*, working with isolated rat hearts and anesthetized guinea pigs treated with toxic or lethal doses of sodium cyanide, found aquocobalamin (vitamin B_{12a}; Aquo-Cytobion), cobalt desferrioxamine (Desferal), and Co_2 EDTA, (cobalt chloride to a lesser extent) far superior to the traditional antidotes such as sodium nitrite and sodium thiosulfate. With regard to toxicity, cobalt desferrioxamine was found to be preferable to Co_2 EDTA. However, aquocobalamin is preferred to the other cobalt compounds since it is not toxic. According to the authors, this compound is *"völlig ungiftig."* The recommended human dose of Aquo-Cytobion is 100 ml of a 10% solution I.V. [*Arch. Toxikol.* **22,** 176 (1966)]. J. T. Bain and E. L. Knowles confirmed these observations with Co_2 EDTA. They injected 300 mg of this compound in 2 evenly divided doses within an interval of 10 minutes in a patient who collapsed in a cyanide plant. Immediately after the first dose, the patient became coherent and the convulsions ceased. The patient recovered [*Brit. Med. J.* **1,** 763 (1967)].

CYANOGEN (Oxalic Nitrile; Ethane Dinitrile; Prussite; Dicyan)

This is a highly toxic gas having an almond-like odor at low concentrations. At high concentrations it is acrid and pungent.

Human subjects exposed to 16 ppm for 6–8 minutes experienced eye and nasal irritation. The odor was not detected at these concentrations or at concentrations of 50–250 ppm.

Effects observed during exposures included asphyxia, lacrimation, upper respiratory tract irritation, pink skin, accentuated poorly coordinated movements, tremors, and prostration.

In skin tests rabbits showed no effects from exposure of the clipped body to 10,000 ppm for 8 hours.

Treatment: See Cyanides, p. 191.

CYANOGEN CHLORIDE

This is a colorless, highly toxic gas. It possesses the same general type of toxicity and mode of action as hydrogen cyanide, but is much more irritating even in low concentrations. It can cause marked irritation of the respiratory tract, producing a hemorrhagic exudate of the bronchi and trachea, and pulmonary edema.

Treatment: See Cyanide, p. 191, and Pulmonary Edema, p. 43.

CYANURIC ACID (2,4,6-Trihydroxy-s-triazine; Isocyanuric Acid; 2,4,6-Trioxohexahydro-s-triazine)

This is a white solid having a low order of toxicity. A 24% aqueous suspension of cyanuric acid did not cause death when given as a single dose to rats at 10 gm/kg and to rabbits at 20 gm/kg; 80 gm/kg given orally over a 4-day period also failed to produce death in rats or rabbits. Most of the compound was excreted unchanged and the animals showed only decreased appetite and activity.

A 0.01% (100 ppm) aqueous solution of cyanuric acid did not produce significant eye irritation when placed in continuous contact with the rabbit eye 30 minutes per day, 5 days per week, for 30 applications.

Twenty milligrams of finely ground cyanuric acid paste (50–60% cyanuric acid) produced mild irritation in the rabbit eye when placed in the conjunctival sac for 24 hours.

Cyanuric acid paste was not irritating when applied to the intact clipped skin of a rabbit for 4 hours.

Treatment: In case of accidental ingestion of large quantities induce vomiting.

CYANURIC CHLORIDE

This hydrolyzes in the presence of water to form hydrochloric acid, which is irritating to the skin and mucous membranes. The dust is particularly irritating to the eye because of rapid liberation of hydrochloric acid, which causes a stinging sensation.

Treatment: See Hydrochloric Acid, p. 317.

CYASORB UV 9 LIGHT ABSORBER

The oral LD_{50} for rats is greater than 5.0 gm/kg. This chemical added to the feed of rats was tolerated at a level of 10,000 ppm for 27 days without apparent toxic effect. Applied to the skin of rabbits, it caused no significant irritation, and doses as high as 16 gm/kg did not cause any evidence of systemic toxicity. The material placed in the eyes of rabbits produced only mild inflammatory reaction of a few hours' duration.

Treatment: In case of eye contact flush with water for 15 minutes.

CYCLAMATE

Cyclamates are used as artificial sweeteners. Sodium cyclamate (Sucaryl), although less potent than saccharin, does not leave the bitter aftertaste characteristic of saccharin. A small percentage of individuals have the capacity to convert and excrete a fraction of ingested cyclamate as cyclohexylamine. These rare exceptions excrete less than 1% (A. J. Lehman, personal communication). The virtually complete absence of adverse effects of this substance among the millions of users, since its introduction nearly 20 years ago, has raised no serious questions as to its safety (Food and Drug Research, No. 55, Jan. 1969). However, it is recommended that adults do not ingest more than 5 gm per day: one hundred 50 mg tablets. The largest selling brands contain from 0.32 to 0.91 gm per 12 fluid ounces (360 ml), the weighted average being 0.45 gm. A child's intake should not exceed 2 such bottles of soft drink per day.

1,4-CYCLOHEXANEDIMETHANOL (1,4-CHIDM)

A 20% aqueous solution administered orally killed 50% or more of the rats and mice dosed with 3.2 gm/kg. Intraperitoneal doses of 1.6 gm/kg killed mice and 0.8 gm/kg was fatal to rats. No abnormalities were found on hematological examination. Only slight skin irritation and no evidence of skin absorption was found in tests with guinea pigs. Rats exposed to atmospheric concentrations of 1.25 mg/l (212 ppm) of the compound showed no signs of apparent injury.

Treatment: In case of eye or skin contact, flood the affected parts with water. For ingestion, induce vomiting.

CYCLOHEXANONE

The acute oral toxicity—LD_{50} (rat)—is approximately 1.6 gm/kg. Five male and 5 female rats survived 208 daily oral doses of 0.16 gm/kg, but growth (especially of the males) was greatly retarded.

Cyclohexanone in undiluted form is highly irritating to the rabbit eye, and vapors have caused irritation to the eyes of exposed personnel. The effects are transient, however, and recovery is complete within 24 hours. Five rabbits dosed with 1 ml/kg on shaved intact skin showed no primary irritation. An intradermal injection of 0.16 mg/kg also caused no reactions.

Ten rats exposed 2 hours a day for 10 days to a vapor concentration of 1,000 ppm showed no serious reactions, and all survived a 10-day observation period. Skin patch tests after the tenth day were negative. The irritation threshold is about 75 ppm, and the recommended threshold limit in air is 50 ppm or 200 mg/m^3.

Treatment: In case of eye or skin contact, flood affected parts with water.

1-CYCLOHEXYL-3-(5-INDANYLSULFONYL)UREA

This is a new blood-sugar-lowering sulfonylurea compound. Studies conducted with this drug in rats, compared favorably with tolbutamide (Orinase). See Sulfonylurea Drugs, p. 563.

CYCLOHEXYLAMINE

This is a highly alkaline colorless liquid with a strong odor and a bitter taste. Contact with the skin has caused necrosis, ulcers, and scarring. Gastric administration of a 3% solution to albino rats produced acute poisoning characterized by spasm and slow labored breathing. The oral LD_{100} is 0.5 gm/kg and the LD_0 is 0.15 gm/kg for the albino rat. Inhalation of a 3 mg/m^3 vapor for 7 hours caused death to some of the experimental animals [R. M. Watrous and H. N. Schulz, *Ind. Med. Surg.* **19**, 317 (1950)]. Cyclohexylamine is a weak methemoglobin-forming substance with cumulative properties capable of producing poisoning [G. N. Lamonova, *Gigiena Truda i Prof. Zabolevaniya* **7**, 51 (1963)].

Treatment: See Ammonia, Aqueous p. 95, and Aniline, p. 102.

N-CYCLOHEXYLMORPHOLINE

The oral LD_{50} of a 10% solution is 178 mg/kg for male rats and 192 mg/kg for female rats. Two out of 10 guinea pigs exposed for 1 hour to an aerosol of 2 mg/liter (2 ppm) died on the seventh and eighth days after exposure. Post mortem findings showed hemorrhagic areas in the lungs. This compound presents an acute inhalation hazard from possible delayed lung damage. N-Cyclohexylmorpholine produces a mild, transient irritation when instilled in the eye of a rabbit. The undiluted compound is a severe skin irritant and systemic intoxication is a definite hazard.

Treatment: In case of inhalation, remove the individual promptly from the contaminated atmosphere. Give artificial respiration and oxygen, if necessary. Observe for premonitory signs of pulmonary edema. For contact with the eyes or skin, flood affected parts with water for 15 minutes. Treat ingestion by the induction of vomiting, gastric lavage, saline cathartics and demulcents.

CYCLOPARAFFINS (Cycloalkanes; Naphthenes)

These are cyclic saturated hydrocarbons such as cyclopropane, cyclobutane, cyclopentane, cyclohexane, etc. In general, their toxicity is comparable to the corresponding aliphatic hydrocarbons. They are central nervous system depressants and excellent lipid solvents. See Petroleum Solvents or Distillates, p. 459.

CYCLOPENTOLATE HYDROCHLORIDE (Cyclogyl)

This drug is used to produce cycloplegia and mydriasis. It has about one half the antispasmodic potency of atropine. The dose for refraction is 2 drops of a 0.5% solution, each drop instilled at 5-minute intervals. When this dose is exceeded, toxic effects (ataxia, dysarthria, incoherent speech) should be expected, particularly in children [*Arch. Ophthalmol.* **67**, 46 (1962)].

CYCLOPHOSPHAMIDE (Cytoxan)

This antineoplastic alkylating agent, a derivative of nitrogen mustard, is administered I.V. and P.O. Usually it is well tolerated, but sometimes it produces nausea and vomiting and, in isolated instances, severe bone marrow depression [*Am. J. Med. Sci.* **254**, 48 (1967)]. Among the more common adverse reactions observed is partial to complete alopecia capitis. One report indicates that this drug may have been responsible for the birth of a child with multiple congenital anomalies [*JAMA* **188**, 423 (1964)]. The drug should not be prescribed when surgery or radiation is the treatment of choice.

Caution: Use drug with caution in the presence of hemopathy, hepatic dysfunction, or in patients who have recently received radiation or other cytotoxic therapy.

CYCLOPROPANE

This is a hydrocarbon gas having a low order of toxicity. It is extensively used as a general gaseous anesthetic. It is the simplest naphthene or cycloparaffin (cycloalkane) hydrocarbon. See Hydrocarbon Gases, p. 316.

Caution: Under certain conditions (via face mask) cyclopropane may be swallowed. Since swallowed gases are known to pass from the stomach to the intestinal tract, the possibility of an explosion should be kept in mind whenever cautery is used on any portion of the enteric tract [Reier and Wu, *Anesthesiology* **28**, 771 (1967)].

CYCLOSERINE (Seromycin; Oxamycin)

This antibiotic is occasionally used alone or in combination with PAS and isoniazid in the therapy of tuberculosis. Central nervous system stimulation, including convulsions, has been noted in a large percentage of patients. A woman who took 30 gm of this drug in a suicidal attempt was admitted in a semi-comatose state and in shock. There were no tremors. Hematology, blood urea, electrolytes, and ECG were normal. She recovered following peritoneal dialysis [*Brit. Med. J.* **1**, 907 (1965)].

Caution: This drug should be reserved for patients in whom PAS, isoniazid, or streptomycin are ineffective [*Tubercle* **38**, 97 (1957)]. According to R. Lich, Jr., administration of cycloserine should always be accompanied by pyridoxine hydrochloride, which prevents the neurotoxic effects of this drug ["Drugs of Choice 1966–1967," V. C. Mosby Company, Saint Louis, Missouri 1966]. As with many other therapeutic agents, kidney function plays an important role in the therapeutic and side effects of cycloserine.

DALAPON SODIUM (2,2-Dichloropropionic Acid, Sodium Salt)

Dalapon sodium, a plant growth regulator, has a low order of acute oral toxicity. Laboratory animals and cattle tolerate large doses without serious effects. Dogs fed 100 mg/kg per day for 1 year and rats given 50 mg/kg per day for 2 years exhibited only slight increases in average kidney weights. Rats receiving 15 mg/kg per day for 2 years and dogs dosed with 50 mg/kg per day for 1 year showed no significant differences from the controls.

Undiluted Dalapon sodium may cause skin irritation if it is allowed to remain on the skin for a prolonged period. Exposures of short durations are not likely to be injurious. Contact with Dalapon dust, particularly when sweating, may cause a mild burning sensation. Prolonged contact with dilute aqueous solutions is not likely to cause any appreciable effect. Systemic effects due to absorption through the skin are not likely to occur.

The material in the solid form or in concentrated solutions is capable of causing appreciable pain and irritation of the eyes, but it is not likely to cause serious damage.

Treatment: For eye, skin, and mucous membrane contact, flood affected area with water.

DEANOL ACETAMIDOBENZOATE (Deaner)

Deaner has been proposed for the relief of a variety of vague complaints. This drug should serve only as an adjuvant to psychotherapy in the treatment of behavior problems severe enough to require medical attention [*Pediatrics* **21**, 325 (1958)].

Treatment: Reduce dose or discontinue use entirely.

DECAMETHONIUM BROMIDE (Syncurine)

Like other curare-type drugs, syncurine is used in anesthesia and in electro-shock therapy. Depolarization of the motor end plates results in a brief period of muscular twitching and fibrillation followed by delayed repolarization at the myoneural junction (due to a delayed rate of metabolism). A toxic dose induces paralysis of skeletal muscles and may cause death by peripheral respiratory failure.

Treatment: Give artificial respiration. Parasympathetic drugs do *not* antagonize the effect of this compound. (Cholinesterase inhibitors actually potentiate the muscle-paralyzing action of the "depolarizers" syncurine and succinylcholine.)

DECHLORANE (Perchloropentacyclodecane)

This is a white, crystalline, free-flowing solid used as a fire retardant additive in thermoplastic and thermosetting resins. Screening tests show that it is nonirritating to the skin. The oral LD_{50} (male rats) is approximately 6.0 gm/kg.

Treatment: In case of skin or eye contact, flood the affected parts with water.

DEF (S,S,S-Tributyl Phosphorotrithioate)

DEF is a defoliant having a moderate degree of toxicity. The acute oral LD_{50} is 325 mg/kg for female rats and 260 mg/kg for male guinea pigs. The intraperitoneal LD_{50} for male rats is 440 mg/kg; female rats, 210 mg/kg; female mice, 290 mg/kg; and male guinea pigs, 150 mg/kg. Rats exposed to concentrations of DEF up to 1610 μg/liter showed no mortality from an inhalation exposure of 60 minutes. Forty-five percent of the mice exposed to a concentration of 3804 μg/liter for 60 minutes died within 10 days.

In cutaneous tests a dosage of 0.4 gm/kg of technical DEF or 50% liquid formulation produced no mortality, whereas 1.0 gm/kg produced 40% mortality in female rats. Measurements of the subacute toxicity of DEF showed that one-half of the acute LD_{50} (100 mg/kg) injected daily by the intraperitoneal route to female rats is fatal in a period of 10 days. One-fourth of the acute intraperitoneal LD_{50} (50 mg/kg) of DEF caused no mortality or symptoms when injected daily for a period of 60 days.

Treatment: Remove from the skin, mucous membranes, and eyes with water. Induce vomiting in case of ingestion and follow with gastric lavage.

DEHYDROACETIC ACID

Animal tests show that this compound has a moderate degree of toxicity. When swallowed it is about twice as toxic as acetic acid. See p. 63. It does not penetrate the skin in harmful amounts and is only slightly irritating after prolonged and repeated skin contact. Tests in humans indicate that dehydroacetic acid is not a skin sensitizer and that it will not irritate the skin of most normal persons. Eyes will be severely irritated by the dust of dehydroacetic acid; in some cases it may cause moderate corneal burns. Breathing the vapors is not considered to be harmful.

Treatment: For eye and skin contact, flood with water for 15 minutes.

DELNAV

This is an organic phosphate pesticide consisting of 70% of the *cis* and *trans* isomers of 2,3-*p*-dioxanedithiol-*S,S*-bis(*O,O*-diethylphosphorodithioate) as the principal ingredient. The remaining 30% consists of other similar insecticides. The oral LD_{50} ranges from 40 to 176 mg/kg, depending on the species. Delnav does not produce myelin degeneration. Oral dosages of 0.075–0.150 mg/kg have been administered daily for up to 60 days to human volunteers. Slight plasma cholinesterase inhibition was observed at the 0.150 mg/kg dosage, but no effect was observed at lower dosages. Clinically, no symptoms of toxicity were produced.

Human volunteers have received 0.075 mg/kg Delnav daily for 60 days and 0.150 mg/kg of malathion daily simultaneously with Delnav for 30 days. Plasma and erythrocyte cholinesterase measurements revealed that potentiation was insignificant at levels of ingestion that were considerably above those resulting from the proper use of both materials as pesticides. Evidence shows that the daily ingestion of up to 0.075 mg/kg of Delnav by humans is without toxic effect [J. P. Frawley *et al.*, *Toxicol. Appl. Pharmacol.* **5**, 605 (1963)].

Treatment: See Organic Phosphates, p. 438.

DEMECARIUM BROMIDE (Humorsol)

This is a potent cholinesterase inhibitor used in the management of glaucoma and accommodative esotropia.

Caution: The drug is contraindicated in narrow-angle glaucoma secondary to iritis. It should not be used in patients in whom less toxic agents yield satisfactory results.

DERRIS (Derris elliptica)

The bark and roots are poisonous; the stems and leaves are toxic to a lesser degree. The principal toxic constituent is rotenone. Ingestion may cause vomiting, respiratory depression, incoordination, clonic convulsions, and death due to central respiratory failure.

Treatment is symptomatic.

DESERPIDINE (Harmonyl)

Side effects noted in some patients who have used this rauwolfia tranquilizer include autonomic reac-

tions, behavioral toxicity, drug potentiation, extrapyramidal syndrome, and hypotension.

Treatment of an overdose is symptomatic.

DESFERRIOXAMINE-B (Desferal; DFOM; DTPA; EDDHA)

This chelating agent is a promising drug in the treatment of iron intoxication [*Lancet* **II**, 708 (1964)]. See
Iron, p. 333.

DESIPRAMINE (Norpramin; Pertofrane)

This tranquilizer, which has actions similar to those
of imipramine (Tofranil), is believed to be a metabolite of imipramine. A 36-year-old woman who took 1.5
gm of desipramine suffered two generalized seizures
followed by cardiorespiratory arrest. Immediate resuscitative measures were successful, but the patient
died 4 days later of irreversible cerebral damage. See
Imipramine, p. 324.

DETERGENTS

Detergents intended for general household use
should not be used in the bath or as hair shampoo because of possible injury to the eyes, hair, and scalp.
Excessive use of detergents to clear oil from beaches
is not recommended. A vast cemetery of marine life, to
a depth of 4 meters, was caused by detergents intended to dissipate the oil liberated by the sinking
Torrey Canyon [*Sci. News* **92**, 230 (1967)]. The three
principal chemical types of detergents are:

Anionic: These materials are sodium salts of sul-
fated higher alcohols and sodium sulfonates of long-
chain alkyl derivatives of benzene. See Alkyl Sodium
Sulfates, p. 85.

Cationic: These are chemically alkyl and/or aryl
quaternary ammonium compounds. In general, this
class of detergents is more toxic than the anionics and
nonionics. See Quaternary Ammonium Compounds,
p. 508.

Nonionic: A multiplicity of molecular types are included in this class, such as polyethylene glycol alkyl
aryl ethers, alkyl aryl polyether sulfates, polyoxethyl-
ene sorbitan monooleate, alkyl phenol polyglycol
ethers, etc. In general, these compounds have a moderate order of toxicity. See p. 710.

DETERGENT GRANULES (Electric Dishwasher Granules)

These powders are mixtures of detergents plus
"builders" consisting of carbonates, silicates, and poly-

phosphates. Because they are alkaline, they may cause mucous membrane irritation and caustic chemical burns. Detergent granules should not be used in place of bubble bath or shampoo. See Table 31, p. 710.

Treatment: See Sodium Hydroxide, p. 543.

DEXON (p-Dimethylaminobenzenediazo Sodium Sulfonate)

This is a seed and soil fungicide. The oral LD_{50} is 60 mg/kg for female rats and 150 mg/kg for male guinea pigs. The intraperitoneal LD_{50} is 13.2 mg/kg for female rats, 10.3 mg/kg for male rats, 60 mg/kg for female mice, and 37 mg/kg for male guinea pigs. The dermal application of 100 mg/kg of the compound to the shaved backs of rats produced no evidence of toxicity or mortality.

Exposure of female rats and mice for 1 hour to an atmosphere containing 200 μg per liter as an aerosol (average particle size 2 μ) revealed no signs of poisoning.

The daily intraperitoneal administration of 0.5, 1.0, and 2.0 mg/kg to female rats for 60 days did not result in any weight losses. At the two lower doses no deaths occurred, while at the 2.0 mg/kg dosage, 1 of 5 rats died during the 60-day period. No significant histopathological effects were found in the animals receiving the above treatment.

Male and female weanling rats were fed a diet containing 80 ppm of Dexon without showing any reduction in growth rate, food consumption, or other toxic effects (Chemagro Corporation, Kansas City, Missouri).

Treatment: For skin, eye, and mucous membrane contact, flush affected area with water. In case of ingestion, induce vomiting and follow with gastric lavage.

DEXTRAN (Gentran)

The dextrans are used to restore circulatory volume after hemorrhage in certain types of shock and in other conditions. They are not substitutes for whole blood, since they cause dilution of blood and its components. They have a low degree of toxicity, but are not devoid of undesirable effects. P. L. McLain and F. R. Franke reported prolongation of bleeding time in almost half of the recipients. This effect, however, is temporary.

The coagulation time is apparently not prolonged ["Drugs of Choice 1966–1967," C. V. Mosby, Saint Louis, Missouri]. In isolated cases, dextran 70 and 75 have induced urticaria, bronchospasm, angioedema, anaphylaxis, and renal injury or failure [*Brit. Med. J.* **2**, 737 (1966); *JAMA* **200**, 889 (1967)]. According to N. P. Couch, the value of low molecular weight dextran (40,000) in clinical medicine and surgery has not yet been established [*Clin. Pharmacol. Therap.* **6**, 656 (1965)].

Caution: The dextrans should be injected slowly. In the event of oliguria, discontinue the infusion and administer an osmotic diuretic such as mannitol or urea. Renal failure or marked dehydration are contraindications to the use of osmotic diuretics [*Med. Letter* **10**, 1 (1968)].

DEXTROMETHORPHAN

Dextromethorphan (Romilar) is used as an antitussive. It is considered to have little or no central depressant or analgesic activity.

Caution: A 23-year-old drug addict developed a toxic psychosis after taking 20 tablets purchased over-the-counter in a drug store. The reaction was characterized by hyperactivity, marked visual and auditory hallucinations, and association of sounds with colors. The experience was likened by the patient to that experienced when he was under the influence of LSD. Physicians should be alerted to the possible misuse of this drug [A. Dodds and E. Revai, *Med. J. Australia* **2**, 231 (1967)]. Preparations that contain dextromethorphan hydrobomide include: Cheracol D, Dextro-Tussin, Endotussin-NN, Lixaminol AT, Naldetuss, Orthoxicol Syrup, Pediatric Phenergan Expectorant with dextromethorphan, Quelidrine Syrup, Robitussin-DM, and Tussagesic Tablets and Suspension [*Clin-Alert* (October 20, 1967)].

DEXTROMORAMIDE (Palfium)

Contrary to earlier reports, this drug is capable of inducing addiction. A number of reports of addiction have appeared in the European literature [R. Seymour-Shove and C. W. M. Wilson, *Brit. Med. J.* **1**, 88 (1967); H. Isbell, *JAMA* (186, 112) (1963)]. Black, who gave Palfium to women in labor in doses of 10–15 mg, noted deep sedation, nausea, vomiting, and severe respiratory depression in the mother. Ten of 30 babies born of these mothers were described as lethargic [*Practitioner* **197**, 348 (1966)].

This drug has no advantages over methadon and related analgesics.

DEXTROSE (Glucose)

Hypertonic solutions of dextrose may cause thrombophlebitis at the site of transfusion. A hypertonic solution of dextrose should not be injected as a mixture with blood because of the tendency to produce hemolysis [*JAMA* **176**, 83 (1961)].

DIALKYLNITROSAMINES

Some dialkylnitrosamines are valuable chemical intermediates or solvents, and their use as insecticides has been suggested. The main acute effect of these compounds is hepatic necrosis, though lung lesions may appear. The compounds also induce tumors in the liver, lung, and kidney. Dimethylnitrosamine has been shown to cause kidney tumors after a single dose. The necrotic and carcinogenic doses of the compounds are closely related. See p. 686.

Treatment: High and barely tolerable doses of cysteine given prophylactically over 2 days doubles the resistance of rats to dimethylnitrosamine. No other treatment has been found which has a marked effect on toxicity [D. F. Heath, *Brit. J. Ind. Med.* **19**, 276 (1962)].

DIALKYLPHOSPHOROCHLORIDOTHIONATES
(Dimethylphosphorochloridothionate; Dimethylthionochlorophosphate; Diethylphosphorochloridothionate; Diethylthionochlorophosphate)

These compounds are capable of undergoing autocatalytic decomposition when heated to temperatures above 120°C. Exposure to vapors can cause severe irritation to eye and lung tissues. See Acid Chlorides, p. 70.

DIAMTHAZOLE (Asterol)

Therapeutic doses of this antifungal agent applied 3 times a day for several weeks to the face, scalp, and body of a 4-week-old girl resulted in convulsions and respiratory difficulties.

Treatment: Discontinue therapy. Treatment with paraldehyde, a barbiturate, and I.V. fluids contributed to the recovery of the child.

DIAPHENYLSULFONE (Dapsone)

This drug has been found useful in the treatment of leprosy. Side effects included hemolysis (reduced life-span of red blood cells) and, much less frequently, various types of anemia and the presence of Heinz bodies in the red blood cells [C. D. R. Pengelly, *Brit. Med. J.* **2**, 662 (1963)]. Profound hemolytic anemia occurred in 3 G-6-PD deficient patients who received 25 mg of this drug as prophylaxis for falciparum malaria.

Caution: While a recent study suggests that a daily dose of 50 mg of Dapsone is the threshold dose for precipitating hemolytic anemia in G-6-PD deficient males, the report by D. Chernof points out that hemolytic anemia may occur in such patients with doses of 25 mg daily [D. Chernof, *JAMA* **201**, 554 (1967)].

DIARRHEA OF TRAVELERS ("Turista"; "Montezuma's Revenge")

"Tourist diarrhea is global in distribution and has a variety of colorful regional aliases; however, whether acquired in Mexico or India, its clinical character is uniform." One out of every three or four Americans who visits Mexico comes down with Tourist's diarrhea, but the disease strikes almost as many Mexicans visiting the United States. Although microbiologists insist that the syndrome is always the result of an infection, there is evidence that it may also be of allergic origin or due to the ingestion of unaccustomed foods. "In its more severe form, it is complicated by nausea, vomiting, fever, chills, cramps, and joint and muscle pain; it is prostrating and may produce serious complications in the debilitated [R. G. Vincent *et al.*, *JAMA* **180**, 367 (1962)]."

Prophylaxis: Avoid ingestion of any food, particularly vegetables, that may have come in contact with a questionable water supply. Also avoid overindulgence in any foods that have not been part of the regular diet. If drugs are to be used for prophylactic purposes, phthalylsulfathiazole (Sulfathalidine) (2 gm per day

P.O.) or neomycin sulphate (1 gm per day, P.O.) are recommended [B. H. Kean *et al.*, *JAMA* **180**, 367 (1962)]. Furazolidone (Furoxone) (100 mg 2–4 times a day P.O.) has also been used. Iodochlorhydroxyquin (Vioform) and sulfamethoxypyridazine (Kynex; Midicel) are not recommended. Prophylactic doses for children must, of course, be reduced and related to body weight.

Treatment: If turista should become a problem, withhold foods except for a bland diet and bottled carbonated beverages. After 12 hours without loose movements, W. Lindau suggests rice, lean meat, apple sauce, toast with jelly (not butter). After another 24 hours without diarrhea, other foods may be eaten with discretion, but fruit juices and highly spiced foods should be avoided. For medication, paregoric (1 teaspoon with every loose bowel movement) is suggested. Lomotil (atropine sulfate, 0.025 mg, plus diphenoxylate hydrochloride, 2.5 mg/tab.) is also recommended; 1 tablet every 6 hours for the treatment of diarrhea and colic. If there is no recovery after 48 hours, a physician should be consulted.

For travel to an area where competent medical care is not readily available, a dozen capsules of tetracycline (250 mg) are recommended for the treatment of diarrhea accompanied by chills, high fever, or blood in stools (for adults: 1 capsule 4 times a day for 2 days). (W. Lindau, University of Miami, personal communication.)

DIATOMACEOUS EARTH

There are three principal forms of diatomaceous earth: crude, calcined, and flux-calcined. The crude form contains no crystalline silica, and the flux-calcined contains about 30% cristobalite. A disease known as diatomaceous earth pneumoconiosis, diatomite silicosis, or diatomite pneumoconiosis may result from prolonged exposure to high concentrations of diatomite dust. See Silicates, p. 530.

Treatment: Discontinue or diminish exposure. Further treatment is symptomatic.

DIAZEPAM (Valium)

This benzodiazepine tranquilizer is chemically and pharmacologically related to chlordiazepoxide

(Librium). For side effects following oral doses, see Chlordiazepoxide, p. 166. Like chlordiazepoxide, this drug is also known to have induced withdrawal symptoms such as tremors, convulsions, and death [*N.Y. State J. Med.* **66**, 1770 (1966); *Brit. Med. J.* **1**, 112 (1967)]. Withdrawal symptoms have been reported particularly in patients who abruptly discontinued therapy subsequent to taking the drug in large doses over a prolonged period.

Intravenous diazepam is apparently very effective when used as the initial drug in the management of prolonged seizure activity associated with idiopathic epilepsy or with old or slowly progressive cerebral diseases. Prensky *et al.*, who administered this drug to 20 patients with acute cerebral disease, experienced severe complications shortly after the injection. One patient suffered cardiac arrest, two had transient hypotensive episodes, and three had demonstrated some degree of respiratory depression. Three of these patients had received barbiturates I.V. shortly before diazepam was given, and this may have been a contributing factor. However, the investigators could not explain the cardiac arrest [*New Engl. J. Med.* **276**, 779 (1967)]. An elderly man undergoing prostatectomy became restless and was given 10 mg of diazepam I.V. He almost immediately lost consciousness and became apneic and cyanotic. He responded to artificial ventilation. A few hours later he again became restless and a similar dose of diazepam was given, but this time I.M. Ten minutes later apnea and cyanosis recurred. Artificial ventilation was again successfully applied. There are also other cases when this drug was used as a sedative during endoscopy; depression of respiration has been noted [Buskop *et al. New Engl. J. Med.* **277**, 316 (1967)].

Caution: Administer this drug cautiously to persons with impaired hepatic or renal function and to elderly, debilitated, agitated, or depressed patients. The drug is contraindicated in infants. It is equally contraindicated in patients with a history of glaucoma, in patients receiving other psychotropic drugs, particularly phenothiazines and monoamine oxidase inhibitors, and during pregnancy. Diazepam should not be administered with alcohol. Some patients who took a dose of diazepam in the afternoon became intoxicated following a cocktail several hours later. See the complete report by A. A. Holbrook, *Med. Times* **94**, 423 (1966). The most recent information indicates that diazepam when administered I.V. or I.M. can cause respiratory and circulatory embarrassment. Particular caution is therefore in order when this drug is used parenterally.

DIAZOMETHANE

Diazomethane is used in laboratory and chemical operations as a methylating agent. It is a gas usually obtained in ethereal solutions by decomposition with alkali of some nitroso-*N*-methyl compounds. It is a pulmonary carcinogen for mice [*Nature* **188**, 420 (1960)].

A 40-year-old-male physician, in good health except for a mild respiratory infection, spilled some diazomethane. After cleaning it up, he had an immediate sensation of weakness and went into the next room and lay down on a table. He experienced a severe generalized headache followed immediately with chest pain, generalized aching of the muscles, and an overwhelming fatigue. Approximately 5 minutes after the exposure he was found by another laboratory worker to be only partially responsive. Physical examination revealed a blood pressure of 150/100; pulse at 120 per minute; oral temperature of 102.2°F; respirations 24 per minute. The patient was markedly flushed and complained of severe headache. An electrocardiogram revealed one ventricular premature contraction and inversion of the T waves in the precordial leads. The chest X-Ray was essentially within normal limits.

Treatment: The patient received 50 mg of Demerol by intramuscular injection, ergotamine (1.0 mg) and caffeine (100 mg) by mouth for relief of headache.

After discharge, exposure to trace amounts of diazomethane caused wheezing, cough, and malaise. He is now affected by concentrations of the gas not detectable by odor [C. E. Lewis, *J. Occupational Med.* **6**, 91 (1964)].

DIBUCAINE (Nupercaine; Nuporals)

This is a local anesthetic used for topical and injection anesthesia. It is more potent than tetracaine

(Pontocaine), cocaine, or procaine [*JAMA* **188**, 711 (1964)]. A 3-year-old child ingested 8 Nuporals lozenges, each containing 1.0 ml of dibucaine hydrochloride. Gastric lavage was started in 20 minutes. Shortly afterwards, hypotension, reduced pulse rate, and anoxia became marked; a generalized nonpitting edema of the entire body was noted. There were no convulsions. The child died in coma 8 hours after ingestion of the drug in spite of symptomatic treatment.

Occasionally, dermatitis is produced by a local anesthetic such as dibucaine, tetracaine, and others [*Practitioner* **197**, 673 (1966)]. According to J. Adriani, allergic responses seldom occur after the initial use of such a drug; usually there is a history of repeated exposure [*JAMA* **196**, 405 (1966)].

Treatment: In case of accidental ingestion, induce vomiting promptly, and follow with symptomatic and supportive therapy. Central excitation is treated by the judicious and cautious use of thiopental sodium or sodium methohexital. These drugs should be administered slowly and in the lowest effective dose to avoid myocardial and respiratory depression. A muscle relaxant is not recommended. The cardiovascular depressant effects of this and other local anesthetics respond to the I.V. injection of vasopressors, preferably those that stimulate the heart muscle, such as ephedrine [J. Adriani, *JAMA* **196**, 405 (1966)].

DIBUTYL FUMARATE

This chemical has a low order of oral toxicity but is irritating to the skin, mucous membranes, and eyes.

Treatment: Flood affected tissues (skin, mucous membranes, and eyes) with water.

DIBUTYL MALEATE

This compound has a relatively low order of toxicity by ingestion and skin application. It is a moderate skin and mucous membrane irritant. Vapors nearly saturated with dibutyl maleate are well tolerated by experimental animals.

Treatment: Discontinue exposure. Flush skin and mucous membranes with water. Induce vomiting and follow with gastric lavage in case of ingestion of large doses.

DICHLORACETIC ACID

This is a strong organic acid which is irritating to the skin, eyes, and mucous membranes.
Treatment: See Acetic Acid, p. 63..

DICHLOROACETYLENE

In the 1940's a number of fatalities were attributed to dichloroacetylene inhalation in patients anesthetized with trichloroethylene. The anesthetic mixture was administered in a closed system with a machine which incorporated a soda-lime carbon dioxide absorber. The soda-lime became hot enough to convert trichloroethylene to dichloroacetylene as a result of the reaction with the moisture and carbon dioxide in the patient's breath.

Anesthetic mixtures of trichloroethylene in air or oxygen (usually 1 % by volume) were reported to give rise to lethal concentrations of dichloroacetylene when administered in this manner. Fatalities were reported after exposures as brief as 45 minutes.

The symptoms of dichloroacetylene poisoning are loss of appetite, extreme nausea, vomiting, symptoms involving the facial muscles, headaches, and facial herpes. This compound also has a pronounced effect on the trigeminal nerve and, with sufficient exposure, gives rise to circumoral herpetiform lesions.

Dichloroacetylene can also be formed in trace quantities from other chlorinated hydrocarbons as a result of pyrolysis and photolysis. Safety respiratory face mask canisters containing alkaline material should not be worn in the presence of vinylidene chloride and trichloroethylene vapors. Uninhibited, medical grade trichloroethylene can undergo considerable decomposition from photolysis. A 1-month exposure to sunlight can generate enough dichloroacetylene to affect the trigeminal nerve of a person inhaling fumes from the container [R. A. Saunders, *Arch. Environ. Health* **14**, 380 (1967)].

DICHLOROBENZENE, ORTHO AND PARA (PDB, Dichlorocide)

Inhalation of *p*-dichlorobenzene vapors may induce eye, skin, and mucous membrane irritation, headache, vertigo, central nervous system stimulation and/or depression, and changes in the formed elements of the blood. The probable lethal oral dose for an adult is 60 gm.

A 69-year-old man sat in a chair which had been treated with *p*-dichlorobenzene crystals. While seated, he developed dyspnea, followed (in 24–48 hours) by swelling, discomfort, petechiae, and purpura in a symmetrical pattern over the upper and lower extremities. There were no other significant features in the history except that he had taken aspirin, phenacetin, and caffeine frequently for years without adverse reactions. Serum antibodies for *p*-dichlorobenzene were still demonstrable in this patient 5 months after the initial exposure.

o-Dichlorobenzene is irritating when applied to the skin of human subjects for 15–60 minutes. The application of undiluted *o*-dichlorobenzene to the eyes of rabbits caused some pain and slight irritation of the conjunctival membranes, which healed completely within 7 days. Rats survived the following exposures to *o*-dichlorobenzene vapors: 977 ppm for 2 hours and 539 ppm for 7 hours.

Treatment: For skin, mucous membrane, or eye contact, flood affected tissues with water. In case of accidental ingestion, induce vomiting and lavage the stomach with water. For inhalation remove victim from contaminated atmosphere; give artificial respiration and oxygen if needed.

In the case cited, treatment was supportive. Prednisolone, 10 mg 4 times a day was given from the seventh to the thirty-first hospital day, at which time the patient had improved and was discharged [R. M. Nalbandian and F. J. F. Pearce, *JAMA* **194**, 238 (1965)].

3,3′-DICHLOROBENZIDINE DIHYDROCHLORIDE

This compound has an oral LD_{50} (rat) of about 3.82 gm/kg. It may cause skin irritation and is definitely an eye irritant. It may be handled safely if precautions are taken to prevent skin and eye contact and breathing of the dust.

Treatment: For skin and eye contact, drench the affected parts with running water for 15 minutes. In case of ingestion, induce vomiting.

1,2-DICHLOROETHANE (DCE)

A painter exposed to DCE vapors lost consciousness and remained unconscious for 3 hours. During this period he had severe tonic-clonic muscle spasms and vomited large amounts of yellow fluid. The next day he had acute conjunctivitis, acute bronchial inflammation, intestinal cramps, anxiety, restlessness, and cardiac pain. The size of the liver was increased. Liver damage was demonstrable 3 months after the acute poisoning [H. Menschick, *Arch. Gewerbepathol. Gewerbehyg.* **15**, 241 (1957)].

Two deaths due to 1,2-dichloroethane have been reported. One was a 79-year-old man and the other a 2-year-old boy, both of whom ingested a liniment that contained 100 gm of 1,2-dichloroethane, 5.8 gm of camphor and pine-needle oils, 0.5 gm of salicylic acid methyl ester, and 18.5 gm of an emulsifier in 100 ml of the mixture. The man died 40 hours after one dose, and the boy died 20 hours after one smaller dose. Autopsy of both patients revealed toxic damage to the hepatic and renal parenchyma. Degenerative changes also were found in the myocardium of the child. Central nervous system disturbances, unconsciousness, spasms, and cardiac and circulatory failure were the predominant signs and symptoms in both patients. Extensive toxic cerebral swelling was observed in the child. See Ethylene Dichloride, p. 257.

Treatment: For inhalation, discontinue exposure. Give artificial respiration and oxygen if necessary. In case of ingestion, induce vomiting and follow with gastric lavage. Thereafter treatment is supportive and symptomatic.

DICHLOROPHENE (G-4)

G-4 is a fungicide and bactericide used to preserve cotton and woolen textiles and other materials. It is generally regarded to be nonirritating to the skin at the usual concentrations of use. In patch tests on humans with a cotton fabric containing 1.0% of G-4, no primary irritation or sensitization of the skin resulted.

Patch tests were also conducted on 194 humans using G-4 at a concentration of 4% in a petrolatum base ointment. The patches were applied to the inside of the forearm and were removed after 48 hours. Out of

194 persons tested, 191 reactions were negative, and 3 were positive.

The oral LD_{50} (guinea pig) is 1.25 gm/kg, and 2.0 g/kg (dog). In chronic toxicity studies on rats, 0.2 % of G-4 was added to the food for a period of 90 days. There was no evidence of toxicity after 90 days. At a concentration of 0.5 % daily in the diet, there was evidence of kidney change at the end of 90 days.

Treatment: Induce vomiting in case of ingestion and follow with gastric lavage.

sym-DICHLOROTETRAFLUOROACETONE (4FK)

4FK is a water-clear, pungent, irritating liquid. It is very toxic when inhaled, ingested, or on skin contact. This compound is a lacrimator which also irritates the skin. The principal effect from inhalation is acute lung inflammation. Contact with the skin or eyes causes burns, particularly if contact is prolonged.

The oral LD_{50} of a 1 % solution is 61 ± 5 mg/kg (albino rat). The percutaneous LD_{50} of a 10 % solution in ethanol is 146 ± 5 mg/kg (rabbit). The inhalation LC_{50} ($\frac{1}{2}$ hour exposure) is 430 ppm, and the LC_{50} (3-hour exposure) is 90 ppm for the albino rat.

Treatment: In case of skin or eye contact, drench affected parts immediately with water and continue irrigating with water for 15 minutes. For inhalation exposure, remove the individual from the contaminated area. Give artificial respiration and oxygen if necessary. Observe victim for premonitory signs of pulmonary edema. Further treatment is symptomatic and supportive.

α,α'-DICHLORO-p-XYLENE

This is a white crystalline solid having a sweet odor and a boiling point of 254°C. The oral LD_{50} for male rats is 1.78 gm/kg. The dermal LD_{50} for albino rabbits is greater than 3.16 gm/kg. The compound produces marked local irritation when applied to the skin or eyes of the rabbits.

Treatment: For skin or eye contact, flood the affected tissues with running water for 15 minutes. In case of ingestion, empty the stomach by inducing vomiting. Further treatment is symptomatic and supportive.

DICYCLOHEXYLAMINE

This is a colorless, oily, highly alkaline liquid. Toxicologically, it is similar to cyclohexylamine, except that it does not form methemoglobin.

Treatment: See Ammonia, Aqueous p. 95.

N,N'-DICYCLOHEXYLCARBODIIMIDE (DCC)

DCC is used as a water scavenger and condensing agent for phosphoramidate synthesis. A chemist who had used this compound for about 1 year gradually noticed skin sensitivity and later acute respiratory difficulty as soon as he opened the DCC bottle. Finally, he had to leave the premises any time the DCC was used in the laboratory. Scientists from two other laboratories have confirmed this sensitizing property of DCC.

DCC probably modifies one or more body proteins which then become highly antigenic. No indication of sensitivity occurs until the DCC bottle is reopened, the antigen is resynthesized, and a violent physiological reaction sets in. The cumulative effect of DCC exposure suggests that the DCC-induced antigen may be a discrete molecule.

Treatment: Avoid exposure. If sensitized, "you've had it."

N,N'-DICYCLOHEXYLTHIOUREA

Guinea pigs exposed to an aerosol of *N,N'*-dicyclohexylthiourea at a concentration of 2.2 kg/liter (2.2 ppm) survived the experiment. Some hyperactivity, with occasional coughing and sneezing, was observed during the exposure. No abnormalities were found at autopsy.

Mild conjunctivitis resulted from the instillation of 0.1 ml of a 10% suspension of *N,N'*-dicyclohexylthiourea in polyethylene glycol 300 into the eyes of rabbits. The conjunctivitis cleared completely in 5 days. Doses of 2000, 632, and 200 mg/kg evenly applied as a powder to the backs of rabbits caused erythema which disappeared after 2 days. No abnormalities were seen at autopsy.

Treatment: Remove from the eyes and skin by flushing with running water.

DIEFFENBACHIA OR DUMB CANE (*Dieffenbachia*)

When chewed or ingested, this and several related decorative plants induce immediate marked salivation and a painful burning sensation in the mouth, followed by vesication and edema of the lips, tongue, and pharynx. Speech may become unintelligible, and in isolated cases, there has been a temporary total loss of the voice — hence the name "dumb cane." Swallowing may become very difficult. Ingestion of parts of the dumb cane plant leads to severe gastroenteritis and systemic effects which may include tremors, cramps, vomiting, diarrhea, respiratory difficulties, bradycardia, and hypotension [G. Drach and W. H. Maloney, *JAMA* **184,** 1047 (1963)].

Other calcium oxalate-containing plants that induce similar but less severe effects include Indian turnip or jack-in-the-pulpit (*Arisaema triphyllum*), green dragon or dragon root (*Arisaema dracontium*), caladium (*Caladium* spp), elephant's ear (*Colocasia* spp), ceriman (*Monstera* spp), philodendron (*Philodendron* spp), and skunk cabbage (*Symplocarpus foetidus*).

Treatment: Prompt removal of the material from the mouth and gastroenteric tract is most important. (See p. 15). Rinse the mouth several times with water, milk or, if available, with a solution of aluminum magnesium hydroxide; follow by an oral dose of about 30 ml of this solution once every hour for several hours. Pain and oral edema may last for a week or longer. The extent of corrosion in the esophagus and gastroenteric tract will depend on the particular plant and on the quantity of the plant material ingested. Administer a bland diet until the patient has recovered. Opiates may have to be administered for severe pain. Additional treatment is symptomatic and supportive.

DIELDRIN (Hexachloroepoxyoctahydroendo-exo-dimethanonaphthalene)

The lethal oral dose of dieldrin in humans is not known. Untoward symptoms have occurred in man after oral doses of 10 mg/kg. In rats, the acute oral LD_{50} of dieldrin ranges from 37 to 87 mg/kg. This difference in values is apparently due to the grade of dieldrin tested, the nature of the solvent and the strain used.

An oral dose of 65 mg/kg is believed to be a reasonable estimate of the lethal dose in man. Dieldrin is twice as toxic by ingestion as by skin absorption. Its oral toxicity is 3 to 5 times greater than that of DDT. A fatality has been reported in a man who ingested an unknown quantity of dieldrin.

The acute dermal toxicity of dieldrin in xylene is approximately 40 times that of DDT. There is considerable difference in the LD_{50} values for different species; the acute dermal LD_{50} value for white rats is 90 mg/kg of body weight for males and 60 mg/kg of body weight for females; for rabbits the range is 400–450 mg/kg. Such inconsistent ranges of dermal toxicity make it difficult to estimate a value for man.

Treatment: See Aldrin, p. 82 and Chlorinated Hydrocarbons, p. 684.

DIESEL OIL AND GREASE GUN INJECTION INJURY

In diesel engines, diesel oil is forced through fine jets at a pressure as high as 6000 psi. At such pressures, the spray may easily penetrate the skin and cause severe injury. A worker received an injection of diesel oil and kerosene into his finger at a pressure of 120 atm (1800 psi) while checking a diesel injector. His finger became tense, swollen, and painful. Incision of the finger failed to relieve the pain and tension, and 8 days later, amputation through the middle phalanx was necessary as the finger tip became gangrenous.

Similar injuries have been reported in mechanics who accidentally injected grease under high pressure into the fingers. The initial injury may appear trivial, but actual subcutaneous tissue injury may be severe and extensive.

Treatment: Immediate bilateral incision of injured areas, inspection of tendon sheaths, and drainage of the wounds are recommended.

2-DIETHYLAMINOETHANOL (DEAE)

This compound is slightly toxic orally for laboratory animals. It is a severe irritant to the skin, and on prolonged contact, can penetrate the intact skin to produce death in test animals at doses of 1.3 ml/kg. For the guinea pig, this compound is a skin sensitizer. The undiluted compound is a severe eye irritant capable of producing permanent eye injury. The vapors are irritating to the respiratory tract; mists generated at 170°C caused death in 1 out of 5 test animals during an 8-hour exposure. A single human exposure to a level below 200 ppm for a few seconds caused nausea and vomiting.

Treatment: For eye and skin contact, flood the affected parts with running water for 15 minutes. In case of inhalation, remove the victim to an uncontaminated atmosphere, give artificial respiration and oxygen if necessary [F. A. Miller *et al.*, *Am. Ind. Hyg. Assoc. J.* **28**, 331 (1967)]. In case of ingestion, induce vomiting and follow with gastric lavage.

N,N-DIETHYLHYDROXYLAMINE (DEHA)

Diethylhydroxylamine is a much weaker base than amines and slightly stronger than amine oxides. DEHA has a low order of acute toxicity. The oral LD_{80} in mice is 2.15 gm/kg; 0.4 gm/kg is nontoxic for rats; the intraperitoneal MLD for mice is approximately 1.75 gm/kg; vapors are nontoxic to mice and rats at more than 320 mg/liter, and 4 mg/liter, respectively. Skin tests on rabbits gave an MLD of 2.0 ml/kg.

Treatment: For ingestion, empty the stomach by inducing vomiting. In case of skin or eye contact, flood the affected tissues with water.

DIETHYL SULFATE

This is a colorless oily liquid having a peppermint odor. It differs markedly from the methyl homologue (dimethyl Sulfate, p. 226), which is highly irritating. It is moderately toxic by ingestion; the LD_{50} is about 900 mg/kg (rats).

Treatment: For accidental ingestion induce vomiting and follow with gastric lavage.

N,N-DIETHYLTOLUAMIDES

The approximate oral LD_{50} for rats is 1.3, 2.0, and 2.4 gm/kg for the ortho, meta, and para isomers, respectively. Intravenous doses above 50 mg/kg of the meta isomer, in the form of an emulsion, were invariably fatal to rabbits. Daily cutaneous application of 200 mg/kg of the ortho and para isomers and 1 gm/kg of the meta isomer in cottonseed oil or isopropanol for 13 weeks produced no serious local or systemic reactions in the rabbits dosed. Continued oral ingestion of diets containing up to 1% meta isomer for approximately 29 weeks was well tolerated by rats. No adverse effects were observed on growth, mortality, hemoglobin, food comsumption, and organ weights. No histological changes in the organs were noted. No acute toxic effects were observed in rats exposed 8 hours per day for 35 days to air saturated with the meta isomer and no toxic effects were observed in rats exposed for 6 hours to an aerosol of meta isomer generated at the rate of 1 ml/hour [A. M. Ambrose, D. K. Huffman, and R. T. Salamone, *Federation Proc.* **17**, No. 1 (1958)]. See OFF, p. 434.

Treatment: In case of accidental ingestion induce vomiting.

DIGITALIS

Digitalis intoxication has become one of the most difficult problems to recognize in clinical medicine. This is because the administration of digitalis continues to depend upon subjective complaints and poorly defined signs in the patient and because of inadequate laboratory tests.

The sensitivity to digitalis varies with the sex and age of the patient. Children tolerate large doses of digitalis before intoxication ensues, and the overdosage may be manifested only by electrocardiographic changes. In elderly patients, digitalis toxicity may disturb the sensorium, and the patient becomes confused, disoriented, or nauseated.

Cardiovascular overdigitalization in its earliest phase is sometimes referred to as a "vagus stage." It results in slowing of the sinus rate or in various degrees of atrioventricular block. When simple rate reduction occurs, the electrocardiogram may be unchanged (except for the rate reduction). Digitalis produces a prolongation of the atrioventricular conduction time or a shortening of the Q-T interval (electrical systole), a depression of the S-T segment, and a symmetrical configuration of the T wave.

With digitalis intoxication, the electrocardiographic alterations become more intense. These changes consist of frank atrioventricular blocking and the development of multiple foci of hyperirritability of the ventricles. This hyperirritability may result only in ventricular premature contractions or in the appearance of unifocal extra systoles. Ventricular tachycardias can begin in an area of ventricular hyperirritability.

Digitalis also affects the gastrointestinal system, causing nausea, vomiting, anorexia, abdominal cramping, and diarrhea. It is particularly important to counteract vomiting and diarrhea, since the electrolyte disturbance that follows results in accentuation of the digitalis overdosage.

The central nervous system is also affected by excessive doses of digitalis. This disturbance may be extremely marked, leading to confusion or delirium, or simply to an alteration in vision. The visual effects may be fleeting spots or distortions causing everything white to assume a yellow cast.

In clinical conditions associated with serum potassium depletion, digitalis sensitivity will be increased. This is most frequently induced by the use of oral diuretics, particularly the chlorothiazide group. Certain metabolic abnormalities may enhance the digitalis effect by disturbing the electrolyte balance. These include diabetes mellitus, chronic renal insufficiency, metabolic alkalosis, pulmonary insufficiency, and excessive catharsis. Certain drugs increase the sensitivity of digitalis, i.e. the catechol substances (epinephrine and ephedrine), calcium, and some tranquilizing antihypertensive drugs, particulary the reserpine group.

Treatment: Discontinue use of digitalis. It is important to understand the duration of the effects of the digitalis compounds. For example, if the patient has been sustained on a short-acting digitalis compound, the physician should anticipate that toxicity would wane after the third or fourth day. However, if the digitalis used is long-acting (as long as 3 weeks), changes may not be expected for weeks after the removal of the drug from the patient's regimen. In the latter instance, it is worthwhile to consider using antidotes. Of these antidotes, the following appear to be the most useful:

Atropine: This drug diminishes nausea and vomiting. However, if a rapid heart rate persists, atropine would be contraindicated. Other drugs with an antiemetic action may be substituted for atropine.

Potassium: If the patient has received chlorothiazides or a long-acting digitalis preparation, it may be necessary to give potassium chloride by mouth 3 to 4 times a day for several days in doses of 1–2 gm. No complications should be anticipated from the potassium therapy unless a low urinary output is present. If the patient is in the hospital, the intravenous potassium — 1.5 gm (20 mEq) in 500 ml of 5% glucose — may be given over a period of 3 or 4 hours. Oral potassium chloride elixir may also be indicated as part of hospital treatment (unless urgency exists). It is important to study the electrocardiogram during the administration of potassium. Frequently, it becomes necessary to use 2 or 3 times the usual amount of potassium, by the intravenous route, over a relatively short period of time (6–8 hours). No danger results from this if monitored by ECG and if the urinary output is adequate. If the patient is taking food by mouth, the diet should include high-potassium foods, such as orange juice, lima beans, apricots, peaches, dates, figs, raisins, almonds and other nuts, prunes, and bananas. Beef broth is also an excellent source of potassium. See p. 38.

Procainamide and quinidine sulfate   When ventricular tachycardia occurs, the use of procainamide, Xylocaine, or quinidine sulfate should be considered. These drugs must be used with *extreme* care. Ventricular tachycardia demands prompt action, and it is imperative that these drugs be effective within a short period of time. Xylocaine (50 mg) or procainamide (100 mg) I.V. are effective for the reversal of ventricular tachycardia. The dose may be repeated within 5–10 minutes, but careful monitoring of the patient's blood pressure and ECG is required.

Quinidine, orally administered in doses of 0.2 gm every 4 hours or intramuscularly administered as a gluconate in doses of 0.6 gm every 4–6 hours, may be useful in restoring a normal sinus rhythm. Quinidine can induce further tachycardia by blocking the digitalis vagal effect. If this occurs, quinidine may be continued if the patient's condition will tolerate it and the rate eventually slows. Quinidine cannot be administered intravenously; intramuscular injections are quite painful.

Molar Sodium Lactate: Molar sodium lactate will accelerate the heart rate.

Chelating agents: The disodium salt of ethylenediaminetetraacetic acid (Na₂ EDTA) has a limited usefulness but it will bind the ionizable form of calcium and reduce the digitalis effect. The chelating agent in doses ranging from 0.5 to 4.0 gm is given by intravenous infusion over periods of 30 minutes to 4 hours. It is imperative that monitoring electrocardiograms be made during this period.

Citrates: Citrates by I.V. drip have been recommended for correcting abnormal rhythms of the heart. This treatment is to be continued until the digitalis is excreted.

Diphenylhydantoin sodium (Dilantin): This is an antiarrhythmic drug that depresses ventricular automaticity and generally enhances AV conduction. Recent evidence suggests that it, like potassium, may specifically counteract certain of the actions of digitalis [*Circulation* **26**, 108, 119 (1967)]. Therefore, potassium and diphenylhydantoin sodium should be considered the drugs of choice for treating arrhythmias caused by digitalis. AV block caused by digitalis may be made worse by all the antiarrhythmic drugs and is best treated simply by withholding digitalis and using electrical means of pacing if needed (Robert J. Boucek, University of Miami, personal communication).

DIGITOXIN

Specific hypersensitivity (thrombocytopenia) to digitoxin, but not to related drugs (digoxin, ouabain, Cedilanid, and digitoxigenin) was reported in a patient by Young *et al.* [*Am. J. Med.* **41**, 605 (1966)].

According to J. Buchanan, 18 cases of self-poisoning have been reported with digitoxin or digoxin. Three of these were fatal. The symptoms included atrial asystole, extreme nodal bradycardia, oliguria, hyperkalemia, and disturbance of liver function [*Brit. Med. J.* **3**, 661 (1967)].

Treatment: F. Navah and M. Honey treated the systemic effects with parenteral atropine and mannitol I.V. #*Brit. Med. J.* **3**, 660 (1967)[. See Digitalis, p. 218.

DIGLYCOLAMINE

This is a colorless, slightly viscous liquid with a mild odor. As with most aliphatic amines, this compound may have some potential as a sensitizer. The vapor pressure of the product is quite low; the boiling point is 221°C. See Amines, Aliphatic, p. 90.

Treatment: In case of eye contact, wash the affected area with water for 15 minutes. Spills on the skin should be washed off promptly with large amounts of water. In case of ingestion induce vomiting and follow with gastric lavage.

DIHYDROCODEINE (Paracodin; Parzone)

A dose of 30 mg of dihydrocodeine, 10 mg of morphine, and 75 mg of meperidine are about equal in analgesic potency. Dihydrocodeine, in this dosage, produces less nausea, euphoria, and respiratory depression than morphine, but as a releaser of histamine it is probably the most potent among the narcotics.

Caution: The drug should not be used in patients with allergies.

Treatment: See Opiates, p. 435.

DIHYDROCODEINONE (Hycodan; Dicodid)

This narcotic is a substitute for codeine but it is more potent and sometimes more addictive than codeine. See Narcotic Drugs, p. 40, and Opiates, p. 435.

β-DIHYDROHEPTACHLOR

β-Dihydroheptachlor is a solid which melts at 135–136°C. No effects could be detected in rats exposed to dietary concentrations of up to 3160 ppm for a period of 90 days. Exposure of mice to 1000 ppm for 90 days produced 10 deaths in the 24 animals exposed. Changes in liver weight and histology were also apparent. The biological half-life of this compound in male mice was estimated to be 4 days, and 8–10 days in the eggs of exposed birds. No signs indicative of organochlorine insecticide intoxication were seen in animals exposed orally. Typical signs could, however, be produced in rats by intravenous injection of the compound in a cotton seed oil.

Treatment: In case of ingestion, empty the stomach by inducing vomiting.

DIHYDROMORPHINONE (Dilaudid)

This narcotic resembles morphine in its action, but it acts more promptly. The side effects are similar to those produced by morphine, except for nausea and vomiting, production of euphoria, and the release of histamine, which are less marked. It apparently does not cause miosis. The drug produces addiction. The probable lethal oral dose for an adult is 100 mg.

Treatment: Nalorphine and levallorphan are effective in antagonizing depression of respiration. See Narcotic Drugs, p. 40, and Opiates, p. 435.

DIISOCYANATES

The diisocyanates are used to make the familiar flexible and rigid polyurethane foams used in upholstery, soft toys, and insulation. The diisocyanates that have so far proved industrially useful are toluene diisocyanate (T.D.I.), diphenylmethane diisocyanate (M.D.I.), hexamethylene diisocyanate (H.D.I.) and naphthalene diisocyanate (N.D.I.). To reduce their toxic effects, T.D.I. and H.D.I. have been used in the form of a reaction product of the diisocyanate and various complex organic materials. These conjugates, although less toxic than the parent diisocyanates, may contain significant amounts of free diisocyanate.

Toxicologically, the diisocyanates cannot all be treated as similar to T.D.I. T.D.I. may irritate the skin and eyes, but its more important actions involve the respiratory system. The clinical picture is usually typified by a gradual onset of throat irritation, with tightness in the chest, breathlessness, and nocturnal cough. A more unusual effect is a frank asthmatic attack. Bronchospasm and recurrence of symptoms on renewed contact suggest an allergic mechanism. However, there has been little evidence to support this view, and some workers have ascribed the action of T.D.I. solely to its irritant effect. The maximum allowable concentration for T.D.I. is 0.02 ppm.

M.D.I. is much less dangerous than T.D.I. Its volatility is low, and at normal room temperatures it is virtually without vapor hazard. The maximum allowable concentration is 0.02 ppm.

H.D.I. has a volatility and toxicity similar to T.D.I. The aliphatic diisocyanates, including H.D.I., act mainly as direct irritants, in contrast to the aromatic compounds which are more likely to produce an allergic response [*Lancet* **I**, 32 (1966)].

Treatment: For respiratory symptoms, avoid further contact with these materials, and treat symptomatically.

DILAURYLTHIODIPROPIONATE

This is a white powder having a low order of toxicity. It is used as an antioxidant in foods in amounts up to 0.02%. When used in packaging material, the allowed limit which may migrate into the food is 0.005%. LD_{50} values are as follows: mice, oral > 2.0 gm/kg; rats, oral > 2.5 gm/kg; mice, intraperitoneal > 2.0 gm/kg.

Treatment: None required.

DIMEFLINE

Dimefline is a potent respiratory stimulant. The LD_{50} (mice) of this compound in 0.9% aqueous sodium chloride is 1.48 mg/kg I.V., and 6.20 mg/kg I.P. [*Toxicol. Appl. Pharmacol.* **6**, 263 (1964)].

DIMERCAPROL (2,3-Dimercaptopropanol; 1,2-Dithioglycerol; BAL; British Antilewisite)

This drug is used in the treatment of certain metal intoxications. The sulfhydryl groups of this dithiol compound compete with the sulfhydryl groups of enzymes for combination with the metal. The complex is excreted.

The systemic toxicity of BAL is relatively high and is related to the dose administered. Side effects can be expected within a few minutes after an injection in about 50% of patients who receive this compound.

The side effects include nausea, lacrimation, salivation, vomiting, headache, constriction of throat and chest, a burning sensation of mouth, throat, and eyes, tingling of nose, mouth, or skin, and in the extremities, abdominal pain and, occasionally, in children, fever. As a rule, the side effects do not last for more than 2 hours.

BAL is the drug of choice in intoxications by arsenic, but not arsine. Prolonged administration is usually required in intoxications by gold. BAL is effective in mercury poisoning, particularly when given early. In subacute intoxications, it is usually of little help. Data based primarily, or entirely, on studies with experimental animals indicate that BAL is worthy of consideration in the treatment of intoxications by antimony, bismuth, cadmium, copper, thallium, tungstate, and dialkyl (but not trialkyl) tin compounds. BAL is not used in intoxications by beryllium, cobalt, iron, lead, manganese, selenium, silver, tellurium, uranium, and vanadium. Two cases of intoxication by lead arsenate responded favorably to the cautious alternated treatment with $CaNa_2$ EDTA and BAL.

Treatment: Reduce the dose or discontinue therapy. It has been suggested that the prior administration of ephedrine (50 mg), diphenhydramine (50 mg), or epinephrine may significantly reduce the incidence and severity of the side reactions.

DIMETHOXANATE HYDROCHLORIDE (Cothera)

This phenothiazine derivative is used as an antitussive agent. Side effects reported include drowsiness, dizziness, and nausea.

Treatment: See Phenothiazines, p. 464.

DIMETHYLHYDRAZINE (Unsymmetrical Dimethylhydrazine; UDMH; 1,1-Dimethylhydrazine)

This is a clear, colorless, weakly basic liquid with a sharp ammoniacal or fishy odor. Contact with the skin and mucous membranes will cause irritation and chemical burns. Inhalation of vapor causes pulmonary irritation, delayed gastrointestinal irritation, hemolysis, and central nervous system stimulation (tremors and convulsions). It may be absorbed through the skin to cause systemic intoxication. The suggested threshold limit is 0.5 ppm.

Methylhydrazine and symmetrical dimethylhydrazine are also respiratory irritants and convulsants. Methylhydrazine vapor is more toxic than the vapors of hydrazine or its dimethyl derivatives and is also hemolytic.

Treatment: For skin or eye contact, flood with water and treat as alkaline burn. See Ammonia, Aqueous, p. 95. For inhalation, remove victim from contaminated area, give artificial respiration and oxygen if necessary. Observe for signs and symptoms of pulmonary edema. See p. 43.

DIMETHYL SULFATE (DMS)

This is an extremely hazardous, colorless, oily liquid. Skin contact causes blistering and necrosis. It is absorbed through intact skin in sufficient quantity to cause systemic intoxication. Inhalation of vapor may cause severe inflammation of mucous membranes and fatal pulmonary injury. Exposure to 97 ppm for 10 minutes can be fatal. The threshold limit is 1 ppm.

Treatment: For inhalation, remove from contaminated atmosphere. Give artificial respiration and oxygen if needed. Watch for pulmonary edema. For skin contact, flood immediately with running water for 15 minutes and treat for chemical burn.

DIMETHYLTRYPTAMINE (DMT)

This compound is present in the seeds of *Piptadenia peregrina* and in the leaves of *Pristonia amazonica*. The pharmacological properties of DMT as well as those of *N,N*-diethyltryptamine (DET) are closely related to those of LSD. However, DMT psychosis appears somewhat more rapidly than that experienced with LSD, and is of shorter duration. DMT is not effective when taken orally. It has been given I.V. or I.M. The two tryptamines are fully as dangerous to the casual thrill seeker as LSD and STP [D. R. Rubin, *JAMA* **201**, 143 (1967)]. Other hallucinogenic compounds that have a potential for abuse include ibogaine, bufotenine (5-hydroxy-*N*-dimethyltryptamine), mescaline and its salts, psilocybin and psilocyn [*Sci. News* **93**, 175 (1968)].

Treatment: See LSD, p. 356.

DI-*n*-HEXYL AZELATE (D*n*HA)

Administered orally in single doses, DHA is a relatively harmless material. The lethal oral dose ranges as follows: mice, 15–45 ml/kg; rats, 15–24 ml/kg; guinea pigs, 6–10 ml/kg; rabbits, 1–3 ml/kg; cats, more than 17 ml/kg.

Treatment: In case of ingestion, induce vomiting.

DINITROBENZENES

Absorption may cause anemia, cyanosis, gastroenteric disturbances, injury to the liver, and neuritis. The meta isomer is more toxic than the ortho and para because it is more potent in converting hemoglobin to methemoglobin. The probable lethal oral dose for an adult is 2 gm.

Treatment: Gastric lavage, saline cathartics, maintenance of fluid balance, glucose I.V., transfusions, and inhalation of oxygen are recommended. See Methemoglobinemia, p. 40.

DINITROPHENOLS

Hyperpyrexia is a prominent sign of intoxication following the absorption of a toxic dose of dinitrophenols and dinitroorthocresol (DNOC), pentachlorophenol, or its sodium salt.

The early signs and symptoms of systemic poisoning by dinitro aromatic compounds include an unusual feeling of well being, sweating (mainly at night), insomnia and restlessness, increased thirst, anorexia, yellow discoloration of the sclerae, chrome-yellow urine, and increased basal metabolic rate. Late effects, which may develop rapidly, less than 1 hour before death, are profuse sweating, intense thirst, yellow skin, air hunger, listlessness and apathy, rising temperature and pulse rate, and a striking increase in basal metabolic rate. Convulsions and coma, probably due to anoxia, precede death [W. F. von Oettingen, *Public Health Bull.* **271**, 131 (1941)]. For an adult the probable Lethal Oral Dose of 2,4-dinitrophenol is 1 gm. See p. 693.

Treatment: Therapy is directed toward promoting loss of heat (ice packs), replacement of fluids and electrolytes, and allaying anxiety. In case of ingestion, gastric lavage and cathartics are indicated. Removal from the skin is best accomplished by thorough washing with soap and water. The administration of 10 ml of a 2.5 % solution of sodium methyl thiouracil I.V. is effective in reducing the basal metabolic rate [Credner and Siedek, *Brit. Med. J.* **2**, 19 (1951)].

DIPHENIDOL (Vontrol)

Vontrol was introduced in 1967 for the relief of vertigo associated with Meniere's disease, motion sickness, nausea associated with surgery or radiation sickness. This new drug has caused auditory and visual hallucinations, drowsiness and confusion in approximately 20 patients. These effects appeared following administration of therapeutic doses and usually within 24–48 hours after initiation of therapy.

Caution: The manufacturer points out that since it is impossible, at this time, to identify the individual in whom the undesirable effects may occur, and because there is no specific treatment for these reactions other than allowing them to run their course (usually 24–48 hours after withdrawal of the drug), the benefit to be derived from the use of Vontrol must be weighed against the risk of serious and potentially dangerous reactions. The use of Vontrol should be limited to hospitalized patients.

DIPHENOXYLATE HYDROCHLORIDE WITH ATROPINE (Lomotil)

Diphenoxylate, a meperidine congener and an exempt narcotic, reduces hypermobility of the gastroenteric tract. Lomotil is used for the relief of certain types of diarrhea, gastroenteric cramps, and hyperacidity associated with peptic ulcer. There have been a few reports of nausea, adynamic paralytic ileus [*Am. J. Gastroenterol.* **42**, 540 (1964)], skin rashes, drowsiness, and restlessness. The lowest effective dose should be used (tablets: 2.5 mg diphenoxylate plus 0.025 mg atropine) to prevent or to reduce side effects. A single large dose of 40–60 mg induces morphine-like euphoria. A 2-year-old boy suffered a nonfatal intoxication after ingestion of 8 tablets. Even though he vomited some of the material, he suffered from mild respiratory difficulties, apnea, cyanosis, and urinary retention [*JAMA* **192**, 920 (1965)].

Caution: The therapeutic dose for infants and children has not been established (New Drugs, evaluated by the A.M.A. Council on Drugs, 1966).

DIPHENYLAMINOCHLOROARSINE

This compound is a sternutator and nauseant. Inhalation of vapors causes burning of the nose, throat, and chest, salivation, severe coughing, and sneezing. In a controlled human exposure study, no adverse permanent effects resulted from a single exposure to an aerosol of 100 mg/minute/m^3 of air [C. L. Punte *et al.*, *Am. Ind. Hyg. Assoc. J.* **23**, 199 (1962)].

Treatment: Discontinue exposure. Further treatment is symptomatic and supportive.

DIPHENYLHYDANTOIN SODIUM (Dilantin)

This drug is important in the treatment of grand mal and psychomotor seizures. Nausea and gastroenteric irritation do not occur if the drug is taken with a meal. It may cause acneiform eruptions of the face, particularly in girls 12–18 years of age. Gingival hyperplasia occurs frequently due to the local action of Dilantin dissolved in saliva. Severe side effects, such as ataxia, bullous exfoliative dermatitis, anemia, agranulocytosis, and lymphadenopathy, are rare. A review of some 80 cases of lymphadenopathy revealed that methylphenylethylhydantoin (Mesantoin) was implicated most frequently, Dilantin less frequently. In 2 cases trimethadione (Tridione) was the drug given. Phensuximide (Milontin) and ethotoin (Peganone) were responsible for one case each [*Med. Letter* **4**, 56 (1962)].

An unusual reaction to Dilantin was characterized by hepatic damage with jaundice and a hemopoietic response simulating infectious mononucleosis [*J. Allergy* **32**, 447 (1961)]. A case of an 11-year-old boy who was hypersensitive to Dilantin was reported by Crawford and Jones. Autopsy revealed severe liver necrosis and hyperplasia of the lymph nodes [*Pediatrics* **30**, 595 (1962)]. Other types of hypersensitivity reactions have also been reported [Heitzman, *Radiology* **89**, 311 (1967)].

Children are quite sensitive to this drug. Nine children, aged 2–13, were hospitalized in Oklahoma City for treatment of overdoses of Dilantin (15–66 mg/kg daily). The signs and symptoms of intoxication included unsteadiness, nausea, severe irritability, vomiting, dizziness, fatigue, hallucinations, insomnia, eyepain, and skin rashes. None had leukopenia.

Caution: Waites and Nicklas treated all forms of convulsions in children with phenobarbital. They used diphenylhydantoin as an adjunct [*Oklahoma State Med. Assoc.* **54**, 95 (1961)]. If lymphadenopathy develops in a patient under anticonvulsant therapy, withdraw the drug and observe the patient closely for possible regression before treating the lymphoma. Prompt diagnosis of aplastic or megaloblastic anemia and use of corrective therapy are important to avoid fatalities. In unrecognized cases, the mortality is about 75% [*Am. J. Diseases Children* **104**, 614 (1962)]. The metabolism of Dilantin is inhibited by phenyramidol (Analexin), hence these two drugs should not be administered concurrently [Solomon and Schrogie, *Clin. Pharmacol. Therap.* 8, 554 (1967)]. See also Barbiturates, p. 119.

Treatment: If side effects become evident, reduce the dose or discontinue the drug. Folic acid or vitamin B_{12} and ascorbic acid usually produce a satisfactory hematological response. Exceptional patients may require injections of vitamin B_{12} at monthly intervals while under Dilantin therapy [*Arch. Internal Med.* 111, 744 (1963)]. After ingestion of an overdose, induce vomiting or administer gastric lavage. Hemodialysis promptly reduced the plasma diphenylhydantoin level from 5.0 to 0.4 mg % in a patient who ingested a toxic dose.

DIPTEREX

This compound is an organic phosphate which produces parasympathetic effects. It is much less toxic than parathion. See Organic Phosphates, p. 438.

DIPYRIDAMOLE (Persantin)

This new oral drug is recommended as a coronary vasodilator, but as pointed out, many drugs have been shown to increase coronary blood flow in animals and human subjects, but have not lessened anginal attacks in patients with coronary disease [*Med. Letter* 8, 25 (1966)]. Side effects appear to be related to dosage, including gastroenteric symptoms, dizziness and weakness. Severe effects, initiated by vasodilatation, may lead to marked hypotension and syncope.

Caution: By weighing the possibility of side effects against the doubtful value of dipyridamole in preventing attacks of angina or in relieving cardiac failure due to coronary disease, renewed emphasis is placed on nitroglycerin and erythrityl tetranitrate (Cardilate) as the preferred drugs for prophylaxis and treatment of angina pectoris and for the relief of symptoms after onset of an attack (*Medical Letter*).

DISULFIRAM (Antabuse; Tetraethylthiuram Disulfide)

A therapeutic dose of this drug interferes with the metabolism of ethyl alcohol resulting in an increased production and retention of acetaldehyde. The increased concentration of acetaldehyde induces a sensation of heat, vasodilatation, flushing, hypotension, palpitation, dizziness, vomiting, unconsciousness, and collapse. The severity of these symptoms is related to the doses of disulfiram and ethyl alcohol and to other factors. (See also Ethyl Alcohol, p. 249). An acute disulfiram intoxication was reported in a 10-year-old girl who ingested 3 gm. Vomiting, drowsiness, and minor motor disturbances were noted the following day. Somnolence and hallucinations followed.

According to Bradley and Hewer, peripheral neuropathy and toxic psychoses are not uncommon after disulfiram therapy. After treatment with 1 gm/day for 7 months, a patient developed a change in gait, symptoms of severe peripheral neuropathy, with paralytic foot drop, clumsy hands, numbness, and paresthesia extending to the elbows and above the knees. The patient, who was a heavy drinker, consumed no alcohol during this period. He recovered slowly after discontinuation of Antabuse therapy [*Brit. Med. J.* **2**, 449 (1966)]. An Antabuse-type of reaction may also be produced by trichloroethylene [Piero Serra, *Securitas* **51**, 89 (1966)] and by certain other drugs. (See Ethyl Alcohol, p. 249).

Treatment: If the alcohol-Antabuse reaction becomes too severe, administer oxygen and large doses of ascorbic acid. Treatment in the acute case cited included administration of intravenous fluids and nikethamide.

Discontinue disulfiram therapy or reduce dose if the patient demonstrates effects of the drug. Antabuse must be given with great caution to alcoholics suffering from kidney or liver injury or from psychoses, diabetes, or epilepsy. Disulfiram should *never* be administered to a patient in a state of alcohol intoxication.

2,6-DI-*tert*-BUTYL-4-NITROPHENOL

This compound is a yellow powder with a melting point of 157°C. It has a relatively low acute toxicity for mammals. The LD_{50} for rats, guinea pigs, and mice exceeds 250 mg/kg when given intraperitoneally. Orally, the compound is about one-half as toxic as it is when given intraperitoneally. When dibutylnitrophenol was applied to the shaved skin of rats and taped to the surface at a dosage level of 1.0 g/kg, there was no mortality, no evidence of systemic toxicity, and no local irritation. After administration of lethal doses of the compound by oral or intraperitoneal routes, animals showed a general depression of activity [D. Vesselinovitch *et al.*, *Toxicol. Appl. Pharmacol* **3**, 713 (1961)].

Treatment: For ingestion of large amounts, empty the stomach by inducing vomiting.

DITHIAZANINE (Delvex; Telmid)

Because of its systemic toxicity, this anthelmintic drug should be reserved for infections not controllable by other drugs, preferably after roentgenographic examinations of the bowel have indicated the absence of gastroenteric diseases. Frequent side effects include nausea, vomiting, diarrhea, and abdominal cramps. Nine fatalities preceded by acidosis, hypotension, and coma have been reported. The autopsy of a 3-year-old child revealed a blue-green discoloration of the heart, kidneys and liver, bronchopneumonia, pulmonary edema, and pancreatitis [Abadie and Samuels, *JAMA* **192**, 326 (1965)].

Caution: This drug should be used with caution in older people and in patients with renal disease.

DITHIOCARB

This chelating agent has been used effectively in the treatment of nickel dermatitis and in intoxications by nickel carbonyl, copper, and thallium [F. W. Sunderman *et al.*, *Am. J. Med. Sci.* **254**, 24 (1967)]. See Nickel, p. 420, Copper, p. 185, and Thallium, p. 582.

DODECENYL ANHYDRIDE

This is a mild primary skin irritant. Inhalation of spray, mist, or fumes causes irritation of the mucous membranes of the respiratory tract. Dodecenylsuccinic anhydride is also irritating to the eyes. It is a moderately toxic compound, having a 48-hour oral LD_{50} (for rats) of 3.8 ml/kg.

Treatment: In case of ingestion induce vomiting and follow with gastric lavage. For skin or eye contact, flood affected tissues with water.

DODECYL BENZENE SODIUM SULFONATE (Santomerse No. 3)

This is a buff-colored, hygroscopic, anionic, surface-active agent of the alkyl aryl sulfonate type. The acute intravenous and oral LD_{50} (mouse) is 105 mg/kg and 2 gm/kg, respectively. One mouse out of 10 died after receiving a dose of 0.1 LD_{50} per os daily, 6 days per week, for 25 doses. No adverse effects were observed with respect to growth, food consumption, survival, hematologic values, organ weights, and organ/body weight ratios when the chemical was fed to male and female albino rats over a 2-year period at dietary levels of 200, 1000, and 2000 ppm. See Detergents, p. 201.

Treatment: In case of accidental ingestion of a large dose empty the stomach by inducing vomiting.

DODECYLBENZYL CHLORIDE (Conoco DBCL)

The oral LD_{50} for rats is greater than 75 ml/kg. The minimum lethal dose (MLD) by skin absorption for rabbits is between 12.5 and 15 ml/kg. Skin irritation for rabbits is found to be mild to moderate, with erythema and considerable loss of hair. After 10 days, drying, cracking, and exfoliation (but no visible damage to the subcutaneous layer of the skin) were observed. Eye irritation for rabbits consisted of reddening and mild swelling of palpebral conjunctivae and lids. The lids displayed mild edema 1 hour after application. Recovery was complete in 72 hours. Vapor inhalation studies demonstrated that 6 rats survived 6 hours of exposure to a saturated atmosphere, showing signs of irritation of the respiratory tract and moderate unsteadiness.

Treatment: Remove from the skin and eyes by flooding the affected tissue with water.

DODECYLBENZYL MERCAPTAN (Branched Chains)

This compound is a mercaptan containing a branched 12-carbon alkyl group. It is a light yellow oil, boiling at 150°C (about 0.5 mm). The oral LD_{50} for rats is above 21.5 ml/kg. The acute dermal LD_{50} for rabbits is more than 10.0 ml/kg. A single application of the undiluted material produced mild to moderate dermal irritation. There was no gross evidence of systemic toxicity from percutaneous absorption. A single application to the eyes of rabbits produced moderate conjunctivitis and complete clearing within 2 to 3 days.

Treatment: In case of eye contact wash the affected area with water for 15 minutes.

DODINE (*n*-Dodecylguanidine Acetate)

Dodine is a cationic surface-active agricultural fungicide. The most conspicuous acute toxic action of the dry material or concentrated solutions is a pronounced irritant effect on the skin and mucous membranes.

The oral LD_{50} for rats is approximately 1 gm/kg, and the LD_{50} of the technical material as an aqueous paste by 24-hour continuous skin contact for rabbits is approximately 2 gm/kg. Skin applications cause severe erythema and edema. Similarly, the dry technical material produced extreme irritation of the rabbit eye.

Rats survived a 100-day feeding of 3200 ppm. Feeding of 800 ppm of Dodine to rats for 2 years was associated with diminution of food intake and retardation of growth. Dietary levels of 200 ppm and 50 ppm of Dodine were well tolerated by rats over a 2-year period.

Feeding 50 ppm, 200 ppm, and 800 ppm for 1 year to dogs revealed no deleterious effects other than slight stimulation of the thyroid gland at 800 ppm [G. J. Levinskas, *et al., Toxicol. Appl. Pharmacol.* 3, 127 (1961)].

Treatment: Remove from the skin, mucous membranes or eyes with large quantities of water. For ingestion induce vomiting and follow with gastric lavage.

DOXAPRAM (Dopram)

Doxapram is a nonspecific central nervous system stimulant. Toxic doses are expected to produce undesirable effects similar to those induced by other analeptics. This drug, in doses of 5, 50, and 100 mg/kg (rat) I.P., induced a marked increase in the concentration of total and esterified hepatic cholesterol, and of all plasma cholesterol fractions in the absence of an increase in plasma triglyceride concentration [G. W. Branham, Jr., and W. R. Wooles, *Toxicol. Appl. Pharmacol.* 9, 347 (1966)].

Treatment: See Picrotoxin, p. 476.

DOXYCYCLINE (Vibramycin)

This new tetracycline has a half-life similar to that of methacycline (Rondomycin), namely about 15 hours. Its common side effects are similar to those of other tetracyclines.

Caution: Photosensitivity reactions have been reported fairly frequently. Hepatotoxicity may be a greater hazard with doxycycline than with other tetracyclines which are more rapidly excreted by the kidneys. Because of the increased risk of liver injury, the longer-acting tetracyclines should not be given to pregnant women, to individuals with hepatic disease, nor to those with renal insufficiency [*Med. Letter* **10**, 13 (1968)[. See Tetracyclines, p. 578.

DRY CLEANERS

These preparations may contain hydrocarbons (Benzene, p. 642; Toluene, p. 663; Xylene, p. 637), Petroleum Solvents or Distillates, p. 459; Stoddard Solvent; halogenated hydrocarbons (Carbon Tetrachloride; Trichloroethylene; Ethylene Dichloride, p. 155, 602, 257); Ketones, p. 344, and Esters, p. 243.

DYLOX (O,O-Dimethyl-2,2,2-trichloro-1-hydroxyethylphosphonate)

This is an organic phosphate having a relatively low order of toxicity. See Organic Phosphates, p. 438.

DYRENE (2,4-Dichloro-6-o-chloroanilino-s-triazine)

This is a foliage fungicide. The oral LD_{50} for female rats is 2.7 gm/kg. For rabbits the LD_{50} is approximately 0.4 gm/kg. No mortality was obtained when male cats received doses of up to 0.62 gm/kg, when female monkeys were given doses of up to 3.2 gm/kg, or when dogs were dosed with 7.1 gm/kg.

In 2-year feeding tests on rats, there was no evidence that 5000 ppm in the diet was harmful. Male and female dogs survived 330–430 repeated oral doses of 250 mg/kg or 1.0 gm/kg during a period of 534–681 days. Some weight loss occurred during the period of approximately 2 years.

The animals given the larger dosage showed enlargement of the liver, kidney, and spleen at necropsy. The dogs given the lower dosage had splenic enlargement at necropsy.

When 9.4 gm/kg of Dyrene paste (in peanut oil or dimethyl phthalate) was kept in contact with the skin of rabbits for 24 hours, a local erythema, edema, ulceration, fissuring, and incrustation occurred. Skin applications also resulted in toxic degenerative changes in the liver and kidneys of the treated rabbits.

Treatment: For skin, eye, and mucous membrane contact, flood affected tissues with water. In case of ingestion induce vomiting and follow with gastric lavage. Further treatment is supportive and symptomatic.

ECHOTHIOPHATE IODIDE (Phospholine)

This is a potent and long-acting cholinesterase inhibitor. Its pharmacological properties and side effects are similar to those of isoflurophate [*Brit. J. Ophthalmol.* **51**, 783 (1967)]. When used in the management of accommodative esotropia or for the control of intraocular pressure in glaucoma, it produces an intense and prolonged miosis, but it may also lower plasma and blood cell cholinesterase activity to less than 50% and cause, in addition, diarrhea, gastroenteric cramps, vomiting, weakness or paresthesia. McGavi observed several patients who showed marked reduction in serum pseudocholinesterase within a few days after initiation of echothiophate therapy [*Brit. Med. J.* **2**, 272 (1965)]. Phospholine is also used to counteract the cycloplegic effects of atropine and scopolamine.

Caution: As with related compounds that induce depression of pseudocholinesterase activity, the administration of succinylcholine as a muscle relaxant is potentially dangerous. This should be kept in mind in the event that patients receiving phospholine undergo surgery. Succinylcholine, procaine, and related local anesthetics are hydrolyzed by the pseudocholinesterases. See Organic Phosphates, p. 438.

EDATHAMIL CALCIUM-DISODIUM (Calcium Disodium Edetate; Calcium Disodium Versenate; Calcium Disodium Ethylenediaminetetraacetic Acid; $CaNa_2$ EDTA)

This is an important drug for the treatment of metal intoxications. It is an effective chelating agent which combines with the metal forming a nonionizable, water-soluble complex that is excreted by the kidneys.

An overdose of EDTA or its sodium salts (Na_2EDTA, Endrate; trisodium edetate; Sodium Versenate) will induce hypocalcemia, which may cause death if not corrected promptly. These drugs are used in the treatment of various types of pathological calcification. A recent publication by C. P. Lamar describes the use of the disodium salt for occlusive atherosclerosis [*J. Am. Geriat. Soc.* **14**, 272 (1966)]. High doses of CaNa$_2$ EDTA will *not* produce hypocalcemia; it is for this reason that this compound is used therapeutically in metal intoxications. In high doses it is known to have induced severe renal tubular lesions in man and animals (M. D. Reuber and C. W. Lee, *Arch. Environ. Health* **13**, 554 (1966)]. Several fatalities have been reported. Side effects occasionally noted include nausea, vomiting, general malaise, numbness and tingling sensations, urinary frequency, chills, fever, and arthralgia.

CaNa$_2$ EDTA therapy is highly effective in lead intoxication; it has been found useful in systemic intoxications due to copper, iron, manganese, and vanadium, and in the local treatment of "chrome" ulcers and nickel eczemas. Even though the drug promotes the urinary excretion of plutonium, thorium, uranium, and yttrium, its use in these intoxications should be approached with considerable caution. (See Plutonium, p. 482). In cadmium intoxications, CaNa$_2$EDTA is moderately effective if used early. It was effective in the treatment of animals given lethal doses of inorganic salts of nickel and cobalt.

CaNa$_2$ EDTA may be administered slowly in doses of 15–25 mg/kg I.V., every 12 hours for 2 days, but not for more than 3 days. After a rest period of 3–7 days, the treatment, adjusted to the patient is repeated if needed. Barie and Wilson recommend that 500 mg of CaNa$_2$ EDTA be dissolved in 250–500 ml of isotonic glucose and *slowly* infused over a period of 12 hours; this procedure to be repeated if necessary [*JAMA* **180**, 244 (1962)]. The drug should not be given by mouth to treat an orally induced intoxication, nor should it be applied to the contaminated skin. (Exceptions are the local treatment of "chrome" ulcer or nickel eczema.) Skin exposure to salts of various metals or radioactive dusty compounds is to be followed by immediate washing with soap and plenty of water. For information on aerosol inhalation of CaNa$_2$ EDTA, refer to *Brit. J. Ind. Med.* **17**, 201 (1960). Renal lesions due to high doses of CaNa₂ EDTA cleared within a week after cessation of treatment [*JAMA* **160,** 1042 (1956)]. CaNa₂ EDTA is ineffective and may cause additional harm in intoxications by beryllium and thallium.

EFOCAINE

This analgesic preparation was withdrawn from the market.

ELASE

The clinical value of *systemic* proteolytic enzymes, such as Elase—a combination of bovine plasmin (fibrinolysin) and bovine pancreatic desoxyribonuclease–has not been established. Local application may be useful in the treatment of some wounds. No adverse reactions have been reported.

ELASTOMER

These are large, stretchy macromolecules such as rubber (Polyisoprene) and polyisobutylene (Vistanex). They are not absorbed from the gastrointestinal tract and have a very low order of toxicity. Ingestion of large quantities could lead to the formation of some rather bizarre bezoars. See Bezoars, p. 643.

EMYLCAMATE (Striatran)

This substituted diol tranquilizer has mild muscle relaxing and sedative properties. Side effects reported have not been of a serious nature [S. Cohen, Mod. Treat. **2,** 505 (1965)].

ENAMELWARE

Lemonade stored overnight in a gray enamelware container poisoned 100 children at a church picnic. Cheap enamel often contains antimony, which is highly toxic. The acid in the lemonade dissolves the enamel on prolonged contact.

Treatment: See Antimony, p. 108.

ENDRIN

Endrin, an isomer of dieldrin, is a widely used, highly toxic insecticide. It can be absorbed through the lungs, intestines, or skin and produces hyperexcitability of the central nervous system [Y. Coble *et al.*, *JAMA* **202,** 489 (1967)].

On May 23, 1956, over 100 people were poisoned in England by flour contaminated with endrin. One to three hours after eating bread made from contaminated flour, signs and symptoms included frothing at the mouth, facial congestion, epileptiform convulsions, opisthotonus, and violent muscular contractions severe enough to cause shoulder dislocation. All recovered without complications. The flour at the bottom of the contaminated sacks was saturated with a solution of endrin dissolved in xylene.

Treatment: See Aldrin, p. 82 and 684.

ENGLISH YEW (Taxus baccata)

Intoxications and fatalities have occurred in children following ingestion of the bright red berry-like fruits of several evergreen plants including the English yew, the Pacific or Western yew (*T. brevifolia*), ground hemlock or American yew (*T. canadensis*), and the Japanese yew (*T. cuspidata*). These plants contain a number of alkaloids, particularly taxine A and B, which are readily absorbed when the berries are chewed. Swallowing of the whole berry causes no harm. Because of the irritant action of taxine, severe gastroenteric irritation, colic, and vomiting follow, together with dizziness, muscular weakness, stupor, coma, hypotension, and convulsions. Red spots may appear on various parts of the body.

Treatment: Since deaths have occurred within the first hour after ingestion of the fruit, it is important to induce vomiting or use gastroenteric lavage promptly. Taxine interferes with myocardial conductivity, therefore, catecholamines should be administered with caution to avoid tachycardia and fibrillation. Further treatment is symptomatic and supportive.

EOSIN DYES (Fluorescein; Lipstick)

Many of the indelible-type lipsticks contain eosin dyes or halogen derivatives of fluorescein. These compounds cause photosensitization more frequently than is recognized. F. G. La Piana recently reported an anaphylactoid reaction after the I.V. injection of 10 ml of 5% sodium fluorescein (Fluorescite) for diagnostic purposes. The patient almost immediately developed nausea, pruritus, progressive hoarseness, and respiratory obstruction. The patient had a childhood history of hay fever. He responded to epinephrine.

Treatment: Discontinue use of a fluorescein-containing lipstick if photosensitization becomes apparent.

EPICHLORHYDRIN

Epichlorhydrin (3-chloro-1,2-propylene oxide; 1-chloro-2,3-epoxypropane) is a clear, colorless liquid miscible with many organic solvents. It is a highly toxic chemical which may prove fatal if inhaled or swallowed. Skin penetration may occur in harmful amounts if contact is prolonged. Covered skin contacts cause severe burns, and uncovered contacts cause some irritation.

Concentrated vapors are highly toxic and a brief exposure kills rapidly. Concentrations of 250 ppm allowed survival after 4-hour exposure, but 500 ppm killed all animals (rats) in 2 hours. Concentrations of 40 ppm cause irritation of the throat in humans in less than 2 hours of exposure. The liquid causes eye injury similar in degree to that caused by liquid hand soaps. Vapors may also be irritating to the eyes.

Treatment: In case of eye or skin contact, immediately flood with water for 15 minutes. For inhalation exposure, remove victim from the contaminated atmosphere. Give artificial respiration and oxygen if necessary.

EPINEPHRINE (Adrenalin)

Oral administration of epinephrine is essentially ineffective. Infusion over a prolonged period may result in severe and irreversible liver damage. Accidental infusion into the tissues has resulted in severe local vasoconstriction and necrosis. An overdose of epinephrine produces a pronounced rise in blood pressure, decreased cardiac output, slowing of the heart, glycosuria, tremors, palpitation, and ventricular fibrillation. (See also Levarterenol, p. 351.

Treatment: As a rule, the effects of epinephrine disappear rather promptly following discontinuation of therapy. Piperoxan (Benodaine) and phentolamine (Regitine) will shorten sympathetic effects induced by epinephrine and related drugs. Hypertension and cardiac distress may also be relieved by sodium nitrite or by Priscoline. Yu-Chen Lee administered 0.4 mg of nitroglycerin sublingually to a patient whose blood pressure was 250/140 mm Hg following an injection of epinephrine. Within 15 seconds, ventricular premature beats disappeared; during the subsequent 30 minutes, the blood pressure dropped to 130/80 mm Hg [*JAMA* **202**, 219 (1967)].

Epinephrine is contraindicated after absorption of drugs or chemicals or in diseases associated with ventricular hyperirritability. Fatal ventricular fibrillation has occurred when epinephrine was used in individuals suffering from poisoning by the chlorinated hydrocarbon pesticides or in patients treated with mercurial diuretics, digitalis, or in cyclopropane anesthesia. According to Matteo *et al.*, epinephrine during cyclopropane-oxygen anesthesia caused ventricular arrhythmias in 30% of patients despite careful attention to adequate ventilation and depth of anesthesia [*Anesthesiology* **19**, 619 (1958); *JAMA* **186**, 811 (1963)].

EPOXY RESINS

Epoxy resins are polyethers prepared by the interaction of epichlorhydrin with a dihydroxy compound such as bis(4-hydroxyphenyl)-dimethylmethane (Bisphenol A). Depending on the type of resin desired, the curing agent may be a polyamine, a phenolic resin, or an acid anhydride.

Some epoxy resins are irritants, sensitizers, or both, but the major problem in handling these materials occurs from the di- or triamine curing agents which are irritants and sensitizers. The workman contacts the epoxy resin and the hardener while mixing the weighed or recommended amounts of these basic ingredients.

Many uncured epoxy resins can be handled without ill effects, but those of the lower molecular weights have irritant properties. On the other hand, almost all amines are irritants and sometimes sensitizers. Their high pH (13–14) damages the keratin or at least severely weakens this protective layer of the skin. At the same time, surface lipids are readily removed. The additional alkaline effect of most industrial cleansers, along with the amines and solvents, leads to marked redness and dryness of the skin. A dermatosis of varying degree usually results. Contact with the fumes has caused not only a dermatitis of the face, eyelids, and neck, but also asthmatic symptoms from breathing the amine-contaminated air. The major cutaneous effects

241

are produced by contact with the liquid stage of the low molecular weight resins, the hardener, or a mixture of these before polymerization or curing is complete. As a general rule, the completely polymerized product is inert with respect to the skin.

It is possible to avert contact dermatitis in working with epoxy resins by educating all concerned on the hazards associated with these materials, by introducing vapor and dust control measures, and by employing protective devices, notably protective gloves and adequate washing facilities and cleansing agents [D. J. Birmingham, *Arch. Ind. Health* **19**, 365 (1961)].

Treatment: Soap and water, and organic solvents such as acetone, may be used to clean skin crevices, nail beds, and mucous membranes. Burow's solution (alum and lead acetate) may be used to neutralize residual free amines. Deep necrotizing injuries are treated like caustic burns. Eye injuries are washed with copious amounts of water. Acute respiratory inhalation is treated like ammonia exposure [Harold H. Borgstedt, *Ind. Med. Surg.* **32**, 426 (1963)].

ERGOT

Ergot, ergotoxin, and to a lesser extent, their closely related compounds exert a marked vasoconstrictive effect on the arterioles. Oral intoxication by ergot or ergotoxin may lead to gastroenteric distress, respiratory and motor disturbances, convulsions, hallucinations, and sometimes gangrene.

There are several reports in the literature on myocardial infarction presumably caused by ergotamine tartrate (Gynergen). Marked nausea is a frequent side effect of this drug; in toxic doses, it may cause vasoconstriction, vascular stasis, and thrombosis leading to gangrene.

Caution: Symptoms of angina or paresis are warning signs for discontinuation of this drug. According to the manufacturers, therapy with Gynergen and related drugs including Cafergot (ergotamine with caffeine) is contraindicated in pregnancy and in patients suffering from sepsis, toxemia, arteriosclerosis, coronary heart disease, hypertension, nephritis and hepatitis. A patient receiving ergotamine-type drugs should be kept under close medical supervision.

Treatment: Withdrawal of Cafergot resulted in rather rapid recovery of several patients [*Am. Heart J.* **70,** 665 (1965); *Can. Med. Assoc. J.* **95,** 1319 (1966)].

ERYTHROMYCIN (Erythrocin; Ilotycin)

Nausea, vomiting, and diarrhea have been noted occasionally after oral administration of this antibiotic. Skin eruptions and urticaria have been reported in less than 1 % of the patients dosed with this drug [*Am. J. Med. Sci.* **243,** 502 (1962)]. An allergic response may follow administration of a single dose [*Oral Surg.* **24,** 323 (1967)]. The drug does not usually produce alteration of the intestinal flora. Reports indicate that in about 12 % of patients, erythromycin propionate lauryl sulfate (Ilosone) may produce cholestatic hepatitis. Whether this effect is specific for this particular form of the antibiotic or only a reflection of the higher blood levels achieved has not been clarified. It appears that this liver toxicity is readily reversible.

Caution: The drug should not be used for minor ailments. Increased transaminase levels, hyperbilirubinemia, and increased eosinophilia are indications of disturbances in liver function suggesting that the use of this drug be discontinued. The prolonged topical use of this antibiotic is not recommended, since there is some indication that this interferes with its subsequent systemic effectiveness against staphylococci [S. Epstein, *JAMA* **202,** 156 (1967)].

ESTERS

In general, these compounds have a low order of toxicity. They are used extensively in industry as solvents and in trace concentrations for food flavoring. Pharmacologically, they are central nervous system depressants similar to ethyl alcohol and ether in their action. Overwhelming doses might cause transient liver and kidney injury. Prolonged contact with the skin will cause tissue defatting and dehydration leading to dermatitis. The direct aspiration of liquid esters into the lung will cause chemical pneumonitis. See also Table 34, p. 715.

Treatment: Remove from the skin and eyes with copious quantities of water. For inhalation remove the victim from the contaminated area, administer artificial respiration and oxygen if necessary. Further treatment is supportive and symptomatic. In case of ingestion, gastric lavage and saline cathartics are indicated.

ESTROGENS

Undesirable effects are likely to occur after use of the synthetic estrogens diethylstilbestrol (stilbestrol), benzestrol, dienestrol, and others. In the adult, these may include gastric distress, nausea, vomiting, headache, retention of salt and production of edema, increase in body weight, uterine bleeding, hyperplasia of the vaginal epithelium, and increase in size of the mammary glands. Adjustment of the dose, or the use of a natural estrogen will usually give relief. Hypercalcemia has been produced by these drugs in individuals suffering osteolytic metastatic mammary carcinoma. Discontinuation of therapy, adequate fluid intake, and infusion of sodium citrate are indicated.

Acute intoxications are rare. Pseudoprecocious puberty as the result of unintentional ingestion of estrogens has been reported. Estrogens given to adolescents may seriously interfere with maturation and ovulation as a result of inhibition of pituitary gonadotropin production.

Menopausal patients given prolonged estrogen therapy may develop nausea, vaginal bleeding, and weight gain; interruption of therapy and downward adjustment of the dose can overcome these effects.

Treatment: Decrease the dose or discontinue use entirely.

ETHACRYNIC ACID (Edecrin)

Ethacrynic acid (dichlorophenoxyacetic acid) and furosemide (Lasix) exert similar diuretic action. They have been used effectively in patients not responding to other diuretics and in cases of impaired renal function [J. C. Hunt and F. T. Mauer, *Am. J. Cardiol.* **17**, 642 (1966)]. [For a preliminary report on the diuretic action of methylenebutyrylphenoxyacetic acid, see *JAMA* **185**, 854 (1963)].

According to G. V. Irons *et al.*, Edecrin side effects are dose-related [*JAMA* **194**, 1348 (1965)]. Following administration of large therapeutic doses, side effects have been rather frequent including nausea, vomiting, severe diarrhea, orthostatic hypotension [*Circulation* **31**, 661 (1964)], hypoglycemia, reduced blood volume, hyponatremia, and hypochloremic alkalosis. Eight of 10 patients, after receiving 150–400 mg daily for 15–30 days, developed hypokalemia [*Circulation* **32**, 11 (1965)]. There have also been reports of transient deafness, tinnitus, and vertigo [*Arch. Internal Med.* **117**, 715 (1966)], and of reversible agranulocytosis, blurred vision, skin rashes, fever, retention of uric acid sufficient to cause articular gout [*Brit. Med. J.* **1**, 124 (1966)], and hepatocellular damage [*Brit. Med. J.* **2**, 152 (1967)]. There have been several deaths due to agranulocytosis [*Ann. Internal Med.* **64**, 1303 (1966)], severe electrolyte disturbances, necrotizing nonhemorrhagic pancreatitis [*N.Y. State J. Med.* **67**, 1438 (1967)], hypotension, oliguria, or a rapidly progressive uremia [*Circulation* **32**, 11 (1965)].

Caution: To avoid or to reduce undesirable effects, administer the lowest effective dose. Intermittent treatment is preferable to daily administration of this potent drug. A patient on ethacrynic acid therapy should remain under a physician's care, preferably in a hospital, to permit frequent checks on electrolytes, serum carbon dioxide, and blood urea nitrogen. Maintenance of serum potassium is of particular importance in digitalized patients and in patients with decompensated liver disease. The forced excretion of sodium by ethacrynic acid, furosemide, thiazides, and organomercurials may increase the excretion of aldosterone, which in turn stimulates an enhanced excretion of potassium at the expense of a subsequently reduced excretion of sodium.

Ethacrynic acid should be avoided during pregnancy. Neither ethacrynic acid nor any other diuretic should be used to promote water loss in the long-term management of overweight patients, nor should diuretics be used to treat peripheral edema resulting from localized venous or lymphatic obstruction [*Med. Letter* **9**, 53, (1967)]. The drug is useful in the treatment of acute pulmonary edema.

Treatment: Reduce the dose or interrupt therapy at the first undesirable sign or symptom. Treatment of an overdose is symptomatic and supportive. Patients who have received doses of 200–400 mg/day for several days may suddenly develop shock (as reported by J. G.

Hilton and K. Kessler), which may be unresponsive to metaraminol, potassium, and glucose in saline. One patient responded to spironolactone [*J. New Drugs* **4**, 93 (1964)]. For hypokalemia consider the use of potassium supplements or an infusion of potassium chloride.

ETHAMIVAN (Emivan; Vanillic Acid Diethylamide)

Ethamivan has been recommended as an adjunctive agent in the treatment of severe respiratory depression secondary to barbiturate poisoning or carbon dioxide narcosis. While this drug in high doses acts as a powerful stimulant to the central nervous system, it cannot be regarded as a specific barbiturate antagonist. Effective doses are likely to add to the difficulties and contribute to additional strain on the central nervous system. Depending on the dosage and the patient's condition, coughing, laryngospasm, dislodging of the endotracheal tube, vomiting, cardiac arrythmias and convulsions may result. In patients suffering from chronic lung diseases, 50 mg I.V. doses of ethamivan were found to be less effective than therapeutic doses of aminophylline. In addition, the I.V. use of this drug has been associated with a high incidence of side effects, including pain at the site of injection, itching, generalized warmth or a burning sensation, apprehension, nervousness, nausea, cough, color hallucinations, and substernal pain. T. Rodman *et al.*, point out that an oral dose of 400 mg (five times the recommended dose) is well tolerated but not effective as a respiratory stimulant [*New Engl. J. Med.* **267**, 1279 (1962)].

Treatment of an oral dose is symptomatic and supportive. See also Barbiturates, p. 119.

ETHANOLAMINE, MONO-, DI-, TRI-

Monoethanolamine and triethanolamine are viscous, high-boiling, relatively stable liquids having an ammoniacal odor. They are very hygroscopic materials and have alkaline strengths comparable to the alkylamines. Diethanolamine has the same general properties except that at normal temperatures it exists either as a white, crystalline solid or a supercooled liquid. See p. 706.

Treatment: See Ammonia, Aqueous, p. 95, and Amines, Aliphatic, p. 90.

ETHCHLORVYNOL (Placidyl)

This is a short-acting sedative. Therapeutic doses have occasionally produced nausea, mental confusion, ataxia, or fixed drug eruption [*Arch. Dermatol.* **92**, 184 (1965)]. Reports indicate that the margin between therapeutic doses (0.5 gm/day) and doses which are liable to induce withdrawal symptoms is less than the margin with short-acting barbiturates [*JAMA* **190**, 154 (1964); *Am. J. Psychiat.* **120**, 1201 (1964)]. A dose of 15 gm has been fatal [*Clin. Pharmacol. Therap.* **5**, 334 (1964)]. A woman who ingested 15–25 gm of this drug was comatose and in shock for 5 days [R. I. Ogilvie *et al.*, *Can. Med. Assoc. J.*, **95**, 954 (1966)].

Caution: This drug does not have the margin of safety originally claimed. Habituation, tolerance, and physical dependence have developed after daily doses of 1.5 gm. In alcoholics, ethchlorvynol is particularly dangerous. In these individuals, doses of 0.5–1.0 gm may suddenly cause collapse and coma lasting for hours.

Treatment The patient of R. I. Ogilvie *et al.* survived after 10 hours of hemodialysis and supportive measures. She responded on the fifth day and complained of weakness and reduced sensation in both limbs. Generalized convulsions, which occurred on the seventh day, were treated with barbiturates and diphenylhydantoin.

ETHERS

These compounds have a low order of toxicity. Pharmacologically, they are central nervous system depressants similar to ethyl alcohol. Diethyl ether and divinyl ether are used as general anesthetics.

Prolonged contact with the skin will cause tissue defatting and dehydration leading to dermatitis. Liquid methyl vinyl ether in contact with the bare skin may cause "frostbite" because of rapid evaporation. The direct aspiration of liquid into the lung will cause chemical pneumonitis.

Accidental arterial injection—instead of injection in the antecubital vein—of a mixture of 0.5 ml of ethyl ether and 0.5 ml of saline caused immediately a severe burning pain in the arm and hand. Massive edema developed in the arm, followed by blotchy cyanosis of fingers and gangrene, necessitating low forearm amputation. Obviously, ether should be used with great *caution* in the measurement of venous circulation time [H. King and D. B. Hawtof, *JAMA* **184**, 241 (1963)].

Treatment: Remove from the skin and eyes with copious quantities of water. For inhalation, remove the victim from the contaminated area and administer artificial respiration and oxygen if necessary. In case of ingestion, gastric lavage and saline cathartics are indicated. Subsequent treatment is symptomatic and supportive.

ETHINAMATE (Valmid)

This drug has found use as a hypnotic. Its toxicity is of a low order and side effects have not been serious.

Caution: Four reports of addiction have appeared. While the minimal oral effective dose is 0.5–1.0 gm, some patients require as much as 2.0 gm to induce sleep. Addiction was undoubtedly related to the dose and frequency of drug administration. E. H. Ellinwood *et al.* reported withdrawal symptoms which included confusion, disorientation, hallucinations, insomnia, hyperactivity, tremors, and convulsions [*New Engl. J. Med.* **266**, 185 (1962)].

ETHIONAMIDE (Thioamide)

This drug which has found some use in the treatment of tuberculosis is considered to be less effective than isoniazid and somewhat more toxic. Early reports indicate that ethionamide may occasionally induce liver damage, purpura, gynecomastia and impotence, effects similar to those produced by ganglionic blocking agents, peripheral neuropathy, possible ototoxicity, psychic depression, drowsiness, acne and severe skin rash, and difficulty in the control of diabetes mellitus [Council on Drugs, *JAMA* **187**, 527 (1964); E. Kuntz *et al.*, *Deut. Med. Wochschr.* **92**, 1718 (1967)].

Caution is in order when this drug is administered to individuals with pre-existing liver damage. As a rule, side effects disappear or are reduced when the dosage is reduced. Urinalysis and blood cell counts, as well as renal and hepatic function tests, should be conducted at regular intervals in a patient on ethionamide therapy. The Council on Drugs recommends that this agent be given only to patients who do not respond to or tolerate the usual combination of streptomycin, aminosalicylic acid, and isoniazid.

ETHOMEENS

The Ethomeens are tertiary amines having one fatty alkyl group (derived from various fatty sources having from 12 to 18 carbon atoms) and two polyoxyethylene groups attached to the nitrogen. They are cationic in nature although by increasing the ethylene oxide content these compounds behave more like nonionics. They have a low order of toxicity. See Detergents, p. 201.

ETHOXYACETYLENE

This compound can produce marked irritation and inflammation of the eyes. Constant irritation by vapors may be harmful to the eyes. Animal studies suggest that the damage is reversible. It can be minimized by immediate and prolonged washing with water following exposure. Ethoxyacetylene can cause local irritation and edema of the skin following prolonged exposure. Systemic effects are noted only when large amounts of the compound are placed in contact with the skin for prolonged periods (6-24 hours). This chemical is toxic on inhalation and prolonged exposure to its vapors should be avoided. In mice the oral LD_{50} is 2.4 gm/kg.

Treatment: In case of inhalation remove individual from the contaminated atmosphere. Give artificial respiration and oxygen if necessary. For skin, mucous membrane, and eye contact flood affected tissues with water for 15 minutes. Induce vomiting, perform gastric lavage, and administer saline cathartics in case of accidental ingestion.

ETHYL ALCOHOL (Ethanol)

"When drink is a man's friend, it is his good friend" — Sir Francis Chichester, Skipper of *Gypsy Moth IV*.

Ethyl alcohol is a central nervous system depressant, not a stimulant. An adult metabolizes approximately 30 ml of whiskey, or the alcohol in one bottle of beer (12 fluid oz.), per hour. With a blood alcohol level of 50–100 mg% (60–120 ml of whiskey, or 3–4 bottles of beer) many adults exhibit impairment of some of the central nervous system functions. In our laboratory, students of medicine showed no increase in reaction time with blood levels below 0.1%. Clinical intoxication is frequently seen after ingesting 150–200 ml of whiskey, or 6–7 bottles of beer [blood alcohol level of 150 mg% (or 0.15%)]. According to H. Moskowitz, "in driving, people are seriously impaired long before the 0.15% blood alcohol level is reached [*Sci. News* **90**, 167 (1966)]." In the average individual, a concentration of 0.15% is associated with partial loss of all higher functions, as well as depression of the centers controlling vasomotor and respiratory activities. With a level of 350 mg%, intoxication is unmistakable. Levels above 550 mg% are usually fatal in untreated patients.

After absorption of a toxic dose, children rapidly fall asleep and remain unconscious for a longer period than adults. They do not show the initial period of agitation (loss of inhibition) which many adults will demonstrate. Occasionally, they will have severe convulsions as a result of marked hypoglycemia. This condition has been misdiagnosed as encephalitis [*Pediat. Clin. N. Am.* **12**, 423 (1965)]. The probable lethal oral dose of 100% alcohol for an adult is 250 ml taken in 30 minutes. For small children the estimated lethal oral dose of 100% alcohol ranges from 6 to 30 ml, indicating a much lower degree of tolerance. Chemical analysis for blood alcohol may be essentially negative 20 hours after ingestion of a lethal dose.

Alcohol has been found to significantly reduce a man's resistance to the effects of hypoxia. Flying skills were markedly impaired by blood alcohol concentrations ranging from 22 to 49 mg% [J. L. Nettles and R. N. Olson, *JAMA* **194**, 1193 (1965)].

Aspiration of alcoholic beverages during swallowing, coughing, or vomiting, may cause pneumonia or fatal pulmonary edema. Individuals reporting severe pain after ingestion of beer, wine, or another alcoholic beverage should be examined for evidence of Hodgkin's disease.

Hypersensitivity to alcohol has been reported in rare instances. Symptoms such as asthma, urticaria, angioneurotic edema, or vasomotor rhinitis may be produced by one or all types or brands of alcoholic beverages. Sensitization to alcohol by thiram and other compounds may be another explanation for hypersensitivity. Barbiturates interfere with the enzymatic action of alcohol dehydrogenase and decrease the body's ability to detoxify alcohol [*Mod. Med.* **32**, 53 (1964)]. There is no evidence that alcohol dilates the coronary arteries. Its tranquilizing effect is useful in tense or worried individuals; it is contraindicated in angina pectoris [A. M. Master and L. A. Kuhn, *Clin. Pharmacol. Therap.* **8**, 603 (1967)].

According to P. Marquardt and H. W. J. Werringloer, many wines, particularly red wines, contain a significant concentration of histamine, up to 22 mg/100 ml [*Food Cosmet. Toxicol.* **3**, 803 (1965)]. This histamine is not a byproduct of alcoholic fermentation, but results from bacterial contamination. For therapeutic purposes, particularly in geriatrics, F. Damran and E. Liddy recommend vodka because it is said to cause less gastric irritation and fewer hangovers than whiskey. It is recognized that vodka is practically free from the whiskey congeners [*Ind. Med. Surg.* **31**, 463 (1962)].

Alcohol can cause increased tolerance and, therefore, true addiction. An individual suffering from chronic alcoholism may go into delirium tremens, either during an acute phase or during withdrawal. Patients with chronic alcoholism are especially susceptible to gout [B. M. Saker *et al.*, *Med. J. Australia* **1**, 1213 (1967)]. Lactic acid, which forms from the metabolism of ethanol, has an effect on the metabolism and retention of uric acid. Plasma triglyceride levels rise within 24 hours after ingestion of alcohol. Persisting high concentrations of blood alcohol eventually lead to a fall of plasma triglyceride concentration, presumably because of deterioration of liver function [P. J. Nestel, *Australian Ann. Med.* **16**, 139 (1967); T. Gebbie and I. A. M. Prior, *Med. J. Australia* **2**, 769 (1967)].

Ethyl alcohol is oxidized to acetaldehyde, then to acetic acid, and finally to carbon dioxide and water. Oxidation beyond acetaldehyde can be blocked by disulfiram (Antabuse), butyraldoxime, cyanamide, chlorpropamide (Diabinese), tolbutamide (Orinase), and presumably also by acetohexamide (Dymelor), and tolazamide (Tolinase). Accumulation of acetaldehyde produces a series of most unpleasant symptoms. Metronidazole (Flagyl) (a systemic trichomonacide), carbutamide (Nadisan; Invenol), furazolidone (Furoxone), and furaltadone (Altafur) have also been reported to have Antabuse-type effects [*New Engl. J. Med.,* July 8, 1965]. See also Amitriptyline (Elavil), p. 94.

Ethyl alcohol was recently recommended for the treatment of ethylene glycol poisoning. Ethyl alcohol displaces ethylene glycol from the active site of the enzyme alcohol dehydrogenase and thus prevents the conversion of ethylene glycol to oxalate, which is the actual toxic agent [*JAMA* **194**, 1231 (1965)].

The odor of ethyl alcohol on an individual's breath does not necessarily mean that he is intoxicated. Other chemical intoxications, head injuries, or concomitant diseases (hemiplegia, diabetes, insulin shock, concussion), may render the individual unconscious and must be ruled out before the diagnosis of an acute alcoholic intoxication is made. See also Lead, p. 347.

Alcohol is absorbed through the skin, hence this factor should be considered in sponging an individual; it may augment an already existing depression. Combinations of alcohol and a tranquilizer may be dangerous. A promising exception appears to be chlordiazepoxide (Librium). Investigators at the Karolinska Institute in Stockholm found that Librium reverses the effects of alcohol in healthy human volunteers and experimental animals. "Sixteen volunteers tested with five ounces (150 ml) of whisky, plus a small dose of Librium, subjectively rated themselves less intoxicated than they normally would feel with that amount of liquor. But with meprobamate (Miltown, Equanil) they rated themselves as drunker [*Sci. News* **94**, 312 (1968)]."

For the significance of blood alcohol levels at autopsy see the report by V. D. Pleuckhahn. He points out that such levels are valid up to 48 hours after death if simple principles were observed in the collection and storage of the blood. Levels up to 0.2% of alcohol may be produced if putrefaction is not prevented [*Med. J. Australia* **2**, 118 (1967)].

According to T. B. Brewin, intolerance to alcohol in women may be a symptom of malignancy some place in the body [*JAMA* **203**, 815 (1968)].

Treatment: Removal of alcohol from the gastroenteric tract is most important. However, vomiting or gastric lavage are of limited, if any, value if hours have passed since ingestion of the alcohol. The treatment of acute poisoning depends on the condition of the patient—excitement or coma. The treatment of excitement requires depressant drugs such as a barbiturate, paraldehyde, chloral hydrate, or one of the tranquilizing agents (chlorpromazine, reserpine, meprobamate). None of these drugs can be administered without some risk to the patient.

If the patient is extremely drowsy or severely depressed, give one of the following: caffeine and sodium benzoate, dextroamphetamine (Dexedrine), amphetamine (Benzedrine), or methylphenidate (Ritalin). In severe hypotension, ephedrine may be administered S.C., I.M., or I.V. Pentylenetetrazol (Metrazol) may be used with caution for a patient in the very severe depressed stage.

Since alcoholic coma may lead to death, it must be regarded as an emergency. The injection of 50% dextrose I.V. in intoxicated children and adults is essential for the treatment of hypoglycemia. Administration of fructose has also been found valuable. The administration of saline I.V. will help to replace the loss of fluid and reestablish electrolyte balance. Correction of the dehydration is of utmost importance. The inclusion of vitamins and pyridoxine in the infusion and the use of insulin may accelerate detoxication. If the patient's respiration is dangerously depressed, a patent airway and the use of artificial respiration may be lifesaving. Studies on the relationship of alcoholic intoxication and anoxemia have shown that inhalation of oxygen and carbon dioxide "tended to sober up the subjects more rapidly." After the recovery from the acute phase, give a "super" protein, high carbohydrate, and low fat diet supplemented with adequate vitamins and minerals.

Treatment of the alcoholic or of delirium tremens includes complete abstinence, search for injuries or infections, administration of fluids to correct electrolyte depletion, drugs to counteract circulatory collapse, and measures to reduce hyperthermia. Sodium diphenylhydantoin (Dilantin) is most effective in aborting grand mal seizures associated with alcohol withdrawal. The usual oral dosage is 100 mg 3 times daily. Chlorpromazine in large doses can also be used successfully in aborting seizures, but the possible hypotensive effect from a phenothiazine derivative can be avoided by the use of sodium diphenylhydantoin [M. E. Chafetz, *JAMA* **200,** 90 (1967)]. C. Muller, comparing three drugs in the follow-up treatment of 131 cases of delirium tremens found chlormethiazole edisylate (Hemineurine) superior to chlordiazepoxide (Librium) and chlorphenoxate HCl (Lucidril) [*Schweiz. Med. Wochschr.* **97,** 1283 (1967)]. See also "Moonshïne," p. 407; "Scrap Iron," p. 407; "White Lightning," p. 407; "Disulfiram," p. 230; C. D. Leake and M. Silverman, "Alcoholic Beverages in Clinical Medicine," Year Book Medical Publishers, 1966; and American Medical Association, "Manual on Alcoholism," 535 N. Dearborn St., Chicago, 60610, Ill.

ETHYL BROMIDE (Bromoethane; Monobromoethane; Bromic or Hydrobromic Ether)

This compound was formerly used as an anesthetic but was abandoned because of its narrow margin of safety. Exposure to a high concentration may cause pulmonary irritation and narcosis.

Treatment: In case of inhalation, remove victim from the contaminated atmosphere. Give artificial respiration and oxygen if necessary. For accidental ingestion, induce vomiting; follow with gastric lavage and symptomatic treatment.

ETHYL CHLORIDE (Chloroethane; Monochlorethane; Chlorethyl; Aethylis Chloridum; Ether Chloratus; Ether Hydrochloric; Ether Muriatic; Kelene; Chelen; Anodynon; Chloryl Anesthetic; Narcotile)

This is a highly volatile flammable gas at room temperature and pressure. It is used as a local anesthetic by freezing the tissue. It should not be sprayed on broken skin. If absorbed it may cause liver injury, ventricular fibrillation, and central nervous system effects (narcosis).

Treatment: Discontinue exposure. Give artificial respiration and oxygen if needed.

ETHYLENEAMINES

Ethyleneamines are compounds with a relatively high order of toxicity, see p. 702. Ethylenediamine, diethylenetriamine, triethylenetetramine, and tetra-ethylenepentamine are slightly viscous water-soluble liquids with a strong ammonia odor. Chemically, they resemble ammonia, with alkaline reactions in water solutions. The vapors also have an unpleasant ammonia odor, and in high concentrations, are painful and irritating to the eyes, nose, throat, and respiratory system. Exposure to vapor concentrations dangerous to life are unlikely to occur because of the warning (irritant) effects of the amine vapors. Vapor concentrations generated at ordinary room temperatures do not present a hazard of serious acute systemic poisoning.

Some of these amines are capable of causing severe skin and eye burns, and precautions to prevent contact are necessary. In addition, human contact has demonstrated that the ethyleneamines have sensitizing properties. It is believed that the lower members of the series are the most active as sensitizers. Sensitization of the skin is common and is easily acquired. Some individuals may develop a hypersensitivity following prolonged or repeated exposure to ethyleneamine vapors or liquid in concentrations well below those which are irritating. This hypersensitivity may manifest itself either as an asthma-like condition or as dermatitis. The threshold limit is 10 ppm. See Table 23, p. 702. Experience has shown that a sensitized individual retains his sensitivity for many years. The sensitized person must generally be transferred to a position where there is no possibility of contact with either liquid ethyleneamines or ethyleneamine vapors. Cross sensitization between members of the series is believed to exist although this has not been proved.

Treatment: In case of skin or eye contact, flood immediately with water for 15 minutes. See Ammonia, Aqueous, p. 95.

ETHYLENE CARBONATE (Dioxolone-2; Glycol Carbonate)

This is an odorless, colorless, noncorrosive, nonhygroscopic solid which has a low acute oral toxicity. Rats survived single doses of 8 gm/kg. The chemical caused essentially no response when applied to rabbit skin, even on repeated prolonged contact. When placed in the rabbit eye, it caused moderate conjunctival irritation and slight transient corneal damage. Tests on inhalation of ethylene carbonate showed no significant toxicity, and patch tests on humans with a 40% aqueous solution showed no instance of skin irritation or skin sensitization.

Treatment: In case of contact with eyes or skin flush immediately with plenty of flowing water.

ETHYLENE CHLOROHYDRIN

Ethylene chlorohydrin (2-chloroethanol-1) is a colorless, mobile aromatic liquid which boils at 128.8°C. It is used in the chemical and textile industries. It may be absorbed through the lungs, the skin, and from the gastrointestinal tract. Exposure to the vapors causes irritation of the mucous membrane of the eyes and nose, nausea and vomiting, giddiness and dizziness, staggering gait and incoordination, numbness of the extremities, and visual disturbances. With more severe exposure there is, in addition, headache, excitement (sometimes passing into delirium), and severe thirst. The pulse becomes soft and thready, and the blood pressure extremely low. There may be profuse perspiration, and the patient may pass into collapse, shock, and coma. He may suffer from spastic contractions of hands and arms and from erythema of the skin of the arms and trunk. Death results from pulmonary edema or from congestion and edema of the brain.

Treatment: Treatment is practically hopeless in severe cases. In subacute poisoning, parenteral administration of hypertonic dextrose solution, cardiac stimulants (caffeine and camphor), and the administration of oxygen (against pressure) have been used successfully. Epinephrine is contraindicated because of the possibility of ventricular fibrillation [W. F. von Oettingen, "Poisoning," Huntington Press, London, 1952].

ETHYLENE DIBROMIDE (1,2-Dibromoethane)

This chemical is used as a soil fumigant for the control of ground pests. It is available in pellet form and is ordinarily dissolved in water for use in the soil. Ethylene dibromide is also used commercially in "leaded" gasoline and as a chemical intermediate.

Liquid and vapor are irritating to skin, eyes, and mucous membranes. Contact of the liquid with tissues may cause erythema, edema, and necrosis, and systemic toxicity due to percutaneous absorption. Inhalation of vapors may produce pulmonary edema. Systemic toxicity is manifested by signs and symptoms of central nervous system depression, and kidney and liver injury. Death may result from respiratory failure and/or pulmonary edema and chemical pneumonitis. The probable lethal oral dose for an adult is 5 ml. Exposure to 10,000 ppm for a few minutes may be dangerous to life.

A 43-year-old white woman ingested 9 capsules of Fumisoil, each containing 0.5 ml of ethylene dibromide. Almost immediately she started to vomit. Twenty-four hours after ingestion of the chemical, watery diarrhea was first noted. Approximately 36 hours after ingestion, there was a decrease in the volume of urine and a darkening in color. By the time of admission to the hospital 48 hours after ingesting the capsules, she was completely anuric. The patient did not improve in spite of supportive therapy. She died 4 hours after admission (54 hours after ingestion of the Fumisoil capsules).

Treatment: In case of inhalation, remove individual from site of exposure and administer artificial respiration and give oxygen if necessary. Observe patient carefully for premonitory signs and symptoms of pulmonary edema. See p. 43. For ingestion, gastric lavage, demulcents and saline cathartics are indicated. For skin and eye contact, wash affected tissues with copious quantities of water for 15 minutes.

ETHYLENE DICHLORIDE (*sym*-Dichloroethane; 1,2-Dichloroethane; Ethylene Chloride; Dutch Liquid; Brocide)

Vapors may produce irritation of mucous membranes, corneal clouding, and central nervous system depression. Deaths due to liver and kidney injury have been reported following ingestion of large amounts. The probable lethal oral dose for an adult is 25 ml. See Table 56, p. 744.

Treatment: For ingestion, prompt induction of vomiting and gastric lavage are indicated. In case of inhalation remove the individual promptly from the contaminated atmosphere and give artificial respiration and oxygen if necessary. Subsequent treatment is supportive and symptomatic.

ETHYLENE GLYCOL ("Permanent" Anti-Freeze; 1,2-Ethanediol)

Ingestion of a toxic dose causes severe abdominal disturbances, malaise, lumbar pain, oliguria, uremia, and central nervous system depression. Death is due to respiratory paralysis and renal failure. The probable lethal oral dose for an adult is 100 ml. It is not hazardous by inhalation or skin contact.

The lethal effects of ethylene glycol in rats and monkeys can be sharply reduced by subsequent administration of ethanol. It appears that protection is dependent on competitive inhibition of the enzymatic oxidation of ethylene glycol thus preventing the formation of metabolic products more toxic than the compound itself. Preliminary studies suggest a similar protection against the toxic effects of other compounds such as chloroethanol and fluoroethanol. The importance of these experiments to the care of patients who have accidentally ingested ethylene glycol is apparent. Early administration of ethanol to patients who have ingested ethylene glycol may prevent its lethal effects by inhibiting oxidation and allowing the compound to be excreted [D. I. Peterson *et al.*, *JAMA* **186**, 956 (1963); W. E. C. Wacker *et al.*, *JAMA* **194**, 1231 (1965)]. See also Glycols, p. 290.

ETHYLENE OXIDE (Epoxyethane; Oxirane; Dimethylene Oxide)

Ethylene oxide is used as an insecticide and sterilant for a wide variety of foodstuffs and medical articles. It is used mainly in vacuum fumigation mixed with varying proportions of carbon dioxide or nonflammable halogenated hydrocarbons, such as dichlordifluoromethane, to provide nonexplosive conditions.

Ethylene oxide is moderately toxic to rats. At a single dose of 0.1 gm/kg all the animals survived. Doses of 0.2 gm/kg killed all the animals. The estimated LC_{50} for 4 hours exposure is approximately 800–1500 ppm (animal studies). The lungs, liver, kidneys, and adrenals show evidence of injury. Repeated exposures to about 100 ppm appear to be safe, but depression of growth in animals and delayed impairment of nervous system functions occur above 200 ppm.

Thirty-seven industrial workers engaged in manufacturing ethylene oxide showed no ill effects at 5–10 ppm levels over an average service of 10 years with an exposure of 8 hours daily. Thiess described the symptoms of 41 cases of ethylene oxide poisoning as follows: after a short exposure, periodic vomiting, irritation of the respiratory passages leading to emphysema, bronchitis, and pulmonary edema. Skin application caused blisters [A. M. Thiess, *Arch. Toxikol.* **20**, 127 (1963)].

Treatment: In case of overexposure by inhalation, remove the victim to an uncontaminated atmosphere. Give artificial respiration if necessary and oxygen. Treat skin burns as thermal burns.

2-ETHYLHEXOIC ACID

This compound has an oral LD_{50} for rats of 3.0 ml/kg, which places it in the same general quantitative toxicity range as acetic acid. Tests on rabbits indicate that it is a minor skin irritant which does not cause skin burns. The liquid causes moderately severe eye injury when instilled in the eyes of rabbits. A single exposure to vapors does not present a hazard since rats exposed to concentrated vapors for 8 hours survived. It is moderately toxic by absorption through the skin.

Treatment: In case of accidental eye contact, the eyes should be flushed with large volumes of water for 15 minutes. Remove from the skin with water.

N-ETHYL-3-PIPERIDYL BENZILATE (JB-318)

This is a very potent hallucinogenic drug. See *d*-Lysergic Acid Diethylamide, p. 356.

ETHYLSULFONYLETHANOL (ESE)

Ethylsulfonylethanol is about half as toxic as ethylene glycol. The rat oral LD_{50} is 18.0 gm/kg. The mouse intraperitoneal MLD is 10.0 gm/kg and the oral MLD is 14.0 gm/kg. No evidence of skin irritancy was found in tests on rabbits.

ESE has been used as a "booster" for isoniazid in the treatment of tuberculosis. Results were satisfactory at an ESE dosage level of 1.5–3 gm per day per patient with no undesirable side effects reported.

Treatment: For accidental ingestion of large doses empty the stomach by inducing vomiting.

ETRYPTAMINE (Monase)

This drug was withdrawn from the market because it has caused agranulocytosis and death.

EUROPIUM CHLORIDE

The symptoms of acute toxicity in mice are arched back, writhing, ataxia, lachrymation, stretching of the hind limbs on walking, and labored and depressed respiration. The intraperitoneal and oral LD_{50}s are 0.55 gm/kg and 5.0 gm/kg, respectively. Feeding various levels of the chemical for 12 weeks produced no effect on growth, the hemogram, or any internal organs. Transient ocular irritation with no permanent ocular damage was observed, but abraded skin showed extensive scar formation. Permanent nodule formation resulted from intradermal injection. Progressive depression was observed, and death was the result of cardiovascular collapse coupled with respiratory paralysis. Neither atropinization nor epinephrine injections could counteract the lethal effects [T. J. Haley *et al.*, *J. Pharm. Sci.* **54**, 643 (1965)].

FARMERS' LUNG

This pulmonary disability among agricultural workers handling moldy hay was first described as a clinical entity in 1932. Farmers' lung develops insidiously. An attack of farmers' lung develops several hours after the handling of moldy hay, in contrast with asthma which develops within minutes of exposure. Acute attacks are characterized by shortness of breath, fever, malaise and unproductive cough. If there is no further exposure, rapid and complete recovery will follow. If exposure is continued, headache, loss of appetite, severe dyspnea, and cyanosis may occur. Radiological examination of the lungs may show a fine mottling, usually more marked in the lower lung fields. If the disease progresses to the chronic stage, with the production of fine interstitial fibrosis frequently accompanied by a honeycomb type of bronchiectasis, then recovery cannot be expected. For more complete information the reader is referred to the reviews by J. Watkins-Pitchford [*Brit. J. Ind. Med.* **23**, 16 (1966)].

Treatment: Removal from the site of exposure is most important. Depending on the severity of the disease, rest and the inhalation of oxygen may be indicated.

FAT

Diets high in fat content will increase the rate of absorption and hence the toxicity of many compounds readily soluble in fats or oils. For this reason, oily cathartics should be given only when clearly indicated.

Fat embolism may be of endogenous or exogenous origin. The endogenous type occurs when fat which originates within the body forms emboli in the cardiovascular system. Exogenous fat embolism may occur when an oily liquid is introduced into the circulation. Two of 5 patients receiving 9 or more liters of a fat emulsion intravenously over periods of 3–9 weeks developed the "fat overloading syndrome" (high fever, rigor, headache, sore throat, anorexia, malaise, cough, confusion, lethargy, irritability, insomnia, thrombocytopenia, anemia) [*Arch. Internal Med.* **107**, 514 (1961)].

Although cholesterol has been blamed for clogging arteries and causing coronary heart disease, triglycerides are the principal form of fat we eat. An average person may eat 100 gm of triclycerides a day, but, by comparison, only half a gram of cholesterol. Recent research has pointed more and more to other fats besides cholesterol as being responsible for clogged arteries. Future studies should resolve the question of whether elevated levels of cholesterol or triglycerides best correlate with ischemic heart disease [*Sci. News* **85**, 40 (1964)].

Treatment: For endogenous fat embolism; oxygen, sedation, and the treatment of shock and circulatory collapse are recommended. Alcohol given prophylactically to patients with fractures reduced the incidence of fat embolism [*JAMA* **178**, 1187 (1961)]. For lowering the blood triglyceride level, see Clofibrate, p. 180.

FERBAM (Fermate; Ferric Dimethyl Dithiocarbamate)

This compound has a low order of toxicity. No cases of human intoxication have been reported. Local irritation may result from contact with eyes, mucous membranes, and skin. Because of its chemical similarity to Antabuse, absorption of Ferbam may potentiate the action of ethyl alcohol. See Thiocarbamates, p. 585.

Treatment: For ingestion of large dose, induce vomiting and follow with gastric lavage.

FERROCYANIDES AND FERRICYANIDES

These salts have a low order of toxicity. Cyanide ion is not formed because it is bound in the ferro- or ferricyanide complex ion. Sodium ferrocyanide (0.5 gm in 10 ml of water) has been injected I.V. to test glomerular function in man. Prussian blue is ferriferrocyanide and Turnbull's blue is ferroferricyanide.

Treatment: None is required except for ingestion of a huge dose in which case the stomach should be emptied by inducing vomiting.

FIBER GLASS (Glass Fiber; Fibrous Glass)

Fiber glass, like all common forms of glass, is a chemically inert substance. It possesses no known toxic properties, although spicules may abrade the skin leading to superficial and transitory irritation. Among fiber glass makers, particularly new workers who are most exposed, skin irritation may occur. Although free silica is a major primary ingredient of the glass batch before melting, no free silica occurs in the glass fibers or in the ultimate products. Silicosis is not a fiber glass hazard. The present consensus is that, because of the particle size, fiber glass is not respirable, and thus is unlikely to reach the tissues of the upper respiratory tract. In animal experiments the introduction of fiber glass particles into the respiratory tract has failed to produce pneumoconiosis. However, some minor tissue changes have been observed, chiefly reflecting a foreign body reaction. No clinical cases of lung cancer have been traced to fiber glass as the source [Ahmed, A.N.M. Nasr, *J. Occupational Med.* **9**, 345 (1967)].

Workers handling glass fiber for the first time often experience skin discomfort and irritation, which is usually temporary, and which disappears when they become "hardened" to the action of the fibers. A number of operators have complained of a typical fiber glass itch and occasionally a fine papular rash in the exposed skin-fold areas, in addition to sneezing, dry throat, and irritation of the facial skin. Clothing contaminated with fiber glass particles produces severe itching with a marked prickling sensation within a few minutes after contact with the skin. Erythema and scratch marks may be present in affected areas. The condition clears rapidly with thorough bathing and the replacement of all affected clothing, towels, and bed linen [*Arch. Dermatol.* **93**, 78 (1966)].

FINGERNAIL-HARDENING PREPARATIONS

Formaldehyde has been known to cause discoloration, pain, dryness, loosening, and even bleeding under the nail, as well as loss of nails. The cuticle and surrounding skin have also been involved. Reactions may persist for weeks or months.

Treatment: Discontinue use.

FIORINAL

Fiorinal is a sedative-analgesic preparation promoted as "the most widely prescribed drug for tension headache." Each tablet or capsule contains butalbital (50 mg), aspirin (200 mg), phenacetin (130 mg), and caffeine (40 mg). The same combination of drugs is also available with varying amounts of codeine (7.5, 15, and 30 mg) as Fiorinal-C for the relief of other painful disorders. Other preparations with similar formulas include Acetabar, Cephalgesic, P-A-C with Cyclopal and Dolor-Plus.

Although Fiorinal has been used for several decades, there is no convincing evidence that the combination of aspirin, phenacetin, and caffeine has greater analgesic effectiveness or fewer side effects than aspirin alone. The ability of sedative doses of barbiturates to potentiate the analgesic effect of aspirin or A.P.C. is not proven [*Med. Letter* **9**, 37 (1967)].

FIRE SALTS

These salts are used to produce multicolored flames on the yule log. The colors result from burning salts of copper, barium, selenium, lead, thallium, arsenic, and antimony. They can cause heavy metal poisoning if swallowed. Gastric irritation usually is severe enough to produce vomiting.

Treatment: See Copper, p. 185.

FISH (Ichthyosarcotoxism)

Ichthyosarcotoxism, or fish poisoning, refers to intoxications resulting from the ingestion of fish that contain toxins of nonbacterial origin. "Toxic" fish (except for the puffer) are usually found in inshore waters in narrow geographical ranges seldom more than a few miles out along coral reefs of islands or along shores in subtropical or tropical waters of the world. Their toxicity fluctuates widely from year to year and from species to species. According to A. H. Banner, unlike reef fish "fish from the high seas, like tuna and mahimahi, are not known to cause the disease, and it is seldom caused by the bottom detrital feeders, like the mullet [*Hawaii Med. J.* **24**, 353 (1965)]."

Puffer Poisoning: Puffer fish, or balloon fish, spiny puffers, and sharp-backed puffers are considered toxic wherever they are found, although specific and seasonal variations are numerous. In most species, the liver and ovary are the most highly toxic, with concentrations of water-soluble toxins (tetrodotoxins) ranging from 100 to 1000 times the amounts present in the flesh. The concentration of toxin in the skin or intestines lies between that of liver and muscles (A. H. Banner, 1967). In Japan, the puffer is esteemed as a gourmet delicacy. It is prepared by licensed fugu handlers who carefully remove the toxic viscera and skin. Since many Chinese and Japanese who are not experienced in the art of puffer-preparation catch and eat these fish, intoxications are frequent. As a result, the puffer presents the greatest single cause of food poisoning in China and Japan. The mortality rate following an acute intoxication is about 60% [Kwan-Ming Li, *Far East Med. J.* **1**, 29 (1965)].

Signs and symptoms of poisoning usually appear within hours after ingestion of "toxic" parts of the fish. Depending upon the severity of an intoxication, some or all of the following effects may be produced: tingling of the lips, tongue, and fingertips, followed by progression of numbness and muscular weakness which may involve the entire body together with nausea, headache, vomiting, profuse sweating, hypothermia, and dyspnea. There may be clonic convulsions. Frequently, the patient rapidly develops a weak, rapid pulse, marked dyspnea, and cyanosis. Death may result from respiratory failure.

Treatment: Institute without delay prompt and vigorous removal of gastroenteric contents followed by a saline cathartic. Artificial respiration has been life saving. No specific antidote is known. Symptomatic treatment, including the administration of central nervous system stimulants, has been effective in some people.

Ciguatera Poisoning: The term ciguatera was introduced by the early Spanish settlers of Cuba to mean intoxications resulting from ingestion of the marine snail, "cigua." Gradually this term expanded to include intoxications caused by ingestion of mollusk and fish caught in Caribbean waters. Today, "ciguatera" is widely accepted as descriptive of the particular type of poisoning by fish caught around coral reefs of the tropics.

Ciguatera poisoning appears to present the most serious fish poisoning problem in the Pacific, but it is also found in the Caribbean. The fish involved include snapper, grouper, marine eel, pompano, jack, reef shark, barracuda, surgeonfish, and occasionally others. A toxin (ciguatoxin) was isolated by P. J. Scheuer, characterized by A. H. Banner as the "principal toxin," and recognized by Li as a potent anticholinesterase [quoted from A. H. Banner, *J. Forensic Sci.* **12**, 180 (1967)].

Symptoms of an intoxication, which may be quite varied, usually appear 2–3 hours after ingestion of "toxic" fish, but occasionally as late as 30 hours. In some patients, the signs and symptoms have been similar to, but not typical of, those induced by organic phosphate pesticides. The following are among the effects that have been noted: nausea and vomiting, followed by tingling and numbness about the lips, tongue, throat, and fingertips, followed by abdominal cramps, diarrhea, arthralgia, muscular weakness, incoordination, numbness and tingling of the extremities, chills, low-grade fever, prostration, hypotension, profuse perspiration, restlessness, marked dyspnea, dizziness, constriction or dilatation of the pupils, ptosis, reduced vision, a metallic taste and dryness of the mouth, and urinary retention. Some patients experience a confusion of temperature sensation; cold objects appear hot and hot objects feel cold. Pruritus, generalized or localized in the palms of the hands and soles of the feet, has also been reported. In severe cases of ciguatera poisoning, shock, convulsions, muscular paralysis, and death have resulted. Most of the gastroenteric effects subside in 24–36 hours, but muscular weakness, tingling, and numbness may last for one or more weeks. Complete recovery, in a severe case, may take months. During the recovery phase, some patients have reported a vague mandibular neuralgic pain, giving the sensation that their teeth were falling out. An attack of ciguatera does not produce immunity; rather, it will render the patient more susceptible to a similar intoxication in later years [A. H. Banner *et. al.*, "Fish Intoxication," Technical Paper No. 141, South Pacific Commission. Noumea, New Caledonia, 1963]. During an outbreak of moray eel poisoning in Saipan, several patients, after recovery from acute effects, suffered from alopecia, foot drop, tongue deviation, and atrophy, as well as an ulnar palsy [C. T. Khlentzos, cited by Li, *Hawaii Med. J.* **24**, 353 (1965)].

Since ciguatoxin is found in a wide variety of fish throughout the Pacific and Caribbean, it appears reasonable to assume that there are variations in the composition of this toxin, with the production of effects which are not necessarily related to cholinesterase inhibition. This is supported by P. J. Scheuer *et al.* who found that ciguatoxin is not a phosphatidic ester, but rather a lipid containing a quaternary nitrogen atom, one or more hydroxyl groups, and a cyclopentanone moiety [*Science* **155**, 1267 (1967)].

Treatment: Immediate treatment may require artificial respiration and oxygen and evacuation of gastroenteric contents. *If* signs and symptoms of excessive parasympathetic stimulation predominate, atropine is the drug of choice. In this case, administration of this drug may be followed by the I.V. injection of 1 gm of pralidoxime chloride (Protopam chloride), or 1 gm of 2-PAM (pyridine aldoxime methochloride). Pralidoxime or 2-PAM, if used, *must be administered within the first few hours of the intoxication.* See 2-PAM, p. 448. The I.V. injection of 5-10 ml of 25% magnesium sulfate may be used to control nicotinic effects such as fasciculations and tremors, but it must be remembered that this drug is likely to make muscular weakness more severe and produce vasodilation and central nervous system depression. Calcium should be available for I.V. dosing to counteract the effects of magnesium. (The use of *d*-tubocurarine is not recommended). Methylphenidate (Ritalin) was used effectively by Okihiro for combatting coma. As is common in intoxications by organic phosphates, some patients suffering from ciguatera tolerate high doses of atropine. A patient treated by M. M. Okihiro *et al.* received 33.6 mg of atropine and 20.25 gm of magnesium sulfate [*Hawaii Med. J.* **24**, 353 (1965)]. Subsequent treatment is symptomatic and may include 10 % calcium gluconate I.V. and fluid therapy.

Clupeoid Poisoning is not widespread. It is caused by ingestion of a variety of tropical sardines (clupeoid fish) found primarily in the Far East waters. Symptoms include nausea, vertigo, abdominal pain, tachycardia, dyspnea, cyanosis, mydriasis, coma, convulsions, and, at times, death within 30 minutes after ingestion. Nothing is known of the nature of the toxin [Kwan-Ming Li, *Far East Med. J.* **1**, 29 (1965)]. Treatment is symptomatic.

Scombroid Poisoning appears to be an allergic type of intoxication, resulting from ingestion of improperly stored tuna and mackeral-like fish. The toxin, or toxins, (histamine-like) causing this type of poisoning are produced by certain strains of bacteria such as *Proteus morganii.* Symptoms usually develop within a few minutes to several hours after ingestion and include erythema of the face, neck, and chest, severe headache, giant urticaria, conjunctivitis, edema of the lips, tongue, and throat, respiratory distress, tachycardia, abdominal pain, and generalized weakness. The acute symptoms usually persist for 8–12 hours, after which the patient experiences a rapid recovery. Few fatalities have been reported.

Treatment: Immediately empty the stomach, then administer antihistaminic drugs [Halstead, (1957), quoted by Li, *Far East Med. J.* **1**, 29 (1965)].

Mullet Poisoning: Mullet, surmullet, or goatfish poisoning has been experienced in specific areas of some Pacific islands, but only during the months of June, July, and August. Symptoms usually persist for a few hours, occasionally up to 24 hours. These include dizziness, loss of equilibrium, lack of coordination, and mental depression. Symptoms, which may begin while the patient is sleeping, include terrifying nightmares and hallucinations [Helfrich (1963), quoted by Li, *Far East Med. J.* **1**, 29 (1965)]. No fatalities have been reported. Poisonings from mullet have been reported only in Hawaii and Norfolk Island.

General Considerations in the Treatment of Fish Poisoning

The tetrodotoxin of the puffer is water soluble, but the toxin causing ciguatera cannot be leeched from the flesh by water. Further, neither cooking nor long periods of refrigeration destroy it. While the concentration of the ciguatoxin may be 50 times greater in the viscera than in the flesh, the concentration in the latter may be sufficiently high to cause coma and death. After fish are caught, they should be kept cool to reduce the chance of scombroid poisoning. Degutting may be expected to reduce the passing of the ciguatoxin from viscera to flesh; obviously this will not influence the toxin already in the flesh. Do not keep or trail live or dead fish in the water. There is no method of recognizing fish that are toxic on ingestion (except by animal feeding studies).

People traveling through tropical islands should avoid eating the viscera even though the fish are considered safe. Where reliable local knowledge is not available, almost all reef fish should be avoided [A. H. Banner, *Hawaii Med. J.* **24**, 353 (1965)].

There may be more than one toxin causing the disease loosely known as "ciguatera," and the barracuda may have a toxin quite dissimilar in pharmacological action to that of the snapper, eel, or other fish [A. H. Banner, University of Hawaii, personal communication (1967)]. *Therefore, the symptoms will indicate whether atropine* (and 2-PAM or Protopam) *should be considered for treatment.* If atropine is used, consideration must be given to the nicotinic effects of excessive parasympathetic stimulation, since these are not antagonized by this drug. The prognosis is favorable if evacuation of the stomach by repeated vomiting or gastric lavage and the administration of a saline cathartic are instituted early. Phenothiazine-type tranquilizers, opiates, and succinylcholine are contraindicated in patients who demonstrate signs and symptoms of excessive parasympathetic stimulation.

FISH STINGS

Catfish, toadfish, surgeon fish, scorpion or stone fish,

ratfish, and rabbit fish are equipped with several sharp spines. Some of these species have spines equipped with rows of sharp teeth that are capable of producing severe lacerations, promoting the absorption of venom. Deaths from the stings of some tropical fish have been reported.

Sharp local pain is the immediate reaction to a fish sting. Redness, local anemia, inflammation, swelling, and hemorrhages usually follow. In severe cases, painful abdominal and muscular cramps, loss of speech, constriction of the throat, marked hypotension, delirium and general muscular paralysis, loss of consciousness, convulsions, respiratory difficulties, and death may follow.

Treatment: Wash the area promptly with sea water. This will tend to remove some of the poison. Soak the injured part in *hot* water for 30–90 minutes. For details, see Stingray Injuries, p. 554.

FLOXURIDINE (FUDR)

There is no agreement on the value of this drug in the I.V. treatment of cancer of the colon or its therapeutic advantage over fluorouracil (5-FU). Among the side effects, leukopenia was reported by one group in 33% of patients, by another group in 65% of patients. According to C. G. Moertel *et al.* the difference in toxicity parallels the difference in the therapeutic effect. This indicates that in the first group an inadequate floxuridine dosage was given, which may account for a low regression rate [*JAMA* **201**, 780 (1967)].

FLUBBER

Flubber is composed of partially polymerized butadiene and mineral oil in a proportion of 70:30. There are minor amounts of polymerization catalysts, antioxidants, and stoppers reported to be present. This product is easily moldable into any shape, and because of its resilience is also used as a bouncing toy.

On May 17, 1963, the manufacturers recalled this product as well as "Roobly Rubber" and "Plubber." At the time of this withdrawal the Food and Drug Administration had accumulated over 1600 reported cases of irritant rashes from Flubber. The rash was described as papular, red, discrete and itching, with some deep-seated vesiculation present on the pad of the hand. In a few cases the rash was present on the forehead and the face, and in one case on the abdomen. All the children affected gave a history of contact with "flubber" for one to several days prior to the appearance of the rash.

FLUORESCENT TUBES

The major manufacturers of fluorescent lighting tubes no longer use beryllium. The following compounds are used today: zinc silicate, calcium lead tungstate, calcium lead manganese silicate, and calcium lead silicate, with an occasional use of magnesium arsenate or a salt of antimony. See p. 108, 350, 530, and 638.

FLUORIDES

Soluble fluorides are rapidly absorbed from the gastrointestinal tract. Insoluble fluorides, when ingested, are slowly and incompletely absorbed. Complexing elements (e.g., calcium, aluminum) retard absorption. Fluoride (absorbed only as the fluoride ion) is rapidly distributed throughout the extracellular body water in a pattern essentially similar to that of chloride. The principal distribution pattern is simple: part goes to bone, the remainder is soon excreted via the kidney. The fluoride concentrations in tissues other than bone and kidney tend to follow blood concentrations but at a lower level, e.g. saliva, milk, fetal blood. Fluoride is a bone seeker; in an unexposed individual up to half of an absorbed dose is rapidly deposited. The larger the daily fluoride intake, the higher the ultimate bone concentration, but not proportionately.

Tooth tissues contain more fluoride, depending on the concentration in drinking water. Surface enamel is rich in fluoride and may also fix some fluoride in the immediate post-eruptive period. Dentine and cementum compare with bone. Fluoride enters bone and tooth mineral by exchange with hydroxyl ions in the hydroxylapatite lattice. Topical applications of concentrated fluoride solutions produce in addition superficial and temporary calcium fluoride deposits. Soft tissue does not store fluoride, while skeletal fluoride is slowly mobilized by haversian reworking.

Fluorides are rapidly excreted principally via the urine, e.g. in 3 hours, $1/7$-$1/4$ of an oral dose of a few milligrams in man. The higher the intake of soluble fluoride, the higher the urinary concentration. The renal mechanism depends on a less efficient (92%) resorption than is usual for chlorides (greater than 99%). Fecal excretion accounts for a small fraction of that absorbed. Excretion in sweat also accounts for a small fraction (more during excessive sweating).

Dental Caries and Fluoridated Water: There is overwhelming evidence that fluoridation of drinking water is both safe and effective. As to the method of administration, communal fluoridation offers optimal benefit (about 1.7 times more cariostasis than with topical fluorides), since it not only reduces incidence of caries approximately 60%, but also lessens its severity. Furthermore, the therapeutic effect of fluoridation is maintained throughout adulthood. In children, the topical use of 2% sodium fluoride, 8% stannous fluoride, or acidulated phosphate-fluoride, or lozenges, chewing gum, or dentifrices, or ingestion of tablets of 1 mg of sodium fluoride, will not duplicate the caries-inhibiting effect of drinking fluoridated water and therefore have limited benefits. Topical fluoride treatment has demonstrated an appreciable caries-inhibiting effect in adults, but, since the rate of caries activity decreases considerably after adolescence, adults should concentrate on good oral hygiene rather than depend on the minimal effects of fluoride, except in extenuating cases.

In areas of nonfluoridated water, extra-dietary fluorides (adjusted to 1 mg of sodium fluoride) may be prescribed postnatally or just prior to tooth eruption in solution, in the form of pediatric drops, or as a lozenge to be sucked, so that it will react with the enamel surface by reducing enamel solubility and will supplement any effect conferred during odontogeny [P. P. Dale, *JAMA* **188**, 92 (1964)].

Some individuals will show undesirable effects with doses below those listed above. The following case history is of interest, even though conclusive evidence has not been presented that sodium fluoride was responsible for the eye effects. A 58-year-old man suffering from spinal osteoporosis developed bilateral optic neuritis after receiving 60 mg sodium fluoride daily for 6 weeks. The right eye was primarily involved, with vision limited to perception of hand movements in the

TOXICITY OF FLUORIDES

Toxicity	Amount of fluoride (F, not NaF)	Dose	Period of administration	Effect
Acute toxicity	2.5 gm or more	Single	2–4 hours	Death
Chronic toxicity				
High grade	20–80 mg or more	Daily	10–20 years	Crippling fluorosis
Low grade	2–8 mg or more	Daily	First 8 years of life	Mottled enamel of teeth
Public health	1 ± ppm[a]	Daily	First 8 years and later	Reduction in dental caries
Kidney changes	±100 ppm	Daily	Months	Dilated tubules; necrosis
Thyroid changes	±50 ppm	Daily	Years	Altered structure or function
Growth retardation	40 ppm (cow)	Daily	Years	Loss of weight

[a] 1 ppm in temperate zone [mean annual temperature 10°C (50°F)]; 0.7 ppm in warm zone [mean annual temperature 21°C (70°F)]

upper temporal periphery of the visual field. Discontinuation of fluoride therapy and administration of prednisone resulted in recovery of the left eye, but the changes in the right eye progressed to optic atrophy. [Geall and Beilin, *British Med. J.* **2**, 355 (1964)].

Treatment: In case of ingestion of an overdose, follow promptly with gastric lavage with lime water or 1% calcium chloride solution. Combat falling blood pressure by intravenous infusion of glucose in isotonic saline. Supply calcium as 10 ml intravenous 10% calcium gluconate solution, this to be repeated in 1 hour or when tetany appears. Support respiration. Prevent chilling. Diuresis increases fluoride excretion (Harold Hodge, personal communication).

FLUORINE

This is the most reactive chemical element known. It has a sharp, penetrating, characteristic odor. In man, at concentrations up to 25 ppm there is very little irritation, but at 100 ppm irritation is marked. The inhalation of "flood" concentrations of fluorine causes asphyxia due to laryngeal and bronchiole spasm and later by bronchiole obstruction and pulmonary edema. The bronchiole obstruction is due to mucous membrane swelling and the secretion of tenacious mucus. Exposure to high concentrations of fluorine is accompanied by gastroenteric symptoms which are secondary in importance to the lung damage, since survival depends on adequate oxygenation of the blood.

A blast of fluorine on the exposed skin or mucous membranes produces a thermal-type burn (similar to that caused by an oxyacetylene flame) by the heat of reaction with the skin and water in the air. Lower concentrations of fluorine on the skin produce chemical-type burns closely resembling those produced by hydrogen fluoride.

After inhalation of gaseous fluorine for 5–60 minutes by experimental animals, the LD_{50} ranges from 150 to 800 ppm. High concentrations cause marked irritation of the eyes and respiratory tract and damage to the lungs, liver and kidneys. The effects of 4 repeated exposures, 1 week apart, are no more severe, and in some instances less severe, than a single exposure to the same concentration [*Am. Ind. Hyg. Assoc. J.* **29,** 10 (1968)].

Treatment: See Hydrofluoric Acid, p. 317.

FLUOROACETATE

Fluoracetate is present in the leaves of *Dichapetalum cynosum* (Gifblaar) and in other species of this genus indigenous to Africa. The toxic dose varies from 0.05 mg/kg for the dog and 5.0 mg/kg for the rat to 500 mg/kg for the toad. Among farm animals, sheep are usually killed with 0.4 mg/kg and rabbits with 0.5 mg/kg. Signs of toxicity differ; the main site of attack is either the central nervous system or the heart. In some animals, such as the dog, central nervous signs predominate, whereas in the sheep and rabbit the main effects are on the heart. There is always a delay in the appearance of toxic signs; in the rat this will vary from about 20 to 40 minutes, when the animal may suddenly have a tonic convulsion resembling that of strychnine. Rabbits or sheep may die of a sudden heart attack.

Fluoroacetate is toxic because it deceives the "condensing enzyme," so that fluoroacetyl-CoA is condensed with oxalacetate to form monofluorocitrate. The latter blocks the enzyme aconitase; hence metabolism of acetyl-CoA (representing the C_2 fragments coming from the pathways of carbohydrate and fat metabolism) is blocked at the citrate stage, causing accumulation of citrate. This occurs *in vivo* and also *in vitro.*

FLUOROACETAMIDE

Fluoroacetamide has about one third the toxicity of fluoroacetate. A small child died after swallowing some fluoroacetamide from a bottle. After a fatal dose (5mg/kg), it may be several hours before symptoms appear. Nausea and apprehension precede muscular twitching, coma, and convulsions. Death finally results from respiratory or cardiac failure. The substance is rapidly excreted in the urine. Chronic poisoning has not been reported.

Treatment: After the stomach has been emptied, treatment is largely symptomatic. A number of substances — acetates, ethyl alcohol, monoacetin, and acetamide — have been found to exert a protective action in laboratory animals, but their clinical value as antidotes is unproven.

FLUOROALCOHOLS, ALIPHATIC

These chemicals are oxidized *in vivo* to fluorocarboxylic acids, which are degraded to fluoroacetic acid (highly toxic) or to nontoxic 3-fluoropropionic acid or its nontoxic metabolites. Compounds with an even number of carbon atoms are highly toxic, whereas those with odd numbers have a relatively low order of toxicity. See Table 36, p. 725 and Table 37, p. 725. For signs and symptoms of toxicity see Sodium Fluoroacetate, p. 542.

FLUOROALKYLAMINES

These are converted *in vivo* to the aldehydes and then to the corresponding carboxylic acid. Consequently, toxicity is similar to the corresponding carboxylic acid depending on even or odd number of carbon atoms in the molecule. See Fluorocarboxylic Acids.

FLUOROCARBONS (Fluorohydrocarbons)

The fluoroalkanes have a low order of toxicity particularly when all the halogens in the molecule are fluorine atoms (perfluoralkanes, C_nF_{2n+2}). Some polyfluoroalkenes (tetrafluoroethylene, $CF_2{=}CF_2$), perfluoroalkenes (perfluoroisobutylene $(CF_3)_2C{=}CF_2$), and perfluoropropylene ($CF_3CF{=}CF_2$) may cause delayed pulmonary edema following exposure to vapors. *Perfluoroisobutylene is ten times more toxic than phosgene.* See p. 471.

Treatment: Remove victim from the contaminated atmosphere and observe for premonitory signs of delayed pulmonary edema. Subsequent treatment is symptomatic and supportive.

FLUOROCARBOXYLIC ACIDS

The fluorocarboxylic acids, $F(CH_2)_nCOOH$, are extremely toxic when n is odd; nontoxic when n is even. See Sodium Fluoroacetate, and p. 542.

FLUOROLUBES AND FLUOROLUBE GR GREASES

These are addition polymers of trifluorovinyl chloride. They have a very low order of toxicity. Pyrolysis products may be toxic. See Fluoropolymers p. 276.

FLUOROPOLYMERS (Teflon; Kel-F)

These macromolecules are pharmacologically inert. Teflons and Kel-F resins are nontoxic when ingested, nonirritating to skin, and nonsensitizing. No fibrotic reaction results from implantation into the peritoneal cavity.

Human exposure to Teflon pyrolysis products causes a syndrome similar clinically to "metal fume fever" (see Metal Fumes), known also as "polymer fume fever." No deaths have resulted from exposure to the thermal decomposition or combustion products of the Teflon resins.

Teflon-coated frying pans present no greater health hazard than the ordinary cooking oils used in metal cooking utensils.

FLUOROSULFUR AND FLUOROCARBON SULFUR COMPOUNDS

Sulfur hexafluoride (SF_6) is pharmacologically inert. Sulfur Decafluoride (S_2F_{10}) and tetrafluoride (SF_4) are highly irritating to the respiratory tract. Sulfur-containing fluorocarbons vary in their inhalation toxicity depending on structure. See p. 728.

FLUOROTHYL (Indoklon)

This drug, which is administered by inhalation, is used to induce convulsions in the treatment of psychiatric illnesses.

Side effects include those commonly seen after the administration of convulsants. The drug is contraindicated in patients suffering from cardiovascular diseases, pregnancy, elevated intracranial pressure, uncontrolled glaucoma, fever, and bone diseases.

Caution: Measures for resuscitation should be available when this drug is used. This is a new drug, not yet fully evaluated [*JAMA* **196**, 29 (1966)].

5-FLUOROURACIL (5-FU)

This antineoplastic drug usually administered I.V. and intra-arterially, is occasionally given by mouth.

I.V. doses are 15 mg/kg or up to 1.0 gm daily for 3 days, followed by 7.5 mg/kg every second day. Dosages in excess of these can be expected to induce severe, sometimes fatal, intoxications. A recent publication calls attention to the usefulness of the topical application of 5-FU for the treatment of basal-cell and squamous skin cancers [*Sci. News* **91**, 181 (1967)].

Caution: 5-FU treatment should be discontinued abruptly as signs or symptoms of toxicity become apparent. If this is not done, serious toxic effects will occur during the following 10–14 days. These may include soreness of the mouth, oral ulcerations, diarrhea, and leukopenia or thrombocytopenia. Continuation of 5-FU therapy will result in severe and extensive oral ulcerations, diarrhea, depression of the bone marrow, and sometimes alopecia and an increased sensitivity to infection.

The dosages should be reduced in debilitated patients and in patients who previously received treatment with an alkylating agent or radiotherapy.

Treatment: Discontinuation of 5-FU therapy will cause remission of most of the side effects in approximately 6–10 days. Recovery from platelet depression and stomatitis is likely to be more rapid than from leukopenia and diarrhea [C. L. Khung *et al., Clin. Pharmacol. Therap.* **7**, 527 (1966)].

FLUPHENAZINE (Permitil; Prolixin)

On a weight basis, this drug is the most potent member of the piperazine group of phenothiazines. Side effects, signs of toxicity, and contraindications are similar to those reported for chlorpromazine and prochlorperazine. All phenothiazine "tranquilizers" show a high incidence of side effects, but extrapyramidal reactions are most likely to occur with fluphenazine and others in the piperazine group (perphenazine, trifluoperazine, prochlorperazine, thiopropazate (Dartal), and carphenazine (Proketazine). Even with the small doses used in minor disorders, the phenothiazines may cause dystonic reactions, uncontrollable restlessness, the Parkinson syndrome, muscular twitching, orthostatic hypotension, and autonomic effects including dry mouth and blurred vision [*Med. Letter* **6**, 99 (1964).

Contraindications and treatment: See Chlorpromazine, p. 464, and Phenothiazines, p. 171.

FLUROXENE (Fluoromar)

This pleasant-smelling, moderately potent inhalation anesthetic has explosive and flammable limits close to the concentrations used in general anesthesia. The drug is less of a depressant to the cardiorespiratory system than halothane. It is relatively nonhepatoxic except in the presence of hypercapnia or in prolonged and severe hypotension.

Caution: There is a slight danger of severe arrhythmias if epinephrine is used. Bleeding time may be prolonged for a few hours. The coagulation time is not altered [A. B. Dobkin and J. Po-Giok Su, *Clin. Pharmacol. Therap.* **7**, 648 (1966)].

FOLIC ACID

Folic acid is used to treat folic acid deficiency. Doses several times in excess of therapeutic doses have not induced signs or symptoms of toxicity.

Folic acid masks the symptoms of pernicious anemia, thereby interfering with the diagnosis, aggravating the disease, and/or precipitating neurologic symptoms.

FORMALDEHYDE (Formalin)

Inhalation of vapors may result in severe irritation and edema of the upper respiratory tract, burning and stinging of the eyes, and headache. The effects are noted particularly during periods of warm weather. Symptoms of bronchial asthma may be due to an allergic response to formaldehyde.

Some phenolformaldehyde resins are potent sensitizers. Retention of some of the material on a worker's clothing has been sufficient to sensitize his entire family. Direct skin contact causes irritation, dermatitis, discoloration, and possibly necrosis, depending on the degree of exposure. Ingestion will induce severe gastroenteric changes and distress. The probable lethal oral dose for an adult is 60 ml.

Treatment: Remove from the skin with soap and water. Following ingestion, induce vomiting or perform gastric lavage with water or with 1% ammonium carbonate or 0.5% ammonium hydroxide; administer demulcents and emollients. Rest and inhalation of oxygen are most important after inhalation exposure. Keep under observation for premonitory signs and symptoms of pulmonary edema. See Pulmonary Edema, p. 43.

FORMAMIDE

This compound has a low order of toxicity (rat oral LD_{50} is 7.5 gm/kg). It is relatively nontoxic by skin absorption.

FORMIC ACID (Formylic Acid; Methanoic Acid)

Formic acid is irritating to mucous membranes. Irritation of the eyes, nose, throat, and upper respiratory tract is accompanied by lacrimation, nasal discharge, discomfort of the throat, and coughing. Skin contact with a concentrated solution causes severe skin irritation and blistering.

Treatment: See Acetic Acid, p. 63.

FOXGLOVE (Digitalis purpurea)

The primary active principles in foxglove and several other plants [lily-of-the-valley (*Convallaria majalis*), oleander (*Nerium oleander*), sweet-scented oleander (*N. indicum*), and yellow oleander—also known as milk bush (*Thevetia peruviana*)] are cardiac glycosides related to digitalis. Intoxications have occurred particularly in children who ingested berries or other parts of the plant, or who consumed water from vases in which the flowers were kept. The severity of an intoxication depends on the quantity and type of plant ingested. Some of these plants also contain saponins or other irritating substances which cause local irritation of the mouth or mucous membranes. Since the glycosides vary in their rate of metabolism, cardiac signs and symptoms may be delayed for days. Unless the intoxication is recognized early, cardiac effects may persist for 2 or 3 weeks.

Treatment: Induce vomiting. See Digitalis, p. 218.

FUMISOIL CAPSULES

These contain 0.5 ml of ethylene dibromide. See p. 256. A 43-year-old woman died following ingestion of 9 capsules.

FURFURAL (2-Furaldehyde; Pyromucic Aldehyde; Artificial Oil of Ants)

The oral LD_{50} for male albino rats is 149 mg/kg; for dogs, approximately 950 mg/kg. The effects of toxic or lethal doses in the dog varied from muscle incoordination to marked retching and vomiting, occasional convulsions, and death.

Furfural is absorbed percutaneously, but causes only slight local irritation in rabbits. Doses up to 500 mg/kg have been applied to the skin of rabbits without fatalities.

The subcutaneous LD_{50} in male albino rats is 148 mg/kg. Lethal doses usually produce terminal convulsions.

The instillation of one drop of undiluted furfural into the eyes of adult white rabbits produces only slight edema of the conjunctiva. Larger quantities cause irritation and opacity of the cornea.

Male albino mice survived one 6-hour exposure to 260 ppm, but mortality was 100% at 370 ppm. Rats survived one 6-hour exposure to 96 ppm but mortality was 100% at 260 ppm. Dogs survived one 6-hour exposure to 240 ppm of furfural. At 370 ppm, the mortality was 50%.

Treatment: For inhalation, use general treatment for overexposure to vapors of toxic chemicals. Keep airway open, give artificial respiration and oxygen if necessary. Observe for premonitory signs and symptoms of pulmonary edema. In case of ingestion, induce vomiting, follow with gastric lavage and saline cathartics. For skin and mucous membrane contact, flood affected tissues with water.

FURFURYL ALCOHOL (2-Furylcarbinol; 2-Furancarbinol; α-Furylcarbinol; Furfuralcohol; 2-Hydroxymethylfuran; FA)

The oral LD_{50} for the rat is 132 mg/kg; convulsions usually occur with lethal doses.

Instillation of one drop of undiluted furfuryl alcohol (FA) produces a reversible irritation of the eyes of adult male rabbits. Two or more drops cause severe but reversible inflammation; the eyes become normal after several weeks.

FA is rapidly and completely absorbed through the skin of the rabbit; the lethal dose by this route is about 400 mg/kg. The subcutaneous LD_{50} for the rat is 85 mg/kg. Lethal doses usually produce terminal convulsions.

Male albino mice survived one 6-hour exposure to 243 ppm; at 597 ppm the mortality was 92%. For rats, an 8% mortality resulted after one 6-hour exposure to 47 ppm, and 100% mortality at 243 ppm. Rabbits survived one 6-hour exposure to 416 ppm, and dogs survived one 6-hour exposure to 349 ppm. A monkey exposed for one 6-hour period to 260 ppm of FA vapor showed no evidence of toxicity other than a slight irritation as evidenced by slight lacrimation.

Treatment: See Furfural, p. 279.

FURNITURE POLISH (20–90% Mineral Seal Oil)

In general, the signs and symptoms following ingestion and aspiration are similar to those produced by kerosene. The pulmonary effects of furniture polish may be more prolonged and the tendency to cause renal damage appears to be greater. See Kerosene, p. 343, and Petroleum Solvents or Distillates, p. 459 and p. 733.

FUROSEMIDE (Lasix)

Prompt onset and short duration of action characterize this new sulfonamide diuretic. Most adverse effects are relatively mild, and resemble those induced by ethacrynic acid and the thiazides. Nausea, vomiting, diarrhea, rash, pruritus, blurring of vision, and postural hypotension may occur. Occasionally, furosemide-induced diuresis has been accompanied by weakness, fatigue, dizziness, muscle cramps, and thirst. A few cases of acute pancreatitis and leukopenia and a single case of thrombocytopenia have been reported [Council on Drugs of the AMA, *JAMA,* **200** 979 (1967)]. The urinary excretion of uric acid is decreased, hence repeated doses may cause hyperuricemia. This is usually asymptomatic. However, one case of acute gout was reported after 2 weeks of furosemide therapy by D. M. Humphres [*Brit. Med. J.* **1**, 1024 (1966)]. S. Kösters and H. Lüllmann reported on the effect of furosemide on experimental edema induced in rats [*Klin. Wochschr.* **24**, 1403 (1966)]. Convulsions and paralysis have been also reported in experimental animals.

Caution: Administration of the lowest effective dose and intermittent treatment will reduce the incidence and severity of side effects. The drug should be used with caution in patients susceptible to gout and in diabetics in whom increased hyperglycemia may be produced [*Practitioner* **199**, 209 (1967)]. Electrolytes should be followed in patients receiving repeated high therapeutic doses of this drug, since it is likely to cause a lowering of the plasma chloride ion and a rise in blood bicarbonate ion concentration [D. E. Hutcheson *et al., Arch. Internal Med.* **115**, 542 (1965)]. The drug must be used with caution in patients receiving other drugs that may induce hypotension. It is contraindicated in the treatment of hypertension. Since furosemide enhances the effects of tubocurarine, the manufacturer cautions against its use one week prior to elective surgery. *Medical Letter* consultants agree that until more is known about furosemide, patients receiving this drug should be hospitalized [*Med. Letter* **9**, 6 (1967)]. The drug should not be given to children and pregnant women.

Treatment: As a rule, side effects clear up after reduction of the dose or discontinuation of therapy. Foods high in potassium will tend to offset potassium loss (see p. 38), but additional potassium supplementation may be indicated. Solutions of potassium chloride are preferable to tablets, and the chloride is preferable to the gluconate or citrate, since it is more likely to control alkalosis (*Medical Letter*). Further treatment is symptomatic and supportive, directed toward correcting electrolyte imbalance, dehydration, reduction in blood volume, and circulatory collapse.

GANGLIONIC BLOCKING AGENTS

The blocking agents induce ganglionic blockage by occupying receptor sites on the ganglion cells and stabilizing the postsynaptic membranes against the actions of acetylcholine liberated from the presynaptic nerve endings [R. L. Volle and G. B. Koelle in "The Pharmacological Basis of Therapeutics," (L. S. Goodman and A. Gilman, eds.). Macmillan, New York, 1965]. These drugs are used for the reduction of blood pressure in hypertensive diseases. They include: (a) Quaternary ammonium compounds such as Banthine (methantheline bromide), chlorisondamine chloride (Ecolid), hexamethonium chloride (Methium; C6), pentolinium tartrate (Ansolysen), and trimethidinium methosulfate (Ostensin); (b) secondary amines such as mecamylamine hydrochloride (Inversine); and (c) tertiary amines; trimethaphan camphorsulfonate (Arfonad).

What is recognized as a side effect depends on the purpose for which the drug is administered. Toxic doses of the ganglionic blocking agents will lower, and even abolish the effects of sympathetic and/or parasympathetic stimulation, resulting in marked hypotension with or without syncope, paralytic ileus, abdominal cramps, and constipation. (Nicotine induces stimulation followed by depression of autonomic ganglia.) In other individuals blurring of vision because of loss of accommodation, dryness of the mouth with decreased appetite, and difficulty in emptying the urinary bladder have been observed.

Caution: When considering therapy with one of these drugs for a patient with renal impairment, the ability of the kidneys to function adequately at a lowered blood pressure should be determined. Repeated determinations of blood urea nitrogen and creatinine are in order. Therapy cannot be expected to be effective when blood urea exceeds 50 mg %. Extreme caution should be exercized when these drugs are used in the presence of cerebrovascular, coronary, or cardiac diseases.

Treatment: To be effective, antidotal drugs must act directly on effector cells. Hypotension is effectively antagonized by neosynephrine. Epinephrine, because of its brief duration of action, is less suitable. Lower-than-normal doses are usually sufficient because of an augmented degree of sensitivity (after ganglionic blockers) of the arteriolar smooth muscles or myocardium. Pilocarpine nitrate, methacholine, or bethanechol (Urecholine) have been found useful in controlling digestive and other disturbances. Neostigmine has also been employed. Mild laxatives are also in order. For palpitation or tachycardia consider digitalis.

GASOLINE

Repeated or prolonged skin contact will remove natural tissue fats and oils and cause dermatitis. Gasoline and other volatile hydrocarbons will cause blistering if the skin is covered and evaporation retarded. Inhalation and ingestion may result in central nervous system depression. Aspiration into the lungs will cause severe chemical pneumonitis which may be fatal.

Various forms of gasoline addiction in children and adults have been reported. The inhalation of gasoline fumes produces hallucinations, erotic sensations, feelings of drifting in space, and giddiness.

Brief exposures to high concentrations of gasoline vapors have caused fatal pulmonary edema, acute exudative tracheobronchitis, passive congestion of the liver and spleen, and acute hemorrhagic pancreatitis.

Ten human volunteers were exposed for 30 minutes to the vapor of each of three nonleaded gasolines at concentrations of 200, 500, and 1000 ppm. The effects of exposure to the vapor were assessed by response to a written questionnaire and by pre-exposure and post-exposure photographs of the eye. The only significant effect noted was conjunctival irritation. At any given concentration, no difference was noted among the three gasoline samples, but for all of the samples the effect increased significantly with increase in concentration.

Treatment: Remove from skin with soap and water. For inhalation give artificial respiration and oxygen if necessary. Caffeine and sodium benzoate may be indicated for collapse. See Kerosene, p. 343.

GENZIODARONE (Cardivix)

This drug has been withdrawn from the British market [*Brit. Med. J.* 2, 882 (1964)].

GERMINE ACETATE

The I.V. and P.O. use of this alkaloid has been revived as a supplemental agent in the treatment of myasthenia gravis. W. Flacke *et al.*, who reintroduced and used this drug in several patients, report that side effects such as transient nausea and tactile, gustatory, and abnormal sensations of heat or cold were related to the infusion rate. After oral administration, these symptoms were mild and not disagreeable. According to the authors, a wider experience with germine acetate is required to establish and delineate the potential place of this drug in the therapy of myasthenia gravis [*New Engl. J. Med.* **275**, 1253 (1966)].

GIBBERELLIC ACIDS (Gibberelin)

This is a plant growth stimulator having a low order of mammalian toxicity.

Treatment: In case of ingestion of large amounts, induce vomiting.

GIN AND TONIC

In a hypersensitive person, minute doses of quinine produced tinnitus, deafness and vertigo, photophobia and diplopia, headache, fever, and gastroenteric disturbances [*JAMA* **164**, 91 (1957)].

GLASS DUST

Flakelike glass dust particles (fiberglass flake) are not toxic and do not irritate the skin and mucous membranes, probably because glass is insoluble and, hence, biologically inert. The particles tend to present flat surfaces rather than sharp edges to the tissue and float upon the surface of any fluid.

Glass dust and flakes did not cause corneal defects in rabbits. Blinking clears the particles effectively from the ocular conjunctiva.

Ingestion of glass flakes by rats did not result in toxicity or trauma to the gastrointestinal tract. When rats ate a diet containing as much ground glass as food, the resultant slight depression in growth rate was due entirely to lower food intake caused by the bulkiness of the ground glass diet.

The pulmonary changes found in guinea pigs and rats exposed to fine glass dust for a year and in rats dosed intratracheally consisted of small focal alveolar dust cell collections without fibrosis. The glass dust does not cause bronchial disease.

GLASS WOOL

Spun glass is a pruritogenic substance capable of causing dermatitis and skin irritation. Angel hair, a spun glass used for Christmas decorations, can cause dermatitis and multiple minor skin abrasions that may become infected.

Inhalation of particles may cause chronic bronchitis, bronchiectasis, emphysema, and reduction in vital capacity.

Treatment: Remove from skin with soap and water. For inhalation, treatment is symptomatic.

GLUCAGON HYDROCHLORIDE

This drug activates liver phosphorylase, which increases glycogenolysis resulting in the formation of endogenous glucose. Glucagon is therefore an antagonist to hypoglycemic reactions, including hypoglycemic coma induced by exogenously administered insulin or drugs acting similarly. It is administered intravenously, intramuscularly, or subcutaneously. In normal and in a few nondiabetic patients, glucagon was found to reduce hunger and food intake and, when administered over a long period, also to reduce body weight [*J. Obesity* **1**, 1 (1964)].

Use glucagon in a patient who cannot take carbohydrates by mouth. Patients who do not respond to this drug within 15–20 minutes should receive dextrose intravenously. While it is recommended that glucagon not be given unless hypoglycemia has been established, H. Elrick *et al.* believe that harmful effects will not result if this drug is administered to a patient with a symptomatology mimicking hypoglycemia. R. S. Kushner *et al.* administered zinc glucagon to a 1-year-old boy with idiopathic hypoglycemia. A 5 mg dose plus feedings at 2- or 3-hour intervals raised the blood glucose level for at least 12 hours [*J. Pediat.* **63**, 1111 (1963)].

Caution: This drug is a polypeptide; therefore, hypersensitivity reactions may occur.

Treatment: An overdose of glucagon responds to insulin, tolbutamide, or chlorpropamide.

GLUES, MUCILAGES, PASTES

These materials, in general, have a low order of toxicity. Large quantities are required to produce systemic intoxication. Their viscosity precludes aspiration of hydrocarbon solvent which may be present.

Treatment: If a large amount has been ingested, induce vomiting and follow with gastric lavage and saline cathartics. See Bezoars, p. 643 and Plastic Model Cement, p. 481.

GLUTARALDEHYDE

Glutaraldehyde is supplied as a stable 25% aqueous solution that has a mild odor and a light color. It is capable of causing severe eye burns when instilled in the eyes of rabbits. It is also a skin irritant. Skin absorption tests on rabbits show that glutaraldehyde readily penetrates the skin in harmful amounts. Care should be taken to avoid contact with the skin, eyes and clothes.

Treatment: In case of skin or eye contact flood the affected parts immediately with water for 15 minutes.

GLUTETHIMIDE (Doriden)

This hypnotic has no real advantages over barbiturates. Side effects noted in some patients, following prolonged use of therapeutic doses, may include tremors, dizziness, hypotonia, nystagmus, ataxia, and a patchy brown discoloration of the skin. As a rule, these undesirable effects disappear upon cessation of therapy. An exception was a 39-year-old patient who had used glutethimide chronically and 4 months after the drug was withdrawn still suffered from sensory neuropathy and cerebellar impairment [*Clin. Pharmacol. Therap.* 8, 283 (1967)].

Signs and symptoms of intoxication may occur in patients who take from 2.5 to 4 gm per day. These may include drowsiness, staggering, hypotension, dilatation of the pupils, and absence of corneal and gag reflexes. Pharmacologically, glutethimide may have barbiturate-like effects after ingestion of an overdose or in its addiction tendency. According to J. F. Maher, *et al.*, higher doses (5–12 gm) may suddenly produce apnea, widely dilated and fixed pupils, and severe hypotension. According to these clinicians, glutethimide differs in action from the barbiturates, in that depression of respiration is infrequent [*Am. J. Med.* 33, 70 (1962)]. There is evidence that this drug can produce tolerance, habituation, and addiction when taken for several months in amounts greater than 2.5 gm per day [*JAMA* 180, 1024 (1962)]. Withdrawal symptoms are similar to those induced by cessation of barbiturate or meprobamate therapy [*JAMA* 180, 1024 (1962); 181, 46 (1962); *Am. J. Psychiat.* 123, 349 (1966)].

The drug is readily soluble in alcohol; a nightcap after glutethimide is likely to induce undesirable effects.

Two fatalities in adults have been reported following ingestion of 10–20 gm; marked pulmonary congestion, edema, bronchopneumonia, and coma were present. Signs of organic brain disorder were still present in one patient 8 months after withdrawal of glutethimide [*Am. J. Psychiat.* **123**, 349 (1966)]. At autopsy (one patient) intraalveolar hemorrhages and a massive hemorrhagic infarct in one adrenal gland were noted. The lethal dose for man is 10–20 gm.

A 39-year-old woman attempted suicide by ingesting approximately twenty 0.5 gm tablets of glutethimide. Signs and symptoms of intoxication included marked hypotension, dilatation of the pupils, and absence of corneal and gag reflexes. The deep tendon reflexes were bilaterally equal and active; deep coma lasted 23 hours.

Treatment: The following treatment and drugs are recommended: gastric lavage, indwelling urinary catheter, pharyngeal airway and suction during deep coma, I.V. fluids, penicillin, ephedrine I.M., neosynephrine, benzedrine I.V., and caffeine and sodium benzoate I.M. Hemodialysis has been lifesaving in some patients. See also Barbiturates, p. 119.

GLYCEROL

In man, the oral toxicity of glycerol is of a low order. In 14 healthy individuals, the ingestion of 30 ml of 95% glycerol, three times daily after each meal for 50 days resulted in increased thirst and a feeling of warmth in the stomach. In another study, ingestion of 100 ml resulted in headache, nausea, and vomiting. Glycerol has found some use when a profound rapid-acting osmotic agent is desired for the transient reduction of intraocular pressure [*Arch. Ophthalmol.* **70**, 625 (1963); **75**, 201 (1966)].

The Approximate Lethal Doses for the rat are as follows: 21 ml/kg, P.O.; 14 ml/kg S.C., and 5 ml/kg I.P. Repeated and extensive application of pure glycerol, or as a 50% aqueous solution, to the skin of rats and rabbits caused mild irritation but no fatalities. Regardless of the mode of administration, toxic or lethal doses of glycerol given to rats and rabbits induced restlessness, mild cyanosis, drop in blood pressure, increased rate and magnitude of respiration, followed by debility, diuresis, tremors, decreased respiration, collapse, clonic convulsions and coma. Absorption of toxic S.C. doses induced reduction in the number of red and white blood cells and hemoglobin concentration. Hemoglobinuria occurred regularly after the S.C. injection, occasionally after the I.V. and I.P. injection, but not after the P.O. administration of glycerol or its application to the skin [Wm. B. Deichmann, *Ind. Med.* **1**, 60 (1940); **2**, 5 (1941)]. Ethyl alcohol reduces or inhibits the metabolism of glycerol [*Science* **150**, 616 (1965)].

Caution: Because of its irritant action, pure glycerol should be applied with caution to the skin or mucous membranes. Inflamed, or sunburned skin is particularly sensitive to concentrated solutions of glycerol. The drug should be administered with caution to older people. It is not surprising that D'Alena and Ferguson noted occipital headache, quivering of the eyes, and nausea in an 82-year old woman after oral administration of 200 ml of 50 % glycerol for the reduction of intraocular pressure [*Arch. Ophthalmol.* **75**, 201 (1966)].

GLYCIDALDEHYDE

In toxic doses glycidaldehyde stimulates the central nervous system. Organ damage consists of pulmonary irritation and injury to the liver, kidney, and testis.

Air concentrations of 5 ppm are unacceptable insofar as comfort is concerned because of nasal irritation. No significant effects were found in the peripheral blood or blood-forming tissues of rats exposed repeatedly.

Sixty 4-hour exposures to 10 ppm of glycidaldehyde vapor had no significant effect on rats. At 20 ppm there was retardation of weight gain and decrease in the number of nucleated cells in the bone marrow. At 40 ppm there was significant change in weight gain, comparative weight of thymus and spleen, and reduction in nucleated marrow cells. Exposure to 80 ppm caused death of 8 of 10 rats before the fifth exposure.

Glycidaldehyde has mild radiomimetic effects, but ample warning is given by the irritation of the skin and mucous membranes on significant acute exposure.

Treatment: Discontinue exposures. Further treatment is supportive and symptomatic.

GLYCOL ETHERS

The glycol ethers as a class are not highly toxic. With the exception of butyl Cellosolve (ethylene glycol monobutyl ether) and hexyl Cellosolve (ethylene glycol monohexyl ether), they do not penetrate the skin in harmful amounts. They are not strong skin irritants, but like all solvents, prolonged and repeated contact is capable of defatting the skin. Overwhelming exposures to high concentrations of vapor may cause central nervous system effects. See p. 729.

Treatment: For inhalation remove victim from contaminated atmosphere. Maintain patent airway, give artificial respiration and oxygen if necessary. Observe for evidence of pulmonary irritation.

GLYCOLONITRILE

Glycolonitrile is a highly toxic compound which forms cyanide *in vivo*. The oral LD_{50} for male albino mice is 10 mg/kg. Deaths occurred within 2 hours after dosing, and survivors made an uneventful recovery. The signs of intoxication resemble those of cyanide poisoning. The acute skin LD_{50} for albino rabbits ranges from 105 mg/kg to 130 mg/kg. Mild dermal irritation of short duration was found in some of the survivors.

A single instillation of 0.05 ml of a 50% solution (26 mg) beneath the eyelid of each of three albino rabbits caused immediate moderate irritation 15–30 minutes after dosing. Later, the animals convulsed, became comatose, and died within 68 minutes of the start of the test.

Seven mice, 7 rats, and 7 guinea pigs were exposed to an average vapor concentration of 27 ppm of glycolonitrile in air for 8 hours. At the end of this time mortalities were 6 of 7 mice, 2 of 7 rats, and none of 7 guinea pigs. Signs of toxicity consisted of lethargy and slight lacrimation. The remaining mouse and four of the rats died within 18 hours after termination of the exposure.

Because of its physical properties, glycolonitrile is a hazard by skin absorption rather than by inhalation.

Treatment: See Cyanides, p. 191.

GLYCOLS

As a chemical class, the glycols have a low to moderate order of toxicity. Their low vapor pressure at room temperature eliminates the inhalation hazard. They do not penetrate the skin and are not skin irritants. Oral toxicity varies with chemical composition. See p. 731. Most human experience with glycol intoxication has been due to ingestion of ethylene glycol in permanent antifreeze formulations. See Ethylene Glycol, p. 258.

GLYMIDINE (Gondafon)

This is a short-acting European oral hypoglycemic agent for the treatment of diabetes mellitus. It is a sulfapyrimidine derivative; its mode of action is similar to that of the sulphonylurea drugs. From 20 to 40% of glymidine is excreted as the demethylated compound which has hypoglycemic properties exceeding those of the original drug. Side effects included leukopenia in 0.5% of patients, skin allergies in 1.2%, and gastroenteric symptoms and malaise in 1.9%.

Caution: This new drug should be used with caution until controlled studies have shown that it is safer than the older hypoglycemia agents. See Acetohexamide, p. 63, and Sulphonylurea Drugs, p. 563.

GLYODIN (2-Heptadecylglyoxalidine Acetate)

This is a fungistatic or fungicidal chemical having a low order of toxicity. Contact with skin or eyes will produce irritation.

Treatment: For skin or eye contact flood affected parts with large volumes of water. For ingestion of large dose, induce vomiting. Further treatment is symptomatic and supportive.

GLYOXAL

Because of its low vapor pressure, commercial glyoxal is not an inhalation hazard, nor is it particularly toxic by skin absorption. The oral LD_{50} for rats is 1.1 gm/kg. A 4-day poultice application of a 40% solution of purified crystalline glyoxal to the clipped abdomen of guinea pigs gave an LD_{50} of 6.6 gm/kg. This application showed no local action. Commercial glyoxal also showed no reaction in the rabbit-belly vesicant test. It is, however, irritating to the rabbit eye.

A 15% dilution produced corneal necrosis, but 3% dilution did not.

If glyoxal is spilled on the skin and allowed to remain for an extended period, the skin will be stained yellow. This is an actual "tanning" of the skin which cannot be removed with solvents or detergents. It will wear off in a few days as the skin in the affected area is renewed.

Treatment: In case of skin and eye contact flood the parts affected with water for 15 minutes.

GOLD

Gold therapy for the treatment of rheumatoid arthritis is again becoming popular. Recently conducted studies call attention to side effects (primarily exfoliative dermatitis) in about 35% of the patients treated. The toxicity of gold sodium thiosulfate (Sanocrysin), gold sodium thiomalate (Myochrysine), or aurothioglucose (Solganal) appears to be related to dosage and individual susceptibility. Toxic effects may include nephritis [*New Engl. J. Med.* **274**, 210 (1966); *JAMA* **195**, 782 (1966)], on rare occasions hepatitis, and blood dyscrasias. McCarty *et al.* reported a fatal case of aplastic anemia secondary to gold salt therapy. A review of the literature disclosed a total of eleven additional fatalities [*JAMA* **179**, 655 (1962)]. Gold storage occurs primarily in the kidneys; it may persist for a year after discontinuation of therapy. A New York court affirmed a judgment in favor of a patient who developed exfoliative dermatitis following therapy because the physician did not make a reasonable disclosure of "the known dangers" incidental to this type of therapy [*Clin-Alert* No. 302 (1965)]. Radioactive gold emits both beta particles and gamma rays; its half-life is 65 hours.

Chronic skin lesions of the fingers were produced in a husband and wife wearing gold wedding rings which contained decay products of radon (radium D and E), emitters of beta radiation with a half-life of more than 20 years. A rash developed after about 1 year. The lesions had not healed some 15 years after removal of the rings. The fact that not all industrial refiners of gold test each batch for radioactivity before processing may explain the observation by jewelers "that some people can wear one type of gold, but another 'type' irritates the skin. . . . Like a wedding ring, a gold dental appliance which is usually worn constantly could result in a significant buccal reaction." Oral reaction to contaminated gold has not been reported [*JAMA* **200,** 254 (1967)].

Treatment: Skin lesions and kidney damage usually disappear after cessation of gold therapy. Gold radiodermatitis in the cases cited above did not respond to treatment. For severe cases of intoxication, BAL is the drug of choice. Hydrocortisone, prednisone or related compounds have also been used with success in reducing signs or symptoms of toxicity. There are reports describing the use of calcium disodium edetate and D-penicillamine for the treatment of gold intoxication [*Presse Med.* **70,** 1523 (1962), and [*Ned. Tijdschr. Geneesk.* **108,** 465 (1964); *Arthritis Rheumat.* **6,** 216 (1963)].

GOLF BALL

The white, thick, liquid or paste in the core of some golf balls may contain sodium hydroxide. Accidental splashing of this material into the eye may cause serious injury. See Sodium Hydroxide, p. 543.

GOSIO GAS (Trimethylarsine)

Gosio gas is found in the air in rooms covered with moldy wallpaper. The gas is believed to be trimethylarsine. This is a more likely source of arsenic than dusts arising from arsenic-containing wallpaper pigments [Challenger, *Chem. Ind. London* p. 657, (1935)].

GRAPHITE

Artificial graphite made from coke is 99% carbon and contains no free silica. Pneumoconiosis from exposure to this form of graphite has not been reported. Natural graphite (plumbago) is a crystalline form of carbon which may contain free silica. Pneumoconiosis (silicographitosis) has occurred following excessive exposure to this form of graphite.

The graphite in lead pencils does not cause lead poisoning.

GRISEOFULVIN (Fulvicin; Grifulvin)

This is a systemically effective antibiotic used primarily for the treatment of fungus infections of the skin, hair, and nails. Its toxicity in therapeutic doses is of a low order. Minor side effects noted occasionally may include gastroenteric disturbances, allergic reactions including skin eruptions, headache, irritability, thirst, urticaria, or pruritus. In a few isolated patients leukopenia, mental confusion, angioneurotic edema, a lupus erythematosus-like syndrome, or generalized exfoliative dermatitis has been reported [Simpson, *Brit. Med. J.* **2**, 1434 (1966); Reaves, *J. Am. Geriat. Soc.* **12**, 884 (1964)]. It has also been observed that griseofulvin can precipitate attacks of porphyria in patients with acute intermittent porphyria in remission [A. Berman and R. L. Franklin, *JAMA* **192**, 163 (1965)], that it is antagonistic to warfarin [S. Cullera and P. M. Catalarro, *JAMA* **199**, 150 (1967)], and that in some individuals there may be a cross-allergy with penicillin [O'Driscoll, *Brit. Med. J.* **2**, 503 (1963)].

The rate of absorption of this antibiotic is augmented considerably by a high fat diet resulting in considerably higher concentrations in the serum. It is believed that inadequate absorption of griseofulvin is one of the mechanisms of clinical failure occasionally noted after therapeutic doses.

Caution: The drug should be used with caution in patients with established porphyria or impaired liver function. The dose should be reduced if hyperpigmentation of mammary areolae and nipples or if enlargement of the breasts becomes apparent in young girls. Until more is known about griseofulvin, it is best not to administer it to pregnant women. Since a few patients under griseofulvin therapy have experienced some degree of mental confusion, it is well to keep this in mind when the drug is used in persons involved in public safety and transportation [*JAMA* **173**, 1402 (1960)].

GROUND-CHERRY (*Physalis* Species)

This ornamental plant with its Chinese lantern-type fruit pods belongs to the family Solanaceae. Most species of this group are not toxic. The poisonous varieties contain solanine, a collective term for a number of glycoalkaloids. The toxicity of the fruit may vary considerably depending on a number of factors. For instance, the ground-cherry and also the black nightshade (*Solanum nigrum*) are harmless when ripe but toxic when ingested green. Other members of this group include the chalice vine (*Solandra* spp), devil's or soda apple (*Solanum dulcamara*), graceful nightshade (*S. gracile*), Jerusalem cherry (*S. Pseudo-capsicum*), apple of sodom or popolo (*S. sodomeum*), and the potato (*S. tuberosum*).

Signs and symptoms of an intoxication may be severe in children; they are relatively mild in adults. Fatalities have been reported but they are rare.

After a latent period of several hours, nausea and a scratchy feeling in the mouth develops, followed by gastroenteric distress (vomiting and diarrhea), increased salivation, perspiration, and fever. In addition, a patient may suffer from headache, dyspnea, muscular weakness, renal damage, gastroenteric hemorrhages, hemoglobinuria, or convulsions. Death is preceded by coma and circulatory and respiratory paralysis. Intoxications are not uniform since the fruit of some members of the solanine group may contain variable amounts of atropine.

Treatment: Induce vomiting. Further treatment is symptomatic. See Crabs-eye, p. 188, and Tung Nut, p. 613.

GUAIACOL (Methyl Catechol; Hydroxyanisol; Methoxyphenol)

Guaiacol and cresol are the primary constituents of creosote. Ingestion of a toxic dose produces effects similar to those caused by phenol, namely, burning in the mouth and throat, gastroenteric distress, tremors, and collapse. The lethal oral dose for an adult ranges from 3 to 10 gm.

Treatment: See Phenol, p. 463.

GUANETHIDINE (Ismelin)

This potent vasodepressor drug exerts its sympatholytic action primarily by reducing the release of norepinephrine. It is used primarily in the treatment of hypertension. Mild orthostatic hypotension must be expected with therapeutic doses. Side effects may include dizziness, weakness, lassitude, dyspnea, bradycardia, mild diarrhea, and edema.

Caution: Postural hypotension is the most frequent and most important undesirable effect. This is noted particularly at abnormal environmental temperatures, after ingestion of alcohol, or shortly after arising from sleep. As a result of lowered blood pressure, decreased myocardial, coronary, or renal function may occur and cause retention of the drug and azotemia. Watch for peptic ulcer. The drug should not be prescribed in pheochromocytoma because of the possibility of producing cardiac arrhythmia [*Can. Med. Assoc. J.* **97**, 1166 (1967)]. If surgery must be performed while under guanethidine therapy, use atropine sulfate to reduce vagal activity. According to the AMA Council on Drugs, "because of its marked hypotensive properties, guanethidine should be used only in patients with severe elevation of diastolic blood pressure (August 16, 1961)." The drug should not be used in the milder forms of hypertension unless the rauwolfia drugs and thiazide compounds have been found ineffective.

GUANOXAN (Envacar)

This antihypertensive drug should be added to the list of drugs capable of precipitating a lupus-like syndrome. A 60-year-old man developed symptoms suggestive of systemic lupus erythematosus after receiving Envacar in a dosage of 40 mg daily for approximately 1 year. There was rapid and dramatic improvement in symptoms on withdrawal of the drug [*Brit. Med. J.* **1**, 111 (1967)].

GUN CLEANER

Typical preparations contain potassium nitrate, sodium nitrate, mercuric chloride, potassium chlorate, and sweet spirits of niter (ethyl nitrite).

Inhalation of ethyl nitrite vapors may cause dizziness and collapse due to hypotension secondary to vasodilation.

Treatment: Recovery is complete following termination of inhalation exposure. For accidental ingestion induce vomiting.

HAFNIUM CHLORIDE

The acute intraperitoneal toxicity of hafnium chloride is of the delayed type with an LD_{50}, after 7 days, of 112 (93.3–134.4) mg/kg. Chronic feeding for 90 days at levels of 1.0, 0.1, and 0.01 % of the diet produced liver changes at the 1.0% level. No changes were observed in the growth rate or the hemogram. Ocular application produced a transient conjunctivitis. Topical application to intact rabbit skin produced a transient irritation, whereas similar studies on abraded skin resulted in nonhealing ulcers. Intradermal injections also produced localized irritation and scar formation [T. J. Haley, *Toxicol. Appl. Pharmacol.* **4**, 238 (1962)].

Treatment: In case of skin or eye contact, flood the affected areas with water for 15 minutes. Induce vomiting in case of ingestion.

HAIR COLORING PREPARATIONS

Hair coloring preparations include (1) aniline products (coloring—temporary to rather permanent); (2) metallic salt dyes (rather permanent dyes); (3) vegetable dyes (rather permanent dyes); (4) acid color rinses (temporary coloring preparations), and (5) bleaches which remove, rather than add, color to the hair. The aniline and bleaching products account for most sales.

1. *Aniline products* are often referred to as tints rather than dyes, to differentiate them from the metallic salts and vegetable dyes which are also permanent dyes. Generally, a tint is a hair coloring preparation containing aniline derivatives and utilizing an oxidizing agent, such as peroxide, to develop hair color. A tint penetrates into the inside layer of the hair shaft to produce a permanent effect. Although the incidence of reaction is low (about 5.5 reactions per million), the products are considered potential sensitizers.

Black hair dyes may contain aromatic diamines (paraphenylenediamine and paratoluylenediamine) which may cause skin reactions due to sensitivity in some individuals. Paraphenylenediamine is considered to be a potent sensitizer. Any individual contemplating hair-dyeing should be patch-tested first.

2. *Metallic salt dyes* usually contain salts of lead or bismuth which undergo chemical changes resulting in the deposition of a colored film along the hair shaft. There is no penetration.

These dyes are probably safer than any other type. Their rate of absorption through the healthy skin is negligible. However, care should be exercised to prevent contact with mucous membranes or skin lesions. There is little if any evidence that persons become sensitized to these metallic salts.

3. *Vegetable dyes.* Henna (*Lawsonia inermis*) is the only one still used today. It consists of the ground-up dried leaves and stems of a shrub found in North Africa and the Near East. This powder is made into a paste with hot water and applied to the hair. Only a reddish color can be produced. The chief virtue of henna is its safety. Apparently henna almost never sensitizes.

4. *Acid color rinses* (primarily organic acid dyes) are available in either a dry or liquid form and are used to tone down gray hair. The color can be removed by shampooing.

5. *Bleaches.* Excessive bleaching will render the hair harsh and strawlike, and it will cause it to lose its elasticity, resilience, and tensile strength. Hair breakage is not uncommon. The damage occurs because peroxide, the bleaching agent, attacks the keratin as well as the hair color pigment. Effects are limited to the hair that is treated; future growth is not affected.

HAIR LOSS

In some instances, emotion and stress seem to precipitate or aggravate alopecia. Loss of hair is fairly common following a severe illness accompanied by high fever. Factors that may contribute to temporary loss of hair include absorption of certain drugs or chemicals such as colchicine, cyclophosphamide, heparin, mepesulfate, selenium, certain sulfonamides, thallium, exposure to ionizing radiation, and in conditions of hypervitaminosis A.

Treatment: There is no specific therapy. Eliminate the offending drug or chemical. "Local agents such as various lotions, counter-irritants, and ultraviolet therapy have generally been discarded. The topical application of various drugs and hormones including estrogens, androgens, and steroid hormones have shown no significant long-range effectiveness. In some instances, the topical nightly application of steroid hormones to the scalp underneath occlusive coverings with plastic caps has shown some degree of regrowth of hair, which is rarely of long-range significance. Local injection of steroid hormones, either via needle or jet spray gun, are similarly of only temporary benefit and both present the hazards of any type of long-range steroid exposure. The systemic administration of various steroid hormones, including several of the newer derivatives still under investigational study, have resulted in partial regrowth of hair in an occasional instance, but the necessity of long-term administration of these hormones is fraught with many dangers.

"The temporary appearance of hair following steroid hormone therapy does not justify their usage during the long periods of time required in the treatment of alopecia totalis. As far as procaine therapy is concerned, this 'cure-all' has been laid to rest in this country and its resurrection is not advisable. Whether it is harmless as well as ineffectual is a moot question [H. T. Behrman, *JAMA* **200**, 188 (1967)]."

HAIR REMOVERS

Depilatories contain compounds that act on the hair protein (keratin) in such a way that it absorbs water and swells. (Some depilatories contain thioglycolates; these liberate H_2S on decomposition.) The hair becomes fragile and breaks off at the surface of the skin.

Caution: To avoid local injury, depilatories should remain on the skin for only a limited time. A chemical depilatory should never be used on the face unless the label specifies that the product may be used for this purpose.

HAIR RINSES

Protein rinses have been suggested as beneficial to damaged hair, but there is little scientific evidence to substantiate such claims.

The extra "body" that beer rinses might give to hair is probably due to the sugars and the proteins it contains. These compounds cling to the hair, giving a sensation of increased "body and manageability." Egg shampoos and creme rinses are used for the same reason. Evidently, no one has ever evaluated the benefits of light beer versus dark beer, although persons with more expensive tastes have used champagne to seek the same results. (When you run out of champagne, try Löwenbräu.)

HAIR SPRAYS

The best known ingredient in hair sprays, aside from freon, ethyl alcohol, lanolin, or perfume, is a synthetic resin polyvinylpyrrolidone (PVP). PVP, as a plasma expander, has been given intravenously to many subjects without producing injury. The material accumulates in macrophages and apparently is not metabolizable. Other natural and synthetic resins, including shellacs and gum arabic, are also used in hair spray.

Persons having heavy exposure to hair spray may acquire pulmonary infiltrates that clear when hair spraying is discontinued. Although the inflammatory, granulomatous, and fibrotic pulmonary lesions have been seen in chest X-rays of individuals exposed, it has not been possible to prove a causal relation by animal experimentation. A number of cases of hair-spray thesaurosis have been reported. Further study is needed to clarify the discrepancy between human experience and the results from animal experiments [*JAMA* **188**, 197 (1964)].

Treatment: Limit or discontinue exposure.

HAIR STRAIGHTENERS

Chemical straighteners contain thioglycolates or alkalies. The thioglycolate curl relaxers require application of a neutralizer (hydrogen peroxide) to the hair to stop the straightening process. Judgment is required to know when to apply the neutralizer. Alkali straighteners, such as sodium hydroxide, are known to have caused first- to third-degree burns. Severe contact dermatitis with swelling of the face and scalp have also been reported. The most serious potential hazard of the alkali straighteners is injury to the eyes.

Treatment: Discontinue exposure. For eye contact rinse eyes with water for 15 minutes.

HAIR-WAVING PREPARATIONS

Thioglycolates are the essential ingredients in cold wave preparations. The permanent waving procedure is initiated by applying a waving lotion to soften the hair, disrupting chemical bonds within the hair protein. The hair, when it is subsequently wound around a curler or formed into a pincurl, accepts a curled position. After 10–20 minutes, it is rinsed with water and "neutralized" (a step that "locks" the hair into the newly curled pattern) by a solution containing an oxidizing agent, such as hydrogen peroxide. Some kits for home use allow for self-neutralization by air oxidation.

A 3-year-old boy ingested an unknown amount of ammonium thioglycolate (a home permanent neutralizer). Immediately after ingestion, the boy gagged, coughed, and vomited. He was cyanotic for 3 or 4 days. About 2 weeks later laryngoscopy revealed an inflammatory reaction of the larynx, trachea, and bronchi.

Caution: The most common complaints from overprocessing are hair damage such as brittleness, frizziness, split ends, and thinning of the hair. Allergic reactions and burns on the scalp or skin have also been reported.

Treatment of an oral intoxication requires prompt removal from the gastroenteric tract. Subsequent treatment is symptomatic and supportive. For eye contact, rinse eyes for 15 minutes with water.

HALLUCINOGENS

Most of the plants which contain delirium or hallucination inducing compounds are usually ingested to escape reality. See LSD, p. 356, Marihuana, p. 363, Nutmeg, p. 433, and Peyote, p. 460. The following plants contain lysergic acid monoethylamide: the ololinqui plant (*Rivea corymbosa*) and the seeds of the heavenly blue and the pearly gates morning glory (*Ipomoea violacea* and *I. alba*). The dried leaves of the periwinkle plant (*Vinca rosea; Catharanthus roseus*) have been smoked. See Periwinkle, p. 459.

HALOGEN FLUORIDES (Chlorine Trifluoride; Bromine Trifluoride; Bromine Pentafluoride; Iodine Pentafluoride)

Chlorine trifluoride is considered to be the most toxic and most hazardous of the halogen fluorides. See Chlorine Trifluoride, p. 651.

HALOPERIDOL (Haldol)

This is a new tranquilizer. See report by McNeil Laboratories, Inc. [*Clin. Pharmacol. Therap.* 8, 770 (1967)] describing the therapeutic usefulness, the rather extensive precautions, and the possible undesirable effects of this drug. Neuromuscular (extrapyramidal) reactions during haloperidol therapy have frequently been reported. Less frequent, but often more severe, are restlessness, dystonia, akathisia, hyper-reflexia, opisthotonos, and oculogyric crisis resulting from the administration of this drug.

Caution: It would be dangerous to use this drug unless the physician is familiar with the conditions that limit its use. See also *Med. Letter* **9**, 69 (1967).

HALOPROPANE

This inhalation anesthetic resembles methoxyflurane in its slow onset of action, good muscle relaxation, and prolonged analgesia after a period of administration. Its analgesic action is much weaker than that of methoxyflurane during the induction period, and it has a marked hypotensive action in the presence of blood volume deficits.

Caution: Troublesome cardiac arrhythmias are the main undesirable effects of this inhalation anesthetic. These side effects have discouraged its use clinically [A. B. Dobkin and J. Po-Giok Su, *Clin. Pharmacol. Therap.* **7**, 648 (1966)].

HALOTHANE (Fluothane)

This is a nonflammable and nonexplosive inhalation anesthetic. It is a very potent hypnotic with rapid induction. Respiratory and circulatory depression are moderate; muscular relaxation and analgesia are slight. Coughing, nausea, and vomiting are limited, and recovery from halothane anesthesia is smooth and rapid.

Halothane is metabolized by liver microsomal enzymes. Apparently, pretreatment with phenobarbital increases the metabolism of this compound. Severe disturbances of liver function have been reported in patients in whom severe respiratory depression or severe hypotension occurred and were permitted to exist [A. B. Dobkin and J. Po-Giok Su, *Clin. Pharmacol. Therap.* **7**, 648 (1966)]. Severe hepatitis and death have occurred only in rare instances. These could usually be explained on the basis of circulatory shock, or hypoxia associated with prolonged use of vasopressors, overwhelming infection, congestive heart failure, or pre-existing liver disease [Report of the Subcommittee on the National Halothane Study of the Committee on Anesthesia, National Academy of Sciences, National Research Council, *JAMA* **197**, 775 (1966)].

Caution: It is dangerous to use epinephrine during halothane anesthesia (Dobkin and Su). Halothane should be used with caution in individuals who have suffered exposure to radiation, to solvents, or to compounds that are known to be hepatotoxic in general [*Brit. Med. J.* **2**, 1529 (1963); *German Med. Monthly* **12**, 490 (1967)].

HANANE

This mixture of bis(dimethylamino)fluorophosphine oxide and bis(dimethylamino)phosphonous anhydrides is used as a systemic insecticide. It is miscible in water and most organic solvents. Inhalation of vapors or skin contact with the liquid will cause signs and symptoms of acetylcholine intoxication due to cholinesterase inhibition, including fatigue, weakness, nausea, vomiting, abdominal pains, diarrhea, confusion, and muscular twitching.

Treatment: See Organic Phosphates, p. 438.

HAND LOTIONS

L. J. Morse and L. E. Schonbeck suggest that all hospitals be alerted to the potential hazard of contaminated hand lotions. Of a total of 26 brands, 4 nationally or regionally distributed brands of skin lotions in unopened bottles were highly contaminated with *Serratia marcescens; Pseudomonas aeruginosa, Escherichia intermedium lebsiella, Klebsiella pneumoniae,* and/or *Alcaligenes faecalis.*

It is suggested that the rise in infections by gram-negative bacteria in hospitalized patients is due to transmission by contaminated hands.

Suggestion: The authors recommend that all hand lotions be checked for sterility and that only bacteria-free lotions be employed [*New Engl. J. Med.* **278**, 376 (1968)].

HARD METAL

The term hard metal is applied to tungsten carbide which is almost as hard as diamond. Two carbides obtained by treating tungsten with carbon black are used to form the cutting edges of tools and other devices. The powdered carbides are mixed with cobalt metal powder and subjected to pressure to produce the required shape. The product is then treated at a temperature that melts the cobalt and binds together the constituent carbides. Final shaping is done by grinding on diamond and carborundum (silicon carbide) wheels. Men working with hard metal may be exposed to dusts containing tungsten carbide, tantalum, titanium, cobalt, silicon carbide, aluminum oxide, and diamond. Of these, the evidence available suggests that only silicon carbide in a high concentration and cobalt are potentially harmful. Changes in the lungs accompanied by symptoms have been reported from exposure to hard metal. Six cases have been reported in Great Britain, one fatal. The symptoms are productive cough, dyspnea, and tightness of the chest. These are seldom disabling, but in a few cases respiratory distress occurs toward the end of the work day, resulting in a fall in ventilatory capacity and increased resistance to airflow in the respiratory airways. The onset of symptoms tends to be sudden, and the duration of exposure varies from 2 to 22 years. The fatality mentioned above was due to anaplastic adenocarcinoma of the bronchus of the right lower lobe, and sections of the left lung showed diffuse interstitial fibrosis and peribronchial and perivascular fibrosis [Editorial, *Brit. Med. J.* **1**, 836 (1963)].

Treatment: Avoid exposure by controlling dust at its origin or by wearing a face mask if necessary.

HEAD AND SHOULDERS

Zinc 2-pyridinethiol-1-oxide, the active ingredient in this proprietary anti-dandruff shampoo, can be irritating to the skin. Irritation in the normal use of the product has not been reported [F. H. Snyder, *Toxicol. Appl. Pharmacol.* **7**, 425 (1965)]. Convincing evidence of the effectiveness of this preparation has not been published [*Med. Letter* **8**, 17 (1966)].

HELLEBORE; FALSE HELLEBORE (Veratrum californicum)

Veratrum is the active ingredient in the false hellebore (also known as corn-lily) and in the green or American white hellebore (*V. viride*). Following ingestion of parts of these plants, the signs and symptoms are similar to the side effects or toxic effects seen after treatment with purified veratrum alkaloids. Effects include salivation, nausea, and epigastric and chest pain. In a severe intoxication, respiratory difficulties, bradycardia, and hypotension develop.

Treatment: Evacuation of enteric contents is most important. Symptomatic treatment may include atropine, vasopressors, and oxygen. Ingestion of hellebore has produced alarming symptoms, but they are rarely life threatening.

HEMIACIDRIN (Renacidin)

In June 1963, the FDA received reports that this drug produces injury when used for the dissolution of kidney stones. A fatality was reported by Kohler. While the cause of death of this patient cannot be ascribed to the drug per se, the production of severe tissue changes in the irrigated kidney was unquestionable [*J. Urol.* **86**, 102 (1962)]. The use of hemiacidrin is limited to irrigation of indwelling urethral catheters and the urinary bladder.

Caution: The drug is contraindicated for therapy or preventive therapy above the urinary bladder, nephrostomy or pyelostomy or lavage for dissolving renal or biliary calculi. The drug may be used only under the close supervision of a physician (D. N. Kilburn, FDA, personal communication).

HEPARIN

The drug is usually administered I.V. in a dose of 5000 units every 4 hours, 10,000 units every 6 hours, or by *slow* infusion. S. Wessler and L. W. Gaston summarized the occurrence of side effects following therapeutic doses: thrombocytopenia occurring occasionally and disappearing when heparin is discontinued; a low incidence of hypersensitivity reactions — sneezing, rhinitis, conjunctivitis, lacrimation, urticaria, bronchospasm, chest pain, hypertension; and a very uncommon occurrence of transient alopecia seen 3-4 months after heparin therapy. Osteoporosis and spontaneous fractures were observed in 10 patients who received 15,000-30,000 units S.C. daily for 6 months or longer, but were not observed in patients receiving 10,000 units, or approximately 100 mg or less per day [*Anesthesiology* **27**, 475 (1966)]. Other reports call attention to distortion of therapeutic effects, such as abnormal bleeding in patients with blood dyscrasias or in those on Coumarin anticoagulants. Such exaggerated reactions were caused by inappropriate dosage in susceptible patients [W. J. Zinn, *Am. J. Cardiol.* **14**, 36 (1964)].

Overdoses of heparin cause hemorrhages, primarily from mucous membranes and open wounds.

Treatment: Reduction of dose or discontinuation of heparin therapy is effective in the treatment of minor hemorrhages. If hemorrhage is severe, the heparin effect can be promptly reversed by the administration of protamine sulfate 50-100 mg I.V. over a period of 25-50 minutes (depending on heparin dose). The injection should be given *slowly* to reduce headache and to detect early signs of impending anaphylactic shock.

HEPTYL ALDEHYDE SODIUM BISULFITE (Hepbisul)

This compound has been administered to experimental animals to produce regression of tumors. Toxic doses cause a generalized depression of the central nervous system. Death is due to respiratory paralysis. Human cases of poisoning have not been reported.

HEROIN

Heroin induces vicious addiction. It is no longer used as a drug. Before the heroin reaches its user, it has been "cut" by the addition of adulterants such as lactose, mannitol, and quinine. Addicts usually dissolve the material in boiling water and inject it I.V., which they call "mainlining." A subcutaneous injection is called "skin popping." Intravenous injection of heroin has resulted, in addition to the effects on the central nervous system, in thrombophlebitis, pulmonary infarction, septicemia, bacterial endocarditis, tetanus, and acutely fatal reactions. Subcutaneous administration has produced ulcerating nodules at injection sites.

Habitual "snorting" or "sniffing" of heroin frequently leads to perforation of the nasal septum. In a series of 2185 addicts examined, almost 5% were found to have perforations ranging in size from that of a pinhead to more than 2 cm. The incidence in females was found to be five times that in the male addict. Messinger, who reported these observations, recommends routine examination of the nasal septum in medicolegal work [*JAMA* **179**, 964 (1962)]. Effects of maternal heroin addiction are more disastrous for the infant than for the mother. Of 18 babies born to women using this narcotic, Krause *et al.* found that the average weight of the newborn was only 2.6 kg. Congenital defects were found in 2 infants and 4 died. Fifteen infants developed characteristic withdrawal symptoms within 1–56 hours [*Am. J. Obstet. Gynecol.* **75**, 754 (1958)].

Treatment: Discontinuation of the use of heroin is essential. Krause's newborn children required methadone treatment; at first 0.5 mg was given every 4–12 hours; then the dose was reduced. See Opiates, p. 435.

HEXACHLOROBENZENE

In southern Turkey, during the period 1955-1959, 600 cases of vesicular and bullous disease resembling porphyria cutanea tarda were reported. The mild cases showed early lesions which were bullous in nature. The vesicles and bullae appeared in areas exposed to sunlight. Subsequently, the lesions became crusted and at times ulcerated. Eventually, healing occurred leaving a depigmented scar. Many clinical variations were noted. These included hyperpigmentation, hypertrichosis, alopecia, corneal opacities, and deformities of the exposed parts, notably the digits. Hepatomegaly was common. Examination of the urine showed the characteristic port wine color associated with porphyria. The explosive occurrence was suggestive of toxic porphyria. Epidemiologists found that a fungicide, hexachlorobenzene, had been used to treat wheat for planting. The diseases occurred in those individuals and families who ate the treated wheat [C. Cam and G. Nigogosyan, *JAMA* **183**, 88 (1963)].

Treatment: Seven unselected cases of hexachlorobenzene-induced porphyria were treated with disodium ethylenediamine tetraacetic acid (EDTA). In four patients the EDTA was administered intravenously in a dosage of 1.5 gm daily for 5 days and 1–2 gm orally and daily over a period of up to 1 year; 3 patients were treated with oral EDTA for periods up to 1 year; and 1 patient was untreated. Improvement observed in all treated patients was characterized by disappearance of light-sensitive skin lesions, marked reduction in hyperpigmentation and hirsutism, and gain in weight [H. A. Peters *et al.*, *Am. J. Med. Sci.* **251**, 314 (1966)].

HEXACHLOROCYCLOPENTADIENE (C-56)

C-56 is a toxic material which is readily absorbed through the skin. The oral LD_{50} for albino rats is 280 mg/kg. The cutaneous LD_{50} ranges from 430 to 610 mg/kg for the rabbit. The vapors are believed to have effects similar to those resulting from exposure to carbon tetrachloride vapors. See Carbon Tetrachloride, p. 155.

α,α'-HEXACHLORO-*m*-XYLENE

The oral LD_{50} for this compound is approximately 3.16 gm/kg for rats. The dermal LD_{50} for rabbits is greater than 3.16 gm/kg. A single application of the moistened material produced a moderate degree of dermal irritation which did not subside completely during an observation period of 7 days. There were definite gross signs of systemic toxicity from percutaneous absorption among the animals at the three higher dosage levels tested, and the majority of the animals showed a loss in body weight.

A single application of 3.0 mg of α,α'-hexachloro-*m*-xylene to the eyes of rabbits produced a mild degree of irritation which subsided completely within 48 hours. There was no evidence of systemic toxicity from mucous membrane absorption.

Treatment: Remove from the eyes and skin by flooding the affected parts with water. In case of ingestion induce vomiting and follow with gastric lavage.

HEXACHLOROPHENE (Gamophen; pHisoHex; Surgi-Cen; Surofene)

This compound is a bacteriostatic agent and is absorbed through the skin. Repeated skin application of hexachlorophene suppresses the growth of normal skin bacteria. The skin of a person with dermatitis cannot be disinfected. Ordinary soap solutions used in the preoperative preparation of a patient's skin remove transient bacteria on the skin surface and in the desquamating epithelium and sebum, but the normal skin flora persists in the deeper layers of epithelial cells and in the ducts of the various glands.

pHisoHex contains 3% hexachlorophene (G-11), Triton-X-100, a surfactant and a vehicle of lanolin, cholesterols and petrolatum. Its oral LD_{50} for mice is 7.3 ml/kg.

A 54-year-old woman was accidentally given 30 ml of pHisoHex in place of milk of magnesia. Within 5 minutes, nausea, abdominal cramps, and emesis developed. Subsequently, several episodes of diarrhea occurred, and dehydration and hypotension were noted. No blood was found in the feces or vomitus and no irritation of the small or large bowel was noted 3 days later at an elective celiotomy for a pancreatic cyst.

Six children who were treated with pHisoHex for burns developed vomiting, abdominal cramps, and convulsions. After changing to a nonhexachlorophene burn-washing solution, these symptoms did not reappear. Hexachlorophene has not been known to cause convulsions in adults, although this compound has been detected in the serum of adults [*Chem. Week* (November 11, 1967)]. See also Soap, p. 538.

Treatment: The woman who drank the pHisoHex was treated with gastric lavage. Subsequently, the problem was that of adequate fluid and electrolyte replacement. This was achieved with the aid of good intake and output records and serum electrolyte determinations. The children were treated symptomatically.

HEXADECANOL (Cetyl Alcohol)

This is a straight-chain 16-carbon alcohol used to reduce the loss of water by evaporation from lakes, reservoirs, etc. The water is covered with a monomolecular film of this alcohol. Reports indicate that the compound has no effect on aquatic life.

Because of its water-binding property, cetyl alcohol has been used in the manufacture of "washable" ointment bases and as an emollient to prevent drying and chapping of the skin.

Treatment: The toxicity is so low that no treatment is necessary.

HEXAFLUOROACETONE (6FK)

This is a colorless, nonflammable, highly reactive, hygroscopic gas which is irritating to the eyes, nose, and throat. The approximate LC_{50} for albino rats is 900 ppm for $\frac{1}{2}$ hour, and 275 ppm for a 3-hour exposure. The gas reacts vigorously with water, liberating heat. Solutions of 6FK dissolved in water may be toxic by skin absorption. At 635°C, 6FK is decomposed to carbonyl fluoride and octafluoroisobutene, which are highly toxic chemicals.

Treatment: In case of inhalation, remove the individual to fresh air and give artificial respiration and oxygen if necessary. Observe subsequently for premonitory signs and symptoms of pulmonary edema. For contact with eyes or skin, flood the affected parts with water for 15 minutes.

1,1,1,4,4,4-HEXAFLUORO-2-CHLORO-2-BUTENE

This compound is highly toxic. Inhalation toxicity studies show that 50% of the rats exposed for 15 minutes to 78 ppm die. This can be extrapolated to give an LC_{50} of 3 ppm for 6 hours. For comparison, the well-known, extremely toxic material perfluoroisobutylene has an LC_{50} of 0.5 ppm for 6 hours.

Two employees became ill after an inadvertent exposure for about 1 hour to less than 10 ppm of this compound. These men suffered drowsiness and shortness of breath for about 4–6 hours after exposure. A day or two later, they recovered completely without treatment [L. L. Ferstandig, Letter to *Chem. Eng. News* (Nov. 28, 1966)].

Treatment: Remove the victim from the contaminated atmosphere. Give artificial respiration and oxygen if necessary. Further treatment is supportive and symptomatic.

HEXAFLUOROISOPROPANOL (HFIP)

This is a volatile, polar, clear, colorless liquid having a high density and low viscosity. The approximate lethal concentration in the rat is 3200 ppm for a 4-hour exposure. Repeated exposure of rats to a concentration of 300 ppm did not result in any gross or microscopic tissue changes after 10 exposures. This concentration did cause lacrimation, salivation, nasal discharge, and hyperemia. When tested in the rabbit eye, HFIP caused severe permanent injury. Washing the eye 20 seconds after exposure did not appreciably lessen the eye damage.

Treatment: For inhalation, remove the victim to fresh air; give artificial respiration and oxygen if necessary. In case of skin or eye contact, immediately flood the affected tissues with water. Hold the eyelids open and irrigate the eyes for 15 minutes. After that, consult an ophthalmologist for further treatment. For ingestion, induce vomiting and follow with gastric lavage.

HEXAMETHYLENIMINE

Hexamethylenimine has an oral Approximate Lethal Dose for rats of 450 mg/kg. When one-fifth of the lethal dose (90 mg/kg) was fed 5 times a week for 2 weeks, cumulative effects were not detected. The approximate lethal concentration for rats exposed to the vapor of hexamethylenimine for 4 hours was found to be 4800 ppm. Hexamethylenimine is irritating to the skin and to the mucous membranes of the nose, throat, and lungs. Concentrated vapor in prolonged contact with the eyes can cause severe injury. At high levels of exposure it produces disturbances of the nervous system.

Treatment: In case of an accidental spill, clothing should be removed at once and the skin thoroughly washed with soap and water. In case of eye contact, irrigate with water for 15 minutes. Further treatment should be given by an ophthalmologist. Treat ingestion by inducing vomiting and administering gastric lavage.

HEXANE

This is an aliphatic saturated hydrocarbon. See Petroleum Solvents or Distillates, p. 459.

1,2,6-HEXANETRIOL

1,2,6-Hexanetriol has a low order of oral toxicity. Toxicologically, it is in the same class as ethanol. When fed to rats for 90 days, 2.5% in the diet had no deleterious effect. This compound does not penetrate the skin in harmful amounts. None of four rabbits was killed when 20 ml/kg was kept in contact with the skin for 24 hours.

It was patch tested on fifty human subjects and caused neither irritation nor sensitization of the skin. See Table 45, p. 731.

Treatment: In case of ingestion of a large dose induce vomiting.

HEXYLENE GLYCOL (2-Methyl-2,4-pentanediol; HG)

This is a watery, white, moderately hygroscopic dihydric alcohol having a mild, sweet odor. Exposure to 50 ppm of the vapor for 15 minutes causes eye irritation. Slight nasal irritation and respiratory discomfort result from exposure to 100 ppm for 5 minutes. Prolonged exposure to high concentrations of the vapor causes deep anesthesia and loss of consciousness. Dermatitis results from frequent or prolonged contact with the skin, and painful irritation follows eye contact with the liquid.

Thirty-six of 605 children admitted to a burn unit developed coma, which lasted for periods varying from 1 to 38 days. Coma developed shortly after the application of dressings impregnated with 80 % hexylene glycol. The mortality in these patients was higher than expected, and coma occurred in 15 of the 30 who died. The condition was due to absorption of hexylene glycol from the dressings—a conclusion supported by the similarity of the toxic signs to those recorded following ingestion of other glycols.

In oral and parenteral therapy toxic effects of drugs are avoided by not exceeding a recommended dosage. Local therapy of burns, however, cannot be standardized by dosage in this way; hence, compounds known to have dangerous toxic effects should not be applied to extensive burns, and all agents considered for local treatment should be investigated for safety as well as clinical value [*Brit. Med. J.* **1**, 590 (1967)].

Treatment: For ingestion, induce vomiting. For skin and eye contact, flood affected tissue with running water for 15 minutes. In case of inhalation, remove victim to fresh air. Give artificial respiration and oxygen if necessary.

HISTAMINE

Histamine is used to stimulate secretion of hydrochloric acid and to test for gastric activity. A therapeutic dose may induce promptly some or all of the following effects: flushing of the skin (it is the most potent capillary dilator known), hypotension, faintness, tachycardia, palpitation, giddiness, bronchoconstriction, temporary headache, and an increased secretion of gastric juice. Absorption of an overdose is followed by cardiovascular collapse or by marked bronchiolar constriction.

Treatment: Side effects of a therapeutic dose are of relatively brief duration. A toxic dose requires symptomatic treatment.

HOLLY; ENGLISH HOLLY (*Ilex aquifolium*)

Ingestion of the berry will induce marked gastroenteric effects.

Treatment; See Tung Nut, p. 613, and Poinciana, p. 483.

HOMATROPINE

This drug produces effects similar to those of atropine. Even though it is considered to be a safer cycloplegic than atropine, severe systemic effects have been noted after instillation of a few drops of 2 % homatropine into one or both eyes of children of 10–12 years.

Treatment: See Atropine Sulfate, p. 116. Catheterization of the bladder is not advisable since the peripheral effects of homatropine are self-limiting. Cholinergic (parasympathetic) drugs are of no value in the treatment of the central effects. Patients should be instructed to stop using homatropine (or atropine) drops at the first indication of side effects.

HONEYSUCKLE (*Lonicera* species)

Ingestion of the berries of *L. periclymenum* has resulted in marked and prolonged vomiting, colic, diarrhea, mydriasis, photophobia, shock, convulsions, and death.

Treatment: See Tung Nut, p. 613, and Poinciana, p. 483.

HORMONE CREAMS

Locally applied hormones do not reverse or correct the aging process or wrinkling of the skin. While the local application of some hormones in sufficient amounts may increase glandular oil production, this increase, when it does occur, has little effect on the appearance or texture of the aging skin. Furthermore, the hormone which causes this glandular oil production is likely to produce undesirable systemic effects. See Adrenocortical Hormones, p. 77.

HORSE CHESTNUT (Plants of the Saponin Group)

There are several groups of plants which, ingested in toxic doses, will induce within 1 hour increased salivation, marked gastroenteritis, colic, vomiting, and diarrhea. The saponins belong to this group. Parts of respective plants that have caused intoxications include the nut of the horse chestnut or buckeye (*Aesculus hippocastanum*), berries of blue cohosh (*Caulophyllum thalictroides*), the fruit of the golden dewdrop or pigeon berry (*Duranta repens*), berries or leaves of English ivy (*Hedera helix*), the orange body of the fruit of the balsam pear (*Momordica charantia*), seeds of the yam bean (*Pachyrhizus erosus*), and the fruit of the mock orange (*Poncirus* spp).

Lacrimation and inflammation of the eyes will result from eye contact with saponin-containing plant material, and sneezing may result from inhalation of the dust. The prognosis is not favorable if effects other than gastroenteric symptoms appear, such as hemolysis, muscular weakness, circulatory changes, incoordination, coma, and convulsions.

Treatment: Prompt removal of the gastroenteric contents is most important. Follow with the administration of demulcents. Exchange transfusions should be considered in a severe intoxication. There is no specific antidote for saponins. Give a bland diet during the recovery phase.

"HOT WATER"

"Hot water" is the term applied by swimmers to bodies of water which cause a sharp stinging sensation. Invisible sea creatures, popularly called "offshore sea lice," are believed to be associated with "hot water" and to be responsible for the stings. The effects are similar to those resulting from contact with large adult coelenterates such as the Portuguese man-of-war (*Physalia physalis*), Stinging Coral (*Millepora alcicornis*), and certain jellyfish. The irritation produced by the sting may disappear in a few minutes, but at other times a wheal, which later becomes pustulous, may appear quickly.

The type of irritation produced is different from that called "sea bather's eruption," which is encountered by bathers in beach areas. This latter type of irritation almost always occurs on parts of the body under the bathing suit and results in an acute form of dermatitis.

Treatment: See Jellyfish, p. 340.

HTH

HTH is a proprietary name for calcium hypochlorite. Calcium hypochlorite is used as a disinfectant, bleach, and deodorizer. Dilute solutions of similar hypochlorites are found under numerous trade names in the home in the form of laundry bleach.

See Bleaching Solution or Powder, p. 139, 167, 181.

HYDRALAZINE (Apresoline)

This antipressor drug has been used in the treatment of essential hypertension, early malignant hypertension, acute glomerulonephritis, and certain types of pregnancy toxemia. Mild side effects have been noted in most patients. These may include tachycardia, palpitation, dizziness, postural hypotension, headache, nausea, anorexia, urticaria, mild edema of the hands and eyes, arthralgia, and conjunctival inflammation. Undesirable effects frequently disappear or decrease in severity as treatment is continued.

A daily dose of 400 mg has been recommended as the upper limit. E. D. Freis, who treated several hundred patients with dosages of 200 mg (or less) daily for periods up to 9 years, observed no serious side effects [*JAMA* **174**, 1651 (1960)]. Approximately 10% of hypertensive patients treated with high doses of hydralazine developed symptoms indistinguishable from systemic lupus erythematosus [*New Engl. J. Med.* **272**, 462 (1965)]. A mild anemia occurs in some patients treated with high doses. See also Procainamide, p. 495

Caution: The drug must be administered with *extreme* caution to individuals suffering from advanced renal damage, existing or incipient cerebral accidents, or diseases of the coronary arteries. All patients receiving hydralazine should remain under constant supervision by the physician.

Treatment: As a rule, minor side effects require no treatment. Aspirin, diphenhydramine (Benadryl), or other antihistaminics may be useful in reducing persisting side effects. Individuals suffering from a severe rheumatic and febrile syndrome may require treatment with corticosteroids or ACTH.

HYDRAULIC FLUIDS

Rats and dogs were exposed for 4 hours to both unpyrolyzed and pyrolyzed aerosols at 520°, 1020°, and 1560°F of the following fluids: OS-40, a phosphate ester; XF-408, a mixture of silicone oil and a fluorochlorohydrocarbon; and MLO-5277, an organosilicate. All aerosols were found to be eye and respiratory irritants. Toxicity was proportional to the nominal concentration of the aerosol (0.3–4.4 mg/liter). XF-408 caused acute tubular nephrosis in dogs exposed to the unheated aerosol and to the aerosol heated to 520°F but not when heated to 1020° or 1560°F. OS-40 produced severe pathologic changes in rats and dogs only when the nominal concentration of the aerosol heated to 1560°F was 3.5–4.3 mg/liter. It was the least toxic of the three fluids tested. MLO-5277 was considered to be the most toxic.

Treatment: Discontinue exposure. Further therapy is symptomatic and supportive.

HYDRAZINE

This is a colorless oily liquid which fumes in air. It has a strong caustic action on skin and mucous membranes causing delayed eye, mucous membrane, and skin irritation. Acute exposure to hydrazine vapor causes respiratory tract irritation and convulsions. It is also a liver poison, causing acute fatty degeneration and hemolysis.

Treatment: See Dimethyl Hydrazine, p. 225.

HYDROCARBON GASES

Hydrocarbons that exist as gases at room temperature include the C_1 to C_4 paraffins: methane, ethane, propane, and butane; the olefins: ethylene, propylene, the butenes, and isobutylene; the diolefins: butadiene, isoprene, and methylacetylene (propadiene) and acetylene. These hydrocarbon gases are simple asphyxiants, irritants, or anesthetics at very high concentrations.

Treatment: Remove promptly from an atmosphere that is irritating or asphyxiating. If symptoms of asphyxiation persist, administer artificial respiration and oxygen. Treat symptomatically thereafter.

HYDROCHLORIC ACID (Muriatic Acid; Hydrogen Chloride; HCl)

Skin contact with concentrated hydrochloric acid will cause tissue irritation and necrosis. Inhalation of hydrogen chloride vapor or mist will result in edema and irritation of the upper respiratory tract. Ingestion of a corrosive dose will cause pain in the mouth, destruction of tissue, salivation, and severe gastroenteric distress. Normal stomach acid is 0.5% hydrochloric acid. Exposure for a few minutes to 1000 ppm of hydrogen chloride gas is dangerous to life.

Treatment: Remove from the skin and mucous membranes by flooding with water. In case of ingestion, gastric lavage with water and emollients are recommended. Do not apply alkalies topically to the skin or mucous membranes or use them for gastric lavage. An exothermic reaction will add to the already existing distress and pathology. In addition, carbonates and bicarbonates, if administered, will liberate carbon dioxide, which is equally undesirable. Observe for signs of peritonitis. If lungs are affected, give antibiotics prophylactically. Rest is important. Observe for pulmonary edema, see p. 43. Consider also using atropine, morphine, and fluid therapy I.V.

HYDROFLUORIC ACID (Hydrogen Fluoride; HF)

Liquid anhydrous HF is colorless, fuming, and corrosive. The aqueous acid is a solution varying between 30 and 80% HF. Contact of HF liquid or vapor with the eyes rapidly causes severe irritation of the eyes and eyelids. If the hydrofluoric acid is not rapidly removed by thorough irrigation with water, there may be prolonged or permanent visual defects or total loss of vision and destruction of tissue. The effects on the skin depend on the concentration of hydrofluoric acid. With lower concentrations (20% or less), burns do not usually appear for several hours. Contact with higher concentrations is usually detected much sooner.

Hydrofluoric acid vapor is extremely irritating to the respiratory tract. Severe exposure will lead to rapid inflammation and congestion of the lungs. The concentration that produces acute effects varies with the exposure; 50 ppm may be fatal when inhaled for 30–60 minutes.

If ingested, hydrofluoric acid will immediately cause severe irritation and damage to the esophagus and the stomach. Coincidentally, severe irritation to the respiratory tract will also occur.

Treatment: Speed is essential. In case of HF inhalation, remove victim to an uncontaminated atmosphere and expose him as quickly as possible to 100% oxygen. C. F. Reinhardt *et al.* have found it helpful to expose even borderline cases to 100% oxygen at half-hour intervals for 3–4 hours. Severely poisoned individuals should receive oxygen under positive pressure for half-hour periods until breathing is easy and the color of the skin and mucous membranes is normal [*Am. Ind. Hyg. Assoc. J.* **27**, 166 (1966)]. The patient should be kept comfortably warm, but not hot. Under no circumstances should a patient be permitted to return home or to work following a severe exposure until examined and discharged by a physician who is aware of the nature of the exposure.

The patient who has ingested hydrofluoric acid should drink a large quantity of water without delay. After the hydrofluoric acid has been diluted with water, administer milk or 60 ml of milk of magnesia as a demulcent.

For skin contact, *flood* with water; remove contaminated clothing rapidly under the shower. Immerse affected part in an ice-cold saturated solution of magnesium sulfate (Epsom salt), iced 70% alcohol, or iced aqueous or alcoholic solution of Hyamine, a high molecular weight quaternary ammonium compound (C. F. Reinhardt, *et al.*). Remove the immersed part for 2–3 minutes every 10 minutes to relieve the discomfort. If the burn is in such an area that it is impracticable to immerse the part, then iced alcohol, magnesium sulfate, or Hyamine solution should be applied in the form of saturated compresses, which should be changed at least every 2 minutes. Continue this treatment for 1–4 hours depending on the extent of the burn. Then cover the area with a generous quantity of paste freshly prepared from powdered magnesium oxide and glycerine. (This is prepared by the addition of U.S.P. glycerine to U.S.P. magnesium oxide to form a thick paste.) This ointment should be applied daily for several days.

If HF has caused injury to the eyes (vapors or local contact with a solution), they should be flushed with water for a period of 15 minutes. This may have to be repeated several times. Ice compresses should be applied when not irrigating. Pain can be relieved by 2 or 3 drops of 0.5% tetracaine (Pontocaine). An ophthalmologist should be consulted for more definitive treatment. See also Fluorine, p. 273.

HYDROGEN PEROXIDE (Anhydrous, 90%, 30%; Superoxol)

Contact with the liquid results in a stinging sensation accompanied by a whitening of the affected tissue. This irritation quickly subsides and the skin gradually regains its color if the contact time is brief. Prolonged contact with concentrated hydrogen peroxide is likely to result in a serious slow-healing burn. Vapors are irritating to the eyes, nose, and throat.

Adverse reactions to bleaching of the hair are primarily limited to the hair shaft itself. Future growth and inherent physical characteristics are not affected. Skin reactions may occur in some persons, but reported cases are few in comparison with the large number who bleach their hair. Bleaching damages the hair because the hydrogen peroxide must penetrate to the cortex of the hair where the pigment is located. In so doing, it often leaves the hair dry, brittle, and more absorbent.

Hydrogen peroxide is dangerous to the newborn infant when used for the lavage of the bowel for removal of meconium. Seven such reports have appeared. There is evidence that the heat of hydrogen peroxide decomposition causes local deleterious effects. The injured tissue then permits oxygen bubbles, hydrogen peroxide, and other bowel contents, including microorganisms to penetrate the disrupted mucosa and thereby gain entrance to the lymphatics and capillaries. Studies in puppies and dogs suggest that oxygen gas embolism in infants can be expected regularly with concentrations exceeding 0.75% of hydrogen peroxide. The eighth report by A. Shaw *et al.* described a fatal intestinal gangrene following introduction of 1.0% hydrogen peroxide into the inspissated meconium. The authors conclude "The clinical and experimental data appear to demand that this potentially dangerous practice be abandoned [*New Engl. J. Med.* **277**, 238 (1967)]."

Treatment: For skin and eye contact, flood affected part with water. Tissue injuries resulting in severe hydrogen peroxide burns are treated as thermal or chemical burns.

HYDROGEN SELENIDE

This is a highly toxic gas with a disagreeable odor; 0.3 ppm killed 50% of the guinea pigs exposed in 8 hours. Acute effects consist of eye, nose, and throat irritation, which may be followed by acute pneumonitis. Subacute and chronic effects include garlicky breath, nausea, vomiting, metallic taste in mouth, dizziness, extreme lassitude, and fatigability. Even brief exposures produced liver damage, weight loss, and general debility in animals.

Treatment: Remove individual at once from contaminated atmosphere. Give artificial respiration and oxygen if necessary. Treatment subsequently is symptomatic and supportive.

HYDROGEN SULFIDE (Sulfuretted Hydrogen; Stink Damp; Hydrosulfuric Acid; H_2S)

In concentrations that do not cause systemic effects, hydrogen sulfide has been known to exert an irritant action on the eyes and mucous membranes. The corneal epithelium may be eroded, and the eyes feel as though grains of sand were on the conjunctiva. There may also be photophobia. Absorption of a toxic dose will produce systemic effects including tremors, convulsions, and collapse. Pneumonia and peripheral neuritis may follow after recovery from an acute intoxication. Death is due to respiratory failure. Exposure to 600 ppm for ½ hour may be fatal.

Treatment: Remove at once from the contaminated atmosphere. Give artificial respiration and oxygen if necessary. Recovery is usually complete without sequelae. Keep under observation for premonitory signs of pulmonary edema.

HYDROGENATED BISPHENOL

Animal toxicity studies indicate that hydrogenated bisphenol is practically innocuous when fed to rats. Animals survived doses up to 25 gm per kilogram of body weight without signs of illness. Rabbits showed no signs of illness following cutaneous doses of 6.5 gm/kg. There was no significant irritation when applied to the eyes of rabbits. It appears that no special precautions are necessary to assure safe handling of this material.

Treatment: In case of ingestion of a large dose, induce vomiting.

HYDROQUINONE (1,4-Dihydroxybenzene; Quinol)

Ingestion of a toxic dose will induce gastroenteric and respiratory difficulties followed by cyanosis and delirium. The probable lethal oral dose for an adult is 2 gm. Hydroquinone vapors are irritating to the eyes and to the respiratory tract. Depigmentation of the skin and eyes and corneal changes have been reported in man. The compound acts as an antioxidant in the presence of fats.

Treatment: After ingestion, induce vomiting, perform gastric lavage, and follow with a saline cathartic and demulcents. In case of eye contact, irrigate the eye with water for at least 15 minutes. Treatment otherwise is symptomatic.

2-HYDROXYADIPALDEHYDE

2-Hydroxyadipaldehyde has a low order of oral toxicity. Administered orally to rats, it is in the same quantitative range of toxicity as ethanol. Tests on rabbit skin indicate that, while it is mildly irritating to the skin, it does not penetrate the skin in harmful amounts. When instilled in rabbit eyes, negligible injury was produced by an excess amount of 2-hydroxyadipaldehyde. Rats survived an 8-hour exposure to vapors saturated at room temperature.

Treatment: In case of skin or eye contact flush the affected parts with water.

HYDROXYCHLOROQUINE (Plaquenil)

This antimalarial agent induces effects closely resembling those of chloroquine. Prolonged use may produce side effects such as anorexia, nausea, vomiting, abdominal cramps, headache, skin reactions, patchy alopecia, bleaching of hair, nervousness, insomnia, and temporary blurring of vision. An 18-year-old boy with discoid lupus erythematosus who was given hydroxychloroquine, in a dosage of 1.2 gm/day for 25 days, developed a painful stomatitis. The leukocyte count was 1050 per cubic millimeter with 150 granulocytes per cubic millimeter. Recovery was complete by the tenth day following withdrawal of the drug [*Lancet* **I**, 1275 (1965)]. Six instances of blood dyscrasias have been reported [*New Engl. J. Med.* **277**, 492 (1967)].

Treatment: Side effects regress upon discontinuation of therapy. The drug should be withdrawn immediately if any of the following adverse effects become apparent: leukopenia or any other severe blood disorder, skin eruptions, or visual haloes. Patients with psoriasis should not receive this drug. See Chloroquine, p. 652.

HYDROXYPHENAMATE (Listica)

This tranquilizer is used as an adjunct in the treatment of anxiety and tension. Side effects reported have not been significant.

Caution: This drug must be used with caution by those who require alertness. Prolonged use should not be discontinued abruptly.

HYDROXYZINE (Atarax; Vistaril)

Hydroxyzine HC1 and hydroxyzine pamoate (Vistaril) are used as calming agents. They also exert antiarrhythmic effects. Their toxicity is of a low order. In doses of 75–400 mg/day they have caused no particular side effects except drowsiness and dryness of the mouth [S. Cohen, *Mod. Treat.* **2**, 550 (1965)]. These drugs are teratogenic in the rat and, obviously, should not be taken during pregnancy [*Am. J. Obstet. Gynecol.* **95**, 109 (1966)].

HYPRIN GP25 (Hydroxypropylglycerine)

Hyprin GP25 has a low order of acute oral toxicity. There is little hazard from the ingestion of single doses. The product also is low in chronic oral toxicity as judged by the results of dietary feeding studies with rats.

Skin contact should cause no irritation even upon repeated prolonged exposure. There is no hazard of systemic toxicity from adsorption through the skin.

Treatment: None required.

HYPROSE SP80 (Octakis (2-hydroxypropyl) Sucrose)

Hyprose SP80 is a viscous, yellowish amber liquid prepared by the reaction of sucrose with propylene oxide. It has a low degree of acute oral toxicity. There seems to be no hazard from ingestion of single doses. The product is low in chronic oral toxicity as judged by the results of 90-day dietary feeding studies with rats.

Contact with Hyprose SP80 has essentially no effect upon the eyes or skin. Any effects that do occur will probably be due to the mechanical action of the thick sticky material.

Treatment: None necessary.

HYTRAST

This iodine-containing preparation for bronchography induced side effects (hyperthermia or marked irritation of the respiratory mucosa) in 28 of 31 patients reported by Misener *et al.* [*Can. Med. Assoc. J.* **92**, 607 (1965)]. Agee and Shires placed 10 ml of this contrast medium in the left lung and then introduced 10 ml into the right main bronchus. The patient died on the sixteenth postbronchographic day. Postmortem examination revealed massive bronchographic crystalline-inclusion pneumonia [*JAMA* **194**, 459 (1965)].

Caution: The absence of coughing or respiratory distress is not necessarily an indication that the patient tolerates Hytrast. This contrast medium should be used with considerable caution.

ICICLES

Icicle decorations for Christmas trees may be hazardous. Although the metals (40% tin and 60% lead) are poorly absorbed from the gastrointestinal tract, the stringy nature of the "icicle" may cause choking and intestinal obstruction. The newer "icicles" are made of plastic.

Treatment: See Bezoars, p. 643.

IDOXURIDINE (IDV; Dendrid; Herplex; Stoxil)

This is a new antiviral agent used topically to treat all forms of herpes simplex infection. Occasionally it may produce a stinging sensation, pruritus, edema or inflammation of the eye, or photophobia. Ey *et al.* reported a high incidence of residual nebular opacities in the anterior corneal stroma following IDV therapy [*Arch. Ophthalmol.* **71**, 325 (1964)].

Caution: According to the Council on Drugs, idoxuridine may delay healing of the deeper lesions [*JAMA* **190**, 535 (1964)].

IGEPONS

This is a group of synthetic surfactants having a low order of toxicity. Prolonged contact may cause skin irritation. See Detergents, p. 201, and Table 31, p. 710.

Treatment: Remove from skin and eyes by washing with large volumes of water. For ingestion induce vomiting and follow with gastric lavage.

IMIPRAMINE (Tofranil)

This drug is used for the management of depression. While the incidence of minor side effects is high, surprisingly few serious adverse effects have been reported [D. G. Friend, *Clin. Pharmacol. Therap.* **6**, 805 (1965)]. Signs and symptoms of toxicity may include dryness of the mouth, blurred vision, tachycardia, constipation, mental confusion, insomnia, a Parkinson-like syndrome, orthostatic hypotension, transient jaundice, and galactorrhea [*New Engl. J. Med.* **271**, 510 (1964)]. Visual hallucinations occurred in about 5% of patients who received this drug for 25-60 days [*Am. J. Psychiat.* **121**, 911 (1965)]. There have been a few reports of leukopenia.

Following ingestion of an overdose, the major effects include convulsions, followed by respiratory depression, circulatory collapse, hypotension (as a rule, not responsive to vasopressor drugs), hyperpyrexia, severe oliguria, and cardiac arrhythmias [*Ther. Umschau* **22**, 180 (1965); *Brit. Med. J.* **2**, 974 (1965)]. Fatalities have been reported in a 16-month-old child following ingestion of approximately 50 mg/kg, and in a woman who ingested 5.0 gm [*Med. J. Australia* **2**, 22 (1967)]. A. S. Curry reported on seven additional fatal cases [*J. Pharm. Pharmacol.* **16**, 265 (1964)]. A 3-year-old boy who ingested approximately 0.4 gm and a 4-year-old girl who swallowed 5–6 mg/kg survived.

Caution: Because of its atropine-like action, this drug should not be used in cases of glaucoma. It should not be given to a patient with coronary artery disease, nor to patients who recently received monoamine oxidase inhibitors. Animal experiments indicate that the drug is capable of causing fetal deformities.

Treatment: Reduce the dose or discontinue treatment if side effects become significant. In case of ingestion of an overdose, induce vomiting or perform gastric lavage promptly. Consider using a saline cathartic. Maintain respiration and administer fluid therapy. Paraldehyde is definitely preferred to barbiturates for the control of convulsions. Lidocaine (Xylocaine) is the drug of choice, but pyridostigmine (Mestinon) may also have a place in the management of arrhythmias, but *hypertensive agents are contraindicated* [C. M. Steel *et al.*, *Brit. Med. J.* **3**, 663 (1967); **1**, 89 (1968)].

The value of forced diuresis is questioned. J. W. Harthorne *et al.* gave a 21-year-old woman 250 gm of mannitol I. V., as a 15% sol., over a period of 14 hours. In this patient, who ingested 5.37 gm of imipramine in a suicidal attempt, mannitol induced an immediate flow of urine (300–400 ml/hr for 14 hours). This patient suffered two episodes of cardiac arrest, which responded to external massage [*New Engl. J. Med.* **268**, 33 (1963)].

C. M. Steel *et al.* advise against forced diuresis because renal excretion of the free drug is of a low order, and because large I.V. infusions are dangerous in imipramine intoxications. Because of the local toxic effect of large doses of imipramine on the myocardium, ECG monitoring should form part of the management of all severely poisoned individuals. Oxygen and/or assisted ventilation should be provided as indicated by the clinical state and blood gas analysis. A slow I.V. drip of an isotonic solution, such as dextrose with half-strength Ringer's lactate, should be given. If arrhythmias or circulatory failure supervene, lidocaine and pyridostigmine (*but no hypertensive agents*) can be added. Maintain sedation as required and keep patient in bed for at least 3 days, or until the ECG is normal (C. M. Steel *et al.*)

INDOMETHACIN (Indocin; Indocid; Indomee)

This drug has analgesic and anti-inflammatory effects. It has been used in the treatment of rheumatoid arthritis (where aspirin is just as effective) and other rheumatic diseases.

Some side effects are produced in approximately 35% of patients. These include severe frontal headache, dizziness, and gastroenteric and psychic disturbances. Approximately 20% of patients cannot tolerate indomethacin. During the past 2 years, reports have appeared describing indomethacin as a pancreotoxic agent [*JAMA* **200**, 552 (1967)], causing hepatitis [*Brit. Med. J.* **1**, 155 (1967)], reactivating infections [*Brit. Med. J.* **1**, 961 (1966)], inducing an asthmatic attack [*Ann. Internal Med.* **66**, 568 (1967)], and causing the death of several children [*JAMA* **199**, 586, 932 (1967)].

Caution: The drug is contraindicated in patients suffering from gastritis, peptic ulcer, or ulcerative or regional colitis. Since the drug may aggravate epilepsy and parkinsonism, it should be used in these patients with caution. Because of limited information, indomethacin should not be prescribed in pregnancy. This drug should not be used in children if a safer drug is available. Like the antihistamines, this drug is contraindicated in any person employed in public transportation.

"INERT INGREDIENTS"

This term found on the labels of commercial products should *not be taken literally.* "Inert ingredients" may include the following substances: glucose, kerosene or other petroleum solvents (p. 459); hydrated or slaked lime, calcium hydroxide, p. 149; calcium carbonate (limestone), low order of toxicity; gypsum (calcium sulfate), low order of toxicity; magnesium carbonate, low order of toxicity; silicates, kaolin, bentonite (clay), diatomaceous earth, p. 206; fuller's earth, walnut shell powder, talc, p. 570; benzene, p. 642; and carbon tetrachloride, p. 155;

INSTANT ICE (Chill-Master Jr.; Kan-O-Frost; Chiller Diller; Invento Freeze)

These freon-containing aerosol preparations are intended for chilling cocktail glasses. At least seven deaths have been attributed to their misuse–inhalation of the aerosol for its intoxicating or psychedelic effect. Death results from asphyxia and freezing of the vocal cords [*New York Times* (Oct. 21, 1967)].

Treatment: Give artificial respiration and oxygen. Perform tracheostomy.

INSULIN

An overdose of insulin produces signs and symptoms of hypoglycemia, which may include some or all of the following: faintness, palpitation, perspiration, headache, marked hunger, a feeling of "hollowness in the stomach," nausea, vomiting, trembling, dilatation of the pupils, double vision, temporary loss of memory, and finally, hypoglycemic coma and death. Occasionally, unconsciousness or grave mental confusion comes on suddenly without the usual warning symptoms. Besides an overdose of insulin, the chief causes of hypoglycemia are delay in eating, change in diet, unusual physical exercise, and a decreased need for insulin after the control of glycosuria or following recovery from complications which temporarily cause an increased insulin requirement.

A hypoglycemic reaction should be suspected whenever a patient receiving insulin complains of unusual sensation, or if he behaves in an unusual manner.

The "jet injection" of insulin appears to be a satisfactory method for administering this drug [*JAMA* **195**, 844 (1966)]; but as F. S. Perkin remarked, time and usage alone will determine its future role in the treatment of diabetics [*JAMA* **195**, 500 (1966)]. Oral insulin is still very much in the experimental stage [*Indian J. Med. Sci.* (July 1966)].

A note in *Clin-Alert* calls attention to stabilized diabetic patients who may experience an enhanced hypoglycemic effect if changed from predominantly bovine insulin to the same dose of a predominantly pork preparation. This hazard is peculiar to the short-acting insulins and mixtures containing them. Until the situation is clarified, doctors, pharmacists, and patients should be aware of the risk of changing brands unless this change is conducted under close supervision [*Clin-Alert* No. 316 (Nov. 1966); Young and Kellock, *Lancet* **II**, 910 (1966)]. George F. Schmitt, M.D., of the University of Miami, has written a new and completely different book for diabetics. According to Dr. Walter Alvarez, it is one "which every diabetic and his relatives, as well as every physician treating diabetes, should own ("Diabetes for Diabetics," Diabetes Press of America, Inc., 30 S.E. Eighth Street, Miami, Florida, 1965)."

There is evidence that some M.A.O. inhibitors potentiate the effects of insulin and sulfonylurea drugs [*Lancet* **I**, 407 (1966)].

Treatment: If a patient is conscious, give orange juice or 1 or 2 lumps of sugar dissolved in water. To maintain relief from the severe reactions of a long-acting insulin, repeated small carbohydrate feedings may be necessary. If a patient is unconscious or otherwise unable to take anything by mouth, administer glucose (50% I.V.). Hypertonic glucose should be used until the patient regains consciousness. A 20% solution of mannitol has also been used in the treatment of prolonged hypoglycemic coma (*Lancet* **I**, 402, (1966). See also Glucagon, p. 286.

INVERTEBRATE STINGS

There are four main groups of invertebrate marine animals that induce injury by contact of "stinging cells."

1. *Portuguese Man O'War (Physalia), sea nettle, sea wasp, sea anemone, sea blubber, elk horn, coral, etc.* The stinging cells (nematocysts) of these marine coelenterates are located primarily in the tentacles, which may reach a length of 20 feet or more. The cells contain threadlike tubes which project upon contact with the skin. The venom (5-hydroxytryptamine and urocanylcholine, not formic acid as commonly believed) is subsequently injected.

2. Among the molluscs are the beautiful *cone shells.* There are more than 400 species, each equipped with a highly-developed venom apparatus capable of inflicting puncture wounds.

Octopus and squid also belong to this group. Each induces injury by biting, followed by injection of venom into the wound. The bites of an octopus may be recognized by two small puncture wounds. These are produced by the animal's sharp parrot-like chitinous jaws [*Quart. J. Florida Acad. Sci.* **29**, 265 (1966)].

3. *Worms,* including the *bloodworm, bristle worm,* and others, either bite or use bristle stinging mechanisms.

4. *Sea urchins, long-spined and other urchins* (*echinoderms*). These are covered either with thin, hollow, venom-filled spines or with solid (nonvenom-containing) spines radiating from the animal, similar to the spines radiating from a porcupine.

The effects induced by stings of any one of the invertebrates may include some or all of the following: local irritation, pain, or a stinging sensation much like that produced by nettles. This may progress to a throbbing pain radiating to other areas of the body. At the site of contact, there is usually redness, sometimes inflammation and edema of the tissues, or blistering and hemorrhages of the more superficial blood vessels. In severe cases, the poison may produce systemic effects including cramps and pain in the muscles and abdomen. There may also be extreme nausea with vomiting, loss of speech, and breathing difficulties because of oncoming muscular paralysis, and even convulsions and death.

Treatment: Remove the stinging material and tentacles immediately, using tweezers, safety razor, soap and water, using caution not to use the uncovered hand to do so. Rinse with ocean water. Then apply one of the following topically: alcohol (or whiskey), calamine lotion, vinegar, corn or olive oil containing 2% phenol, or even wetted baking soda, sugar, gasoline, kerosene, or xylene. Household ammonia may be used if the area involved is not large. Each of these agents or solutions has been employed with partial success, when used promptly. Spray area with a local anesthetic. See p. 352.

For pain give 2 aspirins dissolved in water, repeat in 30 minutes. If pain becomes marked, or if cramps and respiratory difficulties appear, *rush* the patient to a hospital. In an emergency, call for a Coast Guard helicopter if the accident occurred on a boating expedition. Since there is no specific antidote, treatment is symptomatic. If required, apply artificial respiration during transport. J. J. Marr recommends antihistamines I.V. to alleviate not only pain, but also skeletal spasms, visceral cramping, and vasospasm [*JAMA* **199**, 337 (1967)].

IODINE

Skin contact may lead to discoloration, irritation, necrosis, and fever. Iodine vapors are more irritant to the upper and lower respiratory tract than chlorine vapors. In susceptible individuals, traces (or low doses) of iodides have been reported to cause "iodism." Symptoms may include exfoliative dermatitis, edema of the face, abdominal pain, and enlargement of the parotid gland ("iodide mumps"). Ingestion of a toxic dose of an iodine solution will result in gastroenteric distress, disagreeable metallic taste, bloody diarrhea, and collapse. The probable lethal oral dose for an adult is 2–3 gm.

Repeated ingestion of large therapeutic doses of iodine-containing drugs is likely to result in enlargement of the thyroid, salivary, and submaxillary glands and lymph nodes, and in flushing of the face, neck, and upper part of the body [*Nord. Med.* **76**, 1003 (1966)]. Some patients have complained of severe headache. Two asthmatic women who received excessive iodide therapy during pregnancy delivered infants with thyroid goiters and features of cretinism [*New Engl. J. Med.* **267**, 1124 (1962)].

Attention is directed to the occurrence of carcinoma of the thyroid gland following radioactive iodine therapy for hyperthyroidism (*Clin-Alert* No. 295, 1964). Acute leukemia is also known to be associated with the use of this drug; 26 cases were reported since 1960 [*Brit. Med. J.* **2**, 736 (1964)].

Treatment: Discontinue iodide treatment if signs of "iodide mumps" appear. After ingestion of a toxic dose, give demulcents, such as milk, vegetable oil, or starch solution. Perform gastric lavage with caution. Oral administration and lavage with 1–3% sodium thiosulfate is recommended. Sodium chloride has been suggested in doses of 6–12 gm P.O. per day, or 1000 ml of isotonic sodium chloride I.V., or rectally twice a day. The remaining treatment is symptomatic. Following inhalation exposure, remove to fresh air; rest and oxygen are important; wash exposed skin areas with a copious flow of water. (The two infants cited above recovered spontaneously.)

IODIPAMIDE (Cholografin)

This is a radio-opaque iodide contrast medium used for the visualization of the extrahepatic biliary ducts. Both the sodium salt of this compound (Cholografin sodium) and iodipamide methylglucamine (Cholografin methylglucamine), when injected in less than 10 minutes, have induced transient side effects including gastroenteric symptoms and restlessness.

Caution: Patients should be questioned regarding previous allergies (asthma, hayfever) to prevent reactions of hypersensitivity. If it is decided to administer this agent, prior parenteral administration of an antihistamine is indicated [H. Steinberg and T. P. Almy,"Drugs of Choice 1966–1967," C. V. Mosby, St. Louis, Missouri 1966). The drugs should not be administered to patients who are hypersensitive to iodine, nor to those predisposed to renal failure. After injection of iodipamide methylglucamine, a patient with only one kidney developed oliguric renal failure. He recovered within 6 weeks. Another patient with an unsuspected chronic pyelonephritis and a mild degree of jaundice became anuric immediately after cholangiography and died. This patient had received an I.V. dose of 1.75 gm, approximately twice the recommended dose [*Brit. Med. J.*, **2**, 736 (1967)].

IODOFORM (Triiodomethane)

Iodoform is used as a constituent of dusting powder. In contact with diseased or infected tissues, it is believed to result in the liberation of iodine. Application of iodoform to a large skin area or ingestion of a toxic dose will result in nausea, vomiting, headache, diuresis, central nervous system effects, mild convulsions, and possibly death. The probable lethal oral dose for an adult is 3 gm.

Treatment is largely symptomatic. It has been reported that sodium bicarbonate has antidotal effects.

IOPANOIC ACID (Telepaque)

This drug is used for cholecystography in oral doses from 2 to 6 gm the night before the examination. Because of the potential toxicity of this and related contrast media, bunamiodyl (BUN, Orabilex) was withdrawn from the market. The following precautions apply to Telepaque and to other iodine-containing drugs used for similar purposes, including: acetrizoate sodium (Urokon, Thixokon); chloriodized oil (Iodochlorol); diatrizoate (Cardiografin, Gastrografin, Hypaque, Renografin); diprotrizoate sodium (Miokon); iodipamide (Cholografin); iodized oil (Lipiodol); iodoalphionic acid (Priodax); iophendylate (Pantopaque); iophenoxic acid (Teridax); ipodate (Oragrafin); meglumine iothalamate (Conray); and propyliodone (Dionosil). See also p. 392.

Caution: Contrast agents used in radiography should not be administered to patients who are hypersensitive to iodine or to another part of the drug molecule nor to those who suffer from hepatitis or atrophy of the liver or severe renal insufficiency. In these individuals, minimal doses would result in either catastrophic effects or retention and severe signs and symptoms of drug toxicity. These drugs, if used, must be administered with utmost caution to patients suffering from cholangiolitis, marked hyperthyroidism, and circulatory disease. See also Iodipamide, p. 331.

IPECAC (Ipecacuanha)

This centrally acting emetic is composed of emetine, cephaeline, and psychotrine. Severe intoxications and fatalities have occurred because children, by mistake, were given the fluid extract instead of the *syrup of ipecac.* Signs and symptoms include retention of urine, fever, diarrhea, extreme abdominal pain, dehydration, and cardiac irregularities. The fluid extract is 14 times more potent than the *syrup of ipecac.*

The standard dose of *syrup of ipecac* which is used to induce vomiting in children under 2 years of age is 2 teaspoonfuls (8 ml); for children over two, 1 tablespoonful (15 ml). Vomiting is facilitated by prior ingestion of approximately 200 ml of water, milk or tea. Gastric lavage should be performed without delay if a second dose of syrup of ipecac does not induce vomiting in 20-30 minutes.

This drug is not reliable after ingestion of phenothiazines, since these compounds are potent antiemetics.

Treatment of an overdose is symptomatic. See also Acetylsalicylic Acid, p. 63.

IPRONIAZID (Marsilid)

This monoamine oxidase inhibitor was withdrawn because of toxicity.

IRON

Approximately 2000 cases of acute iron poisoning occur yearly in the United States. Severe intoxications and fatalities have been produced in small children who ingested quantities ranging from 40 mg to 1.5 gm of ferrous sulfate. Signs and symptoms of intoxication include nausea, vomiting, diarrhea, tachycardia, rapid, weak or imperceptible pulse, dizziness, shock, and mental confusion. There are at least three critical phases in iron poisoning: an early acute phase of hemorrhagic gastroenteritis and possibly shock occurring a few hours after ingestion of an overdose; a delayed severe shock phase appearing 20–48 hours after ingestion; and a late phase of gastric scarring and contracture, with pyloric obstruction and liver injury and failure appearing about a month later [*J. Pediat.* **64**, 218 (1964)].

Clinical studies show that organic iron preparations such as ferrous gluconate, saccharated iron oxide, and iron choline citrate (Chel-Iron) have a relatively low degree of toxicity. Imferon, an iron-dextran complex, has been on and off the market during the past years. If used, it must be administered as recommended by the manufacturer, with the realization that side effects are likely to occur [*JAMA* **182**, 1334 (1962); *Brit. Med. J.* **1**, 29, 657 (1965)]. Headache, vomiting, and dizziness have occurred in patients receiving iron sorbitol (Jectofer) in doses up to 100 mg daily. More severe effects, palpitation, precordial pain, and severe hypotension have been reported from daily doses of 200 mg [*Med. Letter* (Nov. 19, 1965)]. Iron sorbitol should *not* be injected in patients receiving oral iron therapy. Acetylsalicylic acid (3–4 gm/day) significantly reduces serum iron values [*Blood* **19**, 601 (1962)].

Fatal poisonings occurred aboard ships carrying cargoes of ferrosilicon. When exposed to dampness, this compound emits two extremely toxic gases — phosphine and arsine. Both have an offensive odor similar to that of onions, which should serve as a warning.

Treatment of an oral overdose requires the immediate administration of milk followed by induction of vomiting. This should be repeated. Follow with gastric lavage using a 5% aqueous solution of monosodium phosphate or disodium phosphate. Sixty to 100 ml of this solution should be left in the stomach of a 1- or 2-year-old child. T. J. Covey [*J. Pediat.* **64**, 218 (1964)] recommends that gastric lavage be performed with a solution of sodium bicarbonate and that sodium bicarbonate and a saline cathartic be left in the stomach. He continues, "Intravenous fluids should be given as soon as possible and should contain $CaNa_2$ EDTA, 50–75 mg per kilogram of body weight daily in two doses to chelate free absorbed iron. After the second shock phase, the compound is administered intramuscularly for 4 or 5 days if the amount of ferrous sulfate ingested was 1 gm or more or is unknown. Administration should continue until laboratory data on serum or urinary iron values become available, or, in the absence of such data, until 48 hours pass without further symptoms. Blood, plasma, vasopressors, intravenous fluids, and supportive therapy should be used to treat signs of cardiovascular collapse.

"Peritoneal or hemodialysis should be considered if first-stage symptoms are severe and urine excretion deficient. Intravenous and oral vitamins help prevent liver damage, and oxygen may be advisable during the first 48 hours. Serum proteins should be determined before dialysis. Laparotomy may be necessary if vomiting continues for two weeks and upper gastroenteric findings indicate obstruction. Early continuous antacid and dietary therapy may prevent this complication [T. J. Covey, *J. Pediat.* **64**, 218 (1964)]."

Several publications have appeared recommending both oral and parenteral desferrioxamine (Desferal; DTPA; EDDHA) therapy in iron intoxications [*New Engl. J. Med.* **273**, 1124 (1965); *Nord. Med.* **74**, 985 (1965); *J. Pediat.* **71**, 425 (1967)]. For the treatment of acute iron toxicity from ingestion of ferrous gluconate tablets, F. Henderson *et al.* administered I.V. 0.8 gm of Desferal in 20 ml of water, and P.O. 5.0 gm in 200 ml of isotonic saline to a 14½-month-old child by nasogastric tube. Additional 0.8 gm doses were given

I.V. 12 and 24 hours later [*JAMA* **186,** 1139 (1963)]. W. F. Westlin recommends the following regimen for desferrioxamine: (1) 5.0–10.0 gm via nasogastric tube following gastric lavage (to neutralize the unabsorbed iron); (2) for all patients not in shock or severely intoxicated, 1.0-2.0 gm I.M. every 3-12 hours depending upon the clinical picture, degree of intoxication, and response to therapy; (3) for severely ill patients, and those in a state of cardiovascular collapse, 1.0 gm by *slow* I.V. infusion. The rate of infusion should not exceed 15 mg/kg/hour. The dose is to be repeated depending on the status of the patient. BAL is not effective.

IRON PENTACARBONYL (Iron Carbonyl; Tish)

Iron pentacarbonyl ($Fe(CO)_5$) is a highly flammable yellow-brown liquid at ambient conditions. Its presence may be suspected where high partial pressures of carbon monoxide come in contact with iron or steel vessels. Iron pentacarbonyl (liquid) is used as an antiknock agent in some gasolines.

The oral LD_{50} in rabbits is 0.012 ml/kg, and in guinea pigs 0.022 ml/kg. In rabbits, the percutaneous LD_{50} is 0.24 ml/kg. A 45-minute exposure to iron carbonyl at a concentration of 0.025% by volume (250 ppm) in air was fatal to rabbits. The LC_{50} was found to be 2.19 mg/liter (approximately 275 ppm) for mice, and 0.91 mg/liter (approximately 115 ppm) for rats.

The signs of iron carbonyl poisoning are respiratory distress, cyanosis, tremors, and paralysis of the extremities. Death may be immediate or delayed a few days. Immediately on exposure, giddiness and headache are experienced, occasionally accompanied by dyspnea and vomiting in human subjects. Although these signs may be relieved by removal to fresh air, the dyspnea returns in 12–36 hours, accompanied by cyanosis, fever, and cough. With exposure to lethal concentrations, death usually occurs after four to 11 days [R. S. Brief *et al.*, *Am. Ind. Hyg. Ass. J.*, **28,** 21 (1967)].

Treatment: In case of inhalation exposure, remove individual from contaminated atmosphere. Give artificial respiration and oxygen if necessary. Observe subsequently for premonitory signs and symptoms of pulmonary edema. For eye or skin contact, wash affected tissues with water.

ISOCARBOXAZID (Marplan)

This monoamine oxidase inhibitor is an effective antidepressant drug. It is a hydrazine compound closely related to iproniazid in chemical structure and pharmacological action. Side effects (mild dizziness, weakness, fatigue, constipation, dryness of mouth, blurred vision) may be noted for 2 or 3 weeks after discontinuation of therapy. Rashes, postural hypotension, jaundice, peripheral edema, anemia, leukopenia, and toxic hepatitis have also been reported. Toxic effects on liver and blood, however, are rare [D. G. Friend, *Clin. Pharmacol. Therap.* **6**, 805 (1965)].

Isocarboxazid has been used to give relief in angina. It is prudent *not* to use this drug routinely, except perhaps in instances in which the syndrome has progressed to the severe intractable stage. Contraindications for the use of isocarboxazid are liver disease, renal pathology, or epilepsy. Its continued use during pregnancy is not recommended.

Treatment: See Iproniazid, p. 333, and Monoamine Oxidase Inhibitors, p. 404.

ISOFLUOROPHATE (DFP; Floropryl)

This parasympathomimetic drug is a potent cholinesterase antagonist. It is used as an ophthalmic ointment or solution. The action is more prolonged than that induced by physostigmine or related drugs which cause a reversible inhibition of the enzyme. It is an antidote for atropine. Side effects may include aching of the eyes, headache, photophobia, and blurring of vision. The possibility of an allergic sensitivity reaction to the ointment should be kept in mind. Accidental ingestion of a toxic dose can be expected to produce severe and generalized parasympathetic effects. Chronic exposure has caused demyelination of peripheral nerves.

Treatment: Reduce dose or discontinue treatment if side effects persist. A systemic intoxication (because of ingestion or skin absorption) responds to atropine. Trimethadione, or a barbiturate, is indicated if convulsions should occur or if they are not controlled by atropine. Maintain respiration by whatever method may be required. See Organic Phosphates, p. 438.

ISOLATION

Effects of isolation, or the "toxic effects of a lonely life," were referred to by A. Hatch *et al.* [*Science* **142**, 507 (1963)]. Isolated rats became nervous, aggressive, and intractable in 3 months. Ratios of adrenal and thyroid weights to body weight increased. Reaction to isoproterenol provided a criterion for assessing the development of isolation stress. The LD_{50} of this drug was 850 mg/kg in rats in the community cage. By week 8, the LD_{50} was 118 mg/kg in isolated rats decreasing to less than 50 mg/kg after 3 months. The effect was reversible.

Recommendation: Keep company.

ISOMALIC ACID

Isomalic acid is a colorless, hygroscopic, crystalline powder which melts at 140–142°C. It has a strongly acidic taste. The intraperitoneal LD_{50} for mice is 1.40 gm/kg, which is similar to that of citric acid. By comparison, the intraperitoneal LD_{50} of sodium isomalate is 2.10 gm/kg, a value which approaches the oral LD_{50} of isomalic acid itself (2.45 gm/kg).

Treatment: In case of eye or skin contact, flood with water.

ISONIAZID (Isonicotinic Acid Hydrazide; INH)

Isoniazid is administered alone or in combination with PAS (*p*-aminosalicylic acid), or with both PAS and streptomycin in the treatment of tuberculosis. The drug is also an effective prophylactic agent. Undesirable effects are dose-related. With doses of 3 mg/kg/day, side effects are noted in about 1% of patients. Side effects or signs of toxicity appear in about 17% of patients who receive doses of 10 mg/kg or higher. These effects may include nausea, vomiting, dryness of mouth, restlessness, headache, twitching, paresthesia, and peripheral neuritis [*Geriatrics* **21**, 178 (1966)]. An occasional patient treated with conventional therapeutic doses will have one or more of the following: fever, skin rash, hepatitis, rheumatic syndrome [*Ann. Internal Med.* **63**, 800 (1965)], muscle-twitching, stupor, encephalopathy, convulsions, pancytopenia, thrombocytopenia, granulocytopenia, and gynecomastia [*JAMA* **199**, 942 (1967)]. Ingestion of doses ranging from 10 to 25 gm has induced severe metabolic acidosis, hyperglycemia, perivascular hemorrhage, convulsions, cyanosis, coma, and death.

In response to the possibility that isoniazid may contribute to the production of lung cancer, E. C. Hammond *et al.* conducted an epidemiological study involving a total of 1473 adults and children. They concluded that "the findings give no indication that isoniazid in daily doses of 4 mg per kilogram of body weight increases the risk of cancer occurring in human beings within a period of 10 to 15 years after starting treatment [*Brit. Med. J.* **2**, 792 (1967)]." A possible relationship between the administration of isoniazid during pregnancy and retarded psychomotor activity in the offspring was reported by P. Monnet *et al.* [*Lyon Med.* **218**, 431(1967)].

Most side effects are reduced in intensity or completely disappear upon reduction or discontinuation of therapy. It has been recommended that all patients on prolonged isoniazid therapy, but particularly those with pyridoxine-deficiency anemia, receive supplements of pyridoxine or vitamin B complex [*Brit. Med. J.* **2**, 1177 (1964); *Geriatrics* **21**, 178 (1966)].

Treatment: In case of an acute intoxication resulting from an overdose, perform gastric lavage and administer a saline cathartic, saline and glucose I.V., oxygen, and if necessary, artificial respiration. Control convulsions with paraldehyde or phenobarbital. An exchange transfusion saved the life of a 19-month-old child who swallowed 0.9 gm of isoniazid. Peritoneal dialysis contributed to the survival of a 3-year-old boy who ingested 5 gm of this drug. Since he vomited approximately 2.7 gm, it was assumed that he absorbed 2.3 gm of isoniazid [*New Engl. J. Med.* **269**, 852 (1963)].

ISOPHORONE (Isoacetophorone; 3,5,5-trimethyl-2 cyclohexene-1-one)

This is an unsaturated cyclic ketone; 25 ppm caused irritation of the eyes, nose, and throat of human subjects. See Table 30, p. 709, and Ketones, p. 344.

Treatment: For inhalation, remove the individual promptly from contaminated atmosphere. If breathing has stopped, give artificial respiration and oxygen. In case of skin and eye contact, flood affected parts with water. After ingestion, empty the stomach by inducing vomiting and follow with gastric lavage.

ISOPHTHALOYL AND TEREPHTHALOYL CHLORIDES

These are corrosive skin irritants and lacrimators. The oral LD_{50} of isophthaloyl and terephthaloyl chlorides for male albino rats is higher than 3.16 gm/kg. For albino rabbits, the acute dermal LD_{50} is higher than 3.16 gm/kg. A single application of the moistened form of isophthaloyl or terephthaloyl chloride produced a moderate degree of irritation, and there were definite signs of systemic toxicity from percutaneous absorption in animals at the 3.16 gm/kg dosage level. A single application of 3.0 mg of these chemicals to the eyes of rabbits produced marked irritation which persisted relatively unchanged during a period of 7 days.

Treatment: In case of eye or skin contact, flood with water.

ISOPROPYL ALCOHOL (Isopropanol; Rubbing Alcohol; 2-Propanol; Petrohol)

The single lethal oral dose for an adult is about 250 ml. Ingestion causes gastroenteric pain, cramps, vomiting, and diarrhea. Signs and symptoms of central nervous system depression include dizziness, confusion, stupor, coma, and death from respiratory paralysis. Liver and kidneys are affected, but injury is apparently reversible.

A. W. Freireich *et al.* recently reported the effects following the ingestion of 1 liter of isopropanol by a 54 kg man. His blood pressure rapidly dropped to 60/0, the pulse was 108, and respiration was 16. There was miosis and deep reflexes were absent. At this time extracorporeal hemodialysis was instituted. Within 1 hour he was beginning to swallow and respond weakly to painful stimuli. Blood pressure rose to 40/84, pulse dropped to 88, and respiration rose to 18. After 3 hours of dialysis "the patient was thrashing about." He recovered [*New Engl. J. Med.* **277**, 699 (1967)].

Sponging of the skin with isopropyl alcohol results in absorption in the blood. This may be dangerous in debilitated individuals. The effects are more marked if inhalation of the vapors occurs in addition to skin absorption.

Treatment: After ingestion, induce vomiting and administer gastric lavage, mild central nervous system stimulants, oxygen, and artificial respiration; treat dehydration with I.V. fluids; use antibiotics in case of pneumonia. The above case points out the value of early hemodialysis. The symptomatology and treatment of intoxications due to the higher alcohols (butyl, amyl, hexyl, octyl, etc.) are essentially the same as for isopropyl alcohol. See also Ethyl Alcohol, p. 249.

ISOPROTERENOL HYDROCHLORIDE (Isuprel)

This drug is an effective bronchodilator in the asthmatic or allergic patient and has cardiac-stimulating effects of therapeutic importance. The drug is administered by inhalation or sublingually.

Side effects observed with overdosage arise largely from cardiac stimulation, characterized by subjective discomfort (precordial distress, palpitation, shock, tremors, and nausea). These reactions are similar to those produced by epinephrine and other sympathomimetic amines.

Ball reported an unusual side effect, namely discoloration and severe damage to the permanent incisor and canine teeth of a 12-year-old girl who had used Isuprel tablets for 6 years sublingually for the control of asthma [*Brit. Med. J.* **1**, 1189 (1965)]. See Epinephrine, p. 240.

Caution: This drug should be used with caution in patients with heart disease, especially in patients who have suffered a myocardial occlusion.

JELLYFISH

Marine coelenterates such as jellyfish, living coral, and anemone possess specialized stinging cells called nematocysts, which are capable of penetrating the human skin. Perhaps the best known of this group is the Portuguese man-of-war, *Physalia,* see p. 328.

Treatment: Using a brush, tweezers, safety razor, or soap and water, remove the tentacles and jellylike stinging tissue immediately and completely. Treatment otherwise is symptomatic. See Invertebrate Stings, p. 328. In exceptional instances, the individual may require hospitalization. Treat secondary infections if they occur. Recovery may be slow. Fatalities rarely occur, but the risk is greater in individuals with heart disease [*Arch Dermatol*, **91**, 448 (1965)].

JIMSON WEED: (Datura stramonium)

This annual herb, also known as thorn apple or Jamestown-weed, has been the most frequent cause of intoxications among plants containing the belladonna alkaloids atropine, scopolamine, and hyoscyamine. Other plants of this group include belladonna or deadly nightshade (*Atropa belladonna*), day-blooming jessamine (*Cestrum diurnum*), night-blooming jessamine (*C. nocturnum*), angel's trumpet (*Datura arborea*), fetid nightshade, insane root, poison tobacco or henbane (*Hyoscyamus niger*), and matrimony vine or box thorn (*Lycium halimifoliu.n*).

The severity and the type and onset of symptoms of an intoxication depend primarily on the quantity of plant material or decoction ingested, on the ratio of atropine to scopolamine in leaves, berries, seeds and roots, on the age of the individual, and the quality and quantity of the gastroenteric contents. Briefly, an individual suffering from a typical atropine intoxication may be described as "hot as a hare, blind as a bat, dry as a bone, red as a beet, and mad as a wet hen" [J. M. Arena, *Clin. Pediat.* **2**, *182 (1963);* R. J. Blattner, *J. Pediat.* **61**, 941 (1962); C. J. Polson and R. N. Tattersall, "*Clin. Toxicology,*" pp. 425–442. J. B. Lippincott, Philadelphia, 1951]. See Atropine, p. 116, and Scopolamine, p. 524.

Treatment: Intoxications are most severe in children living in hot climates. Prompt removal of the gastroenteric contents is most important. Repeated vomiting is more effective than gastric lavage. Because of the dryness of the tissues, the gastric lavage tube should be well lubricated. Follow with a saline cathartic. Recovery, except for mydriasis, is usually complete in 24 hours if the plant material was removed promptly from the gastroenteric tract.

KANAMYCIN (Kantrex)

This antibiotic is bacteriologically, clinically, and toxicologically very similar to neomycin. Minor side effects are infrequent; they may include the production of skin rash, headache, paresthesia, and drug fever. Dizziness, tinnitus, and disturbances of equilibrium are early symptoms of ototoxicity. These symptoms, as well as nephrotoxic effects and respiratory paralysis due to neuromuscular blockade, are noted particularly in older people after large doses or prolonged therapy. H. Stupp *et al.* found that kanamycin concentrations in labyrinthine fluid is increased to ototoxic levels, even when the drug is administered at low dosages [*Arch. Otolaryngol.* **86**, 515 (1967)]. As with neomycin, ototoxicity has appeared 2–7 days or later after discontinuation of treatment.

Caution: The drug should be used only for the treatment of serious infections by organisms not susceptible to safer antibiotics. To avoid injury to the auditory portion of the eighth nerve, the drug should be administered to patients who are well hydrated but not in doses exceeding 20 gm/adult over a period of 10–14 days. The patient's hearing should be checked audiometrically during therapy. Withdraw the drug immediately if tinnitus, dizziness, or hearing loss becomes apparent. If, in spite of side effects, the illness requires continuation of kanamycin therapy, lengthen the interval between doses to 3 or 4 days. This is particularly important in patients with reduced renal function. If the need should present itself, kanamycin can be effectively eliminated by hemodialysis or peritoneal dialysis [C. M. Kunin, *JAMA* **202**, 204 (1967)]. See also Neomycin, p. 418, and Streptomycin, p. 555.

KAVA

The roots of the kava plant, which is indigenous to the south sea islands, when dried and ground, yield a powder that upon ingestion produces sleep and muscular relaxation. According to Hans J. Meyer, the effects are due to six different pyrones [*Sci. News* **91**, 138 (1967)].

KEMAMINE N-200 (Propionitrile)

This is an extremely hazardous liquid which is rapidly absorbed through the skin. The vapors are also highly toxic. This is one of the most toxic organic cyanides known. See p. 740.

Treatment: See Cyanides, Inorganic, p. 191.

KENTUCKY COFFEE-TREE (*Gymnocladus dioica*)

Parts of this tree and the golden chain tree or laburnum (*Laburnum anagyroides*), and the shrubs, mescal bean sophora (*Sophora secundiflora*) and necklace-pod sophora (*S. tomentosa*), contain either nicotine, cystisine, coniine, or lobeline. From a toxicological point of view, the difference in pharmacological action of these compounds is not significant. Ingestion of plant material, particularly of the seeds, has led to nicotine-type intoxications. See Nicotine, p. 421. Nausea and vomiting are constant effects which may appear within 10–15 minutes, or be delayed for several hours, after ingestion of several seeds or 1 or 2 pods. In 10 nonfatal cases approximately half of the children had tachycardia, mydriasis, pallor, incoordination, weakness, and drowsiness.

Treatment: Even if the individual has vomited, induce vomiting after administering a dilute solution of potassium permanganate (1:10,000), or a slurry of activated charcoal in water or milk; follow with a cathartic. Complete removal of the gastroenteric contents is important. Symptomatic treatment in a severe intoxication is directed towards restoration of normal blood pressure, normal gastroenteric activity (pilocarpine nitrate, 5 mg P.O. in case of atony), catherization in case of urinary retention, management of convulsions, and inhalation of oxygen. Death due to respiratory failure has been reported one or several hours after ingestion of the seeds, but it may be delayed if green plant material (pods) was chewed and swallowed. Therefore, the early recognition of the intoxication and the prompt removal of the gastroenteric contents may be life-saving.

KEROSENE (Kerosine)

Although kerosene is absorbed from the gastroenteric tract, pulmonary injury after ingestion is due to aspiration of kerosene during swallowing or as a result of gagging and vomiting. The aspiration of a milliliter or less of kerosene into the lungs will produce chemical pneumonitis. Large volumes of kerosene can be tolerated in the stomach without producing pulmonary injury. Gastric lavage is not recommended because aspiration of vomitus containing kerosene may occur during passage of a stomach tube.

Signs and symptoms following ingestion include local irritation of mucous membranes, vomiting, and diarrhea, central nervous system depression, drowsiness, stupor, and coma. Signs of lung involvement include increased rate of respiration, tachycardia, and cyanosis. Kerosene has a defatting action on the skin. The repeated or prolonged use of kerosene on the skin will cause drying and dermatitis.

Treatment: For ingestion or aspiration, do not induce vomiting. Give oxygen if necessary. Use antibiotics to prevent or treat bacterial pneumonia, and saline cathartics to promote elimination from the digestive tract. Corticosteroids may be beneficial. Considerable improvement was observed in an adult following the administration of 15 mg of prednisone 4 times a day. Further treatment is supportive and symptomatic. If the patient survives 24 hours after ingestion of kerosene his chances of recovery are excellent.

KETENE

This is a highly toxic gas. Inhalation may cause severe pulmonary irritation. Death results from delayed pulmonary edema. See Phosgene, p. 471.

KETONES

Ketones are extensively used in industry as solvents. Pharmacologically they are central nervous system depressants similar to ethyl alcohol and ether. Large doses may cause transient liver and kidney injury. Prolonged contact with the skin will cause defatting, dehydration, and dermatitis. The direct aspiration of liquid into the lung will cause chemical pneumonitis. Methyl vinyl ketone is extremely irritating and will produce skin burns on direct contact with tissue. See p. 736.

Treatment: Wash from the skin and eyes with large volumes of water. For inhalation, remove individual from contaminated atmosphere, administer artificial respiration and oxygen if necessary. Further treatment is supportive and symptomatic. In case of ingestion, therapy consists of gastric lavage, saline cathartics, symptomatic and supportive measures.

KEY-PRONE

This is a congener of aminopyrine. See Aminopyrine. p. 93.

LARKSPUR; DELPHINIUM (Delphinium species)

Parts of this plant contain aconitine, which is extremely toxic. Poisonings must be treated as medical emergencies.

Treatment: For signs, symptoms, and treatment, see Monkshead, p. 403.

LARVICIDES

The following are commonly employed as residual larvicides: DDT, dieldrin, BHC, heptachlor, malathion.

LASER

"LASER" is an acronym for "light amplification by the stimulated emission of radiation." Laser radiation from ruby crystals consists of a high-intensity, narrow-beam light of a wavelength of 6943 Å with a band width of less than 1Å. Therefore, a laser produces essentially monochromatic light which is emitted within a cone angle of about 0.1 degree. The brightness of the beam is 10^6 times greater than that of the sun on the surface of the earth. For instance, while a laser produces about 5×10^9 watts/cm², the sun delivers only 10^3 watts/cm².

Operation of the ruby laser is based on four fundamental steps. (1) A light source irradiates a synthetic ruby crystal rod which absorbs energy over a broad band of frequencies. (2) The optical energy excites the atoms in the ruby to a higher energy state from which the energy is reradiated in a narrow band of frequencies. (3) The excited atoms are coupled to an optical resonator and stimulated to emit the resulting radiation together. (This is in contrast to ordinary light sources where the atoms radiate individually at random, and so are responsible for the incoherence of such light sources.) (4) The optical energy released in the form of radiation generates heat in any absorbing object (Aircraft Armaments, Inc., Cockeysville, Maryland). Lasers are capable of cutting diamonds, tungsten, stainless steel, and other hard metals that are difficult to machine by ordinary methods.

Any part of the body exposed to a laser beam may be injured; the eye is particularly vulnerable. At the deep retinal level and immediately adjacent to it, the site of maximum energy density, the incident laser energy is absorbed efficiently, and maximum injury occurs in the form of photocoagulation or thermal injury. A retinal burn is produced when the eye is exposed to as small a quantity of incident laser radiation as 0.1 joule/cm^2 in a 0.5 milli second burst from a ruby laser. Aside from photocoagulation, other biological effects may be produced. Heterogenous distribution of the energy leads to "hot spots," or peaks, within the radiation field producing carbonization, implosions, vapor bubbles, hemorrhages, and scattering of pigment granules into surrounding tissues [M. M. Zaret, *Arch. Environ. Health* **10**, 629 (1965)]. Exposure of mice to pulsed ruby and neodymium irradiation of the head produced damage to the ear on "all or none" basis, suggesting a high potential hazard of laser radiation to the ear. [G. Kelemen *et al., Arch. Otolaryngol.* **86**, 603 (1967)].

Caution and Treatment: Examinations of about 200 persons working with laser beams revealed that 3 individuals had evidence of laser-induced injuries; 2 were minor retinal burns, and the other had subcutaneous burns of the hand with a permanent area of pigmentary changes [*Environ. Health Letter* **1**, No. 15 (May 15, 1962), Ratheon Co., Lexington, Massachusetts]. M. M. Zaret points out that generalized statements in regard to the human hazard from laser may prove of limited value when applied to specific laser systems. Most important in providing protection is an intelligent project leader who is aware of the hazard and who can refer to his safety engineer for guidance in establishing safe operating procedures. The usual burn therapy appears appropriate if this is required.

LAXATIVES

Cascara, senna, and danthron are anthraquinone laxatives. Aloe is also an anthraquinone but it is now rarely prescribed. It is one of the ingredients of Carter's Little Pills and Nature's Remedy. The degradation products of the anthraquinones are excreted by the kidneys, sometimes causing harmless dark coloring in the urine. Melanotic pigmentation of the mucous membrane of the colon has been observed in persons following prolonged use of these agents. This pigmentation is benign and reversible after the treatment is discontinued.

Caution: Since the anthraquinones may be absorbed, they may appear in the milk; these laxatives should not be used by nursing mothers.

LEAD

"Roman culture lost its source of progress when and because its elite, endowed by heredity and/or upbringing. . . . was exterminated by various factors, above all by lead in the diet of the upper-class women . . . ." This led to "sterility, miscarriage, stillbirth, heavy child mortality and permanent mental impairment in the children (S. C. Gilfillan, *The Mankind Quarterly*, Edinburgh, Scotland)." K. B. Hoffman and Rudolf Kobert, between 1883 and 1909, abundantly proved that the lead pots and pipes used only by the wise, intelligent, and rich Romans were primarily responsible for the rapid decline and disintegration of the Roman empire and culture.

In spite of the knowledge that has accumulated in regard to the toxicity and metabolism of lead, intoxications are on the increase. Most of them occur in children, who are more sensitive than adults. In Baltimore, nearly 800 cases of accidental lead poisoning in children occurred during the last 30 years; 124 were fatal.

Ingestion or inhalation of a toxic dose of all the salts of lead, as dust, in solution, or in the form of vapors, will induce symptoms of intoxication. These include headache and weakness, which may progress to paralysis of extensor muscles of the wrists, cramps, and pain in the legs, constipation, collapse, coma, and convulsions. After ingestion, gastroenteric symptoms are predominant. Subacute lead poisoning should be suspected in a child showing irritability, anorexia, anemia, loss of body weight, constipation, and periodic vomiting. Look for these signs and symptoms particularly during hot spells in low income groups living in quarters in which the paint on the walls is 25 years old or older. Skin absorption of lead salts is ordinarily not a problem.

It has become popular in the manufacture of illegal whiskey to use old automobile radiators as condensers in the distillation system. At the temperature of the distillation and under the conditions used, lead is dissolved from the soldered joints in the radiators; this has led to rather frequent cases of lead poisoning. See Scrap Iron, p. 407.

Intoxications from tetraethyl lead differ in several ways from other compounds of lead. L. W. Sanders points out "that tetraethyl lead intoxication exhibits itself as purely a psychotic state, for this is the pattern which invariably is seen, and yet is hardly ever identified by physicians who have not had prior experience with it" [*Arch. Environ. Health* **8**, 270 (1964)]. Tetraethyl lead is readily absorbed through the lungs and the skin. It is quite soluble in fats. "Slight or brief exposure causes insomnia, anorexia, slight fall in blood pressure and body temperature and, if the exposure is more prolonged, stippled red blood cells and leukocytosis, and possibly a lead line [A. Hamilton and H. L. Hardy, 'Industrial Toxicology,' Hoeber, New York 1949]." A severe intoxication results in marked cerebral involvement (insomnia, excitement, maniacal attacks). Death may occur because of exhaustion.

Treatment: Remove the individual from the source of exposure. After ingestion of a potentially toxic dose of a lead compound, induce vomiting and follow with gastric lavage at the earliest possible time. Administer a saline cathartic and an enema. Give calcium gluconate (2 gm), atropine, papaverine, or another antispasmodic for relief of colic. If pain is severe, consider using morphine sulfate. In the case of children, do not give more than 1 mg per 5 kg of body weight. Inject *slowly* I.V. 25 mg/kg of $CaNa_2$ EDTA in divided doses during the first 24 hours. If tolerated, give 75 mg/kg I.V. in divided doses on each of 4 additional days. After a period of about a week, repeat this regimen. (Subcutaneous and intramuscular administrations of this drug have induced less dependable results).

Two severe cases of lead arsenate poisoning at the Jackson Memorial Hospital, Miami, Florida, responded favorably to the cautious alternated treatment with $CaNa_2$ EDTA and BAL. Apparently, only the lead in the blood can be chelated by dimercaprol; the lead in bone and soft tissue is too firmly bound to be mobilized. Therefore, dimercaprol used alone in the treatment of lead poisoning has been abandoned (S. C. Harvey, "The Pharmacological Basis of Therapeutics," Third Ed. The Macmillan Company, New York, 1965).

In treating lead poisoning in children, H. D. Smith prefers edetate rather than dimercaprol, in spite of the fact that after edetate there is frequently an exacerbation of the encephalopathy during the first 24 hours of therapy. He states: "Currently, following the suggestion of Chisholm, we are using dimercaprol together with edetate in the following regimen: dimercaprol 4 mg/kg/dose intramuscularly every four hours for five-six days; edetate 12.5 mg/kg/dose intramuscularly, mixed with procaine, also every four hours for five-six days. The first dose of edetate is given concurrently with the second dose of dimercaprol. Before initiating this therapy, one should make certain that the child is voiding well" [*Arch. Environ. Health* **8**, 256 (1964)]. For additional information, consult the original paper. Oral edetate is not recommended.

H. Mehbod found that the amount of lead removed by peritoneal dialysis is considerably greater than that excreted in the urine, with or without edetate therapy. He recommends the combined treatment of peritoneal dialysis plus edetate: (1) in patients with acute lead intoxication when the speed with which deleading is accomplished is a crucial factor in the outcome, (2) in patients with lead intoxication who also have severe renal functional impairment and azotemia, and (3) in any patients in whom the administration of edetate in high doses may be hazardous [*JAMA* **201**, 972 (1967)].

Oral penicillamine also has been recommended for the treatment of lead intoxication. According to J. Greengard of the Hektoen Institute, penicillamine has the advantage in that it is "apparently less toxic." The initial dose for older children and adults is 250 mg. This may be increased to 250 mg 4 times a day. Subsequent doses depend on the severity of the intoxication and on the amount of lead excreted in the urine [*Can. Med. Assoc. J.*, **88**, 1155 (1963); *Brit. J. Ind. Med.* **23**, 282 (1966); **24**, 272 (1967)].

Tetraethyl Lead. Kerosene has been recommended for the removal of this compound spilled on the skin, followed by a thorough washing with green soap. According to L. W. Sanders, Sr., "No specific therapy for lead encephalography has been developed up to the present time. The treatment therefore, is essentially symptomatic and supportive. Heavy and prolonged sedation with barbiturates has been employed effectively. The short-acting barbiturates are more easily controlled, and there is less likelihood of an unexpected cumulative effect. The water and electrolyte balance of the patient must be maintained, and the maintenance of nourishment is essential, as is the careful cleansing of the air passage" [*Arch. Environ. Health* 8, 270 (1964)]. For additional information consult "Symposium on Lead" R. A. Kehoe, *Arch. Environ. Health* 8, 202–354 (1964).

LEAD NAPHTHENATE

The oral toxicity of lead naphthenate ranges from 3.5 to 5.1 gm/kg (rat). The compound can be absorbed through the skin in toxic quantities. Rasetti *et al.* found evidence of lead absorption in 65% of 14 workers who had prolonged contact with lubricant additives containing 10% lead naphthenate. Skin absorption was found in 3 subjects rubbed with 6 ml of an oil containing 192 mg lead (expressed as metallic lead). Blood samples taken 10 minutes later showed lead absorption. Blood lead levels increased for 60 minutes and then decreased rapidly and became "normal" in 8 hours [L. Rasetti, *Rass. Med. Ind.* 30, 71 (1961)].

LEVALLORPHAN TARTRATE (Lorfan; 1,3-Hydroxy-*N*-allylmorphinan)

This drug, like nalorphine, is used as an antagonist against severe respiratory depression induced by opiates and precipitates the abstinence syndrome in opiate addicts. It produces moderate respiratory depression when administered to individuals who are not under the influence of an opiate and who are not addicted. If depression is due to hypoxia, brain damage, barbiturates, anesthetics, or related drugs, even a low dose of levallorphan will *increase* the respiratory depression. The drug is *not* a narcotic and, therefore, not subject to control by the federal narcotic law.

Treatment: Resuscitation appears to be the best method for combatting respiratory depression. See Narcotic Agents, p. 40, and Opiates, p. 435.

LEVARTERENOL BITARTRATE (Levophed)

This sympathomimetic amine is widely used for the treatment of shock and other conditions characterized by acute or sustained abnormally low blood pressure.

With levarterenol, ventricular arrhythmia may occur. For this reason, the drug is contraindicated during cyclopropane anesthesia and after absorption of other drugs or chemicals that are liable to induce ventricular fibrillation. Prolonged peripheral vasoconstriction may adversely affect the circulation of the central nervous system and kidneys. Sudden withdrawal of Levophed therapy may cause an abnormal drop in blood pressure and a possible loss of responsiveness to this drug.

Subcutaneous extravasation will induce sloughing and tissue necrosis. For this reason and to avoid administration of overdoses, an infusion should be watched *constantly.* A. M. Lands comments as follows: "This phenomenon (necrosis) does not occur frequently; it is almost invariably in the lower extremity; is most likely to occur in patients in whom there is a pathologic process such as arteriosclerosis obliterans, thromboangiitis obliterans, or Raynaud's disease; and is usually found in situations in which infusions have been continued over many hours. If the area proximal to the infusion cannula is watched for blanching, the infusion can be discontinued and set up in another area without danger. Infiltration of this area with Regitine at the first evidence of blanching has been found useful. Perivascular administration should be avoided, and extravasation can be prevented by threading a polyethylene catheter into the vein far enough so that the infused fluid will be picked up and diluted by a good venous flow (Sterling-Winthrop Research Institute)." Apparently, Regitine does not interfere with the maintenance of blood pressure when injected into an area of levarterenol extravasation.

Treatment: Treatment is symptomatic. See Epinephrine, p. 240.

LEVORPHANOL (Levo-Dromoran)

This is a relatively new, potent synthetic narcotic drug. Its properties and side effects are similar to those induced by morphine, except that its action is longer and that it produces less constipation.

LEVULINIC ACID (LA)

This is a white crystalline substance which melts at 37°C. Studies with animals showed levulinic acid to be nontoxic when fed at a level of 5% of their food intake. Its vapors at room temperature are reported to be nontoxic and nonirritating. Normal precautions must be used in handling levulinic acid, since contact of concentrated LA with the eyes results in severe burns similar to those from glacial acetic acid. Concentrated levulinic acid is irritating to the skin.

Treatment: Persons working with levulinic acid should wear protective clothing and goggles. In case of eye or skin contact, the affected areas should be flushed immediately with plenty of water.

LIBRAX

This preparation, containing clidinium bromide and chlordiazepoxide, for the control of hypermotility, hypersecretion and anxiety, after temporary withdrawal, was reinstated by the FDA (9-1-1966).

LICORICE

Compound licorice contains senna, sulfur, glycyrrhizin, and fennel. Individuals who regularly ingested large quantities suffered edema, hypertension, and hypokalemic alkalosis [*Brit. Med. J.* **1**, 1230 (1965)].

LIDOCAINE (Xylocaine)

Lidocaine belongs to the group of important local anesthetics which includes procaine, tetracaine, and dibucaine. The drug is metabolized in the liver by microsomal enzymes. R. Selden and A. A. Sasahara reported severe central nervous system symptoms in a patient with liver disease who had received 600 and 800 mg of lidocaine hydrochloride by I.V. infusion over several hours. Three fatalities were recently reported, one after administration of 200 mg, the second after infiltration of approximately 2500 mg of lidocaine, and the third case, after injection of 1 ml of 5%

tetracaine followed by approximately 150 ml of 2% mepivacaine hydrochloride (Carbocaine) and 2 or 3 injections of lidocaine [Sunshine and Fike, *New Engl. J. Med.* **271**, 487 (1964)].

In animal studies, Akamatsu and Siebold demonstrated that the combination of a local anesthetic with a rapid onset of action and one having a prolonged action is potentially hazardous. They determined the LD_{20} of individual anesthetics in mice, then noted the toxicity of various combinations of LD_{20} doses.

Tetracaine was tested with lidocaine, mepivacaine, chlorprocaine, and propitocaine. Only 10 of 100 animals survived the lidocaine-tetracaine combination. Survival in the other groups ranged from 12 to 20 per groups of 100 mice [*Anesthesiology* **28**, 238 (1967)].

Caution: This and related drugs which are metabolized by the liver should be given with caution. They should not be used in patients with liver diseases [*JAMA* **202**, 908 (1967)]. See Dibucaine, p. 208.

LILY-TYPE PLANTS

These include the spider lily, snowflake, narcissus, jonquil, snowdrop, amaryllis, tuberose, and daffodil. There is only one recorded case of oral poisoning. This occurred because the bulb of the daffodil (*Narcissus pseudo-narcissus*) was mistaken for an onion. Plants of the lily family contain a variety of alkaloids, particularly the heat-stable alkaloid lycorine.

Animal experiments indicate that ingestion of parts of these plants can induce emesis, shivering, narcosis, hypotension, hepatic degeneration, and convulsions.

Treatment is symptomatic following evacuation of the material from the gastroenteric tract.

LIME (Calcium Oxide; Unslaked Lime; Quicklime)

This liberates heat on contact with water. Contact with tissues causes irritation, desquamation and ulceration. Inhalation or ingestion may lead to irritation and ulceration of the respiratory or gastroenteric passages.

Treatment: For ingestion, rapid and thorough gastric lavage is essential. In case of contact with the skin, eyes, and mucous membranes, flood with water. Consult an ophthalmologist for further definitive treatment of eye injury. Treat skin injury and mucous membrane injury subsequently for chemical burn, p. 26.

LIME SULFUR (Calcium Polysulfide)

This compound is irritating on contact with skin, eyes, and mucous membranes. On ingestion, hydrogen sulfide is formed.

Treatment: Remove from skin and eyes with copious quantities of water. In case of ingestion, see Hydrogen Sulfide, p. 320.

LINCOMYCIN (Lincocin)

Lincomycin, erythromycin, and oleandomycin have much the same clinical properties. Few serious toxic effects have been reported. It must be remembered that it has taken many years of clinical experience to appreciate the full toxic potential of the older antibiotics. A few instances of jaundice, abnormal liver function tests (SGOT), and neutropenia, all reversible, have been noted. The drug inhibits protein synthesis, perhaps an ominous portent for the future.

LIPSTICKS

Most lipsticks contain oil-wax mixtures, lanolin, a dye, a perfume, and inorganic color pigments. All of these substances, except the pigments, may cause an allergic reaction.

LIQUEFIED PETROLEUM GAS (LP; LPG)

The liquefied petroleum (LP) gases are composed largely of the following hydrocarbons or their mixtures: propane, propylene, butane, and butene.

See Hydrocarbon Gases, p. 316.

LIQUID MOLLY

Molybdenum disulfide is the principal constituent of a dry lubricant and lubricant additive. See Molybdenum, p. 402.

LITHIUM

Severe intoxications and fatalities have resulted from the use of lithium chloride as a substitute for sodium chloride in low-sodium diets. The symptomatology included nausea, apathy, anorexia, tremors, blurring of vision, polyuria, oliguria, confusion, and coma. The primary toxic action of lithium appears to be in the kidney. A high sodium intake protects animals (up to a point) against the toxic effects of lithium. In the presence of a low sodium intake, the toxicity of lithium is markedly increased.

Lithium carbonate has been used with promising results in the treatment of manic-depressive psychosis. This compound may be the drug of choice as a prophylactic agent in phenothiazine refractory or phenothiazine-allergic manic patients [*Am. J. Psychiat.* **123,** 706 (1966); *Arch. Gen. Psychiat.* **16,** 162 (1967)]. Side effects are not significant. However, lithium therapy cannot be administered indiscriminately, as indicated by a 1957 report in which more or less severe local (cutaneous reactions) and systemic intoxications occurred among 300 psychotic patients treated with lithium [*JAMA* **164,** 1402 (1957); *Am. J. Psychiat.* **124,** 1124 (1968)]. A. Kallos describes the use of lithium bromide as a keratolytic agent in keratoderma and tinea unguium.

Treatment: In acute oral intoxication, induce vomiting promptly; follow with gastric lavage and symptomatic treatment. In the presence of side effects, discontinue lithium therapy, promote diuresis, administer calories I.V. or P.O. to overcome starvation ketosis, and correct acidosis.

LOBELINE

This alkaloid is extracted from the leaves of *Lobelia inflata,* also known as Indian tobacco. Absorption of a toxic dose will produce effects resembling those induced by nicotine. Lobeline has been used to break the tobacco habit.

Treatment: Ingestion of the leaves of *Lobelia inflata* should be followed by prompt vomiting or thorough gastric lavage, administration of cathartics, and replacement of fluids.

LOQUAT; JAPANESE PLUM (*Eriobotrya japonica*)

Chewing and ingestion of the seed kernels of the ripe plum has caused cyanide poisoning. Ingestion of the *whole* seed is harmless. The buds, leaves, trunk or tubers of a number of other plants, bushes or trees contain glycosides that release hydrocyanic acid in the gastroenteric tract. Human intoxications have apparently not been reported except for one instance in which the tubers of the tapioca plant (*Manihot* species) were ingested.

Treatment: See Cyanides, Inorganic, p. 191, for signs, symptoms, and treatment of intoxication. The specific treatment should be preceded by removal of the gastroenteric contents.

LORDS AND LADIES (*Arum maculatum*)

Ingestion of any part of this plant will result in systemic intoxication. Leaves and berries have been primarily implicated. The local effects include painful swelling and inflammation, bleeding of the mucous membranes of the lips, mouth, tongue and epiglottis, and possibly loss of speech. Systemic effects may include the appearance of red spots all over the body, paresthesia, drowsiness, mydriasis, circulatory disturbance, and convulsions preceding death.

Treatment is the same as that outlined under Spurge Laurel, see p. 552.

LOXENE (Loxsit)

This mildew preventive contains a high concentration of sodium pentachlorophenate. Hospital linens treated with Loxene were believed to be responsible for high fever and profuse sweating observed in 9 infants only a few days old. Some of these infants required exchange transfusions. Two died. Loxene (Loxsit) has since been withdrawn from the market.

Treatment: See Dinitrophenols, p. 227.

LSD (Lysergic Acid Diethylamide; LSD-25; Acid; Hawk; The Chief)

This semi-synthetic derivative of the ergot fungus of rye was discovered by the Swiss chemist Albert Hoffmann. Chemically, it is an amine alkaloid resembling ergonovine. It is capable of evoking profound psychic symptoms such as delusions, visual and auditory, hallucinations, depersonalization, impaired judgment, psychosis, euphoria, and depression. Some effects are experienced with an oral dose of 30 μg. Following ingestion of 200–400 μg doses, effects appear in 15–30 minutes. Hard-core "acid heads" inject LSD I.V. for immediate effects. These people, sooner or later, suffer the needle-induced diseases such as local abscesses, phlebitis, hepatitis, endocarditis, and pulmonary foreign-body reactions. Tolerance develops after intake of LSD for several days; this is lost during the next 3 days if the individual witholds this agent.

Accidental ingestion of LSD has occurred. This represents a stressful event because distortions occur without the victim's knowledge that they were drug-induced. Self-destruction or psychotic decompensation may follow such a devastating experience. A child inadvertently ingested a sugar cube containing LSD-25. One month later he was still in a partial state of dissociation [S. Cohen and K. S. Ditman, *JAMA* **181**, 161 (1962)]. A 5-year-old child who ingested 100 μg still suffered after 5 months from abnormal EEG and disorganization of visual-motor functions [D. H. Milman, *JAMA* **201**, 821 (1967)].

Fatalities due to an overdose of LSD have apparently not been reported. However, there is at least one individual who under the influence of LSD jumped to his death because he thought he could fly, and there have been others who under the influence of this agent committed murder [W. C. Alvarez, *Mod. Med.* **35**, 89 (1967)]. An Asiatic elephant given an I.M. dose of LSD died with epileptic seizures [*Sci. News Letter* (Dec. 22, 1962)].

Recent studies show that chromosome damage can result from ingestion of LSD [Council on Mental Health and Committee on Alcoholism and Drug Dependence, *JAMA* **202**, 47 (1967)]. Chromosomal damage has also been reported following the addition of LSD to cultured leukocytes [*Science* **155**, 1417 (1967)]. Injection of LSD into mice in early pregnancy caused a 57% incidence of grossly abnormal embryos [*Science* **157**, 459, 1325 (1967)]. Since chromosomal abnormalities have been reported, there may be a causal relationship between a malformed leg in an infant whose mother took LSD on the 25th day after her last menstrual period and three times between the forty-fifth and ninety-eighth day of her pregnancy [J. S. McDonald and G. Abbs, *Lancet* **II**, 1066 (1967)].

An increasing number of persons who take LSD repeatedly appear to become permanent dropouts from society, abjuring family, friends, and productive activity, embracing instead a hallucinogen-oriented, solipsistic, unproductive existence in which LSD and similar drugs are no longer used merely in attempts to achieve a variety of psychosocial or religious objectives but, rather, become central to existence itself [D. B. Louria, *New Engl. J. Med.* **278**, 436 (1968)].

Treatment: An individual under the influence of LSD responds to phenothiazines and to barbiturates. One of these drugs, preferably a phenothiazine, should be administered early (intramuscularly), since it will assist in establishing the diagnosis. Dr. David Smith of the San Francisco General Hospital administers antipsychotic (chlorpromazine) or antianxiety (chlordiazepoxide) tranquilizers to an individual who is still "high on a lingering trip." He subsequently treats physical disorders, which may include upper respiratory tract infections, hepatitis, and venereal disease. Finally, he talks to the patient and tries to turn him from the myth that LSD or other hallucinogens solve everything [*Look* (Aug. 8, 1967)]. Caution is in order if a phenothiazine and a barbiturate are used in combination. Their effects will be additive. It may take months before all signs and symptoms of the psychotic state have disappeared.

LYSOL

Local and systemic effects are similar to those produced by phenol. See p. 463.

MACHINE OIL (Motor Oil)

Some motor oils contain tri-*o*-cresyl phosphate (TOCP), the chemical that caused the infamous "Jake Ginger paralysis" (extensor paralysis of legs and arms). In Morocco, 10,000 persons became ill and many were paralyzed following ingestion of cooking oil adulterated with aviation oil containing TOCP [*JAMA* **172**, 595 (1960)].

Partial paralysis of all extremities was reported in three sisters, ages 4, 6, and 8, and in a maid after they ingested machine oil instead of castor oil. The oil, almost pure tricresyl phosphate, contained about 5% tri-*o*-cresyl phosphate. After several days of abdominal pain, vomiting, passing of colored urine, and temperature elevation of 103°F, the four victims were stricken with paralysis. Four and a half years later, all showed definite return of function of the affected muscles.

There was complete recovery of the intrinsic muscles of the hands, but the abductors and extensors of the hips were weak. One child had a slight flexion contracture of both hips. The other cleared her feet well, but used a high top shoe, and the third child had more spasticity. The maid had marked foot drop, and abductors and extensors of the hips functioned poorly.

Treatment: After accidental ingestion, induce vomiting *immediately and repeatedly.* Follow with saline cathartics. There is no specific antidote. Recovery from this type of paralysis is extremely slow; some patients never recover. See p. 604.

MADRICIN

This long-acting sulfa drug has been withdrawn because it caused severe blistering and inflammation of the mucous membranes (the Steven-Johnson syndrome) and some deaths.

MAGNESIUM

Slow absorption from the alimentary tract and rapid excretion are responsible for the low toxicity of magnesium salts. Prolonged use of magnesium sulfate (Epsom salt) for cathartic or other purposes will cause dehydration and loss of weight. Pre-existing kidney injury will retard its excretion, and thereby contribute to gastroenteric distress and possibly to acute systemic effects. Signs and symptoms of toxicity have been more frequent following injections of magnesium sulfate. These may include analgesia, muscular and nervous depression, respiratory paralysis, and (after I.V. injection) paralysis of the heart. Magnesium sulfate therapy for pre-eclampsia induced magnesium intoxication in an infant. At no time did the mother show evidence of an intoxication [*Pediatrics* **40**, 100 (1967)].

Magnesium trisilicate is used to treat peptic ulcer. The use of this drug may result in the production of silica concretion (silicon dioxide) in the renal tract.

Fragments of magnesium metal penetrating the skin are likely to produce local irritation, blisters, and ulcers which may become infected. Metal parts should always be removed from the skin. Inhalation of freshly generated magnesium oxide will cause metal fume fever.

Magnesium deficiency has been reported to induce neuromuscular and central nervous system hyperirritability, hallucinations, and cardiovascular disturbances. Malnutrition, magnesium deficiency, and hypocalcemia are closely related, and tetany is likely to occur in patients with low serum magnesium. For a report on the metabolism of magnesium, see W. E. C. Wacker and A. F. Parisi, *New Engl. J. Med.* **278**, 658 (1968).

Treatment: An I.V. injection of magnesium sulfate should *not* be given unless a syringe containing 10 ml of 2–10% calcium chloride in saline is held in readiness to combat respiratory paralysis. Calcium is a direct antagonist to magnesium. Calcium gluconate (P.O. or I.V.) may be used if retention of orally administered magnesium occurs due to poor kidney function. "Magnesium tetany" disappears when serum calcium values return to normal, even when serum magnesium remains low. However, high oral calcium intake may exaggerate a negative magnesium balance [C. C. Booth *et al.*, *Brit. Med. J.*, **2**, 141 (1963)]. In a severe magnesium intoxication, peritoneal dialysis, using a dialysate fluid free of magnesium, or hemodialysis may be necessary. The effect of exchange transfusion was dramatic in the infant suffering from magnesium intoxication.

For immediate relief of pain resulting from silica concretions in the renal tract, meperidine, antispasmodics, and a high fluid intake are recommended. Magnesium trisilicate preparations should not be used indiscriminately.

MAGNESIUM PEMOLINE

Magnesium pemoline (Abbott 30400; Cylert; 2-imino-5-phenyl-4-oxazolidionone and magnesium hydroxide) has been reported to enhance acquisition and retention of a conditioned avoidance response in the rat, to improve attention in humans, to facilitate a complex motor task, and to increase brain RNA synthesis. Recent studies, however, have failed to confirm facilitation of learning, memory, or psychomotor performance in normal adults, or to increase *in vivo* synthesis of brain RNA. The so-called "memory pill" is no more than a stimulant. Rather than enhancing memory, magnesium pemoline, like an amphetamine, stimulates the nervous system. Rats receiving this drug simply work faster (to avoid electric shock), but do not learn better [S. Gelfand *et al.*, *Clin. Pharmacol. Therap.* **9**, 56 (1968)].

MALEIC ANHYDRIDE (Toxilic Anhydride; *cis*-Butenedioic Anhydride; 2,5-Furandione)

This hydrolyzes readily to maleic acid (see Acids, Aliphatic Dicarboxylic, p. 71). Workers exposed to maleic anhydride have symptoms characterized by cough, lacrimation, and respiratory oppression. In nine cases of severe exposure, gastric pain, headache, nausea and vomiting were also reported. Symptomatic treatment brought about recovery in 6–10 days.

MANCHINEEL TREE (*Hippomane mancinella*)

The leaves, branches, fruit, bark and roots of this bushy-type tree contain compounds (not yet identified) which on contact with the skin produce severe irritation, blistering, and desquamation. Ingestion causes severe gastritis, vomiting, bloody diarrhea, loss of body fluids, hypotension, and shock. Eye contact has produced temporary blindness.

Treatment is the same as outlined under poison ivy; see p. 484.

MANDRAX

Mandrax, a combination of methaqualone and diphenhydramine hydrochloride, when administered to 10 ward patients concurrently with thioridazine (Mellaril), induced nosebleed, dryness of the mouth, swelling of the tongue, cracking at the angles of the mouth, dizziness, and disorientation. The symptoms subsided upon withdrawal of Mandrax [A. Kessell, *et al.*, *Med. J. Australia* **2**, 1194 (1967)]. During the 7 months following the introduction of Mandrax, 5% of the "poisoned" patients admitted to the Royal Infirmary in Edinburgh had taken overdoses of Mandrax. They displayed marked hypertonia, myoclonia, shock, hypothermia, and respiratory and renal failure.

Treatment of these patients involved intensive supportive therapy to maintain vital functions. Measures which might have hastened elimination of the drug were not used. All patients survived [*Brit. Med. J.* **2**, 1455 (1966)].

MANEB (Manzate)

This compound has a low order of toxicity and is similar chemically to Ferbam, p. 261. See also Thiocarbamates, p. 585.

MANGANESE

Intoxications from salts of manganese have been rare. Acute inhalation exposure has resulted in respiratory difficulties, increase in hemoglobin, muscular twitchings, and night cramps. Repeated exposures may induce an increased incidence of respiratory disease (manganese pneumonitis), or cause a Parkinsonian syndrome characterized by weakness of the legs, increased muscle tone, slurring of speech, spastic gait, and mental deterioration.

Treatment: Edathamil therapy has been suggested by A. K. Done [*Clin. Pharmacol. Therap.* **2**, 750 (1961)] and by C. M. Whitlock, Jr. *et al.* [*Am. Ind. Hyg. Assoc. J.* **27**, 454 (1966)]. BAL is not effective. The inhalation of oxygen revived animals dying from overdoses of manganese cyclopentadienyltricarbonyl [*Federation Proc.* **23**, T51 (1964)].

MANGO (*Mangifera indica*)

Contact with the sap induces rash, inflammation, and swelling in sensitive individuals.

Treatment is symptomatic.

MANNITOL

This sugar (hexatomic) alcohol obtained from manna and other plant sources has found use as an osmotic diuretic in patients with an acute endogenous or exogenous intoxication due to substances available for renal excretion. Following infusion, it is neither metabolized nor reabsorbed by the tubular cells. (Sucrose is no longer used for this purpose since it may cause renal tubular necrosis.) The maximum dose of mannitol is 200 gm per 24 hours. The infusion should be stopped or reduced if the central venous pressure rises or if there is evidence of circulatory overload. (This drug is not to be confused with mannitol hexanitrate, which is a coronary dilator.)

Caution: Mannitol should be used with caution in patients prone to heart failure because of the hazard of circulatory volume expansion. Urine output and central venous pressure should be watched carefully. If the drug induces a brisk diuresis, electrolyte and water depletion may occur. It has not yet been determined whether this drug is safe for children and pregnant women [G. L. Speath *et al. Arch. Ophthalmol.* **78**, 583 (1967); *Med. Letter* **10**, 5 (1968)]. Mannitol has induced anaphylaxis in a hypersensitive person. Such a reaction occurred 3 minutes after an I.V. infusion of mannitol in a 65-year-old woman who had suffered from bronchial asthma since early childhood. She responded to epinephrine [*Arch. Ophthalmol.* **78**, 583 (1967)]. Roberts and Smith point out that mannitol can cause agglutination and irreversible crenation of red blood cells, that to avoid this, hypertonic solutions of mannitol should never be mixed with blood in a transfusion set, and that intravenous infusions should always be administered at a carefully controlled slow rate [*Lancet* **II**, 421 (1966)]. Ascitic patients with cirrhosis should be carefully observed when on mannitol therapy; if serum sodium increases significantly, the administration of a natriuretic drug may prevent further difficulties [Gipstein and Boyle, *New Engl. J. Med.* **272**, 1116 (1965)].

MARIHUANA (Cannabis; Hashish; Bhang; Khat; Ganga; Dagga; Pot; Grass; Boo)

The narcotic properties of *Cannabis sativa*, the hemp plant, were documented in Chinese writings by 200 A.D. In spite of the fact that the use of marihuana is restricted in almost every civilized country, thrill seekers obtain it illegally and smoke or eat the flowering or fruiting tops of the plant, or drink the extracts. The principal active ingredients of cannabis resin (found in the leaves, flowers and dried tops of the plant) are the tetrahydrocannabinols.

The effects of smoking a "reefer" are evident in a few minutes, and may last for as long as 12 hours. These include a feeling of well-being, hilarity, euphoria, distortion of time and space perception, impaired judgment and memory, and irritability and confusion. The occasional use of cannabis does not cause lasting mental changes.

After repeated administration, or high doses, there is a lowering of the sensory threshold, followed by hallucinations, illusions and delusions, anxiety, and aggressiveness. Symptoms of intoxication frequently include chronic bronchitis, asthma, hypoglycemia, bulimia, and depression of respiration. Particularly severe or prolonged effects, including paranoid behavior, have been reported following the combined use of cannabis plus alcohol or amphetamines. Cannabis has caused a moderate to strong psychological dependence, but no tolerance or physical dependence. According to a recent report, withdrawal symptoms have been reported following the use of the more potent material available in North Africa and now coming to the United States [*Med. Letter* **9**, 73 (1967)].

Treatment: Complete cessation of the use of marihuana is recommended. An acute intoxication requires no specific treatment other than a certain degree of confinement for the purpose of observation. A chronic user of the weed who has acquired a psychological dependence is a sick individual and requires psychiatric help and understanding. In most cases, the prognosis is good for such persons [Council on Mental Health and Committee on Alcoholism and Drug Dependence, *JAMA* **201**, 368 (1967)].

MARKING INK

Aniline dyes are the active ingredients in inks used for marking laundry. Boiling of marked napkins and clothing eliminates the possibility of absorption of the pigment. Absorption of fresh marking ink through the skin has induced severe and fatal intoxications characterized by the formation of methemoglobin, anoxia, and cyanosis.

Treatment: Give antibiotics, oxygen, methylene blue and ascorbic acid. Garments, towels, diapers, etc., newly marked with an ink should not be used before they have been laundered. See Treatment of Aniline, p. 102.

MASCARA

Using someone else's mascara, eye-liner, or similar eye makeup has led to at least one epidemic of severe eye infection and trachoma. The outbreak resulted from schoolgirls borrowing eye-liner pencils. The practice of borrowing or lending mascara and other cosmetics should be discouraged.

MASER

"MASER" stands for "microwave amplification by stimulation of emission of radiation." The biological effects produced result from microwave radiation. See Microwave Radiation, p. 397.

Treatment: Prevention is, of course, the best therapy. Tincture of time supported and abetted with the usual therapy for burns would seem appropriate.

MASKING ODORANTS (Oil of Cloves: Cedar Wood; Cedar Leaf; Citronella; Camphor; Lavender and Wintergreen)

These materials are added in low concentrations to various household or commercial products to impart a pleasant, agreeable odor. At these low concentrations they are essentially harmless. The undiluted oils are irritating to the skin, cause chemical pneumonitis if aspirated into the lung, and, in general, act on the central nervous system because of their lipid solubility.

Treatment: See Citronella, p. 178.

MATCHES

Modern matches contain relatively nontoxic phosphorus sesquisulfide or red phosphorus. In safety matches the phosphorus is used on the striking surface not on the match head. See also Potassium, p. 491.

Treatment: None is required.

MEBUTAMATE (Capla)

Chemically this drug is closely related to meprobamate; it differs pharmacologically, inducing a more pronounced hypnotic effect. It has been used as a centrally acting antihypertensive agent. According to J. A. Janney, Jr. *et al.*, the marked drowsiness produced by a single therapeutic dose of 0.6 gm limits its use. In other words, mebutamate in tolerable doses does not lower the blood pressure effectively [*Clin. Pharmacol. Therap.* **4**, 720 (1963)]. Headache, dryness of mouth, nasal congestion, weakness, and constipation have also been reported.

Caution: Even though mebutamate is useful as an antihypertensive agent (300 mg 4 times a day) in the majority of patients, this type of therapy can not be recommended because of the drowsiness it produces. Administration at bedtime seems appropriate.

Treatment: Reduction of dose is followed by recovery.

MECAMYLAMINE (Inversine)

This ganglionic blocking agent has effects similar to those of pentolinium, trimethiodinium, and chlorisondamine. Side effects may include orthostatic hypotension, constipation, urinary retention, inability to focus, neuromuscular disorders, mental aberrations, and convulsions.

Caution: The drug should be used with caution in patients who cannot tolerate sudden or marked hypotension. According to A. C. Corcoran, salt diuretics usually cut dosage requirements in half, while combined ganglion blockers, diuretics, reserpine, and hydralazine may be required in resistant hypertension ("Drugs of Choice, 1966-1967," C. V. Mosby, St. Louis, Missouri, 1966).

The undesirable effects can be reduced by adjusting the dosage and/or administering neostigmine.

MECLIZINE (Bonine)

This antihistaminic drug, formerly known as Bonamine, is used in the treatment of vertigo and motion sickness. Following therapeutic doses, side effects include drowsiness and sometimes impairment of motor functions. Administration of preparations containing meclizine plus vitamin B_6 (pyridoxine) are not recommended [*Lancet* II, 1334 (1962)].

Meclizine has been shown to be teratogenic in the rat [*Science* 141, 353 (1963); *Am. J. Obstet. Gynecol.* 95, 109 (1966)], and there is presumptive evidence that this drug was responsible for congenital malformations in babies [*Lancet* 1, 675 (1964)].

Caution: This drug should be avoided during pregnancy.

Treatment of overdoses is symptomatic. See Antihistamines, p. 107.

MEDROXYPROGESTERONE ACETATE (Pepo-Provera)

This is a progestational hormone. Of 57 women treated with this drug for threatened abortion, 22 experienced missed abortion and retained a dead fetus for 8 or more weeks. Each of these 22 patients subsequently underwent dilatation and curettage.

Caution: Although Piper *et al.* reported no serious surgical complications, they recommend that medroxyprogesterone not be used in the management of threatened abortion [*Am. J. Obstet. Gynecol.* **97**, 579 (1967)].

MEFENAMIC ACID (Ponstel)

This new analgesic may be hazardous if taken for more than 7 days. The authors agree with the consultants of the Medical Letter that "in view of the limited knowledge of the effects of mefenamic acid, if it cannot safely be used for more than seven days, it should not be used at all [*Med. Letter* **9**, 77 (1967)]."

MELPHALEN (Alkeran)

This anticarcinogenic agent is used primarily for the treatment of multiple myeloma. Oral doses in excess of 0.1–0.2 mg/kg for 7–10 days are likely to produce nausea and vomiting. Another dose-related adverse effect is bone marrow depression. Hyperemia and hemorrhage of the gastoenteric tract have been reported.

Caution: Blood counts should be determined 2 or 3 times a week in patients receiving mephalen. If the white cells drop below 2,000/mm^3 or the platelet count falls below 75,000/mm^3, the drug must be discontinued until the white blood cells rise above 3,000/mm^3 and platelets above 100,000/mm^3. It appears that minimal hematologic toxicity can be expected if the drug is given in *low* doses (approximately 0.085 mg/kg) for 2–3 weeks, and if this regimen is repeated after the blood counts have recovered. For details, see statement by the Council on Drugs, *JAMA* **191**, 547 (1965).

MENTHOL

Excessive ingestion or inhalation of mentholated products has caused abdominal distress and central nervous system depression. Mentholated American cigarettes contain 1–2 mg of menthol. The maximum quantity inhaled per cigarette is 0.7 mg. Hives (urticaria) and/or "hot flashes" occurred over a period of 2 years in two women who were hypersensitive to the menthol in cigarettes and in a face cream [*JAMA* **189**, 546 (1964); *Arch. Dermatol.* **94**, 62 (1966)]. A few isolated instances of menthol contact dermatitis, purpura, and shock-like reactions in children were reported in the older literature. Hypersensitivity is rare considering the extensive use of menthol as a flavoring agent.

Treatment is symptomatic.

MEPAZINE (Pacatal)

This is a phenothiazine tranquilizer. It is noted for its depression of the bone marrow (leukopenia, granulocytopenia, agranulocytosis), production of jaundice, and high incidence of atropine-like effects. It cannot be recommended [S. Cohen, *Mod. Treat.* **2**, 505 (1965)].

MEPERIDINE (Demerol; Isonipecaine; Pethidine)

This is a narcotic analgesic with antispasmodic properties. Overdoses have produced profound shock, irregular pulse, profuse perspiration, and deep coma; the corneal reflex may be absent, and moist rales may be present in both lungs. The drug is highly addictive. According to D. G. Friend, the danger of addiction is very high if the drug is given repeatedly and continuously for 2 weeks. Physicians, nurses and pharmacists head the list of meperidine addicts [*Clin. Pharmacol. Therap.* **7**, 832 (1966)]. In dogs, hypotension due to meperidine is caused by the release of endogenous histamine. Demerol is contraindicated in patients suffering increased intracranial pressure.

Caution: Administration of meperidine with a monoamine oxidase inhibitor is likely to induce collapse, confusion, and cerebral excitement [*Brit. Med. J.* **2**, 822, 1592 (1963)]. I. M. Vigram reported on a patient who received an injection of 100 mg of meperidine and scopolamine hydrobromide (200 μg; 1/300 grain) while on pargyline hydrochloride (Eutonyl) therapy. He became rigid, convulsed and comatose within minutes. The patient responded to oxygen and infusion of dextrose in water [*JAMA* **187**, 953 (1964)]. *Obviously combinations of meperidine, other opiates, and MAO inhibitors should be avoided.* Meperidine should be avoided in toxemia of pregnancy [*Deut. Med. Wochschr.* **90**, 1465 (1965)].

Treatment: In case of an overdose, administer nalorphine or levallorphan. Further treatment is symptomatic and supportive. See Narcotic Agents, p. 40, and Opiates, p. 435.

MEPHENESIN (Tolserol)

This centrally acting muscle relaxant and sedative drug, and mephenesin carbamate (Tolseram), are sold under 20 or more trade names. Side effects following the administration of mephenesin are infrequent. They have included nausea, vomiting, dizziness, muscular weakness, and incoordination. The I.V. injection of this drug is occasionally accompanied by visual and auditory disturbances or by hemolysis and hematuria. While allergic reactions to mephenesin have been reported, D. T. Schwartz *et al.* described a febrile response to Tolseram. A 39-year-old patient with a history of "hay fever" had fever, dyspnea, rales, and wheezes on the fourth day of oral treatment [*JAMA* **190**, 778 (1964)]. Depigmentation of hair during oral treatment with mephenesin carbamate was reviewed by J. D. Spillane. He reported on six such incidents — four women and two men whose hair color became considerably lighter. In the most striking case, while taking 10 gm daily, the hair of a woman turned from dark brown to blonde within 3 months [*Brit. Med. J.* **1**, 997 (1963)].

Treatment: Side effects following I.V. injections are not significant when dilute solutions are used. Oral administration is recommended when possible. Discontinuation of treatment resulted in recovery of the 39-year-old patient in approximately 2 weeks. The new hair color was temporary, and all patients became brunettes again.

MEPHENOXALONE (Trepidone; Lenetran)

This is a new drug with no confirmed activity as an effective tranquilizing agent. The manufacturer warns that in a very small group of patients a tendency to leukopenia and thrombocytopenia has been noticed.

MEPIVACAINE (Carbocaine)

This local anesthetic is used for infiltration and block anesthesia. When the dose is less than 250 mg

(0.5–2.0%), this drug is well tolerated and side effects such as nausea, vomiting, headache, pallor, faintness, hypotension, and drowsiness are not common. When 500 mg or more is infiltrated, respiratory depression, convulsions, and collapse may follow. The drug readily passes the placenta and may cause toxic effects in the infant.

Caution: Mepivacaine like other local anesthetics is contraindicated in patients with emotional instability, severe hypotension, infection in the involved area, and in certain obstetrical complications (placenta previa, pelvic disproportion, and fetal bradycardia) [A. B. Dobkin and J. Po-Giok Su, *Clin, Pharmacol. Therap.* **7**, 648 (1966)].

MEPROBAMATE (Miltown; Equanil)

This substituted diol is a mildly tranquilizing drug. It also relaxes skeletal muscles and has anticonvulsant properties. Side effects and symptoms of toxicity may include hypersensitivity reactions (urticaria, angioneurotic edema, pruritus, purpura simplex, serum sickness often associated with bronchospasms), cardiovascular complications (dizziness, syncope, hypotension), gastroenteric disturbances (nausea, vomiting), abnormal lactation, loss of visual acuity for near objects, central effects (drowsiness, sedation, coma, muscular paralysis, pinpoint or dilated pupils, euphoria, addiction), and blood dyscrasias. Meprobamate is one of several newer nonbarbiturate sedatives that have produced physical dependence similar to that induced by barbiturates. The other drugs are Glutethimide (p. 287), Ethinamate (p. 248), Ethchlorvynol (p. 247), Methylprylon (p. 359), and Chlordiazepoxide (p. 166) [*Clin. Pharmacol. Therap.* **5**, 334 (1964)].

The acute toxicity of this drug is considerably lower than that of most barbiturates. The action of this drug is potentiated by ethyl alcohol. Ingestion of doses ranging from 10 to 40 gm has been followed by recovery, but in some patients, 12 and 16 gm were fatal. In a hypersensitive patient, 0.4 gm induced a severe intoxication. Therapeutic doses range from 0.8 to 2.4 gm/day. In an 11-year-old boy administration of doses increasing to 2.5 and 3 gm/day for several weeks produced nervousness, abdominal pain, and markedly decreased muscle tone and weakness [*New Engl. J. Med.* **267**, 145 (1962)].

Treatment: Prompt vomiting or gastric lavage and a saline cathartic are recommended after ingestion of an acute overdose. The drug is metabolized rather rapidly and usually produces only brief coma, which requires only supportive treatment [R. K. Maddock, Jr. and H. A. Bloomer, *JAMA* **201**, 999 (1967)]. However, depending on the severity of the intoxication, the following may be considered: tracheal aspiration, insertion of an oral airway, forced diuresis, administration of vasopressor substances, I.V. fluids, oxygen, caffeine, and sodium benzoate or an amphetamine. Serious intoxication, with deep coma and a plasma drug level approaching 20 mg%, or overdosage complicated by other drugs or infection require aggressive treatment, including hemodialysis (R. K. Maddock, Jr. and H. A. Bloomer). The 11-year-old boy recovered rapidly when the drug was withdrawn, indicating that significant muscular atrophy did not occur.

Withdrawal of meprobamate should be gradual. B. F. Sorenson recommends that phenobarbital (0.1–0.3 gm, 3 times a day for 2–3 days) be given for treatment of withdrawal symptoms [*JAMA* **184**, 780 (1963)]. Convulsions, if they do occur, may require meprobamate temporarily.

MERCAPTANS, ALKYL (Alkane Thiols; Thio Alcohols; Alkyl Hydrosulfides)

Methyl, ethyl, propyl, and butyl mercaptan are extremely malodorous in concentrations far below the levels that produce toxicological effects. In general, they are central nervous system toxicants causing muscular weakness, convulsions, and respiratory paralysis. High concentrations may cause pulmonary irritation. See p. 739.

Treatment: Remove victim from contaminated atmosphere. Give artificial respiration and oxygen if needed. Observe for premonitory signs of pulmonary edema. In case of ingestion induce vomiting and follow with gastric lavage.

MERCAPTANS, ARYL (Aromatic Thiols)

Thiophenol and toluene thiol are liquids having a penetrating odor and a weakly acidic reaction. Contact with skin and mucous membranes may cause irritation. Excessive exposure to the vapor of thiophenol causes vertigo and headache. See p. 739.

Treatment: Remove victim to fresh air. Give artificial respiration and oxygen if necessary. For ingestion induce vomiting and follow with gastric lavage.

6-MERCAPTOPURINE (Purinethol; 6-MP)

This drug used in adequate dosages will induce remission and prolong life in patients suffering from acute leukemia. In therapeutic doses, 6-MP is generally well tolerated. Prolonged therapy or excessive doses produce severe leukopenia and bone marrow hypoplasia. Liver damage (jaundice, hepatic necrosis), intestinal ulcerations, and skin eruptions have also been reported.

Caution: The dosage of 6-MP is largely dependent upon the effect on the bone marrow; white blood cell and platelet counts should be done at frequent intervals. The drug should be discontinued when definite hematological signs of relapse occur. Jaundice or anorexia, with tenderness in the right hypochondrium, are also indications for withholding the drug.

MERCURY (Quicksilver)

The amount of liquid metal accidentally ingested when a thermometer bulb is broken in the mouth is harmless. Larger amounts may cause systemic toxicity, although this opinion is not shared by all physicians [*JAMA* **182**, 95 (1962); *Med. Welt* **34**, 1768 (1962)].

Vapors of metallic mercury are toxic. A stream of air passing over a 10 cm^2 surface of metallic mercury becomes 15% saturated and contains 3 mg of mercury per cubic meter of air. Globules of mercury, spilled on desks and floors and coming in contact with fat or wax, provide large surfaces for evaporation. [For human experimental inhalation studies, see J. Teisinger and V. Fiserova-Bergerova, *Ind. Med. Surg.* **34**, 580 (1965)]. There have been several outbreaks of mercury poisoning in which the concentration in air ranged from 0.5 to 7.5 mg per cubic meter. Fatalities after 16 hours of exposure were reported by F. T. Matthes. Erosive bronchitis and bronchiolitis with severe interstitial pneumonitis or pulmonary edema were the most outstanding pathological findings. The most obvious effects produced after repeated exposures to toxic or subtoxic concentrations are tremors, damage to the kidneys, mercurialentis and opacity of the cornea, gingival hypertrophy, and areas of dark pigmentation of the gums (deposition of sulphide of mercury) [*J. Occupational Med.* **5**, 157 (1963); *Brit. J. Ind. Med.* **24**, 73 (1967)].

J. T. Buxton *et al.* call attention to the hazard of mercury embolism during blood sampling for blood gas analysis [*JAMA* **193**, 573 (1965)]. The I.V. injection of 10 ml of metallic mercury caused death in 6 months. H. R. M. Johnson *et al.*, in their review covering the past 70 years, reported another fatal case [*Brit. Med. J.* **1**, 340 (1967)]. Leschke reported on an attempted suicide with 2 ml (27 gm) of metallic mercury injected into the right cubital vein. This patient survived for 10 years in good health.

Skin application of ointments of ammoniated mercury, tattooing utilizing pigments containing mercury, or local contact with mercuric chloride or one of many other salts of mercury are likely to induce skin changes including irritation, dermatitis, discoloration of the nails, corrosion and ulceration of mucous membranes and eyes, as well as severe systemic effects [*JAMA* **188**, 830 (1964)].

The lethal oral dose of mercuric chloride for adults is 1–4 gm, although death has followed ingestion of as little as 0.5 gm [*Clin. Pediat.* **2**, 53 (1963)]. The kidneys are affected early, since they are the principal channels of mercury excretion. A patient is expected to recover if he survives for 10 days, although later deaths are not uncommon. An outbreak of neurological disorders and fatalities occurred in Minamata, Japan, following ingestion of fish poisoned by mercuric chloride. The chemical came from a plant for the catalytic processing of vinyl chloride.

Mercurous chloride (calomel or gray powder) has caused systemic intoxications (pink disease, erythredema, polyneuropathy) when used as a cathartic and as a constituent of teething powders. Mercurous chloride is relatively innocuous, but on contact with alkaline digestive juices, it may be converted to the mercuric ion. As a cathartic, calomel should *never* be used with an alkali iodide or an oxidizing and reducing agent; if used, it should be followed within 5–8 hours with a saline cathartic.

Dimethyl mercury and diethyl mercury are extremely toxic compounds which cause cerebellar degeneration, ataxia, delirium, and reduction in the visual fields, depending on the dose. Organic mercury compounds used as disinfectants, germicidal agents, or drugs have a relatively low order of toxicity. These include mercurochrome, phenyl mercuric derivatives, meralluride (Mercuhydrin), mercurophylline (Mercuzanthin), mersalyl sodium (Salyrgan-Theophylline), mercaptomerin sodium (Thiomercin), and chlormerodrin (Neohydrin).

In Iraq, mass poisoning by the fungicide ethyl mercury toluene sulfonanilide (Granosan M) occurred when farmers consumed bread prepared from wheat treated with this compound. Involvement of the nervous system was most constant (disturbance of speech, cerebellar ataxia, spasticity), but the kidneys, gastroenteric tract, skin, heart, and muscles were also affected. There were many fatalities [*Brit. J. Ind. Med.* **18**, 303 (1961)].

Treatment: After ingestion, Solpaw and Alpers recommend gastric lavage with 4% sodium formaldehyde sulfoxalate (reduces mercuric chloride to metallic mercury) in water or in 2–3% aqueous sodium bicarbonate; 200 ml of this solution should be left in the stomach [*J. Lab. Clin. Med.* **27**, 1387 (1942)]. A saturated solution of sodium bicarbonate may also be used for gastric lavage, leaving 200 ml of a saturated solution of magnesium sulfate in the stomach after completion of lavage. Follow with the administration of BAL as outlined under treatment of metal intoxication, p. 224. BAL is most effective when given very early during the course of an intoxication; in subacute cases, it is usually of little help. In these cases, its administration is sometimes followed by increased proteinuria and other undesirable effects. Oral fluid therapy (including 1 teaspoonful of potassium bitartrate and $\frac{1}{2}$ teaspoonful of sodium citrate in water or orange juice) promotes the excretion of mercury. Shock due to peripheral vascular collapse may be treated with whole blood or plasma, dextrose, and saline. Treatment otherwise is symptomatic.

After administration of an overdose of an organomercurial drug, prompt binding of the mercury by BAL is essential. If the mercurial drug has been absorbed and has been present in the body for more than

6 or 7 hours, sloughing of the epithelial cells of the renal tubules can be anticipated. The problem then becomes one of management of the lower nephron syndrome (personal communication, R. Boucek, University of Miami).

Compounds of mercury can be removed from the skin by thorough washing with soap and water.

Patients who suffered from inhalation exposure to mercury vapors were treated by W. J. Burke and J. M. Quagliana with bronchodilators, oxygen mist, and Alevaire (a detergent aerosol) [*J. Occupational Med.* **5**, 157 (1963)]. Of the penicillamine compounds, *N*-acetyl-DL-penicillamine seems to be most effective, but whether this drug should be preferred to the early use of BAL (which apparently is not always effective) has not yet been decided. [*Clin. Pediat.* **2**, 53 (1963); *New Engl. J. Med.* **269**, 889 (1963); *Brit. J. Ind. Med.* **24**, 73 (1967)]. See Penicillamine, p. 452. At this writing, CaNa$_2$ EDTA cannot be recommended. Hemodialysis was used effectively by L. Sanchez-Sicilia *et al.* [*Ann. Internal Med.* **59**, 692 (1963)]. It is of interest that a diet high in sucrose gave considerable protection against the toxic effects of mercuric chloride in rats.

MESITYL OXIDE (Isopropylidene Acetone)

The vapors of this compound (4-methyl-3-pentene-2-one) are irritating to the eyes and mucous membranes. Absorption into the blood stream in sufficient concentration will cause central nervous system effects.

METAL ALKYLS; METAL ARYLS

These compounds, in which a metallic atom is attached directly to the hydrocarbon moiety of the molecule, have marked chemical reactivity. Many burst into flame on contact with air (sodium, potassium, rubidium, cesium, beryllium, magnesium, calcium, strontium, barium, zinc, cadmium, radium, boron, aluminum, gallium, indium, tellurium). Their pyrophoricity depends on the metal and on the hydrocarbon moiety. The decomposition products (vapors or fumes) may cause lung injury and/or fume fever depending on the exposure. Direct contact with skin or mucous membranes results in severe chemical burns.

Treatment: See Alkyl Aluminum Compounds, p. 83, Organotin Compounds, p. 440, and Lead, p. 347.

METAL DUSTS

Metallic dusts used to tint the hair may cause respiratory illness if inhaled. Finely divided metallic dust of alloys of bronze, copper, zinc, tin, and aluminum can cause severe irritation to the nose and lungs.

A tracheostomy had to be performed on a 7-year old boy who inhaled a metallic dust used by a 12-year old neighbor girl to streak her hair. This dust is marketed under several different names by major cosmetics manufacturers.

METAL FUMES (OXIDES)

The industrial disease characterized by chills, fever, muscular pains, nausea, vomiting, and some degree of prostration is commonly called "metal fume fever" (also "galvo," brass founders' ague, and brazier's disease). Inhalation of freshly generated oxides of zinc, copper, or magnesium is the most common cause of metal fume fever, although oxides of other metals such as aluminum, antimony, cadmium, iron, manganese, nickel, selenium, silver, and tin may also produce these symptoms.

Treatment: Discontinue exposure. Recovery is usually spontaneous and complete in 24–48 hours.

METAL HYDRIDES (Sodium, Potassium, Lithium, Magnesium, Calcium, Strontium)

Moisture from the body will convert these chemicals into caustic hydroxides and hydrogen. The hydrides are irritating to the skin, eyes, and mucous membranes of the nose, throat, and lungs. In addition, heat is released from the reaction of the hydrides with the moisture of the skin. Sodium and potassium hydride react explosively with water. Dusts of hydrides are inflammable and can be ignited by sparks or open flames.

Treatment: See Sodium Hydroxide, p. 543.

METARAMINOL BITARTRATE (Aramine; Pressonex)

This drug has actions similar to those induced by neosynephrine. Pressor effects are due to peripheral vasoconstriction. Cardiac stimulation plays a minor role.

Caution: When used as a local nasal decongestant, it is liable to raise the blood pressure—an undesirable effect in certain patients.

METHACHOLINE CHLORIDE (Mecholyl)

This is a true parasympathomimetic agent acting on effector cells, even after complete nerve degeneration. In general, effects are similar to those of physostigmine. Atropine should be readily available whenever this potent drug is administered parenterally.

METHACRYLONITRILE (MAN)

Single-dose rabbit dermal and rat intragastric studies indicate that methacrylonitrile is highly toxic by both routes. The LC_{50} values for single 4-hour inhalation periods varied from 700 ppm of the vapor for female rats to 36 ppm for male mice. Methacrylonitrile formed cyanide ion in the blood of rats and rabbits, and its effects were diminished by the standard therapy for cyanide intoxication. Human sensory response studies showed that the vapor has very poor warning properties. The response of rats and dogs to repeated 7-hour exposures of methacrylonitrile vapor for 91 and 90 days, respectively, suggest that humans should not be allowed to inhale more than 3 ppm vapor for 8 hours per day, 5 days per week. This hygienic standard is an estimate based on experimental data and, therefore, is subject to modification as data are gathered on human experience.

Treatment: Methacrylonitrile on the skin should be removed *immediately* by flushing with large volumes of water. Prolonged exposure to the vapors or ingestion of the liquid requires emergency action. See Acrylonitrile, p. 76, and Cyanide, p. 191.

METHADONE (Amidone; Dolophine)

This drug is a potent narcotic analgesic. Side effects are more severe and more frequent in ambulatory than in hospitalized patients. Respiratory depression will respond to nalorphine and also to levallorphan. See Narcotic Agents, p. 40, and Opiates, p. 435.

METHALLYL CHLORIDE (3-Chloro-2-methyl-1-propene)

Methallyl chloride is a colorless liquid possessing a pungent, penetrating odor. Commercial methallyl chloride contains about 5% of the isomeric isocrotyl chloride (1-chloro-2-methyl-1-propene), which is very difficult to remove by distillation.

Methallyl chloride possesses approximately the same degree of toxicity as allyl chloride. A single 10-minute exposure to 22,000 ppm may be fatal. By comparison a similar exposure is fatal with 20,000 ppm of benzene, 25,000 ppm chloroform, and 50,000 ppm of carbon tetrachloride. Methyl bromide is much more toxic than methallyl chloride. With white rats, a 100% kill resulted from a 1-hour exposure to air containing 16 gm of methyl bromide per cubic meter. Eight such exposures to methallyl chloride resulted in no deaths.

Treatment: See Allyl Chloride, p. 86.

METHAQUALONE (Quaalude)

Methaqualone, which is similar in action to the barbiturates and other hypnotics, appears to have no advantage over the barbiturates; it is used in patients who cannot tolerate the latter drugs. Adverse reactions associated with doses ranging from 0.15 to 0.4 gm have not been important. They have been similar to those observed with other hypnotics [Council on Drugs, American Medical Association, *JAMA* **199**, 749 (1967)]. Several severe and some fatal poisonings following ingestion of 4–30 gm of methaqualone have been reported from Germany. Most of these were suicidal attempts. The signs and symptoms noted following ingestion of these doses included a rapid variation in pupillary width and reaction to light, motor excitation, hyperreflexia, muscle fasciculation, and deep coma. Less frequent were tonic-clonic convulsions, vomiting, salivation, and lacrimation. Characteristic was the *"Nachschlaf"* (sleep from which the patient could be roused), which persisted for 24 or more hours after the regression of other signs or symptoms. Death resulted from pneumonia and acute cardiac failure with terminal shock [S. Gitelson, *JAMA* **201**, 977 (1967)].

Potentiation of the hypnotic effects occur when this drug is administered in combination with barbiturates, ethanol, chlorpromazine, reserpine, meperidine, and other opiates (S. Gitelson).

Treatment: Gastric lavage and perhaps colonic lavage followed by administration of a saline cathartic are recommended. (See Barbiturates, p. 119.) In combined mathaqualone-meprobamate poisoning, hypotension resulting from large doses of meprobamate may aggravate the methaqualone-induced cardiovascular complications, particularly in a patient with pre-existing cardiac disease. Since forced diuresis may further increase the load on the damaged heart, I.V. fluids should be administered in these cases with caution (S. Gitelson).

METHDILAZINE (Tacaryl)

This is a long-acting antihistamine with antipruritic, antiemetic, and sedative effects. An individual who ingested 280 mg in a suicide attempt suffered severe central nervous system depression, labored respiration, obstruction of the respiratory tract (due to edema of the tongue and laryngeal structures), and gastroenteric irritation resulting in hemorrhagic gastritis and vomiting.

Treatment: The patient described above survived after the use of stimulants, steroids, tracheostomy, parenteral fluids, and antibiotics [LeRoy Homer, *J. Med. Soc. N. Jersey* **60**, 115 (1963)].

METHENAMINE MANDELATE (Mandelamine)

This preparation (mandelic acid and methenamine) is used as a urinary antiseptic. To be effective, the urine must be acid (pH 5.5 or less); otherwise, methenamine will not liberate formaldehyde, the primary active agent. According to *Medical Letter* consultants, an acid-ash diet is frequently as effective in producing an acid urine as is ammonium chloride or methionine. Ascorbic acid has also been recommended for this purpose [*Med. Letter* **5**, 53 (1963)]. A related product, Mesulfin, is liable to form an insoluble sulfonamide precipitate in the urine.

Caution: Mandelamine is contraindicated in patients with renal insufficiency or liver disease. Its use should be discontinued if efforts to acidify the urine fail after several days.

METHIMAZOLE (Tapazole)

This is a potent oral antithyroid drug having a prolonged action. Methimazole depresses the formation of thyroxin by the thyroid gland. During treatment the thyroid gland may enlarge, and pre-existing exophthalmos may be aggravated. Other side effects or signs of toxicity may include drug fever, gastroenteric disturbances, pain in joints, hepatitis, loss of taste, cholestasis, neuropathy, and leukopenia.

Caution: An overdose must be avoided, since it may cause enlargement of the thyroid gland. Since blood dyscrasias may develop in certain hypersensitive individuals, patients receiving this drug should have blood counts at regular intervals; they should be told to report sore throat, malaise, and/or fever to the physician immediately.

Treatment: Reduce or discontinue therapy if side effects become significant or threatening. In a recent report, severe cholestasis, without evidence of liver cell damage, cleared up in 10 weeks [*Gastroenterology* **43**, 84 (1962)].

METHIONINE

Although the toxicity of this essential amino acid is of a very low order, neurologic changes have been reported in patients with cirrhosis who received oral methionine therapy. When used for urinary acidification, it is likely to induce gastroenteric irritation and symptoms.

METHIXENE HYDROCHLORIDE (Trest)

This is a new anticholinergic agent (*adult* dose 1–2 mg, 3 times per day) for the symptomatic treatment of functional bowel disorders. Side effects (dry mouth, mydriasis, cycloplegia, rash, and retention of urine) are usually seen after absorption of anticholinergic drugs.

Caution: The drug is contraindicated in the presence of angle-closure glaucoma, pyloric obstruction, prostatic hypertrophy, bladder-neck obstruction, or cardiospasm [*JAMA* **195**, 851 (1966)].

METHOCARBAMOL (Robaxin)

This is a centrally acting skeletal muscle relaxant similar in pharmacological properties and action to mephenesin (Tolserol; Dioloxol).

Treatment of an overdose consists of artificial respiration and use of oxygen if needed.

METHOCEL

This is the trade name for a family of methyl-cellulose ethers. They are colorless, odorless, tasteless, and completely inert. They are extensively used in foods.

METHOHEXITAL SODIUM (Brevital)

This short-acting barbiturate is 2.5 times as potent as thiopental sodium; it has a shorter recovery period and minimal after-effects. It is administered intravenously. See Barbiturates, p. 119.

METHOPHOLINE (Versidine)

This drug and Versidine compound were withdrawn from the market.

METHOTREXATE

Methotrexate is anticarcinogenic; its interference with folic acid function leads to a citrovorum factor deficiency. It is also used in the suppression of psoriasis. One regimen is the daily oral dose of 2.5 ml for 6 days, to be repeated after a rest period of 1 week. The drug may also be injected I.M. or I.V. According to V. H. Witten and R. J. Helfman, this drug should be used only by the experienced physician. Effects of oral toxicity (nausea, gastroenteric ulceration, abdominal pain, anorexia, and alopecia) are fairly common. Because of the inhibition of normal leukocyte response, trivial infections may become severe ("Drugs of Choice, 1966–1967" C. V. Mosby, St. Louis, Missouri, 1966). Hersh *et al.* observed a portal inflammatory reaction in seven of ten patients subjected to liver biopsy [*Cancer* **19**, 600 (1966)]. Adverse effects may not necessarily be reversible. Two psoriatic patients died following oral treatment with methotrexate; one received the drug (5 mg/day) for 5 days, the other for 7 days. In both instances, corticosteroid therapy may have been a complicating factor [*Lancet* **1**, 1165 (1967)].

Caution: When used for the suppression of psoriasis, methotrexate should be administered at a dosage level that does not consistently produce leukopenia, and only in patients in whom psoriasis is seriously disturbing and who do not respond to topical therapy. Before a course of therapy is initiated in any patient, white blood cell and platelet counts and hemoglobin should be determined, and the adequacy of hepatic and renal function should be established. Subsequently, a white blood cell count should be determined before each dose, and the other tests run periodically. During the course of treatment, the risk of toxicity must be weighed constantly against anticipated therapeutic effects.

METHOTRIMEPRAZINE (Levoprome)

This new analgesic is just as effective as morphine and meperidine (Demerol). It is available for intramuscular injection only in a concentration of 20 mg/ml. Adult dosage ranges from 10 to 15 mg; for severe pain it may be increased to 40 mg. The drug is nonaddicting and therefore not subject to the restrictions of the Harrison Narcotic Act. Chemically, methotrimeprazine is a phenothiazine and produces many of the same side effects. The drug produces marked sedation, hypotension, and dry mouth, but this is less severe than that induced by atropine and scopolamine. Occasionally, the drug causes disorientation, nasal stuffiness, and urine retention. Longer use of the drug is required to assess the incidence of pigmentation of the skin and corneal and lens changes. Agranulocytosis and cholestatic jaundice have been reported following long-term, high-dosage use of the drug. Methotrimeperazine induces significantly less respiratory depression than morphine or meperidine [*Med. Letter* **9**, 49 (1967)].

Treatment: Overdoses have not been reported. See Phenothiazines, p. 464.

METHOXYACETALDEHYDE (Methoxyethanal)

Methoxyacetaldehyde has an oral LD_{50} of 2.33 ml/kg for young male albino rats. The dermal LD_{50} for the product held in continuous 24-hour contact with rabbit skin is 1.17 ml/kg. The undiluted product produces a moderate degree of irritation when introduced into the eyes of test rabbits.

The vapor pressure of methoxyacetaldehyde is relatively high at ordinary temperatures, so that high concentrations of vapor can develop if the product is handled carelessly or if ventilation is inadequate.

Treatment: For inhalation, remove the victim to

fresh air. Give artificial respiration and oxygen if necessary. In case of eye or skin contact, flood the affected parts with water.

METHOXYCHLOR. See p. 662

METHOXYFLURANE (Penthrane)

This inhalation anesthetic is a good hypnotic and a potent analgesic. It will not burn in air, nitrous oxide, or oxygen at temperatures below 75°C. Following anesthesia with this compound, recovery is slow, largely because the fat desaturates slowly. Since excretion of methoxyflurane is via the lungs, postoperative respiratory depression will tend to further delay recovery. A recent report describes toxic nephropathy in about 15% of patients. Blood urea nitrogen was elevated in some of these cases [*Anesthesiology* **27**, 591 (1966); **28**, 637 (1967)].

Caution: The possibility of liver injury as well as the respiratory depressant properties of this anesthetic should be kept in mind [A. B. Dobkin and J. Po-Giok Su, *Clin. Pharmacol. Therap.*, **7**, 648 (1966)]. Atropine is helpful in reducing the vagal depressant action and salivation.

METHOXYPROMAZINE (Tentone)

This phenothiazine-type tranquilizer has not been widely used. Little is known of its side effects [S. Cohen, *Mod. Treat.* **2**, 505 (1965)]. See Phenothiazines, p. 464.

METHYL ALCOHOL (Methanol; Methyl Hydroxide; Methyl Hydrate; Columbian Spirits; Wood Naphtha; Wood Spirits; Wood Alcohol; Sterno; Carbinols; Colonial Spirits)

In man, methyl alcohol is oxidized primarily to formaldehyde and formic acid. Ethyl alcohol and methyl alcohol are oxidized mainly by alcohol dehydrogenase, but the rate of oxidation of methanol is about one-seventh that of ethanol. (In mice, acetylsalicylic acid considerably inhibits the oxidation of methanol, thereby reducing the toxicity of this compound) [*Experientia* **22**, 85 (1966)].

Symptoms of intoxication vary with the dose. Outstanding clinical features include rapid or delayed onset of symptoms such as marked gastroenteric and visual complaints and variable neurological abnormalities. The pupils are dilated but do not react to light. Weakness, anorexia, headache, nausea, vomiting, dyspnea, pain in the back, extremities, and abdomen may develop 12–18 hours following partial or complete recovery from inebriation. Late effects may include severe cerebral edema and neuritis. Cyanosis, coma, marked slowing of respiration, and death may follow in several days.

Optic nerve damage and fatalities have been reported after ingestion of 10–250 ml of methyl alcohol and after inhalation of methanol vapors. Based on studies with monkeys, skin absorption of 30 ml may be hazardous to man. Methyl alcohol is present in brandies in concentrations from 0.2 to 1.5 %; in whiskeys in a concentration of about 0.015 %.

Treatment: Prompt removal from the gastroenteric tract by vomiting is important. Gastric lavage may be performed with 1 or 2 % sodium bicarbonate or water. Give 5–10 gm of sodium bicarbonate P.O. every hour until the urine is alkaline. The carbon dioxide combining power must be determined at intervals of a few hours, since acidosis may reappear suddenly. The acidosis produced exceeds that which can be attributed to the oxidation of methanol. Evidently secondary enzymatic inhibitions take place. W. Oaks and C. Heider recommend the immediate I.V. administration of sodium bicarbonate. In a severe intoxication, alkali replacement is calculated on the basis of total body base deficit. One-half to two-thirds the calculated amount is given during the first 3–4 hours. For initial treatment, they recommend 1000 ml of 5 % glucose in water plus 350–400 mEq of bicarbonate. Thereafter, the dose of alkali is based on the serum electrolytes and carbon dioxide combining power. Control of respiratory depression and management of cardiovascular collapse are equally vital [*Penn. Med. J.* **67**, 27 (1964)]. Depending on the severity of the intoxication, this treatment may be followed by the administration of ethyl alcohol to reduce or prevent the formation of formic acid. A concentration of at least 100 mg of ethanol per 100 ml of blood should be maintained for a 70 kg man. Administer 90–120 ml of whiskey (45 % alcohol), followed by 60–90 ml every 4 hours for 1–3 days. Ten milliliters of ethanol per hour is considered the minimum dose required to suppress completely the metabolism of methyl alcohol. A. K. Pfister *et al.* recommend dialysis (preferably extracorporeal) in addition to alkalization and administration of anhydrous ethanol [*JAMA* **197**, 1041 (1966)].

METHYLAL (Formal; Dimethoxymethane)

This is a central nervous system depressant; 15,000 ppm in air is lethal to rats in a few minutes. Excessive exposure may cause liver and kidney injury. See also Dioxane, p. 658.

Treatment: See Ethers, p. 247.

METHYLAMINES (Monomethylamine; Dimethylamine; Trimethylamine)

The presence of methylamines in the air at low concentrations is readily recognized by the fishy odor. At higher concentrations, somewhere in the range of 100–500 ppm, it is hard to distinguish the odor from that of ammonia. The intensity of the odor diminishes after prolonged exposure.

Inhalation of methylamine vapors (>100 ppm) causes irritation of the nose and throat, followed by violent sneezing, burning sensation of the throat, coughing, constriction of the larynx and difficulty in breathing, pulmonary congestion and edema of the lungs.

Methylamine solutions and the anhydrous liquids are highly irritating to the skin and mucous membranes and may cause burns. The physiological effects are similar to those produced by ammonia.

Treatment: For skin contact, remove contaminated clothing immediately and flush the affected parts with large amounts of water. Since the reaction is alkaline, the skin should be washed with a mild acidic solution such as vinegar or 1–2 % acetic acid solution. In case of eye contact, flush the eyes immediately with water. Workers overcome by the gas should be removed to fresh air at once. If breathing has stopped, artificial respiration and oxygen should be administered.

2-METHYLAMINOETHANOL

This compound is slightly toxic orally for laboratory animals. It is a severe skin irritant which penetrates the intact skin, causing death in test animals at doses of 1.0–5.0 mg/kg. It is a very severe eye irritant, and the concentrated compound may cause permanent eye injury. The vapors are irritating to the mucous membranes of the eyes, nose, and throat. Inhalation of mists generated at 170°C did not cause death in test animals on 8-hour exposure [F. A. Miller, *Am. Ind. Hyg. Ass. J.* **28**, 330 (1967)].

Treatment: For eye and skin contact, flood affected parts with water for 15 minutes. Consult an ophthalmologist for more definitive treatment. In case of inhalation, remove the victim to an uncontaminated atmosphere. Give artificial respiration and oxygen if necessary.

METHYL BROMIDE

Following a single exposure to methyl bromide, pulmonary edema and central nervous system symptoms may be delayed for 48 hours. Some or all of the following may be noted after inhalation, ingestion, or skin absorption of a toxic dose of this compound: headache, dizziness, nausea, vomiting, mydriasis, blurred vision, tremors, staggering gait, collapse, respiratory difficulties, and coma. Some individuals complain that objects appear "black," others feel a "scum" over their eyes. Local effects may include vesiculation.

Treatment: Individuals who have inhaled methyl bromide vapors or who have had skin contact with methyl bromide should be moved promptly to fresh air. If skin exposure is extensive, remove clothing under a shower; then wash skin with a solution of sodium bicarbonate. Keep patient under close observation for 48 hours. Prompt bed rest and administration of 100% oxygen is essential if pulmonary edema develops.

METHYL CHLORIDE

Inhalation may cause symptoms similar to those produced by large doses of ethyl alcohol. Mental disturbances and convulsions have also been noted. Delayed symptoms and death have been reported 2–3 weeks after apparent recovery. The main symptoms of poisoning are nausea, stomach pains, halitosis, hiccups, visual disturbances (including diplopia), clonic spasms, and mental confusion. Exposure to 20,000 ppm for 2 hours may be fatal. Contact of the skin with the compressed gas will result in local freezing, formation of blisters, and possibly gangrene. The threshold limit is 100 ppm.

Treatment: For inhalation, remove individual from contaminated atmosphere and give artificial respiration and oxygen if necessary. Subsequent treatment is symptomatic.

METHYLCHLOROFORM

Methylchloroform is one of the least toxic of the chlorinated aliphated hydrocarbons. Excessive absorption through the gastroenteric tract or lungs produces central nervous system depression. Ingestion is followed by vomiting and diarrhea. Mild liver and kidney dysfunction may occur transiently following recovery from central nervous system depression.

Brief vapor exposures above 1700 ppm produce disturbances of equilibrium. Vapor exposures to extremely high concentrations have resulted in four deaths. In each fatality, the individual died shortly after entering an unventilated tank.

The earliest symptoms of a single vapor exposure are lightheadedness and lassitude. The earliest sign of intoxication is an impaired Romberg test. In humans an abnormal Romberg test is usually observed shortly after vapor exposures to 900–1700 ppm. Below the current threshold limit of 350 ppm, no adverse physiological effects have been observed in man during experimental exposures.

The solvent is poorly absorbed through the intact skin, and unless it is trapped against the skin beneath an impermeable barrier, it is unlikely that toxic quantities can be absorbed.

Treatment: There is no specific treatment for methylchloroform intoxication. Prompt supportive treatment should be given to combat the effects of central nervous system depression. Because methylchloroform is primarily eliminated via the lungs, oxygen with carbon dioxide should be administered to facilitate its elimination. Breathing should be assisted if the respiratory center has been depressed.

Severe hypotension may be induced by a combination of central nervous system depression, myocardial anoxia, secondary to poor oxygen uptake. Epinephrine-like drugs must *not* be used to combat hypoten-

387

sion because of the danger of inducing ventricular fibrillation. This danger is not unique to methylchloroform, but exists with chlorinated aliphatic hydrocarbon solvents in general [R. D. Stewart and J. T. Andrews, *JAMA* **195**, 904 (1966)].

N-METHYLCYCLOHEXYLAMINE

The oral LD_{50} of N-methylcyclohexylamine (approximately 10% solution) is 0.52 gm/kg for male rats and 0.40 gm/kg for female rats. Symptoms of intoxication are depression, prostration, ataxia, and muscular tremors.

A 50% mortality was observed in guinea pigs exposed for 1 hour to an aerosol of 7 mg/liter. The following symptoms were observed: ptosis, lacrimation, gasping, irregular respiration, bleeding from the nose and eyes, prostration, and convulsions.

When 0.1 ml of N-methylcyclohexylamine was instilled into the eyes of rabbits, severe eye damage resulted. A 10% solution in polyethylene glycol produced only moderate irritation which subsided in 7 days.

Doses of 200, 632, and 2000 mg/kg were applied to the skin of rabbits. After 1 day, the animals receiving 2.0 gm/kg were dead, and the skin was badly burned. Rabbits receiving the two lower dosages survived, but the skin was severely burned.

Treatment: For skin and eye contact, wash the affected parts with water for 15 minutes. In case of inhalation exposure, give artificial respiration and oxygen.

N-METHYLDICYCLOHEXYLAMINE

The oral LD_{50} of N-methyldicyclohexylamine (approximately 10% solution) is 521 mg/kg (409–664) for male rats; for female rats 446 mg/kg. The following signs were observed: depressed activity and sporadic lung congestion unrelated to the dose level; at 215 mg/kg and above, muscular tremors, ataxia, and convulsions.

Guinea pigs were exposed for one hour to an aerosol of N-methyldicyclohexylamine at a concentration of 2 mg/liter then removed and observed for 14 days. All guinea pigs survived the experiment. Signs of toxicity observed were depression and excessive preening during exposure.

When 0.1 ml of *N*-methyldicyclohexylamine was instilled into the eyes of rabbits, only mild conjunctivitis resulted; this cleared completely in 72 hours. Doses of 200, 632, and 2000 mg/kg were applied to the skin of rabbits. One of the rabbits receiving a 2000 mg/kg dose died the first day. All other rabbits receiving this and lower doses survived. Only slight erythema occurred, and cleared by the fourth day.

Treatment: In case of eye or skin contact, flood affected parts with water for 15 minutes. For inhalation, remove the victim from the contaminated atmosphere; give artificial respiration and oxygen, if necessary.

METHYLDIHYDROMORPHINONE (Metopon)

This narcotic analgesic was recommended particularly for the relief of pain due to cancer; it is not superior to related agents. Tolerance and dependence develop more slowly with metopon than with morphine.

Treatment: Nalorphine and levallorphan are effective in antagonizing respiratory depression. See Narcotic Agents, p. 40, and Opiates, p. 435.

METHYLDOPA (Aldomet)

According to R. Okun *et al.*, tolerance to this drug develops within 9 months in approximately every second patient [*Calif. Med.* **104**, 46 (1966)]. To induce desirable therapeutic effects, doses therefore have to be readjusted from time to time. Serious side effects have been rare. Administration of relatively large daily doses (2–3.7 gm) for 7–13 months caused nonpuerperal lactation in five of fifteen hypertensive women [*Brit. Med. J.* **1**, 1460 (1963)]. Recently three cases of hemolytic anemia were reported which were presumably induced by 9–13 months of treatment with methyldopa [*Lancet* **1**, 549 (1966)]. Occasional side effects noted include headache, fever, nausea, diarrhea, extreme weakness, fluid retention, psychiatric manifestations, acute hepatotoxicity [*N.Y. State J. Med.* **67**, 1897 (1967)], petechiae and ecchymoses on the chest and extremities, thrombocytopenia [*Brit. Med. J.* **2**, 292 (1965)], and extrapyramidal symptoms [*Brit. Med. J.* **1**, 1001 (1963)]. Treatment of a patient with methyldopa and pargyline (Eutonyl), a nonhydrazine monoamine oxidase inhibitor, resulted in visual hallucinations [*Brit. Med. J.* **1**, 803 (1966)]. Disadvantages of methyldopa include slow onset of action and a somewhat unpredictable hypotensive effect.

Treatment: Discontinuation of therapy brought about cessation of lactation and rapid improvement of anemia. Withdrawal of methyldopa and the use of pargyline resulted in the disappearance of mental symptoms.

METHYLENE BLUE

Methylene blue is of value in the treatment of methemoglobinemia, but it must be given in the proper dosage (1–2 mg/kg). Most reports concerning use of the drug either fail to mention toxic effects or imply that methylene blue may be administered intravenously without hazard. Excessive doses of methylene blue will cause methemoglobinemia, hemolysis, and depression of the central nervous system.

Two infants who received methylene blue in relatively high dosage (2 doses each of 0.75–1.0 ml of a 5% methylene blue solution) developed bluish-gray coloration which persisted for approximately 4 days. Both children developed acute hemolytic anemia about 1 week later.

Treatment: Decrease the dose or discontinue therapy.

METHYLENE CHLORIDE (Methylene Dichloride; Methylene Bichloride; Dichloromethane)

This is an inhalation anesthetic used in dentistry and in minor surgery. The probable lethal oral dose for an adult is 25 gm. Ingestion or inhalation of a toxic dose will induce central nervous system depression, followed by convulsions and paresthesia of the extremities.

Treatment: See Methyl Chloride, p. 386.

METHYLENE CHLOROBROMIDE (Bromochloromethane)

The oral LD_{50} for rats is 5–7 gm/kg; the cutaneous LD_{50} for the rabbit is >5 gm/kg. It is moderately irritating to the eyes, and on prolonged skin contact, it has the usual defatting action of solvents. On single inhalation, the maximum exposures causing no mortality were 0.1 hour at 40,000 ppm, 0.4 hour at 20,000 ppm, 1.5 hours at 10,000 ppm, and 7 hours at 5000 ppm. Maximum exposures without liver damage were 0.025

hour at 40,000 ppm, 0.1 hour at 10,000 ppm, 0.3 hour at 5000 ppm, 3 hours at 1500 ppm, and 7 hours at 600 ppm. A 6-month exposure, 7 hours daily, of several species to 370 ppm was without significant effect. The suggested industrial hygiene standard for daily exposures is 200 ppm with 400 ppm as the absolute maximum for peak exposures. The blood bromide concentration at this level is estimated at 40 mg%—well below levels which produce adverse effects [T. R. Torkelson, F. Oyen, and V. K. Rose, *Am. Ind. Hyg. Assoc. J.* **21**, 275 (1960)].

Treatment: See Chloroform, p. 651.

METHYLERGONOVINE (Methergine)

This oxytocic drug has effects similar to those of ergonovine. During recent years, there has been an increasing number of reports concerning vascular complications associated with methylergonovine therapy for severe headache. Many patients took high doses, at times exceeding those recommended by the manufacturer. Most of these difficulties occurred in adults. Fenichel and Battiata reported on a 9-year-old girl who developed thrombophlebitis of the legs 2 weeks after initiation of treatment. She recovered upon discontinuation of therapy [*J. Pediat.* **68**, 632 (1966)]. Several reports have referred to the occurrence of retroperitoneal fibrosis. Presumably, in predisposed patients on prolonged therapy—up to four 2 mg tablets for 3 years—pain in the groin, abdomen, and lumbosacral region, and related symptoms may appear [*JAMA* **191**, 983 (1965); *Med. Ann. District Columbia* **35**, 75 (1966); *Lancet* **I**, 955 (1966); *New Engl. J. Med.* **274**, 359 (1966)]. As pointed out by J. Graham *et al.*, observation of a suspected relationship of methylergonovine to heart murmurs and fibrosis of the aorta, heart valves, and lung tissue has been reported, but further confirmation is necessary to prove this [*Sci. News Letter* (March 5, 1966)].

Caution: Patients who receive methylergonovine should report to the physician at regular intervals. Tests should include urinalysis, renal function test, and excretory urography. The patient should be advised to discontinue the drug for at least 3 months after a 12-months course of therapy even in the absence of side effects. Utz *et al.* believe that these precautions are justified. They add that a direct causal relationship between methylergonovine and fibrosis has not been established, but in view of possible involvement of ureteral function, it would seem wise to avoid this drug in patients with any type of kidney disease [*JAMA* **191**, 983 (1965)]. Other contraindications include: pregnancy, peripheral vascular disease, severe atherosclerosis, severe hypertension, liver and kidney disease, valvular heart disease, rheumatoid arthritis, chronic pulmonary disease, and a history suggestive of collagen-disease diathesis [Graham *et al.*, *New Engl. J. Med.* **274**, 359 (1966)]. Johnson reported on a 44-year-old patient who developed a severe ischemic phenomenon following a 7-day course of treatment with ergonovine and methylergonovine. He advises against the use of this combination therapy [*Arch. Internal Med.* **117**, 237 (1966)]. Reports indicate that in most instances withdrawal of the drug results in gradual recovery. In isolated instances, surgery may be required. Obviously, methylergonovine therapy should be discontinued upon the first appearance of side effects. Steroid therapy has been helpful in the alleviation of pain.

METHYL ETHYL KETONE (2-Butanone)

This is a colorless liquid with a characteristic ketonic odor. It has been widely used as a solvent for resins and lacquers, in paint removers, and in miscellaneous organic syntheses. See Ketones, p. 344, and Table 50, p. 736.

METHYLGLUCAMINE DIATRIZOATE (Cardiografin; Gastrografin; Renografin)

This is a radio-opaque material. A report by Stark and Coburn emphasizes that even small amounts of usually safe contrast media may be followed by serious renal toxicity in the presence of predisposing factors. In one case, a 57-year-old man experienced an abrupt decrease in urinary output following the transfemoral percutaneous injection of 30 ml of 50 % methylglucamine diatrizoate. Approximately 1 year after aortography, renal biopsy revealed focal interstitial nephritis, with tubular atrophy and round cell infiltration. The predisposing factors in this case included azotemia, hypovolemia, and poor collateral runoff. [*J. Urol.* **96**, 848 (1966)]. See also p. 331.

METHYL ISOAMYL KETONE

This ketone is moderately toxic when swallowed. Its oral toxicity is comparable to that of isopropyl alcohol. The compound does not readily penetrate the skin. Uncovered skin contact is not irritating; however, prolonged covered contact may cause skin irritation. The eyes are moderately irritated by contact with the undiluted chemical, but injury is transient.

Inhalation of vapors in a concentration of 4000 ppm killed all the exposed rats after 4 hours, but those exposed to 2000 ppm for 4 hours survived. The deaths were typically narcotic in origin and of a type common to many volatile solvents.

Treatment: For skin or eye contact, wash with water. In case of ingestion, induce vomiting. For inhalation, remove the victim from the contaminated atmosphere; follow with artificial respiration and oxygen if necessary.

METHYL ISOCYANATE

Methyl isocyanate is a potent lacrimator. It is a clear, colorless liquid which boils at 38°C. Dermal irritation may result from topical exposure.

Treatment: In case of skin or eye contact, flood with copious amounts of water.

METHYL NITRITE

This compound is readily formed by the interaction of methanol, sodium nitrite, and hydrochloric acid. It has a sweet odor, boils at −12°C and decomposes rapidly in the presence of water. Methyl nitrite is an extremely potent cyanosing agent. Inhalation rapidly causes palpitation, dizziness, headache, and cyanosis. The consumption of alcohol causes an exacerbation of these symptoms.

Treatment: Bed rest and inhalation of oxygen are recommended. See Amyl Nitrite, p. 100.

METHYL PCT (O,O-Dimethylphosphorochloridothioate); ETHYL PCT (O-Diethylphosphorochloridothioate)

These chemicals are starting materials or intermediates in the manufacture and synthesis of pesticides. The lethal oral dose in rats is approximately 1.0 gm/kg for both Methyl PCT and Ethyl PCT. When applied to the unbroken skin of rabbits, the minimum lethal dose for Methyl PCT is between 750 and 900 mg/kg and in the case of Ethyl PCT, between 250 and 400 mg/kg. Skin and eye irritation studies indicate that both compounds should be classed as severe irritants. The inhalation of an atmosphere saturated with vapors of the samples caused death in rats after 1 or 2 hours of exposure.

Treatment: In case of skin or eye contact, flood affected parts with water for 15 minutes. For inhalation, remove the victim to fresh air and give artificial respiration and oxygen if needed. Further treatment is symptomatic and supportive.

METHYLPHENIDATE (Ritalin)

This cortical stimulant is more potent than caffeine but less potent than amphetamine. Side effects are related to dose.

Treatment: See Amphetamine, p. 98.

METHYLPYRROLIDONE

Methylpyrrolidone has a low order of toxicity. Studies on albino rats gave the following values for acute oral toxicity: LD_0 3 ml/kg; LD_{50} 7 ml/kg; LD_{100} 10 ml/kg.

Methylpyrrolidone is not a primary irritant on skin contact of less than 24 hours, although repeated and prolonged contact produces a mild, transient irritation. It is not a sensitizing agent.

In studies on white rats exposed to methylpyrrolidone vapors for a single 6-hour period, all animals survived the highest concentrations studied. Air was bubbled through a reservoir of methylpyrrolidone held at 110°C and into the animal test chamber. Supersaturation was evidenced by considerable condensation on the chamber walls.

METHYL SALICYLATE (Oil of Wintergreen)

This compound acts somewhat more slowly but is more toxic than acetylsalicylic acid or sodium salicylate. It is too irritating for internal use, but it is used externally as an antirheumatic. The ingestion of toxic doses induces persistent vomiting, perspiration, marked thirst, and dehydration. Symptoms of salicylism appear with blood concentrations of about 25 mg/100 ml. The average lethal dose is 10 ml in children and 30 ml in adults.

Caution: This drug has no real value in modern therapeutics. If used cutaneously, it should not be applied to large areas of the skin.

Treatment of a systemic intoxication is symptomatic and supportive. See the general recommendations outlined in Acetylsalicylic Acid, p. 67.

METHYLTETRAHYDROFURAN (2-Methyltetrahydrofuran)

2-Methyltetrahydrofuran is a colorless mobile liquid having an ether-like odor. The oral LD_{50} for rats is 3.80 gm/kg; the percutaneous LD_{50} for rabbits for a single 24-hour exposure is 4.50 gm/kg. The LD_{50} for rats for a single 4-hour exposure to vapors of 2-methyltetrahydrofuran was 22 mg/liter (6000 ppm).

Eye contact with very small amounts of undiluted methyltetrahydrofuran causes moderate irritation. Absorption of significant amounts by the ocular tissues could result in systemic symptoms of toxicity.

Treatment: For inhalation exposure, remove the individual from the contaminated atmosphere; give artificial respiration and oxygen if necessary. For skin or eye contact, flood with water for 15 minutes. In case of ingestion, induce vomiting; follow with demulcents (milk, vegetable oil, or starch).

METHYL VINYL ETHER

Methyl vinyl ether has a relatively low order of toxicity. The oral LD_{50} for rats is 4.9 ml/kg. At a concentration of 64,000 ppm, none of six rats died during a 4-hour exposure or during a subsequent 96-hour observation period. Instillation of this chemical into the conjunctival sac of the eye of six rabbits produced no corneal, iridial, or conjunctival involvement. Ten rabbits tested showed no erythema, edema, or eschar formation after the application of the compound to the skin.

Treatment: See Ethers, p. 247.

METHYPRYLON (Noludar)

This derivative of piperidine is a non-narcotic sedative. The effects of toxic doses are like those seen after equivalent doses of barbiturates. Approximately thirty-six cases of overdosage have been reported, with one fatality after ingestion of (presumably) 6 gm [*JAMA* **198,** 1213 (1966)]. Because of proper treatment, other patients have survived doses up to 30 gm [*JAMA* **194,** 1139 (1965)]. Addiction (tolerance and withdrawal symptoms) has been produced in an occasional patient [*JAMA* **177,** 133 (1961); *Clin. Pharmacol. Therap.* **5,** 334 (1964)].

Treatment of an overdose is similar to that employed in an intoxication by a barbiturate. G. Xanthaky *et al.* found extracorporeal hemodialysis effective [*JAMA* **198,** 1212 (1966)]. See Barbiturates, p. 119.

METHYSERGIDE MALEATE (Sansert; Deseril)

This oral drug is used to treat chronic migraine headache. It is a serotonin antagonist. Side effects are common. Often they are mild, appear early in the course of treatment, and disappear with continued use or with reduction of the dose. Side effects reported most frequently include nausea, epigastric pain, dizziness, restlessness, drowsiness, vertigo, leg cramps, and psychic disturbances. Occasionally, there may be vomiting, diarrhea or constipation, weakness, peripheral edema, paresthesia in the extremities, dermatitis, and postural hypotension. There have been rare reports of peripheral arterial insufficiency, severe crushing chest pain and ECG evidence of acute myocardial infarction [*Lancet* **I,** 445 (1967)]. Approximately 1 % of patients treated continuously with methysergide for more than 1 year may develop retrolental fibrosis or other fibrotic syndromes [*Med. J. Australia* **1,** 985 (1966)]. However, these effects may develop after less than 5 months of therapy with daily doses not exceeding 8.0 mg [*Radiology* **88,** 976 (1967)]. A recent report describes an unusual type of pleuropulmonary fibrosis in 13 of 36 patients who developed cardiac murmurs while taking methysergide. Some of these patients also suffered retroperitoneal fibrosis [*Am. J. Med. Sci.* **254,** 1 (1967)].

Caution: The drug is contraindicated in renal disease, peripheral vascular disease, serious hypertension, angina, coronary and hepatic insufficiency, and in pregnancy.

Complete regression of the fibrotic syndrome, cardiac enlargement, and partial obstruction of the large arteries have been reported within 2-3 months after withdrawal of the drug [*JAMA* **198**, 808 (1966); *Can. Med. Assoc. J.* **96**, 1420 (1967)]. Methysergide should be reserved for patients with severe migraine not responding to other drugs. The dosage should be kept at a minimum, and reduced to zero for 1 month of the year [*Med. J. Australia* **1**, 985 (1966)].

METOL (p-Methylaminophenol)

This is a photographic developer and hair dye. Contact with skin is likely to cause sensitization leading to itching and weeping dermatitis. Systemic effects are similar to those caused by aniline. See Aniline, p. 102.

METRECAL

Ingestion of Metrecal may cause an increase in the blood levels of protein-bound iodine (PBI) and butanol-extractable iodine. The source of iodine is probably iodocasein [*Texas Rept. Biol. Med.* **23**, 122 (1965)].

METRONIDAZOLE (Flagyl)

This trichomonacide is effective only against *Trichomonas hominis* and *vaginalis*. The drug is administered orally to male patients, and by suppositories to females. A 46-year-old man developed jaundice and evidence of liver enlargement and dysfunction after receiving 250 mg of this drug daily for 5 days. The patient recovered in 2 weeks following discontinuation of therapy [*JAMA* **193**, 1128 (1965)].

MICROWAVE RADIATION

The term microwave generally refers to electromagnetic radiation ranging in frequency from 100 to approximately 30,000 megacycles (Mc). This corresponds to a wavelength of approximately 3 meters to 1 cm. Included in this wide band of frequencies are the very high and ultra-high frequencies (VHF and UHF) of radio communications, certain channels of television, the L, S, and X bands of radar, and one band of medical diathermy utilizing a frequency of 2450 Mc. The same wavelength is also used in microwave ovens, and for the drying of paper photographic prints and leather. At frequencies considerably higher than the 30,000 Mc. of the upper ranges of this band are the frequencies of infrared radiation; beyond them are those of visible light. At the other end of the microwave spectrum are the bands of longer wavelengths, i.e., the frequencies of certain channels of television, short-wave radio, and broadcast band radio (John E. Boysen, USAF, Wright-Patterson AFB).

Microwaves are used extensively in commerce and in the military services. These waves may be directed, focused, reflected, refracted, and concentrated. When striking biological material, they may penetrate, be reflected, or be absorbed. Absorption of microwave radiation by the body releases electrical and magnetic forces which generate heat. Depending on the extent of exposure and on a number of other factors, the heat produced may be local or general; it may be beneficial or harmful.

In 1953, Schwan recommended that a microwave radiation of 10 mw/cm^2 be accepted as a tolerance dose. Studies conducted in recent years have indicated that there are many factors that influence the effects of a specific dose of microwave radiation. These include frequency, period of time of exposure, the "irradiation cycle rate" (that is, the length of individual on-off periods of exposure when total time of *actual* irradiation per minute is kept constant), air currents, environmental temperature, body weight, body type or mass, covering (clothing), size of the area exposed, differences in sensitivity of organs and tissues, orientation or position of the individual in the electromagnetic field, effect of reflections and refractions, and others [W. B. Deichmann, *Ind. Med. Surg.* **30,** 221 (1961); *Arch. Toxikol.* **22,** 24 (1966)].

Results of a recent study showed that power density readings ranged from 3.3 to 5.5 mw/cm^2 in front of the oven area slightly below the perforated oven door of a microwave cooker in operation. It was concluded that there is no hazard to personnel from ionizing or nonionizing radiation in the normal operation of the microwave cooker performed in accordance with the manufacturer's instructions [*Occupational Health Activities*, U.S. Dept. of Health, Education and Welfare, Public Health Service, No. 2 (December 1967)].

Microwave radiation differs from ionizing radiation in several respects. Ionizing radiation occupies the electromagnetic spectrum from the frequency or wavelength of light to cosmic rays. It may be either electromagnetic or corpuscular in nature. Ionizing radiation requires a completely different generating and handling technique than that used for microwave radiation. See Radiation, p. 512, and Laser, p. 345.

Treatment: Treat overexposed or injured area as a thermal burn.

MILK

Allergy to milk or dairy products should be suspected when a child has repeated upper respiratory infections [*JAMA* 198, 605 (1966)].

A patient who treated his gastric ulcer with large doses of alkalies and a gallon of milk per day for 6 months had the following signs and symptoms: marked calcification and severe pain of the wrists, femurs, hip joints, iliac, and radial arteries. The patient became acutely ill and complained of insomnia, hyperirritability, depression, and loss of weight. Polyuria and impairment of renal function with nephrocalcinosis have also been described following prolonged ingestion of excessive quantities of milk and absorbable alkali.

The feeding of excessive volumes of cow or goat milk to infants and children has resulted in iron-deficiency anemia. In four infants with hypochromic microcytic anemia, ingestion of cow's milk was found responsible for significant amounts of fecal blood [*JAMA* 189, 558 (1964); *Med. J. Australia* 2, 212 (1967)]. Several infant deaths have resulted because regurgitated milk was aspirated into the lungs while sleeping.

"Milk is *a* food, not *the* food"; this comment by Dr. Lendon Smith may serve as a warning to dietary faddists [*Time* 89, 62 (1967)].

Attention was recently directed to the lack of vitamin D in nonfat dry milk, a product which is used in significantly increasing amounts in preparing milk for home use for children, and possibly for infants. The American Academy of Pediatrics recommends that infants and children who receive milk from this source also be given a vitamin supplement containing vitamin D to insure consumption of 400 I.U. of the vitamin per day. It may also be noted that nonfat dry milk contains virtually no vitamin A [Committee on

Nutrition, *Pediatrics* **40**, 130 (1967); *Clin-Alert* (Aug. 17, 1967)].

Treatment: In the ulcer patient described above, recovery was complete about 8 weeks after he was placed on a diet free of milk and alkali. In some patients, hypercalcemia continued for months in spite of dietary changes.

MINERAL ACID

This term refers to inorganic acids: hydrohalogen acids (hydrofluoric, hydrochloric, hydrobromic, hydroiodic), sulfuric, phosphoric, and nitric acids. Concentrated solutions are corrosive and destructive to tissue.

Treatment: See Hydrochloric Acid, p. 317.

MINERAL OIL

This complex mixture of aliphatic and alicyclic hydrocarbons has been used as a laxative for many years. Excessive, repeated or prolonged use may diminish absorption of fats and soluble vitamins from the gastrointestinal tract.

Mineral oil nose drops or sprays may spill into the trachea and trickle into the lungs (aspiration) of debilitated individuals causing a low-grade foreign-body reaction "lipoid pneumonia." This is also caused by aspiration of vegetable and animal oils, such as olive oil, cotton seed oil, corn oil, lard oil, peanut oil, etc. Endogenous lipoid pneumonia is due to the hematogenous deposition of cholesterol in the lungs.

Possible ill effects from the repeated inhalation of an oil-contaminated atmosphere (mineral oil mists) are lipoid pneumonia, bronchitis, pulmonary fibrosis, hyperplastic gastritis, rhinitis, sinusitis, pharyngitis, dermatitis, and oil acne.

Mineral oil is removed from the lung with great difficulty by the macrophages. Lipoid pneumonia is entirely different from the fulminating chemical pneumonitis resulting from the aspiration of kerosene, mineral spirits, furniture polish, etc.

Treatment: Symptomatic and supportive.

MISTLETOE

Fatalities have been reported following ingestion of the berries of the American mistletoe (*Phoradendron*

flavescens) or decoctions of the berries used as an ar-
bortifacient. Symptoms in fatal cases included general
malaise, vomiting, copious diarrhea, severe hypertension, respiratory difficulties, hallucinations, and circulatory failure.

Treatment: The importance of the earliest possible
evacuation of the gastroenteric contents cannot be
overemphasized. Repeated vomiting after ingestion of
tap water, salt water, or milk is more effective than gastric lavage. Follow with a saline cathartic. Treatment
should be directed toward correcting dehydration and
the electrolyte imbalance, which are primarily responsible for initiating and causing cardiovascular collapse
and death.

MODELING CLAYS

The ingestion of children's modeling clays may
color the urine and stools. No signs or symptoms of
systemic intoxication have been reported.

Treatment: Tincture of time.

MOLDY BREAD

Bread is capable of supporting the growth of a wide
variety of molds. Mold spores are killed during baking
and the subsequent development of mold on bread is
the result of post-baking contamination with mold
spores derived mainly from the atmosphere. Moldy
bread is usually found to be contaminated with the
mold species commonly present in air. Such molds
include species of *Cladosporium, Penicillium,* and
Aspergillus. Mucor and *Rhizopus* are also frequently
found on moldy bread.

Because of their distinctive appearance or color,
mold colonies on bread are easily detected when very
small, and the products are rejected. Even when incipient mold growth is present, the bread will be unacceptable owing to the development of a "musty" odor
and flavor. For these reasons moldy bread is most unlikely to be eaten. Human disease resulting from the
consumption of moldy bread has not been reported.
See also Mycotoxins, p. 412.

MOLECULAR SIEVES, CHEMICAL LOADED

The volatility of the compound absorbed in a chemical-loaded molecular sieve is reduced considerably

below that of the pure compound. This reduction in volatility lowers the hazards of toxicity and flammability. Since moisture is known to displace virtually all chemicals from molecular sieves, absorbed compounds will be released on contact with the body. For this reason, it is recommended that the same precautions be exercised in handling chemical-loaded molecular sieves as are recommended for the pure chemical. Inhalation of the powder or allowing the powder to contact any part of the body, particularly the eyes, should be avoided.

MOLINDONE (EN-17733A)

Molindone is an indole derivative with antipsychotic activity. In the first clinical pharmacological trial, the drug administered to schizophrenic patients was effective in the second month of therapy. At doses of 50–125 mg per day side effects included marked drowsiness and marked extrapyramidal effects, mainly of an akathisic nature, with occasional tremor and dystonia. These effects, which were controlled with antiparkinsonian medication, were less marked than those produced by trifluperidol, butaperazine, and haloperidol (Serenase). Moderate doses of the drug also induce a definite sedative effect as well as an unusual euphoria.

Caution: This is a new drug. Further studies are indicated to confirm the observations of A. A. Sugarman and J. Herrmann [*Clin. Pharmacol. Therap.* 8, 261 (1967)].

MOLYBDENUM

Acute or chronic poisoning has not been described in man. Cattle ingesting high concentrations of molybdenum (20–100 μg molybdenum per gram matter) have developed a condition known as "teart." This disease is characterized by severe diarrhea, debilitation, and fading of hair color. These effects may be the result of interference with copper metabolism. Molybdenum is an essential trace element in plants, in some bacteria, and possibly in mammals. The total molybdenum content of the body in normal adult humans is approximately 20 mg, and the urinary excretion is about 10–20 μg/liter. Guinea pigs exposed to 200 mg/m^3 of molybdenum trioxide dust (expressed as molybdenum) for 1 hour daily 5 times per week for 5 weeks showed evidence of nasal irritation, diarrhea, loss of weight, and muscular incoordination. Exposure to molybdenite ore dust (MoS_2) at a concentration of 280 mg/m^3 (of molybdenum) caused little effect. Fumes from arcing molybdenum metal caused some mortality at 190 mg/m^3, but little effect at 53 mg/m^3. The pathological findings consisted of bronchial and alveolar irritation and moderate fatty changes in liver and kidneys.

From the standpoint of acute toxicity, salts of molybdenum are relatively unimportant. There is some evidence that this metal increases the hematinic effect of iron. Recent experimental evidence in rats demonstrated that there is apparently also an interaction between molybdenum and zinc. In rats, toxicity to molybdenum was increased through an increased intake of zinc.

MONKSHEAD; WESTERN MONKSHEAD (*Aconitum columbianum*)

Parts of this plant as well as *A. napellus* (monkshead, wolfbane, aconite) contain aconitine, which is very toxic. The leaves have been mistaken for parsley, and the roots for celery or horseradish. The lethal dose for an adult ranges from 2 to 4 gm. Intoxications have also resulted from prolonged skin contact with parts of these plants.

Signs and symptoms may appear shortly after ingestion of the leaves or root. They include a tingling (prickling) or burning sensation in the mouth, throat, and extremities. This leads to constriction of the chest, salivation, nausea and vomiting, and generalized paresthesias particularly involving the face. Numbness follows. In addition, there may be severe headache. Severe or fatal intoxications are characterized by marked muscular weakness, dyspnea, pulmonary edema, tremors and convulsions.

Treatment: Evacuate the gastroenteric contents promptly. Gastric lavage and administration of a dilute solution of potassium permanganate (1:10,000) has been recommended to inactivate aconitine in the gastroenteric tract. Additional treatment may include administration of atropine for bradycardia, and restoration of normal sinus rate by administration of calcium and magnesium salts. In animals, 3% calcium chloride I.V. (10 ml/kg) followed by 12% magnesium sulfate (3 ml/kg) were effective. Paroxysmal supraventricular tachycardia in a patient suffering from aconitine poisoning responded to 40 ml of 10% calcium gluconate followed by 5 ml of magnesium sulfate I.V. Sympathomimetic drugs may have to be administered to support the circulation. Excellent nursing care is important.

MONOAMINE OXIDASE INHIBITORS (MAO Inhibitors)

The monoamine oxidase inhibitors in clinical use include phenelzine sulfate (Nardil), nialamide (Niamid), tranylcypromine sulfate (Parnate), isocarboxazid (Marplan), and pargyline (Eutonyl). Iproniazid (Marsilid), pheniprazine (Catron), and etryptamine (Monase) are no longer used. These drugs, by inhibiting the enzyme monoamine oxidase, cause an accumulation of catecholamines. In a patient with reduced MAO activity, certain foods and beverages which contain certain aromatic amines produce some or all of the following: hypertension accompanied by headache, horrifying nightmares, altered consciousness, atrial and ventricular arrhythmias, cerebrovascular accidents, pulmonary edema, and death. Foods involved—with an increasing tyramine content—are yogurt and camembert, brie, emmentaler, gruyere, and cheddar cheeses. There are also certain beverages, such as beers and wines, which at times contain an augmented tyramine content. Chianti may be considered potentially hazardous but the patient may become "high" before his blood pressure does. [*Nutrition Revs.* **23**, 326 (1965); *Brit. Med. J.* **1**, 1554 (1965)]. In cheeses, tyramine comes from the decarboxylation of tyrosine by tyrosine decarboxylase.

Caution: All sympathomimetic and antihypertensive drugs, as well as alcohol, barbiturates, ether, insulin, procaine, and opiates must be avoided during MAO inhibitor therapy and for at least 2 weeks after cessation of treatment [D. G. Friend, *Clin. Pharmacol. Therap.* **6**, 805 (1965)]. See also Meperidine, p. 368. The MAO inhibitors are contraindicated in patients with a history of impaired liver function, heart failure, and cerebral vascular diseases. In view of the reactions to MAO inhibitors, their use has been abandoned in Germany [*Lancet* **I**, 932 (1964)]. Deaths have been reported when the patient's treatment was changed directly from a MAO inhibitor to an imipramine-type drug. Change in either direction should include a drug-free interval [J. O. Cole, *JAMA* **190**, 448 (1964)].

Treatment: Reduction or withdrawal of therapy with MAO inhibitors will reduce side effects. In case of a hypertensive crisis, administer promptly an α-adrenergic blocking agent such as phentolamine (Regitine); dose: 5.0 mg I.V. followed by 2.5–5.0 mg doses I.M., as required. Carefully avoid sudden hypotension. Levarterenol should be available in the event that this occurs. While phentolamine appears to be the logical choice of treatment, there have been reports of successful reduction of blood pressure with the use of ganglionic blocking agents [L. I. Goldberg, *JAMA* **190**, 456 (1964)]. Hemodialysis was found effective in a patient who ingested 350 mg of tranylcypromine [*Arch. Internal Med.* **116**, 18 (1965)].

MONOBENZONE (Monobenzyl Ether of Hydroquinone)

The depigmenting action of the monobenzyl ether of hydroquinone (monobenzone) was discovered many years ago. The practical usefulness of this compound in the management of pigmentary disorders has been limited due to the high incidence of primary irritation and allergic sensitization. The lack of predictability of its effect on cutaneous pigmentation is another difficulty. Many persons fail to obtain depigmentation from monobenzone, whereas some develop unsightly and sometimes apparently permanent, spotty, complete depigmentation which may even extend to areas not treated. Others may develop hyperpigmentation and spotty leukomelanoderma following application of the substance.

MONOBROMOTRIFLUOROMETHANE (CF$_3$Br)

Monobromotrifluoromethane is a nontoxic gas. In concentrations as high as those of nitrogen in the air (in the presence of 20% oxygen), it did not cause the death of any of the animals exposed (rats, mice, guinea pigs, rabbits, dogs) for 2 hours. This chemical is less toxic than dichlorodifluoromethane. A concentration of 50% in the air (500,000 ppm) causes the oxygen level in the atmosphere to fall to 10 % which is equivalent to that found at an altitude of 5500 meters [(G. Paulet, *Arch Maladies Professionells* **23**, 341 (1962)].

MONOCHLORACETIC ACID (Chloracetic Acid)

This is a fairly strong organic acid which may be irritating to skin and mucous membranes. See Acetic Acid, p. 63.

MONOCHLORAMINE (NH$_2$Cl)

When household cleaning solutions containing sodium hypochlorite and ammonia are mixed, there is a possibility that this toxic chemical may be formed. This gas irritates the eyes and the upper respiratory system and has been reported to cause inflammatory emphysema in animals. Less than 10 ppm is likely to cause eye and respiratory irritation from a few minutes exposure [J. L. Pinkus, *New Engl. J. Med.* **272**, 1133 (1965)].

Treatment: Discontinue exposure. Further therapy is symptomatic and supportive.

MONOCHLORODIFLUOROACETIC ACID (2FA)

This compound, a clear, colorless, pungent liquid dissolves completely in water, liberating heat. It is a strong acid. The liquid is highly corrosive to skin and eyes and should not be permitted to contact tissues.

Treatment: See Hydrochloric Acid, p. 317.

MONOFLUORINATED HYDROCARBONS, ALIPHATIC

1-Fluoroalkanes (CH$_3$(CH$_2$)$_n$F) are believed to be degraded to ω-fluorocarboxylates and thus show an alteration in toxicity. The ω-fluoroalkenes (F(CH$_2$)$_n$—CH=CH$_2$) are toxic irrespective of chain length. See ω-Fluorocarboxylic Acids, p. 275.

MONOMETHYLFORMAMIDE

Administration of this compound to mice on the eleventh day after conception in doses which were not toxic to the pregnant animal caused teratogenic effects in all offspring. Oral administration of this compound produced these effects more markedly than percutaneous treatment [R. Roll and F. Bär, *Arzneimittel-Forsch.* **17**, 610 (1967)].

"MOONSHINE," "WHITE LIGHTNING," "SCRAP IRON"

These alcoholic beverages are produced in moonshine stills, which have remained popular in certain parts of the United States.

Heavy drinkers of moonshine liquor are likely to develop gout and chronic metal poisoning. Certain yeasts in sour mash produce acetic and other organic acids which solubilize the lead of backyard stills, some of which are discarded automobile radiators. Arsenic has also been found in these liquors.

Suggestion: Since illicit liquor is known to be distilled in North Carolina and Kentucky as well as in the New York and New England areas, it may be well for physicians to investigate the drinking habits of any individual afflicted with gout. In the United States in 1965, 7437 illicit stills were seized [Sci. News 90 (1966)].

Treatment: See Ethyl Alcohol, p. 249, and Lead, p. 347.

MORPHINE

This is a potent sedative and analgesic narcotic. It is also used occasionally as an hypnotic, antidiarrheal, or antitussive agent. Side effects are related to the dose and may include respiratory depression, nausea, miosis, increase in intracranial pressure, constipation, spasm of the bile duct and ureter, transient hyperglycemia, hypotension, and release of histamine. Doses which do not markedly depress ventilation may be sufficient to depress the reflex urge to expand the lungs thereby increasing the danger of atelectasis.

Toxic doses cause slow shallow respiration, pinpoint pupils, nausea, vomiting, constipation, urinary retention, weak pulse, muscle twitching and spasms, cyanosis, and coma. Death is due to respiratory paralysis.

Caution: Therapeutic doses of this drug may be dangerous in cases of bronchial asthma, idiosyncrasy, debilitation, increased intracranial pressure, and toxic psychosis. Infants and elderly persons are particularly sensitive to its actions. *The ordinary safe therapeutic dose of morphine may be fatal to persons who have been drinking alcoholic beverages.* Morphine in therapeutic doses resulted in fatalities in individuals whose blood alcohol levels ranged from 0.22 to 0.27%. Morphine is also synergistic with barbiturates and related drugs. The drug is contraindicated in acute diverticulitis [*Brit. Med. J.* **2**, 33 (1963)] and in patients with head injuries.

Treatment: Keep respiratory passages clear; administer oxygen. Administer nalorphine or levallorphan until respiration is normal and the patient is responsive. See Narcotic Agents, p. 40, and Opiates, p. 435.

MOTHBALLS

The original mothball is the hydrocarbon naphthalene. Another moth repellent is *p*-dichlorobenzene. Swimming suits packed in mothballs during the winter should be washed before use to prevent skin rash or allergic reactions. See Naphthalene, p. 416 and *p*-Dichlorobenzene, p. 210.

MOUNTAIN LAUREL (*Kalmia latifolia*)

Ingestion of this shrub (also known as the calico bush or sheep kill) and the honey obtained from its rose-colored flowers have caused intoxications. The toxic ingredients include veratrine and/or andromedotoxin.

Symptoms of intoxication (except for a burning sensation in the mouth and throat) usually appear after 4–6 hours and include salivation, malaise, vomiting, and diarrhea. Like monkshead, laurel will induce a tingling sensation of the skin and sometimes muscular weakness, headache, and difficulties of vision. In a severe or fatal intoxication, bradycardia, severe hypotension, coma, and asphyxial convulsions are produced.

Treatment: Induce vomiting. Further therapy is symptomatic and is directed toward the treatment of hypotension, shock, and respiratory difficulties. Analeptics have been used but are not recommended. Bradycardia noted in some patients is, as a rule, refractory to atropine. In nonfatal cases recovery may be complete in 24–48 hours. Excellent nursing care is important. See also Barbiturates, p. 119.

M-PYROL (*N-Methyl-2-pyrrolidone*)

This compound is a liquid with a mild amine-like odor. It has a low vapor pressure (less than 1 mm Hg) at room temperature. The acute toxicity for albino rats is as follows: LD_0, 3 ml/kg; LD_{50}, 7 ml/kg; LD_{100}, 10 ml/kg. M-pyrol is not a primary irritant when in contact with the skin for less than 24 hours. Repeated and prolonged skin contact produces a mild, transient irritation. It is not a sensitizing agent. White rats survived a 6-hour exposure to air saturated with M-pyrol. The air was bubbled through a reservoir containing M-pyrol heated to 110°C.

Treatment: Remove from the skin and eyes by flooding the affected tissues with water. In case of ingestion, induce vomiting.

MUCOCHLORIC ACID (α, β-Dichloro-β-formylacrylic Acid; 2,3-Dichloromaleic Aldehyde Acid)

This is a very strong primary skin irritant and potent sensitizer in humans. Pulmonary allergy has not been reported.

Treatment: For skin, eye, and mucous membrane contact, flood affected tissues with water. For accidental ingestion, induce vomiting and follow with gastric lavage and saline cathartics. Inhalation should not be a problem because of relatively low vapor pressure at room temperature.

MUSCARINE

This compound is the active ingredient in the poisonous fly mushroom (*Amanita muscaria*). Ingestion will induce effects similar to those produced by physostigmine. See Mushrooms, p. 410.

MUSHROOM MIASMA

This illness may develop in mushroom farm workers who are sensitive to dust liberated when the compost in which mushrooms are cultivated is disturbed. Symptoms may develop a few hours after exposure.

Initial symptoms of the disease are dryness of the nose and throat; skin irritation around the eyes, nose, upper lip, and under the scrotum; nausea; and restlessness. This is followed by dermatitis of the irritated area of the skin, a dry cough, fever between 99° and 100°F., and some increase in pulse rate. The fever often continues for 4–5 days, and between the third and seventh day the patient may have chest pains, severe nose bleed, and inflammation of the nasal mucosa.

Chest radiographs may reveal diffuse miliary mottling. A. Sakula believes that this disease is a variant of "farmer's lung" [*Brit. Med. J.* **3**, 708 (1967)]. Symptoms usually abate within 10–20 days [*Ind. Hyg. Dig.* **26**, 24 (1962)]. See Thesaurosis, p. 584.

Treatment: Prevent exposure by use of air face mask. During actual illness treatment is supportive and symptomatic.

MUSHROOMS

The onset of symptoms resulting from the ingestion of poisonous mushrooms is rapid or delayed, depending on the type ingested.

Onset in 15 minutes to 2 hours: Intoxications of this type may be caused by (a) *Amanita muscaria*, containing ibotenic acid, muscimol (pantherine), and inactive traces of muscarine; (b) *Inocybe* species, containing muscarine; and (c) species of *Agaricus, Boletus, Cantharellus, Lactarius, Paxillus, Rhodophyllus, Russula, Scleroderma, Tricholoma*, and others. Little is known of the active ingredients of this group.

Depending on the specific mushroom, symptoms range from transient nausea and diarrhea to more severe effects including peripheral vasodilation, bradycardia, miosis, colic, diarrhea, and visual hallucinations. Intoxications by *Inocybe* species induce increased lacrimation, perspiration, salivation, and possibly severe gastroenteric effects, but no stimulation of the central nervous system. In fatal cases, death is preceded by respiratory paralysis, delirium, and coma.

Treatment: Amanita muscaria and the *Rhodophyllus* species have caused the most intoxications. In these, little more is required than evacuation of the gastroenteric contents and supportive therapy directed towards lessening gastroenteric effects. *Atropine should be administered only when clearly indicated, that is, in intoxications by Inocybe species.* Chlorpromazine may be considered if agitation or hallucinations become a problem. See also LSD, p. 356.

Onset in 5–12 hours: The second type, with delayed onset, is attributed to *Amanita phalloides, A. verna, A. virosa*, and to the *Galerina* species. Approximately 90% of the fatal mushroom intoxications have been caused by these species. The toxic ingredients in these mushrooms include at least eight peptides including α- and β-amanitin.

Symptoms of an intoxication include severe vomiting and severe abdominal spasms and pain, accompanied by diarrhea of undigested food, mucous, and blood. Extreme thirst follows. The gastroenteric symptoms may subside, and the patient may seem somewhat improved, but after a variable period he may go into shock and prostration, with hypoglycemia and cyanosis. Myocardial abnormalities, jaundice, hypokalemia, lymphopenia, uremia or anuria may also develop. Confusion, delirium, coma, convulsions, or death may follow in 3–7 days.

Treatment: An effort should be made to make certain that the gastroenteric contents have been evacuated. Thioctic (α-lipoic) acid has been used effectively in the treatment of intoxications by *A. phalloides* in a dose of 300 mg per day administered by slow *infusion* in an aqueous solution of dextrose and electrolytes [F. Kubicka, *Prakt. Lekar.* **44**, 702 (1964)].

Onset 12 to 24 hours: Ingestion of cooked *Coprinus atramentarius* is harmless; but if alcohol is consumed 12–24 hours after ingestion of this mushroom, a disulfiram (Antabuse) type of reaction is experienced. See Disulfiram, p. 230. The effects last from 30 minutes to several hours, and have been reported to be severe enough to be quite alarming. The blood pressure may drop considerably.

Treatment: As a rule, no treatment is required other than reasurance. See Disulfiram, p. 230.

Caution: There are no fool-proof tests other than chemical analysis to differentiate between nontoxic and toxic varieties of mushrooms. A particular mushroom grown in one part of the world may be harmless, but when grown in another country, it may be extremely toxic. As a rule, cooking or drying does not destroy the toxic ingredients in mushrooms. It is therefore important to be most discriminative in selecting mushrooms for the table.

MUSTARD

While no proof has been presented, it is noteworthy that sixty-two patients suffering from hypertension, coronary thrombosis, and myocardial infarction had ingested excessive amounts of mustard, pepper, or ginger. Mustard, which contains a minimum of 0.006% of allyl isothiocyanate, is suspected as the toxic agent [Blair, *Ohio State Med. J.* **61**, 732 (1965)].

MYCOTOXINS

Mycotoxins are substances formed during the growth of molds. They show a considerable variety of structures; many of them are comparatively simple compounds. Poisoning by mycotoxins is called mycotoxicosis; it is frequently mediated through the liver, kidneys, or brain, and is thus to be carefully distinguished from mycosis, which refers to a generalized invasion of living tissues by actively growing fungi.

Mycotoxins and mycotoxicosis become especially significant in relation to foodstuffs, which under suitable conditions can provide a favorable medium for mold growth. Once the mycotoxins have been formed, they persist even though the mold is subsequently killed by sterilization. A good example of this is the fungal metabolite aflatoxin, which killed 100,000 turkey poults in 1960. All stricken birds had received feed containing peanut meal. The toxic factor was associated with the presence of a specific mold, *Aspergillus flavus*, which had infected the peanuts from which the meal was prepared.

Four distinct but closely related fungal metabolites, now named "aflatoxin," have been identified chemically. The four compounds occur in varying proportions according to conditions, important factors being the strain of mold and culture medium. In natural sources, aflatoxin B_1 seems to be most frequently encountered. The aflatoxins are extremely potent substances and foodstuff contaminations of the order of a few parts per million may be significant, according to the animal species involved. For example, the peanut meal implicated in the turkey catastrophe contained between 7 and 10 ppm. For a day-old (50 gm) duckling, the LD_{50}s of aflatoxin are: B_1, 18.2 μgm.; G_1, 39.2 μgm., B_2, 84.8 μgm.; and G_2, 172.5 μgm.

In ducklings, one characteristic effect of aflatoxin is the abnormal proliferation of liver bile duct cells, a lesion which can be roughly quantified and made the basis of a useful bioassay. Other animals suffering from aflatoxicosis usually exhibit various pathological

412

changes in the liver. When rats were fed a diet containing 20 % toxic peanut meal for 6 months, 9 out of 11 developed multiple liver tumors. The total intake of aflatoxin was probably 3–5 mg, indicating that the substance is an active carcinogen—more powerful, in fact, than benzpyrene or dimethylnitrosoamine.

Although the intact peanut shell provides a high degree of protection against mold attack, shell damage —by termites or insects, plant disease, or carelessness during harvesting—is all too frequent. The first precaution is to dry the nuts as soon as possible after harvesting to a moisture content not exceeding 8 %. Mold growth will not then occur; but since spores are still present, they will develop under favorable circumstances. Once dried, the nuts must be kept dry and not exposed to conditions that might cause their moisture content to rise above the danger level of 8–9 %. Adequate protection from rain during transport and storage is important.

Aflatoxin poisoning in man has not been reported [A. J. Feuell, *Can. Med. Ass. J.* **94**, 571 (1966)]. Peanut oil, which is the base for margarine manufacture in England, is a safe product for human consumption even when obtained from discolored peanuts. The alkali treatment in oil refinement removes the aflatoxin. It is known that moldy corn is an important ingredient of African native diets. In the male Bantu, hepatomas represent 68 % of carcinomas. Cirrhosis promoters or environmental carcinogens might potentiate the precancerous or cancerous state of the liver. Some speculation has been advanced on the association of moldy diet components with the high rate of Bantu hepatomas. The age-adjusted rate for primary hepatomas per 100,000 population is only 0.18 for Danes, 1.7 for United States whites, 3.2 for United States Negroes, but 14 for the Bantu.

See also Mushrooms, p. 410.

NAIL POLISH (Nail Lacquer, Enamel, or Finish)

Nail polish consists of a resin or plastic (cellulose nitrate) in solvent containing a dye. The principal hazard is associated with the solvents used, although some individuals develop hypersensitivity to the other ingredients present. See list of solvents in nail polish removers, (below). See Table 47, p. 733.

NAIL POLISH REMOVERS

These consist of solvents which may be Esters, (ethyl, butyl, or amyl acetate), p. 243, Ethyl Alcohol, p. 249, Isopropyl Alcohol, p. 339, Acetone, p. 64, or other Ketones, p. 344. See Table 47, p. 733 and Table 50, p. 736.

NALIDIXIC ACID (NegGram)

This antibacterial agent is used orally in the treatment of genitourinary infections. Side effects noted in 3–10% of patients included nausea, vomiting, and weakness. Neurological and visual disturbances, confusion, and hallucinations have also been noted shortly after initiation of nalidixic acid therapy [*New Engl. J. Med.* **275**, 1081 (1966)]. There have been several reports of photosensitivity and two cases of hemolytic anemia. The photoallergic reaction looks like an allergic skin disease with the lesion spreading beyond the areas exposed to sunlight; the phototoxic reaction resembles an excessive sunburn [*Med. J. Australia* **2**, 698 (1966)]. Hemolytic anemia, presumably due to nalidixic acid, occurred in a breast-fed infant, also in an 18-month-old child following 20 days of treatment with a dose of 60 mg/kg. Overdoses can cause transient hyperglycemia and glycosuria, intracranial hypertension or convulsions [*JAMA* **192**, 1100 (1965); *Brit. Med. J.* **2**, 744 (1967); **3**, 370 (1967)]. Resistance to the drug develops rapidly.

Caution: Patients taking nalidixic acid should be cautioned against excessive exposure to sunlight. Its epileptogenic potential and specific undesirable effect in individuals with G-6-PD deficiency should be kept in mind. Renal and hepatic disorders may cause increased retention of nalidixic acid and hence augmented effects or side effects. Routine blood counts are advisable for patients receiving prolonged nalidixic acid therapy.

Treatment: Reduction of the dose or temporary cessation of therapy has usually brought rapid relief from side effects. Overdoses require symptomatic treatment. The child with hemolytic anemia recovered following a transfusion with blood.

NALORPHINE HYDROCHLORIDE (Nalline; N-Allylnormorphine)

This narcotic, respiratory depressant, and analgesic drug is one of the antagonists of choice in the treatment of intoxications by opiates. It antagonizes respiratory depression but does not prevent or abolish opiate convulsions. In a subcutaneous dose of 3 mg it will precipitate an acute abstinence syndrome in persons who have acquired opiate tolerance. For the nalorphine pupil test, see *Clin. Pharmacol. Therap.* **7**, 300 (1966). Nalorphine administration does not prevent addiction to morphine or related drugs.

Nalorphine does not reverse the central nervous system depression induced by barbiturates, anesthetics, and other central nervous system depressants. It may indeed potentiate the effects of these drugs.

Nalorphine is capable of relieving pain; however, it is not used for this purpose because of marked side effects. Toxic doses of nalorphine will induce depression of respiration, severe dysphoria, and hallucinations. The drug is capable of inducing tolerance and severe withdrawal reactions, including convulsions [*J. Pharmacol. Exptl. Therap.* **150**, 437 (1965); *Clin. Pharmacol. Therap.* **7**, 300 (1966)].

Treatment: Resuscitation appears to be the logical method for combatting respiratory depression. The cautious administration of a barbiturate has been recommended for psychic disturbances induced by nalorphine. See Narcotic Agents, p. 40, and Opiates, p. 435.

NALOXONE

This compound is the *N*-allyl derivative of the potent narcotic analgesic oxymorphone (Numorphan). There is some evidence that naloxone is more effective than nalorphine or levallorphan. This is a new drug; use with caution until more is known about it [*Am. J. Med. Sci.* **245**, 23 (1963)].

NAPALM

Napalm is an incendiary substance made by the gelation of gasoline. It gets its name from *na*phthenate and *palm*itate, two constituents of the gelling agent. A powder, consisting of the aluminum soaps of coconut

415

acids, naphthenic acid, and oleic acid, is added to gasoline in amounts varying from 5 to 12% by weight, depending on the desired thickness of the gel. An improved gel, Napalm-B, prepared by combining polystyrene, gasoline and benzene, is currently in production.

Napalm casualties are caused primarily by thermal injury and carbon monoxide poisoning. Napalm burns tend to be deep and extensive. The adhesiveness, prolonged burning time, and high burning temperature of napalm produce third degree burns; coagulation of muscle, fat, and other deep tissues are likely to result. Burns of this depth will probably produce severe scar contractures and deformities, especially under conditions making early skin grafting difficult.

Nephrotoxicity is a serious complication, and the mortality is high in proportion to the total body surface involved. A deep burn of only 10% of the body may result in renal failure. Such burns may indicate primary amputation.

Napalm burns are frequently complicated by carbon monoxide poisoning. Toxic concentrations of carbon monoxide are commonly observed in confined areas during a napalm fire, but lethal levels have been reached in open areas as well. The possibility of carbon monoxide poisoning must be considered whenever unconsciousness occurs in the presence of burning napalm [P. Reich and V. W. Sidel, *New Eng. J. Med.* 277, 86 (1967)].

Treatment: See Carbon Monoxide, p. 154, and Treatment of Burns, p. 26.

NAPHAZOLINE HYDROCHLORIDE (Privine)

This drug is used as a nasal decongestant and a local short-acting vasoconstrictor. Overdoses or prolonged use should be avoided because of possible local and central effects. In sensitive persons, drowsiness and coma have resulted from absorption of a local overdose or accidental ingestion of this drug. See also Epinephrine, p. 240.

NAPHTHALENE (Mothballs)

Ingestion of a toxic dose of napthalene causes gastroenteric distress, tremors, convulsions, fever, changes in the formed elements of the blood, and death from respiratory failure. Fatal hemolytic anemia has been described in a newborn infant whose diapers had been contaminated with naphthalene mothballs. Naphthalene is metabolized to α- and β-naphthols which are hemolytic agents. See Naphthol, p. 417.

Treatment: Thorough gastric lavage, saline cathartics, blood transfusion, oxygen, and fluid therapy are recommended.

NAPHTHALENE ACETIC ACID

This compound and its esters have a low order of toxicity. Contact with skin, eyes, and mucous membranes will cause irritation.

Treatment: Wash eyes and skin with water. Gastric lavage and saline cathartics are recommended for ingestion of an overdose.

NAPHTHENES

This term is synonymous with cycloparaffin hydrocarbons. It is used primarily in the petroleum industry and is not to be confused with the aromatic hydrocarbon naphthalene. See Cycloparaffins, p. 196.

NAPHTHOL

Naphthol (α and β) is capable of producing severe systemic intoxications (kidney injury, jaundice, hemoglobinuria, anemia, convulsions, and coma).

Treatment: Remove from the skin with soap and water. For ingestion, induce vomiting, follow with gastric lavage, cathartics, and fluid therapy. Subsequent treatment is supportive and symptomatic.

NAPHTHYLIMIDAZOLE

A number of intoxications have been reported due to overdosage of this drug in nose drops and nasal sprays. Respiratory difficulties, somnolence, and collapse were noted in infants and children.

Treatment is symptomatic.

NATURAL GAS (Marsh Gas; Cooking Gas)

This gas consists principally of methane, a physiologically inert hydrocarbon. See Hydrocarbon Gases, p. 316. Natural gas can cause asphyxia by replacing oxygen. Manufactured gas contains carbon monoxide, which is highly toxic. See p. 154.

NEO-BORINE

This product was withdrawn from the market.

NEOMYCIN

This antibiotic is used parenterally, topically, and orally. When used I.M., kidney damage (proteinuria, excretion of casts, reduced output of urine), neuromuscular blockade, and eighth cranial nerve injury may occur. These effects are similar to those induced by dihydrostreptomycin, kanamycin, and to a lesser degree, by streptomycin. Ototoxicity may appear following a latent period of 1–4 weeks. Prolonged oral administration should be avoided since this may lead to overgrowth of *Candida* and other nonsusceptible organisms. Occasional less serious side effects include dermatitis, a tingling sensation in the hands and feet, dizziness, and mild fever. Cross sensitization occurs between neomycin, kanamycin, paromomycin, streptomycin, and possibly gentamicin [V. Pirilä and S. Rouhunkoski, *Dermatologica* **125**, 273 (1962); S. Epstein and F. J. Wenzel, *Arch. Dermatol* **86**, 183 (1962)]. Fatal apnea was recently noted during ether anesthesia administered subsequent to the intraperitoneal injection of neomycin.

Pittinger and Long studied the neuromuscular blocking action of neomycin (enhanced by ether) and found that it can be prevented in animals by neostigmine methyl sulfate [*Antibiot. Chemotherapy* **8**, 198 (1958)]. Middleton confirmed this observation in a patient who later died of irreversible shock [*JAMA* **165**, 2186 (1957)]. The slow I.V. injection of calcium gluconate may be similarly effective in preventing neuromuscular blockade [*JAMA* **170**, 943 (1959)].

Caution: This is a highly toxic drug. While nephrotoxicity is usually reversible after discontinuation of therapy, ototoxicity is not. The risk of ototoxicity must be carefully weighed against a beneficial effect. Specific blood and urine tests are indicated for the detection of renal damage. Previous administration of streptomycin or dihydrostreptomycin are contraindications for the use of this drug. An increasing number of reports indicate that skin application of neomycin produces allergic reactions rather frequently and is much more of a problem than was originally recognized.

As to the preferred mode of administration, Harvey Blank puts it this way: "Topical neomycin and its antibiotic combinations are not as effective as systemic antibiotics in ridding wounds of bacteria;" and further, that "adding neomycin to steroid topical preparations does not enhance effectiveness. The addition of neomycin to deodorants incurs many risks and probably should be prohibited. The systemic administration of antibiotics is the treatment of choice for pyoderma."

See also Kanamycin, p. 341, and Streptomycin, p. 555. With regard to the use and value of neomycin patch and intradermal skin tests, refer to *JAMA* **203**, 525 (1968).

NEON LIGHTS

The gases likely to appear in "neon" lights are neon, krypton, argon, xenon, and helium. All of these gases are essentially harmless, acting only as simple asphyxiants. Injury associated with the manufacture of these light tubes is more likely to be due to the phosphors contained in the tubes than the gases. Beryllium-containing phosphors are no longer used in fluorescent lights.

NETTLE

Plants that contain primary mechanical or chemical irritants include the various types of nettle (*Urtica dioica, Laportea canadensis, Cnidoscolus stimulosus*) and the many *Euphorbia* species containing a milky sap which is irritant to sensitive individuals. These plants include the poinsettia or Christmas flower (*E. pulcherrima*), milk bush or pencil tree (*E. tirucalli*), various spurges (*E. peplus, E. helioscopia*, etc), false cactus (*E. lactea*), snow-on-the-mountain (*E. marginata*), and others.

Upon ingestion, the sap produces burning in the mouth and throat, sneezing, emesis, diarrhea, and possibly collapse and death.

Treatment: For skin contact, treat like poison ivy dermatitis. See Poison Ivy, p. 484. In case of ingestion, give milk and egg white, and induce vomiting. Further treatment is symptomatic.

NEUTRONYXES

Nonionic detergents. See Detergents, p. 201, and p. 31 and 710.

NIACATE
[Bis(s-(diethoxyphosphinothioyl)mercapto)methane]

This is an organic phosphate with a relatively low order of toxicity. It is about one-twentieth as toxic as parathion. See Organic Phosphate, p. 438.

NIALAMIDE (Niamid)

The side effects of this monoamine oxidase inhibitor are similar to those caused by isocarboxazid (Marplan); however, hepatic toxicity has not been a problem [D. G. Friend, *Clin. Pharmacol. Therap.* **6**, 805 (1965)].

Treatment: See Iproniazid, p. 333, and Monoamine Oxidase Inhibitors, p. 404.

NICKEL

Nickel-plated objects (garter or brassiere buckles, wrist bands, lighters, etc.) are a common cause of dermatitis in susceptible individuals. Cross sensitivity between nickel and copper has been found in a number of cases. Absorption of inorganic salts of nickel will produce effects resembling those caused by arsenic. Prolonged exposure to nickel dust is known to have induced cancer of the lung and nose in humans.

Nickel carbonyl is extremely toxic. It is a carcinogen for man. Inhalation has induced gastroenteric symptoms, respiratory distress due to delayed pulmonary edema, convulsions, and death. Pathological changes have been produced in the lungs, liver, and brain. Metabolic changes are attributable to extensive damage to lung tissue and to renal insufficiency.

Treatment: For systemic intoxication of inorganic salts of nickel, administer dimercaprol (see p. 224). F. W. Sunderman successfully treated nickel carbonyl intoxications with sodium diethyldithiocarbamate trihydrate (Dithiocarb) [Jefferson Medical College of Philadelphia, personal communication (Jan. 21, 1965); *Am. J. Med.* **34**, 875 (1963); *J. New Drugs* **4**, 154 (1964); *Am. J. Med. Sci.* **254**, 24 (1967)]. Complete bed rest and positive pressure oxygen are indicated for pulmonary edema. Treatment otherwise is symptomatic.

Nickel eczemas may be treated locally with preparations of CaEDTA or with Dithiocarb. (Edathamil calcium disodium was found ineffective as an antidote in experimental animals receiving lethal doses of inorganic nickel salts and nickel carbonyl [B. West and F. W. Sunderman, *A.M.A. Arch. Ind. Health* **18**, 480 (1958)].

NICOTINE

The Federal Trade Commission reported the following concentrations of nicotine and tars in 56 brands of cigarettes: 1.09–1.60 mg nicotine and 17.4–27.1 mg tars per cigarette [*Time* (Dec. 8, 1967)]. Smoking of cigarettes (also of cigars and pipe, but presumably to a lesser extent) causes stimulation of the central nervous system and autonomic ganglia. The effects and tolerance vary considerably in individuals. Increase in sympathetic activity results in acceleration of the heart rate and peripheral vasoconstriction, while augmented parasympathetic activity leads to increased gastroenteric activity, salivation, and perspiration. Prolonged smoking, particularly of cigarettes, contributes to diseases of the circulatory system and may cause "tobacco habituation." In some individuals, abrupt stopping of heavy cigarette smoking has caused irritability, sleep disturbance, impaired concentration and memory, anxiety, a craving for tobacco, and digestive symptoms [R. D. Chessick, *JAMA* **188**, 932 (1964)].

Fatal intoxications have occurred most frequently after ingestion of nicotine-containing insecticides for suicidal purposes. E. Grusz-Harday of Hungary reported 297 fatalities during the years 1959–1966. These individuals ingested many times the lethal dose (approximately 40 mg) of nicotine. Collapse, coma, convulsions, and death frequently occurred within a few minutes [*Arch. Toxikol.* **23**, 35 (1967)]. Intoxications and fatalities have also occurred following occupational or accidental exposure to nicotine sulfate used as an insecticide.

The relationship between excessive cigarette smoking and lung cancer is an established fact. In isolated instances, excessive cigar smoking has produced cancer of the tongue; pipe smoking, cancer of the lips; and chewing tobacco, cancer of the buccal mucosa [N. DeNosaquo, *JAMA* **177**, 588 (1961); P. S. Larson, H. B.

Haag and H. Silvette, "Tobacco, Experimental and Clinical Studies." Williams & Wilkins, Baltimore, Maryland, 1961].

Treatment: Immediate and repeated vomiting is most important after ingestion of nicotine sulfate. Perform gastric lavage with a dilute (1:10,000) solution of potassium permanganate or activated charcoal in water or milk. Further treatment is symptomatic and supportive and may include artificial respiration and measures to combat shock and cardiac arrest. Because of ganglionic blockade, analeptics are not only useless but dangerous. If skin contact has occurred, *flood* affected tissues with water.

NICOTINIC ACID (Niacin)

The value of nicotinic acid as a therapeutic agent has not been established. Repeated doses of approximately 5 gm/day decrease serum cholesterol, but will also cause impairment of hepatic function. There have been reports of hyperglycemia, jaundice, and gastroenteric effects including the development of peptic ulcer. In 1957, an outbreak of food poisoning by nicotinic acid was reported in 145 persons who ate adulterated meat. Signs and symptoms included flushing and itching of the face and neck, perspiration, nausea, and abdominal cramps. The compound was added to the meat to prevent its darkening. (See also Vitamin B Complex, p. 623.)

Caution: Nicotinic acid should be used with some degree of caution if administered in large doses or for prolonged periods of time.

NIOBIUM SALTS (Niobium Pentachloride and Potassium Niobate)

The acute intraperitoneal and oral LD_{50}s for niobium chloride and potassium niobate are 61 and 940 mg/kg, respectively (mice). Niobium chloride is one of the most toxic of the rarer chemicals. Severe localized damage to the skin and transient ocular irritation with no permanent damage are produced by direct contact with the chemical. Niobium chloride produces immediate cardiovascular collapse and respiratory paralysis in the cat at a dose of 5 mg/kg.

The LD_{50} (7 day) value for mice and rats given a single intraperitoneal injection of potassium niobate is 13 and 92 mg of niobium per kilogram, respectively. Renal injury was observed in all species following parenteral injection at doses ranging from 20 to 50 mg of niobium per kilogram. Repeated intraperitoneal injections of 30 mg niobium per kilogram of niobium pentachloride or potassium niobate resulted in renal injury and death. Dietary levels as high as 1 % of either compound were ingested by rats, for a 7-week period, without effect [W. L. Downs, *Am. Ind. Hyg. Ass. J.* **26**, 337 (1965)].

Treatment: In case of ingestion, induce vomiting and follow with gastric lavage. For skin and eye contact, flood the affected areas with water for 15 minutes.

NITRIC ACID

See Hydrochloric Acid, p. 317, for effects of liquid nitric acid, and Nitrogen Oxides, p. 426, for effects of vapors and decomposition products of nitric acid.

NITRITES

Absorption of a toxic dose of inorganic nitrites or organic nitrites and nitrates, such as ethyl nitrite, glyceryl trinitrate (nitroglycerin), erythrityl tetranitrate, mannitol hexanitrate, will induce marked peripheral vasodilation, depression of the heart rate, formation of methemoglobin, confusion, dizziness, and fainting (nitrite syndrome). See Sodium Nitrite, p. 543, Methylene Blue, p. 390, Nitroglycerin, p. 428, and Organic Nitrates, p. 437.

NITROBENZENE

Absorption of a toxic dose will produce marked methemoglobinemia. See Aniline, p. 102.

NITROFURANTOIN (Furadantin)

Nitrofurantoin is used orally and I.V. for genitourinary infections. Furazolidone (Furoxone; Tricofuron) is used occasionally in *Salmonella* infections, both orally and topically. Nitrofurazone (Furacin) has been withdrawn from the market because of marked toxicity.

Side effects noted occasionally after nitrofurantoin therapy include nausea, vomiting, diarrhea, lassitude, and insomnia. In a small percentage of patients, headache, peripheral neuritis, numbness or a tingling sensation, hemolysis, and sensitization (rash, fever) are noted. Hemolytic anemia is found particularly in Negroes and in patients whose racial origin is in the Mediterranian countries.

Martin calls attention to twenty incidents of polyneuropathy that resulted from nitrofurantoin and nitrofurazone therapy. Half of these patients had impaired renal function, some also suffered from anemia. At necropsy, demyelination of peripheral nerves and changes in the ventral horns and the striated muscles were found [*Staff Meetings of the Mayo Clinic* 37, 288 (1962)]. Paresthesias are the first symptoms of impending polyneuropathy. Recovery of a patient can be expected only if Furadantin therapy is discontinued before definite motor involvement has occurred [*Neurosurg. Psychiat.* 29, 224 (1966)]. T. Lindholm reported electromyographic signs of denervation in the peripheral muscles in 23 of 37 patients treated with Furadantin, and in 2 of 11 patients with infections of the urinary tract not receiving this drug. The recurrence of electromyographic abnormalities was not dose related [Neurology 17, 1017 (1967)].

Following topical use, nitrofurazone hypersensitivity reactions (rash) have been a frequent and occasionally severe problem. The overall incidence of sensitization has been reported to range from 1.2 to 5%. Gross hematuria has been noted in 19% of patients [*Med. Letter* 9, 13 (1967)].

Caution: Nitrofurantoin should not be administered to patients suffering from anuria, oliguria or severe kidney damage, or in infants less than 1 month old. This and related drugs should be used with caution in the very young and very old, in debilitated patients, and in persons suffering from electrolyte imbalance, subnormal renal function, diabetes, and anemia. To avoid yellow staining of the teeth, nitrofurantoin should not be given to young children during the period of eruption of the first teeth [*Brit. Med. J.* 2, 1103 (1962)]. Most of the side effects disappear upon reduction of the dose or discontinuation of therapy.

NITROGEN (Caisson Disease; Bends)

Signs and symptoms of caisson disease include itching, and sometimes a macular eruption of the ear lobes and skin of the chest and abdomen, vomiting, deafness, and pain in muscles. Depending on the location of the emboli and the sites affected by the ischemia, additional local effects may be produced, such as a burning sensation in the chest, cough and pulmonary edema, anginal pain, unconsciousness, paralysis, and convulsions. Scuba diving for the obese person is hazardous since fat dissolves almost six times as much nitrogen as blood. See also Diving, p. 31.

It has been reported that a petroleum worker entered a tank purged with nitrogen, intending to simply hold his breath, turn a valve, and leave the tank. However, he was unable to leave the tank, and was found in a coma 4 or 5 minutes later. This man suffered irreversible brain damage. At this writing, he has been in a coma for $5\frac{1}{2}$ months, does not respond to any stimuli except pain, and is being fed sufficient calories via stomach tube to maintain body functions.

Caution: Inert gas (nitrogen) is used in industry to prevent explosions in tanks or other areas undergoing repairs. A man cannot enter such an area expecting to hold his breath while performing some task, because the chances are that he will be unable to leave. Although some men can hold their breath for perhaps a minute, they cannot do this in case of physical exertion, and therein lies the fallacy. A man entering a nitrogen atmosphere must wear an air-supply mask. If the mask does not fit properly, he should not remove it while working in the tank. He should adjust it only after he has left the atmosphere containing nitrogen. Although nitrogen is considered to be physically inert, it must be realized that oxygen is essential to sustain life.

Treatment: To prevent bends, ascension of the diver must be slow and in stages. Recompression with subsequent slow decompression is employed (1) in the treatment of divers who *must* be brought to the surface fairly rapidly and (2) in the treatment of caisson disease (bends). The individual is placed in a steel chamber and subjected to atmospheric air under pressure equivalent to 165 feet (50 meters) until the blood supply to the painful areas has been restored, as indicated by the disappearance of pain, and then gradually brought to a pressure equivalent to 0 feet, or sea level, according to the tables prepared by the U.S. Navy.

Recently, a new regimen of treatment which is less

time-consuming and more effective has come into vogue with the U.S. Navy. This involves recompressing to 60 feet (18.2 meters) and using pure oxygen according to the Navy tables. The *short* (135-minute) schedule is used for treatment of "pain only" bends, if such pain can be completely relieved within 10 minutes of reaching 60 feet. The long (285-minute) schedule is used for all serious symptoms, for recurrence, or if pain is not completely resolved after 10 minutes at 60 feet. However, whichever schedule is used, it is still much less time consuming than the prior 24 or 36 hour time needed with atmospheric air. (Theodore Struhl, private communication, 1968.)

NITROGEN (LIQUID)

Liquid nitrogen, used for the removal of warts or keratotic lesions, must be applied with caution to avoid freezing the superficial nerves underlying the site of nitrogen application. Nix reported two such incidents in *Arch. Dermatol.* **92**, 185 (1965).

NITROGEN MUSTARD

This vesicant used in World War I (tris-β-chloroethylamine) has found some limited use in the palliative treatment of certain neoplastic diseases. Toxic doses will cause anorexia, loss of body weight, vomiting, hemorrhages, enteritis, bone marrow damage, disturbance of water and electrolyte balance, and death. Inhalation of particles or vapors of nitrogen mustard and skin or mucous membrane contact may cause severe local necrotic lesions.

Bone marrow damage can be prevented by the simultaneous administration of sodium thiosulfate (250 mg I.V. per milligram of nitrogen mustard infused into the internal carotid artery). Despite neutralization of the nitrogen mustard, skin discoloration over the ipsilateral supraorbital region, periorbital edema, rapid increase in neurological disturbances, and loss of ipsilateral hair have been noted in some patients.

Treatment: There is no antidote. Discontinue use of the drug. Treatment is entirely symptomatic.

NITROGEN OXIDES

Inhalation of low concentrations of the oxides of nitrogen may cause little or no discomfort to the upper respiratory tract but may result in death hours later due to pulmonary edema. A brief exposure to 200 ppm may be fatal. Industry has been aware of this hazard for many years.

The clinical entity — "bronchiolitis fibrosa obliterans," "silo-fillers' disease," or "silage gas poisoning" due to inhalation of nitrogen dioxide — was first reported in agricultural workers in 1956. The disease is more prevalent among these workers than is generally recognized. Physicians in rural areas should therefore be aware of this hazard. Nitrogen dioxide is formed when nitric oxide in fresh silage comes in contact with oxygen in the air. Gas production is greatest in alfalfa silage, reaching a peak within 24 hours and apparently subsiding in 2–3 days. Nitrogen dioxide is usually visible as a yellowish brown haze and has an irritating odor. However, serious pulmonary injury has been produced with only mildly irritating symptoms. Typical signs and symptoms include respiratory difficulty, feeling of oppression in the chest, dyspnea, cyanosis, and syncope. A farmer had symptoms of a cold and heart pain shortly after filling his silo. Twenty-six days later his shortness of breath became so severe that he had to be hospitalized. He died shortly afterwards of respiratory failure.

Treatment: Avoid remaining for any length of time in a freshly filled silo. Leave a silo at the appearance of the slightest respiratory difficulty. Rest and oxygen are most important in the symptomatic treatment. Antibiotics may be necessary to prevent secondary bacterial pneumonitis.

For effects of long-term continuous exposure of experimental animals to nitrogen dioxide, see reports by B. L. Steadman *et al.* [*Toxicol. Appl. Pharmacol.* **9**, 160 (1966)], and G. Freeman *et al.* [*Arch. Environ. Health* **13**, 454 (1966)]. For teratogenic activity of nitrous oxide in rats, see report by B. R. Fink [*Nature* **214**, 146 (1967)].

NITROGEN TRIFLUORIDE (NF$_3$)

Nitrogen trifluoride is a pulmonary irritant comparable in toxicity to the oxides of nitrogen. LC$_{50}$ (mice) is 2000 ppm (4-hour exposure). See Nitrogen Oxides.

NITROGLYCERIN (Glyceryl Trinitrate)

For the relief of anginal pain, the smallest sublingually effective dose of nitroglycerin should be administered in order to keep the undesirable effects to a minimum and to prevent the development of tolerance. Relief is almost as prompt with nitroglycerin as inhalation of the less safe amyl and octyl nitrites. Oral administration of nitroglycerin is ineffective, because the drug is detoxified in the liver. So-called "sustained-release" oral nitroglycerin and related organic nitrate preparations are often useless because they induce tolerance, are ineffective in an emergency, and at best, are not dependable. An overdose of glyceryl trinitrate and related compounds induces generalized hypotension. Methemoglobinemia becomes a problem only after ingestion of a large dose, i.e., in a child who has swallowed the contents of a nitroglycerin bottle. See Organic Nitrates, p. 437.

Caution: If headache follows the use of nitroglycerin for the relief of anginal pain, the dosage is probably too high. Orthostatic hypotension can be reduced if the patient reclines in an almost horizontal position. For the treatment of severe methemoglobinemia, transfuse with whole blood or administer methylene blue in an I.V. or I.M. dose of 1–2 mg/kg, or in an oral dose of 3–5 mg/kg; the parenteral route is preferred.

β-NITRONAPHTHALENE

No human toxicity data are available. The oral LD_{50}s for rabbits and rats are 2.65 and 4.4 gm/kg, respectively. Oral administration induced degenerative and necrotic lesions in the liver and kidneys and slight degenerative changes in the brain. In rabbits, oral doses resulted in the formation of methemoglobin and large numbers of Heinz bodies and some increase in the clotting time of the peripheral blood. Some degeneration of hepatic cells and renal tubules was observed following contact of abraded skin with β-nitronaphthalene in peanut oil. It is apparent that some percutaneous absorption occurs. Two cats, two guinea pigs, ten mice, and two rats survived when exposed for 7 hours on each of 50 days over a period of 68 days to air that contained 1.91 μg of β-nitronaphthalene per liter.

Treatment: For skin, eye, and mucous membrane contact, flood the affected tissues with water. In case of ingestion, induce vomiting and follow with gastric lavage, demulcents, and saline cathartics. The treatment of methemoglobinemia is described on p. 428.

NITROOLEFINS

The vapors of conjugated nitroolefins produce marked lacrimation and, in high concentration, an intense burning sensation of the eyes and respiratory tract. Liquid nitroolefins cause marked irritation of the skin and mucous membranes. They are readily absorbed through the intact skin, producing pain and systemic effects, including hyperexcitability, tremors, convulsions, and tachycardia followed by a generalized depression, ataxia, cyanosis, dyspnea, and death initiated by respiratory failure. Primary carcinoma was produced in 5 of 27 Swiss mice exposed to 0.2 ppm of 3-nitro-3-hexene for 5 hours per day for 18 months. Similar exposure produced undifferentiated carcinoma in the lungs of 6 of 100 CFN rats exposed to 1.0 ppm, and in 11 of 100 CFN rats exposed to 2.0 ppm for 36 months [*Ind. Med. Surg.* **34**, 800 (1965)]. Decomposition of the nitroolefins is accelerated by water, alkali, and sunlight [*A.M.A. Arch. Ind. Health* **18**, 312 (1958); *Ind. Med. Surg.* **27**, 375 (1958)]. H. E. Stokinger and J. T. Mountain described tests for detecting a blood serum deficiency and its relation to an inherited tendency toward pulmonary emphysema. This test is useful in detecting pulmonary irritants [*J. Occupational Med.* **9**, 537 (1967)].

Treatment: Skin contact is treated with soap and a copious flow of water. Ocular pain and lacrimation resulting from exposure to nitroolefin vapors is relieved within a few minutes after removal to fresh air. If splashed into the eyes, rinse with water for at least 15 minutes. Animal studies indicate that bronchiolar constriction and secretion may be relieved by atropine.

NITROPARAFFINS

Nitromethane: Prolonged or frequently repeated skin exposure may cause a low-grade irritation, but no allergies or other adverse physiological effects have been reported from skin exposure. The oral LD_{50} in white rats is 1.21 gm/kg, and the LD_0 is 0.50 gm/kg. The LD_{100} is 2.0 gm/kg.

Nitropropane: The acute oral minimum lethal dose of 2-nitropropane (2-NP) for rabbits is 0.5–0.75 gm/kg, and the LD_{50} for rats is 0.72 gm/kg. No skin irritation or illness resulted from repeated application to the skin of rabbits and no evidence of significant absorption was observed. No changes occurred in tissues of monkeys, rabbits, guinea pigs, and rats exposed to air containing 328 ppm of 2-NP for 130 periods of 7 hours each (6 months, 5 days per week). In the same series, cats had severe damage to the liver and moderate injury to the kidneys and heart. When cats were exposed to 83 ppm, slight but reversible effects were observed. The MAC is 25 ppm. Earlier work indicated 1-nitropropane to be somewhat more toxic than 2-nitropropane. No skin absorption or injury was noted in animals.

Workers exposed to 2-nitropropane in concentrations ranging from 30 to 300 ppm had headache, dizziness, nausea, vomiting, and diarrhea. Some also complained of respiratory tract irritation. No allergies or other adverse physiological effects have been reported from skin exposure.

Treatment: Remove from skin, mucous membranes, or eyes with copious amounts of water. For ingestion, induce vomiting and follow with gastric lavage. For inhalation, give artificial respiration and oxygen if needed. Further treatment is supportive and symptomatic.

4-NITROPYRIDINE-N-OXIDE

The *Approximate Lethal Oral Doses* are 87 mg/kg as a 0.5% aqueous solution (rats); 8 mg/kg in capsules, 34 mg/kg as 0.5% on grain (dogs); 23 mg/kg as a 1.0% aqueous solution (14–21-day-old chicks). The percutaneous lethal dose for rabbits is 360 mg/kg applied as a paste in tap water. Signs of intoxication include salivation, central nervous system stimulation, respiratory difficulties, and coma. On exposure to light, 4-nitropyridine-N-oxide is changed to a yellow compound having a relatively low toxicity. No cases of human toxicity have been reported.

Treatment: For ingestion, induce vomiting. In case of skin or eye contact, flood affected tissues with water.

NITROUS OXIDE (Dinitrogen Monoxide; Hyponitrous Acid Anhydride; Laughing Gas; Factitious Air)

Nitrous oxide is used as an inhalation anesthetic. Nitrous oxide–oxygen anesthesia almost always causes some degree of hypoxia.

Treatment: Discontinue exposure.

NORBORMIDE (Shoxin)

Norbormide is the active ingredient in a rodenticide (Raticate). The oral LD_{50} for the Norway rat is approximately 10 mg/kg, while mammals other than those in genus *Rattus*, as well as birds, were resistant to this material. For example, in the hamster, the most susceptible of nonrat species, the LD_{50} was 140 mg/kg, while in cats, dogs, pigs, monkeys, mice, birds and others, 1000 mg/kg orally produced neither death nor abnormalities. Indirect dermal studies indicate that man is probably not susceptible to the toxic action of this substance.

Norbormide produces an extreme irreversible peripheral vasoconstriction in rats. It is probable that this vasoconstriction induces local ischemic changes which lead to death of a number of organs and systems and to the death of the animals. Vasoconstriction and circulatory changes do not occur in other species. Norbormide seems to be ideally suited for rodenticidal use. [A. P. Roszkowski, *J. Pharmacol. Exptl. Therap.* **149**, 288 (1965)].

NORCYMETHADOL (Dimephadane)

This is a new analgesic which is expected to be classified as a narcotic. It is somewhat more potent than morphine. When administered to postpartum patients, the side effects noted were nausea, dizziness, drowsiness, and itching. Acutely toxic doses resulted in salivation, ataxia, and respiratory depression. Tolerance to the drug developed more slowly than to morphine or phenazocine (Prinadol) [C. M. Gruber and A. Baptisti, *Clin. Pharmacol. Therap.* **4**, 172 (1963)].

Treatment: Respiratory depression responds to nalorphine and to levallorphan.

NORETHINDRONE (Norlutin)

This orally active semisynthetic drug has been found useful in the treatment of amenorrhea and in causing temporary delay of the menstrual cycle. In the management of habitual or threatened abortion, this drug is not without risk. Of 182 obstetric patients, 10 (5.5%) demonstrated masculinizing side effects. Eighteen percent of the female infants born to these mothers showed some degree of masculinization. The risk of side effects in the fetus is greatest when treatment with norethindrone is initiated during the first trimester of pregnancy.

Caution: "Therapy should always be cyclic and interrupted. Prolonged courses have resulted in extreme hyperplastic changes in the endometrial stroma which are histologically indistinguishable from sarcoma. Doses as small as 2 mg daily may be effective" (New and Nonofficial Drugs, Lippincott, Philadelphia, 1962).

NORMETHADONE (Ticarda)

Ticarda contains normethadone and p-hydroxy-ephedrine. This preparation has respiratory depressant effects similar to those induced by methadone. Several acute intoxications have occurred in children.

Treatment: See Opiates, p. 435.

NORTRIPTYLINE (Aventyl)

Nortriptyline is a potent antidepressant. Experience with this drug has not been extensive; the same adverse effects may be anticipated and the same precautions are recommended for nortriptyline as for amitriptyline (Elavil) [D. G. Friend, *Clin. Pharmacol. Therap.* **6**, 805 (1965)]. The fact that neurotoxic reactions seen in "acute" animals and "chronic" dogs occurred only at doses many times greater than would be considered useful in human patients must be accepted with some degree of reservation, since this and related drugs are frequently administered to patients with subnormal vital functions and with sensitivity exceeding that of healthy rats and dogs [*Toxicol. Appl. Pharmacol.* **9**, 152 (1966)]. A recent report describes three patients who developed paralytic ileus while receiving nortriptyline in therapeutic doses [*Brit. Med. J.* **1**, 841 (1966)]. See also Protriptyline, p. 504, and Amitriptyline, p. 94.

NOVOBIOCIN (Albamycin)

This antibiotic is readily absorbed from the gastroenteric tract. Side effects noted rather frequently include urticaria, erythema, maculopapular eruptions, fever, pruritus, and diarrhea. A yellow tint of the skin, mucous membranes, and sclera are occasionally produced. Resistant strains develop readily. This drug is highly allergenic. A relatively high incidence of leukopenia has been observed after short-term use.

Caution: The drug should not be administered to premature infants or to infants less than 2 weeks old. Its safe use during pregnancy has not been established. Novobiocin should not be used for long-term therapy under any circumstance.

NUTMEG (*Myristica fragrans*)

Nutmeg or mace is used by some individuals in a soft drink, tea, or milk and ingested for its hallucinogenic effect. The toxic constituent is myristicin. One to two nutmegs or one teaspoon of mace may cause serious (rarely fatal) poisoning in an adult. The effects become apparent in 1–6 hours; they include euphoria, central nervous system stimulation and gastroenteric irritation. These symptoms are followed by an acute toxic psychosis and later by central nervous system depression. Recovery is usually complete in 24 hours, although there is a possibility that some hepatic necrosis may have been produced. See p. 301.

Treatment is symptomatic.

NYSTATIN (Mycostatin)

This antibiotic is used only topically or in the form of vaginal tablets for infections caused by *Candida albicans* (*Monilia*) and in other types of monoliasis. The drug is virtually free from side effects.

OCTAFLUOROCYCLOBUTANE (OFCB)

This chemical possesses an extremely low order of acute toxicity. At 80%, with 20% oxygen, there were slight but transient effects on respiration in rats and mice. OFCB does not produce signs of anesthesia or indication of even slight central nervous system depression. Repeated exposure of rats, mice, rabbits, and dogs to 10% for 6 hours daily, 5 days a week, for a minimum of 90 exposures, resulted in no harmful effects as judged by clinical examination of body weight, blood and urine studies, organ weights, and gross and microscopic tissue examination. OFCB is a safe propellant for food products [J. W. Clayton, *et al.*, *Amer. Ind. Hyg. Assoc. J.* **21**, 382 (1960)].

OFF (*N,N*-DIETHYL-*m*-TOLUAMIDE)

OFF contains 15% *N,N*-diethyl-*m*-toluamide in denatured alcohol. Freon is used as the propellant. The dermal LD_{50} in rabbits is 10 ml/kg. In animals, signs of toxicity include depression, labored respiration, ataxia, coma, and clonic convulsions. At autopsy there was evidence of hyperemia of the lungs, intestinal irritation, and renal congestion.

Similar signs and symptoms of toxicity were observed in a $3\frac{1}{2}$-year-old child whose body, night-clothes, and bedding had been sprayed with OFF every evening for 2 weeks. Anticonvulsant therapy and supportive treatment resulted in abatement of symptoms by the third hospital day. See *N,N*-Diethyltoluamides, p. 217.

Treatment: Control central nervous system effects with anticonvulsant therapy. See p. 36. Further treatment is supportive and symptomatic.

OLEFINS (Alkenes; Ethylene Series)

These are unsaturated aliphatic hydrocarbons having a low to moderate degree of toxicity. (See Petroleum Solvents or Distillates, p. 459; and Hydrocarbon Gases, p. 316).

OLIVE OIL

Olive oil or cottonseed oil is a useful emollient and an agent for prolonging the emptying time of the stomach in oral intoxications by corrosive agents. Depending on the dose, they also exert a laxative action. *However, these oils should not be used routinely as cathartics in oral poisonings.* For this purpose a saline cathartic is indicated.

Cottonseed oil has been used I.V. as a "15% oil-in-water emulsion with 4% dextrose" in severely malnourished patients; 500 ml of this solution provides approximately 750 calories. Cottonseed oil (150–180 ml rectally) has also been used for the purpose of softening impacted fecal masses. Wesson oil is hydrogenated cottonseed oil containing 50% linoleic acid (a polyunsaturated fatty acid) and 25% oleic acid (a monounsaturated fatty acid).

OPIATES

In a nonaddicted individual, an overdose of morphine, codeine, or related drugs (except papaverine) will induce signs and symptoms characterized primarily by marked depression of respiration and pinpoint pupils; in addition there is sweating, itching, lightheadedness, headache, nausea, vomiting, and a marked insensibility to pain. Extreme contraction of the pupils is an important diagnostic sign (other central depressants will also produce miosis, but generally less marked); deep coma and a generalized marked depression of the central nervous system predominate in most adults. In some individuals, particularly in women and children, these signs and symptoms may be preceded by a certain degree of central nervous system stimulation, including hyperexcitability, tremors, and tonic convulsions. Death from an overdose is due to respiratory failure. In debilitated patients, even low therapeutic doses have been known to produce alarming respiratory embarrassment.

Caution: Opiates should be administered with particular caution in the very young and very old. Equal consideration should be given to individuals who, in addition to opiates, are treated with tranquilizers, muscle relaxing agents, or barbiturates. Morphine and related drugs are contraindicated in patients with bronchial asthma, pulmonary emphysema, acute and chronic liver diseases, myxedema, adrenal insufficiency, liver disease associated with hepatic encephalopathy, jaundice, ascites, or gastroenteric bleeding.

Repeated or prolonged use of *opiates will almost invariably lead to addiction.* Signs and symptoms of addiction include nervousness, mild tremors, loss of appetite and body weight, diarrhea or constipation, and progressive mental deterioration. An addict behaves normally only under the influence of an opiate.

When an opiate is withheld from an addict, withdrawal symptoms appear; these include yawning, restlessness, respiratory difficulties, abdominal disturbances such as cramps, diarrhea, and vomiting; tremors, marked loss of appetite, and inability to sleep may also be present. Withdrawal symptoms increase in severity for about 3 days, then subside for a week. The infants of addicted mothers have withdrawal symptoms. These symptoms may appear shortly after birth or several hours after delivery. According to Kunstadter and co-workers, signs of addiction in infants are hyperactivity, trembling, twitchings and convulsions, a shrill, high-pitched, prolonged cry, and the appearance of being constantly hungry (sucking of the hands and fingers) [*JAMA* **168**, 1008 (1958); *Mod. Med.* **36**, 145 (1968)].

Treatment: Nausea and vomiting induced by therapeutic doses of morphine and related drugs may be controlled or reduced by lowering the dosage or by administration of cyclizine; amiphenazole is helpful in reducing the sedative action of morphine. Schiffrin recommends the concomitant injection of levallorphan with meperidine in a ratio of 1:100 to prevent the respiratory depression of the latter drug [*Mod. Med.* (Jan. 15, 1958)].

An acute opiate intoxication may be reversed by nalorphine (*N*-allylnormorphine; Nalline) or by levallorphan (1-3-hydroxy-*N*-allylmorphinan; Lorphan; Lorfan). Effects on respiration are almost immediate and last for 30 minutes to 3 hours, depending on the dosage. Done suggests the following I.V. doses: nalorphine, 5–10 mg for adults, 0.1 mg/kg for children, and 0.2–0.4 mg for newborn infants; levallorphan, 1.0–2.0 mg for adults, 0.02 mg/kg for children, and 0.05–0.1 mg for newborn infants [*Clin. Pharmacol. Therap.* **2**, 750 (1961)].

If the opiate has been ingested (for instance a child who took an overdose of paregoric), *gastric lavage* should be carried out with water or with a 1 % solution of potassium permanganate, and followed by a saline cathartic. Emetics, as expected, have little or no effect, since the vomiting center is likely to be depressed. Consider also the use of artificial respiration, oxygen, an antibiotic, and catheterization of the urinary bladder.

Newborn infants exhibiting narcotic addiction were successfully treated by Corbrinik *et al.* with gradually diminishing doses of paregoric and chlorpromazine [*Sci. Newsletter* (Aug. 22, 1959)]; Kunstadter and collaborators recommend the administration of diminishing doses of barbiturates, oxygen, and antibiotics, and fluid and electrolytes parenterally [*JAMA* **168**, 1008

(1958)]. Nalorphine may be given to the mother before severing the umbilical cord. (When given to an addict, nalorphine and levallorphan will promptly precipitate withdrawal symptoms).

Treatment of an addict consists of withdrawal of the drug, substitution therapy, and mental, physical, and sociological rehabilitation. (See also Narcotic Agents, p. 40, and Tripelennamine, p. 610.

ORGANIC NITRATES

Industrial workers handling organic nitrates may absorb sufficient chemical through the surface of the body to produce symptoms, the commonest of which is headache. The syndrome of nitrate-induced headache is characterized by a distressing headache which may be constant and aching but more typically is pulsatile, and which, when severe, is associated with "fullness in the head," palpitations, anorexia, nausea, faintness, tinnitus, mental confusion, flushing of the skin, and occasionally, visual disturbances. The headache is made worse by stooping and lying down.

Popular synonyms for this condition are "nitrate head," "N.G. head," "powder head," and "Monday head." The last-mentioned term derives from the loss of habituation which occurs during a weekend free from exposure.

Workers aware of the ready loss of habituation that occurs during weekends away from the plant rub a little of the nitrate into their hat bands so that they absorb sufficient chemical when off work to maintain the state of habituation.

Prevention: This disorder may be prevented by the use of protective clothing, adequate removal of dust and fumes from the workplace, and by limiting, as much as possible, the dust and fumes produced during milling of the offending material. Prevention is thus a matter of elementary industrial hygiene.

ORGANIC PEROXIDES (Methyl Ethyl Ketone Peroxide; Cumene Hydroperoxide; *t*-Butyl Hydroperoxide; Di-*t*-Butyl Peroxide)

All organic peroxides should be regarded as being potentially explosive. Five grams of acetyl peroxide in a bottle exploded with sufficient force to tear off both of a man's hands. Detonation may be caused by heat, shock, or friction. In general, the stability increases as the proportion of oxygen in the molecule decreases. The methyl, ethyl, hydroxymethyl, and hydroxyethyl hydroperoxides and peroxides, the polymeric alkylidene peroxides derived from low molecular weight aldehydes and ketones, and peroxyacetic acid and diacetyl peroxide should be handled with extreme caution and on a very small scale. Peroxides that are usually regarded as being relatively innocuous may produce detonable mixtures when in combination with other compounds.

Toxicity ratings indicate that the hydroperoxides (ROOH) are "moderately toxic" compounds. Di-*t*-butyl peroxide (ROOR) is the least toxic by all routes of administration. It is classed as relatively harmless to slightly toxic (inhalation). All of the organic peroxides are skin and eye irritants except di-*t*-butyl peroxide.

Inhalation of vapor causes weakness and tremors of the head and neck in animals. See p. 746.

Treatment: For skin, eye, and mucous membrane contact, flood affected tissues with water. In case of ingestion induce vomiting and follow with gastric lavage. For inhalation, remove individual from contaminated atmosphere; give artificial respiration and oxygen if needed.

ORGANIC PHOSPHATES (Alkyl Phosphates; Aryl Phosphates; Alkyl-Aryl Phosphates)

Included in this large class of compounds are some of the most toxic chemicals known. Extensively used today as agricultural chemicals (insecticides, pesticides) are hundreds of molecular types varying in toxicity from highly toxic to essentially nontoxic.

In general, the organic phosphates may be conveniently subdivided into three groups according to their toxicity for man: (1) the highly toxic group, including Tetram, Sarin, Tabun, TEPP, paraoxon, parathion, methyl parathion, Thimet, EPN, Systox, and OMPA, (2) the moderately toxic group, such as EPN, DDVP, and Diazinon; (3) the slightly toxic group, including malathion, chlorthion, and Dipterex.

These compounds are toxic or lethal because they phosphorylate and inactivate cholinesterase. As a consequence, acetylcholine accumulates at the endings of the postganglionic parasympathetic and the skeletal motor nerves. The toxic effects resemble those induced by overdoses of physostigmine (eserine) or neostigmine (Prostigmine). Successive hours or days of unsafe use may cause progressive lowering of the cholinesterase level in the blood and tissues.

The first symptoms of an intoxication are usually anorexia and nausea, often with mental confusion and a sense of unreality. These effects may be experienced during exposure or up to 8 hours later. Vomiting, cramplike abdominal pain, excessive cold sweating, and salivation soon follow. Giddiness, apprehension, and restlessness may also be noticeable. Constriction of the pupil may be seen, but this is not a constant sign of poisoning, nor is it an indication of its severity. It may be caused by the local effect of spray mist in the eye.

As poisoning progresses, muscular twitchings begin in the eyelids and tongue, then other muscles of the face and the neck become involved. Generalized twitching with profound muscle weakness occurs in severely affected persons. Later manifestations include hypoglycemia, diarrhea, tenesmus, involuntary defecation, and pulmonary edema with bronchoconstriction. Ataxia, tremor, convulsions, drowsiness, and respiratory depression follow, gradually advancing to coma.

Treatment: Speed is essential. 1. Flood and wash exposed skin areas *thoroughly* with water. Remove contaminated clothing under a shower. In case of ingestion, administer milk, water or salt-water and induce vomiting repeatedly. In the nonbreathing victim, however, *immediately* institute artificial respiration, using the mouth-to-mouth, the mouth-to-nose, or the mouth-to-oropharyngeal method.

2. Administer atropine, 2 mg (1/30 gr) intramuscularly or intravenously as soon as any local or systemic signs or symptoms of an intoxication are noted. Repeat the administration of atropine every 3–8 minutes until signs of atropinization (mydriasis, dry mouth, rapid pulse, hot and dry skin) occur. Initiate treatment in children with 1 mg of atropine.

3. Watch respiration, and remove bronchial secretions if they appear to be obstructing the airway. Intubate if necessary.

439

4. Give 2-PAM (Pralidoxime; *Protopam*), 2.5 gm in 100 ml of sterile water or in 5% dextrose and water, intravenously, slowly, in 15–30 minutes. If sufficient fluid is not available, give 1 gm of 2-PAM in 3 ml of distilled water by deep intramuscular injection. Repeat this every half hour if respiration weakens or if muscle fasciculation or convulsions recur [Van M. Sim, *JAMA* **192**, 143 (1965)]. Bernstein and Gould recommend giving children 15 mg/kg of Protopam I.V. and slowly [*Mod. Med.* **36**, 115 (1968)].

The patient should be kept fully atropinized and under observation for at least 72 hours, preferably in a hospital. In severe cases, 100 mg or more atropine may be required over the total period of treatment.

Timing is apparently important in the administration of 2-PAM. There is evidence that it should *not* be administered until symptoms of an organic phosphate intoxication have appeared, and not later than 24 hours after the onset of symptoms. Atropine remains the primary drug in the treatment of an organic phosphate intoxication. See p. 116 and p. 448.

The passage of an endotracheal tube and bronchial aspiration should not be delayed if there is any evidence of interference with the airway. Whenever possible, but without sacrificing valuable time, a blood sample should be obtained and analyzed for serum and erythrocyte cholinesterase activity. This will aid the physician in evaluating the severity of the intoxication and predicting the rate of recovery.

ORGANOTIN COMPOUNDS

Most tin compounds are harmless because of their insolubility in body fluids. However, some alkyl derivatives are soluble and quite toxic. Diethyl and triethyl compounds appear to be the most toxic. They produce paresis, tremors, convulsions, and edema of the white matter of the brain and spinal cord.

Higher molecular weight organotin compounds have a lower order of toxicity. Tetrabutyltin, for example, has little acute oral toxicity in rats. In general, of the alkyl compounds, the trialkyls are the most toxic, the dialkyls and tetraalkyls are moderately toxic, and the monoalkyls approach the inorganic tin compounds in toxicity. In rats, the oral LD_{50} of tributyltin oxide (TBTO) is 175 mg/kg, and of dibutyltin oxide is

100–200 mg/kg. TBTO is a primary skin irritant and a skin sensitizer.

Chemical burns have been reported in workers handling dibutyltin dichloride or tributyltin chloride. The skin irritation may not appear for at least an hour and sometimes as long as 8 hours. Sensitization of the skin has not been reported. (See Table 63, p. 753).

Inhalation of vapor or fumes causes sore throat, cough, and retching which may occur several hours after exposure. Symptoms are due to irritation of mucous membranes of the throat.

Diethyltin diiodide combined with lineoleic acid (vitamin F) was used in France for the treatment of furunculosis. It produced severe systemic effects (headaches, disorientation, and encephalopathy) and death.

Treatment: For inhalation, remove victim from contaminated atmosphere. Treat symptomatically and watch for evidence of pulmonary injury. For ingestion, induce vomiting, follow with gastric lavage, and saline cathartics. In case of skin contact, flood affected tissues with water and treat as thermal burn.

OSPOLOT

This is a new anticonvulsant not yet released for general use. E. Overvad, who used it in 104 epileptics for 6–15 months, found it most useful in 53 patients. About one-third of all patients had side effects such as hyperpnea and paresthesia. Caution is in order until more is known about this drug [*Ugeskrift Laeger.* **124**, 1400 (1962)].

OXALIC ACID

Ingestion of rhubarb leaves and other sour grasses has caused fatalities in children. See Rhubarb, p. 519. Sodium and potassium oxalates are used in ink and in stain removers used as bleaching agents. The first signs of intoxication following ingestion of a toxic dose are nausea, vomiting, and gastroenteric pain. The oxalate combines with calcium to form calcium oxalate, which induces central nervous system stimulation (irritability, twitchings, tremors, convulsions). Oxalate crystals in the ureter and bladder may cause pain and hematuria. Death is due to renal obstruction or to hypocalcemia leading to cardiac failure.

Treatment: Evacuate the stomach by repeated vomiting or gastric lavage with milk, limewater, or powdered chalk in water, or by use of 10% solutions of calcium gluconate, calcium lactate, or calcium chloride to produce calcium oxalate in the stomach. Also consider I.V. administration of glucose and saline. If renal function is unimpaired, give up to 4 liters of fluid per day to prevent precipitation of calcium oxalate in the renal tubules.

OXAZEPAM (Serax)

This tranquilizer is chemically, pharmacologically, and toxicologically related to chlordiazepoxide and diazepam (Valium). When compared with these drugs, side effects of oxazepam have been reported to be less frequent and less marked. Signs and symptoms of toxicity were produced in two adults and in one child after doses ranging from 8 to 12 mg per kilogram of body weight. The symptoms, which were particularly severe in the child, included lethargy, ataxia, paradoxical excitation, depressed reflexes, and facial edema [P. M. Shimkin and S. A. Shavitz, *JAMA* **196**, 662 (1966)]. Marked hyperventilation, with respiratory rates over 100 per minute lasting for 2 or 3 days, followed the use of this drug in two elderly patients. Leukopenia and jaundice have also been reported [*Med. Letter* **7**, 93 (1965)]. Withdrawal symptoms after discontinuation of massive doses of this drug were produced in one patient [J. W. Selig, *JAMA* **198**, 951 (1966)].

Caution: The manufacturer warns that this drug should be administered with caution in patients in whom a drop in blood pressure might lead to cardiac complications. Selig's patient responded to sodium pentobarbital.

OXYCODONE (Dihydrohydroxycodeinone; Percodan)

This is a potent narcotic analgesic. It resembles morphine in regard to the production of withdrawal symptoms [*Calif. Med.* **99**, 127 (1963)].

OXYGEN

Oxygen like other agents may result in cellular toxicity if given in too high a concentration over too long a period of time. Although oxygen toxicity has been shown to be a definite entity in animals, there is little evidence of the development of such problems in clinical situations in which high concentrations of oxygen are required to achieve a normal arterial oxygen tension. But when pure oxygen is breathed for 5 hours at sea level, for 3 hours at 3 atmospheres, 30 minutes at 4 atmospheres, or 5 minutes at 7 atmospheres, signs and symptoms of toxicity will follow. These include nausea, dizziness, bronchial irritation, hypothermia, increased depth of respiration, bradycardia, pulmonary discomfort or injury (congestion, bronchitis, edema, pneumonia), peripheral vasoconstriction, amblyopia or loss of vision, syncope, epileptic seizures, and death. Pure oxygen at ⅓ atmospheric pressure can be inhaled for weeks without injury.

Oxygen has been implicated as a cause of retrolental fibroplasia in newborn infants exposed to high concentrations continuously for several days. However, this complication does not develop if the arterial oxygen tension is not markedly elevated.

Prolonged oxygen administration, particularly in high concentrations, may result in other complications. It leads to a washout of nitrogen from the lungs and, should obstruction develop, to the rapid absorption of gas from the obstructed alveoli, thereby causing focal areas of atelectasis. This is accompanied by a more negative transthoracic pressure with consequent engorgement of the capillaries and right-to-left shunting of blood. Such an occurrence can be recognized only by a fall in the arterial pO_2 despite the continued inhalation of a constant concentration of oxygen. Frequent large inflations of the lungs are useful in order to prevent or reverse, at least partially, the lung collapse which may develop during the breathing of high concentrations of oxygen.

Eighty-three autopsies of newborn infants, 75 of them premature, were studied for a possible relationship between therapeutic use of oxygen and the development of pulmonary hemorrhage. Twelve infants were not given oxygen, 11 were given oxygen after 6 hours, 21 were given oxygen before 6 hours, and 39 had received oxygen continuously. The infants receiving oxygen early or continuously showed frequent hemorrhages; those receiving no oxygen and those receiving oxygen later had none. The infants receiving oxygen continuously had nearly twice the frequency of hyaline membrane disease when compared with the other three groups that showed similar effects [D. R. Shanklin and S. L. Wolfson, *New Engl. J. Med.* **277**, 833 (1967)].

Treatment: In all but the most severe cases (pneumonia) recovery is rapid after reduction of oxygen pressure. Supportive treatment should include immediate sedation, anticonvulsive therapy if needed, and rest. Convulsions will not cause permanent injury, but death will follow if the oxygen pressure is not lowered promptly (See also Diving, p. 31; and Nitrogen, p. 424.

OXYGEN DIFLUORIDE (OF$_2$)

Oxygen difluoride is a colorless gas which can be condensed to a pale yellow liquid with a slightly irritating odor. It is the most stable of the compounds of fluorine and oxygen. Inhalation produces effects similar to those of ozone and fluorine. It is a strong irritant to the entire respiratory tract and causes pulmonary edema and hemorrhage when inhaled for a few hours at 0.5 ppm. Development of pulmonary signs leading to death may be delayed several hours after the exposure. Rat inhalation studies at concentrations of 5–40 ppm for 5–15 minutes caused 50% mortality at a CT (concentration × time) of approximately 100. Repeated daily 7-hour exposures of mice, rats, guinea pigs, rabbits and dogs at 0.1 ppm for 30 exposures produced no evidence of toxicity. No signs of irritation of external mucosa of the eye were observed in rats subjected to a lethal exposure of 15 ppm oxygen difluoride for 15 minutes.

Treatment: Remove victim from the contaminated area, administer oxygen, and keep him quiet for 24 hours for observation to detect and combat pulmonary injury. The patient should be examined for skin burns, which can be treated as fluorine burns. The eyes, if affected, should be irrigated with water for at least 15 minutes.

OXYMETAZOLINE HYDROCHLORIDE (Afrin)

Available information does not indicate whether the effects of this new nasal decongestant, including its adverse reactions, are essentially different from those of other nasal decongestants. The data do not permit an unequivocal conclusion that oxymetazoline has a longer duration of action than other nasal decongestants [*JAMA* **193**, 1115 (1965)].

OXYMORPHONE (Numorphan)

This semisynthetic analgesic has properties and side effects similar to those of morphine, but depression of respiration, nausea, vomiting and constipation appear to be more marked.

Treatment: Nalorphine and levallorphan are effective respiratory antagonists. See Narcotic Agents, p. 40, and Opiates, p. 435.

OXYPHENCYCLIMINE HYDROCHLORIDE (Daricon; Vio-Thene)

This anticholinergic agent has been recommended as an adjunct to the management of peptic ulcer. Its effects are closely related to those of atropine.

Treatment: See Atropine Sulfate, p. 116.

OXYTOCIN (Pitocin)

This oxytocic drug is used to induce labor and control postpartum hemorrhage. A 21-year-old woman with incomplete abortion was given oxytocin by I.V. drip — a total of 8 liters of 5% dextrose solution containing 180 U Pitocin. Four hours following D and C, the patient became stuporous, edematous, and experienced a seizure. Mannitol was given to induce urination. She became asymptomatic after the fourth day [*Am. J. Med. Sci.* **252**, 573 (1966)].

Caution: According to M. E. Davis and N. W. Fugo, this drug should be given I.V. extremely slowly for reasons of greater safety and controllability. Other warnings include that (1) oxytocin administration should always be started in extremely small doses and increased cautiously; (2) oxytocin drips should never be used during labor in the presence of any evidence of fetal distress; (3) labor must never be induced with oxytocin if the patient has been subjected to a cesarean section; and (4) that oxytocin must be used with great caution, if at all, if the patient has an extremely irritable uterus or is already in labor ("Drugs of Choice, 1966–1967." C. V. Mosby, Saint Louis, Missouri, 1966).

OZONE

Ozone is a form of oxygen. Under ordinary conditions it is a colorless or pale blue gas with a characteristic pungent odor. In high concentrations it is extremely flammable, and in liquid form it becomes a dangerous explosive.

There are two general sources of exposure to ozone. Ozone is produced by the discharge of high tension electrical equipment, welding operations, ultraviolet light spectrographic equipment, and plasma jet operations. Exposure to ozone may also occur from ozone generators developed for use in industrial processes. Examples of these processes include production of ozone for use as a disinfecting germicide or to control growth of fungus, molds, and bacteria in food processing. The danger of undesirable health effects far outweigh any benefits presumed to be derived from the industrial or institutional use of ozone for control of odors or bacteria in air.

In general, the physiological effects of acute ozone exposure are directly proportional to the atmospheric ozone concentration multiplied by the exposure time. The predominant effect is primary irritation of mucous membranes. Inhalation of a large quantity of ozone can cause sufficient irritation of the lungs to result in pulmonary edema, the onset of which is usually delayed for hours after exposure. Subacute ozone exposures may result in subtle changes, for example, in visual parameters. Thus, ozone is considered to be an insidious toxic agent, especially since the absence, presence, or severity of symptoms at any given time may not prove to be a reliable index of the seriousness of an exposure.

Most normal persons can detect the odor of ozone in concentrations of 0.02–0.05 ppm by volume. These levels are 2–3 times lower than the current TLV for an 8-hour workday and are only slightly higher than the normal background concentration of ozone at the earth's surface.

Olfactory fatigue for the odor of ozone will develop readily. Thus, the odor itself is not a reliable index of atmospheric ozone concentration, particularly of concentrations approximating the TLV range in which the odor is not associated with symptoms of irritation of the nasal passages and other mucous membranes.

Symptoms of acute ozone toxicity appear at a concentration of about 1 ppm by volume. The type and severity of symptoms as well as the time of onset of symptoms depend on the concentration and duration of exposure. In mild cases or in early phases of severe cases, symptoms will include one or more of the following: irritation or burning of the eyes, nose, or throat; lassitude; frontal headache, which may be severe; sensation of substernal pressure, constriction, or oppression; acid in mouth; and anorexia.

In more severe cases dyspnea, cough, choking sensations, tachycardia, vertigo, lowering of blood pressure, severe cramping chest pain which may cause an erroneous diagnosis of myocardial infarction, and generalized body pain may be present. Pulmonary edema may develop; the onset of the edema is usually delayed for one or more hours after exposure.

Following severe acute ozone toxicity, recovery is slow. In the several severe human cases reported, 10–14 days of hospitalization were required. In these cases minimal residual symptoms were present for as long as 9 months. All cases have eventually recovered completely.

The safe level for short human exposure to concentrations of ozone in excess of the TLV is not known with certainty. Probably 2 ppm is safe for several minutes, provided that no respiratory infection—latent or manifest—is present. The atmospheric concentration immediately hazardous to life is likewise not known, but inhalation of 50 ppm for 30 minutes would probably be fatal.

Persons exposed to ozone concentrations as low as 0.2 ppm by volume for 3 hours or more have shown a considerable decrease in night vision. To a lesser degree, these persons also exhibited changes in extraocular muscle balance affecting all but the superior and inferior recti muscles.

Treatment: Remove the patient from exposure. Control restlessness and pain by the administration of sedatives and anodynes orally. Severe cases may require subcutaneous injections of small doses of meperidine hydrochloride (Demerol) for relief of pain. Give oxygen inhalation by face mask and rebreathing bag if dyspnea is acute or accompanied by cyanosis. Keep under observation with symptomatic care until the acute symptoms have subsided. Severe cases require hospitalization since deferred pulmonary edema may develop [Air Force Pamphlet 161-2-4-TB Med 256 (January 1966)].

PAINTS

Paints are complex mixtures of solids and vehicles. Vinyl resins and soya alkyd resins used to give cohesive properties to the paints have a low order of toxicity. The solvents in different types of paint can be responsible for toxic manifestations from paint ingestion. Mineral spirits and turpentine are vehicles for many paints. Other organic solvents are also used, such as alcohol in shellac and ketones and esters in lacquers. In latex-type paint, water is the solvent. The hazards of aspiration pneumonitis and pulmonary edema from small amounts of mineral spirits and other petroleum distillates are well known. Turpentine, too, can be responsible for a serious type of aspiration pneumonitis; in addition, its irritant qualities affect the gastrointestinal and genitourinary systems. Studies have shown that paints may contain high concentrations of hydrocarbon solvents without being an aspiration hazard. This is because the viscosity of the finished paint precludes aspiration. All paint solvents, excluding that of latex paints, can produce some degree of central nervous system depression. See Table 47, p. 733.

Treatment: Emptying of the stomach by gastric lavage is not expected to be effective. Induced emesis is contraindicated. Administer a saline cathartic. Further treatment is supportive and symptomatic.

2-PAM (2-Pyridine Aldoxime Methochloride; 2-PAM Chloride; Pralidoxime Chloride; Protopam Chloride)

2-PAM and several related oximes have been found effective as reactivators of cholinesterase enzymes. It appears, however, that the timing of the treatment is important.

According to D. M. Sanderson, the I.P. administration of atropine plus 2-PAM immediately after oral administration of organophosphorous compounds in rats caused accelerated anticholinesterase effects that were usually lethal, while the administration of this combination *after* the appearance of signs of intoxication was beneficial [*J. Pharm. Pharmacol.* **13**, 435 (1961); **17**, 124 (1965); D. M. Sanderson and E. F. Edson, *J. Pharm. Pharmacol.* **11**, 721 (1959)].

M. M. Okihiro *et al.* administered atropine, promethazine hydrochloride and meperidine to a patient who was suffering from abdominal cramps, severe diarrhea, and other effects related to cholinesterase inhibition. When it was discovered that the patient had ingested a variety of fish and was suffering from ciguatera poisoning, he was given (34 hours after ingestion of the fish) 1 gm of 2-pyridine aldoxime methochloride I.V. over a period of 5 minutes. "The results were startling, unexpected, and almost disastrous." The patient became cyanotic; there was marked bronchoconstriction and he lapsed into coma; the blood pressure rose to 200/120 and the pulse rate to 180 per minute. His color improved following tracheostomy and inhalation of oxygen. There was a marked diuresis; 1200 ml in 3 hours. The patient recovered slowly over a period of 7 days following intensive treatment with atropine. He also received magnesium sulfate and calcium gluconate for the control of fasciculation (nicotinic effects) and methylphenidate (Ritalin) for combatting coma. M. M. Okihiro *et al.* believe that the sudden collapse following the administration of 2-PAM may have been due to an anticholinesterase activity of 2-PAM itself.

Caution: Hobbiger first noted that 2-PAM, to be effective, must be administered early. He theorized that after a period of time the cholinesterase enzyme is phosphorylated in such a way that it cannot be regenerated. This has been termed his "transphosphorylation theory" [*Brit. J. Pharm.* **10**, 356 (1955)]. Large doses of 2-PAM inhibit serum cholinesterase [T. A. Loomis, *J. Pharmacol. Exptl. Therap.* **118**, 123 (1956); A. D. Bergner and P. F. Wagley, *Proc. Soc. Exptl. Biol. Med.* **97**, 90 (1958)], and are liable to produce neuromuscular block [D. Brob and R. J. Johns, *Am. J. Med.* **24**, 497 (1958)]. For human toxicity of various oximes, see report by B. Calesnick *et al.*, *Arch. Environ. Health* **15**, 599 (1967).

Conclusions: It appears that timing is important, and that a delay in the diagnosis of organic phosphate or a cholinesterase-inhibition-type ciguatera fish poisoning precludes the use of 2-PAM and related drugs.

Until more information becomes available, it seems appropriate not to administer 2-PAM until signs or symptoms of an intoxication have become established, and not later than 24 hours after their onset.

PAPAVERINE

This is not a narcotic drug. It does not produce tolerance and addiction even though it is obtained from opium. It is not subject to restrictions of the Harrison Narcotic Act.

PARAFFIN

This is synonymous with "wax," or "paraffin wax," which is a colorless, odorless, tasteless, chemically inert solid hydrocarbon extensively used as a coating material for dairy cartons, paper drinking cups, wax crayons, candles, etc. In England "paraffin" is synonymous with mineral oil. Paraffin is insoluble and essentially nontoxic.

PARAFFIN HYDROCARBONS (Alkanes, Aliphatics, Methane series)

These are saturated straight or branched chain hydrocarbons having a relatively low order of toxicity. See Hydrocarbon Gases, p. 316, and Petroleum Solvents or Distillates, p. 459.

PARALDEHYDE

This drug will induce sedation and hypnosis. It must be given to inebriated individuals with caution. Several fatalities are on record of individuals who received 6–180 ml of paraldehyde while under the influence of alcohol; they died in 12 hours to several days (James C. Munch, University of Miami, personal communication). Paraldehyde must be given with caution to chronic alcoholics during withdrawal of ethyl alcohol since it is relatively easy to induce paraldehyde habituation [*JAMA* 143, 782 (1950)]. Paraldehyde decomposes slowly to form acetaldehyde and acetic acid. Two cases of poisoning and one death have been reported following the use of deteriorated paraldehyde. Paraldehyde should be stored under refrigeration in amber glass bottles. These should be dated when first opened.

The I.M. administration of paraldehyde (labeled for oral use) has been followed by skin sloughing, sterile abscesses, and sciatic nerve damage. An I.V. injection of sterile paraldehyde (Paral) should be given *very slowly*. After an I.M. injection there is frequently pain at the site of the injection until sedation and hypnosis take over. See p. 36 and p. 607.

Treatment of an oral overdose includes vomiting or gastric lavage, followed by symptomatic therapy with particular emphasis on maintaining respiratory exchange and circulatory activity.

PARATHION

This compound is a highly toxic organic phosphate; see Organic Phosphates, p. 438.

PAREGORIC

This is a camphorated tincture containing 130 mg of opium in 30 ml, or 45 mg of morphine in 100 ml of a hydroalcoholic solution. Minor ingredients include anise oil, benzoic acid, and camphor. Addicts frequently concentrate paregoric and add amphetamines, glutethimide, tripelennamine, or a barbiturate before an I.V. injection. Camphor, anise, and benzoic acid are irritants and after injection have led to occlusive sclerosis of the injected veins and a high incidence of infection at the injection sites [F. J. Oerther *et al.*, *JAMA* **190**, 683 (1964)]. See Opiates, p. 435, and Tripelennamine, p. 610].

PARGYLINE (Eutonyl)

Pargyline hydrochloride is a useful drug in the treatment of mild or moderate hypertension associated with depression or angina pectoris. The drug is a nonhydrazine monoamine oxidase inhibitor. Side effects can be reduced by administration of the lowest effective dose. High therapeutic doses have caused weakness, fainting and postural hypotension, nausea, vomiting, constipation, insomnia, nervousness, perspiration, dryness of mouth, nightmares, headache, impotence [*Clin. Pharmacol. Therap.* **5**, 167 (1964)], and atrophy of the optic nerve [*JAMA* **201**, 571 (1967)]. Reports of serious overdosage have been rare [*Am. J. Med. Sci.* **245**, 166 (1963)]. Effects in a $2\frac{1}{2}$-year-old child who ingested seven 25 mg tablets (175 mg) of pargyline included eye rolling, lethargy, mental confusion, staggering gait, abdominal pain, and coma.

Caution: A patient on pargyline therapy should abstain from ingesting ripe or aged cheeses and certain other foods [*Brit. Med. J.* **1**, 803 (1966)]. He should not receive meperidine. See Meperidine, p. 368 and Monoamine Oxidase Inhibitors, p. 404.

Treatment: The child responded favorably and recovered following 24 hours of intermittent repeated peritoneal dialysis.

PARITOL

Paritol is similar in structure and action to heparin.
Treatment of an overdose is similar to that of heparin. See p. 305.

PELARGONIC MORPHOLIDE

Human subjects exposed to an aerosol of 500 mg/m^3 experience a burning sensation of the nose with rhinorrhea, burning of the throat (like swallowing hot pepper), and burning of the eyes with lacrimation. The throat-burning stimulates the cough reflex, and if this can not be controlled, the compound becomes intolerable. Occasionally, nausea follows the coughing spell. Glandular hyperfunction manifested by lacrimation, salivation, and sweating also occurs.

Treatment: Discontinue exposure. Further treatment is symptomatic and supportive.

This compound is nonpersistent in the sense that all symptoms are almost immediately relieved by fresh air. The only sequela noted is belated frontal headache lasting several hours [C. L. Punte *et al.*, *Am. Ind. Hyg. Ass. J.* **23**, 199 (1962)].

PENICILLAMINE (Cuprimine)

This compound is an amino acid derived from penicillin. It is the drug of choice in the treatment of Wilson's disease. It has also been used in the treatment of lead and gold intoxications and, more recently, for reducing the urinary concentration of cystine to levels that do not result in the formation of cystine stones.

In metal intoxications, *N*-acetyl-DL-penicillamine appears to be more effective than D-penicillamine (Cuprimine), but the data available at this time are inconclusive. The initial daily oral dose of Cuprimine for older children and adults is 250 mg. This may be administered in fruit juice. Subsequently, based on the determination of the amount of copper in the urine, the dosage may be increased to 1–2 gm daily in divided doses. Under certain conditions, doses up to 4 and 5 gm/day have been administered.

Undesirable effects with the use of Cuprimine include erythematous skin rash, extravasation of blood into superficial skin layers, fever, leukopenia, thrombocytopenia, agranulocytosis, and the nephrotic syndrome. Except for allergic reactions, the incidence of side effects is low, and usually follows initiation of therapy. Five patients with cystinuria developed marked proteinuria after receiving Cuprimine for 2–36 months. The condition slowly cleared after the drug was withdrawn [*JAMA* **201**, 698 (1967); **203**, 367 (1968)]. Recently, H. R. Kaiser *et al.* reported loss of taste acuity for salt and sweet in 7 of 20 patients with scleroderma and cystinuria. Upon discontinuation of penicillamine therapy, the sense of taste returned to normal within 4–6 weeks in all patients [*JAMA* **203**, 381 (1968)].

Caution: Penicillamine should not be used until the diagnosis of Wilson's disease has been confirmed; it should be given with caution to patients who are sensitive to penicillin. Blood cell counts and urinalysis should be done periodically [Council on Drugs, 1966, American Medical Association, Chicago, *JAMA* **201**, 698 (1967)]. Although penicillamine has less antipyridoxine activity than older forms of the drug, as a precaution, patients on penicillamine should be given 25–50 mg pyridoxine daily [*Med. Letter* **9**, 49 (1967)].

PENICILLIN

Benzylpenicillin (penicillin G) was the earliest and is still probably the most valuable antibiotic. Toxicity, in the usual sense of the word, and the usual minor side effects characteristic of other antibiotics are virtually unknown. A few rare instances of renal tubular dysfunction associated with massive doses or intrathecal injection have been reported Bloomer *et al., JAMA* **200**, 131 (1967); Oldstone and Nelson, *Neurology* **16**, 693 (1966); G. E. Brauninger and J. S. Remington, *JAMA* **203**, 103 (1968).

Because of the highly allergenic nature of the penicillins and their extensive clinical usage (so often needless), an appreciable percentage of the population has unfortunately become allergic to this valuable drug. It is estimated that hypersensitivity reactions occur in 5–10% of those receiving it [Westerman *et al.*, *JAMA* **198**, 173 (1966)].

In the sensitized individual an additional dose may induce a reaction which may be of the acute or delayed type. The most feared acute reaction is anaphylactic shock, which usually occurs within minutes. Symptoms include tightness of the chest, pulmonary edema, circulatory collapse, dizziness, cyanosis, and urticaria; shock and death may follow. Other patients may have angioneurotic edema with swelling of the lips, tongue, or face, and asthmatic breathing. The delayed type of reaction, which may not become apparent until 3 or 4 weeks have elapsed, is commonly the delayed urticarial serum sickness reaction, with or without fever, joint pain, and purpura. A second type of delayed reaction, not infrequently observed, is the erythemato-vesicular reaction beginning with vesicles and bullae on the hands, feet, and in the groin.

Caution: Penicillin is highly allergenic. Anaphylactic shock is usually associated with the parenteral administration, particularly the I.V. injection of penicillin. On rare occasions anaphylactic shock has resulted from oral administration or inhalation [*Arch. Dermatol.* **96**, 687 (1967); *JAMA* **203**, 986 (1968)]. Particular caution is in order when the drug is administered to a patient with a history of allergy. Skin tests cannot be relied upon to demonstrate immediate or delayed penicillin hypersensitivity.

The following measures are essential in minimizing the risks involved in penicillin therapy:

1. Most important is a conscientious effort to uncover any history of a previous penicillin reaction, as well as a prior history of asthma, hay fever, eczema, or hives.

2. The patient should be told that he is being given penicillin.

3. Penicillin should be given orally whenever possible.

4. When penicillin is given I.M., it should be injected in the lateral aspect of the arm, low enough so

that a tourniquet can be applied but not so low to risk injury to the radial nerve.

5. After an injection, the patient should be kept under observation for 1 hour.

6. Drugs and equipment should be available and ready for immediate treatment of a severe penicillin reaction.

7. Care must be taken to avoid accidental intravascular injection. A review of 1000 I.M. injections revealed that blood vessels were inadvertently entered 16 times [Popper, *Public Health Repts. U.S.* **79**, 610 (1964)].

8. The topical use of penicillins in aerosols, ointments, lozenges, and troches should be discontinued.

9. It is advisable to use disposable syringes, since it is practically impossible to destroy completely the antigenic principle of the antibiotic by boiling the syringe used.

When bacterial sensitivity studies indicate the need for penicillin, and when life is threatened, the risk of penicillin therapy in a hypersensitive patient should be discussed with the patient and his family. If it is decided to use this drug, anaphylactic treatment equipment must be immediately available [G. R. Green *et al, Ann. Internal Med.* **67**, 235 (1967)].

Treatment: Emergency treatment for an anaphylactoid reaction includes application of a tourniquet between the site of injection and the heart, injection of epinephrine (1 ml of 1:1000 S.C. or I.M. followed by additional 0.25 ml doses *very slowly* I.V.) and administration of a glucocorticoid I.V., and an antihistamine to inhibit the release of additional histamine.

Tracheal intubation has been found safer and more rapid than tracheostomy. Oxygen should be available. See Anaphylaxis, p. 56.

Aminophylline, adrenal cortical steroids, or ACTH may be used in the management of delayed effects. Antihistamines may be used to treat pruritus. Penicillinase is not recommended for the treatment of delayed effects. Ingestion of dairy products should be avoided.

PENICILLINS, SYNTHETIC AND SEMISYNTHETIC

This group includes phenoxymethylpenicillin potassium (V-Cillin-K), phenethicillin potassium (eight brand products), methicillin (Dimocillin, Staphcillin), oxacillin (Prostaphlin; Resistopen), cloxacillin (Tegopen; Orbenin), nafcillin (Unipen), and ampicillin (Penbritin; Polycillin).

These antibiotics are remarkable for their low order of toxicity. They have not produced serious side effects that were not previously encountered with penicillin G. According to R. Fekety, Jr., each new semisynthetic penicillin was introduced with the hope that cross-hypersensitivity with penicillin G would not become apparent, but eventually "each new derivative has proved just as dangerous as penicillin G" ("Pharmacology for Physicians," Vol. 1. W. B. Saunders, Philadelphia 1967).

Caution: It appears that the synthetic and semisynthetic penicillins should be treated with the same caution afforded penicillin G. See Penicillin, above.

PENICILLINASE (Neutrapen)

This enzyme converts penicillin to penicilloic acid; further hydrolysis yields penicillamine. Penicillinase is no longer used in the treatment of delayed penicillin reactions, since it is capable of inducing severe hypersensitivity reactions and other undesirable effects. Penicillinase was never used in penicillin anaphylaxis.

PENNYROYAL

Pennyroyal is a volatile oil which belongs to the same group as apiol, turpentine, and the oils of savin, tansy, saffron, and rue. Its active constituent, pulegone, is one of several ketones belonging to the monocyclic terpenes. One teaspoonful of the oil has been known to produce convulsions, and at least one case is on record where a patient became comatose following ingestion of 15 ml of the essence of pennyroyal but later recovered.

Treatment: See Turpentine, p. 613.

PENTABORANE

Pentaborane has an unusual degree of toxicity. Animal studies show that rats die with acute symptoms when they are exposed to concentrations of 10 ppm for 2 hours. The animals developed weakness, incoordination, tremors, convulsions, and coma. Repeated exposure to 3.5 ppm for 5 hours a day for 4 days caused 100% mortality. Many organ systems showed impairment. Liver and kidney function were abnormal.

Intoxication may occur from inhalation, ingestion, or absorption through the skin. To maintain a safe working level, the pentaborane concentration should not exceed 0.005 ppm. A strong whiff of the chemical, producing a penetrating feeling in the nose, usually produced symptoms. Complaints after minor exposure included feelings of lethargy, confusion, fatigue, inability to concentrate, feeling of constriction of the chest, headache, and light-headedness. Other symptoms were a detached feeling or sense of day dreaming and lack of coordination.

Treatment: There is no specific treatment. Men with mild intoxication are given no treatment. Those with moderate cases are treated with oxygen and bed rest. In severe poisoning, intravenous fluids are occasionally needed. Intravenous barbiturates are given to control convulsions. Nausea and vomiting are controlled by antiemetics; muscle relaxants give some symptomatic relief.

PENTAERYTHRITOLS

No toxic effect was observed in animals fed 2.5 gm/kg of pentaerythritol daily for 2 weeks. With an oral dose of 20 gm/kg, there was a laxative effect in guinea pigs, but no serious ill effects were noted. Rats fed 1.6 gm of pentaerythritol daily for $3\frac{1}{2}$ months showed no evidence of injury. A saturated aqueous solution of pentaerythritol applied to the skin of an albino rabbit daily for 10 days caused no significant irritation, nor was irritation or inflammation noted when a drop of this solution was instilled into the eye of the rabbit.

Dipentaerythritol and tripentaerythritol are well tolerated when taken orally or when inhaled in large quantities by experimental albino rats. These compounds are nonirritating when applied as aqueous pastes to the skin or when instilled as 10% aqueous suspensions into the eyes of a rabbit.

Treatment: The low order of toxicity in animals indicates that no treatment is necessary in case of accidental ingestion of these materials.

PENTAZOCINE (Talwin)

Pentazocine is a new nonaddicting analgesic, especially useful in the treatment of chronic pain. The drug also acts as a weak opiate antagonist. It is not a narcotic. A 40 mg I.M. dose of pentazocine is equivalent to approximately 10 mg of morphine sulfate. Side effects are similar to but may be somewhat more marked than those induced by equianalgesic doses of morphine or meperidine [*Med. Letter* **9** (1967)]. All undesirable effects are found more frequently in female patients. In a few instances, large I.V. doses have induced epileptiform abnormalities of the electroencephalogram [J. Telford and A. S. Kears, *Clin. Pharmacol. Therap.* **6**, 12 (1965)].

Caution: Pentazocine is a new drug and requires additional evaluation. It should be administered cautiously in patients who have recently been treated with an opiate type drug. It is contraindicated in conditions of increased intracranial pressure, head injury, or in pathologic brain conditions in which clouding of sensorium is undesirable. In these conditions, Talwin-induced sedation, dizziness, nausea or respiratory depression is likely to be misleading. Pentazocine should not be administered to children under 12 years of age, nor during pregnancy until more information has become available.

Treatment: Mild or moderate sedation with respiratory depression responds to nonspecific analeptics, such as methylphenidate (Ritalin) and related analeptics. A severe intoxication requires symptomatic treatment. Nalorphine and levallorphan are not effective in counteracting the respiratory depression of pentazocine.

PENTOBARBITAL (Nembutal)

The period of action of this drug is generally described as "intermediate." See Barbiturates, p. 119.

PENTOLINIUM (Ansolysen)

This is a ganglionic blocking agent. Acute renal failure has been reported in two elderly patients being treated with this drug for hypertension. The usual side effects, postural vertigo, constipation, and dryness did not appear in these individuals. The patient should be alerted to signs of early intoxication—listlessness, drowsiness, and decrease in urine volume—and instructed to stop taking the drug when these signs appear. See Ganglionic Blocking Agents, p. 282.

PERIWINKLE

Smoking of the dried leaves of the periwinkle plant (*Vinca minor* and *V. major, V. rosea*), a current fad among teenagers, produces a tingling or burning sensation in the skin and hallucinations. Excessive smoking induces alopecia, muscular incoordination, followed by a gradual wasting of muscle, and reduction in the number of white blood cells. Vincristine and vinblastine are drugs prepared from *V. rosea*; they are useful because of their antineoplastic activity. Smoking of the leaves can be expected to produce all of the side effects or signs and symptoms of toxicity following overdose of these drugs, including permanent damage and possibly death. See Vinblastine, p. 619.

PERPHENAZINE (Trilafon)

As an antiemetic, this phenothiazine tranquilizer is more potent than chlorpromazine. Side effects are related to dosage, but there are exceptions. Minimal I.M. and oral doses have produced severe or fatal extrapyramidal and epileptiform symptoms [*Brit. Med. J.* **3**, 438 (1967)]. The "neck-face" syndrome was first reported in patients treated with this drug. Hypotension, hepatic pathology, peripheral edema, endocrine disturbances, and skin disorders have also been reported. Several clinicians have noted elevations of protein-bound iodine in patients who were receiving perphenazine but not suffering from disorders of the thyroid. Substantial elevation of PBI was noted long after cessation of therapy [*Am. J. Psychiat.* **122**, 300 (1965)].

Treatment: Reduction of the dose frequently will give relief from side effects. For more detailed information, see Chlorpromazine, p. 171, and Phenothiazines, p. 464.

PETROLEUM SOLVENTS OR DISTILLATES

This is a broad term applied to a complex mixture of hydrocarbon molecules which may be aliphatic (hexane, heptane, octane, etc.), alicyclic (cyclopentane, cyclohexane), aromatic (benzene, toluene, xylene), or all three types. Some examples are Varsol, mineral turpentine, mineral spirits, white spirits, stoddard solvent, kerosene, and mineral seal oil. Repeated skin contact may produce dermatitis due to removal of fat from the skin. In general, the hydrocarbons are not considered to be highly toxic molecules. See p. 316. Benzene (benzol) is the most dangerous hydrocarbon because of its insidious effect on the blood-forming tissue. The liquid hydrocarbons of low viscosity [up to 50 SSU at 37.7°C (100°F)] are readily aspirated into the lung tissue causing endothelial injury. This leads to rapid development of pulmonary edema and hemorrhage.

Treatment: See Kerosene p. 343.

PEYOTE

Peyote, a type of cactus, produces mild, short-lived hallucinations when ingested. It is a sacramental fixture of the Native American Church, which claims upward of 200,000 adherents among Indians of 17 states. This cactus is also referred to as mescal, the button, tops, cactus, big chief, the bad seed, or simply as "P."

The peyote "buttons" used are dried, thin slices of the carrotlike plant. It is very bitter and nauseating to many people but not habit-forming; its use is generally confined to religious ceremonies.

Peyote induces visual hallucinations in which the user retains awareness of where he is and what he is doing. The hallucinations range from elaborate kaleidoscopic patterns of vivid color to visions of personal encounters and a feeling of "looking-at-oneself" detachment. The active ingredient of peyote is mescaline, which can be distilled from the leaves of the plant.

PHENAZOCINE (Prinadol)

This relatively new synthetic narcotic analgesic drug produces the same side effects and addiction as comparable analgesic doses of related potent narcotics [*JAMA* **179**, 56 (1962)]. Respiratory depression is more prolonged than that produced by morphine.

Treatment: Nalorphine and levallorphan are effective respiratory antagonists. See Narcotic Drugs, p. 40, and Opiates, p. 435.

PHENELZINE SULFATE (Nardil)

This antidepressant monoamine oxidase inhibitor is used to treat emotional and psychiatric disorders in which depression is prominent. As with related drugs, since the action of phenelzine is delayed, treatment with this drug is usually continued for about a month before its efficiency is known. Doses over 75 mg/day induce a high incidence of side effects similar to those induced by isocarboxazid. These may include hypotension, constipation, edema (principally of the ankles), headache, and sleeplessness. MacLeod observed a patient under phenelzine therapy who died shortly after experiencing a hypertensive crisis presumably precipitated by ingestion of alcohol [*Brit. Med. J.* **1**, 1554 (1965)]. Four similar but not fatal reactions followed the ingestion of cheese [*Am. J. Psychiat.* **121**, 1012 (1965)]. Overdoses have also produced blurred speech, cool and clammy skin with profuse perspiration, marked piloerection, cyanosis, increased pulse and respiration rate, urinary retention, excitement, agitation, hallucinations, depressed respiration, and convulsions.

Caution: The drug should *not* be used *before, during, or shortly after administration of imipramine, desipramine, nortriptyline, or amitriptyline.* The prolonged use of phenelzine and chlordiazepoxide is not recommended [*Lancet* **I**, 388 (1964)]. Phenelzine must be used with caution in patients with epilepsy, impaired renal function, or suicidal tendency.

Treatment: Minor side effects disappear rather promptly upon reduction of the dose or discontinuation of phenelzine therapy. The *cautious* administration of a phenothiazine, particularly one with a central depressant effect, has been recommended for the treatment of an overdose; treatment otherwise is symptomatic and supportive [quoted by Goldberg, *Diseases Nervous System* **20**, 537 (1959)]. See also Monoamine Oxidase Inhibitors, p. 404.

PHENFORMIN (DBI) (DBI-TD)

Chemically, this antidiabetogenic drug is a biguanide. It is used as phenformin tablets or phenformin-TD (timed-disintegration) capsules. It may be used alone or as a supplement to insulin, acetohexamide, chlorpropamide, or tolbutamide therapy [J. I. Goodman, *Metabolism* **14**, 1153 (1965)].

Side effects noted in some patients include nausea, vomiting, diarrhea, loss of appetite, a metallic taste, and hypoglycemia. J. Lacher and L. Lasagna, in their recent review, concluded that "On the basis of all available evidence, it is suggested that phenformin, both in animals and man, interferes with lactate metabolism and can be an initiating or contributing factor in the syndrome of lactic acidosis [*Clin. Pharmacol.* **7**, 477 (1966)]."

There have been several reports describing the production of severe lactic acidosis; at least six deaths have been reported.

Caution: The urine of patients taking DBI should be routinely checked for ketone bodies as well as for glucose.

Treatment: In phenformin-treated patients, the development of acidosis calls for vigorous sodium bicarbonate (*never* lactate) treatment and supportive measures [*Calif. Med.* **105**, 281 (1966); Davidson *et al.*, *New Eng. J. Med.* **275**, 886 (1966)]. See also Insulin, p. 327.

PHENINDIONE (Danilone; Eridone; Hedulin; Dindevan)

This is a short-acting anticoagulant. In 1962, J. Perkins reviewed the adverse reactions to this drug in 136 patients. The most common complications were a rash (100 patients), fever (34 patients), diarrhea (20 patients), granulocytopenia (18 patients), stomatitis (14 patients), jaundice (10 patients), or nephropathy (5 patients). Occasionally, he found vomiting, misty vision, thrombocytopenia, lymphadenopathy, conjunctivitis, loss of hair, or gangrene of the breast [*Lancet* **I**, 127 (1962)]. A report by Tanser and Keat adds to the list of fatal reactions to phenindione [*Clin-Alert* 125, 175, and 191, (1963); 194 (1964)]. They presented details of two patients in whom hemorrhagic ulcerative colitis followed phenindione therapy in 2 and 7 days. One patient died; the other recovered when phenindione therapy was discontinued. In neither instance was there a history of previous drug hypersensitivity or underlying bowel disorder [*Brit. Med. J.* **1**, 588 (1966)].

Caution: To quote Hollman and Wong, "In view of

these sensitivity reactions we no longer use phenindione in the treatment of new patients [*Brit. Med. J.* **2,**
730 (1964)]." This appears to be good advice. Bishydroxycoumarin, warfarin, and related coumarin drugs
are definitely preferred to phenindione in the management of thrombophlebitis and related thromboem-
bolic disorders. Patients on phenindione therapy
should be instructed to report *promptly* to the physician marked fatigue, chill, sore throat, or fever. See
Bishydroxycoumarin, p. 131.

PHENIPRAZINE (Catron)

This monoamine oxidase inhibitor was withdrawn
because of marked toxicity.

PHENMETRAZINE (Preludin)

This anti-appetite drug is related pharmacologically
to the amphetamines. Widespread misuse of this agent
is common in Sweden. Repeated injections cause
mental and physical deterioration, physical dependence, and addiction. Even though the drug is intended for oral use, addicts inject it intravenously because it rapidly gives them a feeling of well-being,
supreme confidence, and strength [*Med. News London*
228, 4 (1967), quoted in *Clin-Alert* (April 11, 1967);
Brit. Med. J. **2,** 427 (1963)].

PHENOL (Carbolic Acid)

Ingestion of phenol, cresol, or related compounds
causes intense burning of the mouth and throat followed by marked abdominal pain and distress. Lethal
oral doses of phenol for adults have ranged from 1 to
10 gm; for infants from 50 to 500 mg. Cyanosis, muscular weakness, and collapse may occur within a few
minutes after ingestion. Tremors and convulsions are
occasionally observed. If the exposure is sufficiently
severe, local contact with the skin or mucous membranes induces gangrene or corrosion. The use of
phenol for dermatological purposes (removing wrin-
kles, freckles, etc.) should be attempted only by a surgeon who is fully aware of the danger of gangrene,
necrosis, and systemic intoxication. A number of reports on the use of intrathecal phenol for intractable
pain have appeared. Soaps containing phenol should
not be used for enemas. Chronic inhalation may lead

to progressive pulmonary inflammation and injury.

Treatment: Phenol is most efficiently removed from the skin by *flooding* the affected areas with water. To be effective, this must be done promptly. Speed is equally essential in the treatment of oral poisoning. In a conscious patient, induce vomiting. Before or after vomiting, give vegetable oil. If vomiting is not induced readily, employ gastric lavage without delay, using milk or water, or an aqueous solution of 40% bacto-peptone. Do *not* use alcohol. After gastric lavage, administer a vegetable oil. Castor oil may be given if there is no danger of perforation, since the toxicity of phenol in castor oil is greatly decreased. Treatment otherwise is symptomatic. For further information, see F. A. Patty, "Industrial Hygiene and Toxicology," Second Revised Edition, Wiley (Interscience), New York, 1962.

PHENOLPHTHALEIN

Excessive therapeutic doses of this cathartic may, after prolonged administration, produce liver and kidney injury. Certain individuals are hypersensitive to phenolphthalein, and skin changes may be produced. A. C. Kendall reported a fatal encephalomyelitis in a hypersensitive 2-year-old child who ingested approximately 1 gm [*Brit. Med. J.* **2**, 1461 (1954)]. Children have been known to survive a single oral dose of 8 gm. Urine and stools may be red, but this is not caused by bleeding.

Treatment: After ingestion of an overdose, vomiting should *not* be induced nor gastric lavage performed, particularly in children. Give a teaspoon of activated charcoal in water or milk every 1 or 2 hours until diarrhea subsides.

PHENOTHIAZINES

These drugs are used primarily for the treatment of acute and chronic mental disorders. In addition to their tranquilizing action, some exert anticholinergic or antihistaminic effects or an adrenergic blocking action. Each of the phenothiazine derivatives exerts its own characteristic therapeutic effects and side reactions. These may include adverse behavioral, metabolic, or endocrine effects, undesirable stimulation or depression of the central or autonomic nervous system, allergic reactions, and finally, miscellaneous effects such as potentiation of other drugs (for instance alcohol), electrocardiographic abnormalities, anesthetic complications, and unexpected deaths.

Adverse behavioral effects sometimes result, even though most of these drugs are useful as antipsychotic agents. The general rule seems to be that these drugs are better tolerated in more seriously disturbed patients. Those with mild anxiety usually tolerate small doses well; schizophrenics may require and tolerate comparatively large doses. Two safety factors are the following: (1) clinical addiction is unknown, and (2) it is virtually impossible to commit suicide with these drugs as the sole agent.

Central nervous system reactions may be expected with any sedative, but phenothiazines produce several common reactions. Extrapyramidal syndromes are related to the dosage, the age and sex of the patient, and more important, to individual susceptibility. Large doses may produce a syndrome resembling parkinsonism, although some patients do not develop this syndrome. Dystonic syndromes, usually resembling spastic torticollis, are confined to children and young adults, and often occur early in treatment.

Autonomic nervous system effects are predominantly due to adrenergic blockade or anticholinergic actions, distinguishing phenothiazine tranquilizers from other types of centrally-acting sedatives. Older patients are prone to serious complications of this kind.

Allergic or toxic reactions to phenothiazines do not differ particularly from those of other agents. Cholestatic jaundice, found in less than 0.5% of the patients exposed to these drugs, almost always occurs in the first 4–5 weeks of treatment. This illness is usually self-limited. Agranulocytosis is a complication occurring rarely, usually during the first 8 weeks of therapy, probably with an incidence of 0.13–0.7%. Any intercurrent febrile illness occurring early during treatment with these drugs should be considered a possible indication of one of these two complications.

Metabolic and endocrine effects also differentiate these drugs from the conventional sedatives. Feminization is the rule, regardless of the patient's sex. These changes are presumably mediated by an action on the hypothalamic-pituitary system. Abnormal lactation has been reported in female patients treated with thioridazine, trifluoperazine, chlorpromazine, prochlorperazine, meprobamate, and fluphenazine. The higher the dosage, the more marked the tendency to produce galactorrhea [L. E. Hollister, *JAMA* **189**, 311 (1964)].

I. B. Margolis and C. G. Gross recently reported incidents of gynecomastia. One patient developed this syndrome while on chlorpromazine therapy; the second was treated with trifluoperazine (Stelazine); the third with thioridazine (Mellaril) [*JAMA* **199**, 942 (1967)].

Caution: The danger of agranulocytosis is rare, but it does exist. One must therefore be aware of this hazard, particularly during the first 2 months of treatment. Chlorpromazine, mepazine (Pacatal), and promazine have been implicated more often than related drugs. Any complaint of fever, sore throat, stomatitis, malaise, or chills should be followed immediately by a blood count. If no granulocytes are present, intensive treatment with penicillin, and perhaps corticosteroids, should be instituted at once. Most of the side effects appear during the early phase of the treatment, but ocular changes subsequent to the use of phenothiazines have appeared after years of therapy [*Med. News* (April 23, 1965)].

In a recent paper, L. E. Hollister and J. C. Kosek describe six cases of sudden death that occurred in otherwise healthy patients following treatment with chlorpromazine, prochlorperazine and thioridazine. The authors are not certain that excessive dosages played a major role [*JAMA* **192**, 1035 (1965)]. Imipramine and other atropine-like agents, if used at all in patients with glaucoma, must be used with great caution because of their anticholinergic action. Phenothiazine derivatives should be avoided whenever it is possible to use a less hazardous or less potent drug. Children appear to be particularly sensitive to these agents [*Arch. Diseases Childhood* **41**, 551 (1966)].

Phenothiazine and several of its derivatives used in rat studies have shown their capacity to induce high level activity of microsomal systems (benzpyrene hydroxylase) in kidney and lung. These enzymes are capable of detoxifying massive doses of certain polycyclic hydrocarbons [L. W. Wattenberg, *Cancer Res.* **25**, 365 (1965)]. [For additional information, consult "Current Status of Phenothiazines," J. Kinross-Wright, *JAMA* **200**, 461 (1967)]. See Table 7, p. 680.

Treatment: Reduction of the dosage will usually alleviate the side effects of intoxication. An antiparkinsonism drug may be used together with the tranquilizer in severe extrapyramidal disturbances. G. Sheppard and S. Merlis studied the effects of four antiparkinson medications, namely: benztropine (Cogentin), biperiden (Akineton), procyclidine (Kemadrin), and trihexyphenidyl (Artane). These drugs were used to treat extrapyramidal side effects in 378 of 7,110 patients who received chlorpromazine (Thorazine), trifluoperazine (Stelazine), thioridazine (Mellaril), carphenazine (Proketazine), chlorprothixene (Taractan), perphenazine (Trilafon), prochlorperazine (Compazine), or fluphenazine (Prolixin). The agents were similarly effective and relieved or eliminated the side effects in all but 11 patients [*Am. J. Psychiat.* **123**, 886 (1967)].

After ingestion of an overdose, induce vomiting and consider the use of gastric lavage and a saline cathartic. Hypotension and reflex tachycardia may be marked due to partial adrenergic blockage. If a vasopressor drug is needed, administer levarterenol (Levophed) or angiotensin amide (Hypertensin). *Never* give epinephrine. Hypotonic I.V. fluids should be used with caution since they may cause cerebral edema. Exchange transfusions may be lifesaving. Hemodialysis appears to be ineffective [*JAMA* **197**, 142 (1966)].

PHENTERMINE (Ionamin)

This drug is a sympathomimetic amine closely related in pharmacological action and toxicity to amphetamine. See Amphetamine, p. 98.

PHENTOLAMINE (Regitine)

Phentolamine, a potent adrenergic blocking agent, is used I.V. in the diagnosis of pheochromocytosis. This drug given also P.O., and tolazoline (Priscoline) administered P.O. and parenterally, are likely to induce tachycardia, cardiac arrhythmias and anginal pain, as well as gastroenteric symptoms including nausea, vomiting, and diarrhea.

Several reports testify to the risk sometimes involved when this drug is used. A 65-year-old man suffering from hypertension was given 5 mg of Regitine I.V. During the next 3 minutes, his blood pressure dropped from 240/138 to 70/60. He complained of severe and crushing chest pain; he vomited, and his skin became cold and clammy. An electrocardiogram taken 15 minutes after onset of symptoms revealed changes suggestive of an acute inferior myocardial infarction. The patient recovered [*New Engl. J. Med.* **273**, 37 (1965)]. A pregnant woman suffered profound vasomotor shock followed by death shortly after the I.V. administration of 4 mg of this drug. Another patient given a dose of 5 mg experienced a prolonged period of hypotension, ventricular tachycardia, and ventricular fibrillation which terminated in cardiac arrest 30 hours later.

Caution: Both phentolamine and tolazoline should be used cautiously in patients who can ill afford gastroenteric and cardiac stimulation such as patients with a gastric or peptic ulcer, or persons suffering from coronary artery diseases. In one of the patients described above, levarterenol maintained the blood pressure at normotensive values only temporarily, while in the second patient the hypotension responded to this drug, but the patient died of central paralysis. See Levarterenol to increase blood pressure, p. 37.

PHENYLBUTAZONE (Butazolidin)

This drug is administered P.O. and I.M. for the treatment of acute gout, rheumatoid arthritis, and rheumatic fever. It is metabolized slowly and tends to accumulate with repeated doses. Side effects or signs of toxicity noted in 25–60 % of patients include the following: nausea, swelling of the face—particularly of the parotid region (Butazolidin "mumps"), lymphadenopathy [*Lancet* **I**, 448 (1967)], epigastric pain and pericarditis [*Brit. Med. J.* **2**, 795 (1965)], vomiting, dermatitis, hepatic damage, jaundice, hematological disturbances, and retention of fluids. Reactivation of a peptic ulcer is also frequently reported. Agranulocytosis, thrombocytopenia, leukopenia, and exfoliative dermatitis are rare, but more serious. Until 1955, 23 deaths due to this drug were reported [*Deut. Med.*

Wochschr. **87,** 30 (1965); *Med. J. Australia* **1,** 217 (1965); *Brit. Med. J.* **1,** 1673 (1965)]. See Blood Dyscrasias, p. 51. P. M. Aggeler *et al.* are presumably the first to report potentiation of the anticoagulant effect of warfarin by phenylbutazone [*New Engl. J. Med.* **276,** 496 (1967)].

p-Hydroxyphenylbutazone (oxyphenbutazone; Tandearil) has antiinflammatory and toxic properties similar to those of phenylbutazone, but the side effects are produced less frequently. Thrombocytopenic purpura was noted after 5 weeks of treatment with this drug at a dosage of 200 mg per day [*JAMA* **175,** 614 (1961)]. A 35-year-old arthritic received Tandearil in a dose of 100 mg three times a day concurrently with 2.5 mg betamethasone (Celestone). After 2 months, he developed fever and painful ulcers of the tongue, gums, pharynx, and palate. His white cell count dropped to $2800/mm^3$. He recovered rather promptly after discontinuation of Tandearil, increase in steroid dosage, and administration of penicillin.

This drug should be reserved for acutely painful and distressing diseases such as gout, rheumatoid arthritis, and ankylosing sponditis, and only after other measures have failed.

Caution: As side effects become apparent, reduce the dose or discontinue Butazolidin or Tandearil therapy. Discontinue these drugs in any patient if relief is not obtained within 1 week; discontinue *immediately* if symptoms of agranulocytosis, such as fever, sore throat, and lesions of the mouth, become apparent. There are autopsy records that indicate that these drugs can cause severe hepatocellular damage, enlargment and congestion of the spleen, and toxic damage to the brain.

The British Committee on Safety of Drugs has warned all physicians and dentists of the serious side effects of phenylbutazone (Butazolidin), oxyphenbutazone (Tandearil), and nifenazone (Thylin). Since 1964, 50 cases of serious complications with 18 deaths have been reported in patients treated with Butazolidin. There were 16 comparable reports, with 5 deaths, in patients treated with Tandearil and 4 reports of serious complications, none fatal, in which Thylin was involved. There were 5 cases of liver damage and 9 cases of peptic ulceration thought to be due to Butazolidin or Tandearil. Fifty-two patients developed blood dyscrasias while being treated with these drugs. The Committee also advised caution in the use of indomethacin (Indocid; Indocin) [*Lancet* **II**, 396 (1965)].

PHENYLENEDIAMINES

p-Phenylenediamine (*p*-diaminobenzene; ursol D; orsin) may produce dermatitis on skin contact and bronchial asthma if inhaled. When used as a hair dye, it has caused vertigo, anemia, gastritis, exfoliative dermatitis, and death. It is a potent sensitizer. The oral MLD in rabbits is 250 mg/kg.

In industrial use, bulk handling of *m*-phenylenediamine is not considered hazardous. Except under extreme conditions, it is not a skin sensitizer or asthmagenic allergen despite the fact that the para isomer is notable for its activity in both respects. If ingested or administered parenterally it may produce serious liver damage.

Two alkyl phenylenediamines, *N,N'*-bis(1-ethyl-3-methylpentyl)-*p*-phenylenediamine (DOPD-3), and *N,N'*-bis(1-methylheptyl)-*p*-phenylenediamine (DOPD-2), were tolerated at concentrations of at least 0.025 % and 0.1 % in the diet of the pregnant rat without impairment of reproduction. By comparison, *N,N'*-diphenyl-*p*-phenylenediamine (DPPD), which was formerly employed as a feed additive, is toxic at 0.005 %. The presence of 0.1 % of the alkyl compounds caused a temporary depression of food intake and growth, probably as a result of decreased palatability; 0.4 % induced a more severe inhibition. See Amines Aromatic, p. 90.

Treatment: Discontinue exposure. Remove from skin with copious quantities of water. For systemic intoxication treat symptomatically. For pulmonary edema, see p. 43, and for methemoglobinemia, see p. 40.

PHENYLEPHRINE (Neo-Synephrine; Isophrin)

This drug is a vasopressor resembling levarterenol in many of its actions although it is less potent and it has a longer period of action. It is also used as a mydriatic as a substitute for atropine sulfate. It can be injected with local anesthetics, but is incompatible with butacaine (Butyn).

PHENYLHYDRAZINE (Hydrazinobenzene)

Local contact with phenylhydrazine may result in irritation of the skin, eyes, and mucous membranes. Absorption is known to have induced methemoglobinemia, anemia, leukopenia, gastroenteric disturbances, and hepatitis. Phenylhydrazine was formerly used in doses of 0.1–0.2 gm to treat polycythemia vera.

Treatment: In case of ingestion, induce vomiting and follow with gastric lavage. Transfusions of whole blood may be indicated if anemia is severe. Further treatment is symptomatic and supportive. See Methemoglobinemia, p. 40.

PHENYLPROPYLMETHYLAMINE

This sympathomimetic amine is the active agent in a variety of proprietary preparations (Allerest; Contac; Dristan; Vonedrine; etc.).

Caution: Headache, hypertension, and convulsions have been reported in individuals treated with MAO inhibitors and preparations containing phenylpropylmethylamine. In isolated instances, undesirable increase in blood pressure resulted from the use of phenylpropylmethylamine preparations used without MAO inhibitors. See Monoamine Oxidase Inhibitors, p. 404.

PHENYRAMIDOL (Analexin)

This analgesic has a potency comparable to that of the salicylates. It has no antipyretic properties. Occasionally, the drug will induce gastroenteric symptoms, drowsiness, skin rash, and pruritus.

Caution: This drug should be avoided in patients under anticoagulant therapy since severe hypoprothrombinemia has resulted from the concomitant administration of these drugs. Concurrent use of phenyramidol with tolbutamide may result in protracted hypoglycemia since phenyramidol inhibits the metabolism of tolbutamide, and presumably also of related oral diabetogenic drugs [*Metabolism* **16**, 1029 (1967)].

PHOSGENE (Carbonyl Chloride; Choking Gas; CK)

Inhalation of phosgene may result in severe irritation of the membranes of the lower respiratory tract and pulmonary edema several hours after exposure. A brief exposure to 50 ppm may be fatal. Phosgene is formed when halogenated hydrocarbons thermally decompose under oxidative conditions.

Treatment: Remove victim immediately from contaminated atmosphere. Give artificial respiration and oxygen. Observe for 24–48 hours for premonitory signs of pulmonary edema. Subsequent treatment is symptomatic and supportive. See Pulmonary Edema, p. 43.

PHOSPHINE (PH$_3$)

The MAC for phosphine is 0.05 ppm (0.07 mg/m^3). The odor threshold has been set at 0.5–50 ppm, indicating that little reliance can be placed on olfactory detection. The odor has been described as acetylene-like. Acute exposures can cause fatal pulmonary edema, central nervous system depression, and circulatory disturbances. Signs and symptoms of exposure are faintness, weakness and apathy, nausea and vomiting followed by dyspnea, fall in blood pressure, and change in pulse rate. Diarrhea, intense thirst, oppressive sensation in the chest, convulsions, paralysis, and coma precede death. Symptoms of acute phosphine intoxication resemble food poisoning.

The health problem connected with ductile iron machining was discovered in Europe in 1955 when illness was reported among workers machining nodular iron rolls. The workmen complained of pain in the eyes, stomach, and nose, and nosebleeds. The concentrations of phosphine gas produced vary with the depth of the cut and machine speed, a higher concentration of phosphine developing with greater roughing. The use of coolants increases the moisture content at the machining point and increases the amount of phosphine generated.

Control: The hazard can be adequately controlled by efficient exhaust ventilation and efficient collection of the heavier dust particles in a 1 % solution of potassium permanganate.

PHOSPHORIC ACID

Phosphoric acid may cause burns on contact with any part of the body; however, it may not cause an immediate burning sensation on skin contact. In some individuals, no burning sensation is felt unless left in contact indefinitely without rinsing or washing off. Similarly, phosphoric acid may cause local injury if taken internally in a concentrated solution. It is, however, much less hazardous than other mineral acids such as nitric or sulfuric. It has a low vapor pressure and at room temperature is not irritating to the eyes or respiratory tract unless introduced to the atmosphere as a spray or mist.

Treatment: In case of contact with skin or eyes, flush the affected tissues with plenty of water for at least 15 minutes. In case of ingestion, induce vomiting after drinking large volumes of water, and follow with demulcents (milk, vegetable oil, starch suspensions).

PHOSPHORUS

Red phosphorus is nonvolatile and insoluble in water; it has a low order of toxicity. Yellow phosphorus is highly toxic. Tissue surfaces which come in contact with yellow phosphorus will show evidence of irritation and possibly necrosis. Absorption by ingestion or inhalation may lead to severe systemic intoxication characterized by cardiovascular collapse, increased and shallow respiration, coma, and convulsions. Individuals who survive an acute intoxication may have changes in the formed elements of the blood as well as kidney and liver damage. Repeated exposure to yellow phosphorus fumes in the match industry many years ago caused destruction of the mandible ("phossy jaw"). The probable lethal oral dose of yellow phosphorus for an adult is 60 mg. Death usually follows a period of delirium and coma.

Treatment: Remove from the skin by flooding with water; cover with wet dressings until specific burn therapy can be initiated. An oral intoxication is best treated by prompt gastric lavage with a 0.1% copper sulfate solution (forming an insoluble coating of copper phosphide), or a 1:5000 solution of potassium permanganate, which acts as an oxidizing agent. Follow with a saline cathartic and glucose I.V. and, if required, treat dehydration, acidosis, and peripheral vascular collapse. Because of the high mortality rate in oral yellow phosphorus poisoning (about 50%) it is important to keep the patient under close supervision. Rest and a diet high in carbohydrate and protein are important. Do *not* give oily cathartics; avoid fatty foods, including milk.

PHOSPHORUS OXYCHLORIDE (Phosphorus Chloride)

Phosphorus oxychloride is a highly toxic, volatile liquid; its vapors are extremely irritating to the skin and mucous membranes. When heated to decomposition, it emits highly toxic fumes of the chloride and oxides of phosphorus. With water or moisture, it forms hydrochloric and phosphoric acids, both of which can cause severe acid burns.

Treatment: See Hydrochloric Acid, p. 317.

PHOSPHORUS TRICHLORIDE

Phosphorus trichloride is a highly toxic, volatile liquid; its vapors are extremely irritating to the mucous membranes and lungs. When heated to decomposition it emits highly toxic fumes of chlorides and oxides of phosphorus. In the presence of water it hydrolyzes to hydrochloric and phosphorous acids, both of which can cause severe acid burns.

Treatment: See Hydrochloric Acid, p. 317.

PHOSTEX [Mixture of bis(Dialkoxyphosphinothioyl Sulfides)]

This compound has a low order of mammalian toxicity. LD_{50} oral (rat) 2.5 gm/kg. See Organic Phosphates, p. 438.

PHTHALALDEHYDES

The toxicity of *o*-phthalaldehyde is 30 times greater than that of the meta isomer and 40 times greater than that of the para compound in mice. See Aldehydes, p. 81.

PHTHALATES

Esters of phthalic acid are extensively used as plasticizers. They have a low order of toxicity.

Treatment: None required.

PHTHALIC ANHYDRIDE

Phthalic anhydride is a tissue irritant. Its irritant effect occurs rapidly on moist skin and mucous membranes due to the hydrolysis of the anhydride to phthalic acid. The dust and vapor are irritating to the skin, eyes, nose, throat, and upper respiratory tract. If inhaled, the dust may cause coughing, sneezing, and a burning sensation in the throat. If the solid remains in contact with the skin, it may cause superficial chemical burns. The molten material will cause a severe thermal burn.

Treatment: Phthalic anhydride should be washed promptly from the skin with large quantities of water. The eyes should be irrigated with water for at least 15 minutes in case of entry of dust, particulates, or fumes.

Discomfort caused by inhalation can be relieved by gargling with water and taking a sedative cough mixture. If there is difficulty in breathing, administer oxygen. In case of ingestion, induce vomiting and follow with gastric lavage and demulcents (milk, vegetable oil, or starch).

PHTHALOYL CHLORIDES

These acid chlorides hydrolyze on contact with water to form hydrochloric acid and phthalic acid. The oral LD_{50} of terephthaloyl and isophthaloyl chlorides is approximately 2.5 and 2.2 gm/kg, respectively (albino rats).

Treatment: See Acids, Aromatic Mono- and Dicarboxylic, p. 71, and Hydrochloric Acid, p. 317.

PHYSOSTIGMINE (Eserine)

This is a potent anticholinesterase drug used locally for inducing miosis and reduction of intraocular tension and antagonizing effects of atropine. Systemically, it produces muscle fasciculations which are useful in antagonizing the effects of curare. Overdose results in paralysis of striated muscle. The oral dose of physostigmine salicylate ranges from 1 to 3 mg and the S.C. or I.M. dose from 0.6 to 2.0 mg. Topically, 0.1 ml of 0.02–1.0% solutions are used. A 17-year-old girl who ingested 1 gm of physostigmine became nauseated almost immediately; salivation and dyspnea followed. She became comatose in 10 minutes. Subsequent effects included pulmonary edema, miosis, vomiting, and diarrhea. She recovered in approximately 24 hours following gastric lavage, atropine, and supportive treatment [*Med. Klin.* **60**, 1085 (1965)].

Treatment: Atropine sulfate is considered to be the antagonist of choice, but it must be remembered that this drug will block only the muscarinic effects. If the tremors are severe, it may be advisable to give magnesium sulfate or a barbiturate I.V., or ether by inhalation. Treatment otherwise is symptomatic. See Organic Phosphates, p. 438.

PICKLES

There is some evidence that ingestion of heavily salted Japanese fukujinzuke pickles in combination with a low calcium diet may be responsible for the relatively high incidence of stomach cancer among the Japanese [*Sci. News* **92**, 61 (1967)].

PICRIC ACID (2,4,6-Trinitrophenol)

Skin contact will result in staining of the skin and possibly irritation and dermatitis. Ingestion of a toxic dose produces gastroenteric distress, collapse, and kidney and liver injury.

Treatment: Remove from the skin with water. In case of ingestion, induce vomiting and perform stomach lavage with water. Follow with saline cathartics and fluid therapy.

PICROTOXIN (Fish Berry Poison)

This compound is a powerful analeptic particularly stimulating to the respiratory and motor centers. Accidental ingestion has resulted in gastroenteric distress and central excitation, followed by depression of all central functions. The probable lethal oral dose for an adult is 25 mg.

Treatment: Control convulsions with paraldehyde or barbiturates. Induce vomiting or administer gastric lavage and cathartics for the removal of the material from the gastroenteric tract.

PIGEON-BREEDERS' LUNG

The disease, also referred to as "bird breeder's lung," is caused by inhalation of the antigens in avian excreta. Effects include fever, chills, malaise, loss of body weight, coughing, and dyspnea. The acute phase begins 4–6 hours following exposure and recedes within 12 hours. Repeated exposure may cause elevation of γ-globulin and a diffuse nodular interstitial pulmonary lesion.

Three patients had many episodes of an acute interstitial pneumonitis after exposure to pigeons which they bred as a hobby. Laboratory examinations showed leukocytosis and elevated γ-globulin, but no evidence of specific infections. The disease was reproduced in hospitalized patients exposed to aerosols of pigeon serum, pigeon feathers, and droppings. Each patient had high titers of precipitating antibody to extracts of pigeon feathers or droppings and to pigeon serum or eggs. Skin tests with these antigens produced neither immediate nor delayed reactions.

The disease is considered to be of allergic origin, similar to the illness produced by other antigens in farmers' lung, bagassosis, mushroom-pickers' disease, and maple-bark strippers' disease [C. E. Reed *et al.*, *JAMA* **193**, 261 (1965)].

PILOCARPINE NITRATE

This drug is a true parasympathomimetic agent acting on effector cells, even after complete nerve degeneration. The effects are similar to those of physostigmine, p. 475.

PIMELIC ACID

Human toxicity data are not available. The oral LD_{50} of pimelic acid for male albino rats is approximately 7 gm/kg. Pimelic acid is not appreciably irritating to rabbit skin. It is not absorbed through the skin in harmful amounts from a single exposure. A dose of 10 gm/kg in continuous contact with the closely clipped abdominal skin of the albino rabbit for 24 hours did not cause skin irritation or systemic intoxication. Small quantities placed into rabbit eyes caused moderate conjunctivitis with some swelling of the lids. A trace of diffuse corneal opacity was also noted. These signs of irritation gradually subsided 7 days following application of the dose.

Treatment: Wash from skin and eyes with water. In case of ingestion induce vomiting and follow with demulcents.

PIMINODINE (Alvodine)

This relatively new potent narcotic analgesic is chemically and pharmacologically related to meperidine. Its potency and side effects are similar to those of morphine, but it produces little or no drowsiness and euphoria.

Treatment: Nalorphine and levallorphan are effective antagonists. See Narcotic Drugs, p. 40, and Opiates, p. 435.

PIPAMAZINE (Mornidine)

This phenothiazine derivative is an effective antiemetic. Doses exceeding 5 mg per day may cause sedation. A toxic dose can be expected to induce extrapyramidal involvement. This drug was ingested by three 3-year-old children in quantities ranging from 10 to 100 mg. Symptoms included marked central nervous system depression, drowsiness, stupor, and coma.

Treatment: The children recovered after gastric lavage, I.V. fluids, oxygen, and symptomatic treatment. The drug should not be given to a patient suffering from liver disease or hematopoietic tissue malfunction.

PIPERAZINE

This anthelmintic drug is sold as Antepar, Anthalazine, Oxucide, Parazine, Perin, Piperat, Piperazate, Pipzan, and Vermizine. It is accepted as a drug with a relatively low degree of toxicity. In sensitive individuals, however, ingestion of piperazine is likely to cause vomiting, giddiness, blurred vision, diarrhea, urticaria, central nervous system depression, tremors, and collapse. In recent years, there have been increasing incidents of neurotoxicity with several fatalities, occurring almost entirely in young children who received dosages ranging from a single dose of 75–155 mg/kg to doses of approximately 1.5 gm for 3 or more days. The symptoms frequently appeared from the second to the fifth day after the first dose and included somnolence, dizziness, vomiting, hypotonia with severe impairment of gait and petit mal or myoclonic jerks; several children developed status epilepticus. These symptoms were particularly frequent and severe in 10% of 19 children suffering from long-standing diseases of the central nervous system [*Lancet* **I**, 1218 (1966); *JAMA* **195**, 1069 (1966); *Lancet* **I**, 895 (1967)]. A 10-year-old girl who ingested one dose of 4.8 gm of piperazine citrate developed severe purpura with epistaxis and bleeding from the gums in 8 days. She recovered. Adverse effects and fatalities were due primarily to dosages that were too large, to subnormal kidney function, or to the presence of neurological disorders.

Caution: It appears that the undesirable effects in children with normal central and excretory functions are dose-related. The drug should be used with utmost caution in patients with subnormal kidney function and in the presence of neurological disorders. Drug therapy should not exceed 1 week, but may be repeated after a drug-free period of at least 1 week.

PIPOBROMAN (Vercyte)

Pipobroman is an oral antineoplastic drug. Its primary adverse effect is a dose related bone marrow depression; in some patients transient hemolytic anemia has been reported. Reduction of the dosage, or temporary cessation of therapy was often effective in bringing adverse effects under control [*Med. Letter* **9**, 25 (1967)].

Caution: This drug is not fully evaluated. Caution is therefore indicated.

PIPOSULFAN (Ancyte)

This new drug has been found active against various types of tumors in animals and man. In the treatment of patients with malignant lymphomas, leukemias, polycythemia, multiple myeloma, adenocarcinomas, epidermoid carcinomas, and various types of sarcomas, the magnitude of the therapeutic response appeared to be quantitatively inferior to that obtained with current antitumor drugs in wide usage. Of 594 patients treated for varying periods with divided doses of 1–3 mg/kg/day, 118 patients had bone marrow depression and/or gastroenteric disturbances. These effects became evident after 1–267 (mean 36) days of therapy and persisted for 1–166 (mean 14) days following withdrawal of the drug. Adjustment of dose or temporary cessation of therapy was followed by recovery from adverse effects. The toxic effects were reversible in all instances [N. A. Nelson *et al.*, *Clin. Pharmacol. Therap.* **8**, 385 (1967)].

PIVAL (2-Pivalyl-1,3-indandione)

This rodenticide is chemically and toxicologically similar to dicumarol. See Bishydroxycoumarin, p. 131.

PLANT FUME 103

This "smoke generator" contains 15% tetraethyl dithiopyrophosphate (ASP-47). Its toxicity and mechanism of action are similar to parathion. See Organic Phosphates, p. 438.

PLANTS IN A BEDROOM

House plants do not consume sufficient oxygen or release sufficient carbon dioxide to harm a sleeper, even assuming the worst possible conditions with no ventilation and enormous quantities of plant tissue [E. B. Hadley, *JAMA* **201**, 497 (1967)]. Highly odoriferous plants, such as jasmine, should be removed since they may produce nausea and headache.

PLASTER OF PARIS

This compound hardens quickly after absorption of moisture. The ingestion of plaster of paris (anhydrous calcium sulfate or dihydrate with about 5% of water) may result in obstruction of the upper intestinal tract, particularly at the pylorus. See Bezoars, p. 643.

Treatment: Use glycerin or gelatin solutions or large volumes of water to delay the setting process; surgical removal may be necessary.

PLASTIC CHEESE ("Trick Swiss Cheese")

A plastic imitation of a soft slice of Swiss cheese intended to appeal to practical jokers has accounted for at least one fatality in Germany.

Health authorities in the Federal Republic of Germany have demonstrated that this toy, although pliable in its ordinary form, becomes hard, with sharp edges, in contact with gastric juices and can cause serious injury to the intestinal tract.

PLASTIC FINGERNAILS

Methyl methacrylate liquid monomer is a potent sensitizer that can cause an allergic contact type of eczematous reaction of the skin and oral mucosa. Allergic eczematous reactions of the onychial and paronychial tissues have been reported in four patients using acrylic plastic nails. Two of these had normal nails originally. One became sensitized in 2 months and the other in 4 months. Another patient, with onychomycosis, had a very painful reaction and became sensitized in 2 months. The onychomycosis was not influenced by the allergic reaction. The fourth patient had symptoms within 48 hours. Apparently she had previously become sensitized. She still had nail changes 3 months after the initial application of the acrylic resin.

Patch tests revealed that all patients were allergic to methyl methacrylate. None reacted to polymethyl methacrylate. When sensitization occurs, severe onychia and paronychia may follow; dystrophic nail changes may persist for several months. See Acrylates, p. 75.

PLASTIC MODEL CEMENTS (Glue Sniffing)

Some cements used in the construction of model toys contain volatile organic solvents, such as acetone, toluene, xylene, benzene, amyl acetate, butyl alcohol, isopropyl alcohol, and methyl cellosolve acetate. These are not hazardous when properly used, but in recent years there has been an outbreak of deliberate inhalation of the vapors of these substances by adolescents. The toxic effects of sniffing the vapors include a depressant action on the central nervous system resembling acute alcoholic intoxication. Methyl cellosolve acetate has been reported to cause significant damage to the kidney after repeated inhalations of relatively high concentrations. There is also the possibility of kidney and liver damage due to isopropyl alcohol and kidney damage caused by acetone.

The usual technique of glue sniffing is to squeeze the cement from its tube onto a rag or handkerchief and to inhale from this. A few whiffs suffice to stimulate, but soon larger inhalations are needed to get results. Mild euphoria and exhilaration later give place to disorientation and even coma. Habituation, tolerance, and psychological dependence develop in time. The danger is that this habit might lead to more serious forms of misbehavior, such as alcoholism and drug addiction [*N.Y. State J. Med.* **65**, 1984 (1965); *New Engl. J. Med.* **273**, 700 (1965)].

Treatment: See individual solvents listed above.

PLUTONIUM

Plutonium is a radioactive element emitting alpha rays as its principal radiation. According to P. A. Fuqua, the primary hazards and toxicity of plutonium are similar to those of radium, except that plutonium outside the body presents no hazard. This is because plutonium does not emit penetrating beta or gamma radiation. After absorption, plutonium deposits are found primarily in bone and liver. Excretion is very slow, requiring an estimated 200 years to eliminate one-half of the amount absorbed. Plutonium usually enters the body via wounds, but inhalation exposure has also been reported. Ingestion is rare, and absorption through the intact skin is of no practical importance [*Ind. Med. Surg.* **34**, 335 (1965)].

Treatment: In case of a skin or tissue wound, apply a tourniquet to limit absorption. Cautiously cleanse the wound and surrounding area with soap and water, 5 % sodium thiosulfate, a dilute solution of potassium permanganate, or salicylic acid. If decontamination is difficult because of the nature of the injury, excision and debridement may be necessary. According to P. A. Fuqua, prompt excision can result in over 90% removal [*Ind. Med. Surg.* **34**, 335 (1965)]. If surgical removal is not used, local washes and/or I.M. or I.V. administration of DTPA (diethylenetriamine-pentaacetic acid) or the *cautious* use of zirconium citrate [W. D. Norwood *et al., Ind. Med. Surg.* **25**, 135 (1956)] or CaNa$_2$ EDTA are recommended. Fuqua found that 1 gm per day of DTPA is about as effective as twice this dose. The drug is given I.V., but occasionally I.M., in a dilute saline or glucose solution. The drug is not effective when given orally. For ingestion of plutonium, emetics or cathartics are not indicated unless a relatively large amount has been ingested. Depending on the amount involved, I.V. DTPA therapy may be indicated. For details see the original paper cited above. For signs and symptoms of radiation illness, see p. 513.

PODOPHYLLUM RESIN

The dried rhizome and roots of *Podophyllum peltatum* (May apple) have been used as a popular lay remedy for constipation since the medicinal properties of the plant were accidentally discovered about 120 years ago. More recently, podophyllum resin, the resin of *P. peltatum,* has been used principally to treat verrucae vulgaris and condylomata acuminata.

Podophyllum resin is a mixture containing podophyllotoxin, quercitin, α-peltatin, β-peltatin, and two metabolic products of podophyllotoxin, picropodophyllin, and podophyllic acid. Podophyllum resin has colchicine-like effects; for example, in an appropriate dose, it arrests cell mitosis in the metaphase.

A 60-year-old female took approximately 300 mg of podophyllum resin and died after 3 days. The second fatal case was a woman who died after 30 hours from an oral dose of 350 mg of podophyllum resin. In both cases the symptoms were respiratory stimulation, vomiting, diarrhea, ataxia, and coma. The third fatal case followed the use of local application of 25 % podophyllum resin ointment for a condyloma acuminatum of the vulva. This patient also had symptoms of vomiting and respiratory stimulation. The onset appeared 12 hours after the application and coma followed after 24 hours. Death occurred on the seventh day after application of the podophyllum resin.

Treatment: Treatment consists of heavy sedation with morphine sulfate and fluid and electrolyte replacement [M. Balucani and D. D. Zellers, *JAMA* **189**, 639 (1964)].

POI

This popular Polynesian food is prepared from the taro root and is credited with having been responsible for the excellent bone structure and teeth of the early Hawaiians. J. Glaser reported that young infants and premature babies thrive on this carbohydrate as well as control groups fed rice cereal [*Sci. News* **89**, 368 (1966)].

POINCIANA; BIRD-OF-PARADISE (*Poinciana gilliesii*)

Severe gastroenteric effects have been reported after ingestion of several seed pods of this tree and of the dwarf poinciana or Barbados-pride (*Poinciana pulcherrima*).

Treatment is similar as in tung nut intoxication (p. 613). Gastric lavage should be preceded by ingestion of milk, egg white, or another demulcent. Dehydration and electrolyte imbalance requires prompt treatment.

POISON HEMLOCK (*Conium maculatum*)

This plant has caused intoxications because the green material was mistaken for parsley and the seeds for anise. The toxic compounds in the entire plant include coniine, *N*-methylconiine, conhydrine, and several closely related compounds. The signs and symptoms of intoxication are essentially those induced by nicotine. Fool's parsley (*Aethusa cynapium*) contains the same alkaloids.

Treatment: See Kentucky Coffee-Tree, p. 343, and Nicotine, p. 421.

POISON IVY

There are three varieties of the species *Rhus toxicodendron* that are responsible for the majority of poison ivy-like dermatitis in this country. They are poison ivy (*R. toxicodendron radicans*), western poison oak (*R. toxicodendron diversilobum*), and poison sumac (*R. toxicodendron vernix*). When the bark or leaves of any of these plants are cut or injured, an oily fluid or sap exudes containing urushiol (3-*n*-pentadecylcatechol). Contact with this sap or oleoresin in a sensitized individual produces typical poison ivy dermatitis in 24–36 hours. The sensitizing principle is not volatile, but it can be carried in fine particles of leaf with dust or smoke that have come in contact with the injured plant. A frequently mentioned, but rare, source of "poison ivy" is the smoke from a fire containing the leaves or bark of the plant. Cases of mysterious poison ivy attacks can be explained by animal or insect carriers as well as contaminated clothing, gloves, tools, etc.

The sensitivity of an individual to the poison ivy plant varies during his lifetime. The condition of the skin (thickness, temperature, moisture) plays an added role [C. R. Dawson, *Trans. N.Y. Acad. Sci.* 18, 427 (1956)].

Poison ivy and the other *Rhus* belong to the cashew family (Anacardiaceae) along with a number of other plants of worldwide interest. These include such edible fruits as the cashew nut (*Anacardium occidentalis*), the mango (*Mangifera indica*), the pistachio (*Pistacia vera*), and other rare tropical fruits, the Brazil-ian pepper tree (*Schinus terebinthifolius*) which is grown in the southern United States as an ornamental shrub, the lac tree (*Rhus verniciflua*) which is the source of Japanese lacquer, the shrub-like tree "poison wood" (*Metopium toxiferum*) which grows wild in the subtropical United States and the Caribbean area, and the "marking nut" (*Semecarpus anacardium*) used by the dhobies (laundrymen) of India to mark clothing and which causes "dhobie itch." There is a large variety of other plants or trees that induce a similar reaction upon contact. These include litre (*Lithraea caustica*) and primrose (*Primula obconica, P. cortusoides,* and *P. Sieboldii*). "Tulip fingers" and "hop-picker's itch" are other examples of this type of dermatitis which is produced in sensitive individuals. For more complete information on dermatitis-producing plants, the reader is referred to the excellent monograph "Plant Toxicity and Dermatitis" by Kenneth F. Lampe and Rune Fagerstrom, Williams & Wilkins, Baltimore, Maryland, 1968.

Most of the members of the cashew family contain varying amounts of pentadecyl catechols and related phenols which are potent cutaneous allergens.

Signs and symptoms of poison ivy and related intoxications include local redness and swelling followed by vesiculation and formation of bullae. As a rule, these areas heal in about 1 week. Contrary to general belief, blister fluid is not a source of further irritation. Systemic effects are rare but they have been reported.

Treatment: If the affected area is small, allay itching by application of calamine lotion or 1% hydrocortisone lotion. Leave area uncovered. If the area involved is larger, apply a wet dressing of tap water without an occlusive cover to permit evaporation and cooling. Secondary infections must be treated with specific antibiotics.

Desensitization prior to exposure may be considered for individuals who are extremely sensitive to poison ivy and related plants. Injection of poison ivy extracts is *contraindicated* during the period of active disease. See also Zirconium, p. 639.

POISONWOOD TREE (*Metopium toxiferum*)

The poisonwood tree, also known as Florida poison tree, coral sumac, or doctor gum, is abundant in many areas along the borders of hammocks and in pine woods. This tree and the manchineel are the two most poisonous trees in Florida. The milky sap produces dermatitis similar to that of poison ivy. See Poison Ivy, p. 484.

POLYACRYLAMIDE

Polyacrylamide resins (Separan NP10 and AP30 flocculants) are high molecular weight polymers with low acute oral toxicity to rats. Long-term feeding studies of these resins show that these polyacrylamides are quite low in chronic oral toxicity. Laboratory animals tolerated 5–10% in their total diet without effects other than those believed indirectly attributable to the large, hydrophilic, non-nutritive bulkiness of the materials. The unequivocal "no ill effect" levels were 1% in the diet of rats and 5–6% in the diet of dogs.

Studies with carbon-14-tagged resin indicated that negligible amounts of polymer, if any, pass through the walls of the gastrointestinal tract of the rat [D. D. McCollister *et al.*, *Toxicol. Appl. Pharmacol.* **7**, 639 (1965)].

POLYDIMETHYLSILOXANES

These compounds are silicones having a low order of toxicity. See Silicone, p. 530.

POLYETHYLENE AND POLYPROPYLENE GLYCOL

These glycols are bland chemicals having a very low order of toxicity. They do not penetrate the skin in harmful amounts and because of their low vapor pressure, present no inhalation hazard. The higher molecular weight glycols are approved as release agents for food packaging. See p. 747.

POLYFLUOROHYDROCARBONS (Polyfluorinated Hydrocarbons)

The fluoroalkanes have a low order of toxicity, particularly when all the halogens in the molecule are fluorine atoms (perfluoroalkanes, C_nF_{2n+2}). Some polyfluoroalkenes (tetrafluoroethylene, $CF=CF_2$), perfluoroalkenes [perfluoroisobutylene, $(CF_3)_2C=CF_2$ and perfluoropropylene, $CF_3CF=CF_2$] may cause delayed pulmonary edema following exposure to vapors. *Perfluoroisobutylene is ten times more toxic than phos-*

gene. See Table 17, p. 693 (Toxicity of Halogenated Alkenes).

Treatment: Remove the victim from contaminated atmosphere and keep under observation for evidence of delayed pulmonary edema. Treatment is symptomatic and supportive.

POLYMER FUME FEVER

Polymer fume fever is a short-term fever which occurs when polymers of tetrafluoroethylene (Teflon) are heated to above 300°C and toxic fluorocarbons such as isooctofluorobutylene are formed. The following symptoms occur: tightness of the chest, malaise, shortness of breath, headache, chills, fever 100–104°F (37.8–40°C), sore throat, and cough with sputum. The illness follows a latent interval of a few hours and resolves within a day or two with no subsequent ill effects. This may happen, for example, when the polymer is heated to comparatively high temperatures (350–400°C) in an oven, an extruder, or some other equipment used to fabricate it. However, the most frequent cause is probably smoking tobacco that has been contaminated with Teflon powder. Some years ago it was alleged that a workman died as a result of smoking a cigarette placed for a short time in contact with Teflon film. Although subsequently shown to be without foundation in fact, this rumor has continued to circulate [K. Harris, *Brit. Med. J.* **1**, 1146, (1962)].

Thermal degradation of polytetrafluoroethylene occurs only at temperatures above 300–350°C. It has been demonstrated that the maximum temperatures reached in cooking a variety of foods in Teflon-coated pans is 130–195°C. The scorching temperature or smoke point of cooking oils is approximately 200°C. This is obviously well below the decomposition range of Teflon. Should such a pan be neglected on an electric stove, the pyrolysis products released into a normal sized kitchen would not reach harmful concentrations. The average pan is coated with approximately 2 gm of this plastic.

A 50-year-old physician was spraying in the bilge of his boat with an aerosol-propelled lubricant called Slip Spray. He used about $3\frac{1}{2}$ ounces of the lubricant over a period of about 15 minutes. During most of this time he was smoking a cigarette. Shortly thereafter, he began to feel ill. His symptoms consisted of malaise, weakness, numbness and tingling in the arms and fingers, pain in the throat, and some difficulty in breathing. Dyspnea was more marked in a sitting than in a recumbent position. This illness lasted approximately 18 hours and was resolved completely by the next morning.

The label on the can of Slip Spray revealed that the product contained "hexane and fluorocarbotelomer." The latter ingredient is polymerized tetrafluoroethylene (Teflon). The label, which was read after the product was used, warned against using the spray in an unventilated area and warned specifically against smoking during the use of the product.

Caution: Since Teflon decomposition products are toxic, the resin should be stored away from highly flammable materials. In the event of fire, personnel should be provided with a fresh air supply or full-face masks effective against acid gases, organic vapors, and respirable particulate matter. In the event of known exposure to pyrolysis products of Teflon, exposed persons should be kept under observation to rule out the possibility of delayed pulmonary edema. Ventilation is essential in areas where Teflon is heated above 400° F (204°C) or where its processing gives rise to dust. Since the temperature of burning tobacco is sufficient to render Teflon particles hazardous, smoking or carrying tobacco products in areas where plastic is machined or cut should be prohibited [L. B. Tepper, *New Engl. J. Med.* **267**, 349 (1962)].

POLYMERS (Resins)

These macromolecules are poorly absorbed from the gastroenteric tract, and in general, they have a low order of toxicity. Ingestion could lead to the formation of bezoars. See Bezoars, p. 643.

POLYMYXIN B (Aerosporin)

This antibiotic is used intramuscularly, intrathecally, orally, and topically. Signs of toxicity, including neurotoxic and/or nephrotoxic effects, may be expected following single oral doses of 600 mg or intramuscular doses in excess of 3.0 mg/kg/day. In addition to these effects, oral doses may produce nausea, vomiting, and diarrhea. Symptoms of toxicity noted occasionally following injection of polymyxin B include local pain, peripheral paresthesia, vertigo, dizziness, ataxia, and weakness in the legs. Acutely toxic doses have been known to induce a histamine-like reaction including generalized erythema, hyperperistalsis, and paresthesia.

Ten cases of respiratory paralysis associated with therapeutic doses of polymyxin B and E have been recorded in isolated case reports in the literature. These few cases would suggest that this neuromuscular complication is rare. Quite the contrary may be true. L. A. Lindesmith *et al.* encountered 11 such patients during a $2\frac{1}{2}$-year period. Ten patients had either acute or chronic underlying renal disease; one had azotemia without evidence of other renal involvement. The typical clinical syndrome was one of underlying renal abnormality and rapid respiratory fatigability to the point of apnea, occurring 1–26 hours after injection of polymyxin. In five patients, apnea, occurred within 2 hours of the last dose; and in five patients apnea occurred approximately 3–9 hours after injection. Four patients received only one dose of polymyxin, the others received from 2 to 29 injections over a 15-day period. Respiratory fatigability persisted for 10–62 hours and was completely reversed in all patients. Treatment consisted of controlled ventilation and discontinuance of the antibiotic [*Ann. Internal Med.* **68**, 318 (1968); *Clin-Alert* (March 21, 1968)].

Caution: Lindesmith *et al.* warn that one should be alert to the possibility of respiratory paralysis in any patient with renal abnormality receiving a polymyxin drug. Because of the possibility of nephrotoxicity, parenteral use of polymyxin B should be reserved for hospitalized patients. C. M. Kunin *et al.* suggest that uremic patients receive two or three therapeutic doses, in order to achieve high concentrations in blood and tissues, followed by a sharply reduced dosage or withdrawal [*J. Clin. Invest.* **38**, 1498 (1959)]. Antihistamines are effective in relieving histamine-type effects.

POLYOLS (Polyalcohols; Polyhydric Alcohols)

These polyhydroxy compounds include glycerin, numerous glycols, and hundreds of polyglycols varying in molecular weight up to 10,000 or more. See Glycols, p. 290, Ethylene Glycol, p. 258.

POLYURETHANE

This plastic is prepared by reactions between toluene diisocyanate and various polyols. The finished plastic is a nontoxic macromolecule. Ingestion could result in the formation of a bizarre bezoar (see p. 643).

Polyurethane pyrolysis products have caused asphyxia in animals from occlusion of the upper respiratory tract.

A polyurethane foam (*Ostamer*) used to strengthen fractured bones was withdrawn.

Treatment: Following exposure to pyrolysis products of polyurethane, observe for premonitory signs of pulmonary edema. Further treatment is symptomatic and supportive.

POLYVIDONE (PVP; Polyvinylpyrrolidone; PVP-Macrose; Vinisil)

The acute toxicity of PVP is extremely low, and long-term studies have not demonstrated untoward effects. PVP is essentially nontoxic by oral administration, skin absorption, and intravenous or intraperitoneal injection. It is not a primary irritant, skin-fatiguing material, or sensitizer, and it is nonantigenic. Polyvidone is used as a plasma expander—a substitute for plasma or whole blood.

Treatment: If accidentally ingested, no treatment is required.

POLYVINYL TUBING

Of one hundred patients subjected to choledochostomy using polyvinyl T-tubing, four developed nonfatal biliary peritonitis. The tubing was considered a possible factor in the production of this adverse reaction. At the time of insertion, the tubing was soft and pliable, but upon exposure to bile, the plasticizer was removed, resulting in hardening. The removal of such rigid tubing may produce considerable damage to the granulation tissue tract.

Caution: A T-tube of siliconized rubber should be used in long-term drainage of the common bile duct; a T-tube made of latex rubber is probably more suitable for short-term drainage [Winstone *et al.*, *Lancet* **I**, 843 (1965)].

PONSTEL

This new drug has been called a super aspirin. Side effects after administration of therapeutic doses included severe diarrhea, headache, drowsiness, nausea, and nervousness.

Caution: Consultants of *Medical Letter* warn that this drug "may be excessively hazardous if taken for more than seven days" and that it "meets no urgent need" [quoted from *Sci. News* **92**, 445 (1967)].

POTASSIUM (Hyperkalemia; Hypokalemia)

Potassium poisoning has been reported in patients suffering from severe renal insufficiency and, in isolated instances, after the too-rapid administration of a dose of a salt of potassium. Signs and symptoms include mental confusion, numbness and tingling of the extremities, weakness, bradycardia, muscular paralysis, and vascular collapse. Administration of enteric-coated potassium chloride (Esidrex-K) or thiazide potassium chloride (HydroDiuril-Ka) has been responsible for a marked increase in ulcerative lesions of the small intestine [S. J. Boley, *JAMA* **193**, 997 (1965); *Am. J. Surg.* **112**, 97 (1966)].

Hyperkalemia can cause sudden death during renal failure in the absence of overt clinical evidence of uremia and without premonitory clinical signs. Bedside observation of the uremic patient may give no indication of imminent fatal potassium poisoning. Serum potassium measurement is the mainstay of diagnosis and control.

A 14-year old girl consumed several boxes of Swedish matches daily over a period of several months. One box of these matches contained approximately 0.4 gm of potassium chlorate, and smaller quantities of potassium bichromate, potassium permanganate, and sulfur. She was admitted to the hospital with severe anemia and severe serum iron deficiency.

Potassium depletion may be caused by excessive vomiting or diarrhea, following prolonged administration of diuretic agents and mineral corticoids, and may occur in diseases characterized by the increased secretion of glucocorticoids or aldosterone [L. G. Welt, "Pharmacological Basis of Therapeutics" (L. S. Goodman and A. Gilman, Eds.) 3rd ed., MacMillan, New York, 1965].

Caution: Because irreversible damage may already have occurred by the time symptoms appear following oral administration of potassium chloride, enteric-coated potassium therapy should be limited to patients who require thiazides and whose potassium requirements cannot be met by dietary means (S. J. Boley *et al.*). These medications, as well as Hydro-Diuril-Ka, should be discontinued in any patient at the appearance of nausea or abdominal pain and distention.

Treatment: Cardiac massage and use of the artificial kidney were responsible for the survival of a patient who received an overdose of potassium. The management of hyperkalemia includes infusions of glucose with or without insulin. There is some evidence that perfusion with sodium polystyrene sulfonate and divinyl benzene is promising in the treatment of hyperpotassemia [*JAMA* **175**, 704 (1961); **178**, 839 (1961)]. See also Digitalis, p. 218.

In the case of the 14-year old girl, the hemoglobin level rose slowly with iron therapy. Six months after cessation of iron therapy, symptoms of pica and iron-deficiency anemia reappeared. Further treatment with iron brought recovery.

Treatment of potassium deficiency involves the cautious administration of potassium, either orally or I.V. Potassium depletion, in patients on a regimen of salt restriction, is corrected by administration of potassium chloride. For details of treatment see more specific texts. For foods high in potassium content, see p. 38.

POTASSIUM IODATE

Potassium iodate administered orally acts both as a gastroenteric irritant and as a hemolytic agent. Only small amounts of methemoglobin could be found in four dogs given repeated doses of 60–100 mg/kg. This shows that iodate is not an active former of methemoglobin. The minimum lethal dose for potassium iodate administered orally to eight fasted dogs is 200–250 mg/kg. Single doses of this compound at these levels invariably caused emesis. Fatty changes in the viscera, necrotic lesions in the liver, kidneys, mucosa of the gastrointestinal tract and urinary bladder, and retinal degeneration were sometimes present after high doses. All of these changes except retinal degeneration appear to be reversible [S. H. Webster *et al., Toxicol. Appl. Pharmacol.* **8**, 185 (1966)].

Treatment: In case of ingestion, induce vomiting and follow with gastric lavage.

POTASSIUM PERMANGANATE

This compound is a powerful oxidizing agent which may be absorbed through the skin and mucous membranes. Serious local tissue injury and systemic poisoning have resulted from its use as an abortifacient. These include punched-out ulcers and burns of the vagina and cervix, erosion of the vaginal wall, pelvic peritonitis, dynamic ileus, and complete penetration into the cul-de-sac of Douglas.

Ingestion of a toxic dose will result in severe gastroenteric distress, respiratory difficulties, and edema of the glottis. The probable lethal oral dose for an adult is 10 gm.

Treatment: After ingestion, induce vomiting and follow with thorough gastric lavage, demulcents, glucose I.V., fluid therapy, and antibiotics. Tracheostomy may be lifesaving. See p. 13.

PRASEODYMIUM AND NEODYMIUM CHLORIDES

Praseodymium and neodymium chloride have a depressant action and produce death by cardiovascular collapse with respiratory paralysis. Instillation of either chemical into the eye results in transient conjunctival ulceration. Skin damage with scar formation occurs upon application to abraded skin (but not to unabraded skin). Intradermal injection of either chemical produces nodules containing foreign body giant cells and crystals [T. J. Haley *et al., Toxicol. Appl. Pharmacol.* **6**, 614 (1964)].

PREGNANCY: DRUGS

The following is taken from an article by Virginia Apgar [*JAMA* **190**, 840 (1964)]: "The greatest danger of inducing malformations is in the first trimester of pregnancy. Since this includes the period before a woman may be aware that she is pregnant, and since we know very little about the effects of drugs on the fetus, physicians are urged to exercise great restraint in prescribing medications for women of childbearing age, and self-medication by patients in this group should be strongly discouraged . . . .

"Table 8 lists some relationships observed between maternal medication and fetal or neonatal changes. Only a few are proved beyond a shadow of doubt, but until further data are collected, caution should be exercised in administering these substances to pregnant women." See p. 683.

PRILOCAINE (Citanest)

This anesthetic is used for local, spinal, epidural, and nerve-block anesthesia. Its effectiveness is similar to that of lidocaine or mepivacaine. Doses should not exceed 600 mg per 12 hours (8 mg/kg); that is, 20 ml of a 3% solution or 30 ml of the 2% solution of prilocaine hydrochloride. As yet, no maximum safe dose has been established for children [*JAMA* **199**, 837 (1967)]. Several reports have described the production of methemoglobin with a dose of 900 mg. The methemoglobinemia usually disappeared in 24 hours. Destruction of erythrocytes was not observed [D. B. Scott, *et al.*, *Lancet* **I**, Pt. 1, 728 (1964)].

Caution: In obstetrical anesthesia, the relatively low central nervous system toxicity of prilocaine must be weighed against its disadvantage of producing maternal and fetal methemoglobinemia. Prilocaine should be used with caution in anemic patients, particularly in anemic pregnant women [W. E. Spoerel *et al.*, *Can. Anaesthetical Soc. J.* **14**, 1 (1967)]. See also Dibucaine, p. 208, and Mepivacaine, p. 369.

PRIMAQUINE

This is an antimalarial drug. Side effects noted may include gastroenteric pain and distress and methemoglobinemia. The most serious signs of toxicity are acute intravascular hemolysis and granulocytopenia or agranulocytosis. Hemolysis, because of a specific metabolic deficiency in glucose-6-phosphate dehydrogenase (G-6-PD) activity of the red blood cells, is more frequent in Negroes than in white people. About 5% are affected if the daily dose is 30 mg or more. Other drugs or chemicals that occasionally induce this type of hemolysis include acetanilid, acetophenetidin, acetylsalicylic acid, aminopyrine, antipyrine, furazolidone, menadione sodium bisulfite, naphthalene, nitrofurantoin, pamaquine, PAS, pentaquine, phenylhydrazine, probenecid, salicylazosulfapyridine, sulfamethoxypyridazine, sulfanilamide, sulfapyridine, sulfisoxazole, and sulfoxone. See reports by Keller-meyer *et al.*, *JAMA* **180,** 388 (1962); and P. S. Norman and L. E. Cluff, "Drugs of Choice 1966-1967." C. V. Mosby, St. Louis, Missouri, 1966.

PRIMIDONE (Mysoline)

This anticonvulsive agent is used in the treatment of grand mal epilepsy. Side effects (particularly drowsi-ness following therapeutic dose), symptoms of toxici-ty, and treatment are similar to those of phenobarbital and related compounds. See Barbiturates, p. 119.

Caution: The incidence of undesirable effects is reduced if primidone therapy is initiated with low doses and increased after a period of two weeks. Ob-serve for evidence of megaloblastic anemia.

PROBENECID (Benemid)

This uricosuric drug is used in the treatment of gout and gouty arthritis. Oral doses of 0.5 gm, once or twice daily, result in reduction of the blood uric acid con-centration and its excretion in the urine. More recent-ly, probenecid has been found effective as an inhibitor of renal tubular secretion of penicillin [*Arch. Internal Med.* **95,** 83 (1955)]. The drug is generally considered to have a low degree of toxicity. Recently, however, the second case of probenecid-related nephrotic syn-drome was reported [*JAMA* **199,** 43 (1967)]. Hillecke reported what appears to be the first incident of an anaphylactoid reaction following the ingestion of one tablet of probenecid [*JAMA* **193,** 740 (1965)].

Caution: Therapy is recommended with (1) grad-ually increasing doses to prevent a sudden marked uricosuric effect, and (2) high fluid intake to reduce the formation and retention of crystalline-type uric acid material.

PROCAINAMIDE (Pronestyl)

This drug has a cardiac depressant action similar to that of procaine or quinidine. It is administered I.V. and orally. Intravenous injections must be given *slowly* to avoid a sudden drop in blood pressure. Over-dose will induce myocardial depression, which may include conduction block, ventricular tachycardia, fibrillation, and cardiac arrest.

During recent years, there have been reports calling attention to the production of a lupus-like syndrome associated with procainamide therapy in adults and in one child [*Am. J. Diseases Children* **113**, 491 (1967)]. Treatment of these patients ranged from 3 weeks to 2–3 years. Signs and symptoms included one or several of the following: blotchy pruritic rash over the face, chest, or other parts of the body, aching joint pains, numbness in fingers, swelling of the fingers or wrists (polyarthritis), burning of the soles of the feet, muscle soreness, and bilateral chest pain [*New Engl. J. Med.* **186**, 1357 (1962); *Am. J. Med.* **42**, 625 (1967)]. A few isolated patients on procainamide therapy have complained or suffered from nausea, vomiting, fever, leukopenia, eosinophilia, or agranulocytosis [*Michigan Med.* **64**, 655 (1965)].

Caution: The occurrence of rash, joint pain, etc., should alert the physician that the patient may be suffering from a procainamide-induced lupus. Appearance of fever and/or sore throat might indicate evidence of agranulocytosis.

Treatment: Reports indicate that discontinuation of procainamide therapy results, in several weeks, in recovery from the lupus-like state. A 4-year-old girl who received 250 mg three times a day for 1 year followed by 1 gm four times a day for 2 months, and who developed a low grade fever, migratory polyarthritis and a profound neutropenia, recovered in 2 months after discontinuation of therapy.

PROCARBAZINE HYDROCHLORIDE

This monoamine oxidase inhibitor was introduced for the treatment of Hodgkin's disease. Little is known about this agent.

Caution: A. M. Mann and J. L. Hutchison caution that any patient receiving this drug should not use nose drops, cough medicines, tea, coffee, cola, cheese, cigarettes, alcohol, and local anesthetics [Sci. News **92**, 612 (1967)]. See Monoamine Oxidase Inhibitors, p. 404.

PROCHLORPERAZINE (Compazine)

This tranquilizer must be used with the same precautions taken with chlorpromazine. It has been found valuable for the symptomatic relief of vomiting in gastroenteritis and measles in children. Because of its antiemetic action, this drug may obscure the cause of nausea and vomiting. Side effects and signs of toxicity are not always related to dosage. They may include opisthotonus, rolling up of the eyes, protrusion of the tongue, inability to speak, and catatonic posture. Atropine-like effects have been reported; these were particularly noted with a rise in atmospheric temperature and humidity. On rare occasions, hypotension, hepatic pathology, skin disorders, and blood dyscrasias were noted. Hooper *et al.* reported abnormal lactation in certain female psychiatric patients [*Am. J. Psychiat.* **119**, 373 (1962)].

Caution: Patients, particularly children, should be maintained on the lowest effective dose. This drug, like chlorpromazine, may potentiate the effects of hypnotics, anesthetics, alcohol, and other central nervous system depressants. Epinephrine is contraindicated. Five patients with hypoparathyroidism suffered severe dystonic reactions to small I.V. doses of prochlorperazine [*New Eng. J. Med.* **275**, 991 (1966)]. Unless the physician is alert to some of the side effects (trismus, dysarthria, sensory and motor disturbances of the tongue), he may attribute the clinical picture to emotional factors [*JAMA* **193**, 839 (1965)].

Treatment: In children, caffeine and sodium benzoate (0.5 gm I.V.) gave relief in 25–120 seconds. Strong coffee by mouth had some beneficial effect [*JAMA* **170**, 361 (1959)]. For more specific treatment, see Phenothiazines, p. 464, and Chlorpromazine, p. 171.

PROMAZINE (Sparine)

This tranquilizer is chemically and pharmacologically closely related to chlorpromazine. The I.V. injection of this drug is reported to have produced severe vascular disorders, including gangrene of the fingers and hands (*Can. Med. Assoc. J.* **95**, 367 (1966)]. See Chlorpromazine, p. 171, and Phenothiazines, p. 464.

Caution: Avoid giving this drug I.V. If it must be given by this route, be certain that the directions of the manufacturer are followed precisely.

PROMETHAZINE (Phenergan; Fargan)

This potent long-acting antihistamine produces sedation but not true hypnosis. In the presence of promethazine, the effects of central nervous system depressants are potentiated. Undesirable effects have included autonomic reactions and behavioral toxicity.

Treatment: Signs and symptoms resulting from overdoses must be treated symptomatically. See also Phenothiazine Compounds, p. 464.

PROPANESULTONE

Propanesultone is a nearly colorless, odorless, low-melting, crystalline solid. Sultones, a name derived from the structural resemblance of these chemicals to lactones, are the cyclic esters of hydroxysulfonic acids. Propanesultone is the simplest member of the class. On oral administration to rats, it is only slightly toxic. On application to the skin of rabbits, it is slightly toxic; a single application is mildly irritating. It is a strong sensitizer, however, and on repeated application is extremely irritating to the skin. Skin contact should be avoided to prevent sensitization.

Treatment: The material should be washed off the skin immediately with copious quantities of water. In the event of eye contact, flood with water for 15 minutes [R. F. Fischer, *Ind. Eng. Chem.* **56**, 3, 41 (1964)].

PROPANTHELINE BROMIDE (Pro-Banthine)

This anticholinergic depresses gastroenteric activity and gives relief from pain associated with hypermotility. Side effects are less frequent and less severe than with methantheline (Banthine). Occasionally, dryness of mouth, blurring of vision, headache, difficulty in urination, and constipation may be noted.

Caution: Atropine-like drugs are not recommended for patients with protracted fever. In a 20-year-old man with acute pancreatitis the axillary temperature rose to 109°F, ocular movements stopped, and the pupils showed typical atropine-like effects.

Treatment: Reduce dose or discontinue therapy. The young man responded to external cooling and to the administration of chlorpromazine [*Brit. Med. J.* **2**, 119 (1962)].

PROPELLANT FUELS (Missile Fuels; Rocket Fuels; Space Fuels; Rocket Propellants)

This term includes the following: dimethylhydrazine (UDMH); chlorine trifluoride, fluorine, red fuming nitric acid, nitrogen tetroxide, nitrogen dioxide, ozone, HEF-2, HEF-3, Hi Cal-3, pentaborane, and decaborane. For further information see individual chemicals.

β-PROPIOLACTONE (BPL)

β-Propiolactone is an extremely reactive and corrosive chemical. It must be handled with all the precautions used in handling any chemical with properties similar to those of alkalis, acids, and anhydrides. BPL is readily hydrolyzed to the relatively harmless β-hydroxypropionic acid.

Because of the corrosive action of BPL, the greatest potential hazard is skin contact. BPL is a vesicant which causes severe skin irritation and blistering. The burning of the skin is not always immediately felt; minutes to hours later severe blistering may occur. Every precaution should be taken to avoid skin contact.

This compound has been used to sterilize arterial grafts. Sarcomas have been produced in rats by subcutaneous injection. Squamous papillomas and squamous carcinomas have been found in mice after repeated skin applications.

The vapor of BPL is irritating to the eyes and mucous membranes. It is a severe lachrymator. The vapor is also markedly irritating to the nose, throat and the respiratory tract in general.

Treatment: For contact with the skin, mucous membranes or with clothing flood the exposed surfaces with a large quantity of water. For eye contact, flood with water continuously for at least 15 minutes. In case of acute inhalation remove the individual to fresh air. In the event of ingestion, the individual should *immediately* wash the mouth with water, drink several glasses of water, then induce vomiting.

PROPIOMAZINE (Largon)

This drug (administered I.M. and I.V.) was introduced as an adjunct to anesthesia. It has prominent sedative properties. Side effects include dizziness, incoherence, and hypotension.

Caution: The drug should not be given intra-arterially. Intravenous injection may cause perivascular extravasation. When propiomazine is used, reduce the dose or eliminate other central depressants and opiates.

PROPOXYPHENE (Dextropropoxyphene; Darvon)

This drug is a codeine substitute. Although dextro-propoxyphene is not considered to be a narcotic, the World Health Organization has recommended that it be placed under control similar to that of codeine. One instance of addiction has been reported [A. Elson and E. F. Domino, *JAMA* **183**, 482 (1963)]. Side effects noted after therapeutic doses may include nausea and vomiting. A 57-year-old woman with impaired renal function experienced repeated episodes of hypoglycemia following ingestion of therapeutic doses of Darvon [*Neurology* **17**, 703 (1967)].

Approximately 15 cases of acute intoxication have been reported. Two of these were in small children who ingested doses of approximately 1.0 gm. Two died after ingestion of 1.28 and 2.3 gm. In severe poisoning, there is rapid loss of consciousness, respiratory depression, hypoxia, convulsions, and cardiovascular collapse. One patient died as a result of severe cerebral edema that followed persistent, uncontrolled convulsions and resultant hypoxia [*JAMA* **199**, 1006 (1967); *Brit. Med. J.*, **2**, 1324 (1966)].

Treatment: In the cases described above, treatment included the administration of anticonvulsants, nalorphine, oxygen, peritoneal dialysis, and antibiotics. In experimental animals, both nalorphine and levallorphan were found effective. See Opiates, p. 435.

PROPRANOLOL (Inderal)

Waal calls attention to the relatively high incidence of depression (approximately 40%) observed in 89 hypertensive patients who were treated with this drug for cardiac arrhythmias. He found the effects dose-related [*Brit. Med. J.* **2**, 50 (1967)]. Other side effects reported by Kotler *et al.* include a feeling of light-headedness, skin rashes, visual disturbances, purpura and paresthesia; pharmacologic effects such as hypotension, bradycardia, cardiac failure, and dyspnea; and biochemical effects including elevation of blood urea and SGOT, hypoglycemia, and rarely, sodium retention [*Lancet* **II**, 1389 (1966)]. According to a report by W. G. Smith, much of the available evidence on the "safety" of I.V. injections of propranolol is based on its administration to patients who did not suffer from myocardial infarction. He referred to several patients who died during or immediately after an I.V. injection of 5–7.5 mg of this drug [*Lancet* **I**, 165 (1967)].

Caution: Propranolol should be administered with *extreme caution* to patients with acute myocardial infarction [*Brit. Med. J.* **1**, 141 (1967)]. The drug can potentiate the effects of insulin and oral hypoglycemic agents. Therefore, it is contraindicated in patients prone to hypoglycemia. Propranolol may be all the more dangerous because of the absence of the usual hypoglycemic signs associated with the liberation of catecholamine, such as tachycardia and sweating [*Lancet* **I**, 939 (1967)].

PROPYLENE CARBONATE

Propylene carbonate is an odorless, colorless, mobile liquid. It is stable, nonhygroscopic and noncorrosive. Propylene carbonate has a low order of toxicity in large single oral doses by skin absorption and even on repeated feeding of test animals. While it is moderately irritating to the mucous membranes of the eyes and respiratory tract, it presents no serious hazards to health in its handling.

Treatment: In case of skin and eye contact flood affected tissues with water for 15 minutes.

PROPYLENE GLYCOL

Propylene glycol has a very low order of toxicity by all routes of administration. The acute oral toxicity is in the general range of glycerin. Propylene glycol does not penetrate the skin in harmful amounts and is neither an irritant nor a sensitizer. Laboratory animals survived inhalation of concentrated vapors for 8 hours at room temperature; eyes were not harmed by flooding with an excess of the chemical.

Treatment: None required.

PROPYLENE GLYCOL MONOACRYLATE

Propylene glycol monacrylate is a toxic chemical. The oral LD_{50} for rats has been found to be 0.59 gm/kg. The vapors of propylene glycol monoacrylate are irritating to the mucous membranes of the throat, nose, and eyes. Prolonged inhalation of vapors can produce systemic toxic reactions manifested by drowsiness, headache, nausea, vomiting, and weakness.

Liquid propylene glycol monoacrylate is a skin and eye irritant.

Treatment: For skin or eye contact, wash with water for 15 minutes. In case of ingestion, induce vomiting; follow with gastric lavage and demulcents.

PROPYLENE OXIDE

Propylene oxide is a volatile liquid with a boiling point similar to ethyl ether. The oral LD_{50} for rats is approximately 1 gm/kg. The liquid is slightly irritating to uncovered rabbit skin; however, where the application was covered by plastic sheeting, severe skin burns resulted. Small droplets of the liquid are irritating to rabbit eyes. The vapor pressure of propylene oxide is quite high at room temperature, and acutely dangerous vapor concentrations could develop readily in confined spaces. Rats tolerate a concentration of 2000 ppm for 4 hours, although a concentration of 4000 ppm is lethal in the same period of time.

Treatment: In case of eye or skin contact, flood with water. For inhalation exposure, remove the victim from the contaminated area. Give artificial respiration and oxygen if necessary.

PROPYLENIMINE

Propylenimine is a hazardous, toxic, flammable liquid with a boiling point of 66°C (760 mm/Hg). The oral LD_{50} for rats is 19 mg/kg. This low LD_{50} indicates that propylenimine is a poisonous material and extreme care should be used to avoid ingestion. It is also toxic by skin absorption. The percutaneous LD_{50} for guinea pigs is 43 mg; the comparable figure for ethylenimine is 14 mg.

Propylenimine is also toxic by inhalation and is therefore hazardous. In inhalation experiments of 4 hours' duration, five out of six rats were killed by 500 ppm of propylenimine. In contrast, only 62 ppm of ethylenimine killed a comparable proportion of rats in 4 hours. Propylenimine is comparable to ammonium hydroxide with respect to eye injury from fluid contact.

Treatment: For skin contact, immediately flush with large amounts of running water and thoroughly wash affected area for at least 30 minutes. Remove and launder contaminated clothing. For eye contact, flush with plenty of water for at least 30 minutes and obtain prompt medical attention. For ingestion, induce vomiting. Remove to fresh air any person who shows any evidence of illness that may be due to an exposure to vapor of propylenimine. On prolonged exposure, imine vapors tend to redden the whites of the eyes.

PROPYLTHIOURACIL

This drug acts on the thyroid gland, depressing the formation of thyroxin. Drugs having a similar action include carbimazole (Neomercazole), methimazole (Tapazole), methylthiouracil (Methiacil), and iothiouracil. Side effects of propylthiouracil are related to dosage. An overdose can result in enlargement of the thyroid gland and in hypothyroidism. An occasional patient develops hypersensitivity to this drug which may result in blood dyscrasia [*Arch. Internal Med.* **120**, 587 (1967)]. Gilbert reported on a 27-year-old woman who developed severe hypoprothrombinemia and bleeding following administration of propylthiouracil in a dosage of 100 mg every 8 hours for 13 days, followed by 100 mg every 6 hours for 17 days, and 300 mg/day for 10 days [JAMA **189**, 855 (1964)]. Therapeutic doses range from 50 to 200 mg, three to four times daily.

Caution: The drug should be discontinued promptly if these signs or symptoms appear: malaise, sore throat, fever, rash, or jaundice. Blood counts should be determined at regular intervals to detect early hemopoietic changes. According to S. B. Barker, if a true agranulocytosis is encountered, great care must be taken to avoid exposure of the patient to infection. There should be some hesitancy to hospitalize the patient in view of the many resistant organisms now encountered on open hospital wards ["Drill's Pharmacology in Medicine," (J. R. Di Palma, ed.). McGraw-Hill (Blakiston), New York, 1965].

PROTHIPENDYL (Timovan)

The action of this tranquilizer resembles chlorpromazine. See Phenothiazine Compounds, p. 464.

PROTOANEMONIN

This glycoside is the active compound in a variety of perennial herbs and climbing vines including the white baneberry (*Actaea alba; A. pachypoda*), red baneberry (*Actaea rubra*), black baneberry (*Actaea spicata*), anemone (*Anemone spp*), prairie crocus (*Anemone patens*), marsh marigold or cowslip (*Caltha palustris*), clematis (*Clematis spp*), and buttercup or crowfoot (*Ranunculus spp*).

In hypersensitive individuals, skin or mucous membrane contact with some of these plants causes a burning sensation and dermatitis. In some countries, compresses of these plants used to treat arthritis frequently resulted in severe local skin changes including vesiculation.

Ingestion of these plants has caused salivation, pain and vesiculation in the mouth and throat, colic, vomiting and bloody diarrhea, dizziness, weakness, tremors, hematuria, coma, and convulsions. The active principle, which is liberated by enzymatic action, is destroyed by cooking.

Treatment involves prompt removal of the plant material from the mouth and gastroenteric tract. Rinse the mouth with milk, water, or any other available beverage. Administer milk and induce vomiting; repeat several times. Treat systemic effects symptomatically; follow with a bland diet until all symptoms have disappeared.

PROTOKYLOL HYDROCHLORIDE (Caytine)

This sympathomimetic amine has been used as a bronchodilator. In effective doses, it frequently produces cardiovascular and central nervous system side effects.

PROTRIPTYLINE (Vivactil)

This is a dibenzocycloheptine antidepressant drug used in divided dosages of 20–60 mg/day. According to *The Medical Letter*, the effects appear to be the same as those of 50–150 mg of amitriptyline (Elavil). Frequent side effects are dryness of mouth and blurred vision. Dizziness and tremors may occur, particularly in elderly patients. Cardiovascular effects (tachycardia, postural hypotension) may occur more frequently with protriptyline than with other antidepressant drugs.

Caution: This is a new drug. As with imipramine (Tofranil), amitriptyline (Elavil), nortriptyline (Aventyl), and desipramine (Pertofrane; Norpramin), peripheral anticholinergic effects preclude the use of protriptyline in patients with pyloric obstruction, narrow-angle glaucoma, or difficulties of urination.

Each of these drugs is contraindicated in patients taking any of the monoamine oxidase inhibitor antidepressants; nialamide (Niamid), isocarboxazid (Marplan), tranylcypromine (Parnate), and phenelzine (Nardil). To avoid hazardous potentiation of adverse effects of MAO inhibitors, at least 2 weeks should elapse after therapy with an MAO inhibitor before protriptyline or related drug therapy is initiated. Protriptyline and related drugs should not be used concurrently with antihypertensive drugs such as guanethidine (Ismelin) and similarly acting drugs. For more information, see the complete report [*Med. Letter* **10**, 17 (1968)].

PSEUDOEPHEDRINE HYDROCHLORIDE (Sudafed)

An unusual hypersensitivity reaction to the ingestion of pseudoephedrine, an oral nasal decongestant, occurred in a 17-year-old normotensive man who swallowed one 60 mg tablet of this drug for relief from a cold. The usual dosage in adults is one 60 mg tablet, 2–4 times a day. Thirty minutes later he became unconscious and remained so for 1 hour. On hospital admission his blood pressure was 170/110 mm Hg, the pulse 124. The patient recovered in 90 minutes without treatment. In this individual, pseudoephedrine, which is approximately 50% less toxic and has fewer side effects than ephedrine, is believed to have induced a marked stimulatory effect and carotid vasoconstriction to such an extent that there was insufficient blood supply to the brain, resulting in unconsciousness [H. R. Rutstein, *Arch. Otolaryngol.* **77**, 145 (1963)].

PTEROTOLUYLENE

This compound, extracted from the heartwood of *Pterocarpus marsupium*, was found to exert a marked hypoglycemic effect. Toxic doses induce hypoglycemia after an initial period of hyperglycemia [*JAMA* **167**, 1767 (1958)].

PYRAZINAMIDE (Aldinamide)

This is a new drug for the treatment of pulmonary tuberculosis. Cullen *et al.* found it to produce hyperuricemia in tuberculosis patients [*Am. Rev. Tuberculosis* **74**, 289 (1956)].

Caution: Physicians using this drug in the treatment of tuberculosis should be aware that it may cause hyperuricemia [*Clin. Pharmacol. Therap.* **8**, 124 (1967)].

PYRIDINE

Pyridine is a colorless, alkaline liquid with a characteristic odor. The recommended threshold limit is 10 ppm. It has an irritating effect and a nauseating, unpleasant odor. Liver and kidney damage have been produced in animals and in man after oral administration. Lower concentrations cause nausea, headache, insomnia, nervous symptoms, low back or abdominal discomfort, and urinary frequency. It is absorbed through the skin and may cause skin irritation. It is easily detectable by odor at less than 1 ppm, and it is very disagreeable to most individuals at 30 ppm. Odor is an unreliable guide at concentrations exceeding 5 ppm because olfactory fatigue occurs quickly.

Treatment: Wash skin thoroughly with large amounts of water and irrigate eyes with water for at least 15 minutes. In case of ingestion induce vomiting and follow with gastric lavage. For inhalation accidents remove individuals promptly from contaminated area. Give artificial respiration and oxygen if necessary. Subsequent treatment is symptomatic.

PYRIDOSTIGMINE BROMIDE (Mestinon)

This drug is a cholinesterase inhibitor with pharmacological effects similar to those of neostigmine. It has been found useful in the prolonged treatment of myasthenia gravis. As a rule, myasthenic patients tolerate this drug better than patients not suffering from this disease. Patients sensitive to bromides may develop a rash. A toxic dose induces severe muscular weakness simulating the symptoms of myasthenia gravis.

Caution: Do not use this drug in patients suffering from any type of obstruction of the gastroenteric or the urinary tract.

Treatment: Reduce dose if gastroenteric distress becomes annoying. Atropine is the pharmacological antidote if the muscarinic effects of this drug become too marked. Its nicotinic effects (muscle cramps, fasciculations, and weakness) are not antagonized by atropine.

PYRIMETHAMINE (Daraprim)

This antimalarial agent is a folic acid antagonist. There have been a number of reports calling attention to the hematologic side effects of pyrimethamine. The majority of the patients of Kaufman and Geisler showed blood abnormalities such as thrombocytopenia, leukopenia, and normochromic anemia [*A.M.A. Arch Ophthalmol.* **64**, 140 (1960)]. These effects were directly related to dosage. One patient showed evidence of myocarditis and a peculiar bronze pigmentation of the skin. These effects were reversible upon reduction of the dose or cessation of treatment.

Caution: Long-term treatment with this drug should be monitored by platelet counts. In case of severe bone marrow toxicity, large doses of folic acid or folinic acid should be given.

PYRINATE A-200

After applying A-200 pyrinate to the scalp for treatment of lice, chiggers, and flea infestation, two persons were affected by the undiluted product and three by the diluted material. All patients showed similar eye changes including blepharospasm.

Treatment of the eyes included the use of a mydriatic topical anesthetic and local antibiotics. Patients injured with the diluted product were symptom-free within 48 hours. Those injured with the undiluted product recovered after 72 hours [*Arch. Opthalmol.* **68**, 66 (1962)].

PYROGALLOL (Pyrogallic Acid; 1,2,3-Trihydroxybenzene)

This compound is rapidly absorbed through the skin. Ingestion may result in severe gastroenteric symptoms and distress, respiratory difficulties, and convulsions. The probable lethal oral dose for an adult is 2 gm.

Treatment: Remove from the skin with soap and water. In case of ingestion, thorough gastric lavage, saline cathartics and fluid therapy are indicated.

2-PYRROLIDONE

This compound is a colorless solid with a melting point slightly above room temperature. The boiling point at 760 mm Hg is 245°C. 2-Pyrrolidone is a mild primary skin irritant having definite sensitizing properties. Acute oral toxicity studies on white rats and guinea pigs gave the following values: LD_0, 4.0 ml/kg; LD_{50}, 6.5 ml/kg; LD_{100}, 9.5 ml/kg.

Treatment: In case of skin or eye contact, flood with water. In case of accidental ingestion, induce vomiting.

QUATERNARY AMMONIUM COMPOUNDS (QAC)

These are synthetic organic derivatives of ammonium ion of high molecular weight which are extensively used as sanitizing chemicals (germicides, antiseptics, fungicides, deodorants). They are available as solids, liquids, and ointments, usually containing less than 1% of the QAC. Proprietary preparations include the chlorides of benzalkonium (Zephiran), benzethonium (Phemeral), cetylpyridinium (Ceepryn), and cetyldimethylbenzyl ammonium (Triton; K-12). The proprietary products are used as 10% solutions. One human fatality has been reported following the ingestion of 3 gm of a commercial preparation dissolved in 30 ml of water. Skin contact with concentrated solutions will cause local irritation but no systemic toxicity, since percutaneous absorption is negligible.

Treatment: Induce vomiting after giving large volumes of water, milk, or demulcents. Follow with gastric lavage and saline cathartics. Further treatment is symptomatic and supportive.

QUINACRINE HYDROCHLORIDE (Atabrine)

At one time, this drug was used most extensively as an antimalarial drug since it destroys the asexual forms of the malaria parasite. Following oral administration of therapeutic doses, side effects frequently included gastroenteric symptoms, yellow discoloration of the skin, sclera, and urine. Occasional or rarely noted side effects included exfoliative dermatitis, acute hepatic necrosis, agranulocytosis, aplastic anemia, corneal edema, and psychoses. Approximately 300 cases of toxic psychoses due to quinacrine appeared in the literature during 1934–1964 [O. L. Sapp, *JAMA* **187**, 373

(1964)]. Sapp quoted Gaskill and Fitz-Hugh who reported on 35 of 7,604 patients (0.4%) who were treated with quinacrine for malaria and who developed an acute toxic psychosis. Administration of quinacrine to five normal volunteers, in doses which resulted in a plasma level of approximately 100 mg per liter, caused sustained acceleration in the electroencephalographic frequency. These effects became apparent on the third or fourth day and lasted for 6–8 days after cessation of treatment. All EEG abnormalities occurred when plasma levels exceeded 30–40 μg/liter [O. L. Sapp; G. L. Engel *et al.*, *Arch Neurol. Psychiat.* **58**, 337 (1947)].

Recently, quinacrine has been found useful in the control and management of pleural and peritoneal neoplastic effusions. It is instilled intrapleurally or given intraperitoneally. Injections are initiated at low dosage levels: 50–100 mg for pleural effusions, and 100–200 gm for peritoneal effusions. The doses are increased as tolerated by the patient for several days [see report by the Council on Drugs, *JAMA* **195**, 1139 (1966)]. According to I. Borda and M. Krant, symptoms of toxicity after intracavitary administration of this drug are usually transient and dose-related, occurring in approximately 60% of patients [*JAMA* **201**, 1049 (1967)]. According to the Council on Drugs, the most common adverse effects are *fever* and *regional pain*. Increased temperature appears 4–8 hours after administration; it usually lasts only a few hours, but has persisted for as long as 10 days. *The height and duration of the fever are dose-related.* Chest or abdominal pain often follows shortly after treatment. This is believed to be due to the inflammatory response quinacrine induces in the pleural and peritoneal serosa. Temporary dyspnea may also occur. Nausea and vomiting have been noted occasionally, and ileus has been reported following doses of 800 mg or more. Several patients experienced transient hallucinatory episodes. A single case of yellow skin pigmentation, similar to that seen in the therapy of malaria, has been observed [*JAMA* **195**, 1139 (1966)]. I. Borda and M. Krant recently reported convulsions in two patients who received dosages of quinacrine as recommended by the manufacturer. One patient was known to have brain metastases but had been free of convulsive activity prior to quinacrine instillations. The other had had no previous neural abnormality. Both patients also received corticosteroids [*JAMA* **201**, 1049 (1967)].

Caution: When quinacrine is used orally as an antimalarial, vomiting can be reduced by administering also a small dose of sodium bicarbonate. Quinacrine must be used with caution in patients with reduced ventilation or dyspnea, particularly in the presence of bilateral effusions. When used intrapleurally or intraperitoneally, pain can be controlled with analgesics. To reduce local pain and fever, small doses administered more frequently are recommended as helpful.

QUINIDINE

Of the alkaloids found in the cinchona bark (quinine, cinchonidine, cincochonine, and quinidine), quinidine is the most useful for the management of certain cardiac arrhythmias. The drug is given orally or by *very slow* intravenous injection. Side effects may include anorexia, nausea, vomiting, abdominal cramps, and diarrhea. An overdose is likely to produce cinchonism, a syndrome similar to salicylism, characterized by tinnitus, impaired hearing, blurred vision, vertigo, and occasionally by severe emotional reactions. Sensitivity reactions (pyrexia, skin eruptions, thrombocytopenic purpura, asthma, urticaria, acute hemolytic anemia) may require the substitution of another antiarrhythmic agent such as procainamide. Recently, V. S. Barzel described a patient on quinidine and digoxin therapy who developed hypoplastic anemia and agranulocytosis without thrombocytopenia [*JAMA* **201**, 325 (1967)]. Recovery followed the withdrawal of quinidine.

The observations of Bermudez support those of Holland and Klein that quinidine cardiotoxicity is largely dependent on increased potassium retention by the myocardium [*Henry Ford Hosp. Med. Bull.* **13**, 331 (1965); *Circulation Res.* **6**, 516 (1958)]. Cardiotoxicity includes varying degrees of heart block, diminished cardiac output, ventricular tachycardia, and finally ventricular fibrillation or acute ventricular asystole. Syncope, due to paroxysmal ventricular flutter or fibrillation occurred in 3 of 111 patients after quinidine therapy for supraventricular arrhythmia that had been converted to sinus rhythm by electric countershock. All patients had been digitalized before administration of quinidine. A fourth patient developed the same electrocardiographic pattern but suffered no syncope. These arrhythmias occurred with only 1.2 gm of quinidine sulfate [Castellanos, *et al., Am. J. Med. Sci.* **250**, 254 (1965)]. Three similar incidents among 16 patients treated were reported in 1965 [*Brit. Med. J.* **2**, 517], and in 1964 three of 33 patients [*Lancet* **II**, 1184]. Two patients in these three groups died.

Quinidine potentiates the neuromuscular blocking action of both nondepolarizing and depolarizing muscle relaxants. Physicians who use *d*-tubacurarine, succinylcholine, decamethonium, and gallamine concomitantly with quinidine should therefore be aware that increased or prolonged neuromuscular blockade may occur [R. D. Miller, *et al., Anesthesiology* **28**, 1036 (1967)].

Treatment: Quinidine therapy should be discontinued immediately with the onset of premature ventricular contractions or with an increase of over 50% in the duration of the QRS complex. Quinidine cardiotoxicity may be antagonized by altering the sodium gradient between the heart muscle and blood (Bermudez). Severe and progressive cardiotoxicity may be reversed by the intravenous administration of a 1 *M* solution of sodium lactate at a rate of 5-10 ml/minute [Bellet *et al., Am. J. Med. Sci.* **231**, 274 (1956); *Clin. Res.* **6**, 226 (1958)]. Bermudez's studies showed that the administration of THAM and sodium chloride proved effective in reversing the electrocardiographic manifestations of severe quinidine toxicity. He recommends the I.V. infusion of a 0.3 molar solution of THAM in normal saline at a rate of 10 ml/minute until the electrocardiogram shows improvement. This dose is approximately twice that recommended by Kaplan [*Am. J. Diseases Children* **103**, 1, 4 (1962)]. In Bermudez's opinion, administration of THAM in normal saline may prove to be more satisfactory than sodium lactate in the management of adverse cardiac reactions to quinidine.

QUININE

This is an old drug which was used extensively for antipyretic and analgesic purposes and in the treatment of malaria. A typical side effect is "cinchonism," similar to salicylism, which includes ringing in the ears, nausea, vomiting, dizziness, deafness, disturbance of vision, tachycardia, increased respiration, mental dullness, and confusion. Other effects of quinine include local anesthesia, a quinidine-like action on the heart (see Quinidine, above), inhibition of cholinesterase, a curare-like action, and a more-or-less reliable effectiveness against night cramps. Occasional side effects include urticaria, skin rash, and abortion. Recent reports call attention to the development of iris abnormalities which followed quinine-induced amblyopia. The irides showed an abnormal stromal pattern, loss of pupillary margin pigment, patchy transillumination, and nonreaction of the pupil in the areas of pigment defect. The authors point out that this toxic effect of quinine has received little attention since the first case report in 1903 [Knox *et al.*, *Arch. Ophthalmol.* **76**, 359 (1966)].

Caution: Quinine is known to have produced prolonged prothrombin time. The drug should not be given intravenously without the realization that serious adverse effects may follow, such as convulsions, coma, and death. There is suggestive evidence that quinine intake during pregnancy can cause deafness in the infant [G. C. Robinson, *Pediatrics* **32**, 115, (1963)].

RADIATION (Ionizing Radiation; Radioactivity)

The term ionizing radiation refers to electromagnetic waves, such as X rays and gamma rays, and to particulate radiation, such as alpha particles, beta particles, neutrons, and protons.

X rays and gamma rays are extremely penetrating. Alpha particles, which make up the nucleus of the helium atom, have a range of a few centimeters in air and are absorbed by the superficial layers of the skin. Beta particles usually have a range in air of a few feet and may penetrate tissues. Gloves may provide adequate shielding from beta radiation to the skin of the hands. Neutrons penetrate easily but are not readily absorbed by tissues; they produce their ionizing effect indirectly by the release of protons. Biological effects are produced by each of these types of ionizing radiation.

Ionizing radiation always produces some biological effect at the cellular level. There are no "stimulating" effects. What at first appears to be the result of stimulation is in reality a reaction to injury. All cells recover from radiation if the absorbed dose is not excessive; however, changes in the DNA of the genes may be permanent.

The basic unit of radiation exposure is the roentgen (r), and the basic unit of dose is the RAD (Radiation Absorbed Dose expressed as ergs per gram of tissue.) The average dental X-ray exposure of 5 r to the patient delivers about 0.5 RAD to the teeth and a 0.005 RAD stray radiation dose to the gonads.

Tissues differ in their susceptibility to radiation injury. The more rapidly growing and active cells are the most sensitive. These include lymphoid tissue, bone marrow, spleen, the organs of reproduction, and the lining of the gastroenteric tract. Of intermediate sensitivity are the lungs, kidney, liver, and skin. Muscle, nerve tissue, and mature bones are least sensitive.

The introduction of a radioactive isotope into the body becomes a source of internal radiation. The chemical and physical characteristics of the isotope determine the radiation effect. The physical characteristics of half-life and energy and the biological characteristics of distribution and excretion determine the absorbed dose.

Leukopenia is an early indication of excessive exposure. In fatal cases, the leukocytes may almost disappear before death. Serious effects occur within a few days after moderate or severe radiation exposure. Loss of the cells lining the intestine results in denudation of the surface with intractable loss of fluid and salts. This is frequently complicated by ulcerations, spread of infection, and bleeding. The maximum permissible dose of radiation that has no known effect is approximately 1 RAD per year total body.

Acute radiation illness has been grouped by Dunham and co-workers [*JAMA* **147**, 50 (1951)] into three classes of total body radiation severity as follows:

1. Very severe cases (1000 r or more); fatalities up to 100%.

a. First day: Malaise, nausea, and vomiting begin 1–2 hours after exposure and continue for several days or until death; prostration; rapidly developing and persistent severe leukopenia.

b. Next few days: Diarrhea and rising sustained fever.

c. Up to 2 weeks (without therapy): Delirium, and death in coma within 14 days after exposure. Purpura and epilation may appear shortly before death. A few survivors will convalesce for about 6 months. Following an exposure to 1000 r, there will be nausea and vomiting in 1–2 hours, probably with no survivors. With an exposure to 5000 r, incapacitation is almost immediate, and death will occur within 1 week.

2. Severe cases (about 600 r), fatalities about 50%.

a. First day: Nausea and vomiting usually occur a few hours after exposure but rarely persist for more than 24 hours.

b. Second day: Lymphopenia (reduction to about 800 lymphocytes per cubic millimeter).

c. Four days to 3 weeks: One or all of the following signs and symptoms may appear: malaise and easy fatigability; leukopenia, persistent lymphopenia, thrombopenia, anemia, and prolonged bleeding and increased clotting time; fluctuating leukopenia, purpura, and other hemorrhagic complications, such as melena, epistaxis, menorrhagia, and metrorrhagia; oropharyngeal lesions, diarrhea, fever, prostration; infection and breakdown of healing wounds; general sepsis.

d. Three to 6 weeks: Death occurs in 50% of untreated persons with septicemia or with hemorrhagic manifestations dominating the picture.

3. Mild to moderately severe cases (200–500r), fatalities to 20%.

a. First day: Vomiting may occur a few hours after exposure.

b. Next 2 weeks: No definite symptoms; moderate lymphopenia.

c. After 2 weeks: One or more of the following may appear: epilation (chiefly limited to the scalp), malaise, sore throat, petechiae, diarrhea, and weight loss.

More than 80% of these patients can be expected to recover. If death occurs, it is usually the result of complications, such as tuberculosis, bronchiectasis, chronic abscesses, and refractory anemia.

Treatment: Radiation "burns" and flash burns are

treated in the conventional manner for burns: simple dressings, antibiotics, and maintenance of fluid balance.

Therapy is relatively ineffective after a lethal dose of radiation. Symptomatic and supportive therapy consist of properly timed transfusions for hemorrhage and anemia, restoration of water and electrolyte balance by administration of parenteral fluids, antibiotics, and the best possible nursing care. Injection of bone marrow has been successful in some animals.

At present some degree of protection against a lethal dose of radiation may be achieved by the administration of certain drugs, or by procedures applied prior to radiation. These include the use of steroids, estradiol, cysteine, glutathione, or paraminopropiophenone, the production of partial anoxia, and the physical shielding of the spleen.

RADIUM

Radium emits alpha particles and gamma radiation. The half-life of one of the isotopes (^{226}Ra) is approximately 1600 years. After the nucleus loses an alpha particle, the radium is converted to radon, which has a half-life of almost 4 days. Even outside the body, radium is dangerous because of its gamma radiation. External exposure produces local atrophic effects as well as systemic changes similar to those produced by other sources of ionizing radiation (see Radiation, above).

After absorption, the primary biological effect of radium is due to alpha radiation. Following a prolonged latent period, osteogenic sarcoma, anemia, and lung carcinoma have been produced. Lung cancer accounted for 50–80% of all deaths among the uranium miners of Czechoslovakia and East Germany. Signs of poisoning may include spontaneous fractures without evidence of neoplasm at the site of fracture and neoplasms of the paranasal sinuses. (Dr. S. D. Clark is interested in victims of radium poisoning among dial painters and other persons who may have been exposed from 1915 to 1925. He may be contacted at the Radioactivity Center, Massachusetts Institute of Technology.)

Treatment: In case of accidental ingestion, follow the recommendations listed under Plutonium, p. 482.

RAGWEED

The pollen of many plants produces the typical hay fever syndrome in sensitized individuals. Ragweed is a most frequent offender.

Treatment: The only effective prevention is to avoid areas where ragweed grows. Air conditioners remove the pollen to a large extent. In a severe case, treatment includes the use of corticosteroids and desensitization.

RANDOX (2-Chloro-*N*,*N*-diallylacetamide)

A 35-year-old farmer was hospitalized because of marked violaceous discoloration of his severely swollen feet and associated hemorrhagic bullae, crusting, and exudative intertrigo. Similar but milder changes were present on the backs of his hands, pocket areas of each thigh, and buttocks. His history confirmed the clinical diagnosis of dermatitis due to Randox. While planting corn, he spilled the liquid concentrate on his shoes and gloves. He had continued to wear the contaminated shoes and gloves until 3–4 days before his admission, when the eruption had first developed.

In another case, a 21-year-old farmer was hospitalized with marked swelling and a violaceous discoloration of his left foot, along with similar changes noted above. Other sites having violaceous erythema without epidermal eruptive changes included pocket areas of each thigh and a band on his left wrist corresponding to his wrist watch. He had spilled Randox on his left shoe 10 days before admission and had continued to wear the contaminated shoe.

Patch tests with 1% aqueous solutions were done with all the herbicides handled in his work. Violent blistering reactions were caused by the Randox and Randox T (2-chloro-*N*,*N*-diallyacetamide with trichlorobenzyl chloride). A 4+ reaction occurred to Ramrod (2-chloro-*N*-isopropylacetanilide). All three compounds are similar in that one-half of each molecule consists of a chloroacetyl group. The difference between the compounds is in the amine half: that of Randox and Randox-T are diallylamine, and that of Ramrod is *N*-isopropylphenylamine. The chloroacetyl group in all three compounds is quite reactive [M. C. Spencer, *JAMA* **198**, 169 (1966)].

Treatment: Discontinue exposure. Further therapy is supportive and symptomatic.

RATSBANE ("Broke Back")

This is the common name of the shrub *Dichapetalum toxicarium* indigenous to Sierra Leone, Africa. It bears highly toxic fruit believed to contain a long-chain ω-fluorocarboxylic acid. See also Sodium Fluoroacetate, p. 542.

RED SQUILL

Ingestion of a toxic dose has caused severe gastroenteric distress and respiratory and circulatory disturbances.

Treatment: In case of ingestion, the induction of vomiting, thorough gastric lavage, cathartics, and fluid therapy are recommended.

REFRIGERANT GASES

A wide variety of gases may be used as refrigerants. These include ammonia, butane, dichloroethylene, ethyl chloride, isobutane, methyl chloride, methyl formate, propane, sulfur dioxide, and various chlorine-containing fluorocarbons known as freons. For toxic effects, see individual substances listed.

REJUVENATING CREAMS

Ingredients in cosmetic preparations such as orchid pollen, mink oil, turtle oil, "formula X9," placenta extract, "milk serum," or "royal jelly" are useless in rejuvenating creams.

RESCINNAMINE (Moderil)

This is a potent tranquilizer, sedative, and hypotensive agent administered in daily doses ranging from 0.25 to 0.5 mg. Side effects or signs of toxicity are similar to those observed after administration of reserpine, but are usually less severe and occur less frequently. Effects noted most frequently include: sedation, lassitude, transient nasal stuffiness, bradycardia, and diarrhea.

Caution: The drug should be used with caution in

patients having a history of peptic ulcer, in debilitated individuals, or those suffering from cardiac disorders or epilepsy.

RESERPINE (Serpasil)

This alkaloid, obtained from the roots of the shrub *Rauwolfia serpentina,* is used in the treatment of psychotic patients and in mild hypertension. Therapeutic and side effects may last for several weeks after cessation of drug therapy. An overdose may produce a parkinson-like condition and convulsions, and frequently diarrhea, dizziness, fatigue, weakness, headache, insomnia, miosis, ocular pathology [*J. Med. Soc. New Jersey* **60**, 417 (1963)], nasal stuffiness, flushing of the skin, muscular aches and pains, allergic reactions, hypotension, bradycardia or tachycardia, endocrine disturbances, hyperchlorhydria, gastroenteric hemorrhages, and exacerbation of peptic ulcer by augmenting the secretion of hydrochloric acid. The prolonged administration of reserpine significantly lowers myocardial stores of norepinephrine and depresses cardiovascular reflex responses of the human heart. Circulatory effects can be attributed solely to this depleting effect on tissue catecholamines [C. A. Chidsey *et al., New Engl. J. Med.* **269**, 653 (1963)].

Caution: In exceptional instances the parenteral administration of 1–2 mg of this drug has led to severe hypotension. It is therefore recommended that a test dose of 0.25 mg be given I.M. to determine the patient's response before instituting therapy [*New Engl. J. Med.* **268**, 309 (1963)]. The drug should not be used in depressed patients because it tends to augment the depression. In some persons use of this drug may cause systemic lupus erythematosus. Reserpine may potentiate the sedative and hypotensive effects of barbiturates; therefore, these drugs should not be administered together [F. A. Finnerty, Jr., *Am. J. Cardiol.* **17**, 652 (1966)]. Occasionally, anesthesia potentiates the hypotensive effect of reserpine.

This drug is hazardous in patients who have recently suffered strokes; a dose as low as 0.1 mg I.M. has caused severe hypotension in some of these patients [S. C. Leonberg, Jr., *et al. Ann. Internal Med.* **60**, 866 (1964)].

Treatment: Reduction of dosage will usually give relief. For the treatment of severe and unexpected extrapyramidal reactions, discontinue reserpine therapy and follow with a dose of at least 25 mg I.V. of diphenhydramine. For less severe effects 0.4–0.6 gm of diphenhydramine may be given orally [*JAMA* **177**, 665 (1961)]. Consider norepinephrine or phenylephrine if prompt restoration of arterial blood pressure is indicated (F. A. Finnerty, Jr.).

RESORCINOL

Absorption through the skin may result in dermatitis, edema, necrosis, methemoglobinemia, respiratory difficulties, convulsions, and death. Ingestion has induced similar signs of intoxication. The probable lethal oral dose for an adult is 2 gm.

Treatment: Remove thoroughly from the skin with water. If ingested, the induction of vomiting, gastric lavage, cathartics, or enemas are indicated. Further treatment is symptomatic and supportive.

RESORCINOL MONOBENZOATE (RMB)

Resorcinol monobenzoate is a slightly toxic compound when administered orally. It produces moderate skin irritation, but there is no evidence of systemic intoxication by skin absorption. The compound has caused sensitization in some individuals.

RHODAMINE B

This vegetable dye is used to color certain foods and beverages. Ingestion will result in colored urine. An adult who ingested 200 mg of this dye excreted rosy pink urine for 5 days, and a 2-year-old boy after ingesting 10 mg passed pink urine the following day [Pediatrics **36**, 134 (1965)].

Treatment: None required.

RHUBARB (*Rheum rhaponticum*)

Garden rhubarb—also known as pie plant, water plant, or garden sorrel (*Rumex acetosa*)—and Virginia creeper or American ivy (*Psedera quinquefolia*) contain oxalic acid. The concentration varies. In rhubarb, the concentration is highest in the leaves, nearly 1 %.

After some hours, ingestion of toxic quantities of plant material is likely to induce nausea and stupor, followed on the second or third day by vomiting, severe gastroenteritis, and bloody diarrhea. The prolonged illness is due to the relatively slow decomposition of the plant material. Headache, general malaise, and sommolence may also be present, whereas anuria, coma, and convulsions are noted only in severe intoxications.

Treatment: Induce vomiting. Further treatment is directed toward minimizing the local gastroenteric and systemic effects of oxalic acid. Calcium is indicated if signs of tetany and convulsions appear. This may be administered as a large volume of milk or as calcium chloride, 1–2 gm as a 5 % aqueous solution. Repeated administration of fluids is recommended to reduce precipitation and retention of calcium oxalate crystals in the renal tubules and to prevent permanent kidney damage. In a severe intoxication complicated by anuria, hemodialysis has been found to be of value.

RISTOCETIN (Spontin)

This antibiotic is a mixture of ristocetin A and B; it is active against gram-positive cocci. It is administered *only* intravenously. Side effects noted in one of twenty patients included a reduction in the number of circulating white blood cells, and diarrhea or allergic reactions such as skin rash, fever, thrombocytopenia, granulocytopenia, and pancytopenia. Side effects are not usually troublesome if the daily dose does not exceed 3 gm.

Caution: Follow therapy with frequent hematological studies. Therapy should be discontinued immediately when the white blood cell count drops below 5,000/mm³, or if the differential neutrophil count falls below 50 %. Avoid extravasation. The dose must be kept adjusted to kidney function.

RODENTICIDES

Some rodenticides commonly used against mice, roof rats, and Norway rats contain diphacinone, Fumarin, Pival, warfarin, and sodium monofluoroacetate (1080). See p. 626.

ROSIN (Colophony; Yellow Resin; Abietic Anhydride)

This substance has a low order of toxicity. A possible complication following ingestion of a large amount is the development of a bezoar. See Bezoars, p. 643.

ROTENONE

Ingestion of a toxic dose may cause gastroenteric distress and collapse. Skin contact may result in erythema. The probable lethal oral dose for an adult is 10 gm.

Treatment: Remove from the skin with water. In case of ingestion, induce vomiting or perform gastric lavage. Additional treatment, if required, is symptomatic.

"ROYAL JELLY"

Royal jelly is an innocuous secretion of the queen bee whose IQ is apparently higher than that of the consumer who uses it for its alleged miraculous effects.

RUBIDOMYCIN

This antibiotic has some therapeutic effectiveness in the treatment of acute leukemia in man. Remission should be induced by the shortest possible course of treatment. Maintenance therapy is contraindicated because of the toxic effects of the drug on the heart. The average dose before side effects are encountered ranges from 1 to 2 mg/kg/day, until a total of 6–10 mg/kg have been administered. Bone marrow aplasia occurs in a large number of patients. Toxic effects on the heart are evidenced by tachycardia which leads rapidly to terminal pulmonary edema. Death from myocardial degeneration induced by rubidomycin has occurred in about 10% of patients.

Treatment: Bone marrow aplasia commonly appears during the second week of treatment; this requires supportive therapy with antibiotics and transfusions of platelets and white cells. The alternative is to place the patient in a germ-free environment and to administer blood and platelet transfusions when necessary [leading article, *Brit. Med. J.* **1**, 587 (1967)].

RYANIA

This insecticide of botanical origin contains the alkaloid ryanodine. The probable lethal oral dose for an adult is 10 gm. For signs, symptoms, and treatment of overdose see Rotenone, p. 521.

SABADILLA

This insecticide of botanical origin contains alkaloids which produce effects similar to aconite. The probable lethal dose for an adult is 10 gm. See Aconitine, p. 72.

SACCHARIN (Gluside; Sweeta)

This sweetening agent has a low degree of toxicity even when used in maximum amount over a prolonged period of time. It has no food value. Softening of the stool has been reported following the ingestion of high doses. Ingestion of a toxic dose, which may occur if a child drinks the contents of a bottle containing a 20% solution of sodium saccharin (Sweeta), is expected to cause gastroenteric distress and possibly central excitation and motor disturbances.

Treatment: Induce vomiting; treatment otherwise is symptomatic.

SAFROLE (Sassafras Oil)

The use of safrole and oil of sassafras was voluntarily discontinued by certain food and beverage companies when it became known that these materials are weak hepatic carcinogens.

SAGROTAN

This is a mixture of chlorocresol and chloroxylenol in a saponaceous solvent. It is used as a substitute for Lysol.

A mother added "a dash of Sagrotan" to the milk in a child's bottle. The 3-month-old infant, suffering from shock, diarrhea, and vomiting, died a few hours later in the hospital. Autopsy showed slight irritation of the gastroenteric mucosa and fatty degeneration of the liver.

Treatment: See Phenol, p. 463.

SALICYLAMIDE (Salicim; Salrin; Liquiprin)

This drug is an amide of salicylic acid. Its overall properties are similar to those of aspirin; but there are reports indicating that both the analgesic and antipyretic effects of salicylamide are considerably less than those of an equivalent dose of aspirin [*Med. Letter* (Feb. 14, 1964)]. Side effects noted occasionally include dizziness, vomiting, and tachycardia. Serious reactions such as leukopenia and thrombocytopenia have been rare. The drug has no antirheumatic properties, and like acetaminophen, (unlike aspirin), it does not depress blood prothrombin.

Treatment of an overdose, See Acetylsalicylic Acid, p. 67. See also Acetaminophen, p. 61.

SALT SUBSTITUTE

Salt substitutes currently used are mixtures of monopotassium glutamate, glutamic acid, potassium chloride, and sometimes also tricalcium phosphate. See individual compounds.

SANDALWOOD OIL

The commercial oil contains the natural and synthetic products geranium bourbon and synthetic geranium oil. J. C. Starke recently described a case of dermatitis in a man who used an aftershave lotion containing this oil daily for 3 weeks. Discontinuation of use brought little or no relief; there were periodic flare-ups with each exposure to sunlight.

Treatment: Discontinue use if burning or redness of the treated area develops. Starke's patient recovered in 3 months after treatment for 10 days with three 5 mg tablets of trioxsalen (Trisoralen) per day [*Arch. Dermatol.* **96,** 62 (1967)].

SANDBOX TREE (*Hura crepitans*)

The sap of this tree, also known as monkey pistol, contains hurin and crepitan; the seeds contain a toxalbumin. The sap may cause local inflammation, edema, and blistering. Temporary blindness has followed eye contact. Ingestion of seeds or other plant material has induced intoxications similar to those caused by crabs-eye.

Treatment is the same as that described for Crabs-Eye, p. 188, and Castor Bean, p. 158.

SARIN

This is a highly toxic organic phosphate nerve gas. See Organic Phosphates, p. 438.

SAWDUST (Wood)

Lung lesions have been caused by silica dust or the grinding materials used on various types of sand papers (not by the dusts of various woods). In wood workers acute symptoms (bronchitis, emphysema) are sometimes secondary to some lung ailment. See also Wood, p. 636.

Treatment: Discontinue exposure. Treatment is supportive and symptomatic.

SCHRADAN (Octamethylpyrophosphoramide)

This is a highly toxic organic phosphate used as a systemic insecticide and for the treatment of myasthenia gravis. See Organic Phosphates, p. 438.

SCOPOLAMINE

Various proprietary sleeping tablets contain this parasympatholytic drug. Sominex contains 0.5 mg scopolamine aminoxide HBr, 50 mg methapyrilene HCl (an antihistamine), and 200 mg salicylamide. Sleep-Eze contains (per tablet) 0.125 mg. of scopolamine HBr and 25 mg of methapyrilene HCl; Sleep-Tite contains 0.25 mg of scopolamine HBr and 25 mg of methapyrilene HCl [*Clin-Alert* (Oct. 13, 1967)]. At least eight cases of attempted suicide were reported in two individuals who ingested from twelve to a "handful" of Sominex tablets. Signs and symptoms included dilatation of pupils, dry mouth, flushed skin, disturbance of speech and gait, and auditory and visual hallucinations, fever, screaming and severe disorientation, clonic convulsions, and coma [G. O. Beach *et al., New Engl. J. Med.* **270**, 1354 (1964); S. Bernstein and R. Leff, *New Engl. J. Med.* **277**, 638 (1967)]. When compared with atropine, scopolamine causes more marked stupor and delirium, but less central nervous system stimulation.

Caution: It has been stated that approximately 2% of the population over 40 years of age—well over a million persons—suffer from glaucoma and that half of these people are unaware of its presence. Since increased intraocular pressure, incipient or otherwise, does not lend itself to self determination, the effectiveness of a warning on the label that scopolamine or scopolamine aminoxide-containing sleeping tablets should not be used by persons having glaucoma or by children under 12 years of age leaves the decision to the speculation of the reader [*New Engl. J. Med.* **270**, 1354 (1964); *Clin-Alert* No. 176 (1964)].

Treatment: Evacuation of the gastroenteric contents and symptomatic treatment are indicated. See Atropine, p. 116, also Barbiturates, p. 119.

SCORPION STINGS

Scorpion stings can be painful. The sting of the *Tityus trinitatis* is sometimes fatal. The clinical picture includes pain at the site of the sting, salivation, vomiting, epigastric pain and tenderness, extrasystoles, and convulsions. In 45 cases of scorpion sting in patients aged 9–50 years, pain at the site of the sting and excessive salivation were present in 100%, vomiting in 93%, and abdominal cramps in 71%. Half of the patients had tachypnea, 38% tachycardia, and 18% bradycardia. Extrasystoles were present in 24%, drowsiness in 30%, restlessness and shock in 20%, and glycosuria in 42%. All the patients survived. C. J. Marinkelle and H. L. Stahnke, who studied over 1000 cases, found that the venom of scorpions is not highly toxic. The most common symptoms were pain, local edema, and fever 1–20 hours after the sting.

Treatment: There is no specific antidote. Treatment is therefore symptomatic. According to the above authors, antivenin and cryotherapy will probably do more harm than good. Opiates and epinephrine are contraindicated. Local pain may be alleviated with lidocaine (Xylocaine) around the site of venenation [*J. Med. Entomol.* **2**, 197 (1965)].

SEA SNAKE

There are no marine snakes in the Atlantic, but occasionally land snakes will be found swimming offshore. A true sea serpent of the family *Hydrophiidae* is found off the coast of eastern Africa and in the waters from northern Mexico to Equador. In these waters, members of the Miami Institute of Marine Science collected 71 specimens of *Pelamis platurus* [D. R. Paulson, *Sea Frontiers* **13**, 244 (1967)]. Sea snakes are most numerous in tropical regions from Japan southward. Apparently they are not vicious and seldom bite, even when handled roughly. However, accidents, when they do occur, are frequently fatal. H. L. Keegan reports on a visit to Ishigaki Island, where sea snakes were collected alive in shallow water by hand by both men and children. The snakes were killed, smoked on a rack over a slow fire, and shipped in bundles to Okinawa where they are chopped into sections, bottled for shipment to Japan and the Hawaiian Islands, and sold as a delicacy.

In sea snake poisoning, there are two outstanding anomalies: trismus, yet flaccid paresis elsewhere, and hemoglobinuria. There is no pain or local reaction at the site of the bite. The first symptom to appear is muscle pain in 30–60 minutes, followed by paresis, loss of tendon reflexes, and myoglobinuria. Death occurs in about 10% of the victims from cardiac arrest or respiratory failure. After 48 hours, death may be initiated by acute renal failure [*Med. Gen. Lab. 406*, U.S. Army Medical Command, Japan, 1960].

Treatment: There are no antivenins for sea snake bites. For symptomatic treatment, see Snakes, p. 532.

SEAWEED (Kelp)

It is well known that many Swiss and other mountain people suffer from endemic goiter, presumably because of a dietary iodine deficiency. It has been known only recently that excessive dietary intake of iodine in the form of seaweed can induce the same condition. This was reported by K. Mashimo for people who live in the coastal villages of Hokkaido, Japan [*Sci. News* **93**, 148 (1968)].

SELENIUM

Selenium salts are poorly absorbed through the skin. If ingested or inhaled, selenious acid (one of the ingredients in gun-bluing compound), selenium dioxide, the selenites, and the selinates are highly toxic. They induce a marked systemic intoxication resulting in injury to the kidney, liver, and heart muscle. Signs and symptoms of intoxication include nausea, coughing, sternal pain, pallor, gastroenteric disorders, conjunctivitis, and irritability. Absorption may be demonstrated by the presence of selenium in the urine, and by a garlic-like odor of the breath [*Med. J. Australia* **1**, 525 (1966)]. Hydrogen selenide is a highly toxic gas which injures the lungs, liver, and spleen. Wilson reported on the treatment and follow-up of 37 men who suffered accidental exposure to selenium oxide. Inhalation of the vapors induced bronchial spasms and symptoms of asphyxiation. Secondary symptoms included chills, fever, headache, and bronchitis. Pneumonitis and bilateral pulmonary consolidation appeared in 5 men within 12 hours.

The active ingredients in Selsun are sulfides of selenium. This preparation should be used only as directed; unused portions should be destroyed *promptly*. Six cases of partial hair loss in patients using Selsun have been reported. Hair loss ceased after use of Selsun was discontinued. It is significant that hair loss has also been reported in livestock suffering from chronic selenium poisoning. A 46-year-old man who used a selenium shampoo two to three times a week for 8 months developed the following signs and symptoms of toxicity: an eruption of the scalp appearing soon after initiation of treatment, followed by severe generalized tremors, perspiration, metallic taste, and garlicky breath. Discontinuation of treatment resulted in gradual recovery. In animals, selenium appears to be essential for normal liver function. For effects in sheep see *J. Range Management* **15**, 17 (1962). A diabetogenic effect of selenite in rabbits was reported by G. Danon *et al.* [*Pathol. Biol. Paris* **13**, 660 (1965)].

Treatment: After ingestion, induce vomiting, follow with gastric lavage and saline cathartics. In case of eye exposure, flush immediately and thoroughly with water. For inhalation exposure, Wilson treated his patients with oxygen by mask intermittently for 30 minutes, and inhalation of fumes from ammonia-soaked sponges. This treatment was particularly effective in patients who were treated promptly. Discontinue the use of selenium shampoos at the first sign of an undesirable local change or systemic effect. Otherwise, treatment is symptomatic. (In animal experiments, BAL was found to be ineffective.)

SEROTONIN

Serotonin (5-hydroxytryptamine; 5-HT), like norepinephrine, is released from the brain and elsewhere by reserpine. Many of the peripheral effects of 5-HT are antagonized selectively by LSD [L. S. Goodman and A. Gilman, "The Pharmacological Basis of Therapeutics," Third Ed., MacMillan, New York, 1965]. In experimental subjects toxic doses of 5-HT have induced respiratory difficulties, cyanosis, asthma, abdominal cramps, and diarrhea. Injection of large doses in experimental pregnant animals resulted in interruption of pregnancy. Lower doses induced skull, brain, eye, and other defects including abnormalities of the heart in the offspring [*Sci. News Letter* (Feb. 16, 1963)].

SESONE HERBICIDE (Sodium 2,4-Dichlorophenoxyethyl Sulfate)

This chemical is converted at the pH of the stomach to 2,4-dichlorophenoxyethanol and probably metabolized to 2,4-dichlorophenoxyacetic acid.

See 2,4-Dichlorophenoxyacetic Acid (2,4-D), p. 655.

SEVIN

This insecticide, which is not an organic phosphate, is a cholinesterase inhibitor possessing greater anticholinesterase activity against insects than against mammals. It is a wide-spectrum insecticide effective against insects that attack fruit trees, bean and cotton crops, and forests. The technical material is a slightly colored, nearly odorless crystalline solid. Its vapor pressure is less than 0.005 mm of Hg at 26°C. Dogs tolerate as much as 0.5 gm/kg without atropine sulfate, and 0.795 mg/kg with this drug.

Subcutaneous injection of Sevin into the skin of rats resulted in an LD_{50} of 1.4 gm/kg for a 25% suspension in lard. Sevin 85 S is a microfine wettable powder containing 85% active agent by weight. Four rabbits received 85 S at 5.0 gm/kg of a 50% suspension in dimethylphthalate by 24-hour covered application to the skin. No visible ill effects were observed during the 14-day period.

Six guinea pigs gained weight normally following inhalation for 4 hours of a 50% Sevin wettable powder at a concentration of 390 mg/m^3. A 25% aqueous suspension of the microfine material instilled in the rabbit eye caused no injury and 50 mg of the dust caused only traces of corneal necrosis.

Treatment: For skin and eye contact, flood affected tissues with water. In case of ingestion, induce vomiting. See the recent report in *Science* **159**, 1367, (1968).

SHALIMAR PERFUME

Application of Shalimar perfume to the denuded skin of ten volunteers followed by subsequent exposure to ultraviolet light resulted in intense local phototoxic reactions in all subjects. Burdick suggests that manufacturers of perfumes and toiletries utilize a combined stripping-irradiating technic in the evaluation of products for potential phototoxicity [*Arch. Dermatol.* **93**, 424 (1966)].

SHELLAC

Shellac is an insect (*Tachardia lacca*) secretion consisting of condensed polyhydric acids, resin, and wax dissolved in alcohols (methyl, ethyl, propyl).

See Hair Sprays, p. 300, and Alcohols, p. 81, for effects of alcohols, and Bezoars, p. 643, for complications that may arise from ingestion of shellac.

SILICA (Silicon Dioxide)

Inhalation of crystalline forms of silica (quartz, tridymite, and cristobalite) may result in silicosis, a disabling and sometimes fatal pneumoconiosis. The effects of ingestion of silica are purely mechanical.

Treatment: Positive pressure oxygen inhalation, aerosol preparations of bronchodilators (epinephrine

1:1000, phenylephrine 1:100), and the administration of antibiotics have been beneficial.

SILICATES (Potassium, Calcium, Sodium, Aluminum, Magnesium)

These are not to be confused with crystalline forms of silica which cause silicosis. Sodium silicate is "water glass," used in soaps and washing powder. Silica gel is amorphous silica. Naturally occurring silicates are clays, kieselguhr, mica, pumice, fuller's earth, bentonite, diatomaceous earth, and cement. All of these materials have a low order of toxicity on ingestion because of their insolubility. Their effects are purely mechanical, with the exception of sodium silicate, which is alkaline. For signs, symptoms, and treatment of ingestion of large doses of sodium silicate, see Sodium Hydroxide, p. 543.

SILICONE

Silicones have a low order of toxicity. No cases of human oral or cutaneous intoxication have been reported.

The use of liquid silicone as a breast enlarger is apparently widespread among certain groups of dancers and showgirls. After 1–2 years, painful tumor-like nodules frequently form in the breasts. If cancer develops, as it does in 5% of these women, it cannot be recognized early enough for effective treatment. It has been reported that the liquid silicone, which eventually forms a rubbery solid, migrates from the breasts to the chest wall or to soft tissues in the abdomen where it forms cysts. It is believed that most women who received silicone injections were treated with the industrial grade. The purified product has been used by plastic surgeons to correct facial deformities. The use of liquid silicone as a breast enlarger is illegal [*Sci. News* 93, 173 (1968)].

Treatment: If accidentally splashed into the eyes, wash the affected tissues with water for 15 minutes.

SILICONE TETRACHLORIDE (Silicon Chloride)

This compound is used to make smoke screens. It hydrolyzes readily to siliceous acid and hydrochloric acid which are irritating to the eyes and mucous membranes.

Treatment: See Hydrochloric Acid, p. 317.

SILVER

C. A. Moyer *et al.* introduced the application of 0.5% aqueous silver nitrate for the treatment of burns. This is about one-twentieth of the concentration of silver nitrate which was used 50 years ago for this purpose. For details see Treatment of Burns, p. 26.

Local contact with concentrated solutions of silver nitrate (lunar caustic) has produced irritation and ulceration as well as discoloration of the skin. Two infants sustained "permanent" eye damage due to the accidental instillation of a 30% ammoniacal silver nitrate solution in place of the 1% ophthalmic solution. The authors warn that the chance of error in dispensing such solutions may be especially great whenever dental and medical facilities share the same pharmacy, as for instance in military hospitals [R. B. Giffin, *Calif. Med.* **107**, 178 (1967)]. Cauterization of the cervix with silver nitrate may, in some instances, produce cytological changes suggestive of dysplasia. Cytological studies should be postponed 6–8 weeks following silver nitrate cautery to avoid possible misinterpretation of cellular changes seen in subsequent Papanicolaou smears [Hulka and Ison, *Am. J. Obstet. Gynecol.* **90**, 1361 (1964)].

Ingestion of silver nitrate may induce violent abdominal pain and other gastroenteric symptoms. Silver chloride, bromide, iodide, and oxide are essentially nontoxic because they are insoluble. The same is true of silver picrate (Picragol) and silver proteinate (Argyrol). Prolonged absorption of silver salts leads to blue-black pigmentation of the skin called argyria (the blue man in the circus). Low concentrations of silver ion such as are used to sterilize water are harmless.

Treatment: Remove promptly from the skin. For accidental ingestion, gastric lavage with dilute solutions of sodium chloride, followed by cathartics and demulcents are recommended. Otherwise treatment is symptomatic.

SKELLYSOLVES

These are aliphatic hydrocarbons consisting of pentanes, octanes, or mixtures of these hydrocarbons. See Petroleum Solvents or Distillates, p. 459.

SKIN: BROWN SPOTS

Some perfumes may contain photosensitizers. These ingredients, e.g. oil of bergamot, may produce increased skin pigmentation (brown spots) in the areas where the perfume was applied if the user exposes herself to the sun shortly thereafter. This type of spotty pigmentation is often referred to as "Berlocque dermatitis."

Treatment: There is no effective treatment; the pigmentation usually persists for some time.

SMOKE

Smoke, a multivaried substance, is the breakdown product of burning materials. It consists of complex acids which are irritating to the larynx, producing spasm and choking, coughing, and swallowing of smoke. Nausea and vomiting after breathing smoke is actually due to ingestion of smoke. If there has been a great concentration of smoke together with heat and flames, further irritation of the larynx and bronchial mucous membranes may take place with the development of pulmonary edema. If a fireman is brought out from a fire complaining of severe headache without nausea or vomiting, he is in all probability suffering from carbon monoxide poisoning. On the other hand, if his symptoms are nausea and vomiting he has probably ingested considerable quantities of smoke.

Treatment: Emergency tracheostomy may be necessary to provide an airway and to facilitate the removal of secretions. Oxygen is indicated for dyspnea, cyanosis, and progressive hemoconcentration. See carbon monoxide. Use antacids to treat nausea and vomiting.

SNAKES

The four "types" of poisonous snakes native to the United States are the rattlesnake, cottonmouth moccasin, copperhead moccasin, and coral snake [R. L. Ditmars, "The Reptiles of North America," p. 119. Doubleday, Garden City, New York, (1951)]. The first three have heat sensitive organs below and in front of each eye called "pits"; therefore the name pit vipers. The coral snake does not have this feature. It is estimated that between 1500 and 6680 people in the United States are bitten annually by venomous snakes [F. E. Russell, *JAMA* **177**, 903 (1961); H. M. Parrish *et al.*, *Pediatrics* **36**, 251 (1965)]. Approximately 75,000 victims in other countries die from snake venom annually. Although there are few fatalities in the United States, the morbidity resulting in loss of limbs, loss of vision, and loss of various body parts is alarming. Sixty percent of the victims are under 20 years of age and 35% are under 10 years. Ninety-seven percent of snakebites occur in the extremities. All venoms have both neurotoxic and hematoxic factors, although the ratio differs in various species (B. N. Ghosh and N. H. Sarkar, "Active Principles of Snake Venoms, Venoms," Publication No. 44, U.S. Government Printing Office, Washington, D.C., 1956). The venom glands are analogous to the human parotid salivary glands.

Diagnosis: The presence of fang marks in the skin is a diagnostic criterium. There may be only one fang puncture mark (24%), two fang punctures (65%), three (3%), four (6%), or six (2%) [Subcommittee on Snakebite, Fla. Med. Assoc., *J. Florida Med. Assoc.* **55**, 308 (1968)]. Pain is the most common symptom (in 60% of cases) with the average onset within 30 minutes, which may be only slight (40%), moderate (45%), or severe (15%). Edema usually appears within a few minutes and is progressive. The patient may become weak (10%) and dizzy (5%), with nausea (25%), vomiting (15%), sweating (5%), tingling (10%), vesiculations (90%), shock (5%), convulsions (1%), involuntary defecation and melena (1%), involuntary urination and hematuria (1%), petechiae (50%), and ecchymoses (35%). Bites by coral snakes usually do not cause immediate pain or severe local edema. If the patient becomes moribund, the pupils dilate, respiratory exchange is difficult, the pulse is hardly palpable, and unconsciousness follows. Finding the snake is a great help in the diagnosis. It is important to know that the serpent is venomous, because the treatment for a poisonous snake bite may cause complications [E. R. Ellis and R. T. Smith, *JAMA* **193**, 151 (1965)]. Treatment for venomous snake bite is divided into (a) immediate (first aid) treatment in the field, and (b) hospital therapy.

First Aid Treatment: 1. *Localize the antigen, using a flat tourniquet* applied between the bite and the heart, tight enough to impede the superficial venous and lymphatic return but not so tight as to obstruct the arterial supply or produce ischemia. The tourniquet should admit a finger beneath it easily and should *not* be removed and reapplied at short intervals because this perpetuates the spread of the venom [C. C. Snyder *et al.*, Amer. Vet. Pub. Inc., p. 253 Wheaton, Illinois, (1968)]. The patient should be calm and should not elevate his blood pressure by activity, nor accelerate his circulation with stimulant drugs. The affected area should be kept at heart level, without elevation or dependency. The victim should report to a physician or hospital as soon as feasible.

2. *Retrieve the antigen by only one linear incision through the fang marks* [C. C. Snyder and R. P. Knowles, *Consultant* (July-August 1963)], avoiding vital structures such as nerves, tendons, and large vessels. Cruciate incisions are not recommended as they macerate, cause necrosis, and harbor anaerobes [C. C. Snyder, University of Utah, personal communication]. Mechanical suction is advocated for 30 minutes, but not so strenuous as to severely traumatize the surrounding soft tissues.

3. *Neutralize the antigen* using Wyeth's polyvalent antivenin. It is disadvantageous to inject the antivenin into the snakebite area. This is the poorest route of antivenin action because of edema and slow absorption. It is also difficult to retrieve the antivenin or treat the victim if he is allergic to the antivenin. *It is permissible for a lay person to inject the antivenin intramuscularly.* (Intravenous and intra-arterial administration are discussed below). Never inject antivenin into the base of a digit because this may obliterate the vessels by pressure or by spasm and result in loss of the digit.

Hospital Treatment: 1. The emergency room nurse or physician should take a rapid *history* from the patient or friend and learn if the patient has any allergies.

2. With the tourniquet still in position, the *fang marks should be excised* 1 inch (2.5 cm) equidistant

and down to the vital structures beneath the skin [C. C. Snyder and R. P. Knowles, *Norden News* **38**, 6 (1963)].

3. If the patient is not allergic to horse serum, one vial of polyvalent antivenin should be administered *intravenously* [N. C. McCollough and J. F. Gennaro, *J. Florida Med. Assoc.* **49**, 959 (1963)], or *intra-arterially* for rapid neutralization [C. C. Snyder, *et al.* Amer. Vet. Pub. Inc., p. 259, Wheaton, Illinois (1968)] If these two methods of therapy should produce immediate allergic phenomena, the allergic reaction can be counteracted rapidly by the same route. The antivenin is diluted in 100 ml of isotonic saline to which has been added 100 mg Solu-Cortef, and given over a period of 20 minutes. C. C. Snyder favors the intra-arterial route in preference to the intravenous medication, because the antivenin neutralizes the venom faster.

If the patient has many allergies, or the skin test indicates a reaction and therefore requires desensitization, the antivenin must be adjusted to the severity of the snakebite. The initial dose given subcutaneously may be 0.1 ml of a 1:10, 1:100, or 1:1000 dilution of the antisera. Subsequent doses should be doubled and given every 15 minutes until 1 ml of undiluted serum is taken without reaction. The rest of the material is then administered subcutaneously where it may be excised if a reaction ensues.

Epinephrine 1:1000 should be available *only* for allergic or shock-type reactions. Epinephrine is synergistic with envenomation because it increases the spread of the poison and is, therefore, contraindicated as a therapeutic agent. Human antisera are available from C. C. Snyder, University of Utah, Salt Lake City. Antihistamines have also proven to be synergistic with snakebite venom and are also contraindicated [H. M. Parrish and J. E. Scatterday, *Vet. Med.* **52**, 135 (1957)].

The tourniquet should be removed if the extremity is ischemic or cyanotic, although tourniquets are left in position without complications for 2 hours if necessary. Children, because of small blood volume and venom concentration, need more antivenin than adults. If more than one vial of antivenin is necessary it may be administered without hesitation.

4. *Cryotherapy* is beneficial only when used to decrease metabolic processes in the area of the bite. A

frostbite from extensive ice application, superimposed upon a snakebite, changes a serious condition to a critical one. Therefore, cooling this inflammatory process with mild hypothermia is beneficial but to freeze it is detrimental because of local tissue damage and the increased escape of venom when the ice is removed [C. C. Snyder *et al.*, Amer. Vet. Pub. Inc., p. 257, Wheaton, Illinois (1968)].

5. *Ancillary therapy.* Steroid treatment, at one time recommended, is now believed to be of value only to counteract allergic manifestations of the horse serum antivenin [C. C. Snyder *et al.*, *J. Am. Vet. Med. Assoc.* **151**, 1635 (1967)]. Several clinicians and investigators have come to the conclusion that ACTH, cortisone, hydrocortisone, and procaine neither effect absolute recovery nor prevent tissue damage and inflammation [N. C. McCollough and J. F. Gennaro, *J. Florida Med. Assoc.* **69**, 965 (1963)]. Alcoholic beverages are contraindicated because they accelerate circulation and camouflage important symptoms when respiratory depression is present. Tetanus antitoxin or booster, antibiotics, analgesics, oxygen, transfusion, calcium, tracheostomy, fascial incisions, and hemodialysis certainly must be utilized when indications are presented [D. B. Frazier and F. H. Carler, *Calif. Med.* **97**, 177 (1962)]. All victims of venomous snakebite should be hospitalized for observation.

Finally, a word of caution for serpentologists, animal caretakers, and snake bounty hunters: with repeated snakebites, some persons develop an allergy to snake venoms, thus making subsequent bites more dangerous. At the present time, there is no permanent immunity to snake venoms [R. P. Knowles *et al.*, *Small Animal Clinician* **2**, 578 (1962); C. C. Snyder, University of Utah, Salt Lake City, personal communication].

Antivenin may be obtained from the following:

Antivenin (*Crotalidae*) Polyvalent (for bites by Crotalus, Sistrurus, Agkistrodon, Trimeresurus, and Lachesis) is available from Wyeth Laboratories, Inc., Philadelphia, Pennsylvania.

Wyeth Laboratories also produces Antivenin (*Micrurus fulvius*), which neutralizes the venoms of *M. fulvius fulvius*, and *M. fulvius tenere* (the eastern and western varieties of the North American coral snake).

This serum is supplied free of charge to physicians for the treatment of victims of *Micrurus* envenomation in the United States. Supplies are available at the National Communicable Disease Center of the U. S. Public Health Service, Atlanta, Georgia; and also from State Health Departments and Poison Control Centers in North Carolina, South Carolina, Georgia, Florida, Alabama, Mississippi, Louisiana, Texas and Arkansas. This is the only anti-coral snake serum licensed in the United States. When a coral snake-bite accident occurs within the nine-state area described, the hospital or attending physician should notify the State Health Department or the nearest Poison Control Center to arrange for an immediate supply of Antivenin (*Micrurus fulvius*). Any emergency requests for this Antivenin from outside the nine-state area must be referred directly to The National Communicable Disease Center, 1600 Clifton Road, N.E., Atlanta, Georgia [Telephone number: (404) 633-3311].

King cobra (*Ophiophagus hannah*) antivenin may be obtained from the San Diego Zoological Garden or from the Pasteur Institute, Bangkok, Thailand. At this institute the king cobra is not recognized as *O. hannah*, but as *Naja bungarus*. King cobra antivenin ordered from the Pasteur Institute should be referred to as *N. bungarus*.

The polyvalent antivenin for all African snakes is obtained from the South African Institute for Medical Research, Hospital Street, Johannesburg, South Africa, or from the Fitzsimmon's Snake Park Laboratories, Serum Department, P. O. Box 1, Snell Parade, Durban, South Africa, or from the San Diego Zoological Garden.

The antivenin for all Australian snakes, including the tiger snake is available from the Commonwealth Health Department, Commonwealth Serum Laboratories, Parkville, M.2, Victoria, Australia.

The antivenin of the Indian cobra, common krait, Russell's viper, and saw-scaled viper is available from the Haffkine Institute, King Edward's Road, Bombay 12, India.

The antivenin of the South American snakes of the *Elapidae* family may be obtained from the Instituto Butantan or C. Amaral y Cia., Box 2123, Sao Paulo, Brazil. (For further information contact: Wyeth Laboratories, Philadelphia, Pennsylvania; or C. E. Shaw,

Curator of the San Diego Zoological Garden, San Diego, 12, California.)

It is of interest to note that of 1078 cases of snakebite intoxication in which antivenin was used, there were three deaths. [*Pediatrics* **36**, 251 (1965)].

SNOW SPRAY

The "snow" is composed of an inert plastic material and a long-chain fatty acid. The preparation is harmless after the propellent has evaporated. The propellent may consist of halogenated hydrocarbons — methylene chloride and freons. See Methylene Chloride, p. 390, and Fluorocarbons, p. 275.

SOAP (Toilet Bar; Household Soap)

A true soap is a salt of a fatty acid (Na^+, K^+, Ca^{++}, Mg^{++}). Toilet soaps may contain synthetic surfactants. In general, they have a low order of toxicity. When ingested in large amounts, soap may cause gastroenteric irritation, vomiting, and diarrhea.

A. E. Ison and J. B. Tucker recently reported photosensitive dermatitis caused by a soap containing a halogenated salicylanilide. That tetrachlorsalicylanilide can induce photosensitive dermatitis has been known since 1960. In the recent incidents, 12 patients with photosensitive eruptions had histories of using certain soaps. At the time of the study, white Lifebuoy contained 3,4,5-dibromosalicylanilide; Safeguard and Zest contained 3,4,5-tribromosalicylanilide and 3,5-dibromosalicylanilide [*New Engl. J. Med.* **278**, 81 (1968)]. See also Hexachlorophene, p. 308. Antibacterial soaps should not be used routinely, since the active agent may act as a skin sensitizer. See report for use of these soaps in surgical scrub [*Med. Letter* (February 11, 1967)]. See also Bithionol, p. 135.

Treatment: In case of ingestion, give demulcents (e.g., milk); emptying the stomach is not necessary. The patients who suffered photosensitive eruptions recovered upon discontinuation of the specific soaps.

SODIUM ALCOHOLATES (Sodium Methylate; Sodium Ethylate)

The alcoholates are hygroscopic and decompose on exposure to air forming sodium hydroxide and the corresponding alcohol.

Treatment: See Sodium Hydroxide, p. 543. Ethyl Alcohol p. 249, and Methyl Alcohol p. 383.

SODIUM CHLORATE

A 35-year-old woman attempted suicide by ingesting 40 gm of sodium chlorate. She became anoxic because of intense hemolysis and methemoglobinemia. Acute renal failure followed.

Treatment: Exchange transfusions and peritoneal dialysis were used in the case described above. She recovered after prolonged oliguria [*Brit. Med. J.* 3, 601 (1967)].

SODIUM CHLORIDE

In certain areas, drinking water contains an elevated content of sodium ion which may not be detectable by taste. After the use of water softeners (zeolite, soda lime) a level of 530 mg of sodium per liter was reported in Sarasota, Florida. A high level was also reported for Alberta where two cases of recurrent heart failure improved after substitution of low sodium level water. Of 1847 community water supplies sampled for sodium content, nearly 44% had enough to warrant precautions for cardiovascular patients with diet restriction [*Mod. Med.* 32. 222 (1964)]. Hospitals often add much sodium, unwittingly, through their use of water-softener systems. There is an apparent correlation between the quantity of sodium chloride in the diet and the level of arterial blood pressure and the incidence of hypertensive disease. A high incidence of elevated blood pressure and deaths from cerebral hemorrhage coincided with the remarkably high salt intake (27 gm per day) of the natives of Northern Japan. (Animal studies suggest that genetics play a role in addition to a high sodium chloride intake.)

The sodium content in milligrams per 30 ml of certain dietetic carbonated beverages is as follows: Canada Dry black cherry, 3.0 mg; Diet Dr. Pepper, 3.6 mg; Royal Crown Diet-Rite Cola, 3.0 mg; Diet Pepsi Cola, 1.18 mg; and Coca-Cola Tab, 1.0 mg. These values are useful in fitting these beverages into a low-sodium diet [J. Wallace, *JAMA* 195, 236 (1966)].

Less than a tablespoon of sodium chloride (table salt) can severely poison an infant (extensor spasms and coma). This may result in severe brain damage or death [*New Engl. J. Med.* **263**, 1347 (1960)]. Ingestion of unknown quantities of sodium chloride by two 14-month-old twins caused hypernatremic dehydration in 36 hours. Three young women died following thera-peutic abortion induced by the intra-amniotic injec-tion of hypertonic sodium chloride solution. Post mor-tem findings indicated that the cerebral damage was probably due to excessive dehydration of the brain [Cameron and Dayan, *Brit. Med. J.* **1**, 1010 (1966)]. The use of intra-amniotic infusion of hypertonic saline was practiced in Japan for interruption of pregnancy. The success rate was 93%. This method was discarded in 1950 because of too frequent maternal fatalities. Some seventy reports have appeared on this subject, all in Japanese [T. Wagatsuma, *Am. J. Obstet. Gynecol.* **93**, 743 (1965)]. See also *Science News*, **95**, 471 (1969).

Treatment: The value of peritoneal dialysis was demonstrated by J. E. Kiley (personal communication, Albany Medical College) in the treatment of infants with severe sodium chloride poisoning. In small in-fants, peritoneal dialysis is carried out by puncturing the abdominal parietes with a needle for infusion and aspiration of dialysate.

Analysis of the water supply should be carried out from time to time to make it possible to control the in-take of sodium for those on a restricted diet. The twins responded to parenteral fluid therapy (water and electrolytes).

SODIUM DEXTROTHYROXINE (Choloxin)

D-Thyroxine was introduced for lowering serum cholesterol levels. Sodium levothyroxine U.S.P. (thyroxine), thyroid U.S.P., and other thyroid drugs also reduce cholesterol levels. The advantage claimed for D-thyroxine is that it has less metabolic activity; it is, in fact, about one-tenth as active metabolically as L-thyroxine.

Choloxin stimulates the liver to increase oxidative catabolism and excretion of cholesterol and its degra-dation products by the biliary route. Cholesterol syn-thesis is not inhibited. The initial daily P.O. dose of 1.0–2.0 mg is gradually increased. (Follow the direc-tion of the manufacturer.)

In clinical trials of the drug lasting for at least a year, reductions in cholesterol ranging from about 10–35%

were maintained in about half the patients. In many patients, cholesterol levels have reverted to pretreatment levels after several months, even with continued D-thyroxine therapy. At recommended dosage levels, D-thyroxine frequently induces or exacerbates angina, as do the thyroid preparations that are metabolically more active. Side effects noted in less than 1 % of 3000 patients included insomnia, palpitations, tremors, loss of weight, flushing, hair loss, diuresis, menstrual irregularities, gastroenteric complaints, headache, tinnitus, visual disturbances, paresthesia, skin rashes, and muscle pain. Nervousness was noted somewhat more frequently.

Caution: Patients on Choloxin therapy usually show greatly increased serum protein-bound iodine (PBI) levels. The PBI should be interpreted as evidence of hypermetabolism or be used to establish the effective dose of Choloxin. PBI values in the range of 10–25 mcg % in treated subjects are common. A few children with familial hypercholesterolemia have been treated with Choloxin for periods of 1 year or longer with no adverse effects on growth. However, it is recommended that the drug be continued in patients in this age group only if a significant serum cholesterol-lowering effect is observed. R. W. Robinson and R. J. LeBeau found that 4 mg of D-thyroxine caused a definite increase in frequency and severity of angina in 7 of 16 patients [*Circulation* **28**, 531 (1963)]. Arrhythmias and a worsening of peripheral vascular disease have also been reported. The effects of coumarin-type anticoagulants may be potentiated. In diabetic patients, blood sugar levels may rise, requiring larger doses of antidiabetic drugs. The manufacturer cautions against the use of D-thyroxine in pregnant women or nursing mothers [*Med. Letter* **9**, 103 (1968)]. See also Cholesterol, p. 175.

Contraindications include organic heart diseases, hypertensive states (other than mild systolic hypertension), advanced liver or kidney disease, pregnancy, and history of iodism. The drug should not be administered to nursing mothers.

Warning: Choloxin potentiates the effects of anticoagulants, such as warfarin or Dicumarol, or prothrombin time. Reductions of warfarin dosage by as much as 30 % have been required in some patients. Consequently, the dosage of these anticoagulants should be reduced by one-third upon initiation of Choloxin therapy and the dosage subsequently readjusted on the basis of laboratory findings. The prothrombin time of patients receiving anticoagulant therapy concomitantly with Choloxin should be determined weekly or more frequently [Flint Laboratories, *Clin. Pharmacol. Therap.* **8**, 629 (1967)].

SODIUM FLUOROACETATE (1080)

This is a highly toxic chemical. Absorption of a toxic dose will produce hyperexcitability, epileptiform convulsions, premature systoles, and ventricular fibrillation. The toxicity of sodium fluoroacetate is due to the formation of fluorocitric acid. The probable lethal oral dose for an adult is 50 mg.

Treatment: Remove from the skin by thorough washing with water. After ingestion, induce vomiting, perform gastric lavage, and administer cathartics. Do *not* use epinephrine.

Though not yet evaluated in man, monacetin at present appears to be the most promising potential antidote for fluoroacetate poisoning. Doses in man have not been established, but on the basis of monkey experiments, it is suggested that 0.1–0.5 ml/kg may be adequate. These doses should be repeated hourly for several hours, using the electrocardiogram and the clinical cardiac status as criteria of adequacy of treatment; the appearance of pulsus alternans should be prevented if possible. Undesirable side effects of monacetin include sedation, respiratory stimulation, vasodilatation, and local reaction at the site of injection. Some hemolysis may occur, but this usually has not been serious in animal experiments. Deep intramuscular injection would appear to be the route of choice.

SODIUM HYDRIDE

This is a granular, gray, flammable solid which reacts violently with water forming hydrogen and sodium hydroxide. See Sodium Hydroxide, p. 543, and Metal Hydrides, p. 376.

SODIUM HYDROXIDE

Concentrated solutions of sodium hydroxide in contact with any body surface cause irritation and necrosis. Ingestion is followed by pain in the mouth, esophagus, and gastroenteric tract, vomiting, diarrhea, collapse, and coma. Early deaths are due to hemorrhage and shock; later deaths (2–10 days) are due to aspiration pneumonia, asphyxia, edema of glottis, gangrene of the lungs, or pericarditis.

Treatment: Remove immediately from the skin or mucous membranes by flooding with water. For ingestion, perform tracheostomy if laryngeal edema occludes airway. Neutralize alkali in the stomach with liberal oral intake of diluted vinegar, lemon, or orange juice; also give demulcents such as milk, olive oil, or egg white. Do *not* give emetic nor induce vomiting. If indicated, give supportive therapy and sedation for shock. A small, well-lubricated tube is cautiously passed into the stomach and left in place for several days to permit lavage, hydration, and feeding in the event of esophageal stricture. See Removal from Alimentary Tract, p. 15. Ten children who received cortisone and antibiotics following lye ingestion had no evidence of stricture or complications [E. S. Ray and D. L. Morgan, *J. Pediat.* **49**, 394 (1956)]. For management of burns of the esophagus see *JAMA* **160**, 1447 (1956).

SODIUM HYDROXYBUTYRATE

This compound has been proposed as an agent for inducing sedation, sleep (40 mg/kg), and artificial hibernation. Toxicity appears to be of a low order.

SODIUM NITRITE

The older literature refers to a number of acute intoxications that resulted from accidental or intentional ingestion of toxic doses (0.5–2.0 gm) of sodium nitrite. The adult lethal dose is approximately 5.0 gm. Symptoms include nausea, vomiting, methemoglobin formation, collapse, loss of consciousness, and asphyxial convulsions. Most patients recovered because of proper treatment. See Nitroglycerin, p. 428. Methemoglobinemia, as a result of ingestion of nitrates in milk, has occurred in infants fed an artificial formula composed of cow's milk and condensed milk or milk powder diluted with well water. In the gastroenteric tract of the newborn, nitrates are partially or totally converted to nitrites because of the lack of acidity in gastric juice, permitting the growth of nitrate-reducing organisms.

Susceptibility to the production of methemoglobinemia is related to the age of the infant, pH of gastric contents, the concentration of nitrates in water, the boiling period of the water in preparation for use, total quantity consumed per day, number of exposure days, and the infant's general state of health.

Safe concentrations of nitrates in water have apparently not been established; there is no "official" tolerance. The U.S. Public Health Service promulgates the criterion as 10 mg/liter as N for NO_3 plus NO_2. The danger zone begins as a concentration of 40 ppm is exceeded.

The rate of conversion of methemoglobin to hemoglobin is also of importance. This conversion proceeds at a rate approximating 10–15% of the total methemoglobin in the blood per hour. It is of interest to note that normal human blood contains about 0.7% methemoglobin [A. J. Lehman, *Assoc. Food Drug Officials U. S. Quart. Bull.* **22**, 136 (1958)].

Methemoglobinemia as a result of ingestion of nitrates or nitrites in food has occurred because of the addition of excessive amounts of these compounds to meat products. In the curing process of meat the function of nitrates is to fix and to heat-stabilize the red color in meat, as follows:

$$\text{Nitrates} \xrightarrow[\text{reduce it to}]{\text{bacteria in meat}} \text{nitrites}$$

$$\text{Nitrites} + \text{hemoglobin (meat)} \longrightarrow \text{nitric oxide hemoglobin}$$

$$\text{Nitric oxide hemoglobin} \xrightarrow{\text{heat}} \text{nitric oxide hemochromogen} \\ \text{(a red pigment)}$$

An individual consuming 100 gm of corned beef containing 200 ppm of residual nitrite (the concentration permitted by federal regulations) would ingest 20 mg of nitrite. This quantity of nitrite, if all absorbed, could convert approximately 10–40 gm of hemoglobin to methemoglobin, representing 1.4–5.7% of the total blood pigment. In view of the fact that a concentration of 40% methemoglobin in the blood is necessary before compensatory mechanisms of the body are brought into play to increase the oxygen supply to the tissues, the methemoglobin contributed by 20 mg of ingested sodium nitrite is of no significance.

But, because of the low molecular weight of sodium nitrite (69) in relation to the high molecular weight of hemoglobin (64,000), only a small margin of safety exists between the amount of nitrite that is safe and that which is dangerous. The margin of safety is even more reduced when the smaller blood volume and the corresponding smaller quantity of hemoglobin in infants and children is taken into account. This has been emphasized in the recent cases of nitrite poisoning in children who consumed wieners and bologna containing nitrite greatly in excess of the 200 ppm permitted (A. J. Lehman, personal communication).

From 1959 to 1965, 15 cases of nitrite poisoning were reported in Germany which resulted from ingestion of spinach containing an excess of nitrate. Experience gained from these intoxications suggests that infants of up to 3 months of age should not receive spinach; spinach used for older infants should not contain more than 300 mg of nitrate per kilogram of fresh spinach; spinach growers should not use more than 80 kg nitrogen per hectare (2.4 acres), and prepared spinach should be kept in the refrigerator to reduce conversion of the nitrate to nitrite [Sinios and Wodsak, *Deut. Med. Wochschr.* **90**, 1856 (1965); *Clin-Alert* (June 15, 1966)]. See also Spinach, p. 551.

Treatment of an intoxication is comparatively simple. Discontinuance of ingestion of well water and contaminated meat products or spinach is rapidly effective in all but severe intoxications. In mild or moderately severe cases, ascorbic acid by mouth or intravenously reduces the recovery period to 12–24 hours. In severe cases, administer methylene blue I.V., 1–2 mg/kg as a 1% solution. Methylene blue apparently acts as a catalyst in reducing methemoglobin to hemoglobin. (Toxic doses of methylene blue produce methemoglobin.) Administration of oxygen, or oxygen containing 5% carbon dioxide, hastens the breakdown of methemoglobin. Emergency or symptomatic treatment may also include artificial respiration, transfusion with whole blood, cardiac massage, and the administration of caffeine with sodium benzoate (1 gm I.V.). See also Nitrites, p. 423, and Organic Nitrates, p. 437.

SODIUM PEROXIDE (Sodium Dioxide; Sodium Superoxide)

Sodium peroxide is a yellow-white powder that reacts with water to form hydrogen peroxide (see p. 319) and sodium hydroxide (see p. 543). It may ignite and explode in contact with organic matter or readily oxidizable substances.

Treatment: See Sodium Hydroxide, p. 543.

SODIUM SULFOBROMOPHTHALEIN (Bromsulphalein) (BSP)

The rate of elimination of this drug from the circulation after I.V. injection serves as a liver-function test. Side effects have been uncommon, or perhaps not always recognized. Since 1965, a number of reports of toxicity have appeared in the literature. S. Astin reported on 21 cases of adverse reaction, with 8 deaths. A 58-year-old man was given 350 mg in 1 minute. Five minutes later he complained of feeling hot, began to sweat profusely, and lost consciousness, with cardiac and respiratory arrest 12 minutes after the injection. Anaphylactic or allergic phenomena were not observed in this patient [*Brit. Med. J.* 2, 408 (1965)].

Treatment: Resuscitative measures applied by S. Astin resulted in spontaneous cardiac contractions and respiration after $4\frac{1}{2}$ minutes. The 58-year-old patient remained unconscious for 12 hours and then recovered completely.

Note: Patients having an allergic history are a greater risk. A patient who has previously had a BSP retention test may have become sensitized. When the test is repeated, he may have an anaphylactic reaction.

SOLANINE

This compound is a water-soluble alkaloid formed in the parts of the potato having the highest metabolic activity—under the skin and in the sprouts. The average content of solanine in potatoes is 9 mg/100 gm. The upper safe limit is 20 mg/100 gm.

Factors likely to increase the normal solanine content include exposure to light while the tubers are forming or after they have been dug, planting the potatoes near the surface of the soil and not earthing them up during growth, growing in a hot country, and damage to the tops of the growing potatoes by hail or frosts.

Symptoms of solanine intoxications appear about 8 hours after ingestion and consist of vomiting, abdominal pain, diarrhea, and general malaise. On three consecutive Sundays, four people suffered the same symptoms of food poisoning after eating cold meat with baked potatoes. On each occasion, the symptoms developed 8–9 hours after the meal. Analysis of the potatoes from the same batch showed that they contained about 50 mg % of solanine.

Solanine is water-soluble and is diffused by boiling, but not by baking. This explains why potatoes of the same batch had been eaten after boiling for some weeks in a hotel without incident [*J. Med. Soc. New Jersey* **58**, 6 (1961)].

Treatment: The patients described above recovered in 24 hours without specific treatment.

SOLDERING FUMES

The fume composition depends on the flux used and the metal surface involved. When the soldering flux is hydrochloric acid (muriatic acid) or muriatic acid "cut" with zinc to form zinc chloride, the fumes contain, in addition to water vapor, a small amount of hydrochloric acid and zinc or copper in the form of the oxide. In brazing, the flux is usually borax. The concentration of fumes is usually not high enough to injure the cornea.

Treatment: See Hydrochloric Acid, p. 317, and Metal Fumes, p. 376.

SOLOX

Solox is the trade name for a shellac solvent containing ethyl alcohol, denatured grade wood alcohol, gasoline, ethyl acetate, and methyl isobutyl ketone.

The clinical picture of intoxication by Solox ingestion is a foul odor of the breath (similar to wood alcohol with a superimposed sweetish, acetone-like overtone), acidosis, hypoglycemia, and coma. There is a peculiar extensor rigidity of the extremities, apparently related to the hypoglycemia.

Treatment: For ingestion, induce vomiting and follow with gastric lavage. Additional therapy is concerned with the control of acidosis, hypoglycemia, and the prevention of complications [W. J. Hammack, *JAMA* **165**, 24 (1957)].

SOLVENTS

This term covers a wide variety of organic chemicals belonging principally to the following classes: hydrocarbons (aliphatic, aromatic, alicyclic), alcohols, esters, ketones, ethers, and halogenated hydrocarbons. Solvents may consist of a single chemical or of a mixture of chemicals of the various types listed above.

See under categories listed above.

SOLVESSOS

Solvessos are hydrocarbon solvents containing alkylbenzenes as the major hydrocarbon component. See Toluene, p. 663.

SORBIC ACID (2,4-Hexadienoic Acid)

The antimycotic properties of this white, free-flowing powder have proved effective in protecting onions, cheeses, cakes, citrus products, salads, syrups, pickles, salad dressings, and many other products susceptible to spoilage by molds and yeast. A concentration of 0.05–0.1 %, based on the weight of the solids, is usually sufficient and is generally recognized as safe.

Sorbic acid has a very low order of toxicity. It is metabolized to carbon dioxide and water in the same manner as fatty acids normally found in foods. Sorbic acid and potassium sorbate can cause eye irritation. See p. 26.

Treatment: In case of eye contact, flush with plenty of water for 15 minutes.

SPANDEX

H. L. Joseph and H. I. Maibach, and also R. D. Carr reported a total of 19 cases of contact dermatitis from wearing brassieres or girdles containing this stretchable, synthetic fabric. Two of the six manufacturers of spandex advised that in their Lycra and Vyrene brands mercaptobenzothiazole (MBZ)—a rubber additive—is not used [*JAMA* **201**, 880 (1967); *Arch. Dermatol.* **96**, 642 (1967); *Clin-Alert* (January 12, 1968)].

SPARTEINE (Tocosamine)

In Europe, this plant alkaloid has been used for many years as an oxytocic. There have been several reports in American literature calling attention to tetanic contractions and rupturing of the uterus following I.M. use of this drug. Newton *et al.* employed sparteine sulfate for induction or stimulation of labor in 322 patients. Abnormally rapid labor ensued in one-third of these patients and was the cause of cases of fetal distress. Tetanic uterine contractions occurred in four mothers, with one fetal death, and there were four cases of abruptio placentae with one fetal death.

Caution: Newton *et al.* point out that the success or failure of sparteine treatment cannot be predicted by the patient's response to the first I.M. injection. They found the onset of action quite variable, ranging from a few minutes to hours [*Am. J. Obstet. Gynecol.* **94**, 234 (1966)].

SPARTEINE SULFATE

Sparteine sulfate is likely to have an effect on the entire autonomic nervous system, including the bundle of His. A severe case of intoxication occurred in a 4-year-old child who ingested a large dose of this compound.

Treatment: The child survived because of prompt treatment including artificial respiration, cardiac massage, massive doses of calcium, and administration of atropine [G. Landes and R. Robl, *Muench. Med. Wochschr.* **109**, 1729 (1967)].

SPERMINE

This compound (diaminopropyltetramethylenediamine), found as the phosphate in semen and animal tissues, when added to antibiotics prevents drug-resistant strains of bacteria from developing, according to M. G. Sevag and W. T. Drabble of the University of Pennsylvania, Philadelphia. This is based on laboratory studies of the effects of spermine and streptomycin, penicillin, erythromycin, tetracycline, and chloramphenicol upon three bacterial strains: *Staphylococcus aureus, Aerobacter aerogenes,* and *Escherichia coli* [Second Interscience Conference on Antimicrobial Agents and Chemotherapy, Chicago, *Mod. Med.* **31**, 76 (1963)].

SPIDER VENOM (Black Widow Spider; Brown Recluse Spider)

The symptoms resulting from the bite of *Latrodectus mactatus* (the black widow spider) are acute pain, cramps in the abdomen and legs, and a rise in blood pressure. Fatalities have been reported.

Less well known is the brown spider (*Loxosceles reclusus*), size 7–9 mm, whose bite is likely to be more lethal than that of the black widow spider. The initial pain of this brown spider is much less intense but becomes progressively more severe. Hemolysis, thrombocytopenia, and jaundice may follow. The local lesion may progress from a bleb to erythema, ecchymosis, and necrosis, ending in an eschar and ulceration [C. J. Dillaha *et al. JAMA* **188,** 33 (1964)].

Largest of the spiders and most formidable in appearance is the huge tarantula of the tropics. Its poison is not exceptionally virulent, and it is slow to attack.

Treatment: A patient with severe cramping of the trunk muscles and a history of a possible bite or sting should be put to bed immediately and given 10–20 ml of 10% calcium gluconate or lactate intravenously. Calcium neutralizes the action of the black widow spider's toxalbumin on the myoneural junctions. If the calcium solution is administered rapidly enough (2–3 ml in 10 seconds) to cause the patient to flush, or to give rise to a burning sensation in the hands or feet, genital region, or tongue and throat, and if the rate of the injection is then slowed, the pain will be completely relieved in less than 1 minute after the injection is begun. Anxiety and recurring pain may be controlled with morphine sulfate, 15-20 mg S.C. Codeine sulfate in doses of 30-60 mg or meperidine hydrochloride (Demerol) in doses of 50-100 mg may be used.

A 23-year-old male patient was treated successfully with a solution containing 400 mg of succinylcholine chloride in 500 ml of 5% dextrose in saline. Infusion was started at a rate of 30–50 drops per minute. Relief was almost instantaneous. As apnea developed, the infusion was discontinued until spontaneous respiration was resumed. The infusion was then continued for 9 hours at a rate of 10–15 drops per minute. Severe cramping pains occurred deep in thigh and abdominal muscles 2 hours after infusion was resumed. These were relieved by meperidine, atropine, and phenobarbital sodium. Chills developed on the second and third days, but there was no return of muscle spasm.

For treatment of bites by *L. reclusus*, C. J. Dillaha *et al*. recommend the I.M. injection of large doses of corticosteroids (80 mg methylprednisolone). This dose is to be repeated two or three times every other day, then reduced to 40 mg, then 20 mg, and finally 10 mg every second day for 8–10 days. Methocarbamol (Robaxin) (10.0 ml I.V.) has been found to induce immediate relief including relaxation of the tense muscles and loss of pain. This treatment may be followed with calcium gluconate I.V., and methocarbamol by mouth, 1.0 gm every 4 hours.

An immune serum is available (Merck-Sharpe and Dohme, Philadelphia, Pennsylvania). It is imperative to test the patient for hypersensitivity to horse serum before using this antivenin.

SPINACH

Fifteen cases of nitrite poisoning in infants aged 2–15 months were reported in Germany from 1959 to 1965. The principal finding was methemoglobinemia due to the nitrite formed by bacterial reduction of the nitrate in the spinach. Poisoning is possible only if the spinach eaten has contained a high proportion of nitrate, and if it has been prepared in advance and then stored for a long period at room temperature.

The nitrate content of fresh spinach, frozen spinach, and spinach canned for infants varied between 40 and 2100 mg/kg. The high amount of nitrate in spinach can be attributed to excessive use of nitrogen fertilizer. Spinach with a small amount of nitrate is harmless, since only a small amount of nitrite can form, and it can be quickly further reduced to ammonia. Even after being cooked, spinach contains enough bacilli to form nitrite. Canned spinach for infants is free from bacilli.

Treatment: Prevention is the best treatment. Spinach should not be given to infants in the first 3 months of life because at this age nitrate can be reduced in the upper parts of the gastrointestinal tract. Prepared spinach must not be kept for a long period at room temperature [C. Simon, *Lancet* I, 872 (1966)]. See Nitrites, p. 423 and Sodium Nitrite, p. 543.

SPIRONOLACTONE A (Aldactone A)

This drug, and also triamterene (Dyrenium), present a new approach to diuresis through inhibition of the adrenocortical hormone aldosterone. Frequently these drugs are administered in combination with another diuretic. Only when the excretion of potassium is relatively marked will either of these agents be useful as a single diuretic. Patients receiving spironolactone alone should be watched for hyperkalemia. Other occasional side effects noted include drowsiness, mental confusion, and skin eruptions. E. Clark recently reported reversible gynecomastia in four of seven men who took this drug in recommended doses [*Med. Letter* **7**, 105 (1965)]. These drugs are most effective when administered with thiazides (p. 170), organomercurials (p. 374), furosemide (p. 281), or ethacrynic acid (p. 244).

Treatment: See the above drugs for precautions and treatment of overdoses.

SPURGE LAUREL (Resin-Containing Plants)

When ingested, plants of this group induce local and systemic effects similar to those caused by plants of the saponin group (see p. 314). The resin-containing plants include the spurge laurel, also known as the spurge olive or dwarf bay (*Daphne* spp, particularly *D. mezereum*); pokeweed, also known as poke; inkberry or pigeon berry [*Phytolacca americana* (*P. decandra*)]; the rouge plant (*Rivina humilis*); may apple (*Podophyllum peltatum*); and iris, also known as flag (*Iris* spp).

Spurge laurel and pokeweed deserve special attention because of their local effects and systemic toxicity and the large number of intoxications caused by ingestion of parts of these plants. Skin and mucous membrane contact with the sap of these plants has resulted in erythema and blistering. Ingestion of one or two berries of spurge laurel can cause a severe intoxication in a child. The lethal adult dose is approximately twelve berries. Roots of the pokeweed (mistaken for the roots of parsnips or horseradish) have caused serious intoxications. Other parts of the plant, including the berries, have a lower degree of toxicity.

May apple intoxications have been encountered primarily during the industrial processing of various podophyllum preparations for use as cathartics and antimitotics. Skin contact has caused erythema, edema, and alopecia. (See Podophyllum Resin, p. 482).

Systemic effects from ingestion of these resin-containing plants, particularly laurel and pokeweed, may include thirst, abdominal pain, vomiting, severe bloody or watery diarrhea, hematuria, proteinuria, fever, headache, delirium, electrolyte imbalance, tremors, and sometimes convulsions.

Treatment, to be effective, must be instituted promptly and supported by good nursing care. The induction of vomiting, gastric lavage, and administration of a saline cathartic are recommended. Administer demulcents if gastroenteritis is severe and fluids and drugs for electrolyte imbalance and shock. Treatment otherwise is symptomatic and supportive.

STARCH

There are two reports of Negro women who developed severe hypochromic anemia after subsisting on a diet composed essentially of several pounds of laundry starch per day. The condition was rapidly corrected by a change of diet and the administration of iron. The anemia in these women developed as a result of menstrual iron loss without adequate replacement [S. E. Warshauer, *Southern Med. J.* **59**, 538 (1966)]. Starch powder used as dusting powder following surgery caused starch powder granulomas in two cases. Extensive granulomas involving the middle ear and mastoid followed routine stapedectomy. Radical surgery was necessary to remove the granulomas [*Arch. Otolaryngol.* **86**, 8 (1967)]. *Excessive use of powder on the hands and gloves should be avoided* [*Clin.-Alert* (Aug. 17, 1967)]. See also Talc, p. 570.

STEVIOSIDE

This crystalline compound obtained from the leaves of the Paraguayan shrub, *Stevia rebaudiana*, has been found to be about 300 times as sweet as sucrose. It has a low degree of toxicity.

STIBINE (Antimony Hydride)

This is a highly toxic gas; 10 ppm for a few hours is lethal for mice. Compare with Arsine, p. 641.

STINGRAY INJURIES (Manta or Giant Devil Ray, the Bat, and Eagle Ray)

Injuries from a stingray usually occur from stepping on the fish partially buried in a sandy or muddy bottom. When the stinger enters the tissues, the integumentary sheath which surrounds the stinging spine is ruptured, and the venom escapes. When the spine is withdrawn, the sheath may be torn, and parts of it may remain in the wound.

The injury causes excruciating pain and the wound usually bleeds freely. Systemically, there may be marked changes in the cardiovascular, respiratory, and urinary systems, with nausea, weakness, syncope, profuse perspiration, and coma. F. E. Russell *et al.* reported two deaths following stingray injury.

Treatment: F. E. Russell recommends immediate irrigation of the area with salt water and removal of the integumentary sheath. A constriction band may be applied directly above the wound. The affected part should then be submerged in *hot* water (as hot as the patient can tolerate) for 30 minutes to 1 hour. Sodium or magnesium sulfate may be added to the water. If the stinger has entered the abdominal or thoracic cavity, the patient should be hospitalized immediately, and the sheath removed by surgical means.

E. W. Huth's treatment is directed to the immediate control of pain and subsequent prevention of infection. It consists of the following treatment: (1) immediate regional block with Xylocaine; (2) opening of the puncture wound and insertion of a drain; (3) application of a neosporin or wet boric acid dressing; and (4) protection against tetanus.

Primary shock, often noted immediately following the injury, usually responds to supportive measures. When secondary shock develops due to absorbed venom, efforts should be made to maintain cardiovascular and respiratory tone. Use Demerol for the control of pain.

Caution: Since the venom of the stingray contains a potent peripheral vasoconstrictor, vasopressor drugs should not be used unless specifically indicated [F. E. Russell, *JAMA* 195, 708 (1966)].

STP (DOM) (2,5-Dimethoxy-4-methylamphetamine)

For some of the members of the "beatnik" circle,

the letters STP refer to serenity, tranquility, and peace. The compound is chemically related to amphetamine (methylphenethylamine) and to mescaline (3,4,5-trimethoxyphenethylamine) [*Chem. Eng. News* **45**, 39 (1967)]. More than a dozen persons have been hospitalized and a 23-year-old girl nearly died following an STP "trip." Effects included dry mouth, mydriasis, blurred vision, multiple images, increased pulse rate and blood pressure, hallucinations, nightmares, mania, and loss of consciousness. In a controlled study conducted by S. H. Snyder and L. Faillace, oral doses greater than 3 mg caused pronounced hallucinogenic effects lasting about 8 hours, similar to those produced by hallucinogenic doses of LSD, mescaline, and psilocybin. STP is about one-thirtieth as potent as LSD, but 100 times more potent than mescaline [*Science* **158**, 669 (1967)]. However, simultaneous oral administration of STP (10–14 mg) plus chlorpromazine (200 mg) to three subjects produced hallucinogenic effects which "appeared less pronounced than those in subjects who received the same doses without chlorpromazine." According to these authors, the effects of STP are not accentuated by chlorpromazine.

Treatment: Since some of the effects of STP are similar to those induced by anticholinergic compounds such as atropine, a parasympathetic drug, theoretically at least, might provide some relief. However, *caution* is in order since the undesirable or toxic effects of atropine and related drugs are intensified by chlorpromazine. Symptomatic and supportive therapy is recommended.

STREPTOMYCIN

Streptomycin is given I.M. or S.C., and occasionally, intrathecally, intrapleurally, intraperitoneally, or orally.

The primary toxic effect of the parenteral use of this drug is damage to the eighth cranial nerve; this may be irreversible if therapy is not discontinued promptly when vertigo or tinnitus becomes apparent. The drug may also produce disturbances of vestibular function, tinnitus, and impairment of hearing, as well as nausea, vomiting, and diarrhea.

Streptomycin is allergenic. Serum sickness, drug fever, urticaria, skin rash, contact dermatitis, and more severe allergic reactions have been produced in sensitive individuals. In isolated instances streptomycin has caused pancytopenia, thrombocytopenia, leukopenia, and anemia. (See also Blood Dyscrasias, p. 51). Streptomycin is toxic to the kidney, a problem frequently encountered when used in tuberculosis therapy. Along with neomycin, kanamycin, and the polymyxins, it has a blocking action on neuromuscular transmissions [*Brit. Med. J.* **1**, 1111 (1964)].

Caution: Unfortunately, the streptomycin-induced hearing injury is not readily detected, because the first tones lost are beyond the usual conversational range. Audiometer tests should be carried out frequently during long-term administration of this antibiotic. Since the rate of antibiotic excretion is reduced in patients suffering from renal diseases, signs or symptoms of toxicity are more likely to develop in these patients.

Treatment: According to T. W. Bellville, there is a report by Titsche that the effects of streptomycin on the vestibular apparatus can be blocked effectively by dimenhydrinate (Dramamine), and that dizziness is relieved. Cyclizine (Marezine) and meclizine (Bonine) would also probably be effective ["Drugs of Choice 1966–1967," C. V. Mosby, St. Louis, Missouri, (1966)]. See also Kanamycin, p. 341; and Neomycin, p. 418.

STROBANE

This is a chlorinated terpene hydrocarbon about half as toxic as toxaphene. See Toxaphene, p. 598.

STROPHANTHIN K

This drug is a cardiac stimulant used much the same as digitalis; it is administered only parenterally. The effects appear rather promptly but are not lasting. For precautions and treatment, see Digitalis, p. 218.

STRYCHNINE

Strychnine is extracted from the seed of *Strychnos nux vomica* and related plants. The primary effects of strychnine after absorption are on the central nervous system, principally on the motor centers of the spinal cord. The lethal oral dose for adults has been reported to range from 50 to 100 mg. The onset of signs and symptoms of an acute intoxication depends on the dose ingested and may appear in a few minutes. The individual becomes hypersusceptible to a variety of minimal external stimuli, any one of which may precipitate a severe tonic convulsion including opisthotonos. The contraction of the facial muscles is referred to as the *risus sardonicus*. The patient remains conscious and, when he suffers severe pain, is apprehensive of impending death. Periods of convulsion alternate with periods of flaccidity. Death may result during apnea of a convulsion, due to exhaustion of the central nervous system and possibly ventricular fibrillation.

Treatment is directed toward reducing external stimuli to a minimum, control of convulsions, prevention of asphyxia, elimination of the material from the gastroenteric tract, and supportive treatment. Depending on the experience and skill of the physician, convulsions may be controlled by (a) the inhalation of chloroform, (b) the I.V. injection of amobarbital (Amytal, 0.5–0.75 gm) or thiopental sodium (Pentothal, 50–75 mg), or (c) the I.V. injection of *d*-tubacurarine, 3 mg, to be repeated as needed, or succinylcholine (Anectine, 20 mg *slowly*) accompanied by effective artificial respiration. Recently, mephenesin has been recommended, particularly in a dose of 0.5–1.0 gm by *slow* I.V. injection, or in a dose of 1–3 gm by I.V. drip [*Clin. Pharmacol. Therap.* **5**, 136 (1964)].

Opiates are not recommended since they cause respiratory depression and possibly stimulation of the motor centers of the spinal cord. Gastric lavage with a solution of 1:1000 of potassium permanganate may be attempted whenever convulsions and asphyxia are under control. Further treatment is supportive, keeping in mind that the patient should be placed in an isolated area away from such disturbing stimuli as bright light, extreme temperatures, sudden noises, jarring of bed, and touch.

SUCCINIC ANHYDRIDE

This compound is readily hydrolyzed to succinic acid on contact with moisture. It has a relatively low order of toxicity, and the practical hazard from oral ingestion may be regarded as negligible. Large doses

(10 gm) of succinates produce a laxative action, but even prolonged use has no nephrotoxic effect.

Succinic anhydride is a skin and mucous membrane primary irritant. The powder is mildly irritating due to its relatively slow action. Excessive exposure may cause serious eye damage.

Treatment: For skin, eye, or mucous membrane contact, flood affected tissue with water for 15 minutes. Consult an ophthalmologist for further definitive eye treatment. In case of ingestion, induce vomiting and follow with gastric lavage. Further treatment is symptomatic.

SUCCINYLCHOLINE (Anectine; Sucostrin; Quelicin)

This compound is a peripheral-acting muscle relaxant. It depolarizes the motor end-plate, producing an initial brief period of muscle fibrillation and twitching followed by flaccid paralysis. The action of succinylcholine is brief since it is destroyed by pseudocholinesterases. The effects noted in some apparently normal subjects are excessive and prolonged and out of proportion to the decrease in plasma cholinesterase. In patients with liver disease (and low plasma cholinesterase activity), duration of action of a certain dose of succinylcholine may be increased by the factor of three [*JAMA*, **177**, 514 (1961)]. In susceptible patients, namely those with a low pseudocholinesterase activity, a small test-dose may produce potentially fatal respiratory insufficiency [*Arch. Gen. Psychiat.* **9**, 96 (1963)].

SULFAMIC ACID AND AMMONIUM SULFAMATES

The main effect of sulfamic acid is local irritation due to its acidity. Ingestion of solutions more concentrated than 10% will cause lesions of the stomach. The intact skin will be injured by concentrations of 20% or greater.

Ammonium sulfamate is neither very irritating to the skin nor very toxic, but it causes severe irritation and necrosis when 1 ml of a 50% solution is given subcutaneously. The irritant effect on the stomach is also considerably less severe than that of sulfamic acid.

Moderate doses of either chemical have no systemic toxic effects apart from their irritant action.

Sulfamic acid given by intraperitoneal injection is considerably more toxic than ammonium sulfamate. After oral administration of doses of 1.6 gm/kg, sulfamic acid was fatal to 25% of the laboratory rats dosed, whereas ammonium sulfamate caused no fatalities.

The continued oral ingestion of sulfamic acid or ammonium sulfamate by female white rats for 105 days caused an inhibition in growth rates of animals receiving concentrations of 2% in the normal diet, but produced no deleterious effect on animals receiving 1% of either compound.

A 4% solution of sulfamic acid given by subcutaneous injection to rats (2 ml), applied to the conjunctiva of rabbits (0.55 ml), or after cutaneous application in humans, was definitely irritating; ammonium sulfamate did not produce any irritation.

Circulation and respiration were not seriously affected by the compounds after intravenous injection of 100 mg/kg.

Treatment: See Phosphoric Acid, p. 472.

SULFINPYRAZONE (Anturane)

This uricosuric agent is a sulfoxide derivative of phenylbutazone. According to I. H. Krakoff, it is extremely effective and well tolerated. Three percent of patients developed a mild rash, while an occasional patient developed upper gastroenteric discomfort. In rare instances, sulfinpyrazone was found to aggravate peptic ulcers [*Clin. Pharmacol. Therap.* 8, 124 (1967)].

Caution: Considering its relationship to phenylbutazone, it may be well to use this drug cautiously until additional reports have attested to its safety.

SULFOBROMOPHTHALEIN (BSP; Bromsulphalein)

This dye is used as an I.V. test of hepatic parenchymal function in a dose of 5 mg per kilogram of body weight. As a rule, its administration is not associated with undesirable effects, except for rare incidences of fever or anaphylaxis. At least nine fatal anaphylactoid reactions have been reported [*JAMA* **202**, 238 (1967)]. Although there is no common pattern of susceptibility, persons with allergic histories are expected to be more prone to reactions.

Caution: The drug is highly irritant, therefore care must be exercised to avoid extravasation. *Very slow* injection will offer early recognition of an anaphylactic reaction. Drugs and equipment for emergency treatment should be immediately available whenever BSP is injected.

SULFOLANE

Sulfolane is the generic name for hydrogenated sulphones of butadiene (2,3,4,5-tetrahydrothiophene-1,1-dioxide, tetramethylene sulphone, dihydrobutadiene sulphone, thiolane-1,1-dioxide, and sulphoxaline).

It is an unusually inert chemical and under normal conditions does not react with acids or bases. It boils at 285°C. Sulfolane has an acute oral toxicity of 2.1 gm/kg in rats. In mice, the toxicity was found to lie between 1.9 and 2.5 gm/kg. On the skin of rats, a single dose of 3.8 gm/kg produced no apparent systemic effects although the exposure was maintained for 24 hours under cover of an impermeable dressing. Post mortem examination of animals killed by sulfolane did not reveal any specific lesion. Sulfolane appears to be free from skin irritating and sensitizing properties and is only very mildly irritating to the eyes [V. K. H. Brown *et al., Brit. J. Ind. Med.* **23**, 302 (1966)].

Treatment: For ingestion, empty the stomach by inducing vomiting. In case of skin or eye contact, flood with water.

SULFONAMIDES

Acute intoxications have been rare. Side effects are particularly frequent after the administration of sulfanilamide, sulfathiazole, and sulfapyridine. These include dizziness, skin changes, photosensitization, crystalluria, febrile reactions, and gastroenteric disturbances. Peripheral neuritis, muscular paralysis, and blood dyscrasias have also been reported, particularly for sulfanilamide. Loss of hair is common in cases of acquired sensitivity, but the ultimate prognosis is good. These drugs find little or no use today. The adverse effects of these sulfonamides are listed, since they should be kept in mind when the newer drugs of this group are administered, particularly to patients with subnormal renal function.

Broadly speaking, the sulfonamides in current use

may be divided into two groups, those that are rather soluble and more or less rapidly absorbed and excreted, and those that are slowly excreted. The first group includes: sulfaethylthiadiazole (Sul-Spansion), sulfachloropyridazine (Sonilyn), sulfathiazole, sulfadiazine, sulfamerazine, sulfamethazine, sulfisomidine (Elkosin), sulfacetamide (Sulamyd), sulfisoxazole (Gantrisin), sulfaethidole (Sul-Spansion; Sul-Spantab), and sulfamethizole (Thiosulfil). The long-acting sulfonamides include: sulfadimethoxine (Madribon; Madriqid), sulfamethoxypyridazine (Kynex: Lederkyn; Midicel; Retasulfin; also Bimez) and acetylsulfamethoxypyridazine (Kynex Acetyl; Midicel Acetyl). Sulfamethoxazole's (Gantanol) rate of absorption from the gastroenteric tract and excretion of the unconjugated drug in the urine are slower; as a result the drug is retained in the blood for a longer period.

Advantages claimed for the long-acting sulfonamides include smaller daily doses, less frequent administration, and a decreased risk of crystalluria. However, experience has shown that these drugs do not enter the cerebrospinal fluid as readily and tend to accumulate, leading to elevated blood concentrations. This effect is augmented in the presence of renal diseases. In some countries, one or all of the long-acting sulfonamides have been eliminated from their respective formularies because of the increased incidence of the Stevens-Johnson syndrome (a serious variety of erythema multiforme) which followed therapy with long-acting sulfonamides in adults and children. Sulfamethoxypyridazine has been particularly implicated, having caused several deaths [*Lancet* **II**, 593 (1964)]. During the administration of any one of the sulfonamides, the patient should be under constant supervision by the physician in order to detect early adverse effects due to hypersensitivity or direct toxicity, which may include: urticaria, rash, pruritus, nausea, vomiting, diarrhea, jaundice, cyanosis, headache, tinnitus, mental depression, dizziness, and hepatic involvement [*New Engl. J. Med.* **274**, 95 (1966)]. Only occasionally do most sulfonamides cause marked blood dyscrasias. The milder forms, particularly leukopenia, occur more frequently.

The use of a combination of sulfonamides reduces, but does not eliminate, the risk of crystalluria or injury of the renal tubules. The therapeutic effect is that of the sum of the components.

Precautions: To reduce the incidence of undesirable effects, the FDA suggests the use of short-acting sulfa drugs in preference to long-acting ones, since the former are "effective for most of the same conditions" (FDA Report on Enforcement and Compliance, January 1966, p. 15). Blood studies are useful in detecting leukopenia. Appearance of a sore throat, fever, pallor, purpura, or jaundice should be brought promptly to the attention of the physician and therapy discontinued immediately, as these signs represent the early indications of serious blood disorders. The sulfonamides as a group are contraindicated during pregnancy, in premature infants, in infants under 1 month of age, and in nursing mothers. Sulfamethoxypyridazine is teratogenic in rats and mice [*Med. J. Australia* 1, 131 (1965)]. Patients having previously responded to a sulfonamide with a hypersensitivity reaction should receive another member of this group with great caution, if at all. Hypersensitivity reactions to be considered include: drug fever, extensive dermatitis, jaundice, purpura hemorrhagica, and changes in blood cell counts.

To avoid crystalluria, individuals who take sulfonamides, and especially those living in hot climates, should adjust fluid intake to a level that will produce a urinary output of at least 2 liters in 24 hours. Alkalization of the urine increases the solubility of the sulfonamides markedly, and incidentally also supports the therapeutic effects of these drugs.

Treatment: Treatment of an overdose is symptomatic. In case of elevated blood urea or reactions due to toxicity, discontinue treatment and force fluids to eliminate the drug as rapidly as possible. In the presence of oliguria or anuria, give fluids with caution to prevent the production of edema. Except for reported fatalities following the administration of sulfamethoxypyridazine, side effects after use of newer sulfa drugs, as a rule, subside upon discontinuation of therapy.

SULFONATES

These are the metal salts (sodium, calcium, barium) of alkyl aryl sulfuric acids prepared by treating petroleum distillates with sulfuric acid (petroleum sulfonates). Molecular weights range from 200 to 600.

In general, these compounds have a low order of toxicity and are nonirritating to skin and mucous membranes.

Treatment: After ingestion of a large dose (>10 grams), induce vomiting and follow with gastric lavage.

SULFONYLUREA DRUGS

The primary mechanism for the hypoglycemic action of these drugs is the release of preformed insulin and possibly stimulation of secretion. According to S. B. Beaser, this requires at least 30% of normal functioning beta cell tissue ("Drill's Pharmacology in Medicine," 3rd Edition. McGraw-Hill, (Blakiston), New York, 1965). It has now been well established that these drugs are effective only in the adult onset stable type of diabetes, requiring 30 U (but preferably less than 20 U) of insulin a day. Chlorpropamide (Diabinese), in a dose of approximately 250 mg/day, has a therapeutic half-life of approximately 35 hours. The half-life of tolbutamide (Orinase) is about 5 hours; this drug is given in two or three doses totalling 0.5–3 gm/day. The effectiveness of acetohexamide (Dymelor), tolazamide (Tolinase) and carbutamide (Burcol) falls between the first two drugs. While knowledge of the therapeutic half-life is important, it is equally important to realize that these drugs will influence metabolic pathways as long as they, or their metabolites, remain in the body; for chlorpropamide this is in excess of 2 weeks. This factor is of particular importance when these drugs are administered to diabetics of any age who suffer also from subnormal liver or kidney function, and who are therefore unable to metabolize or excrete these drugs normally [*Ann. Internal Med.* **62**, 110 (1965)]. Symptoms of hypoglycemia, which are frequently aggravated because of erratic and unpredictable intake of food, will result. The high incidence of primary failures in patients over 80 years of age confirms these observations.

On the whole, these drugs are well tolerated in carefully selected patients. Side effects have not been alarming and have usually responded to a reduction in dose. Occasionally, more severe reactions have been encountered. Although these were noted primarily in patients treated with the drugs in longest use (tolbutamide; chlorpropamide), they may occur when any one of the sulfonylurea drugs is prescribed. Severe reactions include liver injury, leukopenia, thrombocytopenia, anemia, exfoliative dermatitis, photosensitivity, toxic ambylopia, hypoglycemia (which may simulate a cerebrovascular accident), potentiation of hemolysis (because of glucose-6-phosphate dehydrogenase erythrocytic deficiency) [G. J. Pavlic, *JAMA* **197**, 57 (1966)], hypothyroidism [G. L. Schless, *JAMA* **195**, 1073 (1966); G. Hanno and H. K. Awwad, *J. Endocrinol.* **25**, 343 (1962)], and fatal agranulocytosis. R. B. Hunton *et al.* recently reported that one-fifth of the diabetic patients treated with tolbutamide or chlorpropamide develop hypothyroidism [*Lancet* **II**, 449 (1965)]. Secondary failure of sulfonylurea therapy may result from transient metabolic or emotional stress, from infection, and after anesthesia. "Polypharmacy" is particularly hazardous to patients under sulfonylurea therapy.

Experience has shown that the sulfonylurea drugs may become ineffective, either temporarily or permanently, and that a patient refractory to one drug may respond to one of the others. The use of phenformin with a sulfonylurea drug has broadened the field of usefulness of the oral drugs used in the treatment of diabetes.

Caution: Selection of the patient is most important. The drugs, particularly chlorpropamide, should not be administered to a patient with a history of hepatic or renal dysfunction, nor to a diabetic suffering from ketoacidosis, fever, or trauma. Thiazides must be given with caution, if at all, to diabetics receiving chlorpropamide or related drugs, since these diuretics are likely to aggravate diabetes. Synergistic effects (severe hypoglycemia) have been reported after administration of some of the sulfonylurea drugs with a bacteriostatic sulfonamide, probenecid (Benemid), or phenylbutazone (Butazolidin). M. Kristensen and J. M. Hansen reported that the administration of tolbutamide and Dicumarol increased the half-life of tolbutamide to 17.5 hours [*Diabetes* **16**, 211 (1967)]. "The possibility that phenothiazine-type tranquilizers may cause jaundice or abnormal results in liver function tests should also be borne in mind when these agents are used with acetohexamide [*JAMA* **191**, 127 (1965)]."

During pregnancy, insulin *remains* the drug of choice. Changeover from insulin to an oral drug *must* be made under close medical supervision to avoid an unexpected, severe hypoglycemia.

Clin-Alert called attention to several reports which indicate that a marked variation in dissolution rates exists among eighteen commercially available brands of tolbutamide tablets (May 23, 1964). This means that when a diabetic is adjusted to a particular brand, he should not be switched to another brand without "retitration." See also Blood Dyscrasias, p. 51.

Treatment: Treatment of severe hypoglycemia involves removal of enteric contents and administration of glucose. See Insulin, p. 327. In a patient treated by Davis *et al.*, attempts to elevate blood sugar remained unsuccessful until glucagon was given in addition to glucose [*Lancet* **I**, 363 (1967)].

5-SULFOSALICYLIC ACID

5-Sulfosalicylic acid is a strong acid. As a powder, it appears to be very mildly irritating; a 25 % concentration in corn oil is classified as a moderate irritant; a 25 % aqueous solution is a moderately severe irritant, probably due to the fact that the pH of the aqueous solution is approximately 0.5. Oral ingestion studies in rats and rabbits show that the compound has a local irritant action on the intestinal tract. The oral LD_{50} in rats is 2.45 gm/kg. In rabbits the minimum lethal dose is 1.3–1.5 gm/kg.

Animal studies indicate that the compound is a severe eye irritant, capable of destroying sight unless immediate first aid measures are applied.

Treatment: See Phosphoric Acid, p. 472.

SULFUR

Ingestion of large doses of sulfur (more than 10 gm in a single dose) may induce signs of hydrogen sulfide intoxication. See Hydrogen Sulfide, p. 320.

SULFUR DIOXIDE

The vapors are highly irritating. Inhalation may induce severe respiratory difficulties and pulmonary edema. Exposure to 400 ppm for a few minutes is dangerous to life. The threshold limit is 5 ppm. Liquid sulfur dioxide is corrosive.

Treatment: Remove the victim promptly from contaminated atmosphere. Give artificial respiration and oxygen if necessary. Observe subsequently for premonitory signs of pulmonary edema. (See p. 43.)

SULFUR HEXAFLUORIDE

Pure sulfur hexafluoride is a chemically inert, extremely dense gas. In the production of sulfur hexafluoride, lower fluorides such as S_2F_{10} and SF_4 are by-products. These by-products are extremely toxic. There is an ever-present danger of contamination of sulfur hexafluoride by lower fluorides. Because of the extreme chemical inertness of sulfur hexafluoride, it has been used in some laboratories testing pulmonary function to determine the functional residual capacity as well as to help determine the diffusion capacity of the lung. This gas, or any mixture containing it, is no longer certified for use in humans.

Toxicity studies have shown that the lower fluorides of sulfur hydrolyze to form hydrofluoric acid. It is the chemical attack of hydrofluoric acid on the pulmonary membrane that accounts for the extreme acute toxicity of these compounds. SF_4 is toxic at 10 ppm and S_2F_{10} is toxic at 1 ppm.

In man, inhalation of 80% sulfur hexafluoride and 20% oxygen for 5 minutes produces peripheral tingling and a mild excitement stage with some altered hearing in most subjects. (See Fluorides, p. 270.)

SULFUR TRIOXIDE (Sulfuric Anhydride; Sulfan)

This is the highly corrosive anhydride of sulfuric acid; 1 ppm causes coughing and choking. On contact with water it forms sulfuric acid, liberating heat. It is extremely irritating and corrosive to tissue on contact.

Treatment: See Sulfur Dioxide, p. 565.

SULFURIC ACID (Oil of Vitriol; Battery Acid)

This is a nonvolatile acid which has marked corrosive action depending on the concentration. For signs, symptoms, and treatment see Phosphoric acid, p. 472.

SULFURYL CHLORIDE

This is a liquid with a pungent odor. It reacts with water to form sulfuric acid and hydrochloric acid. See Hydrochloric Acid, p. 317.

SUN RAYS (Ultraviolet Radiation)

It is common knowledge that exposure of the skin to ultraviolet radiation reduces sensitivity to subsequent exposure. Nearly everyone attributes this to the melanin pigment that appears in the skin. It is less well recognized that simultaneously there occurs hyperplasia of the epidermis, followed by thickening of the corneum. At this time, it cannot be stated "how much protection is to be attributed to the amount of melanin and how much to thickness of the corneum . . . This uncertainty is of particular interest . . . because of the general tendency to assume a close correlation between dark color of the skin and refractoriness to sunburn and skin cancer. [H. F. Blum, Conference on Sunlight and Skin Cancer, National Cancer Institute and Princeton University, March 1964]."

The peaks of maximum reactivity for erythema production in human skin were found by Ian A. Magnus to be at about 250 and 300 mμ, and to a lesser extent at 270 and 280 mμ. Animal laboratory experiments set the long wavelength for skin carcinogenesis at about 320 mμ. Wetzel, quoted by Magnus, claimed that neoplasms were not produced in mice by wavelengths 280, 289, and 297 mμ, and only a few with wavelengths 302 and 313 mμ (Conference on Sunlight and Skin Cancer, National Cancer Institute and Princeton University, March 1964).

Sunlight exposure may induce definite systemic effects including reduction of both systolic and diastolic blood pressures. After moderate total body exposure, the maximum vascular effect is noted in 24 hours. Additional effects include a decrease in serum cholesterol, and a low fasting blood sugar level with a flat dextrose tolerance curve [*JAMA* **173**, 1227 (1960)]. Lesions of the macula were reported during World War II in aircraft spotters who frequently had to gaze directly into the sun for prolonged periods.

If solar exposure is excessive some or all of the following may appear: local erythema, edema, increase in melanin pigmentation, thickening and blistering (peeling) of the skin, chills, fever, hypotension, and prostration. Repeated severe exposures contribute to early aging of the skin and to the production of skin cancer. Fair-skinned individuals are particularly sensitive. Negroes are quite resistant to skin cancers.

Prophylaxis and Treatment: Discontinue exposure at the first sign of erythema or edema. The skin should be lubricated by an emollient cream or lotion to prevent excessive drying and more severe effects. Mild or moderate sunburn needs no treatment other than an emollient cream before retiring.

For protection use an ointment containing 5% of phenyl salicylate (Salol) and 5% *p*-aminosalicylic acid. A 15% *p*-aminobenzoic acid cream has been reported to increase the minimal erythema threshold 50–100 times. J. M. Knox *et al.* showed that 10% concentrations of 3-benzoyl-4-hydroxy-6-methoxybenzenesulfonic acid and of *p*-aminobenzoic acid in vanishing cream would increase the minimal erythema dose approximately 100 times, that the benzophenones are also excellent sun screens, and that the best available commercial sun screens increase the minimal erythema threshold only four to sixfold. Certain antimalarials and psoralens have also been recommended. The protection these agents offer is not without disadvantages [Editorial, *JAMA* **195**, 577 (1966)].

"SUNTAN FROM BOTTLES"

When used extensively over large skin areas, dihydroxyacetone (DHA)-containing products have occasionally produced contact dermatitis and a significant elevation of blood sugar, especially in diabetics. Although DHA preparations are relatively harmless, they should not be used as sunburn preventives unless they contain a sunscreening agent [*Today's Health* (June, 1961); *JAMA* **174**, 2072 (1960)].

The chemical reaction between the skin and a mixture of DHA and a naphthoquinone alters the filter mechanism of the skin and effectively blocks ultraviolet radiation. It requires at least 12 hours before this effect becomes apparent. Patients with dermatitis cannot use this method, inasmuch as insufficient amounts of stratum corneum remain intact [Editorial, *JAMA* **195**, 577 (1966)].

Methoxsalen (Oxsoralen; Meloxine) appears to be effective in inducing tanning and therefore protecting against sunburn. Topical application of the drug is effective, but this has also resulted in severe cutaneous lesions. Local treatment followed by overexposure to sunlight has resulted in erythema, edema, blisters and pain. Oral administration has been used, but the effects are not predictable. Side effects noted in a few individuals included nausea, diarrhea, pruritus, restlessness, insomnia, headache, and mild depression [*J. Invest. Dermatol.* **32**, 345 (1959)]. Trioxsalen (Trisoralen) in daily oral doses of 10 mg is used to stimulate repigmentation of vitiliginous areas upon exposure to sun or ultraviolet light [AMA Council on Drugs, *JAMA* **197**, 43 (1966)].

Caution: Do not use DHA-containing products in diabetics. Discontinuation of methoxsalen treatment results in recovery from skin lesions and gastroenteric effects. During the first few days of trioxsalen therapy, patients become photosensitized and subject to more severe sunburn than they might experience under normal circumstances. Continued treatment is often required to retain the new pigment. The recommended dose should *never* be exceeded [AMA Council on Drugs, *JAMA* **197**, 43 (1966)].

SURFYNOLS

These compounds are ditertiary acetylenic glycols. They are surfactants having a low order of toxicity. See Detergents, p. 201.

SURGIBONE (Boplant)

Surgibone is a surgical reconstructive implant material prepared by processing bone or cartilage obtained from the immature bovine. It has been used successfully in such procedures as fusions, fixation of fractures, repair of bony defects, and nasal reconstructive surgery. No antigenic reactions have been reported from its use.

There are no absolute contraindications to the use of surgibone. Although it has been used without incident in patients sensitive to bovine serum, the possibility of a foreign tissue response in persons who react to either bovine or horse serum should not be overlooked [Council on Drugs, *JAMA* **195**, 951 (1966)].

SURITAL

This drug is an ultrashort-acting barbiturate; it is administered intravenously. See Barbiturates, p. 119.

SYROSINGOPINE (Singoserp)

Five milligrams of Singoserp is as effective as 1 mg of reserpine on blood pressure and general autonomic functions, and produces less marked behavioral side effects. See Reserpine, p. 518.

TABUTREX (Di-n-butyl Succinate)

This insect repellent has a low order of toxicity for rats and rabbits. On the basis of its chemical structure and animal data, a low order of toxicity is expected in humans. Large doses might produce central nervous system depression, nausea, vomiting, and transient liver and kidney injury.

Treatment: For overdose by ingestion, induce vomiting.

TALBUTAL (Lotusate)

This barbituric acid derivative is used as a sedative and hypnotic. Therapeutic doses have about the same duration of action as pentobarbital. The same precautions applicable to the use of other barbiturates should be observed with talbutal. See Barbiturates, p. 119.

TALC

Talc is the name for a specific mineral — hydrous magnesium silicate. In industry, the term talc is applied to various mixtures of a group of minerals including talc, serpentine, dolomite, and tremolite that have similar physical properties although they differ in chemical composition. Some commercial talcs contain appreciable quantities of free silica (SiO_2) which may cause silicosis.

Prolonged and heavy exposure to talc may cause pneumoconiosis. The clinical picture of talc pneumoconiosis resembles that of other chronic pulmonary diseases. The onset is insidious, with gradually increasing dyspnea. A dry cough may be present initially, but usually a chronic bronchitis develops and the cough becomes productive. Hemoptysis may also occur. As with other pulmonary diseases, cor pulmonale may appear, with eventual failure of the right ventricle. It is not known whether patients with talc pneumoconiosis have an increased susceptibility to tuberculosis.

Talcum powder aspiration caused the death of a 2-year-old child in 20 hours. Pathological changes included acute bronchitis, bronchiolitis, and obliteration of the medium-sized and small bronchi. Talcum powder containers in the hands of small children are potentially dangerous [*New Engl. J. Med.* **226**, 36 (1962)].

Surgical glove talc can cause granulomas in various intestinal and pelvic organs. In the skin, localized silica granulomas due to glove talc have been observed in surgical scars and as the result of the impregnation of the skin by siliceous particles, such as glass or sand, following an injury. Extensive talc granulomas of the skin have not been reported.

Treatment: There is no specific treatment for talc pneumoconiosis. Control of the frequently superimposed acute and chronic pulmonary infections presents the major problem in the medical care of these patients.

TALL OIL

Tall oil is a mixture of fatty acids and resin acids. The tall oil fatty acids usually contain a minimum of 90% fatty acids with the remainder as resin acids and unsaponifible matter. The fatty acids of tall oil consist of a mixture of linoleic, oleic, and saturated acids. The linoleic occurs in both the conjugated and nonconjugated state. The saturated fatty acids are mainly palmitic, but include minor quantities of stearic, lignoceric, and cerotic acids. See Acids, Fatty, p. 71.

Treatment: None required.

TANNIC ACID

The oral LD_{50} of tannic acid for the albino rat is 2.26 gm/kg. The immediate cause of death is respiratory failure preceded by convulsions when death occurs early, and by hypothermic cachexia when death is delayed. Death is associated with a progressively developing hepatic necrosis and nephritis and a temporary acute gastroenteritis [E. M. Boyd *et al., Can. Med. Assoc. J.* **92**, 1292 (1965)].

In death following the treatment of severe burns with tannic acid, there is a characteristic post mortem picture in the liver — a centrilobular necrosis with polymorph infiltration clearly differing from that of virus hepatitis. Similar lesions can be produced in rat livers by the subcutaneous injection of tannic acid. Tannic acid and sodium tannate were fatal to mice and guinea pigs when given intravenously in a dose of 40 mg/kg. Hepatic necrosis, cirrhosis, hepatoma, and cholangioma have been produced in the livers of young albino rats injected subcutaneously with tannic acid over periods of up to 300 days.

Three patients died after one or two preparatory saline enemas containing 0.75% tannic acid. Vomiting began within a few hours, followed by abdominal pain, coma, and death. Necropsy showed typical liver necrosis and a grossly intact colonic mucosa. Experiments in rats and dogs suggest that tannic acid is absorbed through the intact bowel mucosa.

More effective radiographic examination of the colon is possible if tannic acid is added to a barium enema. Provided that it is not used in a cleansing enema, it may be reasonable to use 1–1.5% in the barium enema. Its use is followed by prompt evacuation of most of the colonic contents, so that little is left to be absorbed [*Lancet* **II**, 34 (1966)].

TAR ACIDS (Coal Tar Acids)

Chemically these are phenols; see Phenol, p. 463, and Alkylphenols, p. 84.

TAR BASES

These consist of pyridine and alkyl pyridines such as methyl pyridines (picolines), dimethyl pyridines (lutidines), and methyl ethyl pyridines (collidines). See Pyridine, p. 506.

TATTOOING

In sensitive individuals, one or several of the pigments used in tattooing have caused local edema, papules, and severe pruritus. Pigments used may include the following: titanium dioxide (white), ferric oxide (yellow), mercuric sulfide (cinnabar) (red), cobalt (blue), iron oxide or carbon (black), and chromium oxide (green). In 15 men, pruritus and nodular or wart-like growths limited to red tattoos — were noted after exposure of the tattooed areas to the sun.

Reproduction of the lesions and a sarcoid-like response was accomplished in mice tattooed with commercial red tattoo pigment only after sun exposure [N. Goldstein, *Ann. Internal Med.* **67**, 984 (1967)].

Treatment: Surgical excision may be required to relieve the edema and to remove the papules. For less severe reactions apply a warm solution of boric acid followed by a zinc oxide ointment, and administer an antihistamine. Avoid direct exposure of tattooed areas to sunlight.

TDE [1,1-Dichloro-2,2-bis(*p*-chlorophenyl)ethane]

This compound is similar to Methoxychlor; see Chlorinated Hydrocarbons, p. 648.

TEA

Tea consists of the dried leaves of *Thea sinensis*. It contains 2–3% caffeine, 1–30% tannin, and traces of theobromine, theophylline, xanthine, adenine, and volatile oils. A cup of tea prepared from 5.0 gm of leaves contains about 60 ml of caffeine.

Excessive ingestion of tea may interfere with digestion and cause gastroenteric distress because of the coagulant action of tannates on proteins. In addition, tannates, because of their astringent action, will lessen gastric secretion, retard absorption, and promote constipation.

According to animal studies, tea — in contrast to coffee — does not increase cholesterol and triglyceride levels; however, other reports indicate that the effects of tea and coffee in elevating blood fat levels in man are very similar (B. Zeitlin, Private Communication). See also Caffeine, p. 147.

TEAK

This is one of the tropical wood species capable of inducing contact eczema. Teak dust will act as a primary irritant, particularly if moistened with water. Workers heavily exposed to this dust may become sensitized. See also Wood, p. 636.

Treatment: Remove teak dust by thorough washing with soap and water. Recovery is complete after removal from the site of exposure. Individuals with predisposing skin conditions should not be employed.

TEAR GASES

The gases used for this purpose are chloraceto-phenone, chloroacetylenone, bromoacetone, ethyl-bromoacetate, bromomethylethylketone, and bromo-benzylcyanide.

A direct blast of tear gas into the eyes may cause severe ocular injury or blindness [*JAMA* **203**, 808 (1968)].

Treatment: Flood eyes with water for at least 15 minutes.

TEFLON

When Teflon (polytetrafluoroethylene) is heated above 300°C., vapors are liberated which are toxic when inhaled. An epidemic of polymer-fume fever (similar to metal-fume fever) involved 36 of 61 employees in one industry over a 90-day period. Several hours after exposure to the products of Teflon pyrolysis, those affected demonstrated the classic influenza-like ("flu") syndrome, with shortness of breath, tightness of chest, malaise, headache, cough, chills, and temperature up to 40°C (104°F). The breakdown products are higher-chain fluorocarbons, the most toxic being isooctafluorobutylene.

Polytetrafluoroethylene is marketed under the trade names of Cadco, Chemelac 300, Chemlon, Fluon, Fluorocomps, Fluoroflex-T, Fluoroplast, Fluorosint, Hostaflon TF, and Polypenco. A close chemical relative, polychlorotrifluorethylene, is also used for somewhat similar purposes and must be regarded as equally toxic under the same conditions. This material is marketed under the trade names of Chemelec 500, Exon, Fiberfil, Fluoroflex-C, Fluron, Fluran, Hostaflon C and Kel-F.

In industry, exposure is preventable by observing certain precautions, namely, (1) adequate ventilation – no recirculation of air in the work area; (2) *no smoking* during working hours, and removal of cigarettes, tobacco, or pipes from working clothes to avoid contamination of tobacco by settling dust or chips which could subsequently be absorbed by inhalation or ingestion; (3) washing hands before eating or smoking; (4) special protection for workers who must use hot-air guns, since such guns have heating elements that reach temperatures considerably above 300°C [C. E. Lewis and G. R. Kerby, *JAMA* **191**, 375 (1965)]. Teflon-covered kitchen utensils provide no danger to the cook, since the maximum temperatures reached in cooking various foods in these pans is between 130 and 195°C. The scorching temperature or smoke point of cooking oils is approximately 200°C, well below the decomposition range of Teflon [Editorial, *JAMA* **191**, 406 (1965)].

Treatment: Polymer-fume fever, like metal-fume fever, is self limiting. A person affected recovers without treatment in approximately 24 hours, *providing* he is removed from the site of exposure. Prolonged exposure to fluorocarbons is likely to induce severe respiratory distress and X-ray symptoms suggestive of pulmonary edema. Such a person requires rest, possibly oxygen, and corticotropin (ACTH) [*New Engl. J. Med.* **271**, 360 (1964)]. Individuals with a past history of hay fever, asthma, or pulmonary disease should avoid exposure to fluorocarbons.

TEFLURANE

Cardiac arrhythmias have been reported in *all* investigations in which teflurane was used as an inhalation anesthetic. There is also one instance involving cardiac arrest in a 45-year-old woman who underwent surgery in the "head up" position to promote deliberate hypotension.

Caution: Epinephrine, norepinephrine, and other vasopressors should *not* be used in conjunction with teflurane anesthesia. These drugs add to the cardiac irritability of teflurane since they tend to induce severe cardiac irregularities [A. B. Dobkin and J. Po-Giok Su, *Clin. Pharacol. Therap.* **7**, 648 (1966)].

TELLURIUM

The effects of tellurium are similar to those induced by salts of arsenic. Absorption imparts a persistent garlic-like odor (due to methyl telluride) to the breath. In addition, there may be nausea, suppression of perspiration, a metallic taste, and somnolence. More severe effects apparently have not been reported in man. In animals, toxic doses of tellurium produce respiratory difficulties, tremors, and convulsions.

Treatment is symptomatic. No specific antidote is known [M. L. Andur, *Occupational Med.* **3**, 386 (1949); *AMA Arch. Ind. Health* **17**, 665 (1958)].

TEREPHTHALOYL CHLORIDE

The acute oral LD_{50} of terephthaloyl chloride for male albino rats is higher than 3.16 gm/kg. The dermal LD_{50} for albino rabbits is higher than 3.16 gm/kg. A single application of the moistened form of terephthaloyl chloride appeared to be poorly absorbed and produced a moderate degree of dermal irritation. There were mild signs of systemic toxicity from percutaneous absorption at the highest dosage level tested.

A single application of 3.0 mg of terephthaloyl chloride to the eyes of albino rabbits produced a moderate degree of irritation, which diminished in intensity; in two of the animals, the eye irritation did not subside completely during an observation period of 7 days. There was no evidence of systemic toxicity from mucous membrane absorption.

Treatment: In case of ingestion induce vomiting. For eye or skin contact, flood the affected areas with water.

TESTOSTERONE

Testosterone is used as a drug in males who suffer from deficiency or absence of this hormone. In boys, side effects may include excessive growth and distribution of hair, growth of external genitalia, change in the voice, and other effects. In high doses, testosterone causes a growth spurt initially, followed by epiphyseal closure resulting in short stature.

In the female, testosterone and related drugs in mild doses have been used for the treatment of breast cancer and dysmenorrhea. Signs of toxicity may include a general masculinizing action leading to hirsutism and deepening and hoarseness of the voice, increase in body weight, flushing of the face or acne, alopecia, and increase in libido. Fluid retention and edema may also occur. Acute intoxications have apparently not been reported.

Treatment: Reduce the dose or discontinue treatment when side effects appear.

TETRACAINE (Pontocaine)

Like all drugs, this local anesthetic must be used in proper dosage. It is rapidly absorbed from mucous membranes, and local overdoses are likely to induce central nervous system stimulation. Ewert recommends that tetracaine hydrochloride (2%) should not be used for surface anesthesia of the respiratory tract, since he found it to cause immediate and complete cessation of ciliary action and flow of mucus. Lidocaine (Xylocaine, 4%) did not have this effect [*Ann. Otol. Rhinol. Laryngol.* **76**, 359 (1967)].

1,1,2,2-TETRACHLOR-1,2-DIFLUOROETHANE AND 1,1,1,2-TETRACHLORO-2,2-DIFLUOROETHANE

Animal exposures showed that these compounds have a low order of oral, dermal, and inhalation toxicity. The symmetric isomer (1,1,2,2) is mildly irritating to rabbit eyes and guinea pig skin. It is not a sensitizer for guinea pig skin. Repeated 4-hour exposures of rats to 3000 ppm for 10 days had slight effects on weight and nervous functions, but no significant pathological changes. Thirty 6-hour exposures of rats, mice, guinea pigs, and rabbits to 1000 ppm produced no toxic signs. Rat hematology revealed slight leukopenia. Slight liver changes were observed histologically in rats. Industrial atmospheric levels of either isomer should not exceed 500 ppm [J. W. Clayton *et al.*, *Am. Ind. Hyg. Ass. J.* **27**, 332 (1966)].

TETRACHLOROETHANE (Acetylene Tetrachloride)

Inhalation, ingestion, or percutaneous absorption of a toxic dose will induce gastroenteric distress, tremors, and convulsions, followed by central nervous system depression of long duration and progressive injury to the liver and kidney. This compound is more toxic than carbon tetrachloride. See p. 155.

Treatment: Remove the individual promptly from the site of exposure. If breathing has stopped give artificial respiration and oxygen. For an oral intoxication, induce vomiting and follow with gastric lavage, saline cathartics. A high-carbohydrate, high-protein, low-fat diet is recommended.

TETRACHLOROETHYLENE (Perchlorethylene; Perclene; Ethylene Tetrachloride; "Perk")

Narcotic effects may be observed at concentrations in excess of 200 ppm. Permanent injury to the nervous system and symptoms of pulmonary edema have been reported from exposure to high concentrations of tetrachloroethylene. Liver injury in men operating tetrachloroethylene degreasers has also been reported.

Treatment: See Chlorinated Hydrocarbons, p. 648.

TETRACYCLINES

Tetracycline Hydrochloride (Achromycin; Tetracyn; Polycycline; Steclin, etc); Tetracycline Phosphate Complex Hydrochloride (Panmycin; Sumycin); Chlortetracycline Hydrochloride (Aureomycin); Oxytetracycline Hydrochloride (Terramycin); Demethylchlortetracycline Hydrochloride (Declomycin); Rolitetracycline Nitrate (Tetriv; Tetrim); Methacycline Hydrochloride (Rondomycin); Doxycycline (Vibramycin)

Because of the high incidence of penicllin reactions, the tetracyclines have been the most commonly used antibiotics for minor infections. They usually are given orally, although I.V. and I.M. administration is not infrequent. The most common side effects noted after oral administration include nausea, vomiting, diarrhea, and candidiasis; but polyuria, polydipsia, glossitis, urticaria, and skin rash are also occasionally produced. Large residues remaining in the gastroenteric tract occasionally will be responsible for secondary infections (overgrowth by tetracycline-resistant bacteria or fungi) resulting from the alteration of the normal bacterial flora.

Of significance was the discovery that these substances, particularly demethylchlortetracycline, chelate with the minerals in the bones and teeth. When given to growing children or animals, they are permanently incorporated in these structures. This results in discoloration, and in severe cases, in deformities. In infants, enamel hypoplasia and retarded skeletal growth can occur. These effects are most marked when the tetracyclines are administered during pregnancy or during the neonatal period.

The tetracyclines accumulate in the skin and nails. No doubt this is the basis for the usefulness of these compounds in the therapy of acne. As a result, after prolonged administration of these drugs, photodermatitis and nail changes may occur. Sunburn and occasionally hyperpigmentation follow if these patients are exposed to sunlight. These reversible effects occur, in some degree, in 10–20 % of patients receiving a tetracycline for a period in excess of the usual 4–5 day course of treatment [H. Stork, *Arch. Dermatol.* **91**, 46 (1965)]. Nine of 10 healthy volunteers given Declomycin (600 mg/day for 1 week) and subsequently exposed to intensive sunlight for 5 hours had photosensitive eruptions within 48 hours. Only 2 of a group of 10 volunteers given doxycycline (200 mg/day for 1 week) reacted abnormally to sunlight [H. Blank *et al., Arch Dermatol.* **97**, 1 (1968)].

Intravenous or I.M. administration of the tetracyclines has frequently resulted in varying degrees of fatty infiltration and jaundice. These effects are rare following oral administration. The tetracyclines have a low order of antigenicity; and allergic reactions, while they do occur, are rare.

Caution: Tetracyclines should not be administered to pregnant women or to the newborn. Administration of tetracyclines to growing children should be of limited duration and only when specifically indicated. Since these drugs are bacteriostatic and will not prevent the subsequent occurrence of rheumatic fever, they should not be used to treat streptococcal throat infections in children. The use of these drugs to treat undiagnosed throat infections in children is not recommended.

When necessary, soluble tetracycline preparations may be given I.M. or I.V., but with caution. The adult oral dose of most of the tetracyclines is 250 mg, four times daily (children: 25 mg/kg daily). The adult dose should not exceed 2.0 gm/day unless the serum concentration is monitored. The dose should be reduced if the concentration exceeds 15 mg per milliliter of serum. The dose should be reduced to one-half or one-quarter in the presence of renal disease and the serum concentration should be maintained well below 15 mg/ml [H. F. Dowering and M. H. Lepper, *JAMA* **188**, 307 (1964)]. To reduce or to avoid nephrotoxic effects, tetracycline hydrochloride and related compounds should not be used if they are outdated or degraded [C. M. Kunin, *JAMA* **202**, 204 (1967)].

The tetracyclines have been shown to interfere with

vitamin K synthesis thereby causing a delay in blood coagulation. Caution is in order in patients receiving certain anticoagulants since the effects may be potentiated by tetracyclines. Patients receiving a tetracycline, particularly demethylchlortetracycline, should avoid direct sunlight [H. Blank *et al.*, *Arch Dermatol.* **97**, 1 (1968)].

TETRAETHYL LEAD (TEL)

This is a highly hazardous, toxic, volatile lead compound. For further details see Lead, p. 347.

TETRAFLUOROHYDRAZINE (N_2F_4)

This is a highly toxic chemical causing pulmonary edema at low vapor concentrations. The approximate lethal concentration for rats (4-hour exposure) is 50 ppm. Kidney injury was also observed at 50–90 ppm and extramedullary hemopoiesis at 25–50 ppm.

Treatment: Discontinue exposure. Treat for pulmonary irritation and pulmonary edema. See Nitrogen Oxides, p. 426.

TETRAHYDROFURAN (THF; Tetramethylene Oxide; Diethylene Oxide)

Liquid THF applied to the skin of 196 persons was found to be essentially nonirritating. Repeated exposure will dehydrate and delipidize the skin and cause dermatitis. Anesthesia is produced at concentrations of 25,000 ppm. Deep narcosis is produced at 60,000 ppm.

Treatment: See Ethers, p. 247.

TETRAHYDROZOLINE (Tyzine; Visine)

This is a potent sympathomimetic drug closely related in action to naphazoline. Therapeutic doses cause a prolonged decongestant effect. Coma and shock have resulted from improper use. Instillation of six drops into the nose of an 8-month-old child induced within 10 minutes, coma, contracted pupils, bradycardia, and Biot's respiration.

Caution: Use the drug only as recommended. A concentration of 0.1 % should *never* be given to infants or children under 6 years; for these patients, 1–3 drops of a 0.05% solution may be instilled in each nostril at intervals of not less than 4–6 hours.

TETRALIN (Tetrahydronaphthalene)

The vapors of these hydrocarbons are irritating to the eyes and mucous membranes and cause nausea, headache, and drowsiness if inhaled in sufficiently large quantities.

Treatment: See Naphthalene, p. 416.

TETRANITROMETHANE

Tetranitromethane is a faintly yellow mobile liquid with a pungent odor similar to the oxides of nitrogen. The inhalation of tetranitromethane causes severe irritation to the lungs and mucous membranes. Human exposure data are limited to the simultaneous exposure to TNT and to the tetranitromethane impurities in munitions manufacture. Light cases of poisoning caused dizziness, dyspnea, pain, and oppression in the chest, associated with scratchy throat, cough, burning eyes, and occasionally skin irritation. Prolonged exposure affects the heart and the nervous system.

Tetranitromethane is a corrosive chemical similar to nitrous acid. Skin absorption is unlikely because of its reactivity with skin surfaces as indicated by the formation of pigmented areas.

Tetranitromethane causes conjunctival inflammation, ulceration, and in more severe contacts, pupillary changes and paralysis of the eye muscles, as well as severe burns.

Treatment: Remove the exposed individual immediately from the contaminated atmosphere, give artificial respiration and oxygen if necessary, and observe for signs and symptoms of pulmonary edema. Contaminated skin or the eyes should be rinsed immediately with copious amounts of running water for 15 minutes. Consult an ophthalmologist for further treatment of eye injury.

TETRAPROPENYLSUCCINIC ANHYDRIDE (TPSA)

Tetrapropenylsuccinic anhydride has an oral LD_{50} of 2.55 gm/kg in rats. Although it is not readily absorbed through the skin, the percutaneous lethal dose ranges from 6.2 to 7.5 gm/kg in rabbits.

Treatment: Acetic Acid, p. 63.

THALIDOMIDE (Distaval; Softenon; Contergan)

This sedative was believed to have a wide margin of safety until reports appeared in the European literature of congenital malformations (phocomelia) in infants born to mothers who had received the drug during pregnancy. Absence or deformities of the extremities and maldevelopment of the viscera were the principal effects. In many instances the damage was done before the woman knew she was pregnant.

The courts of Great Britain approved a judgment against the British manufacturers of thalidomide. The manufacturers must pay damages to sixty-two children born deformed because their mothers took the drug. The amount of damages has not been reported but it is said to be quite substantial [*JAMA* **203**, 1085 (1968)].

THALLIUM

The accidental ingestion of inorganic salts of thallium has induced prompt and severe gastroenteritis, including vomiting, colic, and constipation, followed by respiratory difficulties, tremors, convulsions, motor weakness, polyneuritis, muscular paralysis, loss of hair (head, eyebrows, axilla), loss of nails, and peeling of the skin of the feet. A dose of 0.2 gm may be lethal unless treatment is started promptly. In some intoxications in small children, loss of hair was the only sign. The use of thallium acetate for the treatment of favus cannot be recommended. It has led to severe intoxication [*Muenchen. Med. Wochschr.* **102**, 578 (1960)]. Subacute intoxications are known to have produced encephalopathy. Inhalation exposure to organic thallium compounds produced abdominal pain, loss of weight, pain in legs, and irritability. Thallium readily passes the placental barrier. Thallium was secreted in the milk for 17 weeks and eliminated in the urine for 6 months after an unsuccessful suicide attempt by a nursing mother [*Ned. Tijdschr. Geneesk.* **106**, 1765 (1962)].

Treatment: Immediately and *repeatedly* induce vomiting, and perform gastric lavage with a solution of 1% sodium or potassium iodide (to form the insoluble iodide salt). Activated carbon has been found to be effective if administered shortly after poisoning. Follow with a saline cathartic and a diuretic. *Every effort should be made to eliminate the thallium compound before it is absorbed.* Heat, stimulants, dextrose, and calcium salts are sometimes of value in providing symptomatic relief.

Dithiocarb (sodium diethyldithiocarbamate; dithiocarbamate) appears to be a drug worthy of further trial in the treatment of acute thallium intoxication. The compound was found to be an effective antidote in experimental animals [*Toxicol. Appl. Pharmacol.* **1**, 638 (1959); *Am. J. Med. Sci.* **254**, 24 (1967)]. In 1963, M. Bass found it useful in a patient suffering from thallium poisoning. He administered 25 mg/kg, or 1.7 gm in 500 ml of 5% glucose in saline by I.V. drip over 5 hours. This dose was repeated after 36 hours, and again on each of the following 2 days. Each time the drug was administered, there was marked exacerbation of symptoms which may have been caused by mobilization of thallium. Recently F. W. Sunderman, Jr. reported that Dithiocarb was effective in the treatment of another patient (personal communication, F. W. Sunderman).

Calcium disodium edetate is not effective. BAL deserves a clinical trial. O. Grunfeld reported "dramatic improvement in one and very good results" in two patients [*Arch. Internal Med.* **114**, 132 (1964)]. Reports from other clinicians are less enthusiastic.

The results obtained with diphenylthiocarbazone (dithizon) in thallium poisoning do not look promising. M. R. Zavon, who recently treated two cases, stated "it was not possible to confirm that dithizon exerted any appreciable effect on the course of the illness following the ingestion of significant quantities of thallium [*JAMA* **192**, 786 (1965)]."

THAM (Tromethamine; THAM-E)

THAM is a potent osmotic diuretic which in the presence of normal renal function induces an increased excretion of sodium, potassium, and chloride. Bermudez considers it the antidote of choice in serious quinidine intoxications [*Henry Ford Hosp. Med. Bull.* **13**, 331 (1965)]. THAM shows promise in the treatment of severe acidosis, particularly when this condition does not yield to other drugs or when the intake of sodium is undesirable. In quinidine intoxication, the drug is administered as a 0.3 molar solution in normal saline by I.V. infusion at a rate of 10 ml/minute until the electrocardiogram shows improvement. Otherwise, the dose of a 0.3 molar solution is 5 ml/kg I.V. over a period of 1 hour. Additional doses depend on response in the patient, particularly on acid-base balance. Side effects that have been reported following large doses include depression of respiration and a profound hypoglycemia, meaning that THAM must be used with *particular caution* in diabetics, whether or not they are on insulin or oral therapy. Since solutions of THAM are alkaline, care must be exercised in its administration to avoid extravasation.

THEOBROMINE

This drug has diuretic effects. Excessive doses of theobromine (cocoa beans or cola nut), or salts of theobromine have induced gastroenteric disturbances, hemorrhage, insomnia, tremors, convulsions, and collapse. Fortunately, these manifestations are rare.

Treatment: Symptomatic.

THERMOFAX

Sensitive individuals have experienced contact dermatitis from handling Thermofax copy paper. The toxic agent is believed to be *t*-butylcatechol.

THESAUROSIS

This is a general term defining accumulation of particulate material in the lungs. Some well-known types are silicosis, asbestosis, berylliosis, maplebark disease, bagassosis, and mushroom miasma.

Thesaurosis due to inhalation of hairspray aerosol was first described in 1958. Other reports followed, suggesting that hairspray may incite pathological reactions in the lung, ranging from reticular lymphoid hyperplasia and bronchiectasis to diffuse interstitial fibrosis. Extensive animal experiments have failed to confirm this hypothesis [*JAMA* **193**, 298 (1965)].

Hairsprays consist of vinyl alkylether maleic ester, polyvinylpyrrolidone (PVP), resins, trichlorofluoromethane, dichlorodifluoromethane, dextran, aromatic oils, lanolins, and various types of perfume. The proponents of hair spray thesaurosis contend that intracytoplasmic periodic acid-Schiff (PAS)-positive granules in granulomatous areas in the lungs are particles of PVP. PAS-positive granules are nonspecific. They have been demonstrated in sarcoidosis, in normal animals, in infantile mesenteric lymphadenitis, and in inflammatory cells around brain infarction. It has been shown that about half of the particles in a commercial hairspray are between $10\,\mu$ and $35\,\mu$; only 0.5% are less than $10\,\mu$ and likely to reach the alveoli. Most of the particles probably remain in larger air passages. There is little evidence that exposure to hairspray is associated with significant impairment of pulmonary function or disease [O. P. Sharma and M. H. Williams, Jr., *Arch. Environ. Health* **13**, 616 (1966)].

THIETHYLPERAZINE (Torecan)

This compound is a phenothiazine derivative which has marked antiemetic properties in oral doses of 10–30 mg per day, or by deep I.M. injection in doses of 10 to 15 mg per day. The side effects are similar to those induced by other phenothiazine drugs. Children and young women are especially susceptible. Therapeutic doses of this antiemetic phenothiazine produced intermittent spasm of the face and tongue muscles in a 14-year-old boy. After the sixth dose the spasm became almost continuous. The symptoms subsided upon discontinuation of therapy.

Treatment: Withdrawal of the drug usually eliminates the side effects. See Chlorpromazine, p. 171, and Phenothiazines, p. 464.

THIMET [O,O-Diethyl S-(Ethylthiomethylphosphorodithioate)]

This is a highly toxic organic phosphate systemic insecticide. It is carried in the sap stream of the plant in sufficient concentrations to be lethal to suckling insects feasting on the plant. See Organic Phosphates, p. 438.

THIOCARBAMATES

This is a class of agricultural fungicides which have a moderate order of toxicity. Nabam is disodium ethylene bisdithiocarbamate, Amoban is the corresponding ammonium salt, Ziram the zinc salt, Ferbam the iron salt, and Manzate the manganese salt.

Treatment: See Ferbam, p. 262.

THIOCYANATES (Sulfocyanates; Rhodanates; Sulfocyanides)

Excessive doses of inorganic thiocyanates will induce central nervous system stimulation and depression, ataxia, and possibly collapse and coma. Methyl, ethyl, propyl, and butyl thiocyanates are metabolized to cyanides.

Treatment: Give glucose, I.V.; otherwise, treatment is symptomatic. Sodium and potassium thiocyanates can be removed effectively by hemodialysis. See p. 49. Hemodialysis is about 80 times more efficient than urinary excretion.

THIOGLYCOLATES

The ammonium and sodium salts (3–5%) are used in cold wave preparations (home permanents). The calcium salt is an ingredient of some depilatories. The thioglycolates decompose, liberating hydrogen sulfide.

Ammonium thioglycolate has an exceptionally low sensitizing index. If sensitization does develop, it is of the eczematous contact dermatitis type. Hair damage may occur in some instances in which the hair has been previously altered by dyes and bleaches, particularly when directions for use are not followed and excessive processing times are employed. Damage is apparently limited to the hair shaft, and no inhibition of growth is observed. Direct systemic toxic manifestations after percutaneous application have not been reported. The professional beauty-parlor operator is also exposed to sodium bromate used as the neutralizer for the thioglycolate waving solution.

Treatment: Discontinue exposure.

THIOGLYCOLIC ACID

The oral LD_{50} of thioglycolic acid in rats, rabbits and guinea pigs is 0.126–0.155 ml/kg. See Thioglycolates.

THIOGUANINE

"Thioguanine is an antimetabolite that is comparable in clinical effectiveness to the parent compound, mercaptopurine. It is useful in the treatment of certain leukemias. Its principal adverse effects are depression of marrow activity; jaundice and gastrointestinal disturbances have also been reported [Council on Drugs, American Medical Association, *JAMA* **200**, 620 (1967)]."

THIONYL CHLORIDE (Sulfurous Oxychloride)

This compound is a colorless, fuming liquid which hydrolyzes to hydrochloric acid and sulfur dioxide. The liquid and vapors are highly irritating to tissue. When heated, it decomposes to chlorine, sulfur dioxide, and sulfuryl chloride.

Treatment: See Hydrochloric Acid, p. 317, and Sulfur Dioxide, p. 565.

THIOPERAZINE (Vontil)

This is a phenothiazine derivative used as a tranquilizer. See Phenothiazine Compounds, p. 464.

THIPHENAMIL (Trocinate)

This antispasmodic drug, as well as anisotropine methylbromide (Valpin), has been reviewed by *Medical Letter* consultants with the conclusion that no acceptable evidence has been offered to show that either drug is any more effective than a placebo. When the dose is large enough to exert an anticholinergic effect, it invariably causes one or more typical atropine side effects, such as dryness of the mouth, accelerated heart rate, urinary retention, and impairment in accommodation of the eyes [*Med. Letter* **8**, 89 (1966)].

THIOPHENE (Thiofuran; Thiofurfuran; Thiole; Thiotetrole; Divinylene Sulfide)

The acute toxic action of thiophene is primarily on the central nervous system. It has a selective action on the cerebrum and cerebellum, producing severe ataxia. The inhalation of 2900 ppm caused loss of consciousness and death in mice. Concentrations of 8700 ppm caused death in mice in 20–80 minutes. Repeated daily injection of 2 gm of thiophene in dogs results in locomotor ataxia and paralysis.

Treatment: For skin, eye, and mucous membrane contact, flood affected tissues with water. In case of ingestion, induce vomiting, and follow with gastric lavage and saline cathartics. For inhalation, remove victim from contaminated atmosphere and give artificial respiration and oxygen if necessary. Subsequent treatment is supportive and symptomatic.

THIOPROPAZATE (Dartal)

This tranquilizer is a phenothiazine of the piperazine type. It should be used with the same degree of caution as other phenothiazines.

Contraindications and *treatment:* See Fluphenazine, p. 277, and Phenothiazines, p. 464.

THIORIDAZINE (Mellaril)

The side effects and signs of toxicity of this tranquilizer are similar to those induced by chlorpromazine. They are, as a rule, dose-related. Following therapeutic doses, side effects and signs of toxicity noted occasionally include autonomic reactions, behavioral toxicity, drug potentiation, extrapyramidal syndrome, dyskinesia, hyperflexia, seizures, electrocardiographic changes including ventricular arrhythmias [*Ann. Internal Med.* **65**, 1076 (1966); *Circulation* **34**, III-43 (1966)], hypotension, stimulation of lactation, delayed ejaculation and sexual dysfunction [*JAMA* **188**, 1007 (1964); *Am. J. Psychiat.* **121**, 610 (1964); *JAMA* **200**, 461 (1967)], peripheral edema, jaundice, skin disorders, nasal stuffiness, toxic retinitis [*Am. J. Psychiat.* **120**, 913 (1964); **123**, 97 (1966)], and reversed epinephrine effect. Agranulocytosis, first reported in 1954, is rare, but may be fatal. To our knowledge four incidents of agranulocytosis have occurred following prolonged treatment with this drug. D. S. Rosenthal *et al.* recently added a fifth patient, who recovered upon withdrawal of thioridazine therapy [*JAMA* **200**, 81 (1967)]. A 44-year-old patient experienced a severe near-fatal reaction apparently due to combined thioridazine-amitriptyline therapy [*Am. J. Psychiat.* **121**, 813 (1965)]. Mumps was reported in a 21-year-old girl on thioridazine therapy. It is known that the phenothiazine drugs may induce passive congestion and enlargement of the parotid glands. Discontinuation of therapy resulted in recovery [*Am. J. Psychiat.* **121**, 813 (1965)].

Treatment: Reduced dosage will usually diminish or abolish the side effects including the toxic effects of thioridazine on the bone marrow. Obviously patients receiving this drug should remain under the close supervision of a physician. See also Phenothiazines, p. 464, and Chlorpromazine, p. 171.

THIOTEPA

This nitrogen mustard-like drug is used for the palliative management of a large variety of neoplastic diseases. Bruce and Edgcomb recently reported on an elderly woman who after four 60 mg bladder instillations developed pancytopenia and fatal generalized sepsis. She was treated for transitional cell carcinoma [*J. Urol.* **97**, 482 (1967)]. Based on this observation and unpublished data obtained in dogs in our laboratory (WBD), certain compounds can be absorbed from the urinary bladder in amounts sufficient to cause injury and death.

Caution: The drug is highly toxic to the hematopoietic system and should be reserved for use by a physician experienced in the chemotherapeutic management of malignant diseases.

THIOTHIXANE (Navane)

This new psychotherapeutic agent is a thioxanthene analog of thioproperazine, a phenothiazine drug used widely in Europe. It is capable of inducing extrapyramidal syndromes, tachycardia, hypotension, and convulsions. Prolonged use may result in lenticular pigmentation. Photosensitivity reactions have also been reported [*Med. Letter* **10**, 1 (1968)]. The superiority of Navane over phenothiazines has not been proven.

Caution: Since this is a new drug, the possibility of serious side effects on prolonged use·cannot be disregarded. See Phenothiazines, p. 464.

THIPHENAMIL, see p. 587

THIRAM

This compound is also known as bisdimethylthiocarbamoyl disulfide; bisdimethylthiocarbamyl disulfide; tetramethylthiuram disulfide; TMTD; Thiurad; Thiosan; Thylate; Tiuramyl; Thiuramyl; Puralin; Fernasan; Nomersan; Pomasol; Pomarsol; Tersan; Tuads; Tulisan; and Arasan.

Thiram is irritating to the skin, eyes, and mucous membrane. It may cause allergic eczema in sensitive individuals. The oral LD_{50} in rabbits is 350 mg/kg.

Treatment: For skin, eye, and mucous membrane contact, flood with water for 15 minutes. In case of ingestion induce vomiting and follow with gastric lavage. Treatment thereafter is symptomatic and supportive.

THORIUM DIOXIDE (Thorotrast)

Thorium was used throughout the world as a radiological contrast medium for approximately 20 years. Radioactive thorium is a potent alpha emitter with a half-life of 1.4×10^{10} years. When retained in the body, it presents a potential hazard as a foreign body and because it emits radiation. J. Da Silva Horta *et al.* reviewed the incidence of Thorotrast-induced malignant lesions in Portugal. Between 1930 and 1952, this agent was administered to 2377 individuals; 1107 could be traced, 699 had died and 408 were still living in 1963. The investigators found 22 cases of hemangioendothelioma. This tumor is virtually Thorotrast-specific in the liver. The latent period was 20 years or more with only one exception. They also reported 16 fatal blood dyscrasias, 81 local granulomas, 8 fatalities, 3 local tumors at the edge of granulomas, and liver fibrosis (cirrhosis) in 42 cases; with 17 fatalities [*Lancet* **II**, 201 (1965)]. See also reports in *Arch. Otolaryngol.* **83**, 610 (1966) and in *Can. Med. Assoc. J.* **94**, 1298 (1966).

Caution: Because of the hazard associated with the administration of thorium, its use in man should no longer be considered—not even in those with a presumed life expectancy of only two years. Preparations containing thorium carry the FDA required statement: "Warning—not for administration to man. Not for administration to food-producing animals."

Treatment: For accidental ingestion of a radioactive thorium, consider recommendations under Plutonium (see p. 482). Thorium dust is effectively removed from the skin by thorough washing with soap and water.

TICK PARALYSIS

A 3-year old child bitten by a tick was admitted to the hospital completely paralyzed. According to the child's parents, the paralysis had "gradually crept to her head." Tick paralysis is caused by a venom which the female tick secretes only when producing eggs. Children are more severely affected than adults. The tick proved to be *Dermacentor variabilis*, common in the southeastern United States (other areas have closely related species) and superabundant in the summer season. The bite of a pajaroello tick will produce marked local pain and a swelling (may be large as a hen's egg) with blue and black discoloration of the skin.

A tick may be killed with a layer of fingernail polish, or it may be removed by grasping it with a pair of forceps. Care should be taken not to crush the tick lest bacteria be introduced into the wound. A good tick repellent is *N,N*-diethyltoluamide (50% liquid, or 15% spray). The U.S. Army has used a mixture of *n*-butylacetanilide, 2-butyl-2-ethyl-1,3-propanediol, and benzyl benzoate, with 10% polysorbate 80 as emulsifier. DDT is effective against some species.

Treatment: In the case of the child, treatment consisted of spraying the area with ethyl chloride, which froze the tick *in situ*, and removing it with a pair of tweezers taking care not to break off the head. Within an hour after removal of the tick, the patient was able to more her legs. For removal of ticks use gloves, tweezers, and extreme care to get the head out. Apply soapy water or paint the bite with an antiseptic.

To treat the bite of the pajaroello, L. Osborn (Morrow Bay, California) recommends application of a generous pack of baking soda under a bandage. This reduces the swelling and pain considerably over a period of 12 hours.

TIN

Many tin compounds are harmless because of their insolubility in body fluids; some alkyl derivatives are quite soluble and toxic. According to H. W. Fischer of the Department of Radiology, State University of Iowa, colloidal tin oxide, because of its innocuousness, is an ideal hepatolienographic agent in doses of 500–700 mg tin per kilogram body weight. Chemical burns of the skin have been reported in workers handling dibutyltin dichloride or tributyltin chloride. Skin irritation may not be apparent for at least an hour, and sometimes not before 8 hours. Sensitization of the skin has not been reported. See p. 753. Inhalation of vapors or fumes may cause sore throat, coughing and retching, which may not occur until several hours after exposure. Symptoms are due to irritation of the mucous membranes of the throat. In France diethyltin diiodide combined with linoleic acid was used for the treatment of furunculosis. This compound produced severe systemic effects (headaches, disorientation, and encephalopathy) and death.

Diethyl and triethyltin compounds are highly toxic to experimental animals. In rats, the compounds produce paresis, tremors, convulsions, and interstitial edema of the white matter of the brain and spinal cord. Higher molecular weight organotin compounds have considerably lower mammalian toxicity. Tetrabutyltin, for example, shows little acute oral toxicity in rats. In general, the trialkyltin compounds are the most toxic, the dialkyl and tetraalkyl compounds are moderately toxic, and the monoalkyls approach the inorganic tin compounds in toxicity. The oral LD_{50} for tributyltin oxide for rats is 175 mg/kg, and for dibutyltin oxide the LD_{50} is 100–200 mg/kg. For additional information consult the paper on "The turn of tin" by H. A. Schroeder *et al.*, *J. Chronic Diseases* **17**, 483 (1964). The LD_{50}s of triphenyltin in rats and mice are 8.5 and 7.9 mg/kg I.P., and 491 and 81 mg/kg P.O. The predominant signs of toxicity are progressive weakness and paralysis [H. B. Stoner, *Brit. J. Ind. Med.* **23**, 222 (1966)].

Treatment: For inhalation, remove the individual from the contaminated atmosphere. Treat symptomatically. Watch for evidence of pulmonary injury. For ingestion, induce vomiting and administer a saline cathartic. In case of skin contact, flood affected area with water, and treat the lesion as a thermal burn.

TINNING PAINT

This is a soldering flux paste composed of pulverized tin (50%), pulverized lead (40%), and zinc chloride (10%). This mixture is very corrosive and, if ingested, will induce severe necrosis of the stomach if not diluted and removed immediately. Prompt vomiting did not save an 18-month-old child from total gastrectomy. This child ingested an unknown quantity and rapidly developed marked edema of the mouth, pharynx, and larynx as well as symptoms of systemic intoxication.

Treatment: Immediately administer milk and/or a cup of vegetable oil (*not* mineral oil). Perform gastric lavage with caution. The patient will probably vomit because of the marked emetic action of this preparation. If vomiting occurs, repeat the administration of oil and milk. Symptomatic treatment is directed towards maintaining an open airway, administration of fluids and emollients. Speed is essential in the dilution and removal of tinning paint from the stomach.

TINTEX COLOR REMOVER

This preparation contains sodium hydrosulfite, formaldehyde, oxalates, and tripolyphosphate. See Sulfur Dioxide, p. 565, Formaldehyde, p. 278, Oxalic Acid, p. 441, and Detergents, p. 201.

TITANATES (Barium, Bismuth, Calcium, Lead Titanate)

In general, these compounds are relatively insoluble and chemically inert. They have a low order of acute oral and parenteral toxicity for the rat. The oral LD_{50} exceeds 12 gm for the rat. The intraperitoneal LD_{50} was found to range from 2.0 gm/kg for lead titanate to 5.3 gm/kg for calcium titanate.

Repeated daily administration of 100 mg doses of these titanates to a small group of rats showed no evidence of cumulative effects over a 2-week period.

Treatment: None required.

TITANIUM

Titanium dioxide is a pigment used in white paints. It is insoluble and essentially nontoxic on ingestion. Titanium tetrachloride is a corrosive liquid. On exposure to air, it reacts violently with water, decomposing with the formation of a highly irritant cloud or dust of titanium dioxide and hydrochloric acid. This mixture may self-ignite and explode if the particles are small enough. (Powders must be stored with at least 20% of water.)

Treatment: If splashed on the skin or into the eyes, remove titanium tetrachloride promptly by *dry wiping* with a cloth or soft tissue paper, then follow with washing, using plenty of water. Treat inhalation exposures by immediate removal to fresh air, administration of oxygen, and bed rest. Treatment otherwise is symptomatic.

TOAD *(Bufus marinus)*

A giant tropical night-feeding toad, native of Central and South America, has been found in Florida, Louisiana, and Puerto Rico. The species is not aggressive and does not attack anything. Claims that it is a menace because of the potency of the venom secreted by the glands located directly behind the eyes [E. Larson, *Sci. News* **92**, 38 (1967)] have been vigorously denied by others. When stimulated, the glands secrete a viscous milky substance containing a neurotoxin which oozes out through the secretory glands in the skin. Traces of the venom that have come in contact with human skin have caused one case of hives and painful swelling; and traces that entered a wound (on the thumb) of another individual, caused immediate painful swelling of the hand and paralysis of the muscles of the hand and arm (E. Larson). Over a period of 33 years, I. Velez and his students have caught this toad and used it in the study of zoology without "a single report of poisoning or wart production . . . since 1950 other members of the department have also handled them unreservedly. Students have even had cuts with their scalpels while working with the toads but never with ill effects." However, I. Velez adds, "the effects (of the venom) on cats and dogs are well known here, but never to the extent of killing the mammals [*Sci. News* **92**, 318 (1967)]."

Caution: Avoid contact with *Bufus marinus*. Since the venom has not been identified, treatment is symptomatic.

TOBACCO; TREE TOBACCO *(Nicotiana glauca)*

The tree tobacco, the wild tobacco, or desert tobacco (*N. trigonophylla*), and a variety of other plants of the genus *Nicotina* and *Lobelia* species, contain either nicotine or lobeline as principal toxic agent. Fatalities have occurred because some of the young plants were ingested as salads or because of the ingestion of excessive quantities of home medicines prepared from parts of these plants.

Treatment: For signs, symptoms, and treatment, see Kentucky Coffee-Tree, p. 343 and Nicotine, p. 421.

TOKYO-YOKOHAMA RESPIRATORY DISEASE (Yokohama Asthma)

This disease occurs predominately in the autumn and winter months, and early signs and symptoms are usually nocturnal coughing, very mild sputum production, and mild dyspnea. Individuals affected have had no previous respiratory or allergic disease except for some who have previously suffered with asthma. Pulmonary function studies indicate that this is a severe obstructive disease. It occurs almost exclusively in smokers, and in patients who continue to smoke the recovery rate is very low. Up to 80% of nonsmokers and those who discontinue smoking are cured almost immediately upon vacating the area. A stricken individual who returns to the area, even after a period of full recovery, will have a recurrence.

This disease was first described in 1947 by a U.S. Army official in the Tokyo-Yokohama area. It is uncertain whether air pollutants in this highly industrialized area caused the asthma. However, in some patients the disease is greatly aggravated by residence in Tokyo. The problem is intensified by meteorological conditions leading to air inversions [N. Spotnitz, *Am. Rev. Respirat. Diseases* **92**, 371 (1965)].

TOLAZAMIDE (Tolinase)

At this writing, tolazamide is the newest sulfonylurea drug recommended for the treatment of mild to moderately severe maturity-onset type of diabetes. It is a medium-long acting compound. No serious side effects have been reported. However, more extensive and longer use is required before conclusions can be drawn in regard to its therapeutic importance and safety. For the treatment of overdoses, see Sulfonylurea Drugs, p. 563.

TOLAZOLINE (Priscoline)

Tolazoline (Priscoline), azapetine (Iledar), and phenoxybenzamine (Dibenzyline) are adrenergic blocking agents. Therapeutic doses of tolazoline are likely to cause palpitation, shivering, appearance of goose flesh, and aggravation of the angina. Large or excessive doses of this drug induce marked hypotension, increased gastroenteric activity, secretion of hydrochloric acid, and a curare-like effect. Side effects of Iledar and Dibenzyline include nasal congestion, hypotension and tachycardia. Fever has been reported following Iledar therapy.

Treatment: Ephedrine is preferable to epinephrine or levarterenol for raising the blood pressure. Adiphenine hydrochloride (Trasentin), or other parasympathetic drugs are effective in controlling augmented peristalsis.

TOLBUTAMIDE (Orinase)

This drug is contraindicated in patients whose diabetes had its onset before the age of 20 and in patients with a history of diabetic coma. The drug should not be used in the treatment of patients with Raynaud's disease, impairment of renal, thyroid, or hepatic function, or in persons undergoing surgical procedures. Concurrent treatment of tolbutamide with the analgesic phenyramidol (Analexin), or the anticoagulant bishydroxycoumarin (Dicumarol) may cause protracted hypoglycemia by inhibiting the metabolism of tolbutamide to carboxytolbutamide and hydroxymethyltolbutamide. These metabolites exert no hypoglycemic effect [H. M. Solomon and J. J. Schrogie, *Metabolism* **16**, 1029 (1967)]. See Sulfonylurea Drugs, p. 563.

TOLNAFTATE (Tinactin)

Tolnaftate is used topically as an antifungal agent. In most cases, pruritus disappears within 24–72 hours after the solution is applied, and the lesions usually heal within 2–3 weeks. Thickened lesions of the palms and soles require the concomitant use of keratolytic ointments and orally administered griseofulvin. Tolnaftate is not effective in the treatment of fungal infections of the hair or nails. While the drug is quite effective in chronic infections caused by *Trichophyton rubrum*, relapse is not uncommon. No confirmed adverse reactions have as yet been reported [Council on Drugs, *JAMA* **196**, 1145 (1966)].

TOLUENE-2,4,-DIISOCYANATE (TDI; Tolylene Diisocyanate)

This is used in the manufacture of plastic (poly-urethane) foams of various consistencies, ranging from soft, pillowlike sponges to hard, porous, honeycomb-like products. TDI is a pale yellow, watery liquid with very little odor. Applied to the skin, it produces local skin irritation and sensitization if prolonged contact is permitted. Contact with the eyes causes marked irritation of the eyelids and possibly damage to the corneal epithelium. The foamed plastic itself is not a skin sensitizer. Severe irritation of the respiratory tract is produced by low concentrations of the vapor. Severe cases are characterized by a sensation of con-striction of the chest, cough, dyspnea, and asthma-like attacks.

Treatment: Removal from exposure results in com-plete recovery, with no sequelae. On re-exposure there may be increased sensitivity. Susceptible indi-viduals should be barred permanently from working with this chemical. In case of skin or eye contact, re-move chemical by washing with copious quantities of water for 15 minutes. Consult an ophthalmologist for further definitive treatment of eye injury.

TOLUIDINE (Aminotoluene)

Absorption of *o*-, *m*-, and *p*-toluidine will induce methemoglobinemia. See Aniline, p. 102.

TOLUIDINE BLUE (Tolonium Chloride)

This drug [hexadimethrine bromide (Polybrene) and protamine sulfate (Salmine)] is used to antagonize the anticoagulant effect of heparin. Toluidine blue is usually given in a dose ranging from 3 to 10 mg/kg, by *slow* I.V. injection. A 60-year-old patient with profuse rectal bleeding following hemorrhoidectomy received 3 gm of toluidine blue over a period of 6 days. During this week he experienced nausea, vomiting, and in-creased white blood cell count.

Treatment: With discontinuation of toluidine blue therapy and supportive treatment recovery was prompt in the case cited.

597

TOMATO JUICE

Ingestion of 2 liters of tomato juice daily for 2 years induced an orange-yellow skin color, nausea, vomiting, diarrhea, abdominal pain, and jaundice.

Treatment: Recovery, except for discomfort and pain in the right upper quadrant, was complete 4 weeks after intake of tomato juice was discontinued.

TOXAPHENE (Synthetic 3956; Chlorinated Camphene)

Signs of intoxication (similar to those induced by camphor) include central stimulation, epileptiform convulsions, generalized depression, and loss of consciousness. The onset may be abrupt. This compound is more toxic than DDT. The probable lethal oral dose for an adult is 2 gm. See Chlorinated Hydrocarbons, p. 648.

Treatment: Thorough gastric lavage is recommended after ingestion. Subsequent treatment is symptomatic. Remove from the skin with water.

TRANYLCYPROMINE (Parnate)

Side effects and signs of intoxication noted in some patients receiving this potent monoamine oxidase inhibitor include dizziness, restlessness, insomnia, weakness, nausea, vomiting, anorexia, blurred vision, impotence, drug potentiation, hyperreflexia, and postural hypotension. Liver injury was reported by C. Brandt and F. W. Hoffbauer [*JAMA* 188, 752 (1964)].

A 17-year-old girl died following ingestion of 50 (10 mg) tablets of this drug [*Am. J. Psychiat.* 119, 582 (1962)]. The combined effect of tranylcypromine and cheese is now well documented. The drug—once temporarily withdrawn—should be used only in hospitalized patients suffering from *severe* depression or in office patients who do not respond to other medication. In addition, tranylcypromine should not be administered to individuals over 60 years of age with a history of cardiovascular disease. The drug should not be administered until at least 1 week after discontinuation of amitriptyline (Elavil) or imipramine (Tofranil) therapy [*Med. Letter* 7, 29 (1965)].

Treatment: Many of the side effects can be alleviated by reduction of the dose. For additional information and treatment of overdoses, see Monoamine Oxidase Inhibitors, p. 404.

TRASYLOL (EACA)

Trasylol is an experimental drug which appears useful in the treatment of postoperative hemorrhages. One report indicates that it is valuable in cases of blood-clotting defects occurring in pregnancy. It does not cross the placental barrier and does not affect the fibrinolytic enzyme of the newborn [F. Sicuteri, *Sci. News* **90**, 237 (1966)].

TRIACETYLOLEANDOMYCIN (Cyclamycin)

This acetylated form of oleandomycin (Matromycin) is more rapidly and more completely absorbed from the gastroenteric tract than oleandomycin itself. After administration of oleandomycin, side effects are noted in about 3 % of patients. These include nausea, vomiting, diarrhea, and esophagitis. Skin rash and urticaria have been produced in sensitive individuals. Jaundice and hepatotoxicity have been observed with the ester but not with the free base. Whether this effect is due to the higher blood level produced or to some inherent property of the acetylated form is undetermined [*New Engl. J. Med.* **267**, 964 (1962)].

Caution: To avoid development of resistance, these antibiotics should be administered in minimum dosages sufficient to control the infection.

TRIALKYL BORANES (Alkyl Boranes)

Trimethyl, triethyl, and tributyl boranes burst into flame on contact with air. The pyrophoricity of these compounds decreases as the molecular weight of the alkyl group increases. These chemicals are considered to be highly toxic. See Borohydrides, p. 138.

TRIAMTERENE (Dyrenium)

Triamterene is a new aldosterone antagonist. Its diuretic action is related primarily to the renal tubule itself. It is a promising drug because of its potassium-sparing action. Undesirable effects noted occasionally include nausea, vomiting, mild diarrhea, weakness, headache, dryness of mouth, and skin rash. In a few patients, triamterene alone, and also in combination with hydrochlorothiazide, caused severe *hyperkalemia* with resulting electrocardiographic changes and death [*Ann. Internal Med.* **65**, 521 (1966)]. The report by K. B. Hansen and A. D. Bender summarizes the changes in serum potassium levels in 583 patients treated with triamterene alone, 484 treated with a combination of triamterene and hydrochlorothiazide, and 82 treated with hydrochlorothiazide. The incidence of hypokalemia (<3.5 mEq per liter) in patients treated with a combination of triamterene and hydrochlorothiazide was 6%. Hyperkalemia (>5.4 mEq per liter) developed in 7.5% of subjects to whom the combination was given, in 12–19% of subjects treated with triamterene, and in four percent of patients, especially the severely ill, treated with hydrochlorothiazide [*Clin. Pharmacol. Therap.* **8**, 392 (1967)]. Dyazide is a new proprietary preparation containing triamterene and hydrochlorothiazide.

Caution: Caution is in order until this drug has been more fully evaluated. When used in combination with other diuretics, the serum potassium level should be routinely monitored.

Treatment: Gastroenteric effects and nausea are reduced or eliminated by taking the drug after a meal. An overdose requires symptomatic treatment. For the treatment of hyperkalemia, see Calcium, p. 148.

TRIBROMOETHANOL (Avertin)

This drug, while it is not an analgesic, has sedative and hypnotic properties. It is no longer a "favorite" drug. A toxic dose is likely to produce cyanosis and respiratory and circulatory difficulties as well as injury to the liver and kidneys.

Treatment is symptomatic.

TRIBUTYL ACONITATE

Tributyl aconitate is a light, clear, odorless liquid. The LD_{50} for mice is higher than 50 ml/kg; for rats it is higher than 30 ml/kg.

Treatment: None required.

TRI-*n*-BUTYLPHOSPHINE

Tributylphosphine is a high-boiling, colorless liquid with a garlic-like odor. Following oral administration of tributylphosphine to rats the LD_{50} was approximately 750 mg/kg. In rabbits, dermal application showed an LD_{50} slightly above 2.0 gm/kg. During the 24 hour exposure period, the skin exposed to all doses showed moderate inflammation and occasional swelling. Application of tributylphosphine to the eyes of rabbits showed moderate inflammation and some conjunctival swelling and discharge. There were no corneal or iris effects and no gross evidence of systemic toxicity from mucous membrane absorption. Acute inhalation exposure caused nausea even at fairly low concentrations. At higher concentrations systemic abnormalities appeared in the kidneys and lungs.

Treatment: In case of ingestion induce vomiting. For contact with the eyes or skin, flood with water.

TRICALCIUM PHOSPHATE

H. A. Reimann *et al.* reported on a 48-year-old woman in whom, after years of inadvertent excessive exposure (inhalation and ingestion) to a powdery dentifrice, systemic tricalcium phosphate crystallosis developed. The patient died from alveolar adenocarcinoma. Micron-sized crystals of the salt were found in normal, inflamed, granulomatous and neoplastic areas in the viscera and in the mildly inflamed myocardium and pericardium. Excepting neoplastic changes, similar but more severe lesions were subsequently produced in rats after ingestion of massive doses of tricalcium phosphate, alpha quartz, barium sulfate, bismuth subcarbonate, and magnesium trisilicate. Particles of these substances appeared systemically and in the congested myocardium and pericardium with and without inflammation [*Am. J. Cardiol.* **17,** 269 (1966)].

TRICHLORACETIC ACID (TCA)

This strong organic acid and protein precipitant is immediately irritating on contact with skin, eyes, and mucous membrane.

Treatment: In case of skin, eye, or mucous membrane contact, flood immediately with water and continue washing the affected parts for 15 minutes.

1,1,1-TRICHLOROETHANE (Methyl Chloroform; Chlorothene)

This has a relatively low acute oral toxicity. LD_{50} values range from 5.66 to 12.3 gm/kg (rabbits, guinea pigs, mice, and rats). It is only slightly irritating to the skin even when exposures are prolonged and repeated. Massive exposures for a prolonged period are required to produce adverse systemic effects. There is no danger of the material causing serious injury to the eye, although discomfort can be expected if appreciable contact occurs.

Experiments with human subjects at concentrations indicated below have yielded the following information:

1. At about 500 ppm, the odor was perceptible but not disagreeable to most persons; an exposure period of several hours failed to cause any adverse effects.

2. At about 1000 ppm, the odor was strong and unpleasant; an exposure lasting one-half hour did not cause definite ill effects, but a flushing of the face was noted.

3. At about 2000 ppm, the odor was distinctly disagreeable to most people but might not be sufficiently so to prevent short exposures; definite anesthetic effects occurred in about 5 minutes.

Treatment: For inhalation exposure, remove the victim from the contaminated atmosphere and give artificial respiration and oxygen if necessary. Further treatment is supportive and symptomatic.

TRICHLOROETHYLENE (Trichloroethene; Ethinyl Trichloride; Tri-Clene; Trielene; Trilene; Trichloran; Trichloren; Algylen; Trimar; Triline; Tri; Trethylen; Trethylene; Westrosol; Chlorylen; Gemalgene; Germalgene)

This compound will produce slight central depression to deep narcosis depending on the amount absorbed from the gastroenteric tract or lungs. Repeated exposures have caused anemia, liver injury, respiratory difficulties, and paresis. Ingestion of the material will produce gastroenteric distress. A 22-year-old man recovered after ingesting 150 ml of trichloroethylene cleaning fluid.

Treatment: In case of ingestion, gastric lavage and cathartics are indicated. For inhalation, give artificial respiration and oxygen if necessary. Subsequent treatment is symptomatic.

TRICHLOROMELAMINE (TCM)

Trichloromelamine is an active chlorine compound used to formulate dry-mix sanitizers. When heated to a temperature of 160°C (320°F) or ignited with a spark, pure TCM decomposes with copious evolution of smoke and generation of heat. Mixing with oxidizable or organic matter should be avoided. Once TCM is properly diluted, it can be used with complete safety.

The oral LD_{50} in mice is 490 mg/kg. Chronic toxicity was determined in rats fed a diet containing as high as 0.1% TCM for 14 months. There were no effects on food intake, body weight, or internal organs. As with all active chlorine compounds, care should be taken to avoid contamination of the skin and inhalation of the dust.

Treatment: See Chlorine, p. 650.

2,4,5-TRICHLOROPHENOL (Dowicide)

This is a fungicide having a low order of acute oral toxicity. Excessive exposure to dust and fumes from heated material may cause pain and irritation of the eyes and throat and skin irritation. There is no danger of systemic intoxication from percutaneous absorption.

Treatment: For skin, eye, or mucous membrane contact, flood affected tissues with water. In case of ingestion, induce vomiting; follow with gastric lavage and saline cathartics.

1,1,3-TRICHLOROTRIFLUOROACETONE (3FK)

3FK is a water-clear, pungent liquid that irritates the eyes. The LC_{50} ($\frac{1}{2}$ hour exposure) is 2500 ppm; LC_{50} (3-hour exposure) is 450 ppm for albino rats. The oral LD_{50} (albino rats) is 277 ± 35 mg/kg dosed as a 10% aqueous solution. The acute percutaneous LD_{50} (rabbits) is 770 ± 80 mg/kg when applied undiluted. On ingestion, 3FK is quite toxic. This compound is a lachrymator and irritates the skin and eyes. The principal effect of inhalation is acute lung inflammation. Prolonged skin contact with the liquid may cause burns.

Treatment: For inhalation, remove the victim to fresh air. Give artifical respiration and oxygen if necessary. In case of skin or eye contact, flood with water. For ingestion, induce vomiting and follow with gastric lavage.

TRICRESYL PHOSPHATES

The ingestion of a toxic dose of tri-*o*-cresyl phosphate causes gastroenteric distress followed by skeletal muscle pain, numbness, and paralysis of fingers and toes followed by "footdrop" and later "wristdrop." Recovery is slow and incomplete. This intoxication was first described when tri-*o*-cresyl phosphate, used as an adulterant in ginger extract, caused the so-called "jake" paralysis. The lethal oral dose of TOCP for adults is above 2 gm. The meta and para isomers are not demyelinizing agents and are comparatively nontoxic.

An epidemic of tri-*o*-cresyl phosphate poisoning in 1959 affected 10,000 Moroccans who ate contaminated cooking oil. Within 6 months the clinical picture was predominantly one of peripheral motor paralysis. After 14 months approximately 6000 had recovered, 2000 were still under treatment, 1000 required braces or orthopedic procedures, and 1000 were permanent care patients.

The following compounds produce skeletal muscle pain and paralysis ("footdrop", "wristdrop") similar to that produced by tri-*o*-cresyl phosphate: trimethyl phosphate, triphenyl phosphate, tri-*o*-cresyl thiophosphate, triphenyl phosphite, tri-*o*-cresyl phosphite, tri-*m*-cresyl phosphite, tri-*p*-cresyl phosphite, and catechol phosphate.

The following closely related compounds have *not* induced neurotoxic manifestations: tri-*m*-cresyl phosphate, tri-*p*-cresyl phosphate, monosodium di-*o*-cresyl phosphate, disodium mono-*o*-cresyl phosphate, triphenyl thiophosphate, and guaiacol phosphate.

Treatment: After ingestion of tri-*o*-cresyl phosphate or a related compound, or of an oil or other material containing one of these agents, induce vomiting *immediately* and *repeatedly* and perform gastric lavage. Speed is extremely important in the removal of the material from the gastroenteric tract. Follow with saline cathartics and a diuretic. Treatment otherwise is symptomatic and supportive.

TRIDECYL PHOSPHITE

This compound has an LD_{50} value greater than 10 ml/kg in the rat. Prolonged and repeated skin contact can result in skin irritation even though the chemical is not readily absorbed through the unbroken skin.

Treatment: Prompt flushing with copious quantities of water will reduce irritation in case of accidental contact with the skin or eyes.

TRIETHYLBORANE (TEB)

Triethylborane (TEB) ignites spontaneously in air. Inhalation of TEB vapor in concentrations of 70 ppm for 4 hours caused death in 50% of the rats exposed. The principal toxic effects of inhalation are irritation of the respiratory tract and convulsions.

Treatment: See Boranes, p. 137.

TRIETHYLENE MELAMINE (TEM; Melamine)

The effect of this alkylating agent on the bone marrow and other tissues is similar to that of nitrogen mustard; however, there is no vesication on local contact with tissues, less irritation to the veins when given I.V., and a lower incidence of nausea and vomiting when orally administered. This drug is used in the treatment of inoperable ovarian carcinoma and other malignancies.

Treatment: Reduce dose or discontinue use.

TRIETHYL PHOSPHATE

Triethyl phosphate is a clear, colorless, mobile liquid with a mild, pleasant odor somewhat like that of cider. The major use of triethyl phosphate is as an intermediate in the preparation of tetraethyl pyrophosphate, an effective insecticide.

The LD_{50} in mice, rats, and guinea pigs averages about 800 mg/kg when administered intraperitoneally and 1.60 gm/kg orally. The signs observed with this material are those of anesthesia in the larger dosages. The animals either die promptly from deep anesthesia or recover completely by the next day. In the smaller dosages minimal or no signs are observed.

This material is found to be rather benign as far as effects on the skin are concerned. It has a drying action on the skin similar to that of other solvents, but is very poorly absorbed through the skin. The lethal dose by this route is over 20 gm/kg. It does not cause skin sensitization.

Treatment: In case of eye contact, irrigate with water for 15 minutes.

TRI(2-ETHYLHEXYL) PHOSPHATE (TOF)

This compound is a clear, viscous liquid of low volatility. The oral LD_{50} for rats is 37.08 gm/kg. TOF fed in the diet to rats (0.43 gm/kg/day) caused no effect; 1.55 gm/kg daily reduced the growth rate. When injected subcutaneously into rats, no fibrosing effects were observed. The LD_{50} by skin penetration in rabbits was slightly less than 20 ml/kg. Six rats survived exposure for 8 hours to air nearly saturated with the vapors of TOF. A mist generated from TOF at 170° C, which may contain some thermal degradation products, killed no rats in 30 minutes, but killed two out of six after 1 hour. TOF was instilled into the conjunctival sac of one eye of each of two rabbits at six dosage levels from 0.01 to 0.5 ml. Doses up to 0.05 ml produced slight conjunctivitis; doses from 0.1 to 0.5 ml produced moderate conjunctivitis which cleared up within 24 hours. A dose of 250 mg TOF applied to the clipped skin of the rabbit back produced within 24 hours signs of moderate erythema which persisted for about a week. No evidence of systemic intoxication was observed in the eye and skin tests. No demyelinizing action was found in a study of chickens in which positive results were obtained with tri-*o*-cresyl phosphate [H. N. MacFarland *et al., Arch. Environ. Health* **13**, 13 (1966)].

Treatment: In case of skin or eye contact flood with water.

TRIFLUOPERAZINE (Stelazine)

This tranquilizer is a phenothiazine compound. Sedation is the most common minor side effect. Mild hypotension, blurred vision, jaundice, lactation, weakness, convulsions, the neck-face syndrome, endocrine disturbances, epinephrine reversal, and exacerbation of angina pectoris are among the signs and symptoms of toxicity that have been noted occasionally. Extrapyramidal symptoms have occurred frequently in hospitalized patients (above 50%) given high doses. With doses of 8 mg per day, the incidence was much lower; with 2–4 mg per day, these symptoms were noted in about 2% of patients.

Caution: Central nervous system depressants should be given with caution to patients receiving trifluoperazine therapy. "Two bizarre deaths, apparently from respiratory failure, have occurred in patients who had received large doses of both trifluoperazine and a barbiturate or paraldehyde [*New and Nonofficial Drugs* p. 473 (1962)]." Potentiation does occur. Epinephrine is contraindicated in patients receiving this drug. The usefulness of this agent must be weighed against the production of more lasting side effects. Dystonic reactions of face and neck muscles were still noted in three patients 9, 10, and 36 months after discontinuation of treatment. It has been suggested that patients with brain damage or disease are especially prone to phenothiazine-induced dyskinesia [*Lancet* I, 458 (1965)].

Treatment: Reduction of the dose will usually reduce or eliminate side effects. Administration of antiparkinson drug should be considered if the extrapyramidal disorders are marked, and if treatment with trifluoperazine must be continued. Levarterenol may be considered in cases of prolonged hypotension. See also Phenothiazines, p. 464.

TRIFLUOROETHANOL

In albino rats, oral LD_{50} of trifluoroethanol is 0.24 gm/kg; acute dermal LD_{50} is 1.68 gm/kg; and acute inhalation LCT_{50} is 4600 ppm hrs. This alcohol is not a skin irritant, but contact with skin should be minimized to prevent dermal absorption.

Treatment: In case of eye or skin contact, flood with water. For ingestion, induce vomiting.

TRIFLUOROACETIC ACID (3FA)

3FA is a water-white, pungent liquid. It is a strong acid and the liquid is highly corrosive to skin and eyes. The vapors are irritating. The LC_{50} for a 4-hour exposure (albino rats) is approximately 2000 ppm. This compares with the approximate 4-hour LC_{50} of 1000 ppm for acetic anhydride and chloroacetyl chloride and 2000 ppm for ammonia.

Treatment: See Hydrochloric Acid, p. 317.

TRIFLUPROMAZINE (Vesprin)

This tranquilizer exerts a potent antiemetic effect. It has found use in the control of nausea and vomiting. Side effects are similar to those induced by chlorpromazine but less frequent and less severe. See Phenothiazines, p. 464.

TRIMELLITIC ANHYDRIDE

Animal toxicity tests reveal no major differences between trimellitic anhydride and phthalic anhydride. The minimum oral lethal dose (rat) was 5.6 gm/kg for trimellitic anhydride and 3.1 gm/kg for phthalic anhydride.

Contact with skin, mucous membranes, and eyes causes irritation. Inhalation of fine particles causes respiratory tract irritation and coughing.

Treatment: See Anhydrides, p. 81.

TRIMEPRAZINE (Temaril)

This derivative of phenothiazine has been recommended for treatment of pruritus and other disorders benefited by sedation.

Caution: Three cases of agranulocytosis were reported in 1960. A sex and age predilection has been suggested but additional information is needed to prove this. Although the danger is apparently less in men and younger patients, the physician should be alert for signs of adverse reactions [W. E. Clendenning *et al., Arch. Dermatol.* **82**, 533 (1960)]. Signs of toxicity included autonomic reactions and abnormality in behavior.

Treatment of an overdose is symptomatic. See Phenothiazine, p. 464.

TRIMETHADIONE (Tridione)

The side effects of this anti-petit mal drug may include photophobia, gastroenteric irritation, skin eruptions, photosensitivity, and rarely, alopecia. High doses may cause a generalized depression. Albuminuria and the nephrotic syndrome (four deaths) have also been reported [Am. J. Diseases Children **105**, 196 (1963); *New Engl. J. Med.* **269**, 15 (1963)]. The most serious effects are neutropenia, agranulocytosis, and fatal aplastic anemia. (See Dyscrasias, p. 51.) In a few rare instances trimethadione has caused systemic lupus erythematosus.

Caution: Trimethadione as well as the related oxazolidinedione derivative, paramethadione (Paradione), should not be given to patients suffering from diseases of the liver, kidneys, or optic nerve. Patients receiving these drugs should have frequent urinalyses to detect erythrocytes, casts, and protein. When abnormal urinary findings are obtained, administration of these drugs should be discontinued. In many patients the renal complications apparently will clear spontaneously when this is done [W. Heymann, *JAMA* **202**, 893 (1967)].

Treatment of an overdose is symptomatic. Talamo, Crawford, and Riley (quoted by W. Heymann) recently reported a case of trimethadione nephrosis which was treated successfully with cortisone and mechlorethamine hydrochloride (a nitrogen mustard derivative).

TRIMETHOBENZAMIDE (Tigan)

This is an antiemetic drug. Side effects noted, particularly after prolonged therapeutic doses, include drowsiness, vertigo, diarrhea, pain at the injection site, and local irritation after rectal use. Since the drug induces a drop in blood pressure in animals, this should be kept in mind when it is given I.V. to a patient.

TRIMETHYLOL PROPANE

This is a synthetic polyol containing three primary hydroxyl groups.

Tests on animals show a very low order of oral toxicity. Twenty-four-hour skin contact produced no effects from absorption, and only a slight superficial reddening which disappeared in a few hours. No adverse effects have been reported from its industrial use.

Treatment: See Glycols, p. 290.

TRIMETHYL PHOSPHITE

Human toxicity information has not been reported. The oral LD_{50} (rat) is 2.89 gm/kg. The minimum lethal cutaneous dose for the rabbit is about 2.2 gm/kg. Application of the undiluted material to the skin caused moderately severe irritation persisting for several days. Instilled in the eyes of rabbits, the undiluted material caused severe irritation and swelling which persisted for several days.

In vapor inhalation experiments, rats survived a 6-hour exposure to a saturated atmosphere. The compound produced considerable discomfort and restlessness and severe irritation of the eyes and respiratory tract.

Treatment: For skin, eye or mucous membrane contact, flood affected parts with water. In case of ingestion induce vomiting and follow with gastric lavage.

TRINITROTOLUENE (TNT)

Absorption of a toxic dose of TNT will result in gastroenteric disturbances and distress. This may be followed by toxic hepatitis and nephritis. In addition, the compound may induce anemia, leukocytosis, marked cyanosis, delirium, and convulsions. The probable lethal oral dose for an adult is 2 gm.

Treatment: For inhalation, remove the patient from the site of exposure and give artificial respiration and oxygen if necessary. In case of ingestion, induce vomiting and follow with gastric lavage. Further treatment is symptomatic.

TRIPARANOL (MER-29)

This triphenylethylene derivative was withdrawn from the market.

TRIPELENNAMINE (Pyribenzamine)

"Blue velvet" refers to a mixture of tripelennamine hydrochloride and paregoric used by addicts as follows: 30 ml of paregoric is boiled until about 5 ml of fluid remains; to this is added a crushed 50 mg tripelennamine tablet, giving the mixture a blue color. The mixture is injected I.V., resulting in an immediate euphoria lasting several hours. Tripelennamine tablets contain talcum, magnesium stearate, alcohol, tragacanth, corn starch, petroleum liquid, and coloring substance.

Pulmonary hypertension can be added to the known complications (hepatitis, septicemia, bacterial endocarditis, tetanus) associated with the I.V. injection of drug mixtures *by addicts.* V. E. Wendt *et al.*, who reported this complication, traced it to magnesium silicate crystals (talc), which caused thrombosis of small pulmonary arteries, arterioles, and capillaries, and which subsequently led to pulmonary hypertension and death. They reported two such fatalities; in one, talc emboli were found in the renal glomeruli. V. E. Wendt *et al.* wish to alert clinicians to the effects that may result from the I.V. injection of "blue velvet," which, as shown here, may lead to angiothrombotic hypertension [*JAMA* **188**, 755 (1964)]. See also Talc, p. 570, and Antihistamines, p. 107.

TRIPHENYLMETHANE

The triphenylmethane dye known as Alphazurine 2G was recently introduced to differentiate between second and third degree burns. Reportedly, the dye stains only viable tissues. S. Hepps and M. Dollinger reported on four patients with severe burns who were treated with this compound. There were no difficulties with three patients, but the fourth suffered an anaphylactic reaction after one-third of the calculated dose of 0.1 mg/kg had been slowly injected I.V. The patient, a 44-year-old man, died 5 days later in spite of vigorous treatment. According to the authors, this is the first reported case of a lethal anaphylactic reaction to this agent.

Caution: Hepps and Dollinger warn that this dye should be used with caution until further experimental toxicity studies have been completed and a method has been devised to test a patient's sensitivity before administration [*New Engl. J. Med.* **272**, 1281 (1965)].

TRIPHENYL PHOSPHATE (TPP)

TPP has a low order of acute toxicity for rats, mice, and guinea pigs. It produces delayed generalized illness and paralysis in cats. When administered orally or injected in alcohol solution, it is absorbed slowly. TPP is poorly absorbed through the intact skin and does not produce skin irritation. Although TPP inhibits cholinesterase *in vitro* and *in vivo*, it is not a potent anticholinesterase agent. Large doses do not produce cholinergic symptoms in rats, mice, guinea pigs, or cats. No adverse clinical effects have been found in men exposed for 10 years to TPP vapor mist and dust at an air concentration of 3.5 mg/m³. See Tricresyl Phosphates, p. 604.

TRIPHENYL PHOSPHITE

Prolonged and repeated skin contact can result in skin irritation even though triphenyl phosphite is not readily absorbed through the unbroken skin.

Treatment: See Tridecyl Phosphite, p. 604.

TRIS(β-CHLOROETHYL) PHOSPHITE

This chemical is moderately toxic on ingestion of a single oral dose. The material is absorbed through the unbroken skin in sufficient quantities to cause death in animals. The rate of absorption is such that skin absorption in humans would probably not be a serious hazard from single exposures. Rabbit tests indicate that tris(β-chloroethyl) phosphite is as irritating to the skin as many common detergents.

When applied undiluted into the eyes of rabbits, it caused moderately severe eye irritation. Inhalation studies indicate that the vapors are quite toxic.

Treatment: In case of ingestion, induce vomiting and follow with gastric lavage. For eye, skin, and mucous membrane contact, flood affected parts with water. For inhalation accidents, remove victim promptly from the contaminated atmosphere. If breathing has stopped, administer artificial respiration and oxygen. Further therapy is symptomatic.

TRISODIUM PHOSPHATE

A 5-year-old girl swallowed a wax-remover containing trisodium phosphate. She complained of burning in the mouth and throat and felt sick, but recovered uneventfully. Wax-removers, though not comparable to lye, are strongly alkaline.

Treatment: See Sodium Hydroxide, p. 543.

TRYPTAMINE

Epená, a snuff containing tryptamine-type compounds, is used by some South American Indian tribes in divination, and in the "diagnosis" and treatment of diseases. It is obtained from species of Myristicaceae (*Virola calophylla*) Warburg and *Virola calophylloidea* Markgraf. Absorption of the snuff causes excitation followed by sedation, changes in perception, including macropsia and possibly paresthesia, and sometimes loss of consciousness. The main component of epená is 5-methoxy-*N*,*N*-dimethyltryptamine (5-MeO-DMT). In addition, it contains small amounts of *N*,*N*-dimethyltryptamine (DMT) and 5-hydroxy-*N*,*N*-dimethyltryptamine (Bufotenine). See also Dimethyltryptamine, p. 226. [B. Holmstedt, *Arch. Intern. Pharmacodyn.* **156**, 285 (1965)].

TUNG NUT (*Aleurites fordii*)

The kernels of the tung-oil tree or China wood-oil tree are toxic on ingestion. Contact with the tree, nuts, and crude tung oil has been reported to produce dermatitis in sensitive individuals. Ingestion of three or more nuts results in nausea, vomiting, violent abdominal cramps, diarrhea and tenesmus, followed by thirst, dizziness, lethargy, and disorientation. In a severe intoxication, cramps in arms and legs, mydriasis, fever, respiratory difficulties, and tachycardia have also been reported. A child may have cyanosis. The poison of the tung oil has been found to be a saponin, which can be isolated from the leaves and from commercial tung meal.

Treatment requires removal of the toxic principles (a toxalbumin, a saponin, and an unidentified alcohol-soluble substance) from the gastroenteric tract. Fortunately, the violent vomiting that sometimes follows ingestion of the nut removes most of the material. The patient requires intensive treatment only in a severe intoxication. This may include a saline cathartic, but more frequently, administration of electrolytes and inhalation of oxygen. During the recovery phase, the patient should receive a bland diet.

TUNG SEED

The toxic agent in tung oil is a saponin, which can be isolated from commercial tung meal. Ingestion of tung seeds by three adults caused symptoms of diarrhea and vomiting. The effects in these men were self limiting.

TURPENTINE

Excessive vapor inhalation will induce headache, confusion and respiratory and gastroenteric distress. Skin contact in hypersensitive individuals will result in erythema and itching. Accidental ingestion will induce local irritation of the entire gastroenteric tract and injury to the kidneys if the dose is large. The probable lethal oral dose for an adult is 150 ml. Aspiration into the lungs will cause chemical pneumonitis.

Treatment: Remove from the skin with soap and water. In case of ingestion administer gastric lavage, cathartics, diuretics, and demulcents. Subsequent treatment is symptomatic and supportive.

TURTLE MEAT

Mass poisoning from ingestion of turtle meat was reported in Quilon in 1961. It is believed that the meat became toxic because the turtles (*Eretmochelys imbricata*) had ingested poisonous flagellates. It is interesting to note that individuals who ingested a turtle curry, prepared by boiling and decanting the water from the meat, did not become sick. Symptoms included severe vomiting, pain in the throat, drowsiness, general weakness, and congested eyes. Six pregnant women aborted. Pulmonary edema occurred just before death in 18 patients [*J. Assoc. Physicians India* **10**, 181 (1962); *JAMA* **181**, 802 (1962)].

Attention was recently directed to the danger of pet turtles as a cause of salmonella infection [*Clin-Alert,* No. 280 (1967)]. Therefore, in any unexplained salmonella infection, especially in a child, inquiries should be made as to the possibility of a pet being the vector of the infection [*Brit. Med. J.* **4**, 296 (1967)].

Treatment: Remove gastroenteric contents as soon as the intoxication becomes apparent. Treatment otherwise is symptomatic. See Fish, p. 263, and Clams, p. 179.

TYROTHRICIN

This antibiotic, which contains tyrocidin (80%) and gramicidin (20%), is active primarily against gram-positive organisms. Because of systemic toxicity, its usefulness is restricted to the topical treatment of infections of the nose, throat, and eyes. Absorption of this drug mixture must be avoided because of its marked hemolytic effect. When used as directed, tyrothricin is essentially free from undesirable effects.

Serious side effects noted on rare occasions include anosmia and parosmia [E. M. Seydell and W. P. McKnight, *Arch. Otolaryngol.* **47**, 465 (1948)].

Caution: Because of the danger of producing fatal chemical meningitis, suspensions of tyrothricin must not be used for irrigating nasal sinuses in close proximity to the subarachnoid spaces [F. J. Ohenasek and D. Fairman, *Arch. Otolaryngol.* **47**, 21 (1948)].

ULTRAVIOLET RADIATION

Professional entertainers exposed to radiation from ultraviolet lamps that cause fluorescent materials to glow have complained of eye irritation and mild skin effects resembling sunburn.

Prevention: Reduction of exposure by reducing the number of lamps, location of lamps at a greater distance and installation of partial light shields will reduce eye and skin effects [*Occupational Health Activities,* No. 2, U.S. Dept. of Health, Education and Welfare, (December 1967)]. See also Sun Rays, p. 567.

URANIUM

Many of the soluble uranium salts are highly toxic. In contrast to the more insoluble salts, they are readily absorbed from the lungs, skin, and gastroenteric tract, and may induce local irritation, inflammation of the capillaries, nephritis, hepatitis, acidosis, and edema. Following inhalation, the soluble compounds exert their primary effect on the kidneys; the insoluble compounds act mainly on the lungs. Usually, there is a latent period of 1–4 days between exposure and onset of symptoms. A toxic dose of a uranium compound induces a typical acute intoxication which results either in recovery within 1 month and little or no residual effect, or in early death. Airborne radioactive particles have apparently been responsible for a significantly increased death rate from lung cancer among long-term uranium miners [*Mod. Med.* **31**, 24, (1963)]. (See also Radiation, p. 512.)

Treatment: Uranium dust on the skin is effectively removed by thorough washing with soap and water. In case of an oral intoxication, administer large doses of sodium bicarbonate. This will convert the uranium salt to the bicarbonate, which is much less toxic. Sodium citrate I.V. also has been recommended as an antidote, but it is believed to be less effective. Additional treatment is symptomatic. CaNa$_2$ EDTA has been reported to be useful in increasing the excretion of uranium. BAL is ineffective.

URETHANE (Ethyl Carbamate)

Urethane is a mild hypnotic. It has been used in the treatment of chronic granulocytic leukemia and in chronic lymphocytic leukemia. It is not a cure for leukemia. Following therapeutic doses, side effects such as nausea and vomiting occur in approximately 50%; drowsiness is less frequent. Prolonged oral administration has resulted in gastroenteric hemorrhages. Leukopenia, which occurs occasionally, develops slowly with prolonged treatment. Debilitated patients are more prone to hepatitis or fatal hepatic necrosis, particularly if treatment is for a prolonged period and in relatively large doses. The usual therapeutic dose ranges from 1 to 3 gm daily, taken in three or four doses with meals. The drug, in the same total daily dosage, may also be given parenterally. See Carbamates, Alkyl and Aryl, p. 83, and Polyurethane, p. 490.

Caution: Treatment should be interrupted or discontinued if the leukocyte count drops significantly.

URINE SUGAR TESTING TABLETS

These contain copper sulfate, sodium hydroxide, sodium bicarbonate, and citric acid.

See Sodium Hydroxide, p. 543, and Copper, p. 185.

URUSHIOL

This is a mixture containing catechol derivatives, which are the vesicating agents in poison ivy, poison sumac, and poison oak. See Poison Ivy, p. 484.

VANADIUM PENTOXIDE

In a pilot plant pelletizing operation, eighteen workers processing pure vanadium pentoxide became acutely ill following inhalation of high concentrations of small particle-size vanadium pentoxide dust. The clinical syndrome was characterized by irritation of the eyes, nose, and throat, the presence of rales throughout the lungs, acute bronchospasm (similar in every respect to acute bronchial asthma), and occasional skin symptoms. Urinary vanadium excretion was detectable in twelve workers by spectrographic analysis for periods of up to two weeks. Routine and microscopic urinalysis, chest X-rays, and pulmonary function studies were normal.

Treatment: Removal of the men from the contaminated working environment was effective. A simple cough syrup was given all men for symptomatic relief. Several of the most severely ill were treated with aerosolized bronchodilator agents such as isoproterenol in a dilution of 1:200. Three workers were given oral ephedrine in combination with a mild barbiturate. While on medication, no man was permitted to return to the dusty work area. Recovery in each case was complete [Carl Zenz *et al., Arch. Environ. Health* **5**, 542 (1962)].

VANADIUM TRIOXIDE

This compound is a component of the ash dust formed in the combustion of fuel oils in the boiler furnaces of electric power stations, central heating installations, annealing furnaces, etc. Workers cleaning boilers and furnaces are exposed to the action of this ash dust which has toxic properties due mainly to the vanadium trioxide. The oxide content in the ash dust can reach 10–15% of the total weight of the ash. Vanadium trioxide is a black powder with a high melting point (1900°C). It is practically insoluble in water and in weakly acid and alkaline solutions. Examination of 120 workers exposed to dust containing up to 10% vanadium trioxide and up to 9% vanadium pentoxide revealed three cases of bronchial asthma which had developed after occupational contact of 1–5 years. When contact with vanadium was discontinued, this condition improved but was not completely eliminated. When contact (with the dust) was renewed, the condition of these workers deteriorated acutely [I. V. Roschin *et al., Gigiena Truda i Prof. Zabolevaniya* **28**, 25 (1964)].

Treatment: Discontinue exposure. Further treatment is supportive and symptomatic. See Vanadium Pentoxide.

VANCOMYCIN (Vancocin)

This antibiotic is administered only I.V. and I.M. In an effort to preserve its value, use of vancomycin should be restricted to in-hospital treatment of severe staphylococcal and streptococcal infections that are resistant to other antibiotics. There is no cross resistance, nor cross hypersensitization to other antibiotics. Excessive doses have caused fever, deafness, hypotension, and in exceptional instances renal irritation. This drug is locally irritating and may produce thrombophlebitis; however, little difficulty is usually encountered.

Caution: The directions of the manufacturer should be carefully followed.

VANILLIC ACID DIETHYLAMIDE (Emivan; Vandid; Ethamivan)

Toxic doses of this analeptic produce marked stimulation of the vasomotor and respiratory centers. Depending on the dose, the following may be produced: coughing, vomiting, laryngospasm, cardiac arrhythmias, and convulsions.

Treatment is entirely symptomatic.

VARIDASE

This enzyme preparation, a mixture of streptokinase and streptodornase, is reported to facilitate liquefaction and drainage of fibrinous and purulent exudates.

Caution: The clinical value of systemic proteolytic enzymes has not been established and there is risk of allergic reactions to both topical and systemic preparations, especially the parenteral ones [*Med. Letter* **9**, 17 (1967)].

VIKANE (Sulfuryl Fluoride)

Vikane is the trade name for sulfuryl fluoride, a relatively new fumigant. A 30-year-old white male breathed Vikane for approximately 4 hours under conditions of limited ventilation. The patient noted the onset of nausea, vomiting, crampy abdominal pain, and pruritus, and left the area. Examination revealed normal vital signs, reddened conjunctivae, pharyngeal and nasal mucosa, diffuse rhonchi, and paresthesia (to pin prick) of the lateral border of the right leg.

Treatment: There is no specific treatment for this intoxication. Management of this patient was supportive and symptomatic. He was discharged on the fourth day. Efforts should be directed toward combating respiratory depression, the reversal of which suggests that complete recovery can be expected. Surveillance, however, must be maintained for several weeks to rule out hepatic and renal sequelae.

VINBLASTINE SULFATE (Velban; Vincaleukoblastine)

This alkaloid, derived from the periwinkle plant, has demonstrated varying degrees of antineoplastic activity in the treatment of Hodgkin's disease, lymphosarcoma, reticulum cell carcinoma, mycosis fungoides and chariocarcinoma. N. E. Fusenig *et al.* reported the following side effects in 95 patients: leukopenia <100 cells/mm^3, 12 patients; thrombopenia 50,000, 4 patients; alopecia, 15 patients; vomiting, 11 patients; polyneuritis, 8 patients; paresthesias, 5 patients; diarrhea, 5 patients, and stomatitis, pain in legs, weakness, and thrombophlebitis in 1 to 4 patients [*Intern. J. Clin. Pharm.* **1**, 40 (1967)]. An overdose is liable to produce central nervous system damage or death.

Vincristine sulfate (Oncovin) is closely related to vinblastin. A recent publication describes 20 patients who received this drug and who suffered side effects such as ptosis, ocular muscle paresis, and fifth and seventh nerve involvement. Most patients also had signs of peripheral neuropathy, or cranial nerve palsies, nausea and vomiting, constipation or alopecia [D. M. Albert, *Arch. Ophthal.* **78**, 709 (1967)].

Caution and Treatment: The recommendations of the manufacturer must be followed meticulously. The drugs are given I.V., but no oftener than once in 7 days. Extravasation must be carefully avoided. Side effects usually disappear following decreased dosage. Appearance of frank signs of neurotoxicity require interruption or discontinuation of therapy. See also Periwinkle, p. 459.

VINYL BROMIDE

Vinyl bromide is a colorless, mobile, nonflammable liquid, boiling at 15.8°C (760 mm Hg). The oral LD_{50} value for rats is about 0.5 gm/kg. Because of the high vapor pressure of vinyl bromide, there should be no problem from ingestion incidental to industrial use. Single prolonged exposures may cause slight anesthesia. Repeated inhalation experience indicates that vinyl bromide is not highly toxic but overexposure may cause liver and kidney damage. A level of 50 ppm may be used for control purposes until a threshold limit value is recommended.

Undiluted vinyl bromide is slightly-to-moderately irritating to the eye. Direct contact with the liquid is capable of producing slight-to-moderate conjunctivitis which subsides in a day. Since rapid evaporation of the liquid can cause a frostbite-type injury, eye exposure may result in a burn depending on the extent of exposure.

Undiluted vinyl bromide is nonirritating to the intact or abraded skin if exposure is not excessive. Because of the rapid evaporation, frostbite-type injury can occur if exposure is excessive.

Treatment: In case of inhalation exposure, remove individual to fresh air. If breathing has stopped, start artificial respiration immediately. If eyes are contaminated with vinyl bromide, they should be flushed immediately with copious amounts of flowing water for at least 15 minutes.

VINYL CHLORIDE (Chloroethylene; Chlorethene)

Pure vinyl chloride is a colorless gas at room temperature; its boiling point is 13.9°C. It has a sweetish odor. The vapor has little or no irritating effect. Six human subjects exposed to 4000 ppm for 5 minutes reported no effects; 12,000 ppm under the same conditions caused dizziness in two subjects, but no apparent difference in the reactions of the other four subjects. Two men exposed for approximately 3 minutes to 25,000 ppm experienced dizziness and disorientation as to space and the size of surrounding objects, and complained of a burning sensation in the soles of the feet.

Atmospheric exposure to 10% vinyl chloride produced deep narcosis in mice and rats, but no deaths; 30% concentrations killed these animals. Exposure of guinea pigs to 20% produced deep narcosis; but three of five guinea pigs survived exposures to 40% concentration. The principal pathological changes in animals dying from exposure were congestion of the lungs with pulmonary edema and hemorrhages and congestion of the liver and kidneys.

Thirty-one cases of hand disorder have been reported among 3000 workers involved in vinyl chloride manufacturing and polymerization. These men complained of soreness and tenderness of the fingertips. The great majority were characterized by two common factors: symptoms likened to those ascribed to Raynaud's phenomenon and acroosteolysis of the distal phalanges. A few had no symptoms, but had the roentgenographic evidence of acroosteolysis. In several of the patients, there were external skin lesions on the dorsal surfaces of the hands and forearms, with a rope-like appearance resembling changes sometimes seen in scleroderma. Some had clubbing of the fingers. The disorder is believed to have resulted from the combination of physical injury, chemical insult, and personal idiosyncrasy [R. H. Wilson *et al.*, *JAMA* **201**, 577 (1967)].

VINYLPYRROLIDONE

Vinylpyrrolidone is a clear liquid completely miscible with water and having a boiling point of 193°C (400 mm Hg). The acute oral toxicity for rats is as follows: LD_0, 1.0 ml/kg; LD_{50}, 1.5 ml/kg; LD_{100}, 2.5 ml/kg. Skin tests indicate that this material is neither a sensitizer nor a primary skin irritant.

Treatment: In case of contact with skin or eyes, flush immediately with plenty of water.

VITAMIN A (Oleovitamin A)

Vitamin A deficiency leads to night blindness, changes of the cornea, iris and lens, keratosis, reduced growth in children, and changes in tooth structure.

Hypervitaminosis A is characterized by anorexia, irritability, pruritus, headache, cracking and bleeding of lips, diplopia, and low-grade fever. Signs and symptoms that usually appear later include yellow coloration of the skin (carotenemia), loss of hair, enlargement of the liver, and swelling and pain over the ends of the long bones. Severe gastroenteric upsets were experienced by arctic explorers shortly after ingesting polar bear liver. One pound of this liver contains about 1,000,000 IU of vitamin A. Acute poisoning may occur with doses over 1,000,000 IU. Chronic poisoning occurs more frequently in children than in adults (100,000–500,000 IU/day for months). Infants have shown increased intracranial pressure and desquamation of the skin of the palms and soles.

Bone changes such as premature closure of the epiphyses (affecting one or both legs or other bones) caused by excessive ingestion of vitamin A are longer lasting—indeed they may be irreparable and full longitudinal bone growth may never be attained. The requirement for vitamin A, and the rates of absorption and metabolism vary with the individual. The minimum daily requirement ranges from 1500 to 4000 IU.

A woman who took nearly 150,000 IU daily began to lose hair on the scalp, eyebrows, axilla, and pubic area after 2 years. At the end of 3 years she complained of stiffness and pain in all joints and marked bleeding from the gums; after 4 years, her eyes became inflamed and there was spontaneous oozing of blood from the nose and mucous membranes of the eyes, mouth, and vagina. Another woman who took 600,000 IU/day for 3 years suffered from similar symptoms. It appears that a total of 11 cases of hypervitaminosis have been reported in adults [R. J. Di Benedetto, *JAMA* **201**, 700 (1967)].

Treatment: As a rule no treatment is required. Recovery follows discontinuation of vitamin A intake. Relief from nonspecific and musculoskeletal symptoms occurs within a few weeks; hepatomegaly and alopecia are frequently the last to disappear (Di Benedetto). No statement can be made in regard to recovery from changes in the long bones.

VITAMIN B₁ (Thiamine)

Thiamine deficiency results in beriberi. The toxicity of thiamine is very low. Large I.V. doses (up to 500 mg daily) have been given without ill effects in treatment of deficiency symptoms. Hypersensitivity has been reported, in an occasional patient, particularly after parenteral administration. One hypersensitive patient died after one 10 mg I.V. dose.

VITAMIN B₂ (Riboflavin)

Photophobia, cataracts, abnormal pigmentation of the iris, burning of the eyes, lacrimation, cracking and erosion at the corners of the mouth, and seborrheic dermatitis are some of the signs and symptoms of severe vitamin B_2 deficiency. When these effects appear, the patient usually is in need of other vitamins. Hypervitaminosis has apparently not been observed. In animals, the toxicity of riboflavin is of a low order.

VITAMIN B_6 (Pyridoxine)

Vitamin B_6 deficiency may lead to nausea, vomiting, seborrheic dermatitis, retarded growth, anemia, leukocytopenia, agranulocytosis, neuritis, bone changes, and convulsions. These signs and symptoms have been observed in infants fed a synthetic diet. Pyridoxine deficiency may give rise to seborrheic dermatitis in adults. These incidents are rare; they may be explained on the basis of a deficient diet, subnormal absorption from the gastroenteric tract, or increased requirements. The toxicity of pyridoxine is low. Large doses have not produced harmful effects.

VITAMIN B_{12} (Cyanocobalamin; Cobione)

Prolonged vitamin B_{12} deficiency leads to pernicious anemia. This vitamin combined with the "intrinsic factor" (Bevidox, Cobione, Rametin, Redisol, and Rubramin) promotes the formation of the anti-pernicious anemia substance found in the liver. In persons with pigmented skin, vitamin B_{12} deficiency may lead to hyperpigmentation. S. J. Baker *et al.* described such effects in southern Indian patients, 15 adults and 6 children [*Mod. Med.* **32**, 92 (1964)]. Evidence has not been presented that excessive doses are harmful. Preparations of vitamin B_{12} should be kept refrigerated.

VITAMIN B COMPLEX

The term vitamin B complex refers to a number of compounds which were formerly called vitamin B. Vitamin B complex includes folic acid, nicotinic acid, pyridoxine, riboflavin, thiamine, pantothenic acid, biotin, etc.

VITAMIN C (Ascorbic Acid)

Scurvy results from severe and prolonged vitamin C deficiency. The toxicity of ascorbic acid is of a low order. However, excessive quantities are not recommended since they tend to disturb the vitamin C regularity mechanism which protects the body against loss of this vitamin. Vitamin C has no effect on colds. According to the FDA, drug manufacturers are prohibited from advertising this vitamin as a specific cold remedy [*Sci. News* **92**, 221 (1967)]. Proprietory vitamin C preparations include Cebione and Cevex.

VITAMIN D

In children, vitamin D deficiency causes rickets; in adults it leads to osteomalacia and muscle weakness and occasionally hypocalcemic tetany. A child requires about 400 IU (10 μg) per day. Vitamin D is found in certain fish, liver oils, egg yolk, and milk. Vitamin D is synthesized in the skin under the influence of ultraviolet rays. According to W. F. Loomis, black skin allows only 3–36% of ultraviolet rays to pass, while white skin passes 53–72%. The farther north man went from the equatorial region, the more completely did the light-skinned survive and the dark-skinned die out. United States Negro children suffer far more commonly from rickets than white children [*Time* (Aug. 18, 1967)].

Signs and symptoms of vitamin D toxicity result partially from the ultimate demineralization of the bones and the precipitation of calcium (calcinosis) in various tissues. Toxic effects may be expected from prolonged therapy with doses exceeding 1800 units in infants, 30,000 units in children, and 100,000 units in adults. Tolerance varies considerably. Signs or symptoms have been noted in some individuals with considerably lower doses given for only 1 week.

Tausig points out that some children have the ability to metabolize vitamin D to such an extent that they can be seriously injured by a dose of vitamin D not harmful to others. So-called idiopathic hypercalcemia seems to be related to this unusual ability to metabolize vitamin D and the resulting effect of converting calcium from food to bone calcium. There is also evidence that hypercalcemia is, in turn, related to supravalvular aortic stenosis. Exactly what determines whether an infant with high blood calcium will subsequently develop supravalvular aortic stenosis is not clear. However, present evidence indicates that injury to the cardiovascular system occurs when there is an abnormally high blood calcium and/or abnormality of vitamin D metabolism. Under such conditions, the patient may develop what has generally been considered to be a congenital malformation of the heart. Tausig concludes: "My plea to you all is that, if large doses of vitamin D are not necessary and there is any possibility that they may do harm, do follow the old adage, if you cannot do good, be sure not to do harm [*Ann. Internal Med.* **65**, 1195 (1966)]." The earliest symptoms may include loss of appetite, anorexia, fatigue, nausea, headache, polyuria, and diarrhea. Children frequently become irritated and depressed. The symptoms sometimes resemble those of meningitis. Other undesirable effects may include some or all of the following: anemia, loss of weight, cramps, paresthesia, hyperactive calcification of bone, urinary frequency, nocturia, and finally calcification of the kidneys, arteries, and other organs and tissues.

Treatment of hypervitaminosis includes discontinuation of therapy, high fluid intake, low calcium diet, and administration of cortisone. While chelating agents may be helpful, drastic therapy is not indicated.

VITAMIN K

Normally, vitamin K is produced in the enteric tract from dietary breakdown products. It is required in the formation of prothrombin, which is essential for the clotting of blood. Prothrombin, when acted upon by thromboplastin and calcium ions, is converted to thrombin, which changes soluble fibrinogen to a fibrin clot. Conditions of hypoprothrombinemia may arise because of overdoses of coumarin-type drugs, because of liver disease (this condition is not necessarily benefited by vitamin K), during therapy with antibiotics, and because of dietary insufficiencies in hemorrhagic diseases. In the newborn, gastroenteric activity may be subnormal and hence result in a subnormal formation of vitamin K.

Vitamin K_1 is on the market in the form of two oily liquids: as phytonadione (Mephyton, Aquamephyton, Konakion, Mona-Kay), and as menadione (Menaphthone, Danitanon K, Aquinone, Menaquinone). Water-soluble synthetic vitamin K preparations in clinical use include menadiol sodium diphosphate (Synkayvite; Kappadione; Thylokay) and menadione sodium bisulfite (Hykinone).

M. J. Finkel suggests the following doses:

Vitamin K_1: to mother or to infant, 1–5 mg P.O. or parenterally for prophylaxis, and up to 10 mg (or more if required) to the infant in cases of hemorrhage.

Menadiol sodium diphosphate: to mother during labor, single I.V. dose of 6 mg; to infant, 3 mg. Give slightly larger doses if hemorrhage has occurred.

Menadione sodium bisulfite: to mother, single I.V. dose of 2 mg; to infant, single dose of 1 mg. [*Clin. Pharmacol. Therap.* **2**, 794 (1961)].

In cases of warfarin or bishydroxycoumarin intoxications, vitamin K_1 (phytonadione) is given I.V. *slowly* in a dose ranging from 25 to 100 mg, at a rate not exceeding 10 mg/minute; also consider the same dose of menadione sodium bisulfite. Too rapid injections result in flushing and in a sense of constriction in the chest. In an emergency, when a prompt increase in prothrombin activity is needed, whole fresh blood, or whole plasma should be used.

WARFARIN (Coumadin; Panwarfin; Prothromadin; Warcoumin)

This compound has actions similar to those of bishydroxycoumarin (Dicumarol). The initial oral dose is 40–50 mg, maintenance doses range from 5 to 15 mg/day. Since the compound is readily absorbed from the gastroenteric tract, the dosage is the same whether given orally or intravenously.

Caution: The dosage of warfarin must be controlled and based on determinations of the prothrombin time. At the initiation of therapy, this test should be conducted daily; after a stable dosage schedule has been established, tests may be conducted at 2–4 week intervals.

Treatment of an overdose is the same (vitamin K) as for bishydroxycoumarin, p. 131.

WASHING POWDERS

These preparations may contain borax, sodium carbonate, sodium or calcium hypochlorite, and trisodium phosphate.

WATER

Numerous records are available of men and women surviving long periods of food deprivation. A pilot and female passenger survived 46 days of exposure to extreme cold without food; but there is no authentic report of survival, for even half this period, with total water restriction [N. B. Strydom *et al.,J. Occupational Med.* **7**, 581 (1965)]. Dehydration exhaustion becomes apparent when water deficit reaches 5–6% of body weight. Six to ten per cent dehydration produces high pulse rate, high rectal temperatures, nausea, loss of appetite, difficulty in muscular movements, numbness, and emotional instability. A water deficit of 11–15% causes delirium, deafness, dimness of vision, swollen tongue, anuria and even death (N. B. Strydom *et al.*). To prevent water deficit, ingestion of watery liquids in adequate amounts is essential. Salting of water is not recommended; sodium chloride should be provided at mealtimes, or under certain conditions such as in hot industrial plants; i.e., salt tablets placed near water dispensers. Briefly, the recommendations of Strydom *et al.* for survival with little or no water include: (1) if lost in a desert region, stay where you are so that search parties may find you; (2) make use of any available shelter to reduce effects of sun and wind and do not shed clothing; (3) if moving is essential, this should be done at night; (4) never lie down in the sun, a sitting position will reduce exposed area; (5) if available, drink the radiator water in small sips, do not wait for complete exhaustion; (6) consider ingestion of juices of plants, leaves, roots, or the raw meat of animals, including blood and intestinal juices (See original paper).

H. Lol of the Armour Research Foundation finds that two cups of seawater per day will prolong survival, but he suggests that those stranded at sea do not drink any water at all the first 2 days [*Ensign* (Nov. 1964)]. Seawater, if ingested in larger amounts, is toxic.

Water intoxications have resulted following proctoclysis and the administration of excessive volumes (I.V. drip or ingestion) containing oxytocin used to induce labor. Intoxications have also been precipitated by postoperative administration of excessive amounts of 5% dextrose in water and by administration of hypotonic fluids during mannitol diuresis. Water intoxication can also occur in infants [*Pediatrics* **39**, 418 (1967)] and in normal persons, if the intake is excessive (after profuse sweating) or if the rate of intake temporarily exceeds the ability of the kidneys to maintain isotonicity of body fluids through diuresis.

Certain factors predispose to the development of water intoxication; namely, heart failure, severe liver disease, and renal insufficiency. In the immediate post-operative period, water metabolism is similarly affected. [E. Lipsmeyer and G. L. Ackerman, *JAMA*, **196**, 286 (1966)]. For a report on hypernatremic dehydration from hypotonic enemas, see report by E. W. Fonkalsrud and J. Keen [*JAMA* **199**, 584 (1967)]. The literature on "water intoxication due to oxytocin" includes *New Engl. J. Med.* **269**, 481 (1963); and *Am. J. Med. Sci.* **252**, 573 (1966). P. J. Whalley and J. A. Pritchard warn that it is essential that the volume of electrolyte-free fluid infused be limited by increasing the concentration of oxytocin in the vehicle rather than increasing the rate and volume of water infused [*JAMA* **186**, 601 (1963)]. According to the literature, the prognosis is good with correction of hypotonicity through administration of hypertonic sodium chloride. The report by E. Lipsmeyer and G. A. Ackerman is of interest since they present two patients who suffered irreversible brain damage after prolonged and severe hypotonicity [*JAMA* **196**, 286 (1966)].

Treatment: The oral administration of table salt or injection of solutions of sodium chloride will reverse the state of hypotonicity promptly. For a severe water intoxication, A. V. Wolf recommends the I.V. injection of 200 ml of a 5 % aqueous solution of sodium chloride ("The Urinary Function of the Kidney." Grune and Stratton, New York, 1950). See also Sodium Chloride, p. 539, and Diving, p. 31.

Maintenance Therapy

The following presents, almost verbatim, electrolyte requirements and replacement therapy as prepared by consultants of the *Medical Letter.* In the introduction of this report, it is pointed out that substantial — but by no means unanimous — agreement was reached by the consultants. It is recognized that there are acceptable alternative methods for determining and supplying fluid and electrolyte requirements.

When the patient cannot take fluids orally, as after surgery, intravenous maintenance therapy is indicated to prevent dehydration and electrolyte deficits.

Water: Children and small adults need more water per pound than do larger adults; water requirements are more clearly related to body surface area than to weight. A useful formula for maintenance water, based on studies by Crawford, Butler, and Talbot, is: maintenance water = 1600 ml/per square meter of body surface area/per 24 hours. With obese or edematous patients, surface area should be calculated on the basis of "ideal" rather than actual weight. In the newborn, the volume administered in the first week or two should be half that calculated from surface area. The relationship of surface area to body weight and the corresponding approximate maintenance water requirements are given in Table A.

Table A
Maintenance Water Requirements Based on Surface Area

Body weight		Surface area	Approximate maintenance water
(kg)	(lb)	m²	(ml/24 hours)
3	6.6	0.21	300
6	13.2	0.30	500
10	22.0	0.45	700
20	44.0	0.80	1300
30	66.0	1.05	1700
40	88.0	1.30	2100
50	110.0	1.50	2400
60	132.0	1.65	2600
70	154.0	1.75	2800
80	176.0	1.85	3000

An alternative formula, based on age, is that of W. M. Wallace; it is preferred by some clinicians as simpler and equally reliable, but it is only applicable to patients up to 20 years of age: milliliters of maintenance water/kilogram/24 hours = $100 - (3 \times$ age in years).

Dextrose: All maintenance solutions should contain at least 5% dextrose, since caloric deficits almost always accompany the loss of fluid and electrolytes. The use of dextrose minimizes ketosis and the build-up of "starvation solutes" (urea, phosphate, and other protein-breakdown products), which increase the excretory load. Solutions containing both dextrose and fructose offer no advantage over dextrose alone.

Electrolyte Requirements: Maintenance electrolyte requirements are harder to estimate than water requirements, since renal excretion of sodium, potassium, bicarbonate, and chloride varies enormously in response to variations in such factors as diet, water intake, acid-base balance, and endocrine function. Nevertheless, requirements may be empirically set at about 25 mEq each of sodium, chloride, and either bicarbonate or lactate per liter of maintenance solution. Potassium (15–20 mEq per liter) may also be included if renal function is adequate; when renal function is impaired, potassium should be used very cautiously.

A satisfactory maintenance solution meeting most requirements for patients with good renal function can be made by combining the following ingredients:

1. 150 ml of $\frac{1}{6}$ M sodium lactate *or* isotonic sodium bicarbonate (25 mEq sodium and either lactate or bicarbonate).

2. 20 ml of 1 M potassium chloride (20 mEq potassium and chloride).

3. 830 ml of 5% dextrose in water.

Proprietary solutions with similar electrolyte concentrations are listed in Table B.

Table B
Pre-Mixed Electrolyte Solutions for Maintenance

Solution	Supplier	Milliequivalents per liter					
		Na	K	Cl	HCO_3	Mg	P
Ionosol MB	Abbott	25	20	22	23	3	3
Electrolyte 4	Baxter	35	15	22	20	–	3
Electrolyte 48	Cutter	25	20	22	23	3	3
Electrolyte 4	McGaw	30	15	22	20	–	3
Isolyte P	McGaw	25	20	22	23	3	3

Replacement Therapy

Replacement therapy is indicated when there is considerable loss of water and electrolytes, as in severe vomiting and diarrhea. Solutions resembling extracellular fluid for rapid repair of water and electrolyte deficits include those listed in Table C.

Table C

Solution	Supplier	Milliequivalents per liter					
		Na	K	Cl	HCO$_3$	Ca	Mg
Hartmann's	Abbott; Cutter; McGaw	131	4	110	28	3	—
Ionosol D-CM	Abbott	138	12	108	50	5	3
Normosol R	Abbott	140	5	98	27	—	3
Plasmalyte	Baxter	140	10	103	55	5	3
Polysal	Cutter	140	10	103	55	5	3
Equivisol	McGaw	140	10	103	55	5	3
1-2[a]		150	—	100	50	—	—

[a] 1-2 is a nonproprietary mixture consisting of one part $M/6$ lactate and two parts normal saline.

Rapid Initial Replacement: Rapid restoration of full water and electrolyte balance is seldom necessary. In most instances, replacement of 70 ml of water per kilogram per day in addition to the maintenance water requirement will suffice. Thus, a 50 kg patient would require 3500 ml of replacement fluid plus 2400 ml per day for maintenance. If there is evidence of impaired renal function, an attempt should be made to improve fluid balance rapidly by providing 30 ml of fluid per kilogram in the first hour or two. In the 50 kg patient, therefore, 1500 ml of rapid replacement fluid would be given in the first 2 hours; over the next 24 hours, one of the solutions listed in Table D would be used, in the amount of 2000 ml plus 2400 ml, the calculated maintenance volume.

The solution chosen for rapid replacement therapy in the first hour or two should resemble normal extracellular fluid. Some satisfactory proprietary solutions of this type are shown in Table C. Their use permits rapid expansion of vascular and interstitial volume without undue dilution. If the patient is in shock or if there is no clinical improvement after 2 hours of rapid replacement, whole blood, plasma or dextran should be used.

Subsequent Replacement: After the initial rapid replacement therapy, the estimated daily maintenance requirement plus 40 ml per kg for further repair should be given during the remainder of the first 24 hours and for a second 24-hour period. Solutions useful both for continuation of replacement therapy and to satisfy the maintenance requirements for the day are listed in Table D. Seventy ml/kg/day of these solutions may also be used from the start for replacement therapy in patients not requiring rapid restoration of extracellular volume.

Solutions for repair of fluid and electrolyte deficit during the first 24 to 48 hours, after renal function is restored, include the following:

Table D

Solution	Supplier	Milliequivalents per liter						
		Na	K	Cl	HCO₃	Ca	Mg	P
Darrow's	Abbott; Baxter	121	35	103	53	—	—	—
	Cutter, McGaw	Dilute with equal parts of 10% dextrose						
Ionosol B	Abbott	57	25	49	25	—	5	13
Normosol	Abbott	40	13	40	16	—	3	—
Electrolyte 2	Baxter	61	25	50	25	—	6	13
Polysal M	Cutter	40	16	40	24	5	3	—
Electrolyte 2	McGaw	58	25	51	25	—	6	13
1-2-7[a]		46	—[b]	30	16	—	—	—

[a] 1-2-7 is a non-proprietary mixture consisting of one part M/6 lactate, two parts normal saline, and seven parts 10% dextrose in water.

[b] Add sufficient potassium (preferably as acetate) to provide 25 mEq/liter

While provision of calories is not important during the rapid rehydration of the first few hours, solutions used during the remainder of the first day should contain 5% dextrose for its protein-sparing and antiketogenic effects. Extracellular repair can generally be assumed to be complete after 48 hours of replacement therapy unless there is clinical or laboratory evidence to the contrary. Additional intravenous fluids should therefore be of the maintenance type. Intracellular potassium levels may, however, continue to be low and additional potassium may be necessary. The continued use of repair solutions after deficits have been made up may result in an excess of sodium with edema or heart failure, especially in the elderly or in persons with impaired renal or cardiac function. Reproduced from *Med. Letter* 1, 65–68 (1965) courtesy of Harold Aaron, M.D., Chairman, Editorial Committee.

WATER HEMLOCK (*Cicuta* species)

Cicutoxin is the active agent found primarily in the stem and rhizomes, but also in the leaves and flowers of water hemlock (also known as musquash root or spotted cowbane). Absorption of cicutoxin produces central nervous system stimulation leading to epileptiform convulsions. The onset of symptoms depends on the quantity ingested. One rhizome may be fatal for an adult. General malaise with increased salivation and vomiting may appear in 15–20 minutes and progress rapidly to tremors and convulsions. The cause of death depends partially on the length of the acute illness; it may be due to respiratory failure, ventricular fibrillation, or exhaustion.

Several other plants such as Carolina allspice, strawberry shrub, or sweet shrub (*Calycanthus* spp) contain central nervous system stimulants which have caused intoxications. The seeds contain at least two alkaloids, calycanthidine and calycanthine. The fruit of the chinaberry or Indian lilac (*Melia azedarach*) grown in some regions is very toxic; in other areas it is not. Intoxications are characterized by gastroenteric distress, shock, muscular paralysis, kidney and liver injury, and central excitation. All parts of the nux vomica tree (*Strychnos nux-vomica*) contain strychnine and brucine; the convulsants in pink root (*Spigelia marilandica*) and in the moonseed vine (*Menispermum canadense*) have not been identified.

Treatment: The prevention of convulsions is of primary importance. Move the individual to a semi-dark, quiet room. Induce vomiting and follow with gastric lavage if the intoxication is recognized early. Removal of gastroenteric contents should be attempted only by an anesthesiologist if convulsions are imminent or if they have occurred. A *saline* cathartic may be administered. Sedation with barbiturates is recommended, as well as oxygen. Epinephrine and analeptics are contraindicated. If liver or kidney involvement is suspected (after ingestion of chinaberry) maintain a low-fat, high-carbohydrate, high-protein diet for several weeks after the patient has recovered from the acute effects.

WATER PAINTS

The ingestion of children's water paints may color the urine and stools, but no specific signs or symptoms of systemic intoxication have been reported.

Treatment: Treatment does not seem to be indicated. However, if a large amount of paint has been ingested, empty the stomach by inducing emesis.

WAX CRAYONS

One of the constituents in wax crayons is *p*-nitroaniline, which produces methemoglobin.

Treatment: See Aniline, p. 102.

WEED B GON

This weed-killer contains 2,4,5-trichloro-, and 2,4-dichlorophenoxyacetic acid. See 2,4-Dichlorophenoxyacetic Acid, p. 655.

WEIGHT REDUCTION PILLS (Anorexiants)

Besides the amphetamines, this group includes benzphetamine (*Didrex*), diethylpropion (*Tenuate, Tepanil*), phendimetrazine (*Plegine*), phenmetrazine (*Preludin*), and phentermine resin and hydrochloride (*Ionamin; Wilpo*). These drugs are used as adjuvants to lessen appetite in the management of obesity. The side effects reported have not been significant, but since all of these drugs are sympathomimetic amines, overdoses or excessive or uncontrolled use is likely to produce side effects similar to those produced by the amphetamines (see p. 98).

Caution: Psychogenic dependence has not been reported; however, caution is in order because of the similarity of action of these drugs to the amphetamines. A recent report cautions against the use of proprietary reducing pills. At least six deaths, apparently related to these pills, have been studied by Dr. R. C. Henry of Portland, Oregon. The deaths occurred in individuals who were known to be taking the so-called "rainbow" pills for weight reduction. One of his cases involved a 38-year-old woman who noted a gradual onset of muscle weakness. Over a period of three days, quadriplegia and severe respiratory difficulties developed. The patient was found to have a profound hypokalemia. Another patient, a 35-year-old woman, complained of nervousness, shortness of breath, and palpitation. For a period of 2 months, she had been taking a series of colored weight reduction pills which are known to contain, either singly or in combination, digitalis, thyroid, a thiazide diuretic, a laxative, barbiturates, and amphetamines. When examined, the heart rate was 120 beats per minute. The electrocardiogram displayed ventricular premature beats with runs of ventricular tachycardia and a digitalis-type effect [*JAMA* **201**, 895 (1967)].

Treatment: Discontinuation of therapy will be followed by recovery. The 38-year-old woman responded promptly to potassium therapy. For more specific treatment, refer to the individual compounds involved. See also Thyroid, p. 503.

WELDING (Arc Welding)

Ultraviolet rays and heat produced in electric arc welding and gas welding have caused injury to the eyes and skin. The electrodes used in arc welding produce fumes containing finely divided ferrous and ferric oxides which may be 0.5 μ in diameter. If inhaled, these particles accumulate in the peribronchial and perivascular lymphatic spaces and on alveolar septa. They do not cause secondary fibrosis because they are inert. The condition produced, visible on X-ray examination because of the radio opacity of the iron particles, is known as pulmonary siderosis or "tattooing of the lung."

No association has been found between pulmonary siderosis and chronic bronchitis, pulmonary emphysema, bronchopulmonary neoplasm, or active tuberculosis.

Other potentially hazardous substances produced by various welding operations are nitrogen oxides, ozone, carbon monoxide, carbon dioxide, and the various constituents of rods, rod coatings, and the metal being welded (lead, cadmium, cobalt, and beryllium).

Intoxications and fatalities have occurred because of welding in poorly ventilated rooms.

Caution: Avoid inhalations of fumes and eye injury by use of a face mask. Avoid welding in poorly ventilated spaces.

Treatment consists of immediate removal from the site of exposure, oxygen, and rest.

WHIPCIDE

Whipcide tablets induced severe burning and redness of the conjunctiva in patients treated for whipworm. In some patients keratitis, agonizing photophobia, ocular pain, and dense corneal opacity occurred 24 hours after ingestion of the drug. Some individuals also complained of nausea, buzzing in the ears, and deafness.

Treatment: All signs and symptoms of toxicity, with the exception of the most severe keratitis, disappeared 1 week after the drug was withdrawn. The keratitis disappeared in 3 weeks.

WISTERIA

Intoxications have resulted from ingestion of beans or whole pods of the wisteria vine. The immediate effects include nausea, vomiting, abdominal pain, and sometimes diarrhea.

Treatment: Induce vomiting repeatedly and perform gastric lavage. Treatment otherwise is symptomatic. Consider using chlorpromazine if an antiemetic is indicated. No fatalities have been reported.

WOOD

Sawdust from African boxwood (*Gonioma kamassi*) has been reported to cause local irritation of the eyes and respiratory tract, anemia, hepatitis, and depressed heart action. An alkaloid that produces the same effects as the sawdust has been extracted from the wood. The alkaloid resembles curare in some of its actions.

The Japanese wood called tagayase (tagayasan) is known to cause damage to the eyes and skin, and a dark brown punctate pigmentation of the skin. Systemic effects include abnormal renal and gastroenteric function. The active agent is a phenol-like compound similar to chrysarobin.

East Indian satinwood (*Chloroxylon swientenia*) is well known for its damage to the skin; ingestion has caused gastroenteric disturbances and headache.

S. Milham, Jr. and J. E. Hesser present data which support the hypothesis that Hodgkin's disease, in some cases, may be due to exposure to an environmental agent associated with wood [*Lancet* **II**, 136 (1967)]. This supports a report by E. D. Acheson *et al.* that carcinoma of the nasal cavity and accessory sinuses is more common among woodworkers than among workers in other occupations [*Lancet* **I**, 311 (1967)].

Treatment is symptomatic after removal from the site of exposure.

WORCESTERSHIRE SAUCE

This sauce has been reported to contain a high concentration of acetic acid, as well as garlic, black pepper, ginger, allspice, mace, and cinnamon. Long-continued and excessive ingestion has caused renal damage with glomerular and tubular effects which resulted in aminoaciduria and bilateral stone formation. Discontinuation of ingestion of this sauce does not appear to reduce the renal calculi.

XYLENES (Xylols, Dimethylbenzenes)

Xylenes are mixtures of ortho-, meta-, and para isomers of dimethylbenzene. These chemicals produce the same effects as toluene. See Alkylbenzene, p. 83.

XYLIDENE (Aminodimethylbenzene)

The oral LD_{50} for rabbits is 0.6 gm/kg. Xylidene is toxicologically similar to aniline. See Aniline, p. 102.

YTTRIUM

Yttrium-90 has been used in the treatment of pleural and ascitic effusions due to cancer [E. Siegel *et al.*, *JAMA* **161**, 499 (1956)]. B. Rosoff *et al.* studied the removal of yttrium-90 nitrilotriacetate (Y90-NTA) in patients treated I.V. with this compound. Twenty-four hours after administration of Y90-NTA, 500 mg of the calcium salt of diethylenetriaminepentaacetic acid (Ca DTPA) and equivalent amounts of Na EDTA were administered daily on 4 successive days. Ca DTPA was found to be more effective than Na EDTA. A fourfold increase of either chelate did not result in an appreciably higher excretion of the metal chelate. Similar favorable excretion rates were obtained for the removal of lanthanum [*Health Physics* **6**, 177 (1961)].

ZEN MACROBIOTICS (Food Faddism)

This philosophy includes and revolves around a nutritional system that purports to prevent and cure every disease, including dandruff, psychosis, arthritis, heart disease, and cancer. The diets prescribed are largely vegetarian, with a heavy emphasis on whole-grain cereals and avoidance of sugar and fluid. Reports of deaths of individuals who had been on the more rigid of these diets have appeared in the news media.

A 36-year-old woman in good general health weighing 125 pounds became interested in the philosophy of Zen macrobiotics in the spring of 1964. She began to eliminate meat and milk from her diet, and in September 1964, she eliminated all fruit and drastically decreased her fluid intake. By November 1964, her diet was limited to brown rice, pressure-cooked or boiled, salted, and sprinkled with sesame seeds. She also ate some oatmeal, cornmeal, buckwheat, and bread made from cooked rice. Her maximum liquid intake was 12 ounces per day in the form of soup or tea, never water.

After 8 months on this diet, the patient was hospitalized with many of the manifestations of scurvy: reddish-blue friable, spongy masses in the interdentate papillae, petechiae and perifollicular hemorrhages, broken, brittle, corkscrew hairs, and painful hemarthroses. In addition, she had marked anemia and signs of general malnutrition with edema, weakness, lethargy, and depression.

Treatment: The patient recovered on a diet averaging between 4500 and 5000 calories a day supplemented with ascorbic acid, multivitamins, ferrous gluconate, and folic acid [P. Sherlock and E. O. Rothschild, *JAMA* **199**, 793 (1967)].

ZINC

The soluble zinc salts are astringent, corrosive, and emetic. When ingested in toxic doses, they produce severe gastroenteric irritation, nausea, vomiting, diarrhea, and gastroenteric pain. Intoxications have resulted from drinking fruit juices or from ingestion of sauerkraut kept in galvanized containers. Two recent reports of intoxication indicate again that galvanized pots or tubs should not be used for the preparation or storage of food, especially foods with an acid pH, because of the possibility of conversion of zinc metal into soluble zinc salts [*Arch. Environ. Health* 8, 657 (1964)].

Zinc phosphide is a rodenticide which on ingestion releases toxic hydrogen phosphide (phosphine). A dose of 5 gm has caused death; a 50 gm dose has been survived. There have been 25 deaths (70% suicide) reported from Europe. Besides gastroenteric symptoms, patients suffered from excitement and tightness in the chest. Patients alive after 3 days recovered completely. Those that died suffered severe hepatic, renal, and cardiac damage [J. B. P. Stephenson, *Arch. Environ. Health* 15, 83 (1967)]. Zinc dialkyldithiophosphate is irritating to the skin, eyes, and mucous membranes, but it has a low order of systemic toxicity. It is not a cholinesterase inhibitor. Zinc stearate is used in cosmetics and as a constituent of baby powders. Upon ingestion, it has a low order of toxicity, but repeated or prolonged inhalation of this fine powder has produced pneumonitis as well as fatal pneumonia in infants. Inhalation of zinc oxide vapors has induced metal fume fever.

An antagonistic relationship between dietary zinc and cadmium has been reported by several investigators. Gunn, Gould, and Anderson found that injected zinc inhibits cadmium-induced tumors in rats [*Proc. Soc. Exptl. Biol. Med.* 115, 653 (1964)].

Treatment: For oral intoxication, induce vomiting and follow with prompt and complete gastric lavage, cathartics, and demulcents. Consider specific treatment for metabolic acidosis and hypocalcemic tetany. Maintenance of fluid balance is indicated.

ZINC PHOSPHIDE

This is a rodenticide which on ingestion releases highly toxic phosphine (hydrogen phosphide). See Phosphine p. 472.

ZIRCONIUM

A dermatologic disorder called zirconium deodorant granuloma is the result of an acquired hypersensitivity to the zirconium content in deodorants (antiperspirants). The granulomas are clinically similar and histologically indistinguishable from those of other sarcoid granulomas, such as sarcoidosis and beryllium granulomas. In a sensitized individual, a zirconium deodorant granuloma can be produced locally by intradermal injections of 1:10,000 to 1:1,000,000 dilutions of any water-soluble zirconium salt. W. L. Epstein and J. R. Allen reported a case of granulomatous hypersensitivity which resulted from the local application of Ziradryl, a poison oak medication containing zirconium oxide [*JAMA* **190,** 940 (1964)]. A similar incident was described by Lo Presti and Hambrick involving a 15-year-old boy who applied Ziradryl for a total of 6 days to skin areas affected by poison ivy. Approximately 6 months later, many 2–6 mm, firm, shiny, erythematous, nontender papules appeared over the previously treated area. Many of the granulomatous lesions were still present 18 months later [*Arch. Dermatol.* **92,** 188 (1965)]. For retention in tissues and toxicity in animals, consult O. R. Klimmer and W. Doll [*Arzneimittel-Forsch.* **14,** 1286 (1964)]. Zirconium tetrachloride reacts violently with water to form zirconyl chloride and hydrogen chloride.

Caution: Epstein and Allen point out that the value of zirconium salts in treating poison oak dermatitis is considered nil, and although these preparations rarely induce hypersensitivity, their continued availability constitutes an unnecessary hazard. For exposure to zirconium tetrachloride, see Hydrochloric Acid, p. 317.

ZOXAZOLAMINE (Flexin)

This uricosuric drug has been withdrawn from the market because of toxicity, hepatitis, and fatalities.

Additional Compounds and Items of Interest

ARSINE (Arseniuretted Hydrogen, Hydrogen Arsenide)

Arsine is a colorless gas having a garlicky odor. It is formed when hydrogen is generated in the presence of arsenic-containing substances; it is an extremely toxic hemolytic agent. A 30-minute exposure to 250 ppm may be fatal. Exposure causes fever, diarrhea, vomiting, jaundice, and oliguria. Urine has a "port wine" color (hemoglobinuria).

Treatment: Remove promptly from contaminated atmosphere. Give artificial respiration and oxygen if necessary. Bed rest. Treat anemia, if severe, by transfusion. Treatment otherwise is symptomatic.

ASPHYXIANT

1. Simple asphyxiants: Simple asphyxiants are physiologically inert gases that when breathed in high concentrations act mechanically by excluding oxygen. Examples are nitrogen, helium, hydrogen, neon, argon, and nitrous oxide.

2. Chemical asphyxiants: Chemical asphyxiants are substances that by combining with the hemoglobin of the blood or acting on some constituent of the tissues either prevent oxygen from reaching the tissues or prevent the tissues from using it. Examples are carbon monoxide, cyanogen, hydrogen cyanide, cyanogen bromide, and cyanogen chloride.

AUTOMOBILE EXHAUST

Carbon monoxide is the most toxic component of automobile exhaust. See Carbon Monoxide, p. 154.

BAGASSE DISEASE (Bagassosis)

This is a pneumoconiosis from inhalation of the dust of bagasse (dried pulverized stalks of sugar cane).

Clinical evidence suggests hypersensitivity to an unknown agent. Fever and cough are the outstanding symptoms.

Treatment: Symptoms usually disappear 1-3 months after cessation of exposure. There is no specific treatment. Antihistamines and steroids have been helpful in relieving symptoms due to hypersensitivity [*Am. Rev. Respirat. Diseases* **84**, 582 (1961)].

BALL POINT PEN INK

Numerous types of ink are used in ball point pens, with different colors and different formulations depending on the manufacturer. Some are water soluble, some are not. Purple ink may contain crystals of methyl violet. This dye, also found in indelible pencils, has long been known to cause inflammation, particularly of the eye. Although gentian violet is widely used in therapy, it is a fairly common allergen. Almost any ball point ink that penetrates the skin through puncture wounds may lead to tattoo marks. Some slowly disappear; others prove to be permanent. Even ordinary fountain pen inks may lead to permanent tattooing.

Treatment: It appears desirable to delay debridement for some weeks or months to establish the degree of spontaneous disappearance. For cosmetic purposes, debridement may be warranted if the tattoo marks persist.

BENZENE (Benzol)

Absorption of a toxic dose by inhalation or ingestion causes dizziness, weakness, headache, nausea, vomiting, pain in chest, convulsions, coma, and death from respiratory failure. Late effects from chronic exposure are leukopenia and anemia. See also Blood Dyscrasias, page 51. Contact with skin or mucous membranes causes irritation, drying, a burning sensation, and blistering. Probable lethal oral dose for an adult is 15 ml. Brief inhalation of an atmosphere containing 20,000 ppm may be fatal. Do not use benzene to remove adhesive tape residues from skin. The threshold limit for benzene is 25 ppm.

Treatment: For inhalation, remove individual from exposure area and administer oxygen and give artificial respiration if necessary. For ingestion, give demulcents, saline cathartics, oxygen, and artificial respiration if indicated. Give a balanced diet with vitamin supplements and parenteral fluids if needed. Epinephrine is contraindicated. For skin or eyes, wash with copious quantities of water. Apply bland ointment.

BENZENE HEXACHLORIDE (Lindane; BHC; Hexachlorocyclohexane)

Ingestion, inhalation, or skin absorption may induce nausea, vomiting, hyperexcitability, tremors, micturition, convulsions, and ventricular fibrillation. Oral LD_{50} is 125 mg/kg (rat).

An 18-month-old infant died after ingesting an unknown number of lindane vaporizer pellets. He was in a continuous tetanic state with irregular respirations, superimposed with severe clonic movements during which he screamed and became cyanotic.

Treatment: Prompt removal from the skin by flooding with water, and from the gastroenteric tract by induction of emesis, use of gastric lavage, and saline cathartics. Pentobarbital, phenobarbital, bromides, or ether may be given for the control of CNS stimulation. Carefully avoid all noise, jarring, etc. Keep patient quiet. Do *not* use oily cathartics. Do *not* use epinephrine, since it may induce ventricular fibrillation. Calcium gluconate I.V. has been used with some success as an antidote in conjunction with a barbiturate (*Clinical Memorandum*, Public Health Service, Savannah, Georgia, April 1955).

BEZOARS (Phytobezoars; Trichobezoars; Hair Balls; Concretions)

Trichobezoars are masses containing hair matted together in the stomach, frequently filling the stomach, but in some cases consisting of several separate hair balls. The symptoms usually consist of abdominal pain, nausea, weakness, loss of weight, constipation and diarrhea, and hematemesis.

Phytobezoars result from ingestion of vegetable and plant material of certain types. By far the most common cause of this type of bezoar is the persimmon. The best known species in America is the common or American persimmon (*Diospyros virginiana*), which

643

grows wild in the states between Connecticut and Iowa, and south to the Gulf Coast. The plumlike fruit contains a large amount of an astringent soluble tannin, which upon ripening, undergoes a change in which the tannin becomes coagulated and insoluble. Through ripening, it loses its astringent property and becomes palatable. In the stomach, particularly an empty stomach, dilute mineral acids produce coagulation of the tannin of the fruit, resulting in a sticky precipitate, which is the basis for the bezoar mass. This type of bezoar is frequently encountered as a mass in the stomach, varying considerably in size and shape, and occuring most commonly as an ovoid or spherical object in the stomach. The symptom complex that results from phytobezoars may be similar in some respects to that of a hair ball. In many instances, however, the onset of symptoms is rather abrupt, with intense upper abdominal pain.

Concretions composed of shellac, gums, resins, and similar sticky materials are most commonly encountered among painters and furniture workers where furniture polishes containing strong solutions of shellac are used. This type of concretion develops in individuals after the material has been ingested, usually for the alcohol content of the substance. Concretions have been reported from salol, bismuth, methyl cellulose, carbonates, macaroni, mucilage, sand, biliary calculi, dried peach substance, celery, cherry pits, orange pulp, nail trimmings, raw carrots, and chewing gum. [A. E. Haley, *Ann. Internal Med.* **46**, 30 (1957).]

Treatment: Bezoars and concretions, almost without exception, require surgical removal, although papain-sodium bicarbonate powder (0.5 gm every 3 hours) has been used with success in a case of persimmon bezoar. [D. S. Dann *et al.*, *A.M.A. Arch. Internal Med.* **103**, 598, (1959).]

BHT (Deenax; Butylated Hydroxytoluene; Di-*tert*-butyl-*p*-cresol; DBPC)

This antioxidant is used extensively in fatty foods (200 ppm). It has a low order of toxicity and has been thoroughly tested to ensure safety for repeated ingestion of amounts added to foods [*A.M.A. Arch. Ind. Health* **11**, 93, (1955)].

Treatment: None necessary.

BLEACHING SOLUTION OR POWDER

These preparations usually contain sodium or calcium hypochlorite and calcium chloride (3 to 6%). Ingestion is usually followed by pain in the throat and abdomen, and vomiting. Local injury consists of irritation, edema, and corrosion of the mouth, pharynx, larynx, and stomach. Gastritis and edema may be severe, but perforation of the esophagus or stomach is rare. When household chlorine bleach is combined with an acid or acid-producing substance, as for instance a toilet-bowl cleaner containing sodium acid sulfate or vinegar, there is a sudden release of chlorine gas. Likewise, when a chlorine bleach is mixed with ammonia, lye, or other alkaline substance, the action will liberate highly irritating gases or vapors (chlorine, ammonia, chloramine). In either case, inhalation of the irritant gases or vapors, particularly in a poorly ventilated room, can cause serious injury or death due to pulmonary edema. Accidents of this type have occurred not only in the kitchen and bathroom, but also in swimming pools during cleaning and water treatment operations. *Therefore, a chlorine bleach should never be mixed with a toilet-bowl cleaner, a rust remover, or household ammonia* [H. C. Faigel, *New Engl. J. Med.* **271**, 618, (1964)]. See Table 47, p. 733.

BROMINE

Contact of the liquid or vapors of bromine with the skin may cause acne and slow-healing ulcers. Inhalation of vapors will induce severe irritation of the respiratory passages and pulmonary edema. Probable lethal oral dose for an adult is 1 ml. A brief exposure to 1000 ppm may be fatal.

Treatment: Remove from the skin by washing with aqueous sodium bicarbonate. For alleviation of pulmonary effects following inhalation, see Pulmonary Edema, p. 43.

1,3-BUTYLENE GLYCOL (2,3-Dihydroxybutane; Dimethylene Glycol)

This is one of the least toxic of the glycols. Patch tests for primary skin irritation and sensitivity on 200 human subjects indicate that this compound is less irritating than propylene glycol. Long-term chronic toxicity studies with animals show a low order of toxicity.

CANTHARIDIN

This is a potent ingredient found in the dried and ground Spanish or Russian fly *Cantharis vesicatoria.* According to W. W. Oaks *et al.,* fifteen hundred different species of cantharidin-yielding flies or beetles are estimated to exist throughout the world. Poisonings have occurred, primarily in Europe, because of its intended use for inducing sexual excitement or abortion. The desired results are questionable, while the local and systemic effects are usually severe. The oral lethal dose for man has been reported as 30 mg [*Arch. Toxikol.* **17**, 27, (1958)].

Ingestion (or inhalation of the dust) of a toxic dose may induce, within 10 minutes, marked local irritation and blistering of the mouth, lips, and tongue followed by burning in the mouth, nausea, vomiting, bloody diarrhea, dysuria, frequent urination, gross hematuria, pseudopolycythemia, abortion, coma, renal tubular necrosis, hepatic degeneration, convulsions, and circulatory collapse.

Treatment: The patient will probably have vomited before admission to the hospital; if not, gastric lavage is indicated in oral poisoning. Contol of pain is an immediate problem. Treatment must also be directed to control vomiting and retching, and replacement of fluids by administration of dextrose. "Replacement of sodium is indicated; potassium replacement should be given with caution until it is determined whether or not acute renal failure due to tubular necrosis is going to ensue. If shock is present, therapy must begin with the use of vasopressors to increase the renal blood flow; if renal damage is already present, correcting hypotension with vasopressor agents will have a less dramatic effect on urinary output but it is still of definite value." [W. W. Oaks *et al., A.M.A. Arch. Internal Med.* **105,** 574, (1960).] According to these authors, excessive salivation, dysphagia, and retained secretions present a definite problem, and tracheostomy may have to be performed prophylactically. P. Csiky recommended sodium bicarbonate, homatropine, and application of cool towels to the abdominal area for relief of urinary colic and frequency. He warned against the ingestion of fats, oils, or alcohol because they promote absorption of cantharidin [*Arch. Toxikol.* **17,** 27 (1958)].

CATERPILLAR

Megalopyge opercularis, a stinging caterpillar, has been a public health problem in the southern states of the United States. Stings are usually the result of brushing against the caterpillar or attempting to remove it from the person or clothing. The "toxin" passes into the dermis through hollow spines which penetrate the skin. Symptoms include an intense local burning sensation, pain which may radiate to all extremities, severe headache, nausea, and vomiting. Shock-like symptoms and convulsions have also been reported, but no fatalities.

Treatment: To remove broken spines, apply and remove adhesive or cellophane tape; follow with ice packs to relieve pain. Administer calcium gluconate I.V. and epinephrine if indicated. Opiates may be required for the control of severe pain [J. P. McGovern *et al., JAMA* **175**, 1155 (1961)].

CHENOPODIUM OIL (Wormseed Oil)

This is a relatively safe vermifuge when used to treat roundworm, hookworm, and enteric amebas, but the full therapeutic dose (5-10 drops, 2 or 3 times a day for 2 days; 2 ml per adult) is occasionally toxic. Children and debilitated persons are particularly susceptible. Some side effects appear in about one-third of patients. These are frequently delayed and include nausea, vomiting, ringing in the ears, deafness, headache, tingling of the hands and feet, and impaired vision. Gross overdosage has resulted in severe gastroenteric distress, generalized depression, convulsions, coma, and death by respiratory failure. The lethal oral dose in children is about 3 ml.

Treatment: Induce vomiting. Follow with gastric lavage and saline cathartics. Further treatment is symptomatic.

CHLORATES AND PERCHLORATES

Ingestion of a toxic dose leads to severe gastroenteric pain, vomiting, and diarrhea. Hemoglobin is converted to methemoglobin which may lead to respiratory difficulties and possibly failure of respiration. Kidney and liver injury may also be produced. The lethal oral dose for an adult is approximately 15 gm.

Treatment: Induce vomiting and follow with gastric lavage, saline cathartics, fluid therapy, and oxygen. Methylene blue is not indicated since it promotes the formation of methemoglobin. See Methemoglobinema, p. 40.

CHLORDANE (Chlordane)

The signs and symptoms of acute chlordane intoxication are similar to those caused by DDT—hyperirritability, tremors, ataxia, and convulsions. In chronic intoxication, the liver may be affected. Chlordane is rapidly absorbed through the skin. One ounce (30 gm) spilled on the skin may be fatal. Probable lethal oral dose for an adult is 10 gm. See Chlorinated Hydrocarbons, p. 648.

Treatment: For ingestion, induce vomiting and follow with gastric lavage and administration of saline cathartics. Ether or barbiturates may be used to control convulsions. Oxygen and fluid therapy are also recommended. Do *not* give epinephrine since it may induce ventricular fibrillation. For skin and eye contact, wash with copious amounts of water.

CHLORINATED DIPHENYLS AND POLYPHENYLS (Arochlors)

Arochlor compounds are a series of chlorinated diphenyls and polyphenyls. They range in form from mobile oily liquids to fine white crystals and hard transparent resins. Arochlor 1242 is trichlorodiphenyl and Arochlor 1254 is pentachlorodiphenyl. These compounds are skin irritants and liver poisons. Acute poisoning in man from a single exposure has not been reported. Chronic exposure to vapors causes skin eruptions (chloracne) consisting of straw-colored cysts which plug sebaceous glands. Manifestations of systemic intoxications are nausea, jaundice, digestive disturbances, and weakness. Arochlor 1242 appears to be less toxic than Arochlor 1254.

Treatment: Discontinue exposure. Further treatment is symptomatic.

CHLORINATED HYDROCARBONS

The chlorinated hydrocarbons are central nervous system stimulants which potentiate the action of acetylcholine centrally with stimulation of the vagal centers, leading to hyperreflexia and convulsions. Acute poisoning from the chlorinated hydrocarbons simulates acute strychnine poisoning. Toxicologically, the chlorinated hydrocarbons can be divided into three groups: The first group includes DDT, hexachlorobenzene, lindane, synthetic 3956 (toxaphene), Dilan, 2-4-D, methoxychlor, and chlorbenzilate. Poisoning leads to nausea and vomiting, paresthesia of the tongue, lips, face, and hands, apprehension, muscle weakness, disturbance of equilibrium, dizziness, confusion, anorexia, and weight loss. Death follows from respiratory failure or ventricular fibrillation. Signs and symptoms of intoxication begin 3 or 4 hours after exposure. If recovery occurs it usually takes place within 24 hours.

In 1956, outbreaks of cutaneous porphyria due to ingestion of hexachlorobenzene occurred in southeastern Turkey. Symptoms and signs included photosensitivity, hepatomegaly, and porphyrinuria, without abdominal or neurological symptoms. The suspected cause was poisoning by hexachlorobenzene after eating bread made from treated wheat intended for sowing. This has been verified in experimental animals.

Aldrin, dieldrin, isodrin, endrin, chlordane, and heptachlor form the second group. Intoxication produces a clinical picture similar to that described for DDT, except that paresthesia does not occur. Acute illness may follow as early as 20 minutes after exposure.

D-D soil fumigant and Nemagon typify the third group. Clinical findings include nausea and vomiting, acute gastrointestinal distress, gasping, extreme dyspnea, irritation of the respiratory tract, pulmonary congestion, coughing, and marked depression of the central nervous system.

The adult lethal oral dose of DDT is approximately 30 gm or 500 mg/kg of body weight. The fatal oral dose of toxaphene is 30-100 mg/kg of body weight. The lethal dose of chlordane is estimated to be 50-500 mg/kg. Benzene hexachloride (a mixture of four isomers, including 15% of the γ isomer) is probably lethal at 600 mg/kg. The pure γ isomer (lindane), may be fatal at 100 to 250 mg/kg. Aldrin, dieldrin and endrin, listed in order of increasing toxicity, are 6-40 times more toxic than DDT. See Table 56, p. 744.

The hepatotoxic potency of seven halogenated hydrocarbons in increasing order is 1,1,1-trichloroethane, tetrachloroethylene, trichloroethylene, *sym*-tetrachloroethane, 1,1,2-trichloroethane, chloroform, and carbon tetrachloride. There is no correlation between the dose causing liver damage and the dose causing death. These data on hepatotoxicity should not be used to predict industrial hazard without considering other factors about a compound, such as LD_{50}, vapor pressure, partition distribution between blood and tissues, and rate and route of absorption.

Treatment: In cases of skin contamination, profuse washing with soap and water is required to reduce skin irritation or percutaneous absorption. Ingested material should be removed from the gastrointestinal tract, either by inducing vomiting (unless hydrocarbon solvents are involved and the amount of insecticide is well below the toxic amount) or by gastric lavage with saline solution. Saline cathartics may also be beneficial. Fats and oils should be avoided, both for gastric lavage and as cathartics, since they increase the rate of absorption of all chlorinated hydrocarbons.

Sedation with barbiturates is indicated if signs of CNS irritation are present. The patient should have absolute quiet, expert nursing care and a minimum of external stimuli to reduce the danger of convulsions. Epinephrine is contraindicated in view of the danger of precipitating ventricular fibrillation. If liver or kidney involvement is suspected, a low-fat, high-carbohydrate, high-protein diet should be maintained. If the material ingested was dissolved in a hydrocarbon solvent, the patient should be observed for the possible development of hydrocarbon pneumonitis [*New Engl. J. Med.* **258**, 812 (1958)]. See Kerosene, p. 343.

CHLORINE

Inhalation of chlorine gas causes severe irritation of the upper respiratory tract and pulmonary edema. Skin contact may result in ulceration and necrosis. Exposure to 1000 ppm for a few minutes may be fatal.

Treatment: Remove patient from site of exposure; remove contaminated clothing and wash body with plenty of water. Wash eyes, rinse mouth, and if patient is able, have him gargle with water or dilute aqueous sodium bicarbonate. Keep him warm in a recumbent position and observe carefully for signs and symptoms of pulmonary edema. If necessary, administer oxygen (face mask). Give sodium bicarbonate orally or intravenously to combat acidosis. The inhalation of a spray of a solution containing 2% of sodium hyposulfite and 0.5% sodium carbonate has also been recommended. Codeine is indicated for depression of the cough reflex. Hundreds of cases of chlorine inhalation poisoning have been successfully treated by inhalation of vapors of ethyl alcohol and ether [*Pracovni Lekar:* **7**, 345 (1955)]. See Pulmonary edema, p. 43. Venesection is indicated (280-560 ml) when there is evidence of right heart embarrassment, and nikethamide has been used as a medullary respiratory stimulant.

CHLORINE DIOXIDE

This is a strong respiratory tract and eye irritant. Acute exposures by inhalation cause bronchitis, pulmonary edema, and death. Symptoms can be delayed and recovery may be slow. Symptoms observed in affected workers are coughing, wheezing, respiratory distress, nasal discharge, eye and throat irritation.

Animals survived 2-hour exposures to 200 ppm; 5 ppm is irritating.

Treatment: See Chlorine, p. 650.

CHLORINE TRIFLUORIDE

This is a pale green liquid, which vaporizes to form a colorless gas. It has a somewhat sweet odor and is highly irritating (similar to chlorine or mustard gas) even at low concentrations. With the exception of elemental fluorine, chlorine trifluoride is the most reactive chemical known. It is highly toxic (of the order of hydrogen fluoride) and extremely irritating to the eyes, skin, and respiratory tract. A threshold limit of 3 ppm has been suggested. Concentrations of 50 ppm or more may be fatal in 30 minutes to 2 hours.

Treatment: See Hydrofluoric Acid, p. 317 and Chlorine, p. 650.

CHLOROFORM (Trichloromethane)

Inhalation or ingestion of chloroform will lead to central nervous system depression. In the United States, chloroform is no longer used as an inhalation anesthetic. It has a relatively low margin of safety since it sensitizes the heart to fibrillation. It also induces hepatitis if absorbed for a period exceeding 50 or 60 minutes. Probable lethal oral dose for an adult is 30 ml. Chloroform finds some use as a local (external) stimulant.

Treatment: Diets low in fat and high in carbohydrate and protein provide the best resistance to chloroform.

CHLOROQUINE (Aralen)

Chloroquine is used to suppress and treat certain forms of malaria and gastrointestinal amebiasis. The drug has also been found useful in the treatment of rheumatoid arthritis, and systemic lupus erythematosus. Some patients on prolonged therapy have developed skin reactions (maculopapular, lichenoid, or exfoliative rash and pigmentation); marked graying, bleaching, or loss of hair; ocular lesions including corneal complications; weakness of skeletal muscles, loss of body weight, insomnia, and toxic psychosis [*Brit. Med. J.* **1**, 983 (1966)]. In 1964, a total of 18 deaths due to chloroquine overdosage or accidental ingestion were reported [*JAMA* **190**, 398 (1964)]. In these cases, the amount of drug ingested ranged from 0.5 to 44 gm. Death frequently occurred in less than 2 hours. Symptoms included convulsions and vasomotor, cardiac, and respiratory collapse resulting in sudden death.

Chloroquine-primaquine combinations administered to 10 patients known to have a deficiency of erythrocyte glucose-6-phosphate dehydrogenase caused hemolysis. One patient required a blood transfusion [Ziai *et al., Clin. Pediat.* **6**, 242 (1967)].

Caution: The chloroquine-primaquine combination administered to subjects whose sensitivities are unknown may produce serious ill effects in some patients. Primaquine sensitivity is a genetically acquired error of metabolism characterized by a deficiency in erythrocyte glucose-6-phosphate dehydrogenase. The incidence is approximately 10% among American Negroes. It is common among Jews originating in Mediterranian and Oriental countries but very rare among Ashkenazic Jews [*Clin-Alert* (May 24, 1967)].

Because of the possibility of permanent impairment of vision by chloroquine and other antimalarials, frequent ophthalmologic examinations are recommended for patients who take these drugs. There are several reports of progressive visual damage following discontinuation of the drug. Retinopathy may even appear several years after discontinuation of therapy [R. P. Burns, *New Engl. J. Med.* **275**, 693 (1966)]. The use of chloroquine and hydroxychloroquine (Plaquenil) to treat rheumatoid arthritis and lupus erythematosus is questionable [Rothermich *et al., New Engl. J. Med.* **275**, 1383 (1966)]. A 23-year-old man with discoid lupus erythematosus developed agranulocytosis after treatment with daily doses of slightly less than 600 mg (total 24.2 gm) of hydroxychloroquine sulfate for 6 weeks. Recovery followed withdrawal of the drug. The patient had previously received 300 mg chloroquine weekly for several months. As a result of this treatment, leukopenia preceded the appearance of agranulocytosis and persisted for 6 weeks following clinical recovery [D. Chernof and K. S. Taylor, *Arch. Dermatol.* **97**, 163 (1968)]. Young children are particularly sensitive to chloroquine.

Treatment: Discontinuation of therapy is effective in bringing relief from most of the side effects; however, burning in the mouth and epigastrium, nausea, vomiting, and muscle weakness may persist for weeks after treatment is discontinued.

Treatment of an overdose requires *prompt* and repeated vomiting and/or gastric lavage. Treatment otherwise is symptomatic and directed toward control of convulsions, restoring blood pressure, and maintenance of respiration. *Sudden respiratory and cardiac arrest must be anticipated. This requires immediate artificial respiration and cardiac massage* [Cann and Verhulst, *Pediatrics* **27**, 95 (1961)].

CHRISTMAS TREE CANDLE LIGHT

The fluid bubbling in certain Christmas tree lights is methylene chloride (dichloromethane). Ingestion or inhalation of a toxic dose will induce central depression followed by convulsions and paresthesia of the extremities.

Treatment: Treatment is symptomatic. See Methylene Chloride, p. 390.

CINNAMON

Powdered cinnamon and cinnamon oil have caused contact dermatitis in hypersensitive individuals. Most of these people were employed in the baking and candy industry. There is also a report of a woman with dermatitis of the face, chest, forearm, and hands attributed to cinnamon oil in toothpaste [*A.M.A. Arch. Dermatol.* **81**, 599 (1960)].

Treatment: Discontinuation of exposure and personal hygiene will result in recovery in about 4 weeks.

CRAG FLY REPELLENT (Butoxy Polypropylene Glycol 800; BPG)

Acute animal toxicity studies indicate that this preparation has a low order of toxicity.

Treatment: In case of accidental ingestion of large amounts, empty the stomach by inducing vomiting; for skin contact, remove with water.

CRAYONS

The ingestion of crayons may color the urine and stools. This may be alarming but no signs or symptoms of systemic intoxication have been reported.

Treatment: None is necessary unless a large quantity has been ingested. In this case, empty the stomach by inducing vomiting.

CREAMS (Lotions)

Prolonged use of creams, lotions, and "skin foods" may promote the multiplication of a mite (*Desmodex folliculorum*), normally found in the skin. This may lead to dryness, itching, roughness, and finally pimples and pustules on the skin.

Treatment: Soap and water.

CUTTING OILS

Machine shop operators exposed to cutting oil sprays and mists may develop acne folliculitis, pustular dermatitis, and keratoses. Men with greasy skin and excessive hair on their arms and legs are most frequently affected. Cutting oil additives containing sulfur and chlorine are believed to be partially responsible for these lesions. Some cutting oils contain tricresyl phosphates.

Prevention: Soap and water and barrier creams are helpful only to a limited extent. More effective are reducing the spray by splash guards, reducing the hours of exposure, and using less viscous and less irritating oils. See Tricresyl Phosphate, p. 604.

2,4-DICHLOROPHENOXYACETIC ACID (2,4-D)

This compound has a low order of toxicity. No cases of acute intoxication have been reported in man. The probable lethal oral dose for an adult is 50 gm. Ingestion of a toxic dose causes gastroenteric distress, diarrhea, mild central nervous system depression, dysphagia, and possible transient liver and kidney injury.

Treatment: Induce vomiting and follow with gastric lavage and supportive therapy.

DICUMYL PEROXIDE (Di-Cup)

This compound has a low order of toxicity; the LD_{50} for albino rats is 3.5 gm/kg. Di-cup is a mild skin irritant but not a sensitizer. It does not produce eye irritation. Inhalation of the dust of Di-cup 40 C, the supported form of dicumyl peroxide, had no toxic effect on laboratory animals.

When Di-cup is used to cross-link polyethylene, acetophenone is formed, which has a characteristic sweet pungent odor. This can be reduced to an acceptable level by suitable ventilation. See also Organic Peroxides, p. 437.

Treatment: Remove from skin with water.

DIMETHYLACETAMIDE (DMA)

LD_{50} values range from 2.0 to 5.0 gm/kg depending on the species (mice or rats) and route of administration (oral or intraperitoneal). The dermal LD_{50} in rabbits is from 2.5 to 3.6 ml/kg. Both acute and repeated dermal applications show that the material produces skin irritation and is readily absorbed through the skin. Sublethal doses produce degeneration of the heart, liver, and kidneys. Acute inhalation at 406 and 575 ppm causes some deaths and degeneration of the liver in several species of laboratory animals.

Treatment: Flood affected skin, eye, and mucous membranes with water. For ingestion, induce vomiting and follow with gastric lavage and saline cathartics. Treatment for liver and kidney injury is supportive and symptomatic.

DIMETHYL FORMAMIDE (DMF)

This compound is highly irritating to skin, eyes, and mucous membranes. Rat oral LD_{50} is 7.0 ml/kg; rabbit skin LD_{50} is 5.0 ml/kg. Liver injury has been produced in experimental animals by prolonged exposure to 100 ppm. Vague digestive symptoms—anorexia, nausea, vomiting and a burning sensation in the epigastrium followed by pain and tenderness—were reported in textile manufacture workers. No respiratory symptoms occurred. Edema and desquamation, accompanied by itching, were seen in three cases. One worker had conjunctivitis.

Treatment: In cases of ingestion induce vomiting and follow with gastric lavage. For skin contact, flood affected tissues with water; for vapor inhalation, remove from exposure. Administer artificial respiration and oxygen if necessary. Further treatment is symptomatic and supportive.

DIMETHYLHYDRAZINE (*unsym*-Dimethylhydrazine; UDMH; 1,1-Dimethylhydrazine)

Dimethylhydrazine is a clear, colorless, weakly basic liquid with a sharp ammoniacal or fishy odor. Contact with the skin and mucous membranes will cause irritation and chemical burns. Inhalation of vapor causes pulmonary irritation, delayed gastrointestinal irritation, hemolysis, and central nervous system stimulation (tremors and convulsions). It may be absorbed through the skin to cause systemic intoxication. The suggested threshold limit is 0.5 ppm.

Methylhydrazine and *sym*-dimethylhydrazine are also respiratory irritants and convulsants. Methyl hydrazine vapor is more toxic than the vapors of hydrazine or its dimethyl derivatives and is also hemolytic.

Treatment: For skin or eye contact, flood with water and treat as alkaline burn. See Ammonia, Aqueous, p. 95. For inhalation, remove victim from contaminated area, give artificial respiration and oxygen if necessary. Observe for signs and symptoms of pulmonary edema. See p. 43.

DIMETHYL SULFOXIDE (DMSO)

Dimethyl sulfoxide is a highly polar, stable, hygroscopic organic liquid with exceptional solvent properties. It has an exceptionally low order of toxicity. The acute median lethal dose values for mice are 21.4 gm/kg (oral administration), 3.8 gm/kg (intravenous administration), and 20.5 gm/kg (subcutaneous injection). Its remarkable innocuousness has been demonstrated for a number of other animals, including primates.

Nine milliliters of 90% dimethyl sulfoxide were applied to the entire trunk, from the chin to the pelvic girdle, of 20 men once daily for a period of 26 weeks. Most subjects experienced the disagreeable oyster-like breath odor, to which they eventually became insensitive. Transient erythema was experienced by about one-fourth of the subjects immediately following some of the exposures during the first 2 weeks. Transient burning and stinging were reported by about three-quarters of the subjects during the first few weeks. The dermatitis, which was accompanied by only a moderate inflammation reaction in the dermis, invariably regressed as treatment continued and the skin eventually became histologically normal [A. M. Kligman, *JAMA* **193**, 796, 923 (1965)].

Even with continuous occlusive exposure to 90% dimethyl sulfoxide, which produced an intensive dermatitis in about a week, the skin healed and achieved a remarkable degree of hardening in about 1 month.

The compound is rapidly absorbed and distributed in living material, loses its oxygen, and is excreted in part as dimethyl sulfide, which in mammals may give a garlic-like odor to the breath. Studies with radioactive sulfur in DMSO show that sulfur from the compound may remain in the sulfur pool of the body for several days. Huge doses given orally or topically for several weeks were followed by changes in the refractive power of the lens in swine, dogs, and rabbits. No lens abnormalities were observed in before-and-after ophthalmological examinations in 25 patients treated with up to 30 ml of DMSO topically, applied daily for 19 months for various musculoskeletal disorders [C. D. Leake, *Science* **152**, 1646 (1966)].

In 1965 all clinical trials of DMSO were suspended in the United States. This action was taken by the FDA following reports that the drug caused adverse ocular effects in laboratory animals. Evidence of its value in treating certain skin diseases, however, caused FDA to allow doctors to use DMSO in special cases of serious disorders. FDA is expected to loosen its restrictions once again, allowing investigational use of DMSO in treating minor cuts and bruises.

A recent report by J. J. Kocsis *et al.* suggests considering DMSO as simply an inert solvent unlikely to interact with other agents or to produce toxic effects itself. The investigations found that in rats DMSO markedly potentiated the toxicity of several aromatic hydrocarbons, and that liver preparations from DMSO-treated rats showed an increased capacity to metabolize benzene [*Science* **160**, 427 (1968)].

DIOXANE (1,4-Dioxane; Diethylene 1,4-Dioxide; Diethylene Dioxide; Glycol Ethylene Ether)

In large doses this compound is a weak anesthetic and a renal and hepatic poison.

Fifteen minute exposures to 300 ppm cause mild transient irritation of the eyes, nose, and throat. Animal studies suggest that a single exposure to less than 1000 ppm for a period not over $\frac{1}{2}$ hour would be relatively safe. Several days' exposure to vapor concentrations averaging 470 ppm was believed responsible for the death of a worker. At autopsy, central nervous system damage, bronchopneumonia, and severe liver and kidney injury were found. The liquid may be absorbed through the skin in sufficient quantities to produce injury.

Treatment: For inhalation, remove promptly from contaminated atmosphere. Give artificial respiration and oxygen if necessary. Further treatment is supportive and symptomatic. In case of ingestion, induce vomiting and follow with gastric lavage and saline cathartics.

EPOXY COMPOUNDS

Allyl glycidyl ether, phenyl glycidyl ether, triallyl cyanurate, styrene oxide, and other active diluents having the epoxy group are mildly to severely irritating to the skin. Following excessive body contact and development of contact dermatitis, these compounds may cause sensitization with symptoms similar to those produced by the amine curing agents.

Treatment: See Epoxy Resins, p. 241.

ETHODUOMEENS

The Ethoduomeens are the reaction products of an amine and ethylene oxide. Ethoduomeens are obtained from N-alkyltrimethylenediamines. They are cationic in nature and react as the Ethomeens. Their toxicity is of a relatively low order. See Detergents, p. 201.

ETHYLHEXYL DIPHENYLPHOSPHATE (Saniticizer 141)

This compound has a low order of toxicity. It is used as a plasticizer in food packaging materials.

2-ETHYLHEXYL OCTYLPHENYLPHOSPHITE

This chemical has a low order of toxicity. The oral LD_{50} (rat) ranges from 7.0 to 10.0 gm/kg.

ETHYLHEXANEDIOL (2-Ethylhexanediol-1,3; Rutgers 612)

This compound is an insect repellent having a moderate order of toxicity. On the basis of animal toxicity data, ingestion of a toxic dose would probably cause CNS depression and kidney and liver injury.

Treatment: In case of ingestion empty the stomach by inducing vomiting and follow with gastric lavage.

FURFURAL (2-Furaldehyde; Pyromucic Aldehyde; Artificial Oil of Ants)

The oral LD_{50} of furfural for male albino rats is 149 mg/kg; for dogs, approximately 950 mg/kg. The effects of toxic or lethal doses in the dog range from muscle incoordination to marked retching and vomiting, occasional convulsions, and death.

Furfural is absorbed percutaneously but causes only slight local irritation in rabbits. Doses up to 500 mg/kg have been applied to the skin of rabbits without fatalities.

The subcutaneous LD_{50} in male albino rats is 148 mg/kg. Lethal doses usually produce terminal convulsions.

The instillation of 1 drop of undiluted furfural into the eyes of adult white rabbits produces only slight edema of the conjunctiva. Larger quantities cause irritation and opacity of the cornea.

Male albino mice survived one 6-hour exposure to 260 ppm, but mortality was 100% at 370 ppm. Rats survived one 6-hour exposure to 96 ppm but mortality was 100% at 260 ppm. Dogs survived one 6-hour exposure to 240 ppm of furfural. At 370 ppm the mortality was 50%.

Treatment: For inhalation exposure, use general treatment for overexposure to vapors of toxic chemicals. Keep airway open, give artificial respiration and oxygen if necessary. Observe for premonitory signs and symptoms of pulmonary edema. In case of ingestion, induce vomiting, follow with gastric lavage and saline cathartics. For skin and mucous membrane contact, flood affected part with water.

L-DOPA (Levodihydroxyphenylalanine)

The amino acid L-dopa is still in the investigational stage as far as its effective use is concerned in relieving the symptoms of parkinsonism, including akinesia, rigidity, and tremors. The side effects noted by G. C. Cotzias *et al.* in 26 patients receiving from 4 to 8 gm/day for several months included primarily nausea and vomiting; orthostatic fainting was noted in some patients and transient depression of granulocytes in a few [*New Engl. J. Med.* **276**, 374 (1967)]. Similar undesirable effects were reported by M. D. Yahr *et al.* [quoted in *Med. Letter* **10**, 69 (1968)].

At this time only a few patients have discontinued L-dopa therapy because of the severity of side effects. See also *Science News*, **95**, 476 (1969).

LICORICE

Licorice extract, obtained by aqueous extraction of the root of *Glycyrrhiza glabra* has been used for years as a flavoring agent. Recently reports have appeared of reversible severe hypertension with cardiac sensations, edema, and gain in body weight in adults due to ingestion of large quantities of licorice (100 gm/day in candy form; two to three 36-gm licorice candy bars/day for 6–7 years; 4 kg of licorice over several months; up to 2 pounds weekly). A detailed and comprehensive report by J. W. Conn *et al.* points out that, depending on the doses ingested and the period of time over which the disease progresses, patients may also suffer from hypokalemia and complain of muscular weakness and pain in arms and legs, paralysis, and tetany [*JAMA* **205**, 80 (1968)].

Glycyrrhizic acid, the active principle of crude licorice extract, is similar in its metabolic action to deoxycorticosterone (Molhusen *et al.*, quoted by J. W. Conn *et al.*). The primary effect is on the renal tubules promoting reabsorption of sodium and water at the expense of potassium.

Treatment: J. G. Rausch-Stromann's patient recovered in 14 days after discontinuation of licorice and ingestion of a low-sodium diet [*New Engl. J. Med.* **279**, 606 (1968)]. The patient of J. W. Conn *et al.* required additional and more intensive therapy including potassium supplements and diuretic therapy.

LITHIUM

Severe intoxications and fatalities have resulted from the use of lithium chloride as a substitute for sodium chloride in low-sodium diets. The symptomatology may include nausea, apathy, anorexia, tremors, slurred speech, blurred vision, vomiting, diarrhea, polyuria, oliguria, confusion, and coma. The primary toxic action of lithium appears to be in the kidney. A high sodium intake protects animals (up to a point) against the toxic effects of lithium. A low sodium intake markedly increases the toxicity of lithium.

Lithium carbonate has been used with promising results in the treatment of manic-depressive psychosis. The suggestion has been made that this compound may be the drug of choice as prophylactic agent in phenothiazine refractory or phenothiazine-allergic manic patients [*Am. J. Psychiat.* **123**, 706 (1966); *Arch. Gen. Psychiat.* **16**, 162 (1967)]. Side effects were not significant. However, lithium therapy cannot be administered indiscriminately, as indicated by reports of more-or-less severe intoxications among psychotic patients treated with lithium [*JAMA* **164**, 1402 (1957); *Am. J. Psychiat.* **125**, 520 (1968)]. A. Kallos describes the use of lithium bromide as a keratolytic agent in keratoderma and tinea unguium. According to B. S. Levy, knowledge of the pharmacology of lithium and close attention to dosage and blood level allow this agent to be used with safety [*JAMA* **206**, 1045 (1968)].

LITHIUM METAL

This is a silvery-white metal which reacts with water to form hydrogen and lithium hydroxide, a strong alkali. See Sodium Hydroxide, p. 543.

METAPHOS (O,O-Dimethyl-O-(4-nitrophenyl) Thiophosphate)

Metaphos is also known as Wofatox and Metacide and is highly toxic. See Organic Phosphate, p. 438.

METHOXYCHLOR (Marlate)

The toxicity of this compound is relatively low. A generalized depression is usually observed in an individual who ingests a large dose.

Treatment: See Chlorinated Hydrocarbons, p. 648.

2-METHYLPENTALDEHYDE

The acute oral toxicity is relatively low. Precautions should be taken to prevent spilling or splashing on the skin or into eyes. Prolonged or repeated breathing of 2-methylpentaldehyde is harmful and is to be avoided. Do not use without adequate ventilation.

Treatment: Affected parts should be flushed immediately with large volumes of water. Severe burns may result from covered applications and soiled clothing must be removed to prevent this. In case of accidental ingestion, induce vomiting and follow with gastric lavage. For inhalation, re.nove victim from contaminated atmosphere. If breathing has stopped give artificial respiration and oxygen.

METHYL SALICYLATE (Oil of Wintergreen)

This compound has marked antipyretic and antirheumatic properties. Ingestion of a toxic dose will produce severe gastroenteric distrubances, marked dehydration, cyanosis, and coma. Average lethal dose: 10 ml in children; 30 ml in adults.

Treatment: Thorough gastric lavage and fluid therapy are indicated. Use sodium bicarbonate to combat acidosis. In infants and children exchange transfusions have been lifesaving [A. K. Done and L. J. Otterness, *Pediatrics* 18, 80 (1956)]. See Acetylsalicylic Acid, p. 67.

MORPHOLINE (2,3,5,6-Tetrahydro-1,4-oxazine; Diethylenimide Oxide; Tetrahydro-p-oxazine)

This compound is a colorless, hygroscopic, oily substance with a pepper-like odor. Chemically, morpholine is a secondary amine and behaves as a strong organic base. Liquid morpholine and its vapors are irritating to the skin and respiratory tract. The acute minimum lethal dose for rats is 1.6 gm/kg. Inhalation of air containing 18,000 ppm resulted in excessive lacrimation and mucous secretion from the nose, pulmonary congestion, liver necrosis, and degeneration of the kidney tubules. Exposure for 8 hours to 12,000 ppm produced no permanent changes in animals, although transient alterations in the liver and kidney tubules were noted, see "Morpholine," [*API Toxicol. Rev.* (September 1948)]. See Table 24, p. 706.

Treatment: See Amines, Aliphatic, p. 90.

NITRIC ACID

See Hydrochloric Acid, p. 317, for effects of liquid nitric acid, and Nitrogen Oxides, p. 426, for effects of vapors and decomposition products of nitric acid.

NITROPRUSSIDES (Nitroferricyanides)

These ionize to form cyanide ion. Toxicity is comparable with sodium cyanide although slower in action. See Cyanides, p. 191.

PHOSPHORUS PENTOXIDE (Phosphoric Anhydride; Phosphorus Oxide; Diphosphorus Pentoxide)

This is the highly irritating and corrosive anhydride of phosphoric acid. See Phosphoric Acid, p. 472.

SCHRADAN (Octamethylpyrophosphoramide)

This is a highly toxic organic phosphate used as a systemic insecticide and for the treatment of myasthenia gravis. See Organic Phosphates, p. 438.

TOLUENE (Toluol; Methylbenzene)

Vapors of toluene, xylenes, styrene, and alkylbenzenes may produce irritation of the upper respiratory tract, disturbance of vision, dizziness, nausea, collapse, and coma. Direct contact with skin and eyes has resulted in intense burning. Unlike benzene, these compounds do not affect hemopoietic tissue.

Treatment: Remove from the eyes and skin by thorough washing with water. In case of ingestion administer saline cathartics and demulcents. *Do not induce vomiting.* Subsequent treatment is symptomatic and supportive.

CHAPTER V
TABULAR SUMMARIES

TABLE 1

CHARACTERISTICS OF FOOD-BORNE INTOXICATIONS AND INFECTIONS[a]

Causative organism	Foods commonly involved	Onset of symptoms after ingestion	Symptoms
Staphylococci	Salads Cream puffs Cheddar cheese Dry skim milk Poultry Potato salad Processed meats and fish	Average: 2.5–3 hours (1–6 hours)	Nausea, vomiting, diarrhea, cramps, acute prostration, and sometimes fever
Enterococci (infection) *Bacillus cereus* (infection) *Clostridium perfringens* (infection)	Inadequately refrigerated foods contaminated with enterococci Starchy foods inadequately refrigerated Poultry and meat products cooked and left unrefrigerated	Average: 8–12 hours (2–18 hours)	Nausea, sometimes colicky pains, diarrhea, or vomiting

Clostridium botulinum	Home-canned low acid foods	Average: 1–2 days (2–8 days)	Nausea is often absent, difficulty swallowing, double vision, respiratory difficulties, difficult speech, and loss of reflexes
Salmonella	Inadequately cooked eggs Poultry Dairy products Powdered eggs	7–72 hours	Abdominal pain, diarrhea, and chills; vomiting occasionally; fever, headache, muscular weakness, and sometimes paralysis

[a]From G. M. Dack, *JAMA* **172**, 929 (1960).

TABLE 2

ESTIMATED RELATIVE ACUTE TOXICITY HAZARD OF PESTICIDES TO SPRAYMEN[a]

Most Dangerous	Dangerous	Less Dangerous	Least Dangerous
Demeton (Systox) (OP)	Aldrin (OCC)	BHC (OCC)	Aramite (M)
Di Syston (OP)	Bidrin (OP)	Binapacryl (Morocide) (N)	Captan (M)
Mevinphos (Phosdrin) (OP)	Carbophenothion (Trithion) (OP)	Chlordane (OCC)	Carbaryl (Sevin) (C)
Parathion (OP)	DDVP (OP)	Co-Ral (OP)	Chlorobenzilate (OCC)
Schradan (OMPA) (OP)	Delnav (OP)	Diazinon (OP)	2,4-D (OCC)
TEPP (OP)	Dieldrin (OCC)	Dicapthon (OP)	Diquat (M)
Phorate (Thimet) (OP)	DNOC (N)	Dichloroethyl Ether (M)	DDD (TDE) (OCC)
Zinophos (Cynem) (OP)	DNOSBP (N)	Dimethoate (OP)	DDT (OCC)
	Endrin (OCC)	Dipterex (Dylox) (OP)	Dilan (OCC, N)
	EPN (OP)	Endosulfan (Thiodan) (OCC)	2,4,5-T (OCC)
	Ethion (OP)	Fenthion (Baytex) (OP)	IPC (M)
	Methyl Demeton (Meta-Systox) (OP)	Guthion (OP)	Karathane (N)
	Methyl Parathion (OP)	Heptachlor (OCC)	Kelthane (OCC)
	Nicotine (M)	Lead Arsenate (M)	Malathion (OP)

Pentachlorophenol (M)	Lindane (OCC)	Maneb (M)
Phosphamidon (OP)	Naled (Dibrom) (OP)	Methoxychlor (OCC)
Sodium arsenite (M)	Ruelene (OP)	Mirex (OCC)
Zectran (C)	Toxaphene (OCC)	Morestan (M)
	V-C13 (OP)	NAA (M)
	Vapam (M)	Perthane (OCC)
		Phostex (OP)
		Piperonyl Butoxide (M)
		Romel (Korlan) (OP)
		Rotenone (M)
		Simazine (M)
		Sulphenone (M)
		Tetradifon (Tedion) (OCC)
		Thiram (M)
		Zineb (M)
		Ziram (M)

[a]From H. R. Wolfe and W. F. Durham, *Proceedings of the Second Eastern Washington Fertilizer and Pesticide Conference*, Washington State University, pp. 14–21 (1966). *Key:* OCC = organochlorine compound; OP = organic phosphate; C = carbamate; N = nitro compound; M = miscellaneous.

TABLE 3
BLOOD DYSCRASIAS[a]

Drug	Aplastic anemia with pancytopenia[b]	Multiple cytopenia[c]	Thrombocytopenia[d]	Leukopenia (agranulocytosis)[e]	Erythroid hypoplasia without pancytopenia[f]	Hemolytic anemia[g]
Acetanilid						X
Acetazolamide			X			
Allylisopropylacetylurea			X			
Aminopyrine				X		
Aminosalicylic acid						X
Aprobarbital			X			
Arsphenamine	X	X	X	X	X	
Carbutamide	X	X	X	X	X	
Chloramphenicol	X	X	X	X	X	
Chlordane	X	X	X	X	X	
Chlorothiazide			X	X		
Chlorpromazine				X		
Chlorpropamide	X	X	X	X	X	
Colchicine	X	X	X	X	X	
Dimercaprol						X
Diphenylhydantoin sodium					X	
Dipyrone				X		
Furaltadone						X

Gamma benzene hexachloride	X	X	X	X	X	
Gold	X	X	X	X	X	
Imipramine				X	X	
Lead				X	X	
Lead acetate					X	
Mepazine	X	X		X	X	
Mephenytoin	X	X	X	X		
Methimazole				X		X
Naphthalene						X
Nitrofurantoin						
Parathion	X					
Perphenazine				X		
Phenacetin						X
Phenindione				X	X	
Phenylbutazone	X	X	X	X	X	
Potassium perchlorate	X	X		X		X
Probenecid				X		
Prochlorperazine				X		
Promazine HCl				X		
Promethazine				X		
Pyrimethamine	X			X	X	
Quinacrine HCl		X	X	X	X	
Quinidine			X			X
Quinine			X			
Ristocetin	X			X		
Salicylazosulfapyridine				X		X

TABLE 3 (Continued)

Drug	Aplastic anemia with pancytopenia[b]	Multiple cytopenia[c]	Thrombocytopenia[d]	Leukopenia (agranulocytosis)[e]	Erythroid hypoplasia without pancytopenia[f]	Hemolytic anemia[g]
Sodium sulfoxone						X
Stibophen						X
Streptomycin	X		X	X	X	
Sulfacetamide						X
Sulfadiazine				X		
Sulfamethoxypyridazine	X	X	X	X	X	X
Sulfanilamide				X		X
Sulfapyridine			X			X
Sulfisoxazole				X		X
Sulfonamides				X		X
Thenalidine				X		
Thioridazine HCl				X		
Thiotyr				X		
Thiouracils				X		
Tolbutamide	X	X	X	X		

Trimethadione	X	X		X	X		X	X
Trinitrotoluene	X	X		X	X		X	X	X
Triple Sulfa					X			

[a] This table is a summary prepared by the authors with the permission of Norman De Nosaquo, M.D., Director of Adverse Reactions, from the tabulation of reports compiled by the Panel on Hematology of the Registry on Adverse Reactions, Council on Drugs, American Medical Association. This summary presents data published in the April–May, 1965 and the June 1, 1967 reports. The reader is reminded that the information used in compiling this tabulation is essentially "raw data," obtained from many sources, and that no follow-up investigation has been attempted. The listing of a drug in the tabulation does not necessarily mean that the drug is harmful or that it was responsible for the dyscrasia reported.

[b] Aplastic anemia with pancytopenia – aplastic anemia involving more than one cell type established by bone marrow examination.

[c] Multiple cytopenia – depression of more than one cell type or pancytopenia without bone marrow examination.

[d] Thrombocytopenia – reduction of platelet count to 100,000/mm³ or less.

[e] Leukopenia – reduction of leukocyte count to 3,000/mm³ or less. Agranulocytosis – reduction of neutrophil count to less than 500/mm³ regardless of the total leukocyte count (with associated clinical findings).

[f] Erythroid hypoplasia without pancytopenia – reduction in the erythroid elements without pancytopenia substantiated by bone marrow evidence.

[g] Hemolytic anemia – anemia associated with one or more of the following findings: reticulocytosis, shortened red cell survival time, Heinz bodies, rise in bilirubin and/or fecal and urinary urobilinogen.

TABLE 4

DRUGS AND OTHER AGENTS THAT PRODUCE[a] PHOTOSENSITIVITY REACTIONS

Photosensitizer	Probable mechanism of action	Usual route of exposure
Coal tar derivatives: Anthracene, Acridine, Phenanthrene, Pyridine	Phototoxic	Topical
Antiseptics: Bithionol (bisphenol),	Photoallergic	Topical
Tetrachlorsalicylanilide (Impregon)	Photoallergic	
Diuretics: Thiazides and related sulfonamide compounds	Photoallergic	Oral
Tranquilizers: Chlorpromazine (Thorazine)	Phototoxic[b], Photoallergic	Oral
Antibiotics: Demethylchlortetra- cycline HCl (Declomycin)	Phototoxic[c] (Photoallergic?)	Oral
Sunscreening agents: Digalloyl trioleate (Neo-A-Fil),	Photoallergic	Topical
Aminobenzoic acid	Photoallergic	
Antifungals: Griseofulvin (Fulvicin, Fulvicin U/F, Griful- vin, Grifulvin V, Grisactin, Griseofulvin);	Photoallergic	Oral
N-butyl-4 chlorosalicylamide (jadit)	Photoallergic	
Antihistamines: Promethazine HCl (Phenergan HCl)	Photoallergic	Topical Oral
Antibacterials: Sulfonamides	Phototoxic[b], Photoallergic	Oral Topical
Oral hypoglycemic agents: Chlorpropamide (Diabinese), Tolbutamide (Orinase)	(Photoallergic?)	Oral
Miscellaneous agents: Furocoumarins[c]	Phototoxic	Topical

[a]From R. L. Baer and L. C. Harber, *JAMA* **192**, 989 (1965).
[b]Protection usually afforded by window glass.
[c]Found in fruits, perfumes; used to treat vitiligo.

TABLE 5
SUBSTANCES THAT MAY PRODUCE
SYSTEMIC ANAPHYLACTIC REACTIONS IN MAN[a]

Substance	Route of administration[b]	Fatalities reported
Proteins		
Antiserum (horse)	ID, SC, IM, IV	yes
Hormones		
Relaxin (Releasin)	IM	
Insulin	SC, IV	
Corticotropin (ACTH, Acthar corticotropin)	IV	
Enzymes		
Chymotrypsin	IM	
Trypsin, crystallized (Parenzyme, Tryptar)	IM	
Penicillinase (Neutrapen)	IM	
Hymenoptera sting	SC	yes
Pollen		
Bermuda grass	ID	yes
Ragweed	ID	yes
Food		
Buckwheat	ID	yes
Egg white	ID	yes
Cotton seed	ID	yes
Glue	ID	yes
Hemoglobin (guinea pig)	ID	yes
Polysaccharides		
Acacia	IV	
Dextran (Expandex, Gentran)	IV	
Haptens		
Sodium dehydrocholate (Decholin)	IV	yes
Thiamine	SC, IV	yes
Sulfobromophthalein (BSP)	IV	yes
Procaine (Novocain)	P	yes
Salicylates	PO	
Iodinated organic contrast agents	PO, IV	yes
Antibiotics		
Penicillin	PO, C, IM, IV	yes
Demethylchlortetracycline HCl (Declomycin)	PO	
Nitrofurantoin (Furadantin)	PO	
Streptomycin	IM	
Aminopyrine	PO	

[a]From K. Frank Austen, *JAMA* **192**, 108 (1965).

[b]ID = intradermal; C = conjunctival; PO = oral; SC = subcutaneous; IM = intramuscular; IV = intravenous; P = parenteral, exact route not defined.

TABLE 6

DRWS SUGGESTED FOR ASTRONAUTS IN THE ORBITING RESEARCH LABORATORY[a]

Nonproprietary name	Proprietary name	Use or action
Antiemetics		
Trimethobenzamide HCl	Tigan HCl	Short acting
	Bonadoxin	Prolonged acting
Thioperazine	Vontil	Antiemetic and tranquilizer
Thiethylperazine maleate	Torecan Maleate	Antiemetic and tranquilizer
For operations		
Lidocaine HCl	Xylocaine	Local anesthetic
Tetracaine	Pontocaine	Local anesthetic
Pentothal sodium	Thiopental	General anesthetic
Meperidine HCl	Demerol	Narcotic
Atropine sulfate		Pre-medication
Scopolamine		CNS depressant
Bethanechol chloride	Urecholine	Parasympathetic stimulant
Metaraminol bitartrate	Aramine Bitartrate	Pressor agent
Normal serum albumin		
Electrolyte solution		
Dextrose and water		
Oxygen		

For eyes		
	Dacriose	Sterile ophthalmic irrigating solution
Proparacaine HCl 0.5%	Ophthaine	Short-acting topical anesthetic
Tetracaine ophthalmatic ointment	Pontocaine	Long-acting topical anesthetic
Polymyxin B sulfate	Neosporin	Antibiotic solution
For ears		
Polymyxin B sulfate	Aerosporin otic solution	For external otitis
For nose		
Phenylephrine HCl	Neo-Synephrine	Decongestant
Tripelennamine citrate	Pyribenzamine	Antihistamine
Epinephrine	Adrenalin	For nosebleed
	Trisocort spray pack	For allergy or infection
For enteric tract		
Paregoric		For diarrhea
	Maalox	Antacid for indigestion or ulcer
Propantheline bromide	Pro-Banthine	Parasympatholytic
Magnesia magma	Milk of Magnesia	For constipation
	Kaopectate	Antidiarrheal
Neomycin sulfate		For infectious diarrhea or to reduce flatus
	Fleet's Enema	Cathartic

TABLE 6 (Continued)

Nonproprietary name	Proprietary name	Use or action
For respiratory tract		
Codeine phosphate		For cough
Aspirin		For fever
Chlorpromazine HCl		For treatment of hiccups
Ephedrine		For asthma
For mouth		
Aspirin		For toothache
	Empirin with codeine	For toothache
For genitourinary tract		
	Azo Gantrisin	For infection of tract
For wounds		
Soap	pHisoHex	Antiseptic
Polymyxin B sulfate	Neosporin antibiotic ointment	
For burns		
	Nupercainal ointment	Local anesthetic
	Butesin picrate ointment	Local anesthetic, antiseptic
	Polyethylene glycol ointment	Covering agent

For suturing a wound
Lidocaine HCl | Xylocaine | Local anesthetic

For infections (in general)
Sodium oxacillin | Prostaphlin | For staphylococcal infections
Tetracycline | | Broad spectrum antibiotic
Ampicillin | | Drug of choice in some infections

CNS Stimulants
Caffeine
Detroamphetamine sulfate

Miscellaneous
Prednisone | | For rheumatic disorders and asthma
Prednisolone | Delta Cortef; Hydeltra | For topical application of skin conditions and for treatment of shock of allergic origin

Warfarin sodium | Coumadin sodium | Anticoagulant
Chlordiazepoxide HCl | Librium | Tranquilizer
Meprobamate | Miltown; Equanil | Tranquilizer
Ethyl alcohol | | Tranquilizer

*This list was prepared by one of us (WD) as a member of the Space Medicine Advisory Group of the National Aeronautics and Space Administration, 1964–1965.

TABLE 7

ADVERSE REACTIONS TO PHENOTHIAZINES[a]

Type of reactions	Determining factors	Precautions or treatment
Adverse Behavioral Effects		
Oversedation; impaired psychomotor function	Dose; individual tolerance	Small initial doses; avoid dangerous tasks early
Restlessness, excitement, insomnia, bizarre dreams	Patient personality; type of drug	Conventional sedative or hypnotic drug may be added
Aggravation of schizophrenic symptoms	Patients with insight, somatic complaints	Consider a nonphenothiazine tranquilizer
Toxic confusional state	Dose; age	Stop the drug
Toxic Effects on Central Nervous System		
Extrapyramidal syndromes (parkinsonian syndrome, dystonic reactions, akathisia)	Dose; age; genetic predisposition	Anticholinergic or antihistaminic drugs; reduce dose
Seizures	Dose; prior brain damage	Reduce dose; possibly add phenobarbital
Electroencephalographic slowing, paroxysmal and focal	Dose; duration of treatment; individual susceptibility	Be sure to tell EEG reader of drug history
Disturbed body temperature (hypo- and hyperthermia)	Ambient temperature; midbrain disorder	Avoid extreme temperatures; treat hyperthermia as heat stroke is managed
Respiratory depression	Usually combined with other causes, such as electric convulsive therapy	Use a smaller shock
Various neurologic syndromes	Dose; previous brain damage	Stop drug

680

Toxic Effects on Autonomic Nervous System

Hypotensive crises	Parenteral administration; age; alcohol	Never give drug intravenously; levarterenol intravenously
Tachycardia, blurred vision, aggravation of glaucoma, paralyticileus, fecal impaction, bladder paralysis	Predominant anticholinergic effects	Reduce dose or stop drug; cholinergic drugs, mechanical aids
Nasal congestion	Sympathetic depression	Reassurance
Inhibition of ejaculation	Adrenergic blockade	

Allergic or Toxic Reactions

Cholestatic jaundice	First 4 weeks; uncommon (0.5%)	Stop drug; wait
Xanthomatous biliary cirrhosis	Follows cholestatic jaundice; rare	Might try corticosteroids early in course
Agranulocytosis	Usually first 12 weeks; rare; elderly women	Stop drug; wait; use antibiotic as needed; avoid transfusions or corticosteroids
Eosinophilia	Early in course	No harm
Thrombopenic or nonthrombopenic purpura; hemolytic anemias; pancytopenia	Unusual	Stop drug; may switch to another
Dermatoses; contact dermatitis, photosensitivity	Early in course	Stop drug; may switch to another; avoid exposure to sun

Metabolic or Endocrine Effects

Weight gain	Hypothalamic effect	Small rations
Edema	Increased antidiuretic hormone secretion	Wait
Lactation, gynecomastia, menstrual irregularities	Estrogenic effect	Reassurance

681

TABLE 7 (Continued)

Type of reactions	Determining factors	Precautions or treatment
False pregnancy test	Urinary metabolite (?)	Use immunological tests
Impotency in men, increased libido in women	Estrogenic effect	Reassurance
Miscellaneous		
Unexpected deaths	Dose; previous brain damage or seizures	Completely unpredictable; watch doses in known seizure patients
Hypostatic pneumonia; trophic ulcers	Age; neglect	Adequate nursing care
Anesthetic complications	Blocked pressor reflexes	Stop drug prior to elective surgery
Local inflammation, gangrene	At injection site or perivenous leakage	Avoid parenteral drug when possible
Electrocardiographic abnormalities	Vagolytic, quinidine-like effects	Uncertain
Potentiation of other drugs, alcohol	Dose	Avoid polypharmacy; warn patient
Teratogenic effects	Phocomelia with trifluoperazine; not established	Avoid drugs in fertile or pregnant women as much as possible
Pigmentary retinopathy	Toxic doses	Keep dose under 800 mg daily of thioridazine
Melanin pigmentation; corneal and lens deposits	Chlorpromazine 2 years or more; high dose	Switch to "low-dose" piperazine derivative

TABLE 8
EFFECTS PRODUCED BY DRUGS USED IN PREGNANCY[a]

Maternal medication	Fetal or neonatal effect
Oral progestogens Androgens Estrogens	Masculinization and advanced bone age
Cortisone acetate (Cortogen acetate, Cortone acetate)	Anomalies: cleft palate (?)
Potassium iodide Propylthiouracil Methimazole (Tapazole)	Goiter and mental retardation
Iophenoxic acid (Teridax)	Elevation of P.B.I.
Sodium aminopterin Methotrexate (Amethopterin) Chlorambucil (Leukeran)	Anomalies and abortion
Bishydroxycourmarin (Dicumarol) Ethyl bicoumacetate (Tromexan ethyl acetate) Sodium warfarin (Coumadin sodium, Panwarfin, Prothromadin)	Fetal death; hemorrhage
Salicylates (large amounts)	Neonatal bleeding
Streptomycin	Possible 8th nerve deafness
Sulfonamides Chloramphenicol (Chloromycetin) Sodium novobiocin (Albamycin sodium, Cathomycin sodium)	Kernicterus "Grey" syndrome; death Hyperbilirubinemia
Erythromycin (Ilosone)	Liver damage (?)
Nitrofurantoin (Furadantin)	Hemolysis
Tetracyclines	Inhibition of bone growth Discoloration of teeth
Vitamin K analogues (in excess)	Hyperbilirubinemia
Ammonium chloride	Acidosis
Intravenous fluids (in excess)	Electrolyte abnormalities
Reserpine (Rauloydin, Raurine, Rau-Sed, Reserpoid, Sandril Serfin, Serpasil, Serpate, Vio-Serpine)	Stuffy nose; respiratory obstruction
Hexamethonium bromide (Bistrium bromide)	Neonatal ileus
Heroin and morphine	Neonatal death
Phenobarbital (in excess)	Neonatal bleeding; death
Smoking	Birth of small babies

TABLE 11
TOXIC EFFECTS OF DIALKYLNITROSAMINES AND RELATED COMPOUNDS[a]

Drug	Acute effects		Carcinogenic effects	
	LD_{50} (mg/kg)	ED (mg/kg)	(gm/kg)	Organs affected
Nitrosamines				
dimethyl	27–41	15	0.25	Liver Kidney Lungs
diethyl	216	130	0.25	Liver Kidney
dipropyl		400	2	Liver
dibutyl		800	10	Liver Bladder
diamyl	1750	—	28	Liver Lungs
n-butylmethyl	130	70	0.6	Liver
tert-butylmethyl	700	none at 1800	—	—
ethyl-2-hydroxyethyl	—	none at 3000	—	—
bis(2-hydroxyethyl)	—	9000	160	Liver
piperidine		200	2	Liver and Oesophagus
morpholine	282	200	0.7	Liver
methylphenyl	200	none at 200	none at high doses	
Formamides				
dimethyl	3800	none	none at 13	
diethyl	1740	none	—	
n-butylmethyl	c.500	none	—	
tert-butylmethyl	c.500	none	—	

[a]The acute LD_{50}s are given, and also the dose, ED, which, given singly, causes distinct hepatic necrosis. Under acute effects the lowest doses that have caused tumors in 50% of the rats treated are shown, and the organs in which tumors have been found. Note that carcinogenic doses are in gm/kg, not mg/kg. [From D. F. Heath and P. N. Magee, *Brit. J. Ind. Med.* 19, 278 (1962).]

TABLE 12

ACUTE TOXICITY OF PYRIDINES AND PIPERAZINES[a]

Compound	Single oral LD_{50} dose, rats (gm/kg)	Single skin absorption LD_{50} dose, rabbits (ml/kg)	Single inhalation, rats, saturated vapors	Primary irritation, rabbit skin	Eye injury, rabbits
α-Picoline	1.41	0.41	1 hour killed none of 6 2 hours killed 6 of 6	Mild	Severe
γ-Picoline	1.29	0.27	1 hour killed 1 of 6 2 hours killed 6 of 6	Marked	Severe
2-Methyl-5-ethylpyridine	1.54	1.00	1 hour killed none of 6 4 hours killed 6 of 6	Marked	Severe

TABLE 12 (Continued)

Compound	Single oral LD$_{50}$ dose, rats (gm/kg)	Single skin absorption LD$_{50}$ dose, rabbits (ml/kg)	Single inhalation, rats, saturated vapors	Primary irritation, rabbit skin	Eye injury, rabbits
5-Ethyl-2-methylpiperidine	0.54	0.63	30 minutes killed none of 6 1 hour killed 6 of 6	Causes burns	Severe
Alkyl Pyridine HB	2.14	0.53	4 hours killed none of 6 8 hours killed 5 of 6	None	Moderate
Piperazine	3.80	4	8 hours killed none of 6	Mild	Severe

Compound					
N-Aminoethylpiperazine	2.14	0.88	8 hours killed none of 6	Causes burns	Moderate
N-Hydroxyethylpiperazine	4.92	5.0 ml/kg killed none of 2	8 hours killed none of 6	None	Moderate
N-Methylpiperazine	2.83	1.49	8 hours killed none of 6	Causes burns	Severe
2,5-Dimethylpiperazine	3.2	0.8	8 hours killed none of 6	Minor	Severe
N-Phenylpiperazine	0.21	0.14	8 hours killed none of 6	Causes burns	Severe

[a]Tech. Bull. Union Carbide (1967).

TABLE 13
ORAL LD_{50} VALUES FOR SURFACTANTS (ALBINO RAT)[a]

Surfactant	LD_{50} (mg/kg)
Anionic	
Alkylbenzenesulfonate (tp ABS)[b]	1,220
Linear alkylatesulfonate (LAS)	1,260
Decylbenzenesulfonate	2,320
Ethylphenylphenolsulfonate	2,000
Oleoylmethyl tauride sulfonate	4,000+
Dodecyldiphenylethersulfonate	700
Dioctylsulfosuccinate	1,900
Lauryl glyceryl ether sulfonate	1,820
Lauryl sulfate	1,300
2-Ethylhexyl sulfate	4,125
7-Ethyl-2-methylundecyl-1-4 sulfate	1,250
3,9-Diethyltridecyl-6 sulfate	1,430
Nonionic	
Sulfated Compound	
Lauryl alcohol EO (4)[c]	8,600
Lauryl alcohol EO (23)	8,600
Stearyl alcohol EO (2)	25,000+
Stearyl alcohol EO (10)	2,900
Stearyl alcohol EO (20)	1,900
Oleyl alcohol EO (2)	25,800
Oleyl alcohol EO (10)	2,700
Oleyl alcohol EO (20)	2,800
Octylphenol EO (3)	4,000
Octylphenol EO (10)	1,800
Octylphenol EO (20)	3,600
Octylphenol EO (40)	28,000+
Cationic	
Cetyltrimethylammonium	410
Bromide (quaternary ammonium)	
Cetylpyridinium chloride (quaternary pyridinium)	200
Lauryl imidazodine	3,200

[a] Adapted from J. C. Calandra and Otis E. Fancher, "Cleaning Products and Their Accidental Ingestion."

[b] ABS in which the alkyl group is derived from tetrapropylene. (No longer employed in household detergents.)

[c] EO indicates ethylene oxide condensates in which the numerical designation is the number of moles of EO per mole of base.

TABLE 14
ORAL LD$_{50}$ VALUES FOR CLEANING PRODUCTS (ALBINO RAT)[a]

Product	LD$_{50}$ (mg/kg)
Toilet bar soap	7,000–20,000
General purpose granular detergent	3,000– 7,000
General purpose liquid detergent	5,000– 8,600
Laundry detergent (granular)	6,200
Scouring cleanser	10,000+
Dishwashing detergent (liquid)	7,000
Dishwashing detergent (granular)	3,800
Automatic dishwasher compound with bleach	3,000
Bubble bath	7,600
Bleach (liquid)	10,000+
Fabric softener	5,600–12,000
Fabric whitener	5,000+
Shampoo	5,000–10,000
Shampoo (antidandruff)	3,500
Sodium chloride (table salt)	3,100– 4,200
Sodium bicarbonate (baking soda)	4,300
Ethyl alcohol	13,700
Benzene	5,700
Ethylene glycol	5,500

[a]Adapted from J. C. Calandra and Otis E. Fancher, "Cleaning Products and Their Accidental Ingestion."

TABLE 15
ESTIMATED LD$_{50}$ VALUES FOR A SERIES OF PHTHALATE ESTERS[a]

Phthalate ester	I.P. LD$_{50}$ in mice (gm/kg)	95% confidence limits	Molecular Weight	Solubility in water (gm/100gm)
Dimethyl phthalate	1.58	0.98– 1.99	194	0.45
Diethyl phthalate	2.83	2.42– 3.29	222	0.1
Dibutyl phthalate	4.00	2.94– 5.45	278	Insoluble
Diisobutyl phthalate	4.50	3.36– 6.02	278	0.01
Di(methoxyethyl) phthalate	2.51	1.82– 3.45	282	0.85
Butyl benzyl phthalate	3.16	2.51– 3.98	312	Insoluble
Di(2-ethylhexyl) phthalate	14.19	12.62–15.76	390	0.01
Dicapryl phthalate	14.19	11.21–15.87	390	0.03

[a]From Colley David et al., J. Pharm. Sci. **55**, 58 (1966).

TABLE 16

ACUTE TOXICITY OF ETHYLENEAMINES[a]

	Single oral LD_{50} rats	Single skin penetration, LD_{50} rabbits	Single inhalation concentrated vapors rats	Primary skin irritation, rabbits	Eye injury, rabbits
Ethyleneamine	1.85 gm/kg	0.56 gm/kg	8 hrs. killed none of 6	Severe	Severe
Diethylenetriamine	2.04 ml/kg	1.09 ml/kg	8 hrs. killed none of 6	Severe	Severe
Triethylenetetramine	4.34 gm/kg	0.82 ml/kg	8 hrs. killed one of 6	Severe	Moderate
Tetraethylenepentamine	3.99 gm/kg	0.66 ml/kg	8 hrs. killed none of 6	Severe	Moderate
Polyamine H, special	2.50 ml/kg	0.62 ml/kg	8 hrs. killed none of 6	Minor	Moderate

[a] *Union Carbide Company Technical Bulletin 1967.*

TABLE 17
TOXICITY OF HALOGENATED ALKENES (RATS)[a]

Structure	No. F atoms	No. Cl atoms	ALC[b] (ppm)	LC$_{50}$[c] (ppm)
$CF_2=CH_2$	2	0	128,000	—
$CF_2=CF_2$	4	0	—	40,000
$CF_3-CF=CF_2$	6	0	—	3,000
$(CF_3)_2-C=CF_2$	8	0	—	0.5
$CCl_2=CH_2$	0	2	32,000	—
$CHCl=CCl_2$	0	3	8,000	—
$CCl_2=CCl_2$	0	4	4,000	—
$CCl_2=CF_2$	2	2	1,000	—
$CClF=CF_2$	3	1	—	1,000

[a] From J. Wesley Clayton, Jr., *J. Occupational Med.* **4**, 262 May 1962.

[b] Approximate lethal concentration. Data from C. P. Carpenter *et al.*, *J. Ind. Hyg. Toxicol.* **31**, 343, 1949.

[c] Data from studies at Haskell Laboratory. All are 4-hour exposures with the exception of $(CF_3)_2-C=CF_2$ which was for 6 hours, although a 4-hour exposure at 0.76 ppm was lethal for rats.

TABLE 18

LD$_{50}$ VALUES OF DINITROPHENOLS (MG/KG) FOR RATS AND MICE AT THREE TEMPERATURE RANGES, WITH MLD VALUES FOR DOGS[a]

	Rats	Mice	Mice	Mice	Dogs
Dinitro-phenol	18°–21°	18°–21°	35°–37°	39°–41°	Room temp. (?)
2,3-Dinitro-phenol	190	200	>160 <175	>160 <175	1000
2,4-Dinitro-phenol	35	36	35	<5[b]	30
2,5-Dinitro-phenol	150	273	~250	~200	100
2,6-Dinitro-phenol	38	45	37	<10[b]	50
3,4-Dinitro-phenol	98	112	~115	>100 <110	500
3,5-Dinitro-phenol	45	50	47	50	500

[a] From D. G. Harvey, *J. Pharm. Pharmacol.* **11**, 462–474, 1959.

[b] At these dose levels the mortalities were 100%.

TABLE 19
ACUTE TOXICITY OF STRONTIUM COMPOUNDS ADMINISTERED
INTRAPERITONEALLY TO RATS[a]

Compound	LD_{50} of compound (mg/kg)	LD_{50} of metal (mg/kg)
Strontium nitrate	540	224
Strontium iodide	800	156
Strontium bromide	1000	246
Strontium lactate	900	247
Strontium salicylate	400	88

[a] Data from K. W. Cochran, *et al.*, *Arch. Ind. Hyg. Occupational Med.* **1**, 637–650, June 1950.

TABLE 20
MAXIMUM BIOLOGICAL ALLOWABLE CONCENTRATIONS[a]

Substance	Estimated as	Maximum allowable concentration	Biological material
Lead	Lead	0.15 mg/liter	Urine
Lead	Lead	0.8 mg/liter	Blood
Lead	Coproporphyrin	0.10 mg/liter	Urine
Tetraethyl lead	Lead	0.12 mg/liter	Urine
Tetraethyl lead	Lead	0.07 mg/liter	Blood
Mercury	Mercury	0.10 mg/liter	Urine
Chromium	Chromium	0.04 mg/liter	Urine
Arsenic	Arsenic	0.10 mg/liter	Urine
Arsenic	Arsenic	3 μg/gm	Hair
Benzol	Conjugated sulphates	70%	Urine
Trichloroethylene	Trichloracetic acid	50 mg/liter	Urine
Acetone	Acetone	50 mg/liter	Blood
Acetone	Acetone	100 mg/liter	Urine
Acetone	Acetone	0.12 mg/liter	Expired air
Toluol	Hippuric acid	2.4 gm/24 hours	Urine
Parathion	Cholinesterase activity	reduced by 5%	Blood
CO	COHb	14%	Blood
CO	CO	3 ml%	Blood
CO	CO	0.014%	Expired air
HF	Fluoride	2 mg/liter	Urine

[a] From E. C. Vigliani, *Med. d. Lavoro* **50**, No. 5, pp. 323–327. May, 1959.

TABLE 21

ACUTE TOXICITY OF ALCOHOLS[a]

Name	Single dose oral toxicity to rats: RF LD_{50}	Penetration of rabbit skin:[b] RF LD_{50}	Saturated vapor inhalation by rats: maximum for no death	Inhalation of known vapor concentration		
				Concentration (ppm)	Time (hours)	Mortality in 14 days
	gm/kg	ml/kg				
Phenyl methyl carbinol	0.4	(>15.0)	8 hr.	—	—	—
Undecanol	3.0	(>20.0)	—	—	—	—
Acetaldol	2.18	0.14	30 min.	—	—	—
Diisobutyl carbinol	3.56	5.66	8 hr.	—	—	—
2,6-Dimethyl heptanol-4	3.16	>10	8 hr.	2000	8	0/6
Acetol	2.2	16.0	—	1000	1	4/6
Allyl alcohol	0.064	0.053	—	—	—	—
Diacetone alcohol	4.0	14.5	8 hr.	500	4	2/6
2,3-Dichloropropanol	0.09	0.2	—	16000	8	4/6
Isopropanol	5.84	16.4	—	—	—	—
2-Aminoethoxyethanol	5.66	1.19	8 hr.	1000	8	3/6
Benzyl alcohol	3.10	—	2 hr.	—	—	—
n-Butanol	4.36	—	8 hr.	—	—	—
2-Butyl-1-octanol	12.9	—	8 hr.	—	—	—

695

TABLE 21 (Continued)

Name	Single dose oral toxicity to rats: RF LD$_{50}$	Penetration of rabbit skin:[b] RF LD$_{50}$	Saturated vapor inhalation by rats: maximum for no death	Inhalation of known vapor concentration		
				Concentration (ppm)	Time (hours)	Mortality in 14 days
Decanol (mixed isomers)	9.80	3.56	8 hr.	—	—	—
2-Dimethylaminoethanol	2.34	1.37	8 hr.	—	—	—
3-Heptanol	1.87	4.36	4 hr.	—	—	—
n-Hexanol	4.59	3.10	8 hr.	—	—	—
n-Hexoxyethanol	4.92	1.50	8 hr.	—	—	—
4-Methyl-2-pentanol (methylisobutylcarbinol)	2.59	3.56	2 hr.	2000	8	5/6
Allyl alcohol	0.064	—	—	—	—	—
Propanol-1	1.87	5.04	2 hr.	4000	4	2/6
Butanol-2	6.48	—	—	16000	4	5/6
Isobutyl alcohol	2.46	4.24	2 hr.	8000	4	2/6
Pentanol-3	1.87	2.52	2 hr.	—	—	—
2-Methylpentanol-1	1.41	3.56	8 hr.	—	—	—
2-Methyl-2-pentene-1-ol	4.92	3.00	4 hr.	—	—	—
2-Ethylbutanol-1	1.85	1.26	8 hr.	—	—	—
Heptanol-2	2.58	1.78	8 hr.	—	—	—
2,6,8-Trimethylnonanol-4	17.0	11.22	8 hr.	—	—	—
2,8-Dimethyl-6-isobutylnonanol-4	16.3	—	8 hr.	—	—	—

2-Methylaminoethanol	2.34	—	8 hr.	—	—	—
2-Ethylaminoethanol	1.48	0.36	8 hr.	—	—	—
2-Butylaminoethanol	1.15	—	8 hr.	—	—	—
2-Phenylethylaminoethanol	1.87	3.00	8 hr.	—	—	—
2-Diisopropylaminoethanol	1.07	0.45	8 hr.	—	—	—
2-Dibutylaminoethanol	1.07	1.68	8 hr.	—	—	—
2-Di-(2-ethylhexyl)aminoethanol	4.92	2.52	8 hr.	—	—	—
N-Methyl-2,2'-iminodiethanol	4.78	5.99	8 hr.	—	—	—
	gm/kg	ml/kg				
N-Ethyl-2,2'-iminodiethanol	4.57	—	8 hr.	—	—	—
N-Butyl-2,2'-iminodiethanol	4.25	—	8 hr.	—	—	—
1,1-Dimethylaminopropanol-2	1.89	—	2 hr.	—	—	—
	ml/kg	ml/kg				
2-Butene-1-ol	0.93	1.27	15 min.	1000[e]	4	0/6
Cyclohexanol	2.06	—	8 hr.	—	—	—
2-Cyclopentene-1-ol	0.47	0.18	1 hr.	500[e]	4	0/6
2,2-Dimethylbutanol	2.33	1.77	8 hr.	—	—	—
2,3-Dimethylpentanol	2.38	2.5	8 hr.	—	—	—
1-Ethynylcyclohexanol	0.60	1.00	8 hr.	—	—	—
2-Ethyl-4-methylpentanol	4.29	>5.0	8 hr.	62.5[e]	4	—
Heptadecanol (mixed primary isomers)	51.6	16.8	8 hr.	—	—	—
4-Hexene-1-yne-3-ol	0.034	0.071	1 hr.[d]	—	—	1/6
5-Indanol	3.25	0.45	—	—	—	—
2-Methylbutanol	4.92	3.54	8 hr.	—	—	—
Methylheptanol (mixed primary isomers)	5.16	2.52	4 hr.	—	—	—

TABLE 21 (Continued)

Name	Single dose oral toxicity to rats: RF LD$_{50}$	Penetration of rabbit skin:[b] RF LD$_{50}$	Saturated vapor inhalation by rats: maximum for no death	Inhalation of known vapor concentration		
				Concentration (ppm)	Time (hours)	Mortality in 14 days
4-Methylpentanol	6.50	3.97	8 hr.	—	—	—
2-Propylheptanol	6.73	>10	8 hr.	—	—	—
Tridecanol (mixed primary isomers)	17.2	7.07	8 hr.	—	—	—
2,2,4-Trimethylpentanol	3.73	6.30	8 hr.	—	—	—
2-(4-Chlorophenoxy)ethanol	2.83[c]	0.50	4 hr.	—	—	—
1,3-Dichloro-2-propanol	0.11	0.80	30 min.	125[e]	4	2/6

[a] References:

H. F. Smyth, Jr., *et al.*, "The Place of the Range Finding Test in the Industrial Toxicology Laboratory," *J. Ind. Hyg. Toxicol.* **26**, 269–273, 1944; "Further Experience with the Range Finding Test in the Industrial Toxicology Laboratory," *J. Ind. Hyg. Toxicol.* **30**, 63–68, 1948; "Range-Finding Toxicity Data, List III," *J. Ind. Hyg. Toxicol.* **31**, 60–62, 1949; "Range-Finding Toxicity Data: List IV," *Arch. Ind. Hyg. Occupational Med.* **4**, 119–122, 1951; "Range-Finding Toxicity Data: List V," *Arch. Ind. Hyg. Occupational Med.* **10**, 61–68, 1954; "Range-Finding Toxicity Data: List VI," *Am. Ind. Hyg. Assoc. J.* **23**, 95–107, 1962.

[b] Figures in parentheses were determined by poultices on guinea pigs.

[c] As gm/kg in a suitable vehicle.

[d] The inhalation time shown killed all six rats.

[e] Twice concentration shown killed all six rats.

TABLE 22

ACUTE TOXICITY OF ALDEHYDES[a]

Name	Single dose oral toxicity to rats: RF LD$_{50}$	Penetration of rabbit skin:[b] RF LD$_{50}$	Saturated vapor inhalation by rats: maximum for no death	Inhalation of known vapor concentration by rats		
				Concentration (ppm)	Time (hours)	Mortality in 14 days
	gm/kg	ml/kg				
Acetaldehyde	1.93	—	2 min.[c]	{8000 16000	8 8	0/6} 0/6]
Crotonaldehyde	0.3	(0.03)	1 min.	—	—	—
2-Ethyl, 3 propyl acrolein	3.0	(>20.0)	8 hr.			
Acetal	4.57	10	5 min.	4000	4	2/6
Dimethyl acetal	6.50	20	5 min.	16000	4	3/6
Glyoxal tetrabutyl acetal	8.90	2.24	8 hr.	—		
Methacryl aldehyde	0.14	0.43	—	250	4	5/6
Dichloroethyl formal	0.065	(0.17)	—	{60 120	5 4	0/6} 0/6]
Ethoxy propionaldehyde	0.9	1.0	—	500	4	6/6
Butyraldehyde	5.89	—	5 min.	8000	4	1/6
α-Ethylbutyraldehyde	3.98	—	5 min.	8000	4	5/6
α-Ethylcaproaldehyde	3.73	5.04	—	4000	4	1/6

699

TABLE 22 (Continued)

Name	Single dose oral toxicity to rats: RF LD$_{50}$	Penetration of rabbit skin:[b] RF LD$_{50}$	Saturated vapor inhalation by rats: maximum for no death	Inhalation of known vapor concentration by rats		
				Concentration (ppm)	Time (hours)	Mortality in 14 days
2-Ethylhexyl acrylate	5.66	8.48	8 hr.	—	—	—
Propionaldehyde	1.41	5.04	2 min.	8000	4	5/6
Acrolein	0.046					
Aldol	2.18					
Isobutyraldehyde	3.73	7.13	15 min.	8000	4	1/6
Hexanal	4.89	—	1 hr.	2000	4	1/6
Hexa-2,4-dienal	0.73	0.27	15 min.	2000	4	1/6
2-Methyl-2-pentene-1-al	4.29	4.5	1 hr.	2000	4	3/6
3-Methylglutaraldehyde	0.78	0.30	8 hr.	—	—	—
α-Hydroxyadipaldehyde	17.0	>20	8 hr.	—	—	—
3,3,5-Trimethylcyclohexanecarboxaldehyde	4.14	15.8	8 hr.	—	—	—
3,4-Dihydro-2H-pyran-2-carboxaldehyde	4.92	—	8 hr.	—	—	—
	ml/kg	ml/kg				
4-Cyclohexene-1-carboxaldehyde	2.46	1.77	4 hr.	2000	4	0/6
1-Decanal (mixed isomers)	3.73	5.04	8 hr.	—	—	—
2,3-Dimethyl-4-pentenal	5.66	>10	2 hr.	10,000	4	5/6

	ml/kg	ml/kg				
2,3-Dimethyl valeraldehyde	3.54	7.1	2 hr.	6000	4	0/6
Glutaraldehyde, 25%	2.38	2.56	8 hr.	—	—	—
Glyoxal 29.2%	7.46	>20	8 hr.	—	—	—
1-Hexanal (mixed isomers)	9.51	>10	4 hr.	—	—	—
3-Methoxy butyraldehyde	0.54	0.31	15 min.	500[d]	4	0/6
2-Methyl-4-cyclohexene-1-carboxaldehyde	5.66	3.15	8 hr.	—	—	—
4-Methyl valeraldehyde	5.66	4.46	30 min.	8000[d]	4	0/6
1-Octanal (mixed isomers)	5.63	6.35	8 hr.	—	—	—
1-Pentanal (mixed isomers)	4.76	>20	5 min.	8000	4	3/6
4-Pentenal	0.62	1.59	5 min.	250	4	1/12
2,3-Dichloro-2-methyl-propionaldehyde	1.62	0.36	15 min.	250[d]	4	1/6
2,2,3-Trichloropropionaldehyde	0.24	0.71	2 hr.	—	—	—
2,5-Dimethyl-2-hydroxy-adipaldehyde	5.89	—	8 hr.	—	—	—

[a] References:
H. F. Smyth, Jr., *et al.*, "The Place of the Range Finding Test in the Industrial Toxicology Laboratory," *J. Ind. Hyg. Toxicol.* **26,** 269–273, 1944; "Further Experience with the Range Finding Test in the Industrial Toxicology Laboratory," *J. Ind. Hyg. Toxicol.* **30,** 63–68, 1948; "Range-Finding Toxicity Data, List III," *J. Ind. Hyg. Toxicol.* **31,** 60–62, 1949; "Range-Finding Toxicity Data: List IV," *Arch. Ind. Hyg. Occupational Med.* **4,** 119–122, 1951; "Range-Finding Toxicity Data: List V," *Arch. Ind. Hyg. Occupational Med.* **10,** 61–68, 1954; "Range-Finding Toxicity Data: List VI," *Am. Ind. Hyg. Assoc. J.* **23,** 95–107, 1962.

[b] Figures in parentheses were determined by poultices on guinea pigs.

[c] The inhalation time shown killed all six rats.

[d] Twice concentration shown killed all six rats.

TABLE 23

ACUTE TOXICITY OF ALIPHATIC AND ALICYCLIC AMINES[a]

Name	Single dose oral toxicity to rats: RF LD_{50}	Penetration of rabbit skin:[b] RF LD_{50}	Saturated vapor inhalation by rats: maximum for no death	Inhalation of known vapor concentration by rats		
				Concentration (ppm)	Time (hours)	Mortality in 14 days
	gm/kg	ml/kg				
Aminoethyl ethanolamine	3.0	(1.8)				
n-Butyl amine	0.5	(0.5)	2 min.			
Diethyl ethanolamine	1.3	(1.0)	4 hr.			
Tetramethyl ethylene diamine	1.58	7.0	10 min.			
2-Ethylhexyl amine	0.45	—	1 hr.	$\{125$ $\{250$	4 4	$0/6\}$ $6/6\}$
Hydroxyethyl propylene diamine	4.92	10.	8 hr.	—	—	—
Monoisopropanolamine	4.26	1.64	8 hr.	—	—	—
Tetraethylene pentamine	3.99	0.66	8 hr.	—	—	—
Triethylene tetramine	4.34	0.82	4 hr.	—	—	—
Di(2-cyanoethyl)amine	2.7	10.	—	—	—	—
Diethylene triamine	2.33	1.09	8 hr.	—	—	—
Di(2-ethylhexyl)amine	1.64	—	8 hr.	—	—	—
1,3-Butanediamine	1.35	0.43	8 hr.	—	—	—
Diethylamine	0.54	0.82	5 min.[d]	4000	4	3/6

	ml/kg	ml/kg				
Ethylenediamine	1.16	0.73	—	$\{$2000 / 4000	8 / 8	$\{$0/6 / 6/6$\}$
N-Hydroxyethyl diethylenetriamine	4.92	2.52	8 hr.	—	—	—
Isopropylamine	0.82	0.55	2 min.[d]	$\{$4000 / 8000	4 / 4	$\{$0/6 / 6/6$\}$
α-Methylbenzylamine	0.94	0.78	8 hr.	—	—	—
α-Methylbenzylamine, N-hydroxyethyl	2.83	1.54	8 hr.	—	—	—
Triethylamine	0.46	0.57	—	1000	4	1/6
Ethylamine	0.40	0.39	2 min.[d]	8000	4	2/6
Diisopropylamine	0.77	—	5 min.[d]	1000	4	2/6
Dibutylamine	0.55	1.01	—	250[e]	4	0/6
Hexylamine	0.67	0.42	1 hr.	500	4	2/6
2-Ethylbutylamine	0.39	2.00	15 min.	500[e]	4	0/6
1-Methyl-4-ethyloctylamine	0.73	0.38	8 hr.	—	—	—
N,N-Diethylethylenediamine	2.83	0.82	8 hr.	—	—	—
N,N'-Di(α-methylbenzyl)ethylene-diamine	1.29	0.53	8 hr.	—	—	—
1,2-Diaminopropane	2.23	0.50	4 hr.	—	—	—
N,N-Dimethyl-α-methylbenzylamine	0.42	0.89	30 min.	125	4	2/6
Acrylic acid, N,N-diethylaminoethyl ester	0.89	0.20	2 hr.	—	—	—
7-Aminoheptanoic acid, isopropyl ester	4.00	0.89	8 hr.	—	—	—
3-Aminopropanol	2.83	1.25	8 hr.	—	—	—
Bis-[3-aminopropyl]amine	0.81	0.11	8 hr.	—	—	—
N,N-Bis-[3-aminopropyl]methylamine	1.54	0.14	8 hr.	333	1	6/6
Bis-[2,5-endomethylene-cyclohexylmethyl]amine	1.41[c]	0.11	8 hr.	—	—	—

TABLE 24
ACUTE TOXICITY OF ALKANOLAMINES[a]

Alkanolamine	Single oral LD$_{50}$ dose, rats (gm/kg)	Single skin absorption, rabbits (ml/kg)	Single inhalation rats, saturated vapors	Primary irritation, rabbits skin	Eye injury rabbits
Ammonia (For comparative purposes only)	0.35	1.1 gm/kg	Saturated with 28% NH$_3$ in water, 1 min. killed 2 of 4	None	Severe
Monoethanolamine	2.14–2.74	1.00	4 hr. killed[b] 2 of 6	Mild	Severe
Diethanolamine	1.41–1.82	11.89	8 hr. killed[b] none of 6	Mild	Moderate
Triethanolamine	8.68	20 killed none of 5	8 hr. killed[b] none of 6	Mild	Moderate
Dimethyl ethanolamine	2.34	1.36	8 hr. killed none of 6	None	Severe
Diethyl ethanolamine	2.46	1.26	8 hr. killed 1 of 5	Mild	Severe
Aminoethyl ethanolamine	3.0	3.56	8 hr. killed none of 6	Mild	Moderate
N-Methyl diethanolamine	4.78	5.99	8 hr. killed none of 6	Mild	Moderate
N-Acetyl ethanolamine	27.66	20 killed none of 6	8 hr. killed[b] none of 6	Mild	Mild
Monoisopropanolamine	4.26	1.64	8 hr. killed none of 6	Mild	Severe
Diisopropanolamine	6.72		8 hr. killed[b] none of 6	Mild	Moderate
Triisopropanolamine	6.50	10 gm/kg killed 1 of 4	8 hr. killed none of 6	None	Moderate
Mixed isopropanolamine	5.25	8.90	8 hr. killed[b] none of 6	None	Moderate
Morpholine	1.05	0.50	4 hr. killed 6 of 6	Moderate	Severe
N-Methyl morpholine	2.72	1.35	2 hr. killed 6 of 6	Minor	Moderate
N-Hydroxyethyl morpholine	12.06	14.1	8 hr. killed none of 6	None	Moderate
N-Aminopropyl morpholine	3.56	1.23	8 hr. killed none of 6	Skin burns	Severe
N-Ethyl morpholine	1.78		4 hr. killed 5 of 6	None	Moderate

[a] Data from Union Carbide Chemicals Co., New York, 1958.
[b] Mist from 170°C saturation.

TABLE 25
ACUTE TOXICITY OF ANILINE AND DERIVATIVES[a]

	LD_{50} gm/kg (rat)		
Compound	Intraperitoneal	Peroral	Percutaneous
Aniline	0.42	0.62	1.4
Ethylaniline	0.18	0.28	4.7
Diethylaniline	0.42	0.62	>16.0
Technical ethyl-diethyl-aniline mixture	0.18	0.62	10.7
p-Chloroaniline	0.42	0.42	3.2
p-Anisidine	1.40	1.40	3.2

[a] From M. Sziza and L. Podhragyai, *Arch. Gewerbepathol. Gewerbehy.* **15,** 447–456, 1957.

TABLE 26
ACUTE TOXICITY OF BORANES (RATS)[a]

Borane	Intra-peritoneal (mg/kg)	Oral (mg/kg)	Percu-taneous (mg/kg)	LC_{50}[b] (ppm)
Diborane (B_2H_6)				39
Pentaborane (B_5H_9)	11			18[c]
Decaborane ($B_{10}H_{14}$)	27	64.3	640	95[d]
Dimethylamine borane ($(CH_3)_2NH \cdot BH_3$)	50	59.2		
Trimethylamine borane ($(CH_3)_3N \cdot BH_3$)	175			
Pyridine borane $C_5H_5N \cdot BH_3$	73.6	95.4		

[a] From Roush, G., Jr., *J. of Occup. Med.* **1,** No. 1, 46–52, Jan. 1959.

[b] Four-hour LC_{50}.

[c] Two-hour exposure followed by a two-hour observation.

[d] No animal died after an exposure.

TABLE 27

ACUTE TOXICITY OF CESIUM AND YTTRIUM COMPOUNDS GIVEN
INTRAPERITONEALLY TO RATS[a]

Compound	LD_{50} of compound (mg/kg)	LD_{50} of metal (mg/kg)
Cesium chloride	1500	1118
Cesium hydroxide	100	89
Cesium bromide	1400	874
Cesium iodide	1400	715
Cesium nitrate	1200	817
Yttrium oxide	500	395
Yttrium chloride	450	132
Yttrium nitrate	350	117

[a] From K. W. Cochran *et al.*, *Arch. Ind. Hyg. Occupational Med.* **1,** 637–650, June 1950.

TABLE 28
CARBON MONOXIDE TOXICITY IN AIR

% CO in air	Response
0.01	Allowable for an exposure of several hours
0.04–0.05	Can be inhaled for 1 hour without appreciable effect
0.06–0.07	Causing a just appreciable effect after 1 hour's exposure
0.1–0.12	Causing unpleasant but not dangerous symptoms after 1 hour's exposure
0.15–0.20	Dangerous for exposure of 1 hour
0.4 and above	Fatal in exposure of less than 1 hour

TABLE 29
CARBON MONOXIDE TOXICITY IN BLOOD

% Carboxyhemoglobin	Effect
10	Shortness of breath on vigorous muscular exertion
20	Shortness of breath on moderate exertion; slight headache
30	Decided headache; irritation; ready fatigue; disturbance of judgment
40–50	Headache, confusion, collapse, and fainting on exertion
60–70	Unconsciousness; respiratory failure and death if exposure is long continued
80	Rapidly fatal
Over 80	Immediately fatal

TABLE 30
TOXICITY OF TRADITIONAL CHRISTMAS GREENS[a]

Christmas green	Toxicity
Apple-like fruits or berries	Low
Balsam, juniper, cedar, pine, fir	Low
Bayberry	Low
Bittersweet, American	Low
Bittersweet, European	Very toxic
Boxwood	Low
Eucalyptus (pods and foliage)	Low
Holly	Low
Ivy	Low
Jerusalem cherry	Very toxic
Jequirity bean	Highly toxic[b]
Love apples	Low
Mistletoe, American	Moderately toxic
Mitchella	Low
Yew	Moderately toxic

[a] From *Ind. Med. Surg.*, pp. 522–525, December 1961.
[b] Only if shell is broken.

TABLE 31

DERMAL AND EYE MUCOSA TOLERANCE LIMITS OF SYNTHETIC DETERGENTS[a]

Trade name	Detergent type	Active ingredient	Dermal (20-day subacute)	Eye mucosa (unwashed)
Aldo 33	Nonionic	Glyceryl monostearate	5	100
Arlacel 20	Nonionic	Sorbitan monolaurate	5[b]	100
Arlacel 40	Nonionic	Sorbitan monopalmitate	15[b]	50[b]
Arlacel 60	Nonionic	Sorbitan monostearate	5	75[b]
Arlacel 85	Nonionic	Sorbitan trioleate	15	100
Arlacel C	Nonionic	Sorbitan sesquioleate	5	100
Alromine RA	Anionic	Fatty alkylol amine condensate	2[b]	25
Alrosol C	Nonionic	Fatty alkylol amine condensate	2	5
Atlas G-1702	Nonionic	Polyoxyethylene sorbitol beeswax derivative	5[b]	75[b]
Diglycol Stearate S	Nonionic	Diethylene glycol stearate	5	—
Emulphor VN430	Nonionic	Polyoxyethylated fatty acid	5[b]	50[b]
Hyamine 1622	Cationic	Di-isobutyl phenoxy ethyl dimethyl benzylammonium chloride hydrate	0.5	0.5
Hyamine 2389	Cationic	Alkyl cetyl methyl trimethyl ammonium chloride	0.5[c]	0.5
Igepon TN 74	Anionic	Palmitic and methyl taurine sulfonate	5	10
Intramin WK-33	Anionic	Sodium salt sulfated lorol and myristyl collamide	5	100
Intramin Y	Anionic	Sodium salt sulfated lorol and myristyl collamide	2[b]	25
Lathanol LAL	Anionic	Alkyl aryl sulfoacetate	1	—
Miranol C2M Conc.	Amphoteric	Coconut fatty acid amide condensate	2	50

Trade name	Type	Description		
Miranol 2MCA Modif.	Amphoteric	Coconut fatty acid amide condensate	2	46
Nacconal FSNO	Anionic	Alkyl aryl sodium sulfonate plus sodium sulfate	1	5
Nacconal NRSF	Anionic	Alkyl aryl sodium sulfonate	1	5
Neutronyx 330	Nonionic	Poly alkyl ether condensate of fatty acids	5[b]	95
Neutronyx 600	Nonionic	Aromatic polyglycol ether condensate	5[b]	25
Ninol 2012E	Nonionic	Alkyl amide condensate	0.5	10
Nonisol 100	Nonionic	Polyethylene glycol fatty acid ester	5	100
Nonisol 300	Nonionic	Polyethylene glycol fatty acid ester	5	100
Sipon L20	Anionic	Ammonium lauryl sulfate	2	30
Sipon LS	Anionic	Sodium lauryl sulfate	2	20
Sipon LT	Anionic	Triethanolamine lauryl sulfate	2	40
Sulframin DR	Anionic	Sodium salt of an hydroxy alkyl amido alcohol sulfate	2	25
Sulframin DT	Anionic	Sodium salt of alkyl amino sulfate	1	10[b]
Sulframin LW	Anionic	Sodium salt of alkyl amino sulfate	—	10[b]
Teg acid (regular)	Anionic	Glyceryl monostearate	5	5
Tegin 515	Nonionic	Glyceryl monostearate	5	100
Tegin P	Anionic	Propylene glycol monostearate	5	—
Triton X-200	Anionic	Alkyl aryl polyether sulfonate	2	28
Triton X-301	Anionic	Sodium alkyl aryl polyether sulfate	2	10
Triton X-400	Cationic	Stearyl dimethyl benzyl ammonium chloride	0.5	1.0
Wetanol	Anionic	Modified sodium salt of sulfated fatty alcohol	1	25

[a] From Association of Food & Drug Officials of the U.S., Quarterly Bulletin **23**, No. 3, 151–152, July 1959.

[b] Highest concentration tested. Tolerance is in excess of concentration listed.

[c] Lowest concentration tested. Tolerance is less than 0.5.

TABLE 32

ACUTE TOXICITY OF EPOXY COMPOUNDS[a]

Name	Single dose oral toxicity to rats: RF LD$_{50}$	Penetration of rabbit skin: RF LD$_{50}$	Concentrated vapor inhalation by rats: maximum for no death	Inhalation of known vapor concentration by rats		
				Concentration (ppm)	Time (hours)	Mortality in 14 days
	gm/kg	ml/kg				
1,2,3,4-Diepoxybutane	0.078	0.089	15 min.[c]	—	—	—
Diisobutylene oxide	4.92	14.1	10 min.	4000	4	2/6
Phenyl glycidyl ether	4.26	1.50	8 hr.	—	—	—
Epoxyethylbenzene	4.29	1.06	1 hr.	500	4	2/6
	ml/kg					
2,3-Bis-[2,3-epoxypropoxy]-1,4-dioxane	1.07	1.59	8 hr.	—	—	—
Acetic acid, 3,4-epoxy-6-methylcyclohexylmethyl ester	9.8	7.94	8 hr.	—	—	—
Acrylic acid, 2,3-epoxypropyl ester	0.21	0.40	30 min.	62.5[d]	4	0/6
Bis-[2,3-epoxycyclopentyl] ether	2.14	—	8 hr.	—	—	—
2,2-Bis-[2,2,2-trimethylethyl] oxirane	6.69	14.1	8 hr.	—	—	—
1,4-Dichloro-2,3-epoxybutane	0.71[b]	2.83	2 hr.	—	—	—
1,2-8,9-Diepoxylimonene	5.63[b]	1.77	8 hr.	—	—	—
1,2-7,8-Diepoxyoctane	1.07	0.32	4 hr.	—	—	—
1,2-Epoxybutane	1.41	2.10	—	4000[d]	4	1/6
2,3-Epoxybutyric acid, butyl ester	0.50	2.83	8 hr.	—	—	—

Compound						
3,4-Epoxycyclohexane-carbonitrile	1.23	0.99	8 hr.	—	—	—
4,5-Epoxycyclohexane-1,2-dicarboxylic acid, di-(decyl) ester (mixed isomers)	>64	>20	8 hr.	—	—	—
4,5-Epoxycyclohexane-1,2-dicarboxylic acid, di-(2-ethylhexyl) ester	>64	>20	8 hr.	—	—	—
3,4-Epoxy-2,5-endo-methylene-cyclohexane-carboxylic acid, ethyl ester	4.76	3.54	8 hr.	—	—	—
2-(α,β-Epoxyethyl)-5,6-epoxybenzene	2.83[b]	0.62	8 hr.	—	—	—
2,3-Epoxy-2-ethylhexanol	5.05	3.15	8 hr.	—	—	—
3,4-Epoxy-6-methylcyclohexanecarboxylic acid, allyl ester	0.50	2.83	8 hr.	—	—	—
3,4-Epoxy-6-methylcyclohexanecarboxylic acid, 3,4-epoxy-6-methylcyclohexylmethyl ester	4.92	>10	8 hr.	4000	—	1/6
2,3-Epoxypropyl butyl ether	2.05	2.52	2 hr.	1000[d]	4	0/6
N-(2,3-Epoxypropyl) diethylamine	0.42	0.79	30 min.	—	4	—
9,10-Epoxystearic acid, allyl ester	1.41	15.9	8 hr.	—	—	—
9,10-Epoxystearic acid, 2-ethylhexyl ester	30.8	>20	8 hr.	—	—	—
1,2-Epoxy-4-vinylcyclohexane	2.00	2.83	2 hr.	—	—	—
Ethylene glycol di-(2,3-epoxy-2-methyl-propyl) ether	7.46	3.15	—	—	—	—

[a] References:

H. F. Smyth, Jr., et al., "Range-Finding Toxicity Data: List V," Arch. Ind. Hyg. Occupational Med. 10, 61–68, 1954; "Range-Finding Toxicity Data: List VI," Am. Ind. Hyg. Assoc. J. 23, 95–107, 1962.

[b] As gm/kg in a suitable vehicle.

[c] The inhalation time shown killed all rats.

[d] Twice concentration shown killed all six rats.

TABLE 33

TOXICITY OF EPOXY RESIN CHEMICALS[a]

Material	Physiological classification		Recommendations or precautions[b]
	Primary skin irritant	Sensitizer	
Epon resins (liquid types)	Mild to moderate	Mild to moderate	A
Epon resins (solid types)	Nonirritating	Nonsensitizing	E
Epon resin formulations (pre-cured)	Mild to moderate	Mild to moderate	A, C
Epon resin formulations (fully cured)	Nonirritating	Nonsensitizing	E
Amine curing agents	Mild to strong	Mild to strong	A, B, C
Anhydride curing agents	Mild	Nonsensitizing	A, E
Reactive diluents (epoxy monomers)	Mild to moderate	Mild to strong	A, B, C
Solvents	Defatting only	Nonsensitizing	A, D, E

[a] From *SBS Counselor* **3**, No. 5, October 4, 1957.
[b] Key to recommendations or precautions:

A—Skin protection   B—Goggles or face shield   C—Exhaust ventilation   D—Fire precautions   E—Avoid excessive inhalation of dust or vapor.

TABLE 34

ACUTE TOXICITY OF ESTERS[a]

Name	Single dose oral toxicity to rats: RF LD_{50}	Penetration of rabbit skin:[b] RF LD_{50}	Saturated vapor inhalation by rats: maximum for no death	Inhalation of known vapor concentration by rats		
				Concentration (ppm)	Time (hours)	Mortality in 14 days
	gm/kg	ml/kg				
Ethyl crotonate	3.0	(>10.0)	8 hr.			
2-Ethylhexyl acetate	3.0	(>20.0)	15 min.			
Butyl phthalyl butyl glycolate	14.64					
Calcium ethyl acetoacetate	9.93					
Dibutyl "Cellosolve" phthalate	8.38					
Diethylbutyl "Cellosolve" succinate	3.3					
Glycidyl oleate	3.52					
Methyl Acetyl Ricinoleate	>50					
Methyl phthalyl ethyl glycolate	9.06					
Methyl acetoacetate	3.0	(>10)	8 hr.	—	—	—
Methyl acrylate	0.3	1.3		1000	4	3/6
Methyl "Cellosolve" acetate	3.39	5.25		7000	4	2/6
Methyl diacetoacetate	1.7	(>10)	8 hr.	—	—	—
Vinyl acetate	2.92	2.5		4000	4	3/6

715

TABLE 34 (Continued)

Name	Single dose oral toxicity to rats: RF LD$_{50}$	Penetration of rabbit skin:[b] RF LD$_{50}$	Saturated vapor inhalation by rats: maximum for no death	Inhalation of known vapor concentration by rats		
				Concentration (ppm)	Time (hours)	Mortality in 14 days
Allyl acetate	0.13	1.1	—	1000	1	3/6
Diallyl maleate	0.30	1.15	8 hr.	—	—	—
Di(2-ethylhexyl) maleate	14.2	15.	4 hrs.	—	—	—
Diethyl maleate	3.2	5.	8 hrs.	—	—	—
Dimethyl tetrahydrophthalate	0.7	>10.	—	—	—	—
Ethyl aceto-acetate	3.98	>10.	8 hrs.	—	—	—
Isopropenyl acetate	3.0	—	30 min.	—	—	—
1-Propene-1,3-diol diacetate	0.15	0.67	—	16	4	4/6
n-Butyl acrylate	3.73	3.36	30 min.	1000	4	5/6
2-Chloroallylidene 3,3-diacetate	0.32	0.98	—	8	4	3/6
2-Chloroethyl acrylate	0.18	—	15 min.	125	4	0/6
				250	4	6/6
Dibutyl adipate	12.9	20	8 hr.	—	—	—
Dibutyl fumarate	8.53	15.9	8 hr.	—	—	—
Di(2-ethylhexyl) adipate	9.11	16.3	8 hr.	—	—	—
Diethyl succinate	8.53	—	8 hr.	—	—	—

	gm/kg	ml/kg				
Di(2-methoxyethyl) maleate	3.34	1.94	8 hr.	—	—	1/6
Ethoxypropyl acrylate	0.82	1.41	1 hr.	250	4	—
2-Ethylbutyl acrylate	6.49	5.50	4 hr.	—	—	—
Ethyl-β-ethoxypropionate	5.0	10	8 hr.	—	—	5/6
2-Hydroxyethyl acrylate	1.07	1.01	1 hr.	500	4	—
n-Hexyl benzoate	12.3	21	8 hr.	—	—	—
Isopropyl benzoate	3.73	20	4 hr.	—	—	—
Vinyl butyrate	8.53	—	30 min.	4000	4	3/6
Di(2-ethylhexyl) tetrahydrophthalate	114	>20		—	—	—
Carbonic acid, cyclic ethylene ester	10.40	>20	8 hr.	—	—	—
Carbonic acid, cyclic propylene ester	29.1	>20	8 hr.	8000	4	5/6
Formic acid, ethyl ester	4.29	>20	5 min.	32000	4	5/6
Acetic acid, isopropyl ester	6.75	>20	30 min.	—	—	—
Acetic acid, butyl ester	14.13	—	4 hr.	—	—	—
Acetic acid, 3-methoxybutyl ester	4.21	>20	8 hr.	4000	4	2/6
Acetic acid, 1,3-dimethylbutyl ester	6.16	>20	2 hr.	—	—	—
Acetic acid, 2-methylamyl ester	7.40	>20	8 hr.	—	—	—
Acetic acid, 3-heptanol ester	8.35	—	8 hr.	—	—	—
Acetic acid, 2[2-(2-methoxyethoxy)ethoxy] ethyl ester	11.26	8.00	8 hr.	500	4	5/6
Acrylic acid, 2-ethoxyethanol ester	1.07	1.01	1 hr.	500	4	5/6
Methacrylic acid, 2-butyloctyl ester	25.8	—	8 hr.	—	—	—

TABLE 34 (Continued)

Name	Single dose oral toxicity to rats: RF LD$_{50}$	Penetration of rabbit skin:[b] RF LD$_{50}$	Saturated vapor inhalation by rats: maximum for no death	Inhalation of known vapor concentration by rats		
				Concentration (ppm)	Time (hours)	Mortality in 14 days
Acetoacetic acid, butyl ester	11.26	—	8 hr.	—	—	—
2-Ethylhexoic acid, vinyl ester	4.29	—	8 hr.	—	—	—
Succinic acid, dipropyl ester	6.49	—	8 hr.	—	—	—
Succinic acid, di-2-hexyloxyethyl ester	4.28	12.31	8 hr.	—	—	—
Crotonic acid, vinyl ester	6.50	—	1 hr.	2000[d]	4	0/6
Fumaric acid, diisopropyl ester	3.25	10	8 hr.	—	—	—
Fumaric acid, di(2-ethylhexyl) ester	29.2	>20	8 hr.	—	—	—
Maleic acid, diisopropyl ester	2.14	—	8 hr.	—	—	—
Maleic acid, dibutyl ester	3.73	10.1	—	—	—	—
Maleic acid, di(1,3-dimethylbutyl) ester	7.46	11.9	8 hr.	—	—	—
Maleic acid, mono(hydroxyethyl) ester	2.46	—	8 hr.	—	—	—
Maleic acid, mono(hydroxyethoxyethyl) ester	2.83	7.13	8 hr.	—	—	—
Maleic acid, mono(2-hydroxypropyl) ester	3.73	8.48	8 hr.	—	—	—
Adipic acid, di(2-ethylbutyl) ester	5.62	16.8	8 hr.	—	—	—
Adipic acid, di(2-hexyloxyethyl) ester	4.29	12.31	—	—	—	—
Adipic acid, di(2'2-ethylbutoxyethyl) ester	3.25	4.24	8 hr.	—	—	—

		ml/kg				
Benzoic acid, methyl ester	3.43	—	8 hr.	—	—	—
Benzoic acid, ethyl ester	6.48	—	8 hr.	—	—	—
Benzoic acid, vinyl ester	3.25	—	8 hr.	—	—	—
Benzoic acid, butyl ester	5.14	—	8 hr.	—	—	—
Phthalic acid, dihexyl ester	29.6	>20	8 hr.	—	—	—
1,2-Carbo(2-ethyl)hexyloxy cyclohexane	>60	>20	8 hr.	—	—	—
	ml/kg					
Acetic acid, amyl ester (mixed isomers)	6.50	>20	4 hr.	—	—	—
	ml/kg	ml/kg				
Acetic acid, 1,3-butadienyl ester	0.71	0.42	10 min.[c]	62.5[d]	4	3/6
Acetic acid, 2-butoxyethyl ester	7.46	1.58	8 hr.	—	—	—
Acetic acid, ethyl ester	11.3	>20	15 min.	8000[d]	4	0/6
Acetic acid, isobutyl ester	15.4	>20	1 hr.	8000	4/6	1
Acetic acid, methyl ester	6.97	—	—	16000[d]	4	0/6
Acrylic acid, decyl ester	6.46	6.30	4 hr.	—	—	—
Acrylic acid, tridecyl ester	44.7	6.30	8 hr.	—	—	—
Adipic acid, di-(decyl) ester (mixed isomers)	20.5	8.41	8 hr.	—	—	—
Adipic acid, di-2-propynyl ester	0.20	0.44	—	—	—	—
Azelaic acid, di-(2-ethylhexyl) ester	8.72	20.0	8 hr.	—	—	—
1,2,4-Butanetricarboxylic acid, tri(2-ethylhexyl) ester	>64	20	—	—	—	—
Crotylidene dicrotonate	2.59	—	4 hr.	—	—	—
Decanoic acid, vinyl ester (mixed isomers)	6.17	14.1	8 hr.	—	—	—
Dibenzoyl diethylene glycol ester	2.83	20.0	8 hr.	—	—	—

TABLE 34 (Continued)

Name	Single dose oral toxicity to rats: RF LD$_{50}$	Penetration of rabbit skin:[b] RF LD$_{50}$	Saturated vapor inhalation by rats: maximum for no death	Inhalation of known vapor concentration by rats		
				Concentration (ppm)	Time (hours)	Mortality in 14 days
Dibenzoyl dipropylene glycol ester	9.80	>10	—	—	—	—
Di-(decanoyl)triethylene glycol ester	7.46	11.2	8 hr.	—	—	—
2,5-Endomethylene cyclohexane carboxylic acid, ethyl ester (mixed formyl isomers)	7.46	10	—	—	—	—
2,5-Endomethylene-3-cyclohexene carboxylic acid, ethyl ester	4.29	>5	—	—	—	—
2-Ethylhexanoic acid, 2-ethylhexyl ester	27	>20	8 hr.	—	—	—
Formic acid, vinyl ester	2.82	3.17	5 min.[c]	1000[d]	4	0/6
β-Formyl propionic acid, ethyl ester	9.87	7.1	—	—	—	—
Fumaric acid, diethyl ester	1.78	—	8 hr.	—	—	—
Fumaric acid, di-isobutyl ester	8.12	7.49	8 hr.	—	—	—
Hexanoic acid, vinyl ester (mixed isomers)	19.7	>20	1 hr.	4000	4	5/6
Isophthalic acid, di-(decyl) ester (mixed isomers)	>64	>10	8 hr.	—	—	—
Isophthalic acid, di-(2-ethylhexyl) ester	17.3	7.94	8 hr.	—	—	—
Maleic acid, dihexyl ester	7.34	—	8 hr.	—	—	—
Maleic acid, dimethyl ester	1.41	0.53	4 hr.	—	—	—

Maleic acid, dipentyl ester	4.92	>10	8 hr.	—	—	—	—
Mandelic acid, hexyl ester	17.0	15.4	—	—	—	—	—
Methyl borate	6.14	1.98	—	—	—	—	—
Octanoic acid, vinyl ester (mixed isomers)	7.46	>10	4 hr.	—	—	—	—
Phthalic acid, di-(decyl) ester	>64	16.8	4 hr.	—	—	—	—
Phthalic acid, di-(tridecyl) ester	>64	>20	—	—	—	—	—
Propionic acid, vinyl ester	4.76	10.0	5 min.	4000	4	—	—
6-Chlorohexanoic acid, ethyl ester	4.92	7.07	8 hr.	—	—	4/6	—

[a] References:

H. F. Smyth, Jr., *et al.*, "The Place of the Range Finding Test in the Industrial Toxicology Laboratory," *J. Ind. Hyg. Toxicol.* **26**, 269–273, 1944; "Further Experience with the Range Finding Test in the Industrial Toxicology Laboratory," *J. Ind. Hyg. Toxicol.* **30**, 63–68, 1948; "Range-Finding Toxicity Data: List III," *J. Ind. Hyg. Toxicol.* **31**, 60–62, 1949; "Range-Finding Toxicity Data: List IV," *Arch. Ind. Hyg. Occupational Med.* **4**, 119–122, 1951; "Range-Finding Toxicity Data: List V," *Arch. Ind. Hyg. Occupational Med.* **10**, 61–68, 1954; "Range-Finding Toxicity Data: List VI," *Am. Ind. Hyg. Assoc. J.* **23**, 95–107, 1962.

[b] Figures in parentheses were determined by poultices on guinea pigs.

[c] The inhalation time killed all cats.

[d] Twice concentration shown killed all six rats.

TABLE 35

ACUTE TOXICITY OF ETHERS[a]

Name	Oral toxicity to rats: RF LD$_{50}$	Penetration of rabbit skin:[b] RF LD$_{50}$	Vapor inhalation by rats: maximum for no death	Inhalation of known vapor concentration by rats		
				Concentration (ppm)	Time (hours)	Mortality in 14 days
	gm/kg	ml/kg				
Allyl ether of propylene glycol	0.51	1.1	—	—	—	1/6
2-Chloroethyl vinyl ether	0.25	3.2	—	500	4	1/6
Diallyl ether	0.32	0.6	—	—	—	—
Ethoxyethyl ether of propylene glycol	9.33	11.62	4 hr.	—	—	—
Dichloroethyl ether	0.075	(0.3)	—	1000	3/4	3/6
Dimethyl dioxane	3.0	>10.0	—	8000	4	2/6
Diethylene glycol ethyl ether (pure)	8.69					
Propylene glycol ethyl ether (beta isomer)	8.93					
2-Chloro-1,1,2-trifluoroethyl methyl ether	5.13	0.2	5 min.	1000	4	1/6
2,2'-Dichloroisopropyl ether	0.42	3.00	—	1000	4	0/6
Ethyl butyl ether	1.87	—	5 min.	—	—	—
Tetraethylene glycol dibutyl ether	6.5	10	15 min.	—	—	—
1,3,3-Triethoxy-1-propene	2.46	0.37	2 hr.	250	4	1/6
1,3,3-Triethoxy propane	1.6	8	8 hr.	—	—	—

Butyl ether	7.40	10.08	30 min.	4000	4	2/6
Hexyl ether	30.9	6.9	8 hr.	—	—	—
Di-(2-ethylhexyl)ether	33.9	—	4 hr.	—	—	—
Vinyl butyl ether	10.30	4.24	5 min.	8000[d]	4	0/6
Vinyl 2-ethylhexyl ether	1.35	3.56	4 hr.	—	—	—
Vinyl 2,6,8-trimethylnonyl ether	1.22	5.0	4 hr.	—	—	—
Vinyl 2-methoxyethyl ether	3.90	7.13	1 hr.	8000	4	4/6
2-Ethoxy-4-methyl-2,3-dihydro-4H-pyran	3.40	1.06	4 hr.	—	—	—
1,2-Dibutoxyethane	3.25	3.56	8 hr.	—	—	—
2,2'-Dibutoxyethyl ether	3.90	4.04	8 hr.	—	—	—
1-Butoxy-2-ethoxyethane	2.83	2.12	2 hr.	—	—	—
2-Butoxyethyl vinyl ether	3.10	3.00	4 hr.	2000	4	2/6
1,1-Dibutoxyethane	8.79	—	8 hr.	—	—	—
1,1-Di(2-methoxyethoxy)ethane	3.26	4.24	8 hr.	—	—	—
1,1,3-Trimethoxybutane	1.48	—	2 hr.	2000	4	1/6
	ml/kg	ml/kg				
Allyl vinyl ether	0.55	—	5 min.[c]	8000	4	2/6
Cyclopentyl ether	0.47	1.41	2 hr.	250	4	5/6
1,3-Dimethoxybutane	3.73	10.0	1 hr.	8000	4	4/6
4,4-Dimethyl-1,3-dioxane	3.73	3.54	4 hr.[c]	8000[d]	4	2/6
2-Ethoxy-3,4-dihydro-1,2-pyran	6.16	3.56	—	8000[d]	4	1/6
2-Ethoxy-4-methyl-3,4-dihydropyran	5.63	1.34	2 hr.	—	—	—
Ethyl ether	3.56	>20	5 min.	32,000[d]	4	3/6
2-Ethyl-2-methyl-1,3-dioxolane	2.88	10.0	—	4000	4	4/6
Ethyl-1-propenyl ether	19.0	—	5 min.	8000	4	0/6

TABLE 35 (Continued)

Name	Oral toxicity to rats: RF LD$_{50}$	Penetration of rabbit skin.[b] RF LD$_{50}$	Vapor inhalation by rats: maximum for no death	Inhalation of known vapor concentration by rats		
				Concentration (ppm)	Time (hours)	Mortality in 14 days
	ml/kg	ml/kg				
Isobutyl vinyl ether	17.0	20	10 min.	16,000	4	3/6
1-Methoxy-1,3-butadiene	2.14	—	15 min.[c]	—	—	—
1-Propenyl-2-butene-1-yl ether	8.00	>10	1 hr.	5000[d]	4	2/6
1,1,3-Triethoxybutane	4.92	1.77	2 hr.	2000	4	5/6
1,1,3-Triethoxyhexane	17.0	—	4 hr.	—	—	—

[a] References:
H. F. Smyth, Jr., et al., "Further Experience with the Range Finding Test in the Industrial Toxicology Laboratory," *J. Ind. Hyg. Toxicol.* **30**, 63–68, 1948; "Range-Finding Toxicity Data, List III," *J. Ind. Hyg. Toxicol.* **31**, 60–62, 1949; "Range-Finding Toxicity Data: List IV," *Arch. Ind. Hyg. Occupational Med.* **4**, 119–122, 1951; "Range-Finding Toxicity Data: List V," *Arch. Ind. Hyg. Occupational Med.* **10**, 61–68, 1954; "Range-Finding Toxicity Data: List VI," *Am. Ind. Hyg. Assoc. J.* **23**, 95–107, 1962.

[b] Figures in parentheses were determined by poultices on guinea pigs.
[c] The inhalation time shown killed all rats.
[d] Twice concentration shown killed all six rats.

TABLE 36
TOXICITY OF ω-FLUOROALCOHOLS, $F(CH_2)_nOH$[a]

Formula of alcohol	LD_{50} for mice (intraperitoneal) mg/kg
FCH_2CH_2OH	10
$F(CH_2)_3OH$	46.5
$F(CH_2)_4OH$	0.9
$F(CH_2)_5OH$	>100
$F(CH_2)_6OH$	1.24
$F(CH_2)_7OH$	80
$F(CH_2)_8OH$	0.6
$F(CH_2)_9OH$	32
$F(CH_2)_{10}OH$	1.0
$F(CH_2)_{11}OH$	>100
$F(CH_2)_{12}OH$	1.5
$F(CH_2)_{18}OH$	4.0

[a]From F. L. M. Pattison. "Toxic Aliphatic Fluorine Compounds." Elsevier, Amsterdam, 1959.

TABLE 37
STRUCTURE AND ACUTE TOXICITY OF SEVERAL POLYFLUOROALCOHOLS[a]

Structure	No. of F atoms	ALD^b (mg/kg)	ALC^c (ppm)
$HCF_2-CF_2-CH_2OH$	4	3400	2000
$HCF_2-CF_2-CHOH-CH_3$	4	—	3500
$HCF_2-CF_2-\overset{\mid}{C}OH-CH_3$ (CH₃)	4	670	1000
$CF_3-CF_2-CH_2OH$	5	2250	—
$CF_3-CFH-CF_2-\overset{\mid}{C}H-CH_2OH$ (CH₃)	6	1000	—
$HCF_2(CF_2)_3CH_2OH$	8	—	2500
$HCF_2(CF_2)_7CH_2OH$	16	7500	—

[a] From J. Wesley Clayton, Jr., *J. Occupational Med.* **4**, 262 May 1962.

[b] Approximate lethal dose for rats, oral route.

[c] Approximate lethal concentrations for rats inhaling the compound for 4 hours.

TABLE 38
TOXICITY OF ω-FLUOROCARBOXYLIC ACIDS, F(CH₂)ₙCOOH[a]

Formula of acid	LD$_{50}$ for mice (intraperitoneal) mg/kg
FCH$_2$COOH	6.6
F(CH$_2$)$_2$COOH	60
F(CH$_2$)$_3$COOH	0.65[b]
F(CH$_2$)$_4$COOH	>100
F(CH$_2$)$_5$COOH	1.35
F(CH$_2$)$_6$COOH	40
F(CH$_2$)$_7$COOH	0.64
F(CH$_2$)$_8$COOH	>100
F(CH$_2$)$_9$COOH	1.5[b]
F(CH$_2$)$_{10}$COOH	57.5
F(CH$_2$)$_{11}$COOH	1.25
F(CH$_2$)$_{17}$COOH	5.7

[a] From F. L. M. Pattison, "Toxic Aliphatic Fluorine Compounds," Elsevier, Amsterdam, 1959.

[b] Sodium salt used.

TABLE 39
ACUTE TOXICITY OF FLUOROETHANE VAPORS[a]

Structure	ALC[b]	
	% (Vol.)	Exposure (hours)
CCl$_2$F—CCl$_2$F	1.5	4
CCl$_2$F—CClF$_2$	8.7	6
CClF$_2$—CClF$_2$	>20	8[c]
CClF$_2$—CHF$_2$	>20	2[c]
CClF$_2$—CF$_3$	>20	2
CF$_3$—CF$_3$	>20	2

[a] From J. Wesley Clayton, Jr., *J. Occupational Med.* **4**, 262 May 1962.

[b] Approximate lethal concentration—the lowest concentration which is lethal for one or more of a group of animals exposed for a given time. Animals are rats unless otherwise indicated.

[c] Guinea pig.

TABLE 40
ACUTE TOXICITY OF FLUOROMETHANE VAPORS[a]

| | Animal Studies | | |
Structure	Exposure conc. (%)	No. hours	Fatality
$CHCl_3$	0.4	4	+
$CHCl_2F$	10.0	1	+
$CHClF_2$	20.0	2	−
CHF_3	20.0	2	−
CCl_4	0.8	8	+
CCl_3F	10.0	2	−
CCl_2F_2	20.0	2	−
$CClF_3$	20.0	2	−
CF_4	20.0	2	−
CH_3Cl	0.3	7	+
CH_2Cl_2	1.6	8	+
$CHCl_2F$	10	1	+
CCl_2F_2	20	2	−

[a] From J. Wesley Clayton, Jr., *J. Occupational Med.* **4,** 262 May 1962.

TABLE 41
ACUTE TOXICITY OF FLUOROPROPANE VAPORS[a]

| | Animal Studies[b] | | |
Structure	Anesthetic conc. (%)	Approx. lethal conc. (%)	Convulsions
$HCF_2—CF_2—CClF_2$	10	20	−
$HCF_2—CF_2—CBrF_2$	4	10	+
$HCF_2—CF_2—CHClF$	2.5	3	+
$HCF_2—CF_2—CHCl_2$	0.5	2	+
$CF_2Cl—CF_2—CH_2F$	10	15	+
$CF_2Cl—CF_2—CHF_2$	10	20	−

[a] From J. Wesley Clayton, Jr., *J. Occupational Med.* **4,** 262 May 1962.
[b] Mice.

TABLE 42

ACUTE INHALATION TOXICITY OF SOME FLUOROSULFUR COMPOUNDS[a]

Structure	Exposure		Mortality ratio
	Conc. (ppm)	Time (hour)	
SF_6	170,000	18	0/6
	800,000	2	0/3
S_2F_{10}	1.0	16	6/6
	0.5	18	0/6
	1,780	1	1/1
	10	1	0/3
SF_4	19	4	1/2
	40	1	0/2

[a] From J. Wesley Clayton, Jr., *J. Occupational Med.* **4,** 262 May 1962.

[b] For rats.

TABLE 43
STRUCTURE AND INHALATION TOXICITY OF SOME FLUOROCARBONS CONTAINING SULFUR[a]

Structure	Exposure		Mortality ratio[b]
	Conc. (ppm)	Time (hour)	
(structure)	5	4	0/2
(structure)	2600	3	0/2
(structure)	5	4	2/2
	2.7	4	0/2
(structure)	40000	0.33	4/4
	25000	4	0/4
	25000	4	2/2[c]
	10000	1	0/2[c]

[a] From J. Wesley Clayton, Jr., *J. Occupational Med.* **4,** 262 May 1962.

[b] For rats, unless otherwise indicated.

[c] Mice.

TABLE 44
ACUTE TOXICITY OF GLYCOL ETHERS[a]

Glycol ether	Single oral dose LD_{50} dose rats (gm/kg)	Single skin absorption LD_{50} dose rabbits (ml/kg)	Single inhalation, rats: saturated vapors	Primary irritation, rabbits' skin	Eye injury, rabbits
Methyl CELLOSOLVE[b] (ethylene glycol monomethyl ether)	2.46	1.34	2 hr. killed none of 6 8 hr. killed 6 of 6	Minor	Trace
CELLOSOLVE Solvent (ethylene glycol monoethyl ether)	3.00	3.5	4 hr. killed 1 of 6 8 hr. killed 4 of 6	Minor	Trace
Butyl CELLOSOLVE (ethylene glycol monobutyl ether)	1.48	0.56	2 hr. killed none of 6 8 hr. killed 4 of 6	Minor	Moderate
Phenyl CELLOSOLVE (ethylene glycol monophenyl ether)	2.21		8 hr. killed none of 6	Moderate	Severe
Hexyl CELLOSOLVE (ethylene glycol monohexyl ether)	1.48	0.89	8 hr. killed none of 6	None	Severe
2-Methylpentyl CELLOSOLVE (ethylene glycol monomethylpentyl ether)	3.73	0.44	8 hr. killed 1 of 6	Minor	Severe
Methyl CARBITOL (diethylene glycol monomethyl ether)	9.21	6.54	8 hr. killed none of 6	None	Minor
CARBITOL Solvent (diethylene glycol monoethyl ether)	9.05	16.46	8 hr. killed none of 6	Moderate	Minor

TABLE 44 (Continued)

Glycol ether	Single oral LD$_{50}$ dose rats (gm/kg)	Single skin absorption LD$_{50}$ dose rabbits (ml/kg)	Single inhalation, rats: saturated vapors	Primary irritation, rabbits' skin	Eye injury, rabbits
Butyl CARBITOL (diethylene glycol monobutyl ether)	6.56	4.12	8 hr. killed none of 6	None	Moderate
Hexyl CARBITOL (diethylene glycol monohexyl ether)	4.92	1.50	8 hr. killed none of 6	Minor	Severe
2-Methylpentyl CARBITOL (diethylene glycol monomethylpentyl ether)	5.66	1.58	8 hr. killed none of 6	Minor	Severe
Ethoxytriglycol	10.61	8	—	None	Minor
Methoxytriglycol	11.3		8 hr. killed none of 6	None	None
1-Butoxyethoxy-2-Propanol	5.66	3.00	8 hr. killed none of 5	Minor	Moderate

[a] From Union Carbide Chemicals Company, New York, 1959.

[b] Methyl CELLOSOLVE should be used only with adequate ventilation. Rare cases of severe nervous system injury have occurred after prolonged or repeated breathing of excessive quantities of methyl CELLOSOLVE. Recovery is to be expected, but disability may last for several months.

TABLE 45

ACUTE TOXICITY OF GLYCOLS[a]

Compound	Single oral LD$_{50}$ dose, rats (gm/kg)	Repeated feeding, rats: no-effect dose	Single skin absorption LD$_{50}$, rabbits (ml/kg)	Single inhalation, rats: saturated vapors	Primary irritation, rabbits' skin	Eye injury, rabbits
2,2-Diethyl-1,3-propanediol	0.85	—	4.24	8 hr. killed 1 of 6	Minor	Minor
Diethylene glycol	20.76	0.18 g/kg/day (30 days)	11.89	8 hr. killed none of 6	Minor	None
Dipropylene glycol	14.85	—	More than 20 ml/kg	8 hr. killed none of 6	None	Minor
2-Ethyl-2-butyl-1,3-propanediol	5.04	—	3.81	—	None	Severe
2-Ethyl-1,3-hexanediol	2.71	—	15.2	2 hr. killed none of 6 / 8 hr. killed 6 of 6	Minor	Moderate
Ethylene glycol	8.54	0.18 g/kg/day (30 days)	9.53	8 hr. killed none of 6	None	None
1,2,6-hexanetriol	15.5	1.89 g/kg/day (90 days)	More than 20 ml/kg	8 hr. killed 1 of 6	None	None
Hexylene glycol	4.76	0.31 g/kg/day (90 days)	8.56	8 hr. killed none of 6	Minor	Moderate
1,5-pentanediol	5.89	—	More than 20 ml/kg	8 hr. killed none of 6	None	Minor
Polypropylene glycol 150	14.8	—	More than 20 ml/kg	8 hr. killed none of 6	None	None
Polypropylene glycol 425	2.41	—	More than 20 ml/kg	8 hr. killed none of 6	Minor	Minor
Polypropylene glycol 1025	2.15	—	More than 20 ml/kg	8 hr. killed none of 6	Minor	Minor
Polypropylene glycol 2025	9.76	—	More than 20 ml/kg	8 hr. killed none of 6	Minor	Minor
Propylene glycol	26.38	—	More than 20 ml/kg	8 hr. killed none of 6	None	Trace
Triethylene glycol	22.06	0.83 g/kg/day (30 days)	More than 20 ml/kg	8 hr. killed none of 6	None	None

[a] From Union Carbide Corporation, 1958.

731

TABLE 46
COMPARATIVE LIFE HAZARD OF GASES AND VAPORS[a]

Group	Definition	Examples
1	Gases or vapors which in concentrations of the order of ½ to 1% for durations of exposure of the order of 5 minutes are lethal or produce serious injury	Sulfur dioxide
2	Gases or vapors which in concentrations of the order of ½ to 1% for durations of exposure of the order of ½ hour are lethal or produce serious injury	Ammonia, methyl bromide
3	Gases or vapors which in concentrations of the order of 2 to 2½% for durations of exposure of the order of 1 hour are lethal or produce serious injury	Bromochloromethane, carbon tetrachloride, chloroform, methyl formate
4	Gases or vapors which in concentrations of the order of 2 to 2½% for durations of exposure of the order of 2 hours are lethal or produce serious injury	Dichloroethylene, methyl chloride, ethyl bromide
Between 4 and 5	Appear to classify as somewhat less toxic than Group 4	Methylene chloride, ethyl chloride
	Much less toxic than Group 4 but somewhat more toxic than Group 5	Freon-113, Freon-21
5a	Gases or vapors much less toxic than Group 4 but more toxic than Group 6	Freon-11, Freon-22, Freon-114B2, carbon dioxide
5b	Gases or vapors which available data indicate would classify as either Group 5a or Group 6	Ethane, propane, butane
6	Gases or vapors which in concentrations up to at least about 20% by volume for durations of exposure of the order of 2 hours do not appear to produce injury	Freon-13B1, Freon-12, Freon-114

[a] Underwriters' Laboratories, Chicago, Illinois.

TABLE 47

ACUTE ORAL TOXICITY (RATS) OF SELECTED HOUSEHOLD PRODUCTS[a]

Product[b]	Estimated lethal range on volume basis[c] (ml/kg)
Cleaner, window (solution)	20–35
Cloves (ground)	74->105
Floor wax, liquid	>50
Floor wax, paste	20–50
Ginger (ground)	>29.1
Horseradish (grated, prepared)	31.1->44.5
Mustard (dry)	>37.6
Nutmeg (ground)	>24.4
Pepper, black (ground)	>22.6
Pepper, cayenne (ground)	>27.4
Polish, furniture (liquid)	20->50
Polish, metal (powdered)	27.5->39.6
Polish, shoe (liquid)	>50
Sugar (granulated)	25.3->35.2
Vanilla (extract)	20–35
Whiskey (86 proof, blended)	20–50
Alcohol, rubbing (70% isopropyl alcohol)	5–10
Bleach, liquid (5.25% sodium hypochlorite)	2–10
Cleanser, all purpose (liquid)	10–35
Cleanser (powdered)	7.2–25.8
Cream of tartar	12.3–27.1
Detergent, all purpose (household, granulated)	11.2–25.2
Detergent, light duty, household (liquid)	5–10
Gasoline	10–35
Kerosine	10–35
Nail polish (liquid)	10–35
Nail polish remover	5–10
Paint (house, white)	5–25
Sage (ground)	>31.6
Soap (toilet bar)	7.1->18.9
Wintergreen (essence)	8–10
Aspirin (acetylsalicylic acid)	1.4–4.1
Baking soda (sodium bicarbonate)	2.9–3.9
Bleach (powdered)	8.5–17.0
Carbon tetrachloride	1–3
Disinfectant (alkyl aryl quaternary ammonium compound)	0.5–2
Permanent wave neutralizer (powdered)	1.1–2.7
Permanent wave solution	1–2
Table salt (sodium chloride)	2.4–4.8
Tobacco (cigarette butts)	22.7–30.3
Turpentine	2–3

[a] From H. C. Hodge and W. L. Downs, *Toxicol. Appl. Pharmacol.* **3,** No. 6, 689–695, November, 1961.

[b] Not necessarily representative of all products in each class.

[c] Volume of product administered on basis premix volume per kilogram.

TABLE 48
ACUTE TOXICITY OF HYDROCARBONS[a]

Name	Single dose oral toxicity to rats: RF LD$_{50}$	Penetration of rabbit skin: RF LD$_{50}$	Saturated vapor inhalation by rats: maximum for no death	Inhalation of known vapor concentration by rats		
				Concentration (ppm)	Time (hours)	Mortality in 14 days
	gm/kg	ml/kg				
2-Ethyl hexene-1	80.0	—	15 min.	4000	4	4/6
Tetrahydronaphthalene	2.86	17.3	8 hr.	—	—	—
Cyclopentadiene dimer	0.82	6.72	2 hr.[b]	2000	4	4/6
Cumene (isopropylbenzene)	2.91	12.3	1 hr.	8000	4	4/6
Decahydronaphthalene	4.17	5.90	2 hr.	500	4	4/6
	ml/kg	ml/kg				
Benzene	11.4	—	5 min.	16000	4	4/6
Diethylcyclohexane (mixed isomers)	64.0	2.5	1 hr.	2000	4	2/6
Ethylbenzene	5.46	17.8	1 hr.	4000[c]	4	3/6
Fluoranthene	2.00	3.18	8 hr.	—	—	—
3a,4,7,7a-Tetrahydro-4,7-methanoindene (Dicyclopentadiene)	0.41	4.46	30 min.	500[c]	4	1/6
m-Xylene	7.71	14.1	2 hr.	8000	4	10/12

[a] References:
H. F. Smyth, Jr., et al., "Range-Finding Toxicity Data: List III," J. Ind. Hyg. Toxicol. **31**, 60–62, 1949; "Range-Finding Toxicity Data: List IV," Arch. Ind. Hyg. Occupational Med. **4**, 119–122, 1951; "Range-Finding Toxicity Data: List V," Arch. Ind. Hyg. Occupational Med. **10**, 61–68, 1954; "Range-Finding Toxicity Data: List VI," Am. Ind. Hyg. Assoc. J. **23**, 95–107, 1962.

[b] The inhalation time shown killed all rats.

[c] Twice concentration shown killed all six rats.

TABLE 49
ACUTE TOXICITY OF HYDROXY ETHERS[a]

Name	Single dose oral toxicity to rats: RF LD_{50}	Penetration of rabbit skin: RF LD_{50}	Saturated vapor inhalation by rats: maximum for no death
	gm/kg	ml/kg	
2-(Hexyloxy)ethanol	1.48	0.89	8 hr.
2-(2-Ethylbutoxy)ethanol	1.91	0.32	8 hr.
2-(1-Ethylamyloxy)ethanol	2.28	—	8 hr.
2-(2-Ethylhexyloxy)ethanol	3.08	2.12	8 hr.
2-(Isobutyl-3-methylbutoxy)ethanol	5.41	—	8 hr.
2-(Methoxy-methoxy)ethanol	6.50	4.23	—
2-(2-[1-Ethylamyloxy]ethoxy)ethanol	2.94	—	8 hr.
2-(2-[1-Isobutyl-3-methylbutoxy]ethoxy)ethanol	8.68	3.00	4 hr.
2-(2-Phenoxyethoxy)ethanol	2.14	2.12	8 hr.
3-(2-Ethoxyethoxy)propanol	7.06	—	8 hr.
3-(2-Butoxyethoxy)propanol	5.16	3.00	8 hr.
	ml/kg	ml/kg	
Diethylene glycol divinyl ether	3.73	14.1	4 hr.
Diethylene glycol ethyl methyl ether	6.50	7.07	8 hr.
Diethylene glycol mono-2-methyl-pentyl ether	5.66	1.58	8 hr.
Diethylene glycol ethyl vinyl ether	11.3	8.41	8 hr.
Dipropylene glycol monomethyl ether	5.66	10.0	8 hr.
Ethylene glycol mono-2-methyl-pentyl ether	3.73	0.44	4 hr.
Ethylene glycol mono-2,6,8-trimethyl-4-nonyl ether	5.36	3.15	8 hr.
Propylene glycol monomethyl ether	5.66	14.1	4 hr.
Triethylene glycol monobutyl ether	6.73	3.54	8 hr.
Triethylene glycol monomethyl ether	11.3	7.1	8 hr.

[a] References:

H. F. Smyth, Jr., *et al.*, "Range-Finding Toxicity Data: List V," *Arch. Ind. Hyg. Occupational Med.* **10**, 61–68, 1954; "Range-Finding Toxicity Data: List VI," *Am. Ind. Hyg. Assoc. J.* **23**, 95–107, 1962.

TABLE 50
TOXICITY OF KETONES[a]

Name	Single dose oral toxicity to rats: RF LD$_{50}$	Penetration of rabbit skin:[b] RF LD$_{50}$	Saturated vapor inhalation by rats: maximum for no death	Inhalation of known vapor concentration by rats		
				Concentration (ppm)	Time (hours)	Mortality in 14 days
	gm/kg	ml/kg				
Acetonyl acetone	2.7	(6.6)	1 hr.			
Acetyl acetone	1.0		30 min.			
Phenyl methyl ketone	3.0	>20.0	8 hr.			
Acetophenone	0.90					
Diisobutyl ketone	5.75	20.0	4 hr.	2000	8	5/6
Dypnone (Methyl styryl phenyl ketone)	3.6	6.3	—	—	—	—
Ethylbutyl ketone	2.76	>20.0	30 min.	2000	4	0/5
				4000	4	6/6
Trimethyl nonanone	8.47	11.04	4 hr.	—	—	—
2-Methyl-1-butene-3-one	0.18	0.23	2 min.[c]	125	4	5/6
4-Methyl-2-pentanone	2.08	—	15 min.	2000	4	0/6
				4000	4	6/6
Phenyl xylyl ketone	4.92	20.0	8 hr.	—	—	—
3-Nitroacetophenone	3.25	3.0	8 hr.	—	—	—
Pentanone-3	2.14	20.0	15 min.	8000	4	4/6

Hexanone-2	2.59	5.99	30 min.	4000[d]	4	0/6
5-Ethyl-3-nonen-2-one	8.12	8.48	8 hr.	—	—	—
	ml/kg	ml/kg				
Acetone	10.7	>20	30 min.	16000[d]	4	1/6
2-Butanone	6.86	>10	—	8000[d]	8	3/6
2-Heptanone	1.67	12.6	30 min.	2000[d]	4	0/6
4-Hexene-1-yne-3-one	0.071	0.10	5 min.[c]	12.5	4	2/6
5-Methyl-2-hexanone	4.76	10.0	—	2000[d]	4	0/6
2-Pentanone	3.73	8.00	30 min.	2000[d]	4	1/6

[a] References:

H. F. Smyth, Jr., et al., "The Place of the Range Finding Test in the Industrial Toxicology Laboratory," J. Ind. Hyg. Toxicol. **26**, 269–273, 1944; "Further Experience with the Range Finding Test in the Industrial Toxicology Laboratory," J. Ind. Hyg. Toxicol. **30**, 63–68, 1948; "Range-Finding Toxicity Data: List III," J. Ind. Hyg. Toxicol. **31**, 60–62, 1949; "Range-Finding Toxicity Data: List IV," Arch. Ind. Hyg. Occupational Med. **4**, 119–122, 1951; "Range-Finding Toxicity Data: List V," Arch. Ind. Hyg. Occupational Med. **10**, 61–68, 1954; "Range-Finding Toxicity Data: List VI," Am. Ind. Hyg. Assoc. J. **23**, 95–107, 1962.

[b] Figures in parentheses were determined by poultices on guinea pigs.

[c] The inhalation time shown killed all rats.

[d] Twice concentration shown killed all six rats.

TABLE 51
ACUTE TOXICITY OF LANTHANUM COMPOUNDS[a]

Compound	Concentration	Oral LD$_{50}$		Intraperitoneal LD$_{50}$	
		Compound (mg/kg)	Metal (mg/kg)	Compound (mg/kg)	Metal (mg/kg)
Lanthanum chloride	50% solution	4,200	2,370	350	179
Lanthanum ammonium nitrate	50% solution	3,400	830	625	153
Lanthanum nitrate	50% solution	4,500	1,450	450	145
Lanthanum oxide	50% suspension	>10,000	>8,500	—	—
Lanthanum sulfate	50% suspension	>5,000	>2,450	275	134
Lanthanum acetate	50% suspension	10,000	4,400	475	209

[a] From K. W. Cochran, et al., Arch. Ind. Hyg. Occupational Med. 1, 637–650, June 1950.

TABLE 52
ACUTE TOXICITY OF ALIPHATIC AND AROMATIC MERCAPTANS[a]

Compound	IP LD$_{50}$ mg/kg, rats	Oral LD$_{50}$ mg/kg, rats	Inhal. LC$_{50}$ ppm Mice	Inhal. LC$_{50}$ ppm Rats	Eye irritation, rabbits	Skin LD$_{50}$ mg/kg Rats	Skin LD$_{50}$ mg/kg Rabbits	Toxicity class[c]
Ethanethiol CH$_3$CH$_2$SH	226	682	2770	4420	Slight			Slightly
Propanethiol CH$_3$(CH$_2$)$_2$SH	515	1790	4010	7300	Moderate			Slightly
2-Methyl-1-propanethiol (CH$_3$)$_2$CHCH$_2$SH	917	7168	>25000[b]	>25000[b]	Very slight			Practically nontoxic
2-Methyl-2-propanethiol (CH$_3$)$_3$CSH	590	4729	16500	22200	Slight			Practically nontoxic
Butanethiol CH$_3$(CH$_2$)$_3$SH	399	1500	2500	4020	Slight			Slightly
Hexanethiol CH$_3$(CH$_2$)$_5$SH	396	1254	528	1080	None			Slightly
Methyl heptanethiol C$_8$H$_{17}$SH	12.9	83.5	47	51	Slight	1594	600	Highly
Benzenethiol C$_6$H$_5$SH	9.8	46.2	28	33	Severe	300	134	Highly
α-Toluenethiol C$_6$H$_5$CH$_2$SH	373	493	178	>235[b]	Slight			Moderately

[a] From E. J. Fairchild and H. E. Stokinger, "Toxicologic Studies on Organic Sulfur Compounds. 1. Acute Toxicity of Some Aliphatic and Aromatic Thiols (Mercaptans)," Am. Ind. Hyg. J. 19, 171–188, June 1958.
[b] LC$_{50}$ not calculable.
[c] Toxicity classification of Hine & Jacobson.

TABLE 53

ACUTE TOXICITY OF NITRILES[a]

Name	Single dose oral toxicity to rats: RF LD_{50}	Penetration of rabbit skin:[b] RF LD_{50}	Saturated vapor inhalation by rats: maximum for no death	Inhalation of known vapor concentration by rats		
				Concentration (ppm)	Time (hours)	Mortality in 14 days
	gm/kg	ml/kg				
Acetonitrile	3.8	5.0	—	8000	4	1/6
Acrylonitrile	0.093	(0.25)	1 min.	500	4	0/6
N,N-Diethylaminoacetonitrile	0.16	0.36	8 min.	1000	4	6/6
Propionitrile	0.039	0.21	2 min.[d]	62	4	0/6
3-Butoxypropionitrile	7.46	8.98	8 hr.	125	4	6/6
3-(2-ethylbutoxy)propionitrile	2.46	10	8 hr.	500	4	2/6
3-(2-ethylhexyloxy)propionitrile	4.92	5.99	4 hr.	—	—	—
3-3'-Oxydipropionitrile	2.83	—	8 hr.	—	—	—
3,3'-Iminodipropionitrile	4.92	2.52	8 hr.	—	—	—
N-Methyl-3,3'-iminodipropionitrile	0.89	0.80	8 hr.	—	—	—
2-Hydroxy-3-butenenitrile	0.065	0.0075	—	16	4	3/6
3-Cyclohexene-1-carbonitrile	0.46	9.46	30 min.	62[e]	4	0/6
	ml/kg	ml/kg				
Acetic acid, 1-cyanovinyl ester	0.10	0.14	5 min.	125	4	4/6
2-Acetoxyisosuccinodinitrile	0.12	0.11	1 hr.	—	—	—
Acrylic acid, 2-(2-cyanoethoxy) ethyl ester	1.12	0.75	8 hr.	—	—	—

Acrylic acid, 2-cyanoethyl ester	0.18	0.22	8 hr.	—	—	—
Allyl cyanide	0.12	1.41	5 min.	250[e]	4	0/6
Butyronitrile	0.14	0.50	—	1000	4	5/6
Chloroacetonitrile	0.22	0.071	15 min.[d]	250[e]	4	1/6
4-Cyanoethoxy-2-methyl-2-pentanol	3.2[c]	1.5	—	—	—	—
6-Cyanohexanoic acid, ethyl ester	11.2	7.07	8 hr.	—	—	—
N-Cyanomethylmorpholine, 50%	1.23	0.20	4 hr.	—	—	—
3-Cyanopropionic acid, ethyl ester	10.3	—	4 hr.	—	—	—
Diethylene glycol mono-2-cyanoethyl ether	13.4	—	8 hr.	—	—	—
2,4-Dihydroxy-3,3-dimethylbutyronitrile	0.31	0.13	8 hr.	—	—	—
Dimethylamino acetonitrile	0.050	0.17	10 min.	125[e]	4	0/6
3-(Dimethylamino)propionitrile	2.60	1.41	8 hr.	—	—	—
Glycolonitrile, 70%	0.016	0.0050	8 hr.	250	4	4/6
α-Hydroxyisobutyronitrile	0.017	0.017	5 min.	62.5[e]	4	2/6
Isobutyronitrile	0.10	0.31	10 min.[d]	500[e]	4	0/6
Methacrylonitrile	0.25	0.35	15 min.[d]	1000[e]	4	4/6
3-Methyl-3-butenonitrile	0.54	2.83	15 min.	1000[e]	4	1/6
Trichloroacetonitrile	0.25	0.90	5 min.[d]	125[e]	4	0/6

[a] References:

H. F. Smyth, Jr., *et al.*, "Further Experience with the Range Finding Test in the Industrial Toxicology Laboratory," *J. Ind. Hyg. Toxicol.* **30**, 63–68, 1948; "Range-Finding Toxicity Data: List IV," *Arch. Ind. Hyg. Occupational Med.* **4**, 119–122, 1951; "Range-Finding Toxicity Data: List V," *Arch. Ind. Hyg. Occupational Med.* **10**, 61–68, 1954; "Range-Finding Toxicity Data: List VI," *Am. Ind. Hyg. Assoc. J.* **23**, 95–107, 1962.

[b] Figures in parentheses were determined by poultices on guinea pigs.

[c] As gm/kg in a suitable vehicle.

[d] The inhalation time shown killed all rats.

[e] Twice concentration shown killed all six rats.

TABLE 54
ACUTE TOXICITY OF ORGANIC ACIDS[a]

Name	Single dose oral toxicity to rats: RF LD_{50}	Penetration of rabbit skin:[b] RF LD_{50}	Saturated vapor inhalation by rats: maximum for no death
	gm/kg	ml/kg	
n-Caproic acid	3.0	(5.0)	—
Crotonic acid	1.0	(0.6)	
2-Ethyl hexoic acid	3.0	(6.3)	8 hr.
Sorbic acid	7.36		
Ethoxy propionic acid	4.8	0.75	—
Acetic acid	3.53	—	—
Dichloroacetic acid	2.82	0.51	8 hr.
2-Ethyl-2-hexenoic acid	5.66	2.75	8 hr.
Butyric acid	8.79	6.35	—
3-Methoxybutyric acid	3.03	—	8 hr.
2-Ethylbutyric acid	2.20	0.52	8 hr.
Hexanoic acid	6.44	0.63	8 hr.
2-Methylpentanoic acid	2.04	—	8 hr.
3-Butoxypropionic acid	5.19	0.63	8 hr.
Hexanoic acid, ϵ-lactone	4.29	5.99	8 hr.
3(2-Ethylbutoxy)propionic acid	3.73	0.53	4 hr.
3,5-Dimethyl-3-hydroxy-4-hexanoic acid, β-lactone	2.70	—	4 hr.
3(2-Ethylhexyloxy)propionic acid	3.73	0.75	8 hr.
3-Cyclohexene-1-carboxylic acid	4.26	1.00	4 hr.
	ml/kg	ml/kg	
Acrylic acid, glacial	2.59	0.95	8 hr.
Decanoic acid (mixed isomers)	3.73	1.77	8 hr.
Hexanoic acid (mixed isomers)	2.05	1.05	8 hr.
2-Hydroxy-3-ethyl-heptanoic acid	3.40	1.78	—
2-Methyl propionic acid	0.28	0.50	8 hr.
Octanoic acid (mixed isomers)	1.41	0.71	4 hr.
Pentanoic acid (mixed isomers)	1.12	0.70	8 hr.
Propionic acid	4.29	0.50	8 hr.
6-Chlorohexanoic acid	3.08	—	8 hr.
2,3-Dichloropropionic acid	0.42	0.40	—
2,2,3-Trichloropropionic acid	2.46	1.77	—

[a] References:
H. F. Smyth, Jr., et al., "The Place of the Range Finding Test in the Industrial Toxicology Laboratory," *J. Ind. Hyg. Toxicol.* **26**, 269–273, 1944; "Further Experience with the Range Finding Test in the Industrial Toxicology Laboratory," *J. Ind. Hyg. Toxicol.* **30**, 63–68, 1948; "Range-Finding Toxicity Data: List IV," *Arch. Ind. Hyg. Occupational Med.* **4**, 119–122, 1951; "Range-Finding Toxicity Data: List V," *Arch. Ind. Hyg. Occupational Med.* **10**, 61–68, 1954; "Range-Finding Toxicity Data: List VI," *Am. Ind. Hyg. Assoc. J.* **23**, 95–107, 1962.

[b] Figures in parentheses were determined by poultices on guinea pigs.

TABLE 55
ACUTE TOXICITY OF ORGANIC ANHYDRIDES[a]

Name	Single dose oral toxicity to rats: RF LD$_{50}$	Penetration of rabbit skin:[b] RF LD$_{50}$	Saturated vapor inhalation by rats: maximum for no death	Inhalation of known vapor concentration by rats		
				Concentration (ppm)	Time (hours)	Mortality in 14 days
	gm/kg	ml/kg				
Citraconic anhydride	2.6	(1.0)	4 hr.	—	—	—
Acetic anhydride	1.78	—	5 min.	1000	4	0/6
				2000	4	6/6
Dichloroacetic anhydride	2.82	0.47	8 hr.	—	—	—
Propionic anhydride	2.36	10.0	1 hr.	—	—	—
	ml/kg	ml/kg				
Allylsuccinic anhydride	1.07	0.32	—	—	—	—
Crotonic anhydride	2.83	—	8 hr.	—	—	—
Glutaric anhydride	4.46^c	1.78^c	—	—	—	—

[a] References:
H. F. Smyth, Jr., et al., "The Place of the Range Finding Test in the Industrial Toxicology Laboratory," *J. Ind. Hyg. Toxicol.* **26**, 269–273, 1944; "Range-Finding Toxicity Data: List IV," *Arch. Ind. Hyg. Occupational Med.* **4**, 119–122, 1951; "Range-Finding Toxicity Data: List V," *Arch. Ind. Hyg. Occupational Med.* **10**, 61–68, 1954; "Range-Finding Toxicity Data: List VI," *Am. Ind. Hyg. Assoc. J.* **23**, 95–107, 1962.

[b] Figures in parentheses were determined in poultices on guinea pigs.

[c] As gm/kg in a suitable vehicle.

TABLE 56

ACUTE TOXICITY OF ORGANIC CHLORINE COMPOUNDS[a]

Organic chlorine compounds	Single oral LD_{50} dose rats (gm/kg)	Single skin penetration, LD_{50} dose rabbits (ml/kg)	Single inhalation concentrated vapor or specific concentration in ppm, rats	Primary irritation, rabbits' skin	Eye injury, rabbits
Ethylene dichloride	0.77	3.89	200 ppm, 1 hr. killed 1 of 10	Trace	Minor
CHLORASOL fumigant and solvent (Solvent EDM)	1.64	5.99	2 min. killed 1 of 6 5 min. killed 6 of 6	Trace	Trace
Propylene dichloride	2.27	8.75	15 min. killed 1 of 6 30 min. killed 3 of 6 1 hr. killed 6 of 6	Trace	Trace
1,1,2-Trichlorethane[b]	1.14	3.73	500 ppm, 4 hr. killed 1 of 6 8 hr. killed 4 of 6	Trace	Trace
1,2,3-Trichlorpropane	0.32 ml/kg	1.77	30 min. killed 2 of 6 1 hr. killed 5 of 6	None	Minor
Dichlorethyl ether (CHLOREX solvent)	0.105	0.72	1 hr. killed none of 6 2 hr. killed 6 of 6	Trace	Minor

Dichlorisopropyl ether	0.24	3.00	4 hr. killed none of 6 8 hr. killed 6 of 6	None	Trace
Triglycol dichloride	0.25	1.41	8 hr. killed none of 4	Trace	None
Butyl chloride	2.67	20 ml/kg killed 1 of 4	15 min. killed none of 6	Minor	Trace
2-Ethylhexyl chloride	7.34	15.8	30 min. killed 6 of 6 2000 ppm, 8 hr. killed 4 of 6	Minor	Trace
iso-Decyl chloride (mixed isomers)	45.3 ml/kg	5.7	8 hr. killed 1 of 6	Minor	Trace
Ethylene chlorhydrin	0.089	0.105	30 sec. killed none of 6 10 min. killed 6 of 6	None	Moderate
Epichlorhydrin	0.09	1.3	250 ppm, 4 hr. killed none of 6 8 hr. killed 4 of 6	Trace	Minor

[a] From Union Carbide Chemicals Company, New York, 1960.
[b] Not to be confused with methyl chloroform (1,1,1-trichlorethane).

TABLE 57

TOXICITY LIMITS OF FOUR ORGANIC PEROXIDES[a]

Compound	LD$_{50}$ mg Compound/kg body weight		LC$_{50}$ ppm 4 hours exposure inhalation		Maximal nonirritating strength % peroxide in vehicle	
	Intra-peritoneal rats	Oral (gavage), rats	Rats	Mice	Skin, rabbits	Eye, rabbits
Di-t-butyl peroxide (ROOR)	3210	>25000	>4103	>4103	97	97
t-Butyl hydroperoxide (ROOH)	87	406	500	350	35	7
Cumene hydroperoxide (ROOH)	95	382	220	200	7	1
Methyl ethyl ketone peroxide	65	484	200	170	1.5	0.6

[a] Data from E. P. Floyd, and H. E. Stokinger, *Ind. Hyg. Assoc. J.* **19**, 205, June 1958.

TABLE 58

ACUTE TOXICITY OF POLYETHYLENE GLYCOLS (CARBOWAXES)[a]

Carbowax	Single oral LD_{50} dose rats gm/kg	Repeated feeding rats no-effect dose	Primary irritation, rabbits' skin	Eye injury, rabbits
Polyethylene Glycol 200	28.9 ml/kg	0.88 gm/kg/day (2 years)	None	None
Polyethylene Glycol 300	31.7 ml/kg	5.4 gm/kg/day (90 days)	None	None
Polyethylene Glycol 400	43.62	0.96 gm/kg/day (2 years)	None	Trace
Polyethylene Glycol 600	38.1 ml/kg	2.42 gm/kg/day (90 days)	None	Minor
Polyethylene Glycol 1000	42	—	None	None
Polyethylene Glycol 1500	44.18	0.8 gm/kg/day (2 years)	None	None
Polyethylene Glycol 1540	51.2	2.18 gm/kg/day (2 years)	—	None
Polyethylene Glycol 4000	50	0.88 gm/kg/day (2 years)	—	None
Polyethylene Glycol 6000	50	12 gm/kg/day (90 days)	None	None
Polyethylene Glycol 20M	31.6	1.92 gm/kg/day (90 days)	Minor	Trace
Polyethylene Glycol 350	22 ml/kg	—	None	Minor
Methoxy Polyethylene Glycol 550	39.8 ml/kg	—	Trace	Minor
Methoxy Polyethylene Glycol 750	39.8 ml/kg	—	Trace	Minor

[a] Data from Union Carbide Chemicals Company, New York, 1957.

747

TABLE 59

TOXICITY OF RARE EARTHS AND YTTRIUM IN LABORATORY ANIMALS
(MILLIGRAM OF ELEMENT PER KILOGRAM OF BODY WEIGHT)[a,b]

Rare earth		Mouse		Rat			Guinea pig
Name	Compound	S.C.	I.P.	Oral	I.P.	I.V.	I.P.
Lanthanum	Acetate			4440[e]	209[e]		74[e]
	Chloride	>500[c]	>160[c] 211[e]		106[e] 197[e]	3.5[c]	34[e]
	Chloride citrate		44[e]				
	Ammonium nitrate			830[e]	153[e]		
	Nitrate			1450[e]	145[e]		
	Sulfate			2450[e]	134[e]		
	Oxide			>8500[e]			
Cerium	Chloride	569–2843[d]	201[e]			50–60[d] 3.5[c]	59[e]
Praseodymium	Chloride nitrate		83[e]				32[e]
	Chloride	944[e]	205[e]			3.5[c]	71[e]
	Chloride citrate		80[e]				30[e]
Neodymium	Nitrate					3.5–4.5[c]	
	Chloride	2302[e]	200[e]			3.5[c]	81[e]
	Chloride citrate		80[e]				23[e]

Element	Compound			
Erbium	Nitrate	88[e]	132[e]	30–35[c]
	Chloride		45[e]	>4[c]
Yttrium	Nitrate		117[e]	10[c]
	Oxide		395[e]	20–30[c]

[a] Calculated from published values for the compound.
[b] Data from G. C. Kyker, and E. A. Cress, *A.M.A. Arch. Inc. Health* **16,** 477, Dec. 1957.
[c] M.L.D.
[d] LD.
[e] LD$_{50}$ 10 days.

TABLE 60

ACUTE TOXICITY OF SILICONES[a]

Name	Single dose oral toxicity to rats: RF LD50	Penetration of rabbit skin: RF LD50	Saturated vapor inhalation by rats: maximum for no death	Inhalation of known vapor concentration by rats		
				Concentration (ppm)	Time (hours)	Mortality in 14 days
	gm/kg	ml/kg				
Ethyl trichloro silane	1.33	—	—	4000	4	3/6
Ethyl triethoxy silane	13.72	16	8 hr.	—	—	—
Tetraethoxy silane (ethyl silicate)	6.27	6.3	—	2500	4	4/6
Vinyltriethoxysilane	22.5	10	—	4000	4	2/6
Vinyltrichlorosilane	1.28	0.68	15 min.	2000[d]	4	0/6
Amyltriethoxysilane	19.6	7.13	8 hr.	—	—	—
Tris(2-chloroethoxy)silane	0.19	0.089	8 hr.	—	—	—
Phenyltrichlorosilane	2.39	0.89	8 hr.	—	—	—
	ml/kg					
(4-Aminobutyl)diethoxy(methyl)silane	6.50	0.045	8 hr.	—	—	—
(4-Aminobutyl)triethoxysilane	1.62	2.50	8 hr.	—	—	—
(3-Aminopropyl)diethoxy(methyl)silane	4.76	2.52	8 hr.	—	—	—
(3-Aminopropyl)triethoxysilane	1.78	—	8 hr.	—	—	—
Amyltrichlorosilane	2.34	0.78	4 hr.	1000[d]	8	0/6

(2-Carbethoxyethyl)diethoxy(methyl)silane	20.8	>10	8 hr.	—	—	—
(2-Carbethoxyethyl)triethoxysilane	22.4	—	8 hr.	—	—	—
(2-Carbethoxypropyl)diethoxy(methyl)silane	24.6	—	8 hr.	—	—	—
(3-Carbethoxypropyl)diethoxy(methyl)silane	22.4	—	8 hr.	—	—	—
(2-Cyanoethyl)trichlorosilane	2.00	—	8 hr.	—	—	—
(2-Cyanoethyl)triethoxysilane	5.63[b]	5.95	4 hr.	—	—	—
(3-Cyanopropyl)dichloro(methyl)silane	2.83[b]	1.49	8 hr.	—	—	—
(3-Cyanopropyl)diethoxy(methyl)silane	3.73	—	8 hr.	—	—	—
(3-Cyanopropyl)methylsiloxane, cyclic tetramer	>64	—	8 hr.	—	—	—
(3-Cyanopropyl)trichlorosilane	2.83[b]	—	4 hr.	—	—	—
(3-Cyanopropyl)triethoxysilane	4.92	>10	8 hr.	—	—	—
(3,4-Cyclohexenyl)trichlorosilane	2.83[b]	0.63	8 hr.	—	—	—
Di-(2-ethylhexoxy)-di-(2-ethylbutoxy)silane	56.3	>20	8 hr.	—	—	—
Ethyl(vinyl)dichlorosilane	2.83[b]	0.75	—	4000[d]	4	0/6
(2-Phenylethyl)trichlorosilane	2.83[b]	0.74	8 hr.	—	—	—
(Phenyl)trifluorosilane	0.31	0.64	15 min.[c]	1000[d]	4	1/6
Tetra-(2-ethylhexoxy)silane	>64	>20	8 hr.	—	—	—

[a] References:

H. F. Smyth, Jr., et al. "Range-Finding Toxicity Data, List III," *J. Ind. Hyg. Toxicol.* **31**, 60–62, 1949; "Range-Finding Toxicity Data: List V," *Arch. Ind. Hyg. Occupational Med.* **10**, 61–68, 1954; "Range-Finding Toxicity Data: List VI," *Am. Ind. Hyg. Assoc. J.* **23**, 95–107, 1962.

[b] As gm/kg in a suitable vehicle.

[c] The inhalation time shown killed all rats.

[d] Twice concentration shown killed all rats.

TABLE 61
ACUTE TOXICITY OF TANTALUM AND COLUMBIUM COMPOUNDS[a]

Compound	Concentration	Oral LD$_{50}$		Intraperitoneal LD$_{50}$	
		Compound (mg/kg)	Metal (mg/kg)	Compound (mg/kg)	Metal (mg/kg)
Tantalum oxide	50% suspension	>8000	>6560	—	—
Potassium tantalum fluoride	50% suspension	2500	1150	375	173
Tantalum chloride	50% solution	1900	958	75	38
Potassium columbate	50% solution	3000	1140	225	86
Columbium chloride	50% solution	—	—	40	14

[a] Data from K. W. Cochran, *et al.*, *Arch. Ind. Hyg. Occupational Med.* **1**, 637–650, June, 1950.

TABLE 62

ACUTE TOXICITY OF ALKYL THIOPYROPHOSPHATES[a]

		LD$_{50}$ in mgm/kgm			
R	R'	Mice (I.P.)	Mice (I.M.)	Mice (I.V.)	Mice and rats (I.M.)
CH$_3$	CH$_3$	ca. 1.4			0.25
CH$_3$	C$_2$H$_5$	ca. 1.0			
C$_2$H$_5$	CH$_3$	ca. 1.8			1.0
C$_2$H$_5$	C$_2$H$_5$	0.94	0.5	0.3	0.055
n-C$_3$H$_7$	n-C$_3$H$_7$	7.93	4.41	3.25	
i-C$_3$H$_7$	i-C$_3$H$_7$	ca. 25			50
n-C$_4$H$_9$	n-C$_4$H$_9$	ca. 60			0.25

[a] Data from McIvor, R. A., G. D. McCarthy, and G. A. Grant. *Can. J. Chem.* **34**, 1819–1832, 1956.

TABLE 63

ABILITY OF A GROUP OF BUTYLTIN COMPOUNDS TO CAUSE CHEMICAL BURNS IN MAN ON SINGLE APPLICATION[a]

Compound	Ability to burn (on 1 appl.)
Dibutyltin dichloride	+
Dibutyltin diacetate	−
Dibutyltin dilaurate	−
Dibutyltin oxide	−
Dibutyltin maleate	−
Tributyltin chloride	+
Tributyltin acetate	+
Tributyltin laurate	+
Tributyltin oxide	+
Tetrabutyltin	−

[a] Data from W. H. Lyle, *Brit. J. Ind. Med.* **15**, 193 (1958).

TABLE 64
WOODS THAT HAVE CAUSED DERMATITIS[a]

Acacia

Alder wood

Aroeira (South America)

Bassina (Africa)

Beach Apple (Central America, also called manzanillo and manchineel)

Beech

Birch

Blackwood (acacia melanoxylon)

Blue gum (Mexico)

Boxwood (Africa)

Cajaput (East Indies)

Cedar

Chestnut

Cocobolo (dalbergia, also called bastard mahogany)

Cocus wood (Cuba, grenadil)

Cypress

Dogwood (Australia, West Indies and United States)

Ebony (Africa, diospyros)

Embuia wood (nectandras)

Eucalyptus (hemiphloia)

Eucalyptus (maculata)

Juniper

Lance wood (Australia and Cape)

Macassar

Mahogany (West Indies and West Africa)

Mansonia wood (sterculiacea altissima)

Maple

Melanorrhea Anacardiace (Java, also called Singapore mahogany)

Moa (Australia)

Moule (also called Uganda teak, bush oak and roko)

Muirapenima

Odum (West Africa, also known as roko tree; in East Africa as chlorophora excelsa)

Olive wood

Partridge wood (Tropical America: andira americana)

Pine

Podocarpus (yew family)

Poplar

Quebracho (Central and South America)

Redwood (California, also called sequoia)

Rengas (also rungus, renghas, etc., glauta renghas from Java)

Rosewood (Borneo)

Sabicu (Cuba)

Satinwood (East and West)

Silver Spruce

Tagayasah or Tagayasan (Japan)

Teakwood (East Indies)

Tonquin (East Indies; produces a green skin coloration only)

Ukola (Africa dumeria)

Walnut (Brazil)

Yew (England and Indies)

[a]Data from C. P. McCord, *Ind. Med. Surg.* **27**, 202–204 (1958).

TABLE 65
ACUTE TOXICITY OF ZIRCONIUM COMPOUNDS[a]

Compound	Concentration (% sol.)	Oral LD$_{50}$		Intraperitoneal LD$_{50}$	
		Compound (mg/kg)	Metal (mg/kg)	Compound (mg/kg)	Metal (mg/kg)
Zirconyl acetate	50	4,100	1,660	300	122
Zirconyl chloride	50	3,500	990	400	113
Zirconyl nitrate	50	2,500	853	1,250	426
Zirconium sulfate	25	3,500	1,253	175	63
Sodium zirconyl sulfate	25	10,000	2,290	4,100	939

[a] Data from K. W. Cochran et al., Arch. Ind. Hyg. Occupational Med. **1**, 637–650, June, 1950.

TABLE 66
ACUTE INTRAPERITONEAL TOXICITY OF ALKYL IODIDES (MG/KG)[a]

Compound	Animal	LD_{50}	LD_{16}	LD_{84}
Methyl iodide	Mouse	172.6	154.3	190.8
	Rat	101.0	94.0	108.0
	Guinea pig	51.8	26.2	77.4
n-Butyl iodide	Mouse	101.7	93.6	109.9
	Rat	692.0	573	811
Isobutyl iodide	Mouse	594	475	713
	Rat	1241	786	1695
Isoamyl iodide	Mouse	503	376	629
	Rat	1424	1207	1641
Isopropyl iodide	Mouse	1300	566	2133
	Rat	1850	1612	2088
n-Amyl iodide	Mouse	489	410	569
	Rat	948	793	1083
n-Octyl iodide	Mouse	1416	646	2184
	Rat	1982	1114	2852
Methylene diiodide	Mouse	467.2	364.4	570.6
	Rat	402.6	314.8	493

TABLE 67
ACUTE INHALATION TOXICITY OF ALKYL IODIDES
(4 HR EXPOSURE RATS) (MG/LITER)

Compound	LC_{50}	LC_{16}	LC_{84}
Methyl iodide	1.30	0.9	1.55
n-Butyl iodide	6.1	4.25	8.8
Isobutyl iodide	6.7	3.3	13.5

[a]Courtesy Boris Shugaev, Yaroslavl, U.S.S.R.

TABLE 68
ACTION OF DRUGS ON COUMARIN ANTICOAGULANTS[a]

Coumarin effect decreased by	Coumarin effect increased by
Barbiturates	Anabolic steroids
Phenobarbital	Antibiotics, broad-spectrum
Sodium amobarbital (Amytal)	Phenyramidol HCl (Analexin)
Secobarbital sodium (Seconal)	Clofibrate (Atromid S)
Chloral hydrate	Phenylbutazone (Butazolidin)
Glutethimide (Doriden)	Oxyphenbutazone (Tandearil)
Griseofulvin	Diphenylhydantoin (Dilantin)
Meprobamate (Miltown, etc.)	Methylthiouracil
Ethchlorvynol (Placidyl)	Quinidine
	Quinine
Increased anticoagulant dosage	Radioactive compounds and X ray
required for therapeutic effect.	Salicylates
	d-Thyroxine
Decreased anticoagulant dosage	
required when above drugs	*Hemorrhage* may occur if above
are withdrawn.	drugs are added to stabilized
	anticoagulant regimen.
Decreased prothrombin time.	*Increased* prothrombin time.

[a] Taken from *Clin-Alert* (May 8, 1968).

Index

Proprietary names for drugs appear in italic type.

Drugs or compounds listed alphabetically in Chapter IV (pp. 59-641) are not repeated in the index. Drugs are discussed in Chapter IV under their nonproprietary names.

Aminodimethylbenzene, 637
N-Aminoethylpiperazine, 687
2-Amino-2-methyl-1,3-propane-diol, 91
2-Amino-2-methyl-1-propanol, 91
Aminopterin, see Aminopteroyl-glutamate, 22
Aminopyrine (*Amidopyrine, Pyramidon*), *93*, 494, 670, 675
Aminosalicylic Acid, *94*, 337, 568, 670
o-Aminothiophenol, 90
Aminotoluene, *see* Toluidine, 597
Amiphenazole HCl (*Daptazole*) 436
Amitriptyline HCl (*Elavil*), *94*, *461*, 504, 588, 598, 685
Ammonia, 95, 96, 406, 645, 732
Ammonium chloride, *39*, *96*, 379, 683
Ammonium hydroxide, 95
Ammonium lauryl sulfate, 711
Ammonium salts, *see* Thioglyco-lates, 586
Ammonium sulfamates, 558
Ammonium thioglycolate, 301
Amobarbital (*Amytal*), *36*, *557*, 757
Amosite, 114
Amphetamine sulfate (*Benzedrine*), *36*, *98*, 555, 635
Amphojel, see Antacids, 105
Ampicillin (*Penbritin, Polycil-lin*), *100*, *453*, 455
Amygdalin, 87
Amyl iodide, 756
Amyl nitrite, *100*, 191
Amytal, see Amobarbital
Analeptics, *see* Central nervous system stimulants
Analexin, see Phenyramidol
Analgesics, *see* Pain, treatment of
Anaphylaxis, treatment of, *56*, *454*, 495, 559, 611
Ancyte, see Piposulfan, 479
Androgens, 683
Andromedotoxin, 408
Anectine, see Succinylcholine
Anemone, 504

Anesthetic hyperthermia, 101
Anesthetics, 178, 210, 241, 278, 351, 370, 383, 404, 431, 494, 497, 499, 518, 575, 577
Angel's trumpet, 341
Anhydrides, organic, 102, 743
Anileridine (*Leritine*), *41*, *102*
Aniline, *102*, 297, 364
  and derivatives, 707
Anise, 484
Anisondione (*Miradon*), 131
Anisotropine methylbromide (*Valpin*), 587
Anodynon, 254
Anorexiants, *see* Weight reduc-tion
Anovulatory drugs, 103
Ansolysen, see Pentolinium, 283
Antabuse, see Disulfiram
Antacids, 105
Antagonistic, additive, or syner-gistic effects, 120, 133, 146, 164, 207, 252, 258, 282, 289, 294, 302, 328, 355, 358, 360, 364, 366, 368, 370, 375, 378, 389, 392, 403, 405, 407, 411, 418, 435, 458, 465, 469, 471, 497, 499, 501, 511, 518, 535, 536, 541, 542, 555, 558, 564, 580, 588, 596, 598, 607, 639, 658, 661
Antepar, see Piperazine
Anthalazine, see Piperazine
Anthophyllite, 114
Anthracene, 674
Anthraquinone, 142, 346
Anti-appetite drugs, 36, 98, 245, 634
Antibiotics
  broad spectrum, 757
  cutaneous reactions, 106
Anticoagulants, 103, *131*, 305, 452, 541, 564, 580, 596, 597, 683, 757, *see also* Blood clotting
Antidiarrheals, 35, 40, 45
Antidote, "Universal," 35
Antiemetics, 45, 227, 459, 497, 585, 608, 609
Antifebrin, see Acetanilid, 62, *494*, 670
Antifungal agent, 548, 596
Antihemorrhagics, 91, 580, 597, 599, 625, 626, 683

761

Dodecyl boric acid, 84
n-Dodecylguanidine acetate, 234
Dogwood, 754
Dolomite, 570
Dolophine, see Methadone HCl
Dolor-Plus, see Fiorinal, 263
DOM, *see* STP, 226, **554**
Dopa, *see* L-Dopa, 660
DOPD-2, *see also* Phenylenediamines, 470
DOPD-3, *see also* Phenylenediamines, 470
Dopram, see Doxapram, 234
Doriden, see Glutethimide
Dowicide, 603
Doxycycline (*Vibramycin*), 235, 578
DPPD, *see also* Phenylenediamines, 470
Dragon root, *see* Dieffenbachia, 215
Dristan, 471
Drowning, treatment of, 33, *see also* Salt water, Fresh water, Diving
Dr. Pepper, 539
Drug-induced phototoxicity, *see* Sun rays, Sensitization, 674
Drug sensitivity, *see* Sensitization, 674
Drugs
    narcotic, *see* Narcotics, 2, **40**, 431
    non-narcotic, *see* Non-narcotics, analgesics
DTPA, 482
Dumb cane, 215
Dust, *see* Sawdust, Teak, Wood, Lungs, Thesaurosis
Dutch liquid, 257
Dusting powder, 331, 553
Dwarf bay, 552
Dyes, *see* Congo Red, Eosin, Hair coloring, Aniline (marking ink), Ball point pen ink, Rhodamine B, Alphazurine, Triphenylmethane
Dylox (Dipterex), 230, 438, 668
Dymelor, see Acetohexamide, Sulfonylurea drugs, **563**, 684
Dyrenium, see Triamterene

E

EACA, 91, **599**
Eagle ray, 554
East Indian sattinwood, 637
Ebony, 754
Ecolid, see Chlorisondamine, Ganglionic blocking agents, 282
Ecotrin, see Buffered aspirin, 143
Edathamil calcium disodium, 236, 349
Edecrin, see Ethacrynic acid
Edema, 127, 330, 516, 533, 572, 588, 591, 592, 594, 615, 645, 656, 660, 663
    peripheral (treatment), 245
    pulmonary (pneumonitis), 73, 95, 110, 129, 137, 146, 163, 168, 183, 192, 226, 256, 273, 275, 301, 318, 320, 343, 362, 386, 420, 427, 429, 443, 444, 447, 472, 528, 565, 580, 581, 593, 597, 603, 614, 621, 639, 645, 649, 650, 656, 660
Edetic acid, *see* Edathamil, calcium disodium, 236, 349
Edrophonium Cl (*Tensilon*), 38
EDTA, 236, 349
Efocaine, 238
Egg white, 675
Eighth cranial nerve damage, *see* Auditory apparatus, 342, 418, 555, 683
Elavil, see Amitriptyline
Electric dishwasher granules, 201
Electrocortin, *see* Aldosterone, 552, *also* Adrenocortical hormones
Electrolyte balance, imbalance, and treatment, 33, 47, 628-632
Elephant's ear, 215
Elipten, see Aminoglutethimide, 91
Elkosin, see Sulfisomidine, 561
Emetics, 110, 332
Emetine, 332
Emivan, see Ethamivan
Emodin, 142

Girdles, 548

Glass fiber, *see* Fiber glass, 262

Glaucoma, 525

Glory lilly, 189

G-6-PD, *see* Glucose-6-phosphate dehydrogenase

Glucocorticosteroids, *see* Adrenocortical hormones, **76**, **551**, 675, 683

Glucose, *see* Dextrose, **204**, 627

Glucose-6-phosphate dehydrogenase (G-6-PD), 53, 414, 424, 494, 564, 652

Glue-sniffing, 481

Gluside, see Saccharin

Glutamic acid, 523

Glutaric acid, 71

Glutethimide (*Doriden*), 133, **287**, 757

Glycerol, **288**, 489

Glyceryl monostearate, 710, 711

Glyceryl trinitrate, *see* Nitroglycerin, 423, **428**

Glycol carbonate, 255

Glycol ethers, 291, 729, 730

Glycol ethylene ether, 658

Glycols, 290, 729-731

Glycyrrhizic acid, 660

Glymidine (*Gondafon*), 291

Goiter, *see* Seaweed, 526

Gold, 292, 671

Golden chain tree, 343

Golden dewdrop, 314

Gold sodium thiomalate (*Myochrysine*), 292

Gold sodium thiosulfate (*Sanocrysin*), 292

"Goof-balls," *see* Barbiturates

Gout, 85, 170, 184, 245, 251, 281, 282, 394, 407, 468, 495, 559

GP-25, 322

Graceful nightshade, *see* Ground-cherry, 294

Gramicidin, *see* Tyrothricin, 614

Granosan M, 374

"Grass," 363

Gray powder, 373

"Gray syndrome," 165

Grease gun injection injury, *see* Diesel oil, 216, 276

Green dragon, *see* Dieffenbachia, 215

Green hellebore, *see* Hellebore, 304

Grifulvin, see Griseofulvin

Griseofulvin (*Fulvicin, Grifulvin*), 106, **293**, 674, 757

Ground hemlock, 239

Grouper, *see* Fish, 263

Guaiacol phosphate, 604

Guanethidine (*Ismelin*), 295, 505

Gum camphor, 150

Gun-bluing compound, 527

Guthion, 668

Gynecomastia, 172, 248, 466, 552

Gynergen, see Ergot, 242

H

Habit forming, *see* Addiction

Hair (dyes), 297

Hair, loss of, or excessive growth, 77, 85, 152, 184, 196, 277, **298**, 305, 307, 322, 369, 381, 426, 459, 514, 527, 541, 553, 560, 582, 608, 619, 621, 622, 652

Hair balls, *see* Bezoars, 643

Hair bleaches, 319, *see also* Bleaches

Hair, color changes, 369, 652

Hair removers, 122, **299**

Hair shampoo, 201

Hair sprays, 300, 584

Hair-waving, 300, **586**

Haldol, see Haloperidol

Haldrone, see Paramethasone

Hallucinogens, 40, 226, **301**, 433, 460, 613

Halogenated alkenes, 693

Halogenated hydrocarbons, *see* Solvents

Halogenated salicylanilide, *see* Soap, 127, **538**

Haloperidol (*Haldol*), 301, 402

Halothane (*Fluothane*), 101, **302**

Harmonyl, see Deserpidine, 200

Hashish, 363

"Hawk," *see* LSD, 356

Hearing loss, *see* Auditory apparatus

Heart failure, (cardiac massage), 6, 8

Heavenly blue morning glory, 301, *see also* Hallucinogens

Hydrochlorothiazide (*Esidrix, Hydro-Diuril, Oretic*), 170
Hydrocortisone, *see* Adrenocortical hormones, **76, 551**, 675, 683
Hydrocortone, see Hydrocortisone
Hydrocyanic acid, 191, 641
Hydro-Diuril, see Hydrochlorothiazide, 170
Hydro-Diuril-Ka, 170, 171, 491, 492
Hydrofluoric acid, 26, **317**
Hydrogen (gas), 641
Hydrogen arsenide, 641
Hydrogen chloride, 317
Hydrogen cyanide, 191, 192, 641
Hydrogen fluoride, 651
Hydrogen peroxide, 319, 546
Hydrogen phosphide (phosphine), *see* Zinc, 638
Hydrogen selenide, 320, 527
Hydrogen sulfide, 320, 586
Hydrogenated sulfones, *see* Sulfolane, 560
Hydrohalogen acids, *see* Mineral acid, 400
Hydroiodic acid, *see* Mineral acid, 400
Hydroperoxides, 438
Hydroquinone, 76, **321**
Hydrosulfuric acid, 320
p-Hydroxyacetanilid, *see* Acetaminophen, 66, 523
Hydroxy alkyl amido alcohol sulfate, sodium salt, 710
1,3-Hydroxy-*N*-allylmorphinan, *see* Levallorphan tartrate, 41, 436
Hydroxyanisol, 295
5-Hydroxy-*N*,*N*-dimethyltryptamine, *see* Bufotenine, 226, 613
Hydroxyephedrine, 432
Hydroxy ethers, 735
N-Hydroxyethylpiperazine, 687
Hydroxymethyltolbutamide, 596
Hydroxyphenylbutazone (*Oxazolidin*), 469
p-Hydroxyphenylbutazone (oxyphenbutazone, *Tandearil*), *see* Phenylbutazone, 468, *also* 133, 564, 671, 757
β-Hydroxypropionic acid, 498
5-Hydroxytryptamine (Serotonin), 328, 396, **528**
Hygroton, see Chlorthalidone, 174
Hykinone, see Vitamin K, 625
Hyoscine HBr (scopolamine HBr), 341, **524**
Hyoscyamine (*Bellafoline*), 341
Hypaque, see Iopanoic acid, 331
Hypercalcemia, 148, 624
Hyperglycemia, *see* Diabetes
Hyperkalemia, 491, **492**, 552, 599
Hyperpyrexia and treatment, **40, 227**, 324, 337, 409, 510, 514, 524
Hypersensitivity, *see* Sensitization
Hypertensin, 101
Hypertonic sodium chloride sol., *see* Sodium chloride, 539
Hyperuricemia, *see* Gout
Hyperventilation, 31
Hypocalcemia, 148, 624, 625
Hypoglycemia, *see* Diabetes
Hypokalemia, **491, 492**, 600, 635, 660
Hyponitrous acid anhydride, 431
Hypoprothrombonemia, 625
Hypothermia and induction of, **12**, 40, 536

I

Ibogaine, 226
Ibotinic acid, 410
Ice, 327
Icewater and treatment of burn, **27**, 28, 31, 318
Ichthyosarcotoxism, **263**
Idoxuridine (IDV, *Dendrid, Herplex, Stoxil*), 324
IDV, 324
Iledar, see Tolazoline
Ilosone, see Erythromycin propionate lauryl sulfate
Ilotycin, see Erythromycin, 243
Imferon (Iron dextran complex), *see* Iron, 333

779

Midicel Acetyl, see Sulfonamides

Mienie-Mienie Indian bead, see Crabs-eye, 188

Mikedimide, see Bemegride, 126

Milk bush, 279, 419

Milkcup chalice vine, 295

Milk of Magnesia, 105

Milontin, see Phensuximide, 229

Miltown, see Meprobamate

Mineralo-corticosteroids, see Adrenocortical hormones, 76, 551, 675, 683

Mineral (seal) oil, see Furniture polish, 281; Petroleum solvents, 448, 459

Mineral spirits, see Paints, Petroleum solvents, 448, 459

Miokon, see Diprotrizoate

Miradon, see Anisindione, 131

Miranols, 710, 711

Missile fuels, 498

Miticide (Bayer 30686), 124

Moccasin (copperhead and cottonmouth), see Snakes, 532

Mock orange, see Horse chestnut, 314

Moderil, see Rescinnamine, 517

Molds (moldy bread), 401, 412, 548

Molluscs, see Clams, 179

Molybdenum, 354, 402

Monacetin, 542

Mona-Kay, see Phytonadione, 625

Monase, see Etryptamine

"Monday head," 437

Monkey pistol, see Sandbox tree, 523

Monkshead, 403, 408

Monoalkyl compounds, see Tin, 591

Monoamine oxidase inhibitors, 325, 328, 333, 336, 368, 404, 451, 461, 471, 505, 598

Monobenzyl ether of hydroquinone, 405

Monobromethane, 254

Monochlorobenzene, 168

Monochlorethane, 254

Monoethanolamine, see Ethanolamine, 246

Mo ofluorocitrate, 274

Monomethylamine, 385

Monopotassium glutamate, 523

Monosodium di-o-cresyl phosphate, 604

"Montezuma's revenge," 205

Moon face, 77

Moonseed vine, see Water hemlock, 633

Mornidine, see Pipamazine, 478

Morning Glory, 301

Morocide (Binapacryl), 668

Morphine sulfate, 18, 40, 228, 407

Morpholine, 92, 662

Mosatil, see Edathamil calcium disodium, 236, 349

Mothballs, 408, 416

Motion sickness, treatment of, 227, 366

Motor oil, 358 see also Tricresyl phosphates, 263

Mouth-to-mouth breathing, see Resuscitation, 2-8

Mouth-to-nose breathing, see Resuscitation, 2-8

6-MP, 372

Mucilages, 286

Mucomyst, see Acetylcysteine, 66

Mullet poisoning, 267

Multifuge, see Piperazine

"Mumps," 330, 468

"Münchener Bierherz," 182

Muriatic acid (HCl), 317

Muscarine, 409, 410

Muscimol, 410

Muscle (skeletal) cramps, pain, stimulants, relaxants, 46, 89, 148, 157, 171, 190, 198, 277, 281, 284, 329, 342, 347, 358, 362, 366, 370, 380, 394, 396, 418, 424, 439, 459, 478, 491, 496, 506, 511, 512, 526, 541, 550, 551, 557, 558, 560, 582, 594, 596, 604, 613, 622, 624, 635, 649, 652, 660

Mushroom miasma, 409, 584

Musquash root, see Water hemlock, 633

Myambutol, see Ethambutol HCl

Myasthenia gravis, see Muscle (skeletal) etc.

Paramethadione (*Paradione*), 609

Paramethasone acetate (*Haldrone*), **78**

Paraminyl Maleate, see Pyrilamine maleate, 107

Paraoxon, 438

Paraphenylenediamine, 297

Parasal, see Aminosalicylic acid

Parathion, 438, 450, 669, 671, 694

Parazine, see Piperazine, 478

Paregoric, *36*, *40*, *451*, 610

Parenzyme (Tryptar), 675

Pargyline (*Eutonyl*), *404*, *451*, 684

Parnate, see Tranylcypromine

Paromomycin, *see* Neomycin, 418

Parpanit HCl, see Caramiphen HCl

Parsley, 403, 484

Parsnip, 552

Partridge wood, 754

Parzone, see Dihydrocodeine, 40

PAS, 197, 494, *see also* Aminosalicylic acid, 670; Primaquine, *494*, 652

Pasem, see Aminosalicylic acid, 670

Pastes (glues), 286

PBI (protein-bound iodine), 459

PDB, *see* Dichlorobenzene, 210

Peanut, 412

Peanut oil, meal, 400, 412, 413

Pearly gates morning glory, *see* Hallucinogens, 301

Pediatric *Phenergan*, 203

Peganone, see Ethotoin, 229

Penbritin, see Ampicillin, Penicillins

Pencil tree, *see* Nettle, 419

Penicillamine (*Cuprimine*), 349, 452

Penicillin, 106, *453*, 495, 675

Penicillins, synthetic and semi-synthetics, 455

Penicillinase (*Neutrapen*), 456, 676

Pentaborane, 137, *456*

Pentachlorophenol, 227, 356, 669

Pentadecyl catechols, 485

Pentaquine, 494

Penthrane, see Methoxyflurane, 383

Pentolinium (*Ansolysen*), 283, *458*

Pentothal, see Thiopental sodium

Pentylenetetrazol (*Metrazol*), 36

Pepo-Provera, see Medroxyprogesterone, 366

Pepper, 412

Perazil, see Chlorcyclizine, 166

Perchlorates, 647

Perchlorethylene, 578

Perchloropentacyclodecane, 198

Perclene, 578

Percodan, see Oxycodone, 442

Perfluoroacetone, *see* Hexafluoroacetone, 309

Perfluoroisobutylene, 275

Perfume (*Shalimar*), 529

Perganol, 181

Perin, see Piperazine, 478

Peritoneal dialysis, *see* Dialytic therapy, 49

Peritoneal effusion, 509

Periwinkle, 301, 459

"Perk," 578

"Permanent" anti-freeze, 252, 258

Permanent wave neutralizer, 300

Permanent wave solutions, 586

Permitil, see Fluphenazine

Peroxides, organic, 746

Perphenazine (*Trilafon*), 277, *459*, 467, 671, 685

Persantin, see Dipyridamole, 230

Persimmon, 643

Perthane, 669

Pertofrane, see Desipramine

Pesticides, 110, 124, 177, 183, 200, 215, 230, 238, 256, 258, 278, 434, 507, 521, 522, 542, 598, 643, 648, 662, *669*
safe handling, 19

Pethidine HCl, *see* Meperidine HCl

Petrohol, 339

Petroleum pitch, 136

Petroleum solvents or distillates, 448, *459*

2-Pyridine aldoxime methiodide, 440
Pyridine borane, 89
Pyridoxine, *see* Vitamin B$_6$, 623
Pyrilamine maleate (*Neo-Antergan Maleate, Paraminyl Maleate*), 107
Pyrimethamine (*Daraprim*), **507**, 671
Pyrogallic acid, 507
Pyromucic aldehyde, 279

Q

QAC, 508
Quaalude, see Methaqualone
Quantril, see Benzquinamide, 129
Quartz, *see* Silica, 529
Quaternary pyridinium, 690
Quelicin, see Succinylcholine
Quelidrine (syrup), 203
Quicklime, 26, 353
Quicksilver, *see* Mercury, 372
Quinacrine HCl (*Atabrine*), **508**, 671
Quina-Glute, see Quinidine
Quinidine, **220**, **510**, 583, 671, 757
Quinine, 510, **511**, 671, 684, 757
Quinoform, see Iodochlorohydroxyquin, 206
Quinol, 321
2,3-Quinoxalinedithiol cyclic trithiocarbonate, 124
Quintox, see Dieldrin, **215**, 284, 649, 668

R

Rabbit fish, *see* Fish stings, 268
Radiation, ionizing, 292, 482, **512**, 757, *see also* Laser, 345; Microwave radiation, 397
Radio-opaque (contrast media), 144, 323, 331, 332, 392, 590, 675
Radium, 515
"Rainbow-pills," 635
Rametin, see Vitamin B$_{12}$, 623
Ramrod, 516
Ran-Sed, 683

Rapacodin, see Dihydrocodeine, 40
Rare earths, 748
Ratfish, *see* Fish stings, 268
Raticate, 431
Rattlesnake, 532
Rauloydin, 683
Rautrax, see Flumethiazide, 170
Raynaud's disease, *see* Tolbutamide, 563, 596
Recompression 33, 425
Red Baneberry, *see* Protoanemonin, 503
"Red-birds," *see* Barbiturates, 119
Redisol, see Vitamin B$_{12}$, 623
Redwood, 754
Reef shark, *see* Fish, 263
Regitine, see Phentolamine
Rela, see Carisoprodol, 157
Relaxin (Releasin), 675
Relay, 68, 143
Releasin, 675
Renacidin, see Hemiacidrin, 305
Renese, see Chlorothiazides, 170
Renografin, see Methylglucamine, 332, 392; Iopanoic acid, 331
Reproduction, *see* Ovulation
Reserpine, **37**, 378, **518**, 528, 683
Resin-containing plants, *see* Spurge laurel, 419, **552**
Resins, 488
Resistopen, see Penicillins, 455
Respiration, 43
Respiratory stimulants (treatment), 38, 43
Restrol, see Estrogens, **244**, 683
Resuscitation, cardiac 6, **8**, **12** mouth-to-mouth, mouth to nose, 2–8
Silvester method, 8
Retasulfin, see Sulfamethoxypyridazine, 206, 495, **561**, 672
Rexall powder *see* Bithionol, 135
Rhodanates, 586
Rhubarb, 441, **519**
Riboflavin, *see* Vitamin B$_2$, 622

V

n-Valeraldehyde, *see* Aldehydes, 81
Valium, *see* Diazepam
Valmid, *see* Ethinamate, 248
Valpin, *see* Anisotropine methylbromide, 587
Vancocin, *see* Vancomycin, 618
Vandid, *see* Ethamivan
Vapam, 669
Varsol, 460
Vasodepressors (antihypertensives), 37, 100, 139, 144, 230, 295, 296, 315, 366, 425, 428, 451, 543
Vasopressors, 11, 37, 44, 101, 117, 147, 150, 240, 351, 376, 416, 470, 471, 505, 580
VAZO, 117
V-C13, 669
V-Cillin K, *see* Penicillins, 455
Vegetable dyes, *see* Hair coloring, 519
Velban, *see* Vinblastine sulfate
Ventricular defibrillation, 45
Veratrum, 304, 408
Vercyte, *see* Pipobroman, 479
Vermizine, *see* Piperazine, 478
Versene, *see* Edathamil calcium disodium, 236, 349
Versidine, *see* Methopholine, 381
Vesprin, *see* Triflupromazine, 608
Vibramycin, *see* Doxycycline
Vinblastine sulfate, 459, *619*
Vincaleukoblastine (*Velban*, *Vikane*), 618, 619
Vincristine (*Oncovin*), 459, 619
Vinisil, *see* Polyvinylpyrrolidone
Vikane, 618
Vinyl acetate, 715
Vinyl alkylether maleic ester, 584
Vinyl chloride, 373, 620
Vinyl cyanide, 76
Vinylformic acid, 76
Vinylidene chloride, 210
Vinyl resins, 448
Vioform, *see* Iodochlorhydroxyquin, 206
Vio-Serpine, 683

Vio-Thene, *see* Oxyphencyclimine HCl, 445
Virginia creeper, *see* Oxalic acid, 441; Rhubarb, 519
Visine, *see* Tetrahydrozoline, 580
Vistanex, *see* Elastomer, 238
Vistaril, *see* Hydroxyzine HCl, 322
Vitamin B₁ (Thiamine), *622*, 623
Vitamin C (ascorbic acid), 27, *40, 545, 623*
Vitamin D, 399, *624*
Vitamin K, 580, *625*
Vitamin K analogues (menadiol sodium diphosphate: *Synkayvite*, *Thylokay*, *Kappadione*; menadione sodium bisulfite: *Hykinone*), 625, 626, 683
Vitamin K₁ (phytonadione: *Mephyton, Aquamephyton, Konakion, Mona-Kay*; menadione: *Menaphthone, Danitanon K, Aquinone, Menaquinone*), 625, 626
Vitriol, oil of, 566
Vivactil, *see* Protriptyline, 504
Vomiting, induction of, 1, 15, 110, 332
"Vomiting sickness," 72
Vonedrine, 471
Vontil, *see* Thioperazine, 587
Vontrol, *see* Diphenidol, 227

W

Walnut, 754
Warcoumin, *see* Warfarin sodium
Warfarin sodium (*Coumadin, Panwarfin, Prothromadin, Warcoumin*), 132, 294, 469, 521, 541, 580, *626*, 683
Wasps, 124
Water, balance, maintenance, replacement therapy, 33, 47, *627*
"Water glass," 530
Water hemlock, 633
Water intoxication, 47, 627, *see also* Salt water, 33; Fresh water, 33; Diving, 31, 425